High-Performance Oracle®
Proven Methods for Achieving
Optimum Performance and Availability

High-Performance Oracle®

Proven Methods for Achieving
Optimum Performance and Availability

Geoff Ingram

Wiley Publishing, Inc.

Publisher: Robert Ipsen
Executive Editor: Robert M. Elliott
Assistant Editor: Emilie Herman
Managing Editor: John Atkins
New Media Editor: Brian Snapp
Text Design & Composition: MacAllister Publishing Services, LLC

Published by Wiley Publishing, Inc., Indianapolis, Indiana
Published simultaneously in Canada

For general information on our other products and services please contact our Customer Care Department within the United States at (800) 762-2974, outside the United States at (317) 572-3993 or fax (317) 572-4002.

Wiley also publishes its books in a variety of electronic formats. Some content that appears in print may not be available in electronic books.

Library of Congress Cataloging-in-Publication Data:

Ingram, Geoff, 1962-
   High performance Oracle : proven methods for achieving optimum
performance and availability / Geoff Ingram.
         p.   cm.
"Wiley Computer Publishing."
Includes index.
   ISBN 0-471-22436-7
   1. Oracle (Computer file) 2. Relational databases. 3. Software
maintenance.   I. Title.
   QA76.9.D3 I53422 2002
   005.75'85--dc21

Printed in the United States of America.

10 9 8 7 6 5 4 3 2 1

This book is dedicated to my wife Renata; to my children Rosalind, Alexandra, Alice, and Sebastian; to my father Vincent; and to the memory of my mother Muriel.

Acknowledgments

Special thanks go to Mark Clark, whose vision ultimately made the book possible, and to Steve Shaw.

Special thanks also go to Bob Elliott and Emilie Herman at Wiley Publishing, Inc. Bob turned the book proposal into something of a book in its own right. Hopefully the end result justifies that. Emilie, in her own words, "edits with a heavy red pen," which is not actually as painful as it sounds and has definitely led to more concise content, better organization, and improved readability. Thanks also to John Atkins for the final polish, and Brian Snapp.

Honorable mentions go to colleagues and others, past and present, whose input influenced the content in large and small ways. In no particular order: Wai Lee, Glen Howell, Sheck Cho, Chris Chandler, Nisit Kotecha, Anoop Marld, Richard Dutton, Arthur Muir, Susan Gruebel, Jose Garcia, Matt Solomon, Pradeep Malhotra, Michael Wang, Ping Huang, Anna Lam, Peter Chellone, Mike Bean, Tony Way, Andy Knight, Richard Kirkwood, Jenny Scott, Iain Beckingham, Carlos Tubau-Gamble, Simon Gregory, Adrian Cockcroft, and Ray Leah.

Finally, thanks go to all those Oracle technologists, such as Thomas Kyte and Jonathan Lewis, who contribute to bulletin boards and news groups on the Web, both at Oracle and elsewhere. Without such people prepared to share their expertise free of charge, the Oracle world would be a much poorer place.

Contents

Introduction

The purpose of this book is to help organizations deploy Oracle8*i* and Oracle9*i* (including Release 2) systems that meet the key end-user requirements of performance and availability at the same time. The ability to deliver on these twin requirements requires a holistic approach to the design and build of the end-to-end Oracle system, and this holistic approach is at the heart of this book. Too often, insufficient emphasis is given to components that are not related to the server. For example, consider a scenario where an Oracle end-user application uses a local configuration file (tnsnames.ora) to locate an Oracle database. If the database relocates to a new server one weekend, and the configuration file change is overlooked, end users won't be able to connect on Monday morning. The database may as well be down. From the end-user perspective, it is. In the worst case, the outage could affect the organization's bottom line. Appropriate network configuration, based on a centralized naming service, is a critical success factor for delivering availability. A similar emphasis is required on all aspects of the Oracle configuration, from initial installation to production support, in order to meet performance and availability requirements.

Overview of the Book and Technology

One of the strengths and weaknesses of Oracle is its sheer flexibility. This is a strength because you can always (or nearly always) achieve your goal. It's a weakness because the number of options available for meeting a straightforward requirement can be overwhelming and the need to evaluate all the available options can delay deployment. For example, if you need a high-availability Oracle system, do you choose Oracle replication, Real Application Clusters (RAC), or Oracle Data Guard, or a combination of all three?

In contrast, Microsoft SQL Server reduces choices for out-of-the-box deployment through the use of wizards, leading to faster delivery of applications with lower

demands on the database administrator's (DBA's) time for cases where the more eso-
teric features are not required. Oracle certainly provides more wizards than ever
before, especially in Oracle9*i* Release 2, in order to assist the user in choosing the right
approach for the problem in hand, but the Microsoft wizard-for-everything approach
isn't there yet. What can help is information on how to choose the right approach.

This book sets out to reduce deployment time by choosing approaches in each area
of significance that are proven to work in the real world. In some cases, the approach is
based on a qualitative discussion of requirements against available features. In others,
it requires a step-by-step, hands-on example or code snippet. I have tried to avoid providing page after page of code, while at the same time attempting to make code examples self-contained.

Oracle server command-line examples are based on Sun Solaris, which is the most
popular platform for commercial Oracle deployment on UNIX today. These command-
line examples are for illustration only and shouldn't be viewed as reflecting a personal
preference for Sun. In any case, due to the POSIX compliance of most UNIX flavors
today, the examples are pretty much interoperable with most popular UNIX systems
on which Oracle is deployed. For example,nearly all of them will work unchanged on
Linux. The sheer openness of Oracle's architecture means that many third-party tools
exist for meeting performance and availability requirements. For example, VERITAS
provides offerings that potentially deliver both enhanced performance and availability
for Oracle. These are covered in Chapter 20. When I recommend or cover a third-party
vendor tool, it is based on a carefully chosen set of vendor-neutral requirements. I also
try to cover Oracle's own offering as a comparison. In some cases, such as Oracle
Change Manager (which is covered in a separate white paper on the companion Web
site for this book), Oracle provides the best-of-breed offering. However, that doesn't
mean that there aren't other tools that could do the job.

What's most important when choosing third-party software for your Oracle deployment operating system is a complete set of requirements. Once the requirements are
clear, there are usually several options available to meet them at varying price points.
If the requirements are correct, you can choose a solution to fit your budget.

I've emphasized where Oracle features are different or improved in Oracle9*i* compared to Oracle8*i*. This is a significant task in itself because Oracle9*i* contains many
great new features to enhance performance and availability, including the following:

- Resumable space management, which enables operations to suspend rather
  than abort when space shortages exist. As a result, processing can work the
  first time rather than following the traditional (and time-consuming) abort and
  then repeat approach.

- Flashback query, which enables data to be viewed at a previous point in time
  without requiring an expensive restore and recover operation.

- Configurable DBA-controlled undo retention means that the legendary ORA-
  01555 "snapshot too old . . . " error becomes a thing of the past.

- Standby features in Oracle9*i* Data Guard (including the long-awaited logical
  standby in Release 2) represent a quantum leap forward in providing Oracle
  data availability (without data loss) in the face of disasters.

- Oracle RAC, which provides a huge step toward delivering performance and availability at the same time. When deployed on Linux running on Intel, the price/performance combination becomes very attractive.

How This Book Is Organized

This book is divided into six parts, which are intended to cover subjects in the order you might address them when setting up an Oracle configuration from scratch. In order to get the most out of the book, the best approach is to read it from cover to cover in sequential order. The detail is important, and a lack of attention to detail in all relevant areas of the technology is—based on personal experience—a significant reason why Oracle systems don't meet end-user performance and availability requirements.

For example, Chapter 16, which discusses using performance management tools, is somewhat meaningless without first understanding end-to-end performance management (see Chapter 8), the factors that most influence performance (see Chapter 9), and the definition of criteria for choosing performance management tools (also Chapter 16). Similarly, production tasks (which are covered in Part Six) are likely to be carried out more efficiently with reduced outages based on a standard Oracle network configuration (see Chapter 3) and server configuration (which is covered in Part One).

In the final analysis, all the subjects covered are related. Some of the relationships are obvious. You might only become aware of others when it's too late, unless you understand them in advance. For example, the use of unrecoverable (NOLOGGING) operations can speed up the performance of your production system. If you run a standby database without understanding the side effects of NOLOGGING operations, your standby may be unusable when you need to activate it, following a disaster. As another example, consider a disaster that requires you to reinstall your Oracle software. If you can't find the CDs (or they were destroyed), you have a problem. Maybe you can restore from tape, if that option is available. However, if you follow the recommendations in Chapter 1, your complete Oracle software library will always be available on disk across redundant sites. Therefore, it's not really appropriate to say that some chapters contain information that's more important than others. But it would be more convenient.

The following is a list of all the chapters and the key topics that each one covers. Part One covers the fundamentals of an Oracle configuration:

Chapter 1: Installing Oracle.   Topics covered include UNIX configuration for Oracle, installation via the network file system (NFS), silent installation using the Oracle Installer, and client installation using Microsoft Systems Management Server.

Chapter 2: Database Creation.   Topics covered include a new layout approach for manageability based on Oracle-Managed Files (OMF), the use of Oracle9*i* automatic undo management and server parameter files, Redundant Array of Independent Disks (RAID) layout for performance, raw partitions versus file systems, and the benefits of storage area networks (SANs) and network attached storage (NAS).

Chapter 3: Configuring Oracle Networking.   Topics covered include networking fundamentals, dynamic registration, network failover and load balancing, complete instructions for running Oracle Names, considerations for running Lightweight Directory Access Protocol (LDAP), and shared server and transparent gateway configuration.

Chapter 4: Environment Standards and Tools.   Topics covered include how to set a standard login environment, how to stop and start Oracle services using some downloadable Perl scripts, and Apache Web server basics for DBAs.

Chapter 5: Securing Your Database.   Topics covered include logon authentication options, password management policies, reducing the cost of user administration through Oracle9i enterprise users and Oracle Internet Directory, application security, and how to perform a security audit using a downloadable script.

Part Two shows you how to design fast and supportable applications:

Chapter 6: Designing Supportable Applications.   Topics covered include the provision of tracing facilities, error reporting and logging, run-time application configuration, and avoiding outages using Oracle9i resumable operations.

Chapter 7: Choosing Third-Party Software.   Topics covered include a checklist of all the things you need to consider to ensure that the third-party software you purchase meets your immediate and future needs.

Part Three offers performance management and tuning techniques:

Chapter 8: End-to-End Performance Management.   Topics covered include the challenges of end-to-end performance management including a detailed example of a three-tier application, the cost of identifying and fixing performance issues, the measurement and collection of transaction times, and an estimate of the return on investment.

Chapter 9: Fundamentals of SQL Tuning.   Topics covered include tuning and its place in the application lifecycle, Oracle statistics and events, tools for measuring statistics and events, how to view the Oracle buffer cache and control its contents, how to detect full table scans and the SQL performing them, viewing and stepping through SQL execution plans, parallel operations, identifying which SQL to tune, making SQL faster with and without code changes through the use of hints and stored outlines, tuning SQL for the network, and defining server memory requirements using the advisories in Oracle9i Release 2.

Chapter 10: Collecting and Using Optimizer Statistics.   Topics covered include basic table and index statistics, column statistics and skewed data, the ANALYZE command, statistics collection with DBMS_STATS, system statistics in Oracle9i, and statistics tables.

Chapter 11: Partitioning.   Topics covered include an overview of partitioning performance and availability features, partition creation examples using range, list, hash, and composite methods, partition indexing techniques, and availability considerations for global indexes.

Chapter 12: Managing Indexes. Topics covered include estimating the cost of index management, understanding index types, identifying which columns to index including Oracle9*i* skip scans, identifying unused indexes in Oracle8*i* and Oracle9*i*, determining when to rebuild indexes, and building function-based indexes.

Chapter 13: Managing Space Growth. Topics covered include collecting space growth information, presenting space growth information using Microsoft Excel charts, identifying space waste, minimizing space waste, measuring the effects of row migration and chaining, and correcting space waste.

Chapter 14: Stress Testing and Benchmarks. Topics covered include how to run a basic stress test, an overview of the TPC-C benchmark, and the use of a benchmark to compare Oracle on running two operating systems.

Chapter 15: Server Consolidation and Resource Management. Topics covered include an overview of server consolidation, the use of Oracle profiles for resource control of a single Oracle session, the use of Oracle Resource Manager for resource control of an Oracle instance, the use of Solaris Resource Manager (SRM) for resource control on a Sun server, and server consolidation using IBM zSeries mainframes.

Chapter 16: Selecting and Using Performance Management Tools. Topics covered include defining roles and responsibilities for those involved in performance management, setting performance goals and tool requirements, using Oracle Expert and Precise/Indepth, and comparing Oracle Expert with Precise/Indepth.

Part Four covers the best way to perform backups, restores, and recoveries:

Chapter 17: Fundamentals of Oracle Recovery. Topics covered include understanding the system change number (SCN), recovering from an instance crash, recovering from a media failure, using and viewing Oracle redo with LogMiner, and using Oracle9*i* Flashback Query to recover without a restore.

Chapter 18: Backup and Recovery Using Recovery Manager (RMAN). Topics covered include backup and recovery requirements, how RMAN addresses the risks of in-house scripts, a simple backup using RMAN, backing up using a backup catalog, cloning a database with the RMAN DUPLICATE command, managing archived redo logs on disk, using RMAN with Legato NetWorker, maximizing backup throughput, performing RMAN restore, and backup and restore troubleshooting.

Chapter 19: Backup and Restore Using Export and Import. Topics covered include using preexport checks to reduce the chance of import errors, using parameter files for export, national language support (NLS) considerations, exporting to a point in time using Oracle9*i* Flashback Query, maximizing export performance using direct path, identifying limitations and security considerations for direct path, controlling the size of export files using UNIX file compression, using transportable tablespaces to speed up restore, and running import for maximum performance including an import benchmark.

Part Five covers high-availability solutions:

Chapter 20: VERITAS High Availability (HA) for Oracle.   Topics covered include Oracle Disk Manager, and an overview of the following VERITAS products and features with respect to Oracle HA—VERITAS File System (VxFS) and Volume Manager, Storage Rollback, VERITAS Cluster Server (VCS), FlashSnap, and VERITAS Volume Replication Facility (VVRF).

Chapter 21: Oracle Replication.   Topics covered include a comparison of multimaster replication and standby database for disaster recovery, synchronous and asynchronous replication, conflict resolution and notification, issues associated with sequences in a replicated environment, prerequisites for a multimaster configuration, and the setup and execution of a multimaster configuration using Oracle Enterprise Manager (OEM).

Chapter 22: Real Application Clusters (RAC).   Topics covered include the functionality gaps in Oracle Parallel Server (OPS) that RAC solves, the components of a RAC configuration, a description of cache fusion improvements, installation improvements and manageability enhancements, interconnect configuration, parameter differences between RAC and single instance configuration, a complete set of initialization parameters for a two-node cluster, the client network configuration for load balancing and failover, considerations for choosing your Oracle operating system, and choosing to run RAC on Linux.

Chapter 23: Protecting Data Using Standby Databases.   Topics covered include creating and running a physical standby database in Oracle8*i*, creating and running a physical standby database using Oracle9*i* Data Guard, creating and running a logical standby database using Oracle9*i* Data Guard, and improving standby management using Oracle9*i* Data Guard Manager and broker.

Part Six shows you how to maintain your Oracle system:

Chapter 24: Guidelines for Health Checks and Monitoring.   Topics covered include health checks for physical layout, health checks for tablespace and rollback segment definitions, defining monitoring requirements, implementing monitoring using database jobs, sending alerts from within the database using UNIX sendmail, implementing monitoring using OEM and Oracle Intelligent Agent (OIA), creating customized monitoring scripts using Tool Control Language (Tcl), and performing fixit jobs.

Chapter 25: Auditing Techniques.   Topics covered include enabling the database audit trail, relocating the audit trail and changing ownership, understanding the audit session identifier, choosing audit options, identifying suspicious activity, using the audit trail to track input/output (I/O) trends, using triggers to audit data content changes, and using fine-grained access control to audit SELECT statements in Oracle9*i* using the DBMS_FGA package.

Chapter 26: Migration and Upgrade.   Topics covered include a migration prerequisites checklist, using Oracle Data Migration Assistant (ODMA) to perform migration, and post-migration tasks.

Chapter 27: Working Effectively with Oracle Support. Topics covered include benefits and drawbacks of problem reporting via the Web, the Oracle Support Services (OSS) view of the customer's role in the support process, the escalation process, the use of Oracle STATSPACK and Remote Diagnostic Agent to standardize support, and the choice of your Oracle product set for supportability.

Chapter 28: Troubleshooting Oracle DBMS Problems. Topics covered include understanding the UNIX system log, identifying Oracle shared memory, using UNIX kernel tracing, using Oracle and operating system network tracing, using Oracle event tracing, and utilizing operating system performance diagnostics.

Who Should Read This Book?

One theme that emerges strongly from the book is that both DBAs and developers have a strong influence on whether systems meet performance and availability goals. Organizations where developers and DBAs have a rigid view of their respective roles and responsibilities often deliver production applications that don't meet end-user requirements.

At different times, I've been both a professional Oracle DBA and a product developer at Oracle Corporation, so I've seen the situation from both sides. The best approach is one where an organization employs Oracle professionals with a mixture of skills, where some have an emphasis on development and others have an emphasis on production DBA support. A secondary goal of this book is to try to break down the traditional walls between developers and DBAs by giving visibility to the kind of tasks that each performs. From my experience, a poor relationship between DBA and development groups often results from a poor understanding of what the other group does.

Therefore, this book is intended for both DBAs and developers of all levels. In many ways, the term *advanced* in the Oracle world is something of a misnomer. The scope of what Oracle provides is very extensive: There's a lot to know, but most of it is not especially complex. Anyone who understands Oracle fundamentals can understand and benefit from the contents of this book and Oracle's own Concepts Guide is a great place to start. The challenge comes in deploying systems based on techniques that work from the many techniques available. This book sets out to provide a fast track to deploying systems with performance and availability built in.

Tools You Will Need

This book contains many SQL code examples, and you need a suitable tool to execute them. DbCool (www.dbcool.com) is a tool you might consider using as a companion to this book. It was used to run all SQL and generate all SQL output referenced in the text. One advantage of DbCool is that all SQL output column widths are automatically sized to fit the width of the data in output. Another is that output results can be grouped and sorted on the client without re-executing the original SQL. There is no obligation to use DbCool, which is free and runs on Windows platforms. SQL*Plus and *i*SQL*Plus work just as well in many cases, except in situations where line-mode output is incompatible with the requirement, such as stepping through a SQL execution plan. All SQL examples in the text contain the statement terminator required when you submit SQL or PL/SQL from SQL*Plus.

Some examples are based on C code, and you will need a C compiler to build the shared libraries from source code. All code compiles with the free Gnu C compiler (gcc).

It's assumed that you have access to an Oracle database running the Oracle Enterprise Edition, as this is required for some of the more advanced Oracle features. It is noted in the text when the Enterprise Edition is required.

What's on the Companion Web Site?

The companion Web site for this book (www.wiley.com/compbooks/ingram) includes updates on techniques found in the book, links to useful resources, and full source code for several examples referenced in this book, including the following:

dbcool_perl.tar. A UNIX tar file containing all the scripts required to implement the Perl-based Oracle management scripts covered in Chapter 4.

dbcool_mon.sql. A PL/SQL package for the collection of Oracle events and statistics metrics

dbcool_tkprof.sql and dbcool_tkprof.c. A PL/SQL package and external procedure to enable TKPROF to be executed from a client-side application

dbcool_audit.pl. A Perl script to provide a basic database security audit

dbcool_rman_gen.pl and dbcool_legato_gen.pl. Perl scripts to generate a selection of different backup types for Oracle RMAN backups and Legato Networker for Oracle backups.

dbcool_space.sql and dbcool_space.xls. A PL/SQL package for collecting database space growth statistics and an Excel spreadsheet for producing JPEG images charting growth based on the collected statistics

dbcool_utl.sql and dbcool_utl.c. A PL/SQL package and external C code for performing UNIX-style pattern matching in SQL, and presenting database-server file system space information. Full details are available in a related paper on the companion web site.

dbcool_gen_standby.pl. A Perl script to help generate physical and logical standby databases

dbcool_arch_to_standby.pl. A Perl script to copy archived redo logs from a primary server to a standby server

dbcool_ora_healthcheck.pl. A Perl script to check database conformance with layout standards and other configuration issues

dbcool_2pc_pending.pl. A Perl script to notify OEM of a critical severity problem

High-Performance Oracle®
**Proven Methods for Achieving
Optimum Performance and Availability**

PART

One

Fundamentals of an Oracle Configuration

Installing Oracle

What could be simpler than installing Oracle on UNIX from the installation media? Place the CD-ROM in the mounted drive, follow the instructions in the Installation and User Guide, and you're done. It's as simple as that, isn't it? Long-time Oracle users know that rarely are things that simple. Even before you unpack the CD-ROM, you must read and digest the installation documentation for your platform. If you have an active support contract, check Oracle's Metalink Web site (metalink.oracle.com) for late-breaking news on installation issues.

As a database administrator (DBA) or developer, you should begin with a set of requirements that will help you build a system to meet those requirements. The following are the requirements for your Oracle installation:

- First, all Oracle software in your organization should be installed the same way on all machines. That way, DBAs know how their installed environment looks and will feel comfortable with it, no matter what machine they log onto. They will be able to do their job faster and with fewer mistakes, which is especially important during an emergency callout or after a hardware failure that requires a reinstallation of the Oracle software.

- Second, you want to install the software right the first time. Then your Oracle software and database instances will be available to your business users in the shortest possible time.

- Third, you need to adopt a service-based approach, founded on standards. By defining clearly the role of the DBA group, you can set expectations for the people you provide the service to.

Before any of this happens, though, the Oracle DBA requires the services of the UNIX system administrator (SA) for some basic system configuration to support Oracle. To enable this service-based approach, you need to document and publish what services you provide and the services you require from other groups. But if you're in the DBA group, be prepared to standardize first, and not wait for others.

This chapter covers the following topics:

- UNIX configuration for Oracle
- Installation via the Network File System (NFS)
- How to perform a silent installation
- Using Microsoft Systems Management Server for client installation

USING REMOTE COPY COMMANDS, REMOTE SHELLS, AND .RHOSTS

Several examples in this book use UNIX remote copy (rcp) and shell (rsh) commands to copy files between your systems and run remote commands between them. In some cases, this is an Oracle requirement. For example, Oracle Data Guard Broker (covered in Chapter 23) enables you to configure a standby database from a primary database by using the rcp command to copy the primary database files to the standby site. Using these commands requires the configuration of a .rhosts file to authenticate the local machine running the command to the remote server that runs the rsh command (or is the target of an rcp).

To run either an rsh or rcp command against a remote server from a local server, log onto the remote server and create a file named .rhosts in the remote $HOME directory. Insert the following line into this file to enable remote operations from the server named local and account oracle:

```
local oracle
```

If you aren't concerned about security (although you should be!), you can instead add the line:

```
+ oracle
```

This allows remote connections onto the remote server from all other servers, provided that the remote account is named oracle. The security concern here is that anyone who can create a local oracle account on any UNIX server on your network, or log onto such an account, can then access the remote server as the Oracle DBA account without providing a password. After you've configured authentication in the .rhosts file, the rsh command provides a fast way to check the configuration. For example, to test the connection to a machine named remote, run:

```
$ rsh remote
```

If you connect without being prompted for a password, the rsh and rcp commands are working as required. If you are prompted for a password, you might need to specify the host name in the remote .rhosts file using a fully qualified host name, such as remote.uk.dbcool.com. Finally, check that the remote .rhosts file is owned by the login account, and that only the login account has write access to the file. If this is not the case, UNIX denies access for security reasons. If a password prompt still appears, consult your SA group. They might have disabled all rsh services for security reasons.

The Oracle DBA Group Cluster

Until now, you've probably used a local CD-ROM drive to install Oracle software, or requested that an SA remote mount the drive onto your machine. This book proposes that you unload the software from the CD-ROM once, and that the DBA group build a minimum of two UNIX servers to provide redundant Oracle services, including:

- Oracle Names address resolution services
- Oracle DBA group repository and warehouse
- DBA group Web site
- Oracle Recovery Manager (RMAN) backup catalog
- Oracle software releases

By providing each of the listed services on two different servers, all the services can remain available if a single server is down. Ideally, these two servers should be on different sites to provide a disaster recovery (DR) capability as well as redundancy against scheduled site outages. It's best to dedicate the two servers solely for the provision of Oracle services: If you allow other groups to co-host with you, you run the risk that their downtime requirements might impact your database services. Throughout the rest of this chapter, we'll refer to this pair of machines as the DBA Cluster, and the two servers in it as ora1.uk.dbcool.com and ora2.uk.dbcool.com. The following sections are based on this configuration.

UNIX System Requirements

This section covers the Oracle standard build for your UNIX servers. It's based on Sun Solaris, which is the most popular platform used to run commercial Oracle systems. However, the operating-system-specific details are as critical as covering the same areas for your organization's strategic platform.

You should document your standard configuration and publish it on the DBA group's Web site on the DBA Cluster so that any UNIX SA knows where to find your standard build information. With this approach, the DBA is not even involved in a system build. Don't email the details because over time the requirements might change, and you will have to resend them. Instead, refer people to the DBA Group Web site for the latest version. Developing this standard build requires a liaison with your SA team. It might be difficult, as DBAs and SAs sometimes regard each other with suspicion, but it will save countless hours in the future.

TIP **If you don't know how to set up a Web site, you should learn. Oracle makes this easy by shipping Apache Web server with the Oracle database management system (DBMS), starting with Oracle8i Release 3. Chapter 4 covers basic Apache configuration.**

Oracle UNIX Account Details

The goal of the following sections is to provide you with sufficient information to create a standard build document for the UNIX SA group that configures your servers. You should begin by configuring the UNIX account that owns the Oracle software, as shown in Table 1.1.

Usually, you can simply use the default options for choosing an account name and group. The Korn shell (ksh) is chosen because it's very similar to the Bourne shell (sh) (which Oracle uses to develop its own scripts) with some extra facilities such as a command history. No DBA should be expected to work in a shell without a command history. Standardizing the shell makes it possible to standardize a set of aliases for common commands. If you ever wondered why Oracle doesn't use the Korn shell, it's because Oracle was shipping UNIX systems before ksh existed. On some non-Sun systems (such as Linux) where ksh is not available, the Bash shell provides similar capabilities.

The Oracle account UNIX home directory should be set to the value of $ORACLE_BASE, where $ORACLE_BASE is traditionally set to /u01/app/oracle as defined by the Oracle Optimal Flexible Architecture (OFA) standard. The OFA standard should be followed religiously for all your Oracle software and database layouts. This book assumes that you are familiar with it. It's well documented at www.oracle.com.

A local password file should be used to authenticate the account rather than a network account, and you should consider giving the Oracle account a different password on each server. This means more effort for the DBA because a repository is required to

Table 1.1   Oracle UNIX Account Details

SETTING	VALUE
Oracle UNIX account name	oracle
Oracle UNIX group	dba
Login shell	ksh
Oracle configuration files directory	/var/opt/oracle or /etc (owner oracle, group dba)
Oracle $HOME	$ORACLE_BASE (owner oracle, group dba)
Authentication	local password file

track all the passwords. But if you use a single network logon and someone cracks the password, they have DBA access to all your databases. Your security audit group might want to talk to you about that. But security isn't necessarily about making life easy for the DBA; it's about protecting your systems.

Oracle UNIX Memory Requirements

Ensure that at least 400MB are free in /tmp because the Oracle Installer uses temporary space. Ensure that the system has an absolute minimum of 256MB of RAM. Determining your memory requirements is discussed later in the book. Make sure that at least double the amount of physical memory is available in swap space. To avoid excessive paging, which severely degrades performance, you don't want your memory requirements to exceed physical available memory by much. Chapter 28 explains how to detect when excessive paging is taking place.

Oracle UNIX Kernel Requirements

Set the following UNIX kernel parameters as below, and ensure that the system is booted with these in effect. These settings are needed for your database creation (covered in detail in Chapter 2) to succeed:

```
set shmsys:shminfo_shmmax=4294967295
set shmsys:shminfo_shmmin=1
set shmsys:shminfo_shmseg=10
set shmsys:shminfo_shmmni=100
set semsys:seminfo_semmns=1000
set semsys:seminfo_semmni=100
set semsys:seminfo_semmsl=250
```

The values listed above relate to Sun Solaris, but most UNIX flavors use similar terminology. Note that shmsys:shminfo_shmmax is not the size of shared memory to allocate; it's a high watermark value, so you can set it higher for 64-bit versions of Oracle if required. By building in a high value, you avoid having to increase it and reboot the system later if more real memory is added. It's the DBA's responsibility to ensure that any shared memory allocated by Oracle fits appropriately into available memory.

Operating System Release

Consult the Oracle Operating System documentation to check the patches required, and ask your SA to patch the system if necessary. If this step is overlooked, it can result in mystifying and intermittent errors.

Oracle Software Installation Directory

The OFA recommendation is to use a top-level directory of:

```
/u01
Minimum size 4Gb, >100000 inodes
```

Use an $ORACLE_BASE (top-level directory for the Oracle software tree) of:

```
/u01/app/oracle
```

The OFA standard is flexible enough to allow other choices for the top-level directory. For example, if the file system contains only Oracle software, you might choose /ora01 instead, to indicate the Oracle-specific contents. This book uses the Oracle OFA default of /u*nn* (where *nn* is a two-digit number) in all examples to indicate file systems containing Oracle databases and software.

It's essential that the /u01 file system is configured by your SA with sufficient UNIX inodes to hold all the Oracle installation files. Oracle 9*i* includes more than 100,000 files. If the number of inodes is not sufficient, the installation proceeds until the number of inodes is exhausted, at which point an error is reported. The installation then needs to be repeated after the number of available inodes has been increased.

NOTE Every Oracle DBA should be familiar with OFA. We will be adopting it along with some extensions not covered by the standard throughout the book.

An OFA-style installation of Oracle software based on a top level of /u01 is shown in Figure 1.1.

The contents of /u01 must contain only Oracle software under /product and Oracle database instance-related files under /admin. All contents below /u01 are maintained by the Oracle DBA group and this requirement must be enforced through UNIX privileges. No other group should have write access to the underlying file system. This is because you need to monitor space on the file system to ensure that Oracle has space for its log and trace files. To do that, you need total control of the contents. If you allow write access to other groups, the temptation to dump scratch data and junk on what is apparently available space might be too good to resist.

Your UNIX SA Group might prefer to install the Oracle software under /usr/local, or another standard UNIX directory. That doesn't sound unreasonable at first, but it doesn't meet the OFA standard, which is based on very sound principles that are

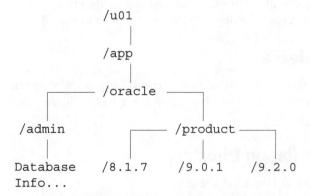

Figure 1.1   An OFA directory structure for Oracle software.

proven to work. In this scenario, you need to sell the OFA standard to your SA Group. Here's one advantage of OFA: By installing Oracle under a unique name (/u01), you pretty much guarantee that if you merge your organization at a later time with another division or company, the others can adopt your /u01 name without any problems. It is almost certain that /u01 won't already be in use for a different purpose.

Request a file system with at least 4GB of free space to allow for a complete installation of Oracle Server Enterprise Edition (a minimum of 2.6GB for Oracle9*i*) and associated logs. Seriously consider allocating space up front for two complete Oracle software versions to coexist, ensuring that when upgrade time comes around, you don't have to request additional space. You'll find that migration is easier as a result.

Installation of Oracle Software via NFS

Traditionally, before you run the Oracle Installer, you need to arrange for a local CD-ROM drive to be mounted, or a CD-ROM drive to be remote mounted from another server (assuming that your server has no local drive). You might have to wait for an SA to become available to do the work and, depending on your organization, you might be required to follow a Change Control procedure that introduces further delay. This could happen each time you install Oracle on a server.

By copying the CD contents onto disk first and using this disk copy as the basis for all installs, you can avoid this SA dependency in the future and speed up your installations. Installing the Oracle software from the CD-ROM just one time makes the Oracle software (and subsequent patches) available for installation on all the UNIX servers on your network without any dependency on the availability of the CD media or an SA.

The key to this approach is the NFS. Every major operating system has an NFS implementation, and it is used in almost every UNIX environment worldwide. It provides a convenient mechanism for sharing data across platforms, particularly in read-only situations such as the delivery of software. As such, it is an excellent fit with our requirements for installing Oracle quickly and reliably on all servers, and providing an identical configuration on each one.

WARNING   Using NFS to run the installed Oracle software is often the subject of debate. I don't recommend it and I'll explain why in the *Running Oracle Software over NFS* section later in this chapter.

After the SA has mounted the first CD in the Oracle ship set onto one server in the DBA Cluster (ora1.uk.dbcool.com), use the UNIX recursive copy command to copy the mounted CD contents onto the following disk directory structure, assuming that a local CD drive has been mounted under the name /cdrom:

```
$ cd /cdrom/orcl901_1

$ mkdir -p /u01/app/oracle/admin/cdrom/9.0.1/Disk1

$ cp -pr . /u01/app/oracle/admin/cdrom/9.0.1/Disk1
```

Repeat the process for each CD-ROM, copying each one into a separate directory (Disk1, Disk2, Disk3). After this exercise is completed, you have the Oracle installation contents on disk in a format that can be mounted onto other systems for installation purposes, or copied onto a local disk first and installed from there.

The choice of Disk1, Disk2, and Disk3 as the directory names is important. These names enable the Oracle Installer to identify the location of the next CD contents on disk automatically during installation without prompting you for them. That's actually an improvement on a CD-based installation because the disk-based version doesn't require you to change the CDs. As a result, you avoid potential Device Busy messages that occur because the current working directory of the session is set to the CD-ROM mount point. Your operating-system-specific Installation and User Guide (IUG) should include notes that warn you not to start installation from the CD directory, but it's easy to overlook them.

After you have the CD contents on disk on one node in the DBA Cluster, you can file the CD-ROM away in your software library. From ora1.uk.dbcool.com, copy the whole tree to the other server in the DBA Cluster, making sure you've configured rcp connectivity as described earlier in the chapter:

```
$ cd /u01/app/oracle/admin/cdrom/9.0.1

$ rsh ora2.uk.dbcool.com "mkdir -p /u01/app/oracle/admin/cdrom/9.0.1"

$ rcp -pr . ora2.uk.dbcool.com:/u01/app/oracle/admin/cdrom/9.0.1
```

You now have two binary-identical copies of the CD installation media on the two servers in the DBA Cluster. I strongly recommend at this point that you plan to retrospectively copy *all* your Oracle CD installation media (including previous versions) onto these two servers. It can be very unsettling to find yourself in a disaster recovery situation that needs the reinstallation of some long forgotten version of Oracle for which the installation CDs can't be located. The solution is to make sure that you have on disk all the media for all versions of Oracle that you run, and that you cross-check the versions of Oracle in use by your applications with the media on disk. As this stage, the Oracle installation software is available on two different servers and needs to be made available to the local server where the install is required. One approach is for the SA to mount the software explicitly from one server in the DBA Cluster. However, if the software is mounted from ora1.uk.dbcool.com, and that server is not available, an install isn't possible without having an SA change the mount to use ora2.uk.dbcool.com instead. What's needed is for the software to be available at all times from whichever server is available, without requiring the DBA to know which one is currently in use. Your SA can provide the solution to this problem through the features furnished by UNIX automount, and the replication facilities of NFS. A detailed discussion of these features is beyond the scope of this book. However, it's simple to explain what happens when such a configuration is in place. When automount and NFS replication are used to provide access to the Oracle software, the DBA can change to the following automount directory on the local server and find the Oracle software available read only at:

```
/u01/app/oracle/admin/cdrom
```

In this case, automount and NFS work together (as configured by the SA) to ensure that the remote software is mounted automatically from whichever of the following directories is available:

```
ora1.uk.dbcool.com:/u01/app/oracle/admin/cdrom/9.0.1

ora2.uk.dbcool.com:/u01/app/oracle/admin/cdrom/9.0.1
```

As a result, if ora1.uk.dbcool.com is down, the software is made available to the local server from ora2.uk.dbcool.com under the same local directory (/u01/app/oracle/admin/cdrom).

Your OFA software configuration on the installation machine has now been extended to include an additional automount directory (/u01/app/oracle/admin/cdrom) through which the Oracle CD-ROM installation media (held on disk on the DBA Cluster servers) is always available (as shown in Figure 1.2). The implementation

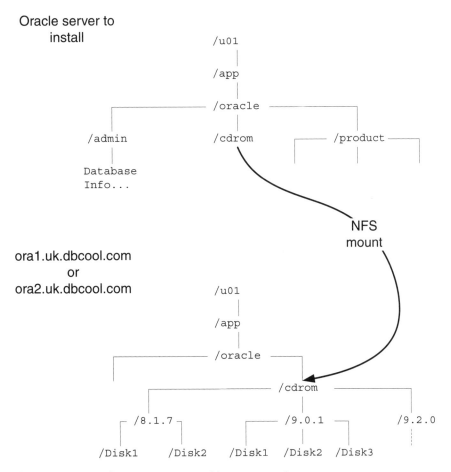

Figure 1.2 OFA directory structure with NFS extensions.

of the cdrom directory as a remote NFS mount onto one or the other of two machines is completely transparent to the local user.

NFS replication transparently ensures that one of the remote file systems is always automounted on the local directory. Provided that you've designed the DBA Cluster so that at least one server is always available, the Oracle software is always available.

Before running the Installer, you might choose to protect yourself from a lack of temporary space in /tmp during your install by pointing the Installer to use a different temporary directory with more available space. The shell you use determines the environment variable you need to set. Running the following commands in whatever shell you use guarantees that sufficient temporary space is available during installation:

```
$ mkdir /u01/oradata/tmp
$ TMPDIR=/u01/oradata/tmp; export TMPDIR
$ TEMP=/u01/oradata/tmp; export TEMP
$ TMP=/u01/oradata/tmp; export TMP
```

Setting the following environment variables and making sure that the required directories exist saves you from typing them again when you run the Installer:

```
$ mkdir /u01/app/oracle/product/9.0.1
$ export ORACLE_HOME=/u01/app/oracle/product/9.0.1
$ export ORACLE_BASE=/u01/app/oracle
$ export PATH=/usr/ccs/bin:$ORACLE_HOME/bin:$PATH
```

If your UNIX system uses /usr/ccs/bin (and Solaris is an example), this directory must appear first in the path to ensure that Oracle uses the correct UNIX link loader and archive commands when the software is relinked during the installation. If you use a different version, you receive an error message when you start up a database. If this procedure seems convoluted, it is. Chapter 4 covers how to set up a standard Oracle UNIX runtime environment, enabling you to set the environment for a given Oracle version or database instance using a single command.

The Oracle installation program on UNIX is a Java program that requires an X Windows display. Set your UNIX DISPLAY environment variable to the X Windows server running the screen from where you'll run the Installer and check that it's a valid X display using xdpyinfo:

```
$ export DISPLAY=yourdisplay.uk.dbcool.com:0.0
$ /usr/openwin/bin/xdpyinfo
```

TIP If you are using the popular Hummingbird Exceed X Server on a Microsoft Windows PC, set the Window Manager for the screen display to Native and make sure you are running version 7.0 (or later) for best results. This ensures that screen windows for Oracle's Java-based graphical applications, such as Oracle Enterprise Manager and Oracle Installer, display correctly.

You're almost ready to run the Installer. Before you start, warn an SA that they'll need to run the root.sh script that Oracle creates during installation. If you forget,

Oracle reminds you during the installation, and it can certainly be irritating to have to delay completion of the installation because there's no one on hand to run the script. Don't ignore the requirement to run root.sh because it changes the UNIX permissions on the Oracle Intelligent Agent so that it runs as setuid root, and this is required for later tasks covered in this book. Now change to the installation media directory on the NFS mount and run the Installer:

```
$ cd /u01/app/oracle/admin/cdrom/9.0.1/Disk1
$ ./runInstaller
```

Continue by using the default responses until you reach the screen requesting the Oracle software install destination, where you should find the $ORACLE_HOME directory and the installation products list (products.jar) set already. Proceed with the installation and, if possible, avoid a custom install of the software. Pick a complete installation of the DBMS, choosing the Enterprise version only if you are licensed to run it. Note that Oracle9*i* installations are simpler than previous versions because fewer installations options are presented, and that's a good thing.

Do not create a database as part of the installation. First we must define a standard for creating the database, which is covered in Chapter 2. You should also bypass the network configuration stage during the installation, because we'll be covering networking configuration as a separate step in Chapter 3.

After the installation is complete, you might want to inspect the installation log file, although the Oracle Installer should make you aware of any errors, their causes, and possible resolutions.

Cloning the Installed Oracle Software

In the days of Oracle7, it was quite simple to take an installed Oracle software tree and copy it to another server, saving on the installation time. You simply performed a recursive copy (using rcp -pr) of the complete contents of the software under the $ORACLE_HOME directory onto the cloned server. You can still clone a software installation with Oracle8*i* and Oracle9*i*, provided that you also copy the additional files and directories that Oracle uses to run its Java engine and to keep an inventory of the installed products. These directories fall outside the $ORACLE_HOME directory. By copying these directories and files, you ensure that Oracle will work, but also (and just as important) you ensure that you're able to perform patches and upgrades in the future. These are the additional files and directories you need:

```
/var/opt/oracle/oraInst.loc   # contains the location of the inventory
/u01/app/oracle/jre           # Java runtime engine
/u01/app/oracle/oui           # Oracle Universal Installer
/u01/app/oracle/oraInventory  # inventory of installed software
```

Also, if you're running the Apache Web server from Oracle, you need to change the ServerName setting to the name of the cloned server in the Web server configuration file:

```
/u01/app/oracle/product/9.0.1/Apache/Apache/conf/httpd.conf
```

If your $ORACLE_BASE directory on both machines is different, don't attempt to clone the installation. Install it from the media or from disk copies of the media. However, if you are following the recommendations in this book, cloning is possible because your Oracle software is in the same location on all servers. After you have cloned the software, remember to relink the software using the Oracle Installer, and also remember to have the root.sh script reexecuted by the SA on the cloned machine. Relinking can be performed as a separate step by the Installer. However, product directories contain a Make file that can be used to perform a manual link without the Installer. For example, the relational DBMS (RDBMS) and related products can be relinked using the following commands:

```
$ cd $ORACLE_HOME/rdbms/lib

$ make -f ins_rdbms.mk  install
```

Performing a Silent Installation

The Oracle Installer is a graphical user interface (GUI) program that by default requires the DBA to enter configuration information during the install process. After you have standardized your local installation directory (based on OFA) and the location of the CD-ROM media on disk (based on the NFS), it's possible to run a silent installation that doesn't require user input. This results in installations with lower cost because DBAs don't need to be present during the whole installation process. Silent installation requires that you create a response (.rsp) file ahead of time to provide the input that the Installer requires.

Silent installation is essential if you need to install Oracle from a terminal that's connected to the installation server across a wide area network (WAN). For example, if you try installing Oracle using the GUI running on a PC display in India onto a server in London, you might find that the installation takes several hours. That's because the Oracle Installer GUI uses X Windows to communicate between the Installer program on the server and the X Windows screen display running on the user's terminal. X Windows is an unsuitable protocol for running over a WAN because it sends and receives lots of small packets. Using X Windows across a WAN, you can expect response times of several seconds for every keypress you make during the Installer session, and screen redrawing can take several minutes. Using a silent install based on an .rsp file solves this problem. Keep in mind that it's still necessary to set a valid X Windows DISPLAY variable on the server where the installation takes place, and to use the UNIX xhost+ command on the workstation running the X server enabling the Installer to access the display. The X display is required to initialize some Java classes in the Oracle Installer. When the silent install is running, no X Windows traffic is generated.

The construction of the .rsp file is covered in detail in the "Oracle Universal Installer Concepts Guide." Several .rsp file settings are mandatory for a silent installation, including the following, which are shown with sample values based on previous examples:

```
FROM_LOCATION="/u01/app/oracle/admin/cdrom/9.0.1/Disk1/stage/
products.jar"
```

```
LOCATION_FOR_DISK2="="/u01/app/oracle/admin/cdrom/9.0.1/Disk2"
LOCATION_FOR_DISK3="="/u01/app/oracle/admin/cdrom/9.0.1/Disk3"
ORACLE_HOME="/u01/app/oracle/product/9.0.1"
```

After the .rsp file has been created, a silent installation is initiated using a command line like this one:

```
$ ./runInstaller -silent -responseFile /tmp/901install.rsp
```

Actions performed during installation can be monitored by inspecting the contents of the following files located in oraInventory/logs:

```
installActions.log
silentInstall.log
oraInstall.err
oraInstall.out
```

Running Oracle Software over NFS

On Web discussion groups and bulletin boards, you frequently see discussions about whether it's a good idea to run Oracle software from an NFS mount. Keep in mind that at this stage, the scope of Oracle software sharing has been limited to the sharing of the installation media, followed by installation of the Oracle software onto a local file system. I believe that sharing the installation media is a very good idea. However, running Oracle software from an NFS mount is a completely different requirement. At first, it has a significant attraction because it means that you install the software only once, and then run it on multiple servers, reducing maintenance. On deeper investigation, I believe that running Oracle software from an NFS mount is a bad idea, and that, far from reducing maintenance, it leads to maintenance problems. The rest of this section presents issues (listed below) that you should consider before running Oracle software via NFS:

- Oracle version dependencies
- Network dependencies
- Delayed write-caching problems
- Time synchronization problems

Side Effects of Oracle Version Dependencies

Recall that in Figure 1.1, the Oracle software is installed under directories using three digits to identify the Oracle version number (for example, 9.0.1). Oracle defines the fourth digit in the version number as a patch release on which you don't need to regression test your software. The first three digits are the most significant when you take the delivery of Oracle applications because they identify the release used to develop and test the application.

This means that when one application running NFS-mounted Oracle software needs an Oracle code patch upgrade, all applications automatically take the same patch.

This upgrade requires an outage of all applications sharing the code. Also, problems sometimes occur when application code regresses (that is, fails to work correctly) where a fourth digit patch is made. So, for applications requiring the highest availability, you can't afford to have them sharing Oracle software releases. If you're like me, you probably don't even apply fourth-digit patches without insisting on regression testing your applications because you've been stung by this in the past.

You could install Oracle to the fourth digit under the . . . /product directory and upgrade your Oracle applications that need the new version individually, leaving the third-digit installation unchanged. The downside in that case is that you need to change the $ORACLE_HOME of that application, the Oracle network listener, and possibly the scripts that depend on the $ORACLE_HOME. All those changes introduce the risk of a mistake followed by an unplanned application outage. If you use a local disk installation of the Oracle software, you don't need to worry about these issues because they don't apply.

Introduction of Network Dependencies

If you run Oracle software via NFS, a network outage prevents Oracle sessions from starting. This introduces the possibility of causing Oracle application outages that would simply not occur when running software installed on the local disk. The possibility might be small, but it is finite.

Delayed Write Caching

In an effort to improve efficiency, some NFS implementations cache write operations on the local machine to batch them before sending the large packages more efficiently across the network. This means that information might not be written to the server holding the information for several seconds, with a potential for loss of data, such as logging and trace information written to database instance log and alert files.

Time Synchronization

NFS does not synchronize the time between the local machine and server. This makes for the possibility that the timestamps on log and trace files on the NFS server can differ from the time the client wrote the information. This can lead to confusion when you are analyzing trace and log files on the server, where the chronology of events is important. Of course, you can synchronize the time between servers (usually via the UNIX NTP command), and your organization probably has time servers in place to do that, but once again this is a nonissue when running locally installed software.

Installing Client Software with Microsoft Systems Management Server (SMS)

The previous section covered how to install Oracle DBMS software onto your UNIX servers. This section describes how to efficiently install the Oracle client software for

PCs using Microsoft Systems Management Server (SMS). SMS is a technology that companies use to perform hardware and software inventory, software distribution, and remote diagnostic services for the Windows desktops in the organization. The decision to invest in SMS is typically made by senior technical architects in an organization (not the DBA group), usually to save costs on managing PCs across the enterprise. If your company manages hundreds or even thousands of Windows desktops manually, it stands to gain massive savings by standardizing its desktops as a result of controlling how all software is delivered and supported.

The DBA group can take advantage of SMS deployment by using its software distribution services. Delivery of the packaged Oracle software is as simple as the SMS administrator using a GUI to drag an icon (representing the package) from the SMS and drop it onto an icon representing a group of PCs. These PCs are SMS clients, running a software agent that communicates with the SMS server and enables the PC to take delivery of packages.

The same delivery effort is required whether the group represents all the PCs in your organization or just a subset. This voids the need for site visits to install Oracle or troubleshoot problems resulting from manual installation. At last, the direct relationship between the number of desktops and the number of people required to support them is broken. The outcome is a more reliable desktop, and fewer outages arising from business user application failures. These outages escalate support costs and, if the business function compromised by the outage generates revenue, they can affect your company's bottom line directly.

As with any piece of infrastructure that you implement at the organization level, it has a greater cost up front in terms of planning and design. Microsoft offers real-life case studies to help you demonstrate the cost savings.

From the DBA's point of view, using SMS means that the DBA group must take responsibility for specifying (as opposed to actually creating) the SMS package required to standardize the Oracle client software delivered to the desktop. Creating SMS packages requires a certain expertise, and the DBA group can expect to work closely with the SMS technicians. As any package, it is likely to be deployed across the organization as part of the standard build for all PCs, so the time invested pays off quickly. If your DBA staff spends many hours a week, most weeks, diagnosing Oracle database connectivity issues from the desktop, you are in a prime position for taking advantage of SMS. If your user sites are spread across many locations, the savings are even greater because you can eliminate the overhead of traveling time.

Using SMS Packages

SMS uses a before-and-after snapshot technique to identify all changes made to the desktop during the running of a product installation script. For example, during an Oracle client installation, the Oracle Installer makes changes to the Windows registry, creates disk folders and files, and modifies the Windows environment. An SMS package, at the most simplistic level, stores the desktop changes for the installation process in a single set of instructions that can then be replayed onto another PC on demand. In addition, other changes to the desktop can be programmed into the package. For example, you can set the TNS_ADMIN environment symbol to point to a particular folder and provide a sqlnet.ora file to reside there. As a result, you can always find Oracle's network configuration files in the same place, no matter how many versions of the Oracle client software exist on the desktop.

A basic SMS package for an Oracle Windows client should include the following products as a minimum:

- Oracle software for TCP/IP support
- SQL*Plus
- Oracle Installer

The base Oracle networking software is noted for its reliability. SQL*Plus enables connectivity to be tested, and the Oracle Installer enables you to find out the installed list of Oracle products. The DBA simply needs to provide the SMS team with the Oracle software installation media and documented instructions to run the Installer for the products listed. The SMS team creates the package. Testing is performed by the Oracle team and typically consists of a series of connectivity tests from popular Oracle-based applications in the organization onto the back-end Oracle database servers. These components are not likely to require updating in the short to midterm, avoiding changes to the desktop environment that are notorious for causing support issues and instability.

At least some of your Oracle desktop applications are likely to have a dependency on one or more of the Oracle programmatic interfaces. These products are more likely to require patch releases. The recommendation is to package them separately and have them dependent on the base package. This additional package might contain:

- The latest Open Database Connectivity (ODBC) driver
- The latest Java Database Connectivity (JDBC) driver
- Oracle Data Objects for Windows (formerly Oracle Objects for OLE)

You might even decide to create separate packages for these products so that you can release them separately and independently. The base package should be configured to make additional changes to the Oracle client environment, on top of those made by the Oracle Installer in the areas of folders and environment symbols. Table 1.2 shows the extra folders that should be created by your Oracle client package, above and beyond the folders created by the Oracle Installer.

Table 1.2 Additional Oracle Folders for an SMS Client Package

FOLDER NAME	PURPOSE
c:\var\opt\oracle	Location of the sqlnet.ora file
c:\u01\app\oracle\network\trace	Location of network trace files
c:\u01\app\oracle\network\log	Location of network log files
c:\u01\app\oracle\product\9.0.1 c:\u01\app\oracle\product\8.1.7	Version-specific installation folder for each Oracle software release, specified during Oracle Installer session

Table 1.3 Additional Environment and Registry Settings

SETTING	VALUE
TNS_ADMIN environment variable	c:\var\opt\oracle
TcpMaxConnectRetransmissions	1

Table 1.3 shows the additional environment and registry setting that should be created by your Oracle client package, above and beyond those created by the Oracle Installer.

TcpMaxConnectRetransmissions is a registry key used to minimize the time for Oracle name-to-address resolution requests to fallback to the next Oracle Names server, when the first one is not available. Oracle Names is covered in Chapter 3. The retransmission setting is set in the following registry location:

```
\HKEY_LOCAL_MACHINE\SYSTEM\CurrentControlSet\Services\Tcpip\Parameters
```

Fixing the locations of trace files, log files, and the location of Oracle's names directory list (sqlnet.ora) ensures that—in the case of a problem—the Oracle DBA knows where to find the files. By default, the network log files are placed in the folder from which any Oracle-enabled application is launched. As a result, they can be difficult to locate, more so on a machine that uses many network shares. The sqlnet.ora file is placed by default in an Oracle software version-specific directory, which can lead to multiple copies of the file coexisting on disk if multiple versions of the Oracle client software exist. If a problem occurs on the client, what inevitably follows is the problem of determining which file is actually used by which application. By fixing the location of the sqlnet.ora file through the TNS_ADMIN setting, only one sqlnet.ora needs to be present on the PC, and this can be shared by all applications irrespective of the Oracle software version they are using. The contents of the sqlnet.ora file are explored in detail in Chapter 3, but here's a sneak preview that shows how the locations of the log and trace files can be specified (given the previously created folders):

```
AUTOMATIC_IPC = OFF
trace_directory_client = c:\u01\app\oracle\network\trace
LOG_DIRECTORY_CLIENT=c:\u01\app\oracle\network\log
names.directory_path = (TNSNAMES,ONAMES)
names.preferred_servers=
(address_list =
    (address =
        (protocol = TCP)
        (port = 1575)
        (host = oranames1.uk.dbcool.com)
    )
    (address =
        (protocol = TCP)
        (port = 1575)
        (host = oranames2.uk.dbcool.com)
    )
)
```

Notice that the folder names I've chosen for the installation location of the Oracle software match those for the installation of the Oracle DBMS software on the UNIX server (apart from the direction of the slashes). Your organization might have naming standards in place that don't allow this. If it doesn't, what could be simpler from a support perspective than using the same directories on the client and server?

It's worth mentioning before closing this discussion that Oracle does not support the installation of Oracle software using SMS. Before you throw up your hands in horror, what this actually means is that if you encounter any problems resulting from your SMS-installed Oracle software, Oracle Worldwide Support (WWS) won't resolve or submit bugs for those problems unless the same problems can be demonstrated by installing the software via the Oracle Installer. My personal experience is that Oracle software installed via SMS offers nothing but benefits, and by thorough testing of your SMS Oracle packages before deployment, you'll get the same degree of confidence in the process that I have. Finally, remember that the snapshot technique used to create the package is a record of what the Oracle Installer itself does during an installation, so in effect, an SMS drop of the Oracle client software onto a PC is the same as running the Installer manually.

Running Terminal Server Applications

Standardizing your PC build through the use of SMS might introduce logistical issues with installing and running applications. For example, consider a situation where your organization has outsourced a development project to an offshore data center (ODC), the environment doesn't support SMS, and the ODC has no intention of adopting it. Or consider a situation where the packaged applications themselves are several hundred MB in size, and the clients are situated over a WAN where delivery of the software could take several hours for each PC. In either case, even if you could install the software via SMS, you still have the possibility that those applications might be sending many thousands of database records across the network for display in the client application at runtime.

In this case, the use of Citrix Metaframe and Microsoft Windows Terminal Server might be a solution to these concerns. In this configuration, all application processing is performed on a server running Windows 2000 or Windows NT Terminal Server Edition. A special client application known as the Citrix Independent Computing Architecture (ICA) client simply provides the application display, and the only information transferred across the network consists of screen frames, and keyboard and mouse movements. This can result in applications using as little as 10 percent of their usual network bandwidth, and the application looks and behaves exactly as if you were running it from a local PC. Problems with Terminal Server usually relate to product installation issues, often involving the Windows registry settings. If you understand the concept of running a UNIX X Windows application (such as the Oracle Installer) using a PC for the X Server display, the concept is similar with the ICA client taking the place of the X display. Figure 1.3 shows how network bandwidth can be saved using a Citrix Metaframe configuration.

The Citrix/Microsoft infrastructure typically provides load balancing by making a collection of servers (referred to as a server farm) available to service requests from

(a) Traditional Two-Tier Application

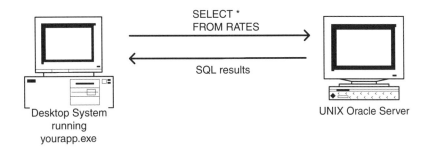

(b) Same Application on Citrix

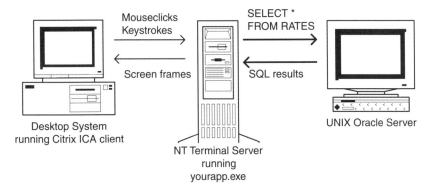

Figure 1.3   Standard versus Citrix configuration.

potentially many users running applications on the same server at the same time. The support implications from Oracle's perspective are the same as using SMS to deliver Oracle software: Oracle expects you to duplicate the problem in a non-Citrix environment first. Once again, I can personally vouch for the success of many projects running applications on Terminal Server. Oracle actually does support the use of Citrix for running the Application Desktop Integrator (ADI) component of Oracle Financials, so this solution is not a totally unknown quantity for Oracle Support.

Unfortunately, it's not possible to deliver software to your Terminal Servers via SMS 2.0. Microsoft is likely to address this at some point, as it seems reasonable to use SMS to deliver packaged software onto any Windows platform in your organization. In any case, the lack of SMS delivery isn't the drawback it might first appear to be. The number of Terminal Servers you run is probably orders of magnitude less than the number of user desktops you support, so the number of manual installations of the Oracle software is limited.

Summary

You should now be able to create a standard build document for your UNIX SA group that will become the basis for the initial configuration of all Oracle server builds in your organization, as well as a companion document that contains a requirements specification for an Oracle SMS client package for the desktop. Using a DBA Cluster of at least two servers, you also have a step-by-step guide to configuring the environment to support the installation. You now have your Oracle software installed on the client and the server, and you are ready to create a database (which is covered in Chapter 2).

Database Creation

This chapter covers how to create an Oracle database to meet the requirements of performance and availability. This involves covering subjects such as defining naming standards for the file components of the database, designing a physical layout, choosing a character set, and determining a block size. This chapter is one of the longer chapters in the book because much has changed in terms of Oracle9*i* features and the underlying hardware architectures that are available for deploying an Oracle database. Oracle has made claims of a 40 percent reduction in administration costs in Oracle9*i*, and although the actual figure is contentious, it's certainly true that Oracle has added features that can reduce administration costs. Along the way, we'll consider the age-old debate of using raw partitions versus UNIX file systems. This is often presented as a religious-style argument with both camps firmly entrenched, armed, and ready for a war of attrition. I don't believe that needs to be the case, and like anything else having to do with physical layout, you simply need to make a call based on the costs and benefits of each approach. The discussion comes down to the relative importance of performance versus availability for your application.

Storage area network (SAN) and network-attached storage (NAS) technologies represent the future for storage in most organizations and will lead to a fundamental change in the role of a database administrator (DBA) with respect to the physical layout of the database.

This chapter covers the following topics:

- Oracle file types
- Traditional Oracle physical layout

- A new layout approach for manageability based on Oracle-Managed Files (OMF)

- Server parameter files (spfiles)

- The physical layout for performance based on Redundant Array of Independent Disks (RAID)

- SAN and NAS for Oracle databases

An Overview of Oracle File Types

It's useful to briefly review the distinct types of files and their functions in an Oracle database because the file types have historically had a close association with physical storage. These types can be grouped under the following headings:

- Control files

- Tablespace datafiles

- Online redo log files

- Archived redo logs

- Rollback segments, if not using Oracle9i undo tablespaces

- Temporary segments

Control Files

Control files maintain a list of the other files in the database, the database name, and system change number (SCN). The SCN is a number (internally generated and maintained by the database) that increases with each data change made by end-user applications; a unique SCN is assigned to every committed transaction. Chapter 17 on backup and recovery fundamentals describes the SCN in more depth. From Oracle8i on, the control file also maintains a list of Recovery Manager (RMAN) backups. This explains why the control file can increase in size over time as more backup information is stored in it. Loss of the control file means that the database stops working, so a database usually uses a minimum of two, which Oracle maintains as mirrors of each other. The database can continue to operate provided that one control file is available. Traditionally, each control file is stored on a separate disk; however, with the increasing virtualization of storage space presented by volume managers, it can be difficult for the DBA to control the placement at the physical disk level because such information is not readily available.

Tablespaces

An Oracle database is divided into logical units of storage called *tablespaces*. Tablespaces themselves consist of operating system disk files or raw partitions. All database objects (such as tables and indexes) in an Oracle database are stored in tablespaces. From the DBA's perspective, tablespaces have the capability to control disk allocation for data objects and therefore enable the distribution of data across physical devices for the purpose of input/output (I/O) balancing. The tablespace is the largest unit of data that can be taken offline as a single unit (with the exception of the whole database, which can be taken offline by a database shutdown). This is useful if you need to rebuild parts of a database while keeping the rest online. In an index-driven type of application, where the design is intended to avoid table scans, the I/O patterns on tablespaces tend to be random on both the table and indexes. To manage space efficiently, the DBA needs to play close attention to the FREELIST, FREELIST GROUPS, PCTFREE, and PTCUSED settings for objects in a given tablespace, as well as the OPTIMAL setting for rollback segments. These are covered in more detail in Chapter 13 on managing space growth.

Every Oracle database contains a special tablespace called SYSTEM, which is created at database creation time to hold the data dictionary. The SYSTEM tablespace is *always* online when the database is open and should never be used to store user objects.

Online Redo Log Files

Every Oracle database must have a set of a least two online redo log file groups. Each group can contain one or more members. The members in a group are mirrors of each other. The database continues to run provided that at least one member in each group is accessible. Traditionally, each member in a group is located on a separate disk (to avoid a single point of failure), but storage virtualization presents the same challenge to placement as that posed to control files. The set of log groups can be viewed as a circular queue: When one redo log group is filled, the system moves on to the next and eventually circulates back to the first. Redo logs are written in a sequential fashion: The next write begins where the last one left off.

Archived Redo Logs

To protect the database from a media failure, a database must run in ARCHIVELOG mode. In this mode, as online redo logs are filled, they are archived to a disk directory before they can be reused. These files are referred to as *archived redo logs*. In the event of a media failure, the most recent database backup can be restored and all changes can be made because the backup can be applied from the archived redo logs to recover the database. Oracle's archiving of logs takes place in the background. It is managed by the ARCH process, is designed to be fast enough that it completes before an online redo log needs to be reused, and is at a low enough priority that it doesn't affect the overall system performance.

The size of the online redo logs influences the online performance and recovery time. During a log switch, a checkpoint that flushes dirty buffers to disk occurs. As checkpoints can degrade performance, many DBAs choose to allocate large online redo logs (sometimes hundreds of megabytes in size) to minimize the number of checkpoints. The improved performance from large online redo logs leads to potentially slower recovery after an instance crash, due to the requirement for Oracle to apply a redo in the logs before the database can open. It's also possible to run an Oracle database in NOARCHIVELOG mode, but if you do that, you have no protection from disk failures that require point-in-time recovery.

Rollback Segments

A database usually has several rollback segments in a dedicated tablespace. These have a dual purpose. On one hand, they store prechange data to provide a rollback of uncommitted transactions. On the other hand, they provide read-consistent views of data for queries.

Transactions are assigned to a rollback segment based on two simple rules. First, Oracle tries to assign a new transaction to a rollback segment that has the fewest number of active transactions. If no single segment meets this requirement, then the transaction is assigned to a segment in order to keep undo information available for the longest possible time for use in a read-consistent view. Read consistency guarantees that a query either returns data as it was at the time the query began or it fails. For that reason, data for committed transactions in rollback segments can be very valuable. This is why Oracle tries to keep it for as long as possible rather than freeing it immediately after a transaction commits.

The extents in a rollback segment are used in a circular fashion, moving from one to the next after the current extent is full. Multiple transactions can exist in a single extent at the same time. A transaction writes a record to the current location (the head) of the rollback segment and moves the head to the next location. When the head wraps around and catches up with the tail (the location of the oldest active transaction), the rollback segment allocates a new extent because undo data for active transactions can't be reused until either a commit or rollback takes place. However, if the data in the segment is no longer active, because it has been committed or rolled back, then the space can be reused. This reuse takes place even if the inactive data is required to generate a read-consistent view of old data for a long-running query that's still in progress. At the point when the long-running query realizes that the old data no longer exists (because a newer transaction overwrote it), then the famous "ORA-01555: snapshot too old" error is reported. This is Oracle's way of telling the user that it couldn't keep the old data long enough and had to reuse it for another transaction.

Oracle's action for this error is to use larger rollback segments. This is somewhat misleading as you probably have space available in other segments that you could free up instead.

Historically, Oracle's rollback segment design has given the DBA a performance and availability headache due to the dual purpose of the data in the segment. The story goes something like this. For performance, it's a good idea to have several rollback segments in order to support several concurrent transactions and avoid rollback segment contention. As transactions can't span rollback segments, the total pool of rollback space must be fragmented across several smaller segments. Fragmenting the total space into smaller parts has the side effect of limiting the size of the largest transaction because the total pool of free space is never available to a single transaction. To address this, you can set an OPTIMAL value on a rollback segment to cause rollback segments to shrink by freeing up inactive extents back to the total pool of free space at appropriate times. However, freeing up inactive extents to make room for large transactions can inadvertently free up old inactive data required for read-consistent views, resulting in ORA-01555.

Every Oracle DBA has experienced the frustration of having to repeat a long-running operation that failed with an ORA-01555 or ran out of rollback space. For example, an

ORA-01555 can result from an index build that failed after a long period of time. The read-consistent view of the table data needed to create the index could not be generated due to the changing data in the table and other short concurrent transactions that caused the read-consistent prechange data to be overwritten in the rollback segment. Even more frustrating, the fragmentation of the pool of rollback space across several segments can cause a large transaction to run out of rollback space, causing a massive amount of redo information to be generated upon rollback, followed by a similar amount upon a repeat of the transaction after extending the space or manually shrinking the segments. The traditional solutions to these problems include a combination of a massive overallocation of rollback space, a reduction in the number of rollback segments, manual shrinking, or database "babysitting" to monitor the rollback segments to ensure that they don't fill up. It's possible to use the SET TRANSACTION USE ROLLBACK SEGMENT command to explicitly associate a given transaction with a specific rollback segment. In this case, a large rollback segment is kept offline until it's needed for a particularly large transaction, when it's then placed online for use by the large transaction. Using this approach, you need to keep in mind that after it's online, you can't prevent Oracle from assigning other transactions to that same rollback segment.

Clearly, rollback segments present a management challenge for the DBA. With Oracle9*i*, there's excellent news because Oracle provides a special undo tablespace, which is covered later in the chapter, to solve the problems of rollback segment management by managing them automatically, banishing ORA-01555 to the history books.

Temporary Segments

During query processing, Oracle might require disk space for various intermediate stages of processing that require a sort. Sorting is required during query processing for statements containing, for example, GROUP BY and ORDER BY statements. The creation of large indexes also typically requires large amounts of sort space. Oracle attempts to perform sort operations in memory if resources are available using a memory buffer whose size, by default, is determined by the sort_area_size parameter. The sort_area_size parameter can be set dynamically using the ALTER SESSION command; otherwise, the default initialization parameter value is used. Default parameter values can be found in the v$parameter view. If the sort buffer is not sufficiently large, Oracle allocates temporary segments on disk on behalf of the user performing the Structured Query Language (SQL) operation. By default, an Oracle account uses the SYSTEM tablespace for sorting unless the DBA remembers to assign a temporary tablespace to the user at creation time. The use of SYSTEM for user sorting can cause severe performance degradation or fill up the SYSTEM tablespace so that data dictionary objects can't extend, causing the database to stop.

Oracle9*i* provides two new initialization parameters—pga_aggregate_target and workarea_size_policy—that enable the database to autotune the sort area size. These parameters together enable an appropriate value to be chosen to meet the sort requirements based on the current memory available and the maximum associated with pga_aggregate_target. By default, autotuning is off and is enabled by setting workarea_size_policy=true. It's worth mentioning that the hash_area_size, bitmap_merge_size, and create_bitmap_area_size can also take advantage of autotuning facilities.

Traditional Oracle Physical Layout

Given the types of files described earlier in this chapter, an optimal layout for the best Oracle performance would necessarily involve many disks. One disk would be needed for each redo log group, a set of disks would be required for table data (with data striped across them), and another set of disks would be required for indexes (with data striped across them). Striping involves splitting logical volumes of storage into fixed-sized chunks of data across multiple physical disks to balance I/O and improve performance. Another disk would be needed for archived redo logs and yet another for rollback segment data. Physical disks are then grouped into discrete pools of independently managed space at the UNIX operating system level through the creation of several file systems. I've set up databases like this myself, but not for a long time.

The reason for my change of heart came over time as I noticed the support issues of fragmenting the total available database space across many relatively small files and file systems. The issues with this fragmentation seemed to cause more outages for users and more administration issues for DBAs than performance problems cause. In any case, in the long term, it usually turned out that the 9GB disk (remember that this was the mid- to late 1990s—nowadays it's 36GB or higher) allocated to the redo logs would eventually have to be "sacrificed" to hold table and index data; the business people wouldn't countenance the waste of disk space. This turned out to be a forerunner of the cost issues that have come to the fore with the implementation of SANs. All of a sudden the business people are charged for every gigabyte of storage they rent, and they want to be sure they aren't overpaying because space isn't used efficiently.

Oracle Layout for Manageability

Let's take a step back for a moment and look at the DBA's requirements for Oracle physical layout. These requirements are for performance and availability. You could add manageability to that list, but in my opinion, manageability is synonymous with availability. When I use those two terms, they're almost interchangeable. Let's concentrate on availability first and see what happens.

The easiest and most flexible way to lay out an Oracle database for the highest availability from a DBA's perspective is to put all the files on a single, large file system. The following are some of the areas that show enhanced manageability when you do this. You'll almost certainly find that there other potential issues that suddenly become non-issues simply because you keep all the space for databases on a server available in a single file system, where it's available to any datafile or any database on that server that needs the space. Nothing is wasted.

AUTOEXTEND

You can turn AUTOEXTEND on for your files. This reduces the possibly that an application will fail because an object can't extend. All datafiles can use all available space. It doesn't matter if your TRADES table suddenly experiences 10 times the expected growth rates because your company decides to take on some extra data processing work. The reason it doesn't matter is because all the space on the file system is available for the TRADES table to grow into. This doesn't mean that you stop monitoring database growth. However, it does mean that you can reduce outages from lack of space because they should never happen unless the disk is full. Availability is improved. Using AUTOEXTEND means that you don't have to add datafiles to your database; you can just let them grow. Your datafiles are no longer restricted to the size of a small file system. Adding datafiles to a database is a potentially risky operation because there's always a chance that the operation will fail because you've reached the maxdatafiles limit for the control file. In this case, you need to recreate the control file, which is an outage to your database, followed by a tricky control file rebuild. You can avoid it by not adding files, and you can avoid adding files by making sure that existing files have space to grow.

Archive Logs

When a large transaction rolls back, the archived redo logs generated no longer need to fill the disk, causing the database to freeze, because the whole space of the file system is available to hold the extra logs, which can be backed up and removed in good time.

Database Restores

When you suddenly need to restore or copy another database onto your server, you know that if the total size of the database is less than the available space on the file system, then the database is guaranteed to fit. This is a simple piece of arithmetic you can do in your head. You don't need to get a spreadsheet out and spend a couple of hours working out how to remap the backup files onto the restore file systems in a way that makes them fit as you would do with multiple smaller file systems. As a result, you can get the task done faster and your restored or copied system is available sooner.

Database Backups and Exports

You know that an RMAN database backup to disk fits by checking if the file system free space is less than the physical size of the database you're backing up. The same goes for an export: If file system space is fragmented across several smaller file systems, you don't know in advance if the output file fits; you need to either spend extra time checking that it fits or rerun the command if it fills the space, wasting valuable time.

Duplicate Databases on the Same Server

Using a single file system, you know that you can create a clone of a database on your server using the RMAN DUPLICATE command if space is available for the source database. Better still, you can run the command knowing that the process will almost certainly work the first time because all you need to do is change the $ORACLE_SID value in the source database to the $ORACLE_SID of the cloned database in each datafilename in the source database. This is a single change to the init.ora file of the cloned database to set up the duplicate. Once again, no complicated remapping of the files to different file systems is required.

OMF

So now that you've had the opportunity to consider a new way of Oracle physical layout, you're probably holding up your hands in horror. Certain thoughts are going through your mind—thoughts like "I must have raw partitions" or "I must have my redo logs on a dedicated disk for sequential access." To add weight to the manageability benefits of a single (or just a few) large file systems, let's explore a new feature of Oracle9i called OMF.

The goal of OMF is to make database administration easier and less prone to mistakes. Using OMF means that you no longer need to specify names and locations for tablespace datafiles, online redo logs, and control files. Instead, you define a directory in your init.ora file as the default for your datafiles and one or more directories for your redo logs, with each group having a member in each of the directories you provide. Oracle then takes responsibility for naming the files in an appropriate way to identify the type of data in the files and for creating the file in the appropriate directory. For the redo log groups, it means you no longer have to deal with the hassle of locating each group member in the correct location: Oracle does it for you and ensures that you can identify the group from the generated filename.

Oracle also takes responsibility for removing the files when you drop the object that uses them. This feature alone causes many DBAs to breathe a sigh of relief. If you've ever run a DROP TABLESPACE command, you know that afterwards you should remove the underlying operating system files in the tablespace to free the physical space. However, you need to be 100 percent sure you're removing the correct files, and on a system supporting many databases, this can cause paranoia. You know that if you remove the wrong files, you've trashed the database. On the other hand, if that tablespace contains OMF, Oracle removes the constituent files for you. Even if you're not using OMF, Oracle9i provides a new option—DROP TABLESPACE INCLUDING CONTENTS *AND DATAFILES*—to enable datafiles to be removed automatically at the time a tablespace is dropped. OMF provides an automatic file remove facility for online redo log files when you use the DROP REDO LOG GROUP command. The power of OMF is easily demonstrated. In this example, you create a new database named omfd1 with an instance name of omfd1. Create the following directories first to hold the OMF because Oracle doesn't create them for you:

```
$ mkdir -p /u02/oradata/omfd1
$ mkdir -p /u03/oradata/omfd1
```

Create an init.ora file containing *nothing else* but the following entries:

```
db_name=omfd1
DB_CREATE_FILE_DEST=/u02/oradata/omfd1
DB_CREATE_ONLINE_LOG_DEST_1=/u02/oradata/omfd1
DB_CREATE_ONLINE_LOG_DEST_2=/u03/oradata/omfd1
```

Now use SQL*Plus to create the database as follows:

```
SQL> connect / as sysdba;
Connected to an idle instance.
SQL> startup nomount
 .
 .
 .
SQL> create database omfd1;
Database created.
```

Hopefully, you're suitably stunned. This takes less than a couple of minutes of preparation. Of course, for a production database, you wouldn't allow all the other parameters to inherit default values in the init.ora, but the example demonstrates the power of OMF beautifully. For a test or development database, many of the defaults might be quite acceptable. Now run the following files from SQL*Plus while connected as SYSDBA exactly as you would after a non-OMF database creation to install the standard Oracle data dictionary views and packages, where "?" is shorthand for the current $ORACLE_HOME:

```
@?/rdbms/admin/catalog.sql
@?/rdbms/admin/catproc.sql
```

It is possible that your catalog SQL failed due to insufficient rollback space, but the Oracle dictionary should be in sufficiently good shape to continue for the purposes of this example. Now let's investigate what Oracle has actually created on our behalf using OMF in terms of control files, redo logs, and tablespace datafiles. It's also useful to know that both DB_CREATE_FILE_DEST and DB_CREATE_ONLINE_LOG_DEST_n are dynamic parameters that can be set using ALTER SYSTEM or ALTER SESSION while the database is up and running.

Control Files

OMF has created two controls files for our database, one in each of the locations specified in DB_CREATE_ONLINE_LOG_DEST_1 and DB_CREATE_ONLINE_LOG_DEST_2, which you can see using the query SELECT NAME FROM V$CONTROLFILE:

```
/u02/oradata/omfd1/ora_xwqz36p4.ctl
/u03/oradata/omfd1/ora_xwqz36wg.ctl
```

The names are clearly identified as belonging to Oracle because of the prefix ora_. The files are clearly identified as control files because the file type is .ctl. As we aren't using an Oracle spfile in our example, it's necessary to manually add a line to the init.ora file to make sure that the database starts up the next time:

```
control_files=("/u02/oradata/omfd1/ora_xwqz36p4.ctl",
               "/u03/oradata/omfd1/ora_xwqz36wg.ctl")
```

This requirement is no longer necessary if you use an spfile instead of an init.ora file. spfiles are discussed shortly.

Online Redo Logs

If you reverse engineer the redo log file creation SQL, using DbCool, for example, you can see that OMF has resulted in the creation of two log file groups, with a member in each of the locations specified in DB_CREATE_ONLINE_LOG_DEST_1 and DB_CREATE_ONLINE_LOG_DEST_2 and sized at 100MB each:

```
ALTER DATABASE ADD LOGFILE GROUP 1
(
  '/u02/oradata/omfd1/ora_1_xwqz3784.log',
  '/u03/oradata/omfd1/ora_1_xwqz3f7b.log'
) SIZE 100M
/
ALTER DATABASE ADD LOGFILE GROUP 2
(
  '/u02/oradata/omfd1/ora_2_xwqz3m80.log',
  '/u03/oradata/omfd1/ora_2_xwqz3ryk.log'
) SIZE 100M
/
```

The files are identified as Oracle files by the ora_ prefix and as redo log files by the use of the .log file type. You can add another log file group without specifying the log filenames by running the following:

```
ALTER DATABASE ADD LOGFILE GROUP 3;
```

As you can guess, this adds another group with the log file members multiplexed across the two destinations just like the other groups, as if you had run the following SQL:

```
ALTER DATABASE ADD LOGFILE GROUP 3
(
  '/u02/oradata/omfd1/ora_3_xwr2ymf3.log',
  '/u03/oradata/omfd1/ora_3_xwr2ysgx.log'
) SIZE 104857600
```

If you drop a log file group by running the ALTER DATABASE DROP LOGFILE GROUP 3, for example, you find that the member files have been removed for you. You can check this as follows to prove that the files are no longer present:

```
$ ls -l /u02/oradata/omfd1/ora_3_xwr2ymf3.log
$ ls -l /u03/oradata/omfd1/ora_3_xwr2ysgx.log
```

In a pre-OMF situation where you had to remove the operating system files, you might first query V$LOG and V$LOGFILE several times to make *absolutely* sure the files were no longer in use before removing them. Even then, people have removed the wrong files and sometimes destroyed a production database as a result. Human error always occurs, but by using OMF, you reduce the chances of these kinds of human errors.

NOTE **The naming format of OMF files changed to use a different prefix after the initial release of Oracle9*i*, and Oracle does not guarantee that the format won't change again in the future.**

Tablespaces

Now let's take a look at the OMF-style SYSTEM tablespace that is created at database creation time. This is created as if you had run the following SQL:

```
create tablespace system
datafile '/u02/oradata/omfd1/ora_system_xwqz461n.dbf'
size 104857600 autoextend on
next 2048 maxsize unlimited
default storage
(initial 10240 next 10240 minextents 1 maxextents 121 pctincrease 50)
online permanent;
```

The file is identified as an Oracle database file by the ora_ prefix and as a datafile by the use of the .dbf file type. Oracle uses the first eight characters of the tablespace name in the filename, so you need to restrict your tablespace names to eight characters or less to take maximum advantage of the OMF-generated association between the tablespace name and filename. The default attributes of an OMF-created datafile use AUTOEX-TEND with an unlimited maximum size, an initial size of 100MB, and dictionary-managed extents. Using OMF, you can create a tablespace without specifying a datafile. For example, running CREATE TABLESPACE TABLE_DATA creates a tablespace as if you had run the following SQL:

```
create tablespace table_data
datafile '/u02/oradata/omfd1/ora_table_da_xwr4fvxp.dbf'
size 104857600 autoextend on
next 2048 maxsize unlimited
default storage
(initial 10240 next 10240 minextents 1 maxextents 121 pctincrease50)
online permanent
```

You can drop the tablespace with DROP TABLESPACE TABLE_DATA and Oracle removes the datafiles for you. You can also modify the default parameters at tablespace creation time and still have the files as OMF. For example, CREATE TABLESPACE INDEX3 EXTENT MANAGEMENT LOCAL creates an OMF datafile with local as opposed to dictionary-managed extents, and CREATE TABLESPACE INDEX4 DE-FAULT STORAGE (PCTINCREASE 0) creates a dictionary-managed tablespace with PCTINCREASE 0 instead of the default PCTINCREASE 50. You can identify OMF tablespaces by the following SQL:

```
select tablespace_name from dba_tablespaces
where user_management='SYSTEM'
```

To enable easier segment space management, Oracle9*i* introduces the concept of automatic segment space management for a locally managed tablespace. This feature removes the need for the DBA to specify the FREELIST, FREELIST GROUPS, and PCTUSED settings for tablespace objects. Through information stored in a bitmap, Oracle maintains the free space available in blocks, which determines the blocks that are available for insert. As a result, Oracle can manage the space efficiently without DBA assistance. An OMF tablespace that would require the lowest DBA administration overhead might look like the following, where the SEGMENT SPACE MANAGEMENT AUTO specifies that Oracle and not the DBA should manage segment space:

```
create tablespace tabauto
extent management local uniform size 128k
segment space management auto
```

Server Parameter Files (spfiles)

Server parameter files (spfiles) represent another manageability improvement for your Oracle databases and make some of Oracle9*i*'s self-tuning features possible. For the moment, let's concentrate on the manageability aspects. This example is based on the same instance as the previous example, omfd1. To remove this database in preparation for this exercise, you can generate a list of UNIX commands as follows to remove the files:

```
select 'rm '||name RM_COMMAND from
(
select f.member name from v$logfile f
Union select name from v$controlfile c
Union select f.file_name from dba_data_files f
union select tf.file_name from dba_temp_files tf
);
RM_COMMAND
-------------------------------------------------
rm /u02/oradata/omfd1/ora_1_xwrk4zv2.log
rm /u02/oradata/omfd1/ora_2_xwrk5c4k.log
rm /u02/oradata/omfd1/ora_system_xwrk5w6p.dbf
rm /u02/oradata/omfd1/ora_temp1_xwrk7p5o.tmp
rm /u02/oradata/omfd1/ora_undo1_xwrk7gx3.dbf
rm /u02/oradata/omfd1/ora_xwrk4zgp.ctl
rm /u03/oradata/omfd1/ora_1_xwrk55gr.log
rm /u03/oradata/omfd1/ora_2_xwrk5jqg.log
rm /u03/oradata/omfd1/ora_xwrk4zko.ctl
```

Then you need to SHUTDOWN ABORT the instance before you run the rm commands. In the previous section, we added settings to the Oracle init.ora file prior to database creation and manually added the control_files section to the init.ora file afterwards by hand. If you forgot to do that, your next database restart would fail because Oracle would be unable to identify the location of the control files. Oracle9*i* addresses this problem by enabling you to use an spfile instead of an init.ora file. The major difference between the two is that when you run ALTER SYSTEM commands, you can optionally persist the data into the spfile so that it automatically takes effect the next time you start the database. You can't do that with an init.ora parameter file. When such functionality is in use, it also gives the Oracle database management system (DBMS) the capability to manage some of the dynamic settings itself, such as increasing or reducing buffer cache sizes depending on usage patterns. So spfiles are a key enabling factor for self-tuning.

Let's repeat the database creation exercise in the previous section using an spfile instead of an init.ora file and use two more Oracle9*i* features for manageability: automatic undo and the default temporary tablespace. The goals of the exercise are to create a database using the simplest process possible and to incorporate several important manageability features that we might want to use in a production database for the resulting database.

When the automatic undo feature is operational, as determined by the undo_management=auto setting in the init.ora file, you can create a special type of tablespace using the CREATE UNDO TABLESPACE statement. When you have an undo tablespace combined with undo_management=auto, Oracle manages undo for you without requiring you to explicitly create rollback segments, alleviating some of the earlier issues raised by DBA-managed rollback segments. You can create several undo tablespaces, although only one can be active at any time. The ALTER SYSTEM SET UNDO_TABLESPACE=*tablespace_name* command can be used to switch between them. When you use automatic undo management, you control the time that Oracle retains committed undo information through the use of the undo_retention parameter. This is set in the init.ora file or can be changed dynamically at run time through the ALTER SYSTEM command. For example, to keep committed undo information for 1 hour, you would enter the following:

```
alter system set undo_retention=3600
```

Keep in mind that if an active transaction requires undo space, it takes precedence over the undo_retention time, and redo space is reused if more space can't be allocated. When used carefully and provided you are prepared to live with the additional undo space required, you can eliminate the ORA-01555 snapshot too old error that has irritated DBAs and users for many years.

The default temporary tablespace feature creates a temporary tablespace with tempfiles to be used for all users at user creation time in cases where the TEMPORARY TABLESPACE clause is omitted. This tablespace is created using OMF in our example. The default temporary tablespace feature fixes one of the major problems with temporary tablespaces described earlier, where the temporary tablespace defaults to the SYSTEM tablespace at user creation time, if the DBA doesn't specify it.

To demonstrate these features, we need to make an spfile first. This requires an init.ora file. The spfile should never be modified directly with an editor and has built-in checks to detect tampering. To create an spfile, make a file called undo.ora in $ORACLE_HOME/dbs that contains nothing but the following parameters:

```
db_name=omfd1
compatible='9.0.0.0.0'
undo_management=auto
```

> **NOTE** The compatible parameter is required for the OMF features to work during database creation in combination with the undo and default temporary tablespace statements.

Next, create an spfile from the init.ora file, using the CREATE SPFILE statement in SQL*Plus:

```
connect / as sysdba;
create spfile from pfile='undo.ora';
```

At this stage, the database instance hasn't been started yet. When you start an Oracle9*i* instance, it searches for spfiles and init.ora files in the following order:

1. spfileomfd1.ora

2. spfile.ora

3. initomfd1.ora

In our example, now that we have an spfile for the instance (spfileomfd1.ora), it will be used when the instance is started. Now let's start the instance, staying in SQL*Plus, and use the ALTER SYSTEM command to set up the directories required for OMF:

```
startup nomount
alter system set DB_CREATE_FILE_DEST='/u02/oradata/omfd1'
          scope=both;
alter system set DB_CREATE_ONLINE_LOG_DEST_1='/u02/oradata/omfd1'
          scope=both;
alter system set DB_CREATE_ONLINE_LOG_DEST_2='/u03/oradata/omfd1'
          scope=both;
create database omfd1;
```

The SCOPE qualifier takes one of the values SPFILE, MEMORY, or BOTH. In this case, the use of BOTH causes the setting to take effect in both MEMORY (the current session) and SPFILE so that it remains in effect across database shutdown and startup. You can now shut down Oracle and restart it after database creation without a problem because the manual settings that were required in the init.ora file are now stored in the spfile by Oracle automatically. If you want to go the other way, you can create an init.ora in SQL*Plus from an spfile as follows:

```
create pfile='fromspfile.ora' from spfile;
```

Now we're ready to create the database. The database uses OMF for all its tablespaces as determined by the spfile settings. In addition, an OMF undo tablespace named undo1 is created during database creation, along with an OMF default temporary tablespace. All of this is performed with the following single command:

```
create database omfd1
default temporary tablespace temp1
undo tablespace undo1;
```

It's worth mentioning at this point that on UNIX, when temporary tablespaces are specified using tempfiles (whether OMF or not), Oracle creates the files as sparse files. UNIX doesn't actually allocate blocks in a sparse file until the blocks are used. The advantage of sparse files is that they can be created almost instantaneously. As a result, tablespace creation of a temporary tablespace that specifies a tempfile is much faster than the creation of a tablespace that uses a regular datafile whose blocks are initialized by the DBMS at creation time. The behavior of sparse files can be demonstrated with an example. The following temporary tablespace creation statement uses a tempfile apparently of size 2000MB:

```
REM this takes only a few seconds...
create temporary tablespace temp2
tempfile '/u02/oradata/d3/temp02.dbf' size 2000m
autoextend on next 1280k extent management local uniform size 128k
/
```

Although the UNIX ls -l command shows the file to be 2000MB in size, the du -sk command (which shows the size of blocks actually used, in 1KB units) reports a much smaller size because the file is sparse:

```
$ du -sk /u02/oradata/d3/temp02.dbf
96      /u02/oradata/d3/temp02.dbf
```

By running a SQL statement that forces a disk sort using the tempfile, you can force blocks to be allocated in the file to demonstrate that the number of used blocks increases. Oracle tracks the number of blocks used in tempfiles through the v$temp_space_header view:

```
select blocks_used from v$temp_space_header where
tablespace_name='TEMP2';
  BLOCKS_USED
-------------
          16

REM run some SQL that performs a large sort on disk...
select sum(length(text)) from all_source;

REM confirm that blocks have been used...
select blocks_used from v$temp_space_header where
tablespace_name='TEMP2';

  BLOCKS_USED
-------------
        4672
```

The du -sk command can then be used to confirm that blocks have actually been allocated from the file system holding the tempfile:

```
$ du -sk /u02/oradata/d3/temp02.dbf
37272   /u02/oradata/d3/temp02.dbf
```

Although sparse files allow the rapid creation of temporary tablespaces that use tempfiles, they introduce the possibility that the full 2000MB of physical space may no longer be available when it's actually needed by a sort operation. To force the physical space for the tempfile to be allocated in the file system, you can pre-create the file (for example, using the UNIX dd command) and then add this to the tablespace by specifying the REUSE option in the tablespace creation SQL:

```
$ dd if=/dev/zero of=/u02/oradata/d3/temp02.dbf bs=1000k count=2000
create temporary tablespace temp2
tempfile '/u02/oradata/d3/temp02.dbf' reuse
autoextend on next 1280k extent management local uniform size 128k
/
```

Oracle Layout for Performance

Hopefully, the manageability of OMF is obvious, and you are now seriously considering placing your Oracle database onto one or two large file systems. This still leaves the issue of performance, which you need to address. Having fantastic manageability is pointless if users have to wait an unacceptably long time for their SQL to complete. If that happens, you've just reduced the availability of the users' data.

It's clear that using the large file system approach means that the DBA no longer has a direct influence on I/O performance at the hardware level. Instead, the available I/O throughput is determined by the characteristics of the file system on which the database files are created. As a result, the DBA becomes less involved in hardware performance issues: Disk and hardware performance in general become a service provided to the DBAs by either the system administrator (SA) group or, in the case of managed SAN storage, possibly a third-party company dedicated to the role.

Performance and availability at the hardware level are now requirements rather than the responsibility of a DBA. Given the complex nature of modern hardware architecture and the role of the DBA, it seems likely that the DBA will become further removed from hardware considerations in the future. Personally, I welcome that. The complexity of deploying Oracle9*i* in the most efficient way is quite enough for a DBA. In the long run, the environment that a DBA sees on a UNIX server will be an abstraction of something much more complicated and powerful underneath. However, none of this means that the DBA shouldn't be interested in the underlying technology or that the DBA can't contribute to the requirements. If you're like me, you want to understand the end-to-end infrastructure because any information might help you deliver a better database service to business users. No one in the organization probably understands data usage patterns and requirements better than the DBA. The following is an overview of the hardware technologies that meet the performance and availability requirements of a production Oracle system.

RAID Overview

The term RAID was first coined in 1987 by academics at the University of California at Berkeley. Originally, it stood for Redundant Array of Inexpensive Disks, although today it stands for Redundant Array of Independent Disks. As the name suggests, this aims to provide higher availability to disk data by introducing redundancy that enables the data to remain available in the event of a single disk failure and therefore increases the mean time between failure (MTBF) for disks. At the same time, the data in the collection of disks, or the array, should appear as a single logical piece of space at the operating level for usability. Originally, five different levels were defined, with each providing fault tolerance in a different way to provide a range of cost/performance combinations for different types of customers. A nonredundant architecture (RAID 0) was included.

Disk drives in a RAID group are partitioned into chunks known as *stripes*, whose size can range from tens of kilobytes up to several megabytes. Stripes are sized optimally for performance when individual application I/O requests fit into a single stripe. This means that all disks can work on a different I/O operation at the same time, and through this parallel operation, throughput is maximized. RAID can be implemented in hardware or software. Hardware RAID is generally faster and more expensive than software RAID, and it's completely transparent to the server it's running on. RAID is best understood using simple examples. The most commonly used RAID levels—0, 1, 4, and 5—are shown in Figure 2.1. For simplicity, the example in the discussion considers a file system made out of just six blocks on a host.

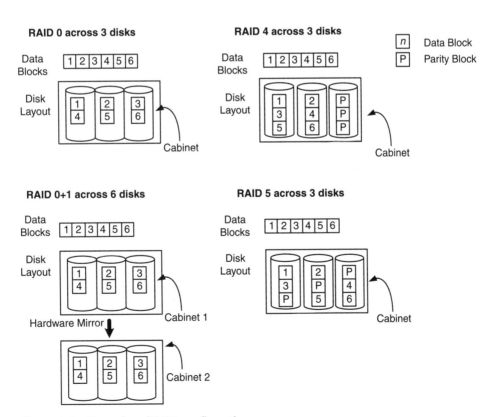

Figure 2.1 Examples of RAID configurations.

RAID 0

In the RAID 0 example, the data blocks are distributed, or striped, across three disks. There is no redundancy, and if a disk is lost, data is irretrievably lost and the system can't continue. From an I/O performance standpoint, all three disks can service I/O operations at the same time. The disk space overhead to provide protection is meaningless in this case so the available data capacity is 100 percent of the total space allocated.

RAID 0+1

In the RAID 0+1 example, the striped array is mirrored across to an identical array using hardware mirroring. Writes have extra overhead to maintain the mirroring, but reads show an increased throughput because they run against either cabinet. If any single disk is lost, the system continues to run. In this configuration, the available data capacity is 50 percent of the total space allocated.

RAID 4

In the RAID 4 example, the use of error checking codes (ECCs) to store parity information about the data is shown. When data blocks are written, an extra parity block is written containing information that can be used to derive the contents of the original data if a single disk is lost. For example, if the middle disk is lost, then the parity information in the third disk along with the data information in the first disk can be used to regenerate it. Writes take an extra operation to generate the parity information each time, and reads benefit because the data is striped across multiple disks. The available data is $N–1/N$ of the total capacity (where N is the number of disks), which for this three-disk configuration works out to be 66 percent of the total space allocated.

RAID 5

In the RAID 4 configuration, the parity information is kept on a single drive, which can become a bottleneck during high write requests. On writes, the parity must be regenerated each time. RAID 5 is very similar to RAID 4. The difference, however, is that parity information is distributed across all the available drives. The overhead of the ECC information in the parity block and the performance characteristics are broadly similar to RAID 4. In the past, RAID 5 has been associated with poorer performance for write-intensive applications. My advice is to not accept information related to RAID 5 on the basis of hearsay: Check it out for yourself. Due to the sophistication of nonvolatile hardware disk caches and write back caching (where the disk returns a write-complete message to an application as soon as data is in the cache), the poor write performance of RAID 5 is greatly overstated from my experience and not actually evident in many cases. As you'll soon see in the section *SANs and NAS*, some of the most popular SAN solutions are implemented over RAID 5 storage, so the decision on RAID levels is no longer a customer decision.

Advantages of RAID

Using RAID on your disks protects your organization against an application outage caused by a single disk drive failure. For RAID 0+1, it might protect you against more than one disk failure depending on the actual disks that fail. The economic cost of an application outage depends on the organization and application, but includes factors such as lost sales, data reentry time, and data restore time. As a DBA, you should confirm that all of your production systems are protected against a single disk failure; this requirement is usually implemented with RAID. Keep in mind that if you lose a disk, your system might no longer be tolerant to a single disk failure (if it's RAID 4 or RAID 5) so hot-swappable disks are a good idea. These typically reside in a spare slot in the disk cabinet and are automatically regenerated with data along with an email alert to the SA team; they are enabled if a drive is lost.

Remember that your hardware requires protection against types of hardware failures other than just simple disk media failure. This protection involves items such as redundant power supplies, disk controller cards, and cooling fans. Failure of any of these can cause a server outage if no redundancy is built in, so systems with high availability requirements are usually configured to hot swap these components without a server outage.

Raw Partitions versus UNIX File Systems

In terms of manageability, which ultimately translates into availability, raw partitions are at the opposite end of the spectrum from the single UNIX file system approach I've just discussed. Due to the complex nature of setting up a database to use raw devices, the DBA is dependent on the SA for the initial configuration and long-term management. A lot of planning needs to be done up front on the predicted growth of the system because each raw partition can only be used for one datafile. Any space not allocated for the datafile is wasted. If your system doesn't grow as predicted, and many if not most systems probably fall into this category, you're heading for severe maintenance headaches. With raw devices, it just isn't that easy to move free space where it's needed. Keep in mind also that you can't use OMF with raw partitions.

Of course, you sometimes have to use raw partitions, for example, when using Oracle Real Application Clusters (RAC) on some versions of UNIX. It's interesting to note that Oracle Parallel Server (the forerunner to RAC) is definitely easier to manage on the VMS operating system, rather than UNIX because the VMS clustering enables you to use standard files for your Oracle database, which you can extend on demand.

Oracle's own UNIX Performance Tuning Tips guides usually quote a 5 to 40 percent increase in disk throughput resulting from the use of raw partitions. However, remember that disk I/O is just one part of the overall performance equation and might not be relevant to your particular performance problem. Your requirement as a DBA is actually to deliver performance that meets the business requirements of today and the future to the business user. You can usually find many different (and easier) ways to achieve that than using raw partitions.

In my experience with a large number of different types of Oracle systems, from real-time credit-card billing to warehouses for equity settlements data, I've never come across a performance problem that could be solved by using raw partitions. This includes situations where raw partitions have been used as a last resort to alleviate perceived I/O problems.

It's interesting to examine the reasons why raw partitions are supposed to give better performance than the UNIX file system. One of the reasons given is that using raw partitions bypasses the UNIX buffer cache for Oracle reads and writes, and avoids the central processing unit (CPU) overhead of moving database blocks between the disk and the UNIX buffer cache. Instead, data goes directly from the disk to the Oracle System Global Area (SGA). On operating systems where free memory is made available for caching file blocks, the UNIX buffer cache can actually *improve* performance. In this case, when Oracle performs a physical read because a data block is not present in the SGA data block buffer cache, a physical read request is made to the operating system. If this block is in the operating system buffer cache, the Oracle physical read is not actually a physical read at all. The point about the operating system buffer cache in this case is that it makes sure that real memory is used to cache data, if any memory is available. Solaris is an example of such an operating system. Of course, you could allocate more memory to the Oracle SGA instead, but if your application causes many table scans (and if you have any free memory available), leaving the caching to the operating system can be more flexible. Figure 2.2 shows the screen output for a free Solaris utility called memtool, showing that some of the Oracle database files are cached in the operating system buffer cache.

A second reason given for using raw partitions is that they avoid a file system lock that UNIX takes out to serialize access to data on a file system. For an Oracle application with large physical I/O requirements, this serialization can cause a bottleneck. Other solutions to this problem are available that don't require using raw partitions; they were developed precisely to provide the benefits of file system-style usability with the performance of raw partitions. For example, Quick I/O from VERITAS Software Corporation is designed to overcome file system locking through a VERITAS file that can be extended more flexibly than a raw partition. Operating system vendors are

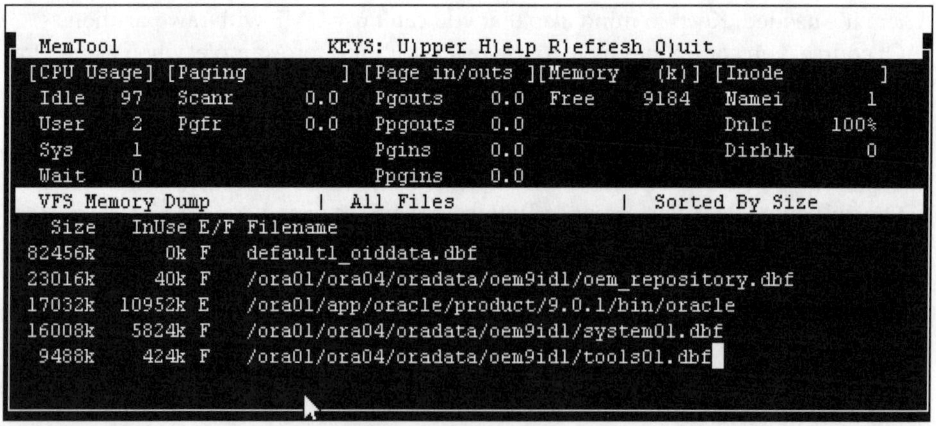

```
  MemTool                      KEYS: U)pper H)elp R)efresh Q)uit
 [CPU Usage] [Paging         ] [Page in/outs ][Memory  (k)] [Inode        ]
   Idle   97  Scanr     0.0   Pgouts    0.0  Free   9184   Namei       1
   User    2  Pgfr      0.0   Ppgouts   0.0               Dnlc     100%
   Sys     1             Pgins     0.0               Dirblk      0
   Wait    0             Ppgins    0.0
   VFS Memory Dump          |  All Files             |  Sorted By Size
   Size    InUse E/F  Filename
   82456k     0k  F   defaultl_oiddata.dbf
   23016k    40k  F   /ora01/ora04/oradata/oem9idl/oem_repository.dbf
   17032k 10952k  E   /ora01/app/oracle/product/9.0.1/bin/oracle
   16008k  5824k  F   /ora01/ora04/oradata/oem9idl/system01.dbf
    9488k   424k  F   /ora01/ora04/oradata/oem9idl/tools01.dbf
```

Figure 2.2 Solaris file data in the UNIX buffer cache.

also looking to make such features available as standard through their file systems. From Release 3 on, Sun Solaris 8 includes improved file system direct I/O concurrency (Quick I/O style functionality) for which Sun claims I/O performance approaching 90 percent of raw partition access speeds. The performance of Solaris direct I/O, which is used by database applications to access unbuffered file system data, is improved by providing concurrent read and write access to regular files on a UNIX file system and is specifically aimed at database customers. On the subject of file system caching, VER-ITAS additionally has a Cached Quick I/O feature, which sets out to provide the I/O write throughput of raw partitions (Quick I/O) with configurable read buffering for individually named files. Remember that to increase read buffering, you can control it through Oracle by increasing the memory allocated to the Oracle data block buffer cache. From Oracle9*i* on, you can change the cache size on the fly.

To sum up, raw partitions are options for improving I/O throughput at the cost of manageability and flexibility. Before you consider using them, be absolutely sure that your application performance issue is due to an I/O bottleneck that can only be solved by using raw partitions. Even then, consider whether file system features in your operating system or through a third-party vendor such as VERITAS can provide the throughput you require without resorting to raw partitions. It might be helpful to read the sections in this book on tuning first before you make such a commitment because you need to identify the root cause of your performance problem first. If you need orders of magnitude performance improvements, you're unlikely to get them through using raw partitions. As a final note, you might have noticed that hardware vendor benchmarks running Oracle nearly always use raw partitions for performance. You can see some examples at www.tpc.org. Luckily for the Oracle DBA, real-world business applications hardly ever have the sole goal of running Online Transaction Processing (OLTP) transactions as fast as possible at the cost of everything else.

Tablespaces and Fragmentation

Since Oracle7, database fragmentation seemed to be an obsession for many DBAs. Extent fragmentation exists in two forms. In the first form, any segment containing a large number of extents was said to be fragmented, and this was deemed to be inefficient from an I/O standpoint. The second form of fragmentation occurs when a tablespace has enough total space to satisfy a space request, but the space is fragmented across multiple smaller extents that are noncontiguous. In this case, a request for a 10MB extent would fail if the available space was distributed across 10 extents that were 1MB. This scenario can occur when lots of segments with different extent sizes are mixed in the same tablespace, effectively creating holes in the available free space that can't be used by any segment. As a result of both types of fragmentation, DBAs were at the office every weekend exporting and importing the database to defragment the data into large extents to create more efficient I/O and free wasted space.

From the discussion of storage technologies such as RAID, it's clear that it's actually a good idea to distribute apparently contiguous blocks of data across multiple physical disks for I/O balancing. Therefore, by definition, RAID is introducing fragmentation. This leads to the conclusion that fragmentation is good for I/O throughput if the I/O characteristics of the application can be represented as multiple random concurrent requests for relatively small chunks of data. This description of I/O characteristics probably fits any Online Transaction Processing (OLTP) type of application where the user's data requests are index driven rather than requiring the full table scans found in a Decision Support System (DSS) type of application. The conclusion is that the existence of many small extents for a given segment is not only unavoidable with modern disk storage architectures, but actually beneficial to performance. So the first form of fragmentation (the existence of many small extents) isn't actually a problem that needs to be fixed.

NOTE **DSS applications are characterized by mainly read-only activity on historical data and are used for reporting and forecasting. For example, a company might store all its historical sales data in a data warehouse to identify sales trends by region, by quarter, by department, and so forth. DSS applications usually require processing of all the rows in very large database tables (referred to as full table scans). DSS applications contrast with OLTP applications. OLTP applications are characterized by many simultaneous, small, real-time transactions on small subsets of table rows, which are accessed via indexes. The ATM machine you use at your bank is a front end to an OLTP application.**

On the other hand, the wastage of space caused by extent fragmentation is a valid concern, especially if your space is allocated from a managed service like a SAN and you pay for the amount used on a regular basis. If you still think that having a few large extents is good and that defragmenting your database is a way of life, then take the time to read the classic Oracle white paper "How to Stop Defragmenting and Start Living: The Definitive Word on Fragmentation," which is available from Oracle's corporate Web site. Every Oracle DBA should be familiar with the contents of this paper. To save you from having to read it, the conclusions of the paper are provided in the following list:

- The performance of Data Manipulation Language (DML) is largely independent of the number of extents in the segment.
- Segments smaller than 128MB should be placed in 128KB extent tablespaces.
- Segments between 128MB and 4GB should be placed in 4MB extent tablespaces.
- Segments larger than 4GB should be placed in 128MB extent tablespaces.

It's worth emphasizing these conclusions: It's not necessary for good DML performance to have all your objects allocated across a few very large extents, and you can avoid space wasted from fragmentation by ensuring that all segments in a given tablespace use the same extent size.

The choice of extent size is designed to restrict the maximum number of extents in an object to 1,024, which is deemed to be the maximum that's efficient for Data Definition Language (DDL) operations. It should be stated that the experience of the authors of the white paper, and mine personally, is that performance with a few thousand extents is not much different.

Now that we have buried the myth of fragmentation and performance, and have avoided space wastage, we return to an Oracle physical layout where we create tablespaces with a uniform extent size and never set storage parameters at the object level. The result is that extent fragmentation and the wastage that goes with it simply disappear.

Performance is good because of the underlying RAID technology that distributes I/O across all disks, and DBA management of space is minimal because datafiles can autoextend into a large pool of available space on a single, large file system. Database creation is simplified because file creation is managed by OMF. Automatic undo allocation takes care of the rollback segment headaches we had in the past. Come to think of it, maybe the Oracle claim of a 40 percent savings in administration costs isn't so far fetched after all.

SANs and NAS

SANs and NAS are modern data storage technologies that most organizations are likely to adopt in the long term, possibly alongside each other.

SAN technology sets out to provide reduced costs, higher availability, improved performance, and better asset utilization for an organization's storage. It almost sounds too good to be true and it's definitely not cheap to implement. Deciding to implement a SAN is usually a strategic corporate-level decision. By choosing a SAN, an organization makes the decision that storage is a strategic enterprise technology that can be used for competitive advantage, not just a bunch of disks.

To the DBA, and actually to the whole organization, this means that storage is no longer attached to the database server by a Small Computer Systems Interface (SCSI) cable. Instead, storage is actually physically located remotely from the server and typically attached to the server by a dedicated Fibre Channel network for performance reasons, with the Fibre Channel network isolated from the normal production data highway used to transfer data between servers.

One important component that enables high performance for storage attached via a SAN is the host bus adapter (HBA) card. This plugs in to the host, where the storage is accessed and contains an intelligent I/O processor. HBAs process block-level I/O without requiring many CPU cycles from the host processors. The existence of an HBA provides higher performance for SAN compared to NAS, which typically uses a standard Transmission Control Protocol/Internet Protocol (TCP/IP) network interface card to attach the host to remote storage devices and therefore requires CPU resources from the host itself in order to handle data transfer.

The SAN architecture is a collection, referred to as a *fabric*, of Fibre Channel hubs, switches, and gateways connecting servers to storage in a many-to-many relationship. The actual disks where your data is stored might be shared with other applications or databases on other servers. You no longer have visibility of the underlying physical layout. The storage is now a managed service and the database server is just another client of the managed service. The underlying physical disk used to store your data might be located in a unit such as an IBM Enterprise Storage Server (ESS), known as Shark, providing up to several terabytes of storage using RAID 5. The traditional DBA reluctance to deploy a database on RAID 5 is now a relic because it isn't relevant to a managed storage architecture on a SAN. The DBA can concentrate on what a DBA does best, which is running databases—managing the storage is left to a dedicated team.

As a DBA using a SAN for your storage, your relationship with database storage can be expressed as a simple requirement: You need the storage to deliver performance and availability. That's all. Storage matters are out of your hands and are now managed by a group dedicated to meeting your requirements. In the old days, if your database server was short of space, you would have probably followed a somewhat tedious procurement process involving your SAs and business users to purchase a new disk. When the disk arrived, an outage would be arranged to install the new disks. With a SAN, you submit a request to increase your database file system by 9GB, and the next day, the file system is bigger. No outage is needed. Because your storage is now managed by a dedicated team, you can rest assured that performance of the storage is being monitored for you. Data might be relocated behind the scenes to balance I/O. However, it's all transparent to the DBA: You see only the benefits of the flexible management of database space, and performance and availability are guaranteed. Many companies use an internal charge-back model to account for storage space on a SAN, where business groups rent space and pay monthly per gigabyte. As a DBA, the use of storage space for your databases is likely to be more carefully scrutinized in the future as a result. If a third party provides your SAN as a managed service, what your organization pays is dictated by how much you use, so good housekeeping of space is critical for keeping costs down. As well as providing raw space, SANs can actually provide benefits that are not available from locally attached storage—such as the near-real-time mirroring of data to a remote site (for disaster recovery) or flash copy for instantaneous backups— completely transparently to the server that runs the application.

It can't be emphasized enough that you should be absolutely sure that the end results don't compromise the integrity of your database before you use any of these SAN valued-added features. The Oracle Storage Certification Program (OSCP) on Oracle's corporate Web site is a good place to start.

NAS, on the other hand, is a fundamentally different technology. The key element of a NAS system is a dedicated storage appliance directly attached to the corporate production data highway. The storage appliance manages storage operations and disk array. NAS uses standard local area network (LAN) and wide area network (WAN) protocols such as the Network File System (NFS). This leads to the age-old question of whether you can run Oracle databases in a NAS configuration. In the past, the accepted wisdom was that you couldn't run Oracle databases on NFS because NFS is based on the unreliable User Datagram Protocol (UDP) (used to send email); therefore, writes couldn't be guaranteed. Actually, NFS can run on top of the guaranteed delivery of TCP/IP if configured to do so, but as it turns out, that's a moot point. In reality, Oracle provides the OSCP to enable vendors to certify their storage according to Oracle's defined requirements for storage compatibility. One of the most popular platforms for running Oracle on NAS is through the NetApp filer (file server appliance) from Network Appliance Inc. If you're concerned about the reliability and compatibility of such a solution, the fact that Oracle uses NetApp to run its ebusiness should put your mind at rest. NAS uses the corporate production data highway for data, so it follows that you need to make sure your network has sufficient bandwidth to cope with the extra traffic resulting from using NAS for database storage.

Naming Standards and Physical Layout

The original Optimal Flexible Architecture (OFA) layout for managing Oracle databases was based on the existence of several real file systems. So how does OFA fit into the picture if the database actually resides on only a single file system? My approach to this is to continue to use OFA names when laying out the database.

In this situation, OFA becomes more of a logical layout, but by continuing to use it, you're making a statement that you are laying out Oracle in a standard way, but without making any assumptions about the underlying hardware. So, if you query the files in the Oracle data dictionary, you'll have no clue that the database actually resides on a single file system. This has two main advantages. The first is that OFA is a published standard, and if you recruit new staff, they will be familiar with it. The second is that if for any reason you have to relocate your database onto a different hardware platform that actually has multiple smaller file systems, you don't have to change the file paths because they are also compatible with that layout.

Here's one way to create directories to mimic an OFA layout when you have a single, large file system called /bigfs for your Oracle database instance OFAD1. In this case, you arrange for your SA to create three top-level links—/u02, /u03, /u04—which are links to bigfs, and request that all directory trees matching the pattern u* below /bigfs are owned by oracle, group dba:

```
$ mkdir -p /bigfs/u02/oradata/OFAD1
$ mkdir -p /bigfs/u03/oradata/OFAD1
$ mkdir -p /bigfs/u04/oradata/OFAD1
$ ln -s /bigfs/u02 /u02
$ ln -s /bigfs/u03 /u03
$ ln -s /bigfs/u04 /u04
```

When you create your database, use the /u* links as if they were file system names. Place the redo log groups on /u02 and /u03, with one member on each, and the tablespaces in /u04. You should still multiplex the redo log files at the Oracle level and keep multiple copies of the control file: Ignore the fact that the /bigfs file system is configured as RAID 0+1, which means that all the files on it are actually mirrored at the hardware level. By not making assumptions about the underlying hardware, you protect yourself against the accidental human removal of those files or write corruption, because RAID doesn't protect you from those kinds of problems. In terms of datafile naming, the files should be OFA compliant. Therefore, the first two datafiles in tablespace TRADES would be the following:

```
/u04/oradata/OFAD1/trades01.dbf
/u04/oradata/OFAD1/trades02.dbf
```

The important point is that no reference to /bigfs exists anywhere in the Oracle configuration. Some DBAs like to prefix the name of the datafile with the instance name (in this case, OFAD1), which would give the following:

```
/u04/oradata/OFAD1/OFAD1_trades01.dbf
/u04/oradata/OFAD1/OFAD1_trades02.dbf
```

Other DBAs view this as overkill, but it's not unreasonable to give each file a unique name. After all, this is exactly what OMF does for you. In the event where you're running many instances on a consolidated server, anything that makes the DBA feel more comfortable must be a good thing. For example, without using the instance name in such a scenario, all SYSTEM tablespaces in all databases would have the name system01.dbf. This might cause paranoia in restore situations, due to the concern of overwriting the wrong file.

The use of upper- or lowercase characters for instance names can cause some unresolvable arguments. In some ways, it's like trying to argue that right is better than left, or vice versa. If pushed, I would choose uppercase names because they make the directories and datafile names (if you include the instance in the names) stand out from other UNIX files, which tend to have all lowercase names. The examples in this book use both.

Choosing a DB_BLOCK SIZE Value

Before Oracle9i, choosing a db_block_size value for your database required careful consideration because after being created with the chosen size, it could only be changed with a time-consuming complete database build. The choice is quite difficult to make because, in general, a fixed block size is not flexible enough to address the various requirements of a typical application.

Smaller block sizes are usually more suitable to OLTP-type applications. In a typical OLTP application, row sizes are small, blocks hold many rows, and many transactions typically take place at any one time. Because Oracle protects blocks with latches during access, the larger the block size in such a situation, the higher the chance that a session has to wait while another session holds the latch for a row in the same block. The problem is exacerbated as the number of concurrent sessions and transaction volumes increases. So , as a rule, smaller blocks result in less block contention; this applies to index blocks also.

Considering space usage rather than contention by using smaller blocks increases the depth of an index tree for the same number of indexed rows, requiring potentially more physical I/O operations to read the index data. Small blocks are also less space efficient. This is because Oracle blocks have a fixed overhead, so smaller blocks waste more space than larger blocks for the same amount of data. Larger blocks are more efficient for physical I/O, so DSS systems or warehouses that scan tables and don't modify data are more suited to large block sizes. However, the decision to use a large block size for the tables forces you to use the same block size for your indexes (prior to Oracle9i), and that isn't always a good thing.

It's clear from the previous discussion that a mixture of block sizes might be appropriate for many applications, with the block size chosen to meet the usage profile of the data. Oracle9i enables you to choose a block size at the tablespace level and create separate buffer caches for blocks of a particular size. So you are no longer stuck with a fixed block size, and as a result, the choice of the block size at database creation time is no longer so critical. The most important side effect of this Oracle9i feature is that you must stop using db_block_buffers in init.ora to specify the size of the database block buffer cache. This parameter cannot be changed when the database is running and is considered obsolete. Instead, you should use the db_cache_size and db_nk_cache_size initialization parameter settings (where n is the block size that the cache stores data for), as in the following example of an init.ora file:

```
db_cache_size=60m
db_2k_cache_size=20m
db_8k_cache_size=20m
```

The db_cache_size value refers to the cache for the db_block_size used to create the database. As you can see, you can now use the user-friendlier M unit to specify the sizes. As the parameters are dynamic, you can change the settings while the database is running using the ALTER SYSTEM command to change the distribution of total cache space between buffers of different block sizes. The total cache space available is controlled by the fixed parameter sga_max_size at instance startup time. Both 4KB or 8KB are typical values used for db_block_size at the initial database creation. After database creation, you can specify block sizes for application tablespaces according to the I/O characteristics of your application.

Choosing a Storage Character Set

When you create a database, you need to specify a storage character set for the database in the CHARACTER SET clause of the CREATE DATABASE statement. The choice is important because it determines what languages client applications can use to store and display information from the database. On the client, the NLS_LANG environment variable can be used to control the character used by the client application. The rule is that the client character set must be a subset of the database storage character set for your application to work correctly.

For example, if you create a database with a storage character set of US7ASCII and a client application in Paris tries to insert a French name containing accented characters, then information would be lost at storage time because those accented characters are represented in 8 bits of information per character and the database stores only 7 bits. To address this, you might create the database with the storage character set of WE8ISO8859P1, which stores characters in 8 bits, but is limited to handling Western European languages. If you then extend your client base to include Russia and Poland, which use Cyrillic characters, or Japan, you are back to your original problem.

Oracle provides a storage character set called UTF8 to act as a universal storage character set for all languages. Unlike WE8ISO8859P1 and US7ASCII, which store characters in a single byte, UTF8 stores characters in a variable number of bytes. This has an impact on the physical size of your database and the way that VARCHAR2 columns need to be sized. VARCHAR2 column sizes store a number of bytes. So if you use UTF8 as the storage character set, you might increase the column sizes depending on the languages that you intend to support.

Oracle does provide the ALTER DATABASE CHARACTER SET command, enabling you to change from one character set to another when the old character set is a subset of the new one. For example, a conversion from US7ASCII to UTF8 would work because all characters in US7ASCII are also defined in UTF8. If the subset requirement doesn't apply, you need to perform an expensive export, database rebuild, and import to change the character set. So here's the lesson: Choose your storage character set carefully at database creation time with all your possible long-term client user languages in mind.

You can check for possible data conversion issues introduced by ALTER DATABASE CHARACTER SET in advance using the Character Set Scanner utility csscan. Using csscan, you can check all existing data and dictionary data for conversion issues by running the utility, which scans data and then produces a summary of an exception report on completion. During the scan, objects are placed into three categories with respect to convertibility:

- CHANGELESS objects require no conversion.

- CONVERTIBLE objects require conversion by using a full export followed by a full import into a database built with the new character set.

- EXCEPTIONAL objects contain data that requires a manual change before conversion.

Creating the Database

Now we that we've covered all the various aspects of database creation, it's time to create the database itself. Database creation means that we don't just create a skeleton database with the CREATE DATABASE command, but we install the database schema components for all products that have a database dependency, such as the Java Virtual Machine, Intermedia, Oracle Replication, and others.

The best tool for creating a database is the Database Configuration Assistant program, which has the name dbca on UNIX. As it's a graphical user interface (GUI) program, you need to set the X server display in the usual way before running it. Using dbca has two main advantages. The most important one is that you can save the database creation steps into a series of scripts and modify them before running them. This is what I do by choosing the New Database template name. This template means you can change the tablespace and redo log creation to use OMF, set the local extent management and uniform extent allocation for your tablespaces, configure automatic undo management, and alter the storage character set. In short, you can make sure your database is created exactly how you want it, and you get to keep the original scripts used. During configuration, if you select the Generate Database Creation Scripts option, then a set of files is created in the OFA-compliant $ORACLE_BASE/admin/ $ORACLE_SID/scripts directory. For example, using an Oracle SID of OMFD1, the following files are among those created in $ORACLE_BASE/admin/OMFD1/scripts:

```
init.ora
OMFD1.sh
CreateDB.sql
CreateDBFiles.sql
CreateDBCatalog.sql
```

```
JServer.sql
ordinst.sql
spatial.sql
ultraSearch.sql
```

The top-level script OMFD1.sh is the one you run to create your database. This calls the other scripts in the order shown. Be sure to check whether a stored parameter file is created as part of the process. If it is and you're not aware of that, you'll find yourself making changes to the init.ora file that have no effect. You can modify the scripts to meet your own requirements first and you'll probably do that. All scripts after CreateDBCatalog.sql install other products. For any product that you don't require, comment out the entry in OMFD1.sh that calls it. By default, dbca configures an undo tablespace and enables automatic undo management, which is fine because that's the most easily managed way to handle undo. The following tablespace creation statement is a template for the changes you might make to the dbca-generated tablespace creation scripts in CreateDBFiles.sql and puts into practice the recommendations of this chapter:

```
create tablespace oltp_tab blocksize 8kextent management local uniform
size 128k
segment space management auto;
```

The pre-Oracle9i DBA wouldn't recognize parts such as the blocksize clause, the automatic extent management, and the missing datafile specification due to the use of OMF. Assuming your db_block_size is not 8KB, you must set a cache for 8KB blocks first before running this statement—for example, ALTER SYSTEM SET DB_8K_CACHE_SIZE=4M. In a nutshell, this statement encapsulates the path of the Oracle physical layout in the future. It looks a lot less complicated than the old creation statement looks, and at the same time, it produces a much more manageable database.

The other benefit of dbca is that you can create templates that can be reused for the future creation of other databases. For example, you might create a template called No Java for databases that you don't want to install Java support into.

Summary

New Oracle9i features—such as OMF, automatic undo management, spfiles, default temporary tablespaces, variable block sizes, and dynamic cache sizes—reduce administration overhead. The resulting database should be easier to create and administer than ever before and perform just as well.

After the discussion of RAID, SAN, and NAS technology, it seems likely that the DBA will be insulated from issues of hardware performance and availability in the long term and can concentrate on delivering those requirements at the database level instead.

Configuring Oracle Networking

Consider an Oracle network that is configured so that all client users have hard-coded database name-to-address configuration files (tnsnames.ora) residing on each client PC. One weekend the database moves to a different server, the change management process is flawed, and the configuration files aren't updated. On Monday, the users can't access the database. The database itself is fine, but the users (they could be real-time traders) can't connect to the database. Availability is compromised, and the company loses money.

Another situation you might find yourself in is a disaster that destroys one of your main data centers. In this case, you'll need to relocate many of your databases onto different servers, and the resulting mess of trying to readdress all of the clients to find the new database locations is a nightmare. To reiterate, high performance on the server alone is meaningless unless your infrastructure is set up to make that server available at all times on the network without requiring configuration changes on the client.

This chapter explains, step by step, how to migrate from your existing tnsnames.ora-based configuration to a centralized Oracle Names configuration based on a predefined naming standard and how to take advantage of the failover and load-balancing capabilities of Oracle's networking software.

The following topics are covered:

- Oracle networking fundamentals
- Dynamic registration
- Network failover and load balancing
- Running Oracle Names

- Considerations for running the Lightweight Directory Access Protocol (LDAP)
- Shared server configuration
- Transparent gateway configuration

Oracle Networking Fundamentals

Starting from Oracle8i, Oracle's networking capabilities took a significant step forward and new terminology appeared. As was always the case with Oracle networking, the old configuration files still work and many database administrators (DBAs) probably still use the old configuration unchanged. That's not a problem. This section covers the changes from the old configuration to the new, how the changes manifest themselves, and the potential benefits that result.

A traditional pre-Oracle8i network configuration where the client is a desktop PC running Microsoft Windows and the server is running an Oracle database might use a tnsnames.ora configuration file on the client as follows:

```
mydb.dbcool.com=
  (DESCRIPTION =
    (ADDRESS_LIST =
      (ADDRESS=(PROTOCOL=TCP)
      (HOST=srv1.dbcool.com)
      (PORT=1521)
        )
    )
    (CONNECT_DATA =
     (SID = mydb)
    )
  )
```

The file is located in either C:\$ORACLE_HOME\network\admin, by default, or in a standard directory you define (such as C:\var\opt\oracle), which is controlled by setting the TNS_ADMIN environment variable. The use of a standard directory is better because the tnsnames.ora file can be shared between all Oracle client versions on the PC.

A user application specifies the Transparent Network Substrate (TNS) alias mydb.dbcool.com at connect time, and the Oracle networking software that is linked into the application executable searches the tnsnames.ora file for a match on the alias. If it finds a match, it identifies the server where the database is located using the HOST=srv1.dbcool.com entry and attempts a Transmission Control Protocol/Internet Protocol (TCP/IP) connection to the Oracle listener process on the server, on TCP/IP port 1521, passing the SID=mydb information to the server. This System ID (SID) value identifies the database for which the connection request is intended.

The listener process ($ORACLE_HOME/bin/tnslsnr) on the UNIX server is listening for TCP/IP connections on port 1521. This port is identified from the listener.ora file located in TNS_ADMIN when the listener was started. For the purpose of this example, we'll run an Oracle9i listener. Remember that if you have multiple versions of Oracle software on your server, you should always run the listener from the most recent release. The listener.ora contains the following contents, which haven't changed in format since Oracle7:

```
LISTENER =
  (ADDRESS_LIST=
  (ADDRESS=(PROTOCOL=TCP)(HOST=srv1.dbcool.com)(PORT=1521))
  )

STARTUP_WAIT_TIME_LISTENER = 1
CONNECT_TIMEOUT_LISTENER    = 10
LOG_DIRECTORY_LISTENER      = /u01/app/oracle/admin/log
TRACE_LEVEL_LISTENER        = OFF
TRACE_DIRECTORY_LISTENER    = /u01/app/oracle/admin/trace
SID_LIST_LISTENER =
    (SID_LIST =
      (SID_DESC =
        (SID_NAME = mydb)
        (ORACLE_HOME = /u01/app/oracle/product/9.0.1)
      )
    )
```

When the listener receives a client request containing an SID value, it first completes a TCP/IP connection with the client program. This connection uses a newly created TCP/IP port on the server. Once a connection is established, the listener searches the SID_LIST looking for the SID value passed from the client connection request in an SID_NAME entry. When the listener finds a match, it spawns an Oracle process using the executable located in the ORACLE_HOME for the SID_DESC (in this case, . . . /9.0.1/oracle). It also renames the spawned process to include the name of the SID. At this point, the listener process bequeaths its connection with the client onto the spawned process and returns to listening for new requests on the advertised port 1521. A TCP/IP virtual circuit or connection is now established between the application and the Oracle database, and the SID name passed is used to identify the Oracle shared memory segment of the database on the server. If you run the UNIX ps command, you'll see something like this for the spawned process, which is referred to as the *Oracle shadow process*:

```
UID     PID    PPID  C   STIME TTY     TIME CMD
oracle 18434    1    0   19:25:13 ?    0:01 oraclemydb (LOCAL=NO)
```

Hopefully what I've said so far is old news. This is all about to change.

Understanding Dynamic Registration

After shutting down and restarting the mydb database in the previous example and querying the status of the listener using lsnrctl status at the UNIX prompt, the following output appears:

```
STATUS of the LISTENER
  .
  .
```

```
.
Service "mydb" has 1 instance(s).

  Instance "mydb", status UNKNOWN, has 1 handler(s) for this service
 . . .

Service "mydb.dbcool.com", has 1 instance(s).

  Instance "mydb", status READY, has 1 handler(s) for this service . . .

The command completed successfully
```

This is the first clue to the difference in behavior of the Oracle9*i* listener because Instance "mydb" appears twice. The extra entry occurs because the database registers information with the listener at database startup time through a process referred to as dynamic registration. In contrast, databases that are registered with the listener through information from the listener.ora file are referred to as statically registered. In the previous output, the status UNKNOWN refers to the statically registered setting. That's the listener's way of indicating that it doesn't know anything about that instance and will only check for its existence when a connection request is made by a client.

Dynamically registered databases are indicated by status READY or status BLOCKED (for a standby database) in the status information. A dynamically registered database also dynamically unregisters from the listener whenever that database shuts down, and its information disappears from the status list. As result, the listener always knows the state of the database, whether it's up or down. This information is used in the fallback and load balancing of connection requests. You can't turn self-registration off (in any documented way at least) and that's no bad thing due to the benefits. If you're wondering why you need a static registered entry in the listener.ora when you get self-registration for free, the answer is that you don't need to do static registration at all, except for a couple of anomalous situations. The result is that, provided you use the default listener port of 1521, you no longer need a listener.ora file. However, you'll probably still use one, if only to direct log and trace information to a standard directory, as in the earlier example. If you do persist with static registration, you can remove the ORACLE_HOME entry from the SID_DESC section if your database is Oracle9*i*. Therefore, it looks like this:

```
(SID_LIST =
    (SID_DESC =
       (SID_NAME = mydb)
     )
  )
```

Here's what happens during self-registration, assuming your listener is up and running before the databases are started. Whenever you start a database, two pieces of information are by default registered with the listener: the instance and the service.

The instance value registered with the listener takes its value from the instance _name parameter in the init.ora file. If this is not set, then the db_name value from the init.ora file is used. During single instance operation, you don't have to set this parameter, but it's best to set it to the value of db_name to take full value advantage of dynamic registration. However, if you are running Oracle in a Real Application Clusters (RAC) configuration, you must set the instance_name parameter to a unique value for each instance in the cluster.

The service value registered with the listener takes its value from the service_names parameter in the init.ora file. If this is not set, the database registers itself using the concatenation of the db_name and db_domain values from the init.ora file. If you choose to provide the service_names value, you can use either a fully qualified name (such as mydb.dbcool.com) or a short name (such as mydb). If you choose a short name and the db_domain parameter is set, the service registered with the listener is a concatenation of the service_names value and the db_domain value. For example, the following settings will result in the service mydb.dbcool.com being registered with the listener:

```
db_domain=dbcool.com
service_names=mydb
```

Optionally, you can specify multiple service values in the service_names parameter, separating each by a comma, which is useful in shared server configurations as explained later in the section "Using Shared Server." The use of service_names is *mandatory* when you need to do connection-time failover or load balancing, or want to distribute connections transparently between instances in a RAC configuration. To enable these facilities, you simply set service_names in the database parameter file for each instance to the same value and refer to that in the service_name setting in the connection request from the client. The following section on load balancing and failover provides examples.

It's good practice to set explicit values for the service_names and instance_name initialization parameters even though Oracle will generate default values for dynamic registration (based on db_name and db_domain) if you don't set them. The reason is that there is a subtle difference in dynamic registration behavior if your listener is restarted after the databases are up. If your listener is restarted after the databases are up, then the PMON process for each database will reregister it automatically after a short time *only* if you explicitly set service_names and instance_name in the init.ora file. If you don't set service_names and instance_name explicitly, then dynamic registration takes place only when the database is started after the listener is running. If the listener is subsequently restarted in this case, dynamic registration information is lost.

Clearly, it's best to start the listener on a server prior to starting any databases and avoid listener restarts altogether in order to prevent the possibility of losing dynamically registered database service information. At the same time, you need to recognize that it's possible for the listener to fail, which inevitably requires a listener restart. Setting explicit values for service_names and instance_name provides protection from a listener restart by ensuring that your databases automatically remain registered with the listener as long as they are running. It's worth keeping in mind that you can also register service values manually with the listener at any time while the database is open using the ALTER SYSTEM REGISTER command from SQL*Plus. This command is useful to replace service values that have been lost as a result of a listener restart, and it registers exactly the same values as those set by dynamic registration at database startup.

To summarize, for a non-RAC configuration, as a general rule you should always set db_domain in your init.ora file and set instance_name and service_names based on the values of db_name and db_domain. Don't register static information using the listener.ora file because dynamic registration will do that for you. Here's an example of the relevant part of an init.ora file where the naming meets these requirements:

```
db_name=mydb
db_domain=dbcool.com

instance_name=mydb
service_names=mydb.dbcool.com
```

If you use the Oracle Database Configuration Assistant program to create your databases, which is recommended, then this information will be automatically generated in the init.ora file for you. For the client connection description, stop using the old-style SID = entry and replace it with the service_name value, as shown in Table 3.1.

The new style has a pleasing symmetry because the same name is used for all the following values:

- mydb.dbcool.com is the TNS name that end-user applications use in connection requests. This is specified in the first line of the client connection description.

- mydb.dbcool.com is the service_name value used in the CONNECT_DATA section of the client connection description. At connection time, service_name is passed to the database listener on the server, which attempts to match it with the name of a database service registered with the listener using the service_names initialization parameter.

- mydb.dbcool.com is the service_names value specified in the database initialization file on the database server, used to dynamically register the database with the listener at database startup time.

Table 3.1 Old- and New-Style Client Connection Descriptions

OLD STYLE	NEW STYLE
mydb.dbcool.com=	mydb.dbcool.com=
(DESCRIPTION =	(DESCRIPTION =
(ADDRESS_LIST =	(ADDRESS_LIST =
(ADDRESS=(PROTOCOL=TCP)	(ADDRESS=(PROTOCOL=TCP
(HOST=srv1.dbcool.com)	(HOST=srv1.dbcool.com)
(PORT=1521)	(PORT=1521)
)	)
)	)
(CONNECT_DATA =	(CONNECT_DATA =
(SID = mydb)	(service_name=mydb.dbcool.com)
)	)
)	)

Keep in mind that the old-style CONNECT_DATA using a SID value continues to work.

What about those anomalies mentioned earlier? Unfortunately, Oracle software doesn't always obey its own rules for service naming across all products. For example, Oracle Enterprise Manager (OEM) uses the tnsnames.ora file to locate database services on the current server. One of our goals is to get rid of that by replacing the tnsnames.ora file with an Oracle Names server. However, OEM won't recognize a Names server. Therefore, on one hand, you want to ditch tnsnames.ora and on the other hand you want to use OEM. To work around this, you can statically register a service name with the listener through the use of the GLOBAL_DBNAME parameter in the listener.ora file:

```
SID_LIST_LISTENER =
  (SID_LIST =
    (SID_DESC =
       (SID_NAME = mydb)
       (GLOBAL_DBNAME = mydb.dbcool.com)
    )
  )
```

If you don't do this, OEM will identify your database using a combination of the host name and instance name (srv1_mydb), which is annoying when you've already created a unique name for it that obeys your naming standard, which in this case is mydb.dbcool.com. To compound matters, using GLOBAL_DBNAME itself has a side effect. It breaks Transparent Application Failover in RAC, so you should not use GLOBAL_DBNAME in a RAC configuration.

You've probably got a headache by now so let's move on to the benefits of using a network configuration based on dynamic listener registration on the server (through the service_names initialization parameter) and service_name in the client connection description. This is referred to as the service-name-based approach in the following examples.

Using Failover and Load Balancing

The behavior of the service-name-based failover and load-balancing capabilities are best shown using real-world examples.

Failover to a Different Server

For the first failover example, let's use an example that we'll actually put to use when configuring Oracle Recovery Manager (RMAN). In this scenario, your company has three data centers on different sites that are subject to periodic scheduled power outages for building maintenance. All of the data centers contain Oracle databases. Company policy dictates that only one site can be out at any time.

The DBA group has a requirement to back up and restore databases 24×7, and all backups are based on an RMAN backup catalog. This means that the RMAN backup catalog database needs to be available pretty much at all times so the backup and restore service is available at the other two sites during a site outage. A solution to this problem is as follows. The DBA group identifies two servers—site1.dbcool.com and site2.dbcool.com—each on a different site to hold the backup catalog database. This database is only up and running on one site or the other. The DBA group manages this switchover manually by shutting down the database on one site, according to the outage requirements, and physically copying it to the other site. The init.ora parameters for the database are the same on both sites and include the following information, relevant to failover:

```
db_name=rmanp1
db_domain=dbcool.com

instance_name=rmanp1
service_names=rmanp1.dbcool.com
```

The failover capability is provided through a TNS alias as follows:

```
rmanp1.dbcool.com  =
  (description =
    (address_list =
      (address=(protocol=tcp)(host = site1.dbcool.com)(port = 1521))
      (address=(protocol=tcp)(host = site2.dbcool.com)(port = 1521))
      (load_balance = false)
      (failover = true)
    )
    (connect_data =
      (service_name = rmanp1.dbcool.com)
    )
  )
```

NOTE **All keyword values in a connection description are case insensitive, so failover=true, FAILOVER=TRUE, and FAILOVER=true are all equivalent.**

All backup clients connect to the catalog database using the TNS alias rmanp1 .dbcool.com, and the connection is made to the service name, which actually comprises one of the databases on site1 or site2. The list of servers where the database can be found is provided by the ADDRESS values in the ADDRESS_LIST, and the FAILOVER=TRUE value means that the client connection fails over to the database at address site2.dbcool.com if the database is down at site1.dbcool.com. No configuration change is required on the client system (the server where the database to be backed up resides) whenever the backup catalog is relocated due to a site outage; the failover feature takes care of the reconnection. The meaning of LOAD_BALANCE and FAILOVER are described in the matrix in Table 3.2.

In our case, we use load_balance=false and failover=true to indicate that only one of our databases is operational at any time. If the first one in the list (on site1.dbcool .com) is down, then the second one (on site2.dbcool.com) should be contacted as failover and should be up. There is actually a small outage to the availability of the cat-

Table 3.2 LOAD_BALANCE and FAILOVER Connection Options

	FAILOVER=TRUE	FAILOVER=FALSE
LOAD_BALANCE=TRUE	Try one address at random from the ADDRESS_LIST and attempt a connection. If it fails, try the other address.	Try one address at random from the ADDRESS_LIST and attempt a connection. If it fails, return an error message to the client.
LOAD_BALANCE=FALSE	Try the first address from the ADDRESS_LIST and attempt a connection. If it fails, try the next address.	Meaningless.

alog database due to the need to relocate it to a different site, but because this is under the control of the DBA group, the relocation can be scheduled at a time when the backup server is not in use.

NOTE This outage can actually be reduced to almost zero using Oracle9*i* standby database technology, which is covered in Chapter 23.

Understanding When Failover Takes Place

It's important to understand exactly when a connection attempt fails over and when it doesn't. As a side effect of this investigation, you'll see why the service-name-based approach provides superior capabilities compared to failover that was available prior to Oracle8*i*. Three main failover scenarios are of interest:

- The database is down.
- The listener is down.
- The server is down.

If the Oracle database instance is down on the first connection attempt (ORA-01034 message from the server), failover will take place instantaneously to the second if service names are in use. Prior to the existence of the service names feature (for example, using SQL*Net 2.3.4 client failover) the client would receive an ORA-01034 message, and no failover would take place. So the service-name-based failover is a significant improvement on older versions because the underlying database self-registration means that the listener knows if the database is up or down and can use this information.

If the target machine is up but there is no tnslsnr process listening on the specified port, then the remote TCP module responds immediately, indicating that it can't make a connection and the client process knows right away that it's time to failover. In this case, when the Oracle client application tries to establish a TCP connection, it sends a message (specifically, an SYN packet) to the TCP module on the target machine asking for a connection to a particular port (which by default is 1521 for the Oracle listener) and this request is rejected.

If the target machine is shut down or not available on the network (that is, a ping request fails), then the time to failover is determined by the operating system TCP/IP configuration setting. On Solaris, this is given by the following:

```
tcp_ip_abort_cinterval
```

By default, this is set to 180,000 milliseconds (3 minutes). This time can be reduced to approximately 10 seconds by placing the following command in the Solaris initialization scripts, which are controlled by the root account:

```
ndd -set /dev/tcp tcp_ip_abort_cinterval 10000
```

Before you make this change, be aware that it affects all TCP/IP connections on the server, and if you have some very slow links, then these might time out too quickly. On the other hand, 3 minutes is a long time to wait for a connection, and many users will simply give up and call the helpdesk, adding to your support burden.

Failover to an Instance on the Same Server

In a second scenario, say that we have two instances on the same server srv1.dbcool .com and we want to connect to either one that is up. This is somewhat different from the previous example because we are not failing over between sites, so the load-balancing and failover capabilities from the ADDRESS_LIST are not available. However, we still have a failover capability through the use of service names. In this case, we register both databases with the listener using the same service name, even though they have different instance names, as shown in the init.ora parameters in Table 3.3.

If you run the lnsrctl status command, you'll clearly see the two instances associated with a single service name:

```
Service "mydb.dbcool.com" has 2 instance(s).
   Instance "mydbp1", status READY, has 1 handler(s) for this
service . . .
   Instance "mydbp2", status READY, has 1 handler(s) for this
service . . .
```

Table 3.3 init.ora Details for Failover to Different Databases on a Server

INITMYDBP1.ORA FILE CONTENTS	INITMYDBP2.ORA FILE CONTENTS
db_name=mydbp1	db_name=mydbp2
db_domain=dbcool.com	db_domain=dbcool.com
instance_name=mydbp1	instance_name=mydbp2
service_names=mydb.dbcool.com	service_names=mydb.dbcool.com

All client applications connect to the service using the following alias:

```
mydb.dbcool.com  =
  (description =
    (address_list =
      (address=(protocol=tcp)(host = srv1.dbcool.com)(port = 1521)))
    (connect_data =
      (service_name = mydb.dbcool.com)
    )
  )
```

The instance to which the first connection attempt is made is determined by the one that registered first with the listener. If that instance is down, then the other is contacted.

Failover with Load Balancing

Finally, let's see an example of load balancing and failover together using an RAC configuration with two instances, one on each node in a two-node cluster. The server names are rac1.dbcool.com and rac2.dbcool.com. We want to load balance all users across both instances in the cluster and make sure that connection requests are transparently redirected to other instances in the cluster when one instance is down. Note that the load-balancing capabilities are actually more sophisticated than a random selection of the server address. These capabilities are determined by the actual server loading on each instance.

Before we begin, it's helpful to distinguish between the Oracle SID value that you specify in the UNIX environment to identify the instance and the instance_name parameter you use in the init.ora file. The SID (specified by the $ORACLE_SID UNIX environment variable) is used by the Oracle software to determine the shared memory segment, background processes, and init.ora file used when you start an instance on the server. The instance_name in the init.ora file is used to identify the instance to the Oracle listener process. In a RAC environment, it's mandated that each instance in the RAC has a different instance_name. Therefore, our /var/opt/oracle/oratab file (or /etc/oratab on some UNIX variants) that identifies the $ORACLE_SID present on the node looks like this on each node:

```
mydbp11:/u01/app/oracle/product/9.0.1:N   # on rac1.dbcool.com
mydbp12:/u01/app/oracle/product/9.0.1:N   # on rac2.dbcool.com
```

The init.ora files on each node of the cluster (in the example) share the service_names value, but use different instance names, as shown in Table 3.4.

To support connections to the service mydbp1.dbcool.com, the TNS alias used by all clients to connect would use the following mydbp1.dbcool.com entry, which specifies both load balancing and failover, but has no reference to the individual instance on either node. This means that the Oracle networking software can decide on the instance that the client application connects to, both for load balancing or failover to

Table 3.4 init.ora Differences for a Two-Node RAC Configuration

INITMYDBP11.ORA ON RAC1.DBCOOL.COM	INITMYDBP12.ORA ON RAC2.DBCOOL.COM
db_name=mydbp1	db_name=mydbp1
instance_number=1	instance_number=2
db_domain=dbcool.com	db_domain=dbcool.com
instance_name=mydbp11	instance_name=mydbp12
service_names=mydbp1.dbcool.com	service_names=mydbp1.dbcool.com

the other instance if the first one is down while being completely transparent to the client application:

```
mydbp1.dbcool.com=
   (description=
   (address_list=
     (address=(protocol=tcp)(host=rac1.dbcool.com)(port=1521))
     (address=(protocol=tcp)(host=rac2.dbcool.com)(port=1521)))
       (connect_data=
         (service_name=mydbp1.dbcool.com)
       )
     (load_balance=on)
     (failover=on)
   )
```

Of course, it's sometimes necessary to provide a facility to connect specifically to one instance or the other. This is facilitated by providing individual aliases that specify the same service_name but different instance_name values, as shown in Table 3.5.

The TNS aliases can be named any way you choose. The previous examples have a naming standard that appends the instance_number in each init.ora file to the db_name component of the name in order to identify the instance—for example, 1 and 2. This

Table 3.5 TNS Aliases for Instance-Specific RAC Connections

CONNECTION TO INSTANCE ON RAC1	CONNECTION TO INSTANCE ON RAC2
mydbp11.dbcool.com=	mydbp12.dbcool.com=
(description=	(description=
(address=	(address=
(protocol=tcp)	(protocol=tcp)
(host=rac1.dbcool.com)	(host=rac2.dbcool.com)
(port=1521)	(port=1521)
)	)
(connect_data=	(connect_data=
(service_name=mydbp1.dbcool.com)	(service_name=mydbp1.dbcool.com)
(instance_name=mydbp11)	(instance_name=mydbp12)
)	)

naming convention is used by the Oracle Database Configuration Assistant when creating a cluster database. Whatever you choose, stick to a standard and you'll be able to connect to any of your instances without needing to look up the names.

Running an Oracle Names Server

In my experience, no other Oracle product provides such significant benefits with such little effort as Oracle Names. If you use Oracle Names and set up the configuration so that it's redundant against a single point of failure, then you no longer need to use a tnsnames.ora file on the client. This means that whenever you create a new Oracle service in your organization or relocate an Oracle database onto a different server, no configuration change is required on the client. In fact, the clients won't even be aware of the change. This reduces support costs as you should be able to eliminate Oracle connectivity problems from your workload altogether. Provided that you run Oracle Names on a minimum of two sites, you will still have an Oracle name-to-address service available even in the case of a site disaster. You'll be able to relocate the database to other servers, possible even in different countries, and the client application won't detect a thing. If you use Oracle Names to resolve Oracle service aliases, then by definition you are centralizing your Oracle name-to-address service. At this point, you should implement a global naming standard for your Oracle database TNS aliases. This doesn't mean that you need to convert the old names; it just means that all names from this point should obey the standard. You should put a task on your list to convert the old names over time.

> **WARNING** Be forewarned that Oracle is not releasing Oracle Names after Oracle9*i*. That's fine for now, and Oracle Names will continue to work for several years. However, the demise of Oracle Names in the long term means we need to investigate the use of LDAP to resolve Oracle service names in the future. This is covered in the next section. LDAP is Oracle's directory protocol of choice, and Oracle is increasing the number of features available via LDAP over time. Oracle name resolution using LDAP requires Oracle8*i* or higher client software.

A Naming Standard for Oracle Databases

The point of a database-naming standard is to guarantee that you can address every Oracle database in your organization by a unique name. This means using a fully qualified name for the connection alias, changing the global_name value that's stored persistently in the database to match the connection alias, and enforcing the naming standard. Using this naming schema means that the external name used to connect to the database on the network matches the database's internal global name. Why is this important? Let's take an example of a poor name choice and fix it to meet the standard after identifying the problems. For purposes of the example, let's say that Big Inc is a global organization with a Domain Name Service (DNS) name of big.com and has offices in London, New York, and Tokyo. A London DBA creates a database, names it sales, and uses a default domain of world. This is how the relevant part of the init.ora file looks:

```
db_name=sales
db_domain=world
```

The TNS alias used by clients to connect to the database is sales.world. The DBA group duly adds this to the tnsnames.ora file and delivers the changed file to all London PCs:

```
sales.world=
  (description=
  (address=
     (protocol=tcp)
     (host=srv1.uk.big.com)
     (port=1521)
  )
  (connect_data=
  (service_name=sales.world)
  )
```

Logging onto SQL*Plus and selecting the global name of the database gives the following:

```
SQL> select * from global_name;

GLOBAL_NAME
------------------------------------
SALES.WORLD
```

Then a DBA in New York creates a database with the same global name (sales.world) on a New York server. The connection alias in the tnsnames.ora file that's shipped to New York users looks like this:

```
sales.world=
  (description=
  (address=
     (protocol=tcp)
     (host=ny.us.big.com)
     (port=1521)
  )
  (connect_data=
  (service_name=sales.world)
  )
```

Everything's fine until someone in New York needs to access the London server. Now there's a problem because the name that London uses to refer to the London database (sales.world) is already in use in New York to refer to the New York database. The problem can be fixed in ad hoc ways by modifying the TNS name of one of the databases and changing its global name; however, that's not a well-thought-out solution. A better solution is to use a global naming scheme based on a top-down notation like DNS. DNS fixes the problems involved in resolving host names centrally and uniquely, and you can use a similar approach to name your database services.

To resolve this problem, Big Inc has a meeting with its DBAs and they come up with a global naming standard for Oracle databases that prevents the names from clashing in the future. They decide that all database global names and TNS aliases must include the region in the name, giving the tnsnames.ora entries shown in Table 3.6, which can be safely copied into the tnsnames.ora files on both sites.

The DBAs agree that the last three components of each name will be used to identify the region where the service is located, so New York will use us.big.com and London will use uk.big.com. Tokyo is informed that it should start using jp.big.com for its databases. This is a simple and flexible naming scheme that enables further subdivisions of the name in a top-down fashion. For example, when the London trading department wants an equities trading database and an equities warehouse, there's nothing to stop the London DBA group from choosing the following names because they meet the standard, even though the names have five components:

```
trading.equities.uk.big.com
warehouse.equities.uk.big.com
```

Additional benefits that no one thought of in advance come about when the New York and London DBAs have a requirement to connect their databases together for the purposes of replication using Oracle database links. Now it's very straightforward to link the systems together because they already have names that are guaranteed to be globally unique, and no one needs to struggle with thinking up appropriate names. With the naming standard in place, it's a no-brainer. At this point, it's worth explaining the exact purposes of the database global_name value, the db_domain init.ora parameter, the global_names init.ora parameter, and the names.default_domain setting in the sqlnet.ora on the client. The relationships between these settings can be confusing.

Table 3.6 TNS Aliases in a Global Naming Scheme

NEW YORK ALIAS	LONDON ALIAS
`sales.us.big.com=`	`sales.uk.big.com=`
`  (description=`	`  (description=`
`  (address=`	`  (address=`
`    (protocol=tcp)`	`    (protocol=tcp)`
`    (host=ny1.us.big.com)`	`    (host=srv1.uk.big.com)`
`    (port=1521)`	`    (port=1521)`
`  )`	`  )`
`  (connect_data=`	`  (connect_data=`
`  (service_name=sales.us.big.com)`	`  (service_name=sales.uk.big.com)`
`  )`	`  )`

The DB_DOMAIN Parameter

The db_domain setting from the init.ora file is used as the default setting for the domain part of any database link you create. If the db_domain setting in your init.ora file is uk.dbcool.com, then the following two Structured Query Language (SQL) statements will create the same link, sales.uk.dbcool.com (which you can check by selecting from the USER_DB_LINKS table):

```
create database link sales;
create database link sales.uk.big.com;
```

A database link has two components—a link name, which is stored in the local data dictionary, and an associated TNS alias, which is the external name that Oracle uses to connect to the remote database associated with the link name. You've probably noticed that the two link creation statements didn't specify a TNS alias to identify the remote database to connect to because there is no USING clause present in the SQL. That's another advantage of this naming standard. If you don't specify the USING clause, then Oracle silently defaults it to be the same as the link name. So if you create a link named sales.uk.big.com and use it in a query, Oracle will connect to the remote database identified by the alias sales.uk.big.com. That's exactly what we want based on our naming standard. The db_domain setting is also used if you select from the database link without using a fully qualified link name. In this case, Oracle will silently suffix the db_domain setting for you. So the following SQL statements are equivalent, using a db_domain value of uk.big.com:

```
select * from all_users@sales;
select * from all_users@sales.uk.big.com;
```

From my experiences of working in a global environment, I strongly recommend that you don't rely on default domains on links and always specify domain-qualified names when you create links or use them. If you don't, there's the possibility that in a globally replicated system, where the databases all have the same names and differ only in the value of the db_domain, you'll end up running SQL against the wrong database by mistake.

GLOBAL_NAME and GLOBAL_NAMES

Sometimes Oracle seems determined to confuse the DBA, and the existence of both global_name and global_names is an excellent example. It is possible that enforce_global_names would have been a better choice than global_names. Anyway, the global_name setting is a persistent setting in the database, and you can view and set it using the following SQL:

```
select * from global_name;
alter database rename global_name to sales.us.big.com;
```

Although the name implies that it's somehow related to the db_domain value in the init.ora file, you can set the global_name and db_domain independently, which isn't really a good thing. In reality, you'll endeavor to make sure that the global_name value is identical to the db_name and db_domain values from the init.ora file, joined with a ".".

The global_name has two main purposes. It's often used by developers of Oracle applications to tell the user which database he or she is connected to, usually by putting the value in the caption of the application window after connection. DbCool does this. More importantly, the global_name can be used to enforce the global naming standard for database link names when used in combination with the init.ora setting global_names=true. Here's an example of how it works, given that global_names= false at the start. In the New York database, a DBA creates a database link to the London database, and the London database has a global_name setting of sales.uk.big.com:

```
create database link sales.uk.big.com;
```

Another New York DBA comes along and creates another link to the London database:

```
create database link nonstandard.uk.big.com;
```

Both these links will work perfectly fine, but you want to disallow the nonstandard one. To do this, you need to make sure that the global_names=true setting is on the New York database when you start it up. In this case, a query against the nonstandard link will return a runtime error:

```
select * from all_users@nonstandard.uk.big.com;

ORA-02085: database link NONSTANDARD.UK.BIG.COM connects to
SALES.UK.BIG.COM
```

By setting global_names=true in your init.ora file, you enforce the global naming standard that any database link name in the local database must match the global_name of the remote database. If it doesn't, Oracle will refuse to run the SQL and return an ORA-02085 error. If you're familiar with database links, you'll know that you might have several database links to a remote database, each with different authentication at the remote end. For example, one link might connect to the SALES account at the remote end and one might connect to the MANAGERS account. How do you enforce the global naming standard while still allowing multiple links with different authentication? The answer is that you use connection qualifiers. Connection qualifiers enable you to enforce global naming and at the same time allow multiple links with different properties connecting to the same remote database. You create such qualified links as follows and use them just like a regular link:

```
create database link sales.uk.big.com@q1
       connect to managers identified by sz7123
       using 'sales.uk.big.com';

select * from commission@sales.uk.big.com@q1;
```

In the example, the link qualifier is q1. Note that the link name still obeys the global standard. The qualifier could be any string you choose. When you create a link with a connection qualifier, you must provide the connection alias in the link create statement in the USING clause. You might think that Oracle could just strip the qualifier off the end of the link name and use what's left (sales.uk.big.com) as the connection alias. However, it doesn't, and if you forget to provide it, you'll receive the following message:

```
ORA-02019: connection description for remote database not found
```

You can see the database link information best by querying the SYS.LINK$ table, which includes the passwords for any link connections in cleartext. For that reason, if you're using links, be extra vigilant about security. Also, remember that the HOST column is not the remote server where the remote database is located; it's the TNS alias for the remote database. It's set to HOST for long forgotten historical reasons. Here are the contents for the links we created in the examples:

```
select name,host,userid,password from sys.link;

NAME                   HOST                 USERID    PASSWORD
-------------------- ------------------- -------- ----------
SALES.UK.BIG.COM@Q1  sales.uk.big.com    MANAGERS    SZ7123
SALES.UK.BIG.COM     sales.uk.big.com
```

NAMES.DEFAULT_DOMAIN

Recall the TNS alias we used to identify the New York database:

```
sales.us.big.com=
  (description=
      .
      .
      .
```

Any client application needing to connect to this database would need to specify the name sales.us.big.com at connect time. Actually, that's not entirely true. We've already seen that the db_domain value in the database init.ora file can be used to default the domain used when you create a database link. In a similar way, the names.default_domain setting can be used to default the domain part of the connection alias during an Oracle connection. The names.default_domain setting is found in the sqlnet.ora file that holds client-side Oracle connection settings.

If you set names.default_domain=us.big.com to the sqlnet.ora file on an Oracle client, then a client application could provide the unqualified name sales at connect time and the connection would succeed because us.big.com would be silently appended before connection.

The use of names.default_domain is very strongly discouraged. Its use can result in DBAs accidentally connecting to the wrong database in replicated environments where the default domain depends on the location of the client machine. In most graphical user interface (GUI) applications, either the user chooses a connection from a list of names or the connect string is built into the application. So the only benefit of using names.default_domain appears to be in saving a DBA from typing in a few extra characters when connecting to a database using command-line tools like SQL*Plus. So it's not much of a sacrifice to give it up.

Now we have our global naming standard for databases in place. We've agreed to use global_names=true in all our databases, use fully qualified names for our database connect aliases, and ensure that the db_name and db_domain settings in our init.ora file match the global_name of the database.

Finally, all host names specified in our TNS connection descriptions should also use fully qualified domain names. Although the DBA can't implement this, as it's a service provided by the system administrator (SA) group, there's absolutely no point in the DBA group implementing domain-qualified names if the underlying host names are not domain qualified. If this is the case in your organization, encourage your group to adopt DNS immediately.

Using an Oracle Names Service on the Client

Now we'll set up an Oracle Names service based on installing an Oracle Names server on two hosts. You could use the two hosts in the DBA Cluster discussed in Chapter 1. The concept of Oracle Names is extremely simple.

To connect to an Oracle database, a client application needs to resolve an Oracle TNS alias like this:

```
sales.uk.big.com=
  (description=
   (address=
     (protocol=tcp)
     (host=srv1.uk.big.com)
     (port=1521)
   )
   (connect_data=
   (service_name=sales.uk.big.com)
   )
```

In the early days, this was done through a lookup in a local tnsnames.ora file on the client. To use a Names server, load up all the tnsnames.ora entries into the Names server, remove the tnsnames.ora file on the client, and change the sqlnet.ora file on the client to use the two Names servers to resolve the aliases instead. In simple terms, the Oracle Names servers hold a list of database TNS descriptions, which are indexed by the TNS alias names. So the client application sends sales.uk.big.com to the Names server at connect time, the Names server returns the description part, and the client uses the host and service_name values returned in the description to identify the server and database to connect to. That's all there is to it.

You can actually verify that a description is all you need to connect to an Oracle database. You don't actually need to provide a TNS alias to connect at all. You can connect using the description instead, making sure it's enclosed in quotes. It's a bit awkward to enter the following all on one line instead of sales.uk.big.com, but it does work using SQL*Plus:

```
'(description=(address_list=(address=(protocol=tcp)(host=srv1.uk.big.com
)(port=1521)))(connect_data=(service=sales.uk.big.com)))'
```

That's how some of Oracle's tools, and DbCool for that matter, enable you connect to an Oracle database just by providing an Oracle service or SID, a host name, and a port number: They create a description based on those details and connect using that. This is what the sqlnet.ora file used by all clients in London looks like, after changing it to use the Names servers:

```
names.directory_path = (TNSNAMES,ONAMES)

names.preferred_servers=
(address_list =
    (address =
        (protocol = TCP)
        (port = 1575)
        (host = oran1.uk.big.com)
    )
    (address =
        (protocol = TCP)
        (port = 1575)
        (host = oran2.uk.big.com)
    )
)
```

The names.directory_path specifies that a local tnsnames.ora file should be used to resolve an Oracle TNS alias before using the Names server. As there is no tnsnames.ora (we've removed it), the Names server will be used. The purpose of leaving the tnsnames.ora file as a possibility is so that the DBA can manually add entries to the file in an emergency and override the Names server. This is a very unlikely scenario.

The names.preferred_servers value specifies the two Names servers to be used to resolve names. The first server is contacted, and if it's down, the second one is used. Provided the servers are never both down at once, which must be a key feature of your design, you have a 24×7 service. The names for the hosts in the client sqlnet.ora files should be DNS aliases and not the real host names. This means that in the unlikely event that you lose both your servers, you can redirect the aliases to two new servers without having to change the sqlnet.ora file on each client. There's no need to stop at two servers. If you want more redundancy, you can add more preferred servers. Two is a minimum.

Once you're using an Oracle Names server, you'll get a very useful feature, known as a *global database link*, for free. For example, if you're connected to sales.uk.big.com and you want to query SELECT * FROM TRADES@sales.us.big.com, then provided that your local session logon and password exist on the remote database, you can go ahead and run the SQL without creating the database link. Oracle looks in the Names server for a TNS alias matching the database link you specified. If one exists, it uses it to connect.

Building an Oracle Names Server

You need to designate a minimum of two hosts on which to run Oracle Names to ensure that the service is maintained if you have an outage on one site or the other, planned or otherwise. As is often the case, Oracle gives you too much choice in the configuration. The one I've chosen means that you hold all of your Oracle TNS entries in an Oracle database, which gives you all the protection and security that comes with an Oracle database.

Ensure that you have installed Oracle Names. You can check this by looking for the $ORACLE_HOME/bin/names executable. Designate a database to hold the TNS entries, one that has 24×7 availability. For our example, we use the instance onamesp1 located on server s24x7.uk.big.com. Create a schema within the database as follows using SQL*Plus:

```
create user names identified by names901
temporary tablespace temp default tablespace tools quota unlimited on
tools;

grant create session to names;

grant resource to names;

revoke unlimited tablespace from names;

grant create synonym to names;

connect names/names901

@/u01/app/oracle/product/9.0.1/network/admin/namesini
```

Now create a names.ora file on each of your chosen hosts. Our example uses srv1.uk.big.com and srv2.uk.big.com. Remember that the host name oran1.uk.big.com used in the client sqlnet.ora file shown previously should be a DNS alias for the real host name srv1.uk.big.com, and the same relationship exists between oran2.uk .big.com and srv2.uk.vig.com. The names.ora file is located in the TNS_ADMIN directory. Table 3.7 shows the contents of the Names services' names.ora files on each site.

Note that each Names server has a different name, listens for requests on port 1575 (to match the port specified in the sqlnet.ora file on the client sites), and shares the same REGION database for storing the TNS entries. Table 3.8 shows the contents of the sqlnet.ora files on the Names server sites. These are different from the client versions and different across the Names server sites. This is because we want the namesctl command-line utility (used to stop and start the Names servers) to default to the Names server on the local site first. The order is determined by the order of the preferred servers in the sqlnet.ora file. The clients have a different requirement: They simply need to access any Names server that is available so the lookup order does not matter.

To start the Names server on each site, use the namesctl utility. Don't worry about messages involving problems contacting the default server (the first in the sqlnet.ora file) because the server is not up yet.

```
namesctl start
```

Table 3.7 Contents of the names.ora File on Names Server Sites

FILE NAMES.ORA FILE ON FIRST SITE	FILE NAMES.ORA FILE ON SECOND SITE
NAMES.SERVER_NAME = NS_SRV1.UK.BIG.COM	NAMES.SERVER_NAME = NS_SRV2.UK.BIG.COM

NAMES.ADDRESSES =
  (ADDRESS = (PROTOCOL = TCP)
         (HOST = srv1.uk.big.com)
 	
         (PORT = 1575))
	NAMES.ADDRESSES =
	  (ADDRESS = (PROTOCOL = TCP)
	          (HOST = srv2.uk.big.com)
	
	          (PORT = 1575))

NAMES.ADMIN_REGION =
  (REGION =
    (DESCRIPTION =
      (ADDRESS = (PROTOCOL = TCP)
      (HOST = s24x7.uk.big.com)
      (PORT = 1521))
      (CONNECT_DATA =
        (SID = onamesp1)
        (Server = Dedicated)
)
)
    (USERID = names)
    (PASSWORD = names901)
    (NAME = LOCAL_REGION)
    (REFRESH = 86400)
    (RETRY = 60)
    (EXPIRE = 600)
    (VERSION = 134230016)
)
	NAMES.ADMIN_REGION =
	  (REGION =
	    (DESCRIPTION =
	      (ADDRESS = (PROTOCOL = TCP)
	      (HOST = s24x7.uk.big.com)
	      (PORT = 1521))
	      (CONNECT_DATA =
	        (SID = onamesp1)
	        (Server = Dedicated)
	      )
	    )
	    (USERID = names)
	    (PASSWORD = names901)
	    (NAME = LOCAL_REGION)
	    (REFRESH = 86400)
	    (RETRY = 60)
	    (EXPIRE = 600)
	    (VERSION = 134230016)
	  )

Table 3.8 Contents of sqlnet.ora File on Names Server Sites

FILE SQLNET.ORA FILE ON SRV1.UK.BIG.COM	FILE SQLNET.ORA FILE ON SRV2.UK.BIG.COM

names.directory_path =
(TNSNAMES,ONAMES)
names.preferred_servers=
(address_list =
    (address =
        (protocol = TCP)
        (port = 1575)
        (host = srv1.uk.big.com)
)
    (address =
        (protocol = TCP)
        (port = 1575)
        (host = srv2.uk.big.com)
)
)
	names.directory_path =
	(TNSNAMES,ONAMES)
	names.preferred_servers=
	(address_list =
	    (address =
	        (protocol = TCP)
	        (port = 1575)
	        (host = srv2.uk.big.com)
	    )
	    (address =
	        (protocol = TCP)
	        (port = 1575)
	        (host = srv1.uk.big.com)
	    )
	)

On one site and as a one-off task, load up your TNS entries from the tnsnames.ora that you've removed from client sites. You can provide the path to the file if it's not in the TNS_ADMIN directory. Otherwise, Oracle looks for the tnsnames.ora file:

```
load_tnsnames
```

Now start the Names server on the other site. Your Names service is now up and running on both sites, providing 24×7 service.

Other Oracle Names Configurations

Oracle provides other configurations for running a Names server. One uses a method referred to as *continuous replication*, which doesn't use an Oracle database for holding names. Instead, it uses only a checkpoint file. As it's potentially less robust as a result, I recommend the *repository database configuration*.

Another configuration means that you run a Names server in each region with its own Names database repository. In our example, uk.big.com and us.big.com would run their own repository databases. Local requests for remote services would be met through an additional Names server (the root domain server) in the hierarchy, and the root domain server is used only for delegation purposes. This would forward requests between regions so that a U.S. request for sales.uk.big.com that could not be resolved locally would be delegated to the United Kingdom Names server by the root domain server. A configuration based on delegation adds complexity to running the Names service. If your goal is to provide the most reliable service, it makes much more sense to reengineer your separate DBA groups to act as a global team, running a single repository, rather than adding complexity to the service in order to workaround the management issues of poor communication between your teams. Of course, you need to locate the single repository in one region or the other. If your U.S. and U.K. teams use the same standard, the decision on where to locate the repository effectively comes down to the toss of a coin, where the result doesn't matter.

A single repository configuration does not stop the Names servers in all regions from running during a repository outage. It just prevents changes from being made during the repository outage. It's also worth remembering that when a Names server starts, it loads up all names into its cache; therefore, even if a single repository is shared across countries, the name-to-address resolution can be configured to take place locally so that it doesn't require a lookup across a wide area network (WAN). So, in our example, U.S. clients would use a sqlnet.ora that referred only to their own local Names servers rather than the London version given earlier.

```
names.preferred_servers=
(address_list =
    (address =
        (protocol = TCP)
        (port = 1575)
        (host = oran1.us.big.com)
    )
    (address =
        (protocol = TCP)
```

```
        (port = 1575)
        (host = oran2.us.big.com)
    )
  )
```

The fact that the Names servers in London and New York share a common repository is transparent to client requests and is only visible through the names.ora files on each Names server site. You could make the system more robust by allowing New York requests to failover to London, and vice versa. This protects against a failure of the service on both sites in a single region. In this case, the sqlnet.ora file for New York clients would look like this:

```
names.preferred_servers=
(address_list =
    (address =
        (protocol = TCP)
        (port = 1575)
        (host = oran1.us.big.com)
    )
    (address =
        (protocol = TCP)
        (port = 1575)
        (host = oran2.us.big.com)
    )
    (address =
        (protocol = TCP)
        (port = 1575)
        (host = oran1.uk.big.com)
    )
    (address =
        (protocol = TCP)
        (port = 1575)
        (host = oran2.uk.big.com)
    )
  )
```

London clients would use a similar file with the London servers appearing before the New York servers.

Oracle Names Support Tips

You should be aware of what happens if you lose your Names repository database due to a scheduled or unscheduled outage. In this case, your Names servers will continue to run, but you won't be able to modify or remove existing TNS definitions in the server or insert new ones. If you try, you'll receive the following message:

```
Response status:        NNC-00430: Database not accessible
```

However, you can still stop and restart the Names server itself, or restart it after a crash, and it will continue to work because it caches the contents of the Names database on disk as a protection measure against repository outages. It's a good idea to take periodic dumps of the Names server contents by using the dump_tnsnames command. This dumps the contents in a format that is suitable for loading into another Names repository with the load_tnsnames command. You'll need to implement monitoring on the server where the Names server runs, to ensure that a Names server is restarted immediately after an unexpected crash. When connected to one Names server, you can connect to the other by using the SET SERVER command using the server name specified in the names.ora file.

Oracle Names enforces the uniqueness of entries by using the combination of a TNS alias and description as a unique key. This means you can enter the same alias twice by accident if the description parts don't match. The most reliable way to enter and remove TNS aliases is to use the netmgr program. This enables you to query entries before you remove them. You can also query aliases by using the dump_tnsnames command and searching the output file or entering a query command within namesctl. For example, to query the description of sales.uk.big.com, you would enter the following:

```
query sales.uk.big.com a.smd
```

If you register or unregister entries using the namesctl utility, you need to run the RELOAD command on the other Names servers in order to load the changes into the other Names servers' caches. It's better to use netmgr, which can issue a RELOAD command on all Names servers for you.

Using LDAP to Resolve Names

The introduction to the section on Oracle Names stated that Oracle Names will not be provided after Oracle9i. Oracle Names is very good at what it does, which is providing a 24×7 Oracle name-to-address resolution service with a very low setup and management cost. In effect, it's a directory of Oracle TNS aliases. However, the limitations of Oracle Names include the proprietary protocol used to access the service and the restriction on servicing requests for Oracle TNS aliases alone. The future of Oracle directory services is based on LDAP. LDAP addresses the deficiencies in Oracle Names because it's defined by the Internet Engineering Task Force (IETF) and as such represents an open standard that many other large companies like Microsoft support. As the IETF is also responsible for Hypertext Transfer Protocol (HTTP) and TCP/IP standards among others, you can rely on the standard not changing frequently and not without an extensive consultation process.

LDAP provides access to a distributed directory containing a broad range of information about different types of objects, including TNS aliases. The information in the directory exists in a directory information tree (DIT), and LDAP contains features to query and modify information in the tree. As you would expect, an LDAP-compliant directory can support the resolution of Oracle names to addresses in the same way that Oracle Names does. The difference is that LDAP uses an open standard network protocol. For the purposes of this book, we're interested in the using LDAP to resolve Oracle TNS aliases and support centralized user management and enterprise role management and retrieval, which is discussed in Chapter 5.

Chapter 5 contains details on how to set up Oracle Internet Directory (OID), which is Oracle's LDAP-compliant directory. My recommendation is to wait for a later release of OID before deploying it and to consider using Microsoft's LDAP-compliant directory as an alternative. A decision to use OID simply to provide an Oracle name resolution service is an overengineered solution. A directory is much more complicated to configure and manage than Oracle Names.

Migrating to LDAP

Oracle provides tools to help you migrate your TNS entries from an Oracle Names server into an LDAP-compliant directory such as OID. The namesctl utility provides the dump_ldap command to dump TNS entries into a file in LDAP interchange format. With minor changes to the output, the dumped data can be modified into a format suitable for loading into an LDAP directory. The following command when executed at the namesctl prompt dumps all TNS aliases ending in uk.dbcool.com into a file uk.dbcool.com.ldif:

```
dump_ldap uk.dbcool.com -f uk.dbcool.com.ldif
```

The following example shows the dumped output for a single TNS alias orad1.uk.dbcool.com modified with the addition of the line "changetype: add" to make it suitable for loading into an LDAP directory:

```
dn: cn=orad1,cn=OracleContext,dc=UK,dc=DBCOOL,dc=COM
changetype: add
objectclass: top
objectclass: orclNetService
cn: orad1
orclNetDescString:(DESCRIPTION=(ADDRESS_LIST=(ADDRESS=(PROTOCOL=tcp)(HOS
T=ldn1.dbcool.com)(PORT=1521)))(CONNECT_DATA=(SID=orad1)))
```

The OracleContext entry in the first line determines the location of the entry in the DIT as specified by the domain components dc=UK, dc=DBCOOL, and dc=COM. If your Oracle TNS aliases include names with different numbers of components or component names, then you need to create multiple OracleContext entries in the DIT to hold the names. For example, the following aliases would all require new OracleContext entries in the DIT, in addition to dc=UK, dc=DBCOOL, and dc=COM:

- trading.dbcool.com
- debt.us.dbcool.com
- debt.standby.dbcool.com

Therefore, to simplify migration to LDAP, you might consider requiring all of your aliases to consist of three-part names ending in dbcool.com and modifying those that don't in order to avoid the need to create multiple OracleContext entries in the DIT. Although using simple names makes LDAP migration easier, it reduces the descriptiveness of the names. For that reason, you should not migrate to LDAP without considering whether to modify your existing names to make migration easier. Until you do that, it's best to stick with Oracle Names.

In order to load names into LDAP, you use the ldapmodify command. The following example loads an LDAP-formatted TNS entry in the file orad1.ldif into the OID running on TCP/IP port 389 on server srv1, where the connection to the directory is authenticated by the username orcladmin and the password welcome:

```
$ ldapmodify -D cn=orcladmin -w welcome -h srv1 -p 389 -f orad1.ldif
```

The example assumes that orad1.ldif contains the LDAP description of orad1.uk.dbcool.com shown previously and that an OracleContext for dc=UK, dc=DBCOOL, and dc=COM exists in the directory. Chapter 5 contains a step-by-step example of how to install OID and create the OracleContext entries and the orclNet-Service class required to store the aliases in the directory.

As well as the dump_ldap command, Oracle provides the Oracle Names LDAP Proxy in Oracle9*i* to enable client applications that can't use directory naming to use a Names server that acts as a proxy for an LDAP directory. All Names servers must be upgraded to Oracle9*i* first. The LDAP Proxy enables the process of migrating from Oracle Names to LDAP to be performed in two stages. In the first stage, the server is modified to use LDAP with changing the client configuration. When this stage is successfully implemented, client configurations can be modified to use the LDAP server directly.

Using Shared Server

In a standard Oracle configuration, each client connection has a corresponding process on the UNIX database server, which is known as a *shadow process*. Such connections are referred to as *dedicated server connections* because each client has its own server process. When thousands of users connect concurrently, performance often degrades because UNIX uses a lot of central processing unit (CPU) cycles' context-switching between the processes rather than running SQL requests. To address this, Oracle provides a shared server architecture that enables a pool of server processes to be shared between multiple clients in order to help performance levels be maintained when the number of users increases. Shared server processes can be started on demand to satisfy end-user requests. In previous versions, Oracle called this architecture a multithreaded server (MTS). MTS was a bad name choice because the rest of the computing community uses the term *multithreaded* to refer to lightweight threads of execution running within a single process. Shared server is a much better description.

Configuring Dispatchers

Using shared server, many user processes connect to a dispatcher, which directs incoming network session requests to a common queue. An idle shared server process in the pool picks up the request from the queue. The initial number of dispatchers to start and the maximum network connections for each are specified in the DISPATCHERS initialization parameter as follows:

```
dispatchers="(protocol=tcp)(dispatchers=2)(connections=200)"
```

The max_dispatchers initialization parameter controls the maximum number of dispatchers and can be altered dynamically using the ALTER SYSTEM command. To control resource allocation, a pool of dispatchers can be associated with a specific service name registered with the listener through the service_names parameter. That way, resource allocation to different groups of clients can be controlled according to business requirements. In the following example, two services are defined, where one contains 2 dispatchers and the other 10:

```
service_names=(g1.db1.big.com, g2.db1.big.com)
dispatchers="(protocol=tcp)(dispatchers=2)(service=g1.d1.big.com)"
dispatchers="(protocol=tcp)(dispatchers=10)(service=g2.d1.big.com)"
```

In effect, this configuration provides a higher service level for clients that specify g2.d1.big.com in their connection requests because that service has more dispatchers allocated to it, enabling requests using that service to be allocated more quickly from the request queue.

Connection Pooling

In order to make better use of resources, shared server provides connection pooling to allow an idle session to time out, enabling the connection to be used by an active session. This can be useful for interactive Web applications where only a few of several hundred client connections may be active at any time. When an idle session becomes active, the physical connection is transparently reconnected. Connection pooling introduces the concept of a network tick, which is a measurement of time (in seconds) that is used to specify the idle timeout interval. The following example shows a dispatcher configuration where connection pooling is enabled for idle connections after 3 ticks (specified by POOL=3), where each tick is 2 seconds long (identified by TICK=2):

```
dispatchers="(protocol=tcp)(dispatchers=1)(pool=3)(tick=2)
(connections=100)(sessions=400)"
```

The values of ON and TRUE can be used for POOL in which case the default time of 10 ticks is used. The SESSIONS value specifies the maximum number of network sessions to allow for each dispatcher. Oracle recommends the use of low tick values (such as 1) for local area networks (LANs) and higher tick values (such as 15) for WANs.

Specifying Shared and Dedicated Server Connections

The sqlnet.ora file can be configured with use_dedicated_server=on to enforce the use of a dedicated (that is, nonshared) connection in a shared server configuration. This overrides other methods. Alternatively, the server=shared or server=dedicated settings can be used in the connect_data section of a TNS alias description to control the choice of a shared or dedicated server connection according to the end-user application requirements. The following example explicitly requests a dedicated server connection:

```
trading.dbcool.com=
(description=
  (address=(protocol=tcp)(host=trading)(port=1521))
  (connect_data=
     (service_name=trading.dbcool.com)
     (server=dedicated)
  )
)
```

Using Transparent Gateways

Many organizations run database management system (DBMS) technologies from more than one company in order to meet business requirements. Oracle's transparent gateways enable Oracle applications to reference data in Microsoft SQL Server and Sybase databases (and several others) directly from SQL running in the Oracle database and transparently to the end-user application. This section discusses the Oracle Transparent Gateway for Microsoft SQL Server.

Server Configuration

The transparent gateway for Microsoft SQL Server needs to be installed on a Windows server where the Microsoft SQL Server client tools have been installed previously. The gateway behaves like a standard Oracle listener in the sense that it listens for connection requests from clients. However, rather than using TCP/IP port 1521 (as used by an Oracle database), the gateway uses port 1541 by default. The following example shows the contents of the listener.ora file for a Microsoft SQL Server transparent gateway installed on server mssql1.dbcool.com and listening for connection requests on port 1541:

```
LISTENER =
 (ADDRESS_LIST=
   (ADDRESS=(PROTOCOL=tcp)(HOST= mssql1.dbcool.com)(PORT=1541)))

SID_LIST_LISTENER=
   (SID_LIST=
      (SID_DESC=
         (SID_NAME=tg4msql)
         (ORACLE_HOME=c:\oracle)
         (PROGRAM=tg4msql)
      )
   )
```

The example uses the default SID_NAME value of tg4msql. The value for SID_NAME can be chosen by the DBA if desired. Whatever value is chosen must match the corresponding value used in the client TNS alias exactly as it must for a regular connection to any Oracle listener and client application. Associated with the SID_NAME is a file that identifies the SQL Server database to which the listener forwards SQL requests from the Oracle client. In the following example, the file inittq4msql.ora identifies the SQL Server database named mssql1.mdsdb:

```
# inittg4msql.ora
# This is a sample agent init file.
# It contains the HS parameters that are
# needed for the gateway Agent.

#
# HS init parameters
#
HS_FDS_CONNECT_INFO=mssql1.mdsdb
HS_FDS_TRACE_LEVEL=ON
```

The use of HS_FDS_TRACE_LEVEL=ON enables the tracing of the original Oracle SQL requests into SQL Server format, which can be useful for problem diagnosis. The configuration file doesn't contain authentication information for connection to the SQL Server database. This information is passed from the database link definition used by the Oracle client application, as shown in the next section. Once the configuration files are in place, the gateway listener is started using a Windows service in the same way as an Oracle listener on Windows.

Client Configuration

When an Oracle database references data in a SQL Server database, the Oracle database is the client. Data location transparency in the client is typically enabled through the use of views created in the Oracle database that reference remote SQL Server objects via database links. These links are used in exactly the same way as they would be used to connect to another Oracle database. The difference is that the link specifies a gateway running on a Microsoft Windows server rather than an Oracle database listener. The gateway acts as a proxy between the Oracle and Microsoft databases, forwarding SQL requests from the Oracle side, submitting them to a SQL Server database, and then returning the results to Oracle. The following SQL shows an example of a database link used to connect to a SQL Server database via a gateway:

```
create public database link "TG4MSQL.MSSQL1.MDSDB.DBCOOL.COM"
connect to mds2 identified by xyk791 using
'tg4msql.mssql1.mdsdb.dbcool.com';
```

There's nothing to distinguish this link from one you would use to connect to an Oracle database, except for the naming convention used. My preferred naming convention is to prefix all SQL Server database link names with TG4MSQL to indicate that the link refers to a SQL Server database. The next part of the name, MSSQL1, is the host name where the SQL Server database is located, and MDSDB is the name of the database. You can choose your own naming conventions if you don't like this one. As usual, the TNS alias used in the link creation statement needs to resolve to a database server through a tnsnames.ora file, LDAP directory, or Oracle Names server. The TNS alias for the SQL Server connection in the previous example is shown in the following:

```
tg4msql.mssql1.mdsdb.dbcool.com =
   (description =
         (address =
            (protocol=tcp)
            (host=mssql1.dbcool.com)
            (port=1541)
         )
      (connect_data=(sid=tg4msql))
      (hs=ok))
```

This alias bears a close resemblance to an Oracle TNS alias with two significant differences. The use of port=1541 and hs=ok together indicate that the alias refers to a transparent gateway. By default, transparent gateways use TCP/IP port 1541. The connection can be tested using a simple query against the SQL Server data dictionary from the Oracle database. For example, the following SQL shows some of the accounts in the remote SQL Server database if the link is working:

```
select * from all_users@tg4msql.mssql1.mdsdb.dbcool.com where username
like 'db%' and rownum <=5;
```

```
USERNAME              USER_ID CREATED
------------------ --------- ---------
db_accessadmin         16385
db_backupoperator      16389
db_datareader          16390
db_datawriter          16391
db_ddladmin            16387
```

The gateway can translate queries on many of the Oracle data dictionary tables into queries on the corresponding SQL Server objects. Once the database link exists, views can be created using the link to enable applications to transparently reference SQL Server data.

Summary

Oracle provides comprehensive networking facilities that can enhance the performance and availability of your applications. The centralizing of naming services provided by Oracle Names ensures that your Oracle network names are defined in one place. If you implement the service across multiple sites, the service is available 24×7 even when a single-site outage occurs due to either a disaster or scheduled outage.

Using Oracle Names enables you to change the database location details in one place so that all clients see the change instantaneously without a single configuration change on the client. Whenever Names is implemented, organizations experience higher availability and lower support costs for Oracle services. Eventually, you need to move away from Oracle Names to an LDAP-compliant directory. However, you must understand the challenges of migrating to LDAP and the extra complexity of managing a directory service before you consider upgrading.

Oracle Net provides built-in load-balancing and failover capabilities that you can use to ensure that client connections are transparently redirected to available servers where resources are available. The shared server capabilities enable thousands of client connections to be managed efficiently. If you are in the habit of transferring data between heterogeneous databases in your organization using file transfer, then you should seriously consider switching to the Oracle transparent gateways, which allow access to data from other DBMSs directly from an Oracle database, without the overhead of file copy.

Environment Standards and Tools

There are gaps in what Oracle offers to help you manage database servers. For example, Oracle has always provided two scripts—dbstart and dbshut—to stop and start your databases whenever a UNIX server boots up or shuts down. Oracle has always made it clear that dbstart should only be run at system boot time, as you can see from the comment in the following code:

```
It should ONLY be executed as part of the system boot procedure
```

Countless database administrators (DBAs) found that running dbstart under Oracle7 while a server was up would not only start databases that were down, but would actually shut down and restart any databases that were already up! So the comment in the code was of little assistance. In other early releases of Oracle, dbstart and dbshut weren't upgraded by Oracle and failed to work properly, which perhaps suggests that the need to provide a standard interface for starting and stopping Oracle databases wasn't high on the list of priorities. Given that these scripts do eventually work properly, what about all the other Oracle services you might like to start on server boot, such as the listener, gateways, Names servers, and the Oracle Intelligent Agent?

Clearly, the boot-time functionality provided by dbstart and dbshut is nowhere near enough. It's not uncommon to need to restart or shut down a database outside the server reboot sequence, or start a database in a nonstandard mode, such as managed standby. You can do all those things, but they typically involve writing custom scripts using one of the UNIX command shells or consulting the documentation to find out the exact order of commands. If you're running a backup through a third-party media manager, you might need to automatically shutdown and startup mount your database as part of the backup process and open it afterwards. In that case, you want your script to have a well-defined interface and return code so that it can interface it with third-party software such as scheduling tools. In general, you want to be able to embed your scripts in other scripts easily.

This chapter describes a set of standards and tools for the UNIX environment in which you manage Oracle database servers. It covers the following topics:

- How to set a login environment
- How to use the set_env alias
- Why Perl is a good choice for Oracle scripting
- How to build a Perl interpreter, including an Oracle interface
- Standard tools for managing Oracle
- Configuring and running Apache
- How to integrate Oracle services with machine boot

This chapter defines the requirements that a set of scripts needs to do all these things and provides the code for you. These scripts are written in Perl. Before we run the scripts, we'll set up a standard UNIX login environment that enables you to set Oracle environments for all instances on the server with a single command.

Setting a Login Environment

Any DBA who logs onto any UNIX Oracle account on any database server in your organization should find the same initial environment. That way, all DBAs can manage databases on all servers because the environment is standardized. To do this, you need to standardize the environment through settings in the $HOME/.profile file that UNIX runs when you log on. We've already standardized on ksh as our login shell (although bash on Linux works just as well), as described in Chapter 1, so a minimal $HOME/.profile file looks like this:

```
# --------- ORACLE_BASE setting
# Set $ORACLE_BASE from special oratab entry e.g.
#      #ORACLE_BASE:/u01/app/oracle
MYORATAB=/var/opt/oracle/oratab
if [ ! -f $MYORATAB ] ; then
    echo "Please create $MYORATAB" exit 1
fi

ORACLE_BASE='grep "^#ORACLE_BASE:/.*$" $MYORATAB|awk -F: '{ print $2 }''
echo $ORACLE_BASE
if [ ! -d "$ORACLE_BASE" ] ; then
    echo "ORACLE_BASE is missing from /var/opt/oracle/oratab"
    exit 1
else
    export ORACLE_BASE
fi
```

```
#--------- end ORACLE_BASE setting

# use emacs on set -o if you prefer the emacs editor
set -o vi # enable vi mode for command line editing

export ORACLE_PATH=.:$ORACLE_BASE/sql  # to locate useful SQL scripts

export EXINIT="set tabstop=3 ic"       # enable case insensitive search
in vi

# set X DISPLAY to telnet client machine
export DISPLAY='who am i | awk '{print $6}' | sed 's/(//' | sed
's/)//'':0.0

# On Solaris, you must have /usr/ccs/bin first in the path.
# Without it, Oracle re-links will fail.
if [ -d /usr/ccs/bin ] ; then
PATH=/usr/ccs/bin:$ORACLE_BASE/oraperl/bin:$ORACLE_BASE/perl:$PATH:.
fi

# Useful aliases
alias tal='tail -f
$ORACLE_BASE/admin/$ORACLE_SID/bdump/alert_$ORACLE_SID.log'
alias dba='sqlplus "/ as SYSDBA"'

#  Alias to set up Oracle environments based on oratab
alias set_env='. $ORACLE_BASE/admin/scripts/set_environment'
```

The first section of .profile sets the $ORACLE_BASE environment variable by using a special entry that we add to the oratab file. As the $ORACLE_BASE setting is so fundamental to a working Oracle configuration, it needs to be accessible in a well-known place and defined only once. The setting needs to be available in such a way that all of the tools and scripts that need to set it (and all of ours do) know where to find the value. The natural place to define $ORACLE_BASE is the oratab file because the file already contains the location and name of all Oracle instances on the server, and every DBA should understand the contents of the file and know where to find it.

Changes to the contents of the oratab file need to be treated with care. As defined by Oracle, lines in the oratab file identify two types of content. Lines that start with a # are treated as comments by Oracle scripts and ignored, and any others identify Oracle instances on the server that are to be started and stopped by the Oracle-supplied dbstart and dbshut on server boot:

```
# this line is a comment. Next identifies a database instance . . .
OMFD1:/u01/app/oracle/product/9.0.1:Y
```

The oratab file is a natural place to add extra information to identify other Oracle services to start and stop on server boot, as well as the location of $ORACLE_BASE. Provided that this extra information is added on lines starting with a #, then they will safely be ignored by Oracle's own scripts, and we can make use of the extra information in our scripts. Our scripts, including .profile, identify the ORACLE_BASE value for the server by looking for a line that starts with the string #ORACLE_BASE, followed by a ":" followed by the $ORACLE_BASE directory:

```
#ORACLE_BASE:/u01/app/oracle
```

On UNIX variants where the /usr/ccs/bin directory exists (such as Solaris), the PATH setting requires that /usr/ccs/bin appears first to ensure that any Oracle code relinks, including those at install time, use the correct versions of the linker and archiver commands. There may be several versions of these on a server, and Oracle requires that you use the /usr/ccs/bin versions on those platforms where they exist. If you don't, your code might link okay, but when you start up the database you'll get errors that don't have an obvious cause. The same applies to Perl interpreters. We'll be building one later. It's important that our Perl interpreter takes precedence over any other one found on the server, so $ORACLE_BASE/oraperl/bin should appear in the path before any other directories that might contain another Perl interpreter.

The set_env alias is described in the following section. It's the only command you'll ever use to set up your Oracle environment from the UNIX command line.

The set_env Alias

The set_env alias is designed to let you set Oracle environments based solely on the contents of the oratab file. This is located in either /var/opt/oracle/oratab or /etc/oratab depending on your UNIX platform. This section assumes /var/opt/oracle/oratab. If you run set_env without any arguments, it presents you with a list of Oracle instances on the server and a list of Oracle client versions. If you choose a version or System ID (SID) from the list, that environment is set for you as follows:

```
$ set_env
SIDs on this machine are: OMFD1 WS817D1
Versions on this machine are: 8.1.7 9.0.1

 Enter SID or Version: OMFD1

srv1.dbcool.com:OMFD1 >
```

Once the environment is set, the UNIX command prompt is changed to reflect the server you are logged onto and the SID in the environment that you set. The appearance of the server name in the prompt is particularly useful if you are running Oracle in a clustered environment. If you know the environment you want in advance, you can pass it on the command line directly:

```
$ set_env OMFD1
srv1.dbcool.com:OMFD1 >
```

The Versions list enables you to set an Oracle client environment. This is useful if your UNIX server has no databases installed and you just need to run Oracle client software of a particular version against a remote database. This is enabled through special entries in the /var/opt/oracle/oratab file, that are introduced with # followed by the three dot-separated digits to identify the version as follows:

```
#
# These are our special entries that Oracle's tools ignore
#
#ORACLE_BASE:/u01/app/oracle
#9.0.1:/u01/app/oracle/product/9.0.1:N
#8.1.7:/u01/app/oracle/product/8.1.7:N
#net:9.0.1:Y

# these are real SID entries understood by Oracle's tools
WS817D1:/u01/app/oracle/product/8.1.7:Y
OMFD1:/u01/app/oracle/product/9.0.1:Y
```

You can also see other lines with a special meaning, for example:

```
#net:9.0.1:Y
```

The line #net:9.0.1:Y tells our Oracle service startup script (covered later) to start the 9.0.1 tnslsnr process on machine boot rather than the 8.1.7 version. Because there are two Oracle versions on this server, you need to specify which listener to start. By using the oratab file to hold information about your Oracle services to start and stop on machine boot and shutdown, you make the service startup and shutdown process data driven. That means you can change the behavior of the Oracle services at server boot time without changing your scripts, resulting in a more robust environment. For example, when Oracle9.2 is released, you won't need your system administrator (SA) to be involved in the process of changing the environment at server startup time. You will simply change the oratab entry as follows to start the Oracle9.2 version of the network listener on machine boot:

```
#net:9.2.0:Y
```

The use of set_env sets the UNIX CDPATH environment variable, making it easier to navigate to Optimal Flexible Architecture (OFA) directories for the database instance by avoiding the need to specify a full path. For example, running set_env OMFD1 sets CDPATH as follows:

```
CDPATH=/u01/app/oracle/admin/OMFD1:.
```

As a result, navigating to any of the OFA directories for an instance, such as bdump, cdump, arch, and pfile (or scripts in 9*i*) can be done using a simple cd command without specifying a full path. For example, the following command takes you to the alert log directory without the need to specify the full path:

```
srv1.dbcool.com:OMFD1 > cd bdump
/u01/app/oracle/admin/OMFD1/bdump
```

If you provide 24×7 support, the ability to navigate easily to the OFA directories without needing to specify a full path can save time during a crisis.

Using Perl for Scripts

If you've never used Perl before, you might reasonably ask the question "Why Perl?" In some ways, you don't need to know because you can treat all of the provided scripts as a black box that take certain inputs—for example, an $ORACLE_SID—and perform well-defined actions—for example, database shutdown. But it's definitely worth knowing more—once you've seen what the scripts can do for you, it's quite likely that you'll want to extend them or use them as a basis for others.

Speaking as a programmer writing a standard set of Oracle DBA scripts, Perl has several things going for it. It's excellent for text processing, so it's easy to process the structure of the oratab file, parse output from SQL*Plus that may contain Oracle error messages, or handle command-line arguments. It makes error handling so easy that it encourages you to do error handling. Error handling may be left out because it's tedious to code sometimes with disastrous consequences. It also has built-in functionality for handling networking, directories, files, and just about everything else you might want to do. In short, Perl also makes routine programming tasks easy.

The fact that Perl is free raises doubts in some people's minds about supportability. Actually, you'll find fantastic support available free on the Web, although you should be warned that the average Perl guru is pretty intolerant of beginners asking the same basic questions in a newsgroup over and over again without reading the documentation first. Another strength of Perl is that programmers with knowledge of an existing scripting language can start writing useful scripts immediately. This usually means that a page of code written by a beginner could be written by an expert in a couple of lines, but that's all part of the fun, and both versions do the job. In fact, the beginner's version may be more readable, which is important for maintainability, if not performance.

Last, but definitely not least, the Perl interpreter that we're using will have a built-in Oracle interface. That means you can write Oracle-enabled programs from a scripting language, and, as a result, you can create useful Oracle utilities without any compiling or linking. As an alternative to Perl, you might consider using Tool Control Language (Tcl) instead. The relative merits of Perl and Tcl are covered briefly in Chapter 24. In many ways, the choice is a religious discussion, which I prefer to avoid. Both languages provide excellent features for managing Oracle environments compared to a standard UNIX shell.

Building a Perl Interpreter

In order for the scripts to run, you need to install a Perl interpreter on each server. It's quite possible that your server already has an existing Perl interpreter installed, but we're going to build one anyway. The installed server might not have the Oracle functionality built in, and it's not possible to add it without access to the source code. In any case, the Perl interpreter should be installed in a predefined location so that all the scripts can find it, and it's not a good idea to tamper with any preinstalled software.

The interpreter that we build will be installed under $ORACLE_BASE on all of our UNIX Oracle servers and should be considered as part of the standard Oracle script

Table 4.1 Perl Interpreter Software Components

SOFTWARE	SITE
Perl interpreter source code v5.6.1	www.activestate.com
Gnu gcc C compiler Solaris package v2.95.3	www.sunfreeware.com
DBI module: Database-independent interface for Perl	http://search.cpan.org/search?module=DBI
DBD-Oracle-1.12: Database-dependent interface for Oracle	http://search.cpan.org/search?dist=DBD-Oracle

toolkit. Once you've built it on one server, you can package it and ship it to all of the others so that the build cost is a one off.

In order to build the Perl interpreter, you'll need to download, build, and install various software packages. Versions are provided in Table 4.1, along with the Web sites where you can find the software.

All of the previous sites have existed for several years, and it's possible that more recent releases of some of the components may be available at the time of this writing. If so, you may choose to use the more recent releases. If you want to guarantee success, it's probably better to use the versions listed. In order to build the Perl interpreter with Oracle, you need to do things in the following order:

1. On Solaris, install the C compiler Solaris package first. This requires root privileges.

2. Compile, link, and test the Perl interpreter using the C compiler.

3. Compile and link the Database-independent (DBI) module into the Perl interpreter and then test.

4. Compile and link the Database-dependent (DBD) module into the Perl interpreter and then test.

Installing the C Compiler

You need a C compiler to build the Perl components from source code. If you're on Solaris, you can use the Sun C compiler if it's installed. However, the Solaris C compiler package is an extra-cost option. If you don't have it, then you can download the gcc compiler package from www.sunfreeware.com and use that instead. The package is a prebuilt installable of the gcc compiler for Solaris that is ready to run. If you're not running Solaris or Linux, then you have two options. You can use a different C compiler than gcc, or you can use your existing C compiler to build the gcc version from source code. If you're running Oracle on Linux, you have a head start because the gcc compiler comes installed with the operating system and no separate install is required. The following examples assume you are using gcc.

If you're a DBA who is new to C compiling, don't worry—the software components compile, build, and even *test* themselves from a couple of simple commands. To those people who think that nothing that is free has any value, you'll be amazed at the quality of this free software. Life would be much easier if all commercial software was so well engineered.

To install gcc on Solaris, place the Solaris package from www.sunfreeware.com in /tmp, for example, and ask the SA to install it as root. Assuming that the file containing your gcc package is *gcc_package_name*, this uses a command like the following:

```
$ pkgadd -d /tmp/gcc_package_name
```

This installs the gcc executable into /usr/local/bin. Make sure this directory is in your path and then run gcc -v to check that the compiler is available. Now create a simple test program, gcctest.c, with the following contents:

```
main()
{
   printf("hello world\n");
}
```

Compile and link the test program using the following command:

```
$ gcc -o gcctest gcctest.c
```

Run the program gcctest and the string "hello world" should appear on the screen. This confirms that the C compiler is working. Now you can build the Perl interpreter from source code.

Building the Perl Interpreter

Unpack the source code for the interpreter on your disk into a directory—for example, /u01/ActiveState5.6.1. Now read the install notes for your server platform in the top-level directory—for example, README.solaris. Chances are there are no issues for the platform. Now read the INSTALL file in the top-level directory. In our case, we aren't installing Perl into the standard directories of /usr/local or /opt. Perl supports two types of install: a default one and a locally configurable one. We'll be using the latter.

The two differences from the defaults that we'll be making are the use of gcc rather than cc as the C compiler and the use of /u01/app/oracle/oraperl as our installation directory for the built interpreter. By default, Perl attempts to create a symbolic link from /usr/bin/perl to the newly built version. We don't want to do that, so we'll turn that functionality off.

When building Perl, first run a program called Configure that stores the configuration settings in two files: config.sh and Policy.sh. We'll remove them first and then build the interpreter with gcc and install into /u01/app/oracle/oraperl as follows:

```
$ mkdir -p /u01/app/oracle/oraperl

$ cd /u01/ActiveState5.6.1

$ rm -f config.sh Policy.sh
```

```
# note: -des stops lots of prompts from the build script
$ sh Configure -Dcc=gcc \
-Dprefix=/u01/app/oracle/oraperl -Uinstallusrbinperl -des

# compile and link the interpreter
$ make

# test the interpreter
$ make test

# install the interpreter into /u01/app/oracle/oraperl
$ make install
```

This process will probably take well under 1 hour.

Adding Oracle Support to Perl

Before building the DBI and DBD modules, make sure that the Perl interpreter in your path is the one just built. You can do this on Solaris or Linux by running the UNIX which command, which shows you the path to the Perl interpreter:

```
$ which perl
/u01/app/oracle/oraperl/bin/perl
```

Next, unpack the DBI module into a directory of your choice—for example, /u01/DBI-1.20. Then build, compile, and test the code as follows:

```
$ cd /u01/DBI-1.20
$ perl Makefile.PL
$ make
$ make test
$ make install
```

The DBI generic module is required to enable Perl access for any database supported by Perl. Both Oracle and Sybase are very popular. Next, unpack the DBD module into a directory of your choice—for example, /u01/DBD-Oracle-1.12. Set an environment using set_env for a database instance that Perl can use to log on and run some Oracle SQL tests. Specify the Oracle account to use by setting the ORACLE_USERID environment symbol. Build, compile, and test DBD as follows:

```
# set a database to test DBD Perl
$ set_env ORA817D1

# set a database logon to run the tests
$ export ORACLE_USERID=scott/tiger

$ cd /u01/DBD-Oracle-1.12
$ perl Makefile.PL
```

```
$ make
$ make test
$ make install
```

If the test stage shows any errors, be sure to check the README documents. You now have a Perl interpreter with a built-in Oracle interface. The tools in the next section are all based on this interpreter.

Standard Tools

This section describes a standard set of tools used for performing the following functions:

- Shutting down a database: dbcool_db_shut.pl
- Starting up a database: dbcool_db_start.pl
- Testing if a database is up: dbcool_db_up.pl
- Starting Oracle services on machine boot: dbcool_ora_startup.pl
- Stopping Oracle services on machine shutdown: dbcool_ora_shutdown.pl

All the tools have a common design philosophy incorporating a standard set of features, making them easy to use. The features are made available as subroutines in a common library (dbcool_util.pl), so you can easily embed them into your own scripts to enforce a common approach.

All Environments Are Based on oratab

Without a standard approach, if you want to shut down a database from a script and have several Oracle versions on your server, you need to set the Oracle environment correctly before shutdown to match the database. This can result in confusion if a shutdown is run from the environment of the wrong Oracle version. When developers or DBAs write Oracle scripts using sh or ksh, Oracle environments are often hard coded within the scripts. Therefore, if the $ORACLE_HOME for a database changes, then the script breaks.

All the Perl scripts use a few simple functions to set the environment for an SID based on the oratab file contents. So if you upgrade your database from one version to another and change oratab to reflect the change, all scripts will continue to work. Here are some examples that are based on the hard-coded SID name OMFD1. In reality, most scripts read the SID value from the command line:

```
set_oracle_env('OMFD1'); # set Oracle environment for SID
$oracle_home = get_oracle_home('OMFD1'); # get home for SID
$oracle_base = get_oracle_base(); # get $ORACLE_BASE
```

Command-Line Arguments

All scripts take arguments in the form of name=value pairs like Oracle's export and import command-line utilities rather than the terse and hard-to-remember UNIX format that uses single-character argument names introduced with the hyphen character. You can run all commands with a single argument help=y to see what arguments are available for the script. All argument processing is performed using the standard Perl CGI.pm package. This package was designed for use in Common Gateway Interface (CGI) Web scripts, but the interface is so easy to use that I use it for all my scripts, whether or not they are intended for use on the Web. One side effect of this approach is that you can enable a script to run from the UNIX command line or Web server with hardly any effort, and output plain text or HTML-tagged output depending on the calling environment.

Logging

All the scripts send output to a log file every time they are executed. The location of the log directory is predictable, making it easy find. If the script runs on behalf of a particular SID, then the log file is given by $ORACLE_BASE/admin/$ORACLE_SID/log/*scriptname*.log. For example, you can run the following command to shut down your OMFD1 database:

```
$ dbcool_db_shut.pl sid=OMFD1
```

In this case, the log file will be /u01/app/oracle/admin/OMFD1/dbcool_db_shut.pl.log. Logging is important for all Oracle startup and shutdown operations. If your script isn't specific to any particular instance, then the log is written to $ORACLE_BASE/admin/log/*scriptname*.log. The Perl scripts make logging easy. You can use the logging facilities in your own scripts by using the following subroutine:

```
set_logging_on($sid);
```

Single Instance at a Time

The scripts protect you from running more than one instance at a time through functions in the dbcool_lock.pl library. For example, if you are shutting down a database, you don't want to allow another shutdown at the same time. These lock features are designed to embed into other scripts easily using a single function call. The locking is 100 percent guaranteed to make your scripts single threaded. For example, you can run the following script to shut down your OMFD1 database:

```
srv1.dbcool.com:OMFD1 >dbcool_ora_shut.pl sid=OMFD1
```

If you run the same script at the same time from another session, you'll receive a message that informs you that the second attempt failed because the script is running from another session already:

```
logfile is: /u01/app/oracle/admin/OMFD1/log/dbcool_ora_shut.pl.log

ERROR: dbcool_ora_shut.pl is already running
INFO: lockfile=/u01/app/oracle/admin/OMFD1/lock/dbcool_ora_shut.pl
```

To use this feature in your own Perl programs, simply add the following calls near the top of the code:

```
require("dbcool_lock.pl");
.
.
.
# exit if current script already running for this sid
exit_if_running($sid);
```

Stopping a Script from Running

All scripts can be stopped from running by creating a stop file. Each script checks for the existence of the well-known stop file before the script begins its actions. If the stop file exists, then the script exits immediately with a message. This feature enables you to temporarily stop a scheduled script from executing without making a potentially risky code change to the script itself and without having to make a change somewhere else in your infrastructure—for example, to disable the job scheduler.

Say you have an Oracle Recovery Manager (RMAN) (covered in Chapter 18) closed database backup scheduled to run at 13:00 every Saturday from a centralized backup server. One Saturday you need to do some maintenance and therefore need to stop the database from being shut down at the usual time. Because you always use the dbcool_db_shut.pl script to shut down the database, you can create a stop file, which stops the shutdown without impacting any other facilities. The stop file has a predictable name and location based on the name of the script and the SID, so for the previous example you would create a stop file in the stop directory for the instance and the script that you want to stop like this:

```
touch /u01/app/oracle/admin/OMFD1/stop/dbcool_ora_shut.pl
```

Any attempts to shut down the database while the stop file exists result in an error message:

```
srv1.dbcool.com:OMFD1 >dbcool_db_shut.pl sid=OMFD1
logfile is: /u01/app/oracle/admin/OMFD1/log/dbcool_db_shut.pl.log

ERROR: dbcool_db_shut.pl is stopped
INFO: stopfile=/u01/app/oracle/admin/OMFD1/stop/dbcool_db_shut.pl
```

You still need to remember to remove the stop file when you want shutdown operations to continue as normal. To use this feature in your own programs, simply add the following calls near the top of the code:

```
require("dbcool_util.pl");
.
.
.
# exit if current script is stopped for this sid
exit_if_stopped($sid);
```

Predictable Return Codes

All scripts return one of two values to the operating system upon completion just like many UNIX commands. A value of zero means that the operation was a complete success. A value of one means the operation failed. This enables you to interface your scripts with other tools—for example, job schedulers—that need to know whether the previous operation in the schedule succeeded before they continue processing.

Standard Tools Reference

This section is a reference guide for the standard Perl scripts, which can be downloaded in full from the companion Web site. It describes the command-line interface and behavior. Mandatory arguments are shown in { . . . }. Optional arguments are shown in [. . .] and choices are separated by |. All commands take a help=y argument that shows the usage message; this is not shown for clarity. All scripts take log=y|n. It's recommended that logging is always used. Arguments that are environment specific and need to be supplied by the user appear in italics. All scripts return a 0 if the script succeeded and return a 1 if it did not.

dbcool_db_up.pl

The command-line description for dbcool_db_up.pl is as follows:

```
dbcool_db_up.pl {sid=ORACLE_SID|tns=TNS_ALIAS} [log=y|n]
```

The dbcool_db_up.pl script checks if a local database given by sid, or a remote database given by tns, is up. To check if the database is up, an attempt is made to connect to the database with SQL*Plus using a dummy username. If an Oracle ORA-01017 message is returned, it is used to confirm that the database is up. The script is secure because a real Oracle logon is not hard coded into it. The following is an example of its usage:

```
dbcool_db_up.pl sid=OMFD1
dbcool_db_up.pl tns=omfd1.dbcool.com
```

dbcool_db_start.pl

The command-line description for dbcool_db_start.pl is as follows:

```
dbcool_ora_start.pl {sid=ORACLE_SID} [mode=mode] [log=y|n]

mode=startup nomount|startup mount|mount|open|managed standby
```

The dbcool_db_start.pl script starts a local database given by sid, but only if the database is not already up. If the database is up, then the command returns an error. The mode options are useful for starting the database up into various states. The code does not perform the sanity checking of states. For example, mode=mount only works if the database is in nomount state, and mode=open only works if the database is in a mounted state. The following is an example of its usage:

```
dbcool_db_start.pl sid=OMFD1 mode='startup nomount'
dbcool_db_start.pl sid=OMFD1 mode='managed standby'
```

dbcool_db_shut.pl

The command-line description for dbcool_db_shut.pl is as follows:

```
dbcool_ora_start.pl {sid=ORACLE_SID} [mode=mode] [startup=mount]
[log=y|n]

mode=abort|immediate
```

The dbcool_db_shut.pl script with only the sid argument does a clean database shutdown by performing a shutdown abort, followed by a startup restrict, followed by a shutdown normal. The mode argument can be used to shut down the database with the abort or immediate options. The startup=mount argument starts the database up in mount mode immediately after a clean shutdown and is useful before running an RMAN-closed database backup. The following are examples of its usage:

```
dbcool_db_shut.pl sid=OMFD1 mode=abort
dbcool_db_shut.pl sid=OMFD1 startup=mount
```

dbcool_db_restart.pl

The command-line description for dbcool_db_restart.pl is as follows:

```
dbcool_ora_restart.pl {sid=ORACLE_SID} [log=y|n]
```

The dbcool_db_restart.pl script does a shutdown abort and then startup, and is useful if a database requires a restart for a parameter change to take effect. The following is an example of its usage:

```
dbcool_db_restart.pl sid=OMFD1
```

dbcool_ora_startup.pl

The command-line description for dbcool_ora_startup.pl is as follows:

```
dbcool_ora_startup.pl
```

The dbcool_ora_startup.pl script is typically called by the UNIX boot sequence init process to start all Oracle-related services defined in the oratab file. This script can take advantage of the oratab extensions covered earlier in this chapter, so it can start up Oracle Names servers, gateways, databases, and the network listener.

As the general framework is now in place, you can easily add extra information to the oratab file yourself, provided you add it on lines that appear as comments. Recall that comment lines start with a # character. The information in these new lines can be used to start up other Oracle-dependent services at boot time. All you need to do is modify the script to reference the oratab lines you've added and take appropriate actions. For example, you might want to start the Oracle9*i* Intelligent Agent on machine boot. To enable this, you would define a line in oratab to identify the agent and version you want to start:

```
#oia:9.0.1:Y
```

Then you would modify dbcool_ora_startup.pl to look for a line beginning #oia, followed by a three-digit Oracle version number. Having found such a line in oratab, you would set the Oracle environment to 9.0.1 using set_oracle_env('9.0.1') and then run the following command to start the agent:

```
$ agentctl start agent
```

If you're not completely sure how to do it, take a look at how the existing code works for databases or Oracle Names servers, and then copy and modify it as required. Nearly all programmers write code by cutting and pasting existing code, and this is no exception.

dbcool_ora_shutdown.pl

The command-line description for dbcool_ora_shutdown.pl is as follows:

```
dbcool_ora_shutdown.pl [when=time-in-seconds]
```

The dbcool_ora_shutdown.pl script is typically called by the UNIX shutdown sequence to shut down all Oracle-related services defined in the oratab file. This script can take advantage of the oratab extensions covered earlier in this chapter, so it can shut down Oracle Names servers, gateways, databases, and the network listener. You must supply a time in seconds to wait before activating the shut down.

Integrating Oracle Services with UNIX

Now that we have some building blocks for stopping and starting Oracle services, these can be added to the UNIX server boot sequence so that all our Oracle services will start up and shut down in synchronization with the UNIX server. To accomplish this, the UNIX SA needs to create a file /etc/init.d/dbora with the following contents:

```
ORACLE_OWNER=oracle

case "$1" in
'start')

su $ORACLE_OWNER -c "/u01/app/oracle/perl/dbcool_ora_startup.pl"

;;

'stop')

su $ORACLE_OWNER -c "/u01/app/oracle/perl/dbcool_ora_shutdown.pl when=0"

;;
```

After the creation of this file, the SA needs to create two links to it using names that will be called at the appropriate point during the UNIX server boot and startup sequence. For Sun Solaris, the following links will do the job:

```
$ cd /etc/rc0.d
$ ln -s /etc/init.d/dbora K10dbora  # K... means shutdown

$ cd /etc/rc2.d
$ ln -s /etc/init.d/dbora S99dbora  # S... means startup
```

You should test the startup and shutdown of your Oracle services by arranging for the server to be rebooted after checking first that dbcool_ora_startup.pl and dbcool_ora_shutdown.pl run successfully from the Oracle UNIX account. You can find the logs for dbcool_ora_startup.pl and dbcool_ora_shutdown.pl in the $ORACLE_BASE/admin/log directory.

Configuring and Running Apache

All DBAs should have an appreciation of how scripts can be called from a Web browser using the CGI, especially as Oracle now ships a standard Apache Web server with the Oracle database management system (DBMS). This section describes the basics of Apache configuration and shows you how to run the dbcool_db_up.pl script over the Web in a secure way.

Starting and Stopping Apache

Use the following commands to start and stop the Apache Web server (httpd) processes:

```
$ $ORACLE_HOME/Apache/Apache/bin/apachectl start

$ $ORACLE_HOME/Apache/Apache/bin/apachectl stop
```

The CGI

CGI is just a fancy term for giving a user the ability to run a script on a Web server by initiating it from a browser and passing any screen output back to the browser. Typically, a user fills in Hypertext Markup Language (HTML) fields in a form. When the user presses the form submit button, the fields in the form become arguments passed to the script. The Web server takes the command string and arguments, runs the script, and sends output back to the client, which is usually tagged in HTML format, but sometimes in plain text.

For example, we could take the dbcool_db_up.pl script and run it from a Web browser to save us the effort of logging onto the server and running it from there. In general, Web execution is much more convenient than other methods because most PCs have a browser installed, and it's quite straightforward to take the existing Perl scripts and run them over the Web.

Virtual Directories

The location used to specify an executable script from the browser is known as a *virtual directory*, and the Web server maintains a configuration file, httpd.conf, to hold the mapping between the virtual directory and the actual server directory where the script resides. For example, the server path for dbcool_db_up.pl might be /u01/app/ oracle/perl/bin/dbcool_db_up.pl, whereas a Netscape user might call the script using the URL http://srv1.dbcool.com/cgi-bin/db_cool_db_up.pl. In this example, the virtual directory /cgi-bin/ maps to the real directory /u01/app/oracle/perl/bin/. If you installed Oracle's Apache Web server into a $ORACLE_HOME of /u01/product/9.0.1 using the default settings, then the directory to hold executable scripts would be as follows:

```
ScriptAlias /cgi-bin/ "/u01/product/9.0.1//Apache/Apache/cgi-bin/"
```

Apache provides a trivial script called printenv to test the functionality of your CGI scripts. This script simply shows all the UNIX environment symbols for the environment in which your script runs. You can run this using the following URL after installing Apache onto srv1.dbcool.com using the default port settings:

```
http://srv1.dbcool.com:7777/cgi-bin/printenv
```

Web Enabling a Perl Script

Perl is one of the most popular scripting languages used on the Web. Provided you use the CGI.pm package (and the standard scripts developed here already do), you can Web enable any script with minimal effort. First your script needs to detect if it's being called from a Web server or from the UNIX command line. If you check for the GATEWAY_INTERFACE environment symbol and it's set, that's a very good indicator that the script is being called from a Web server and not the command line. In this case, it's necessary to send an HTML header back to the browser in order for the standard output of the script to appear in the browser. This code fragment demonstrates what you need to do:

```
# test if this is running from a web browser
if ($ENV{'GATEWAY_INTERFACE'})
{
    # send a header back to the browser to text is returned, not HTML
    print $query->header('text/plain');
}
.
.
.
```

All the Perl scripts described in this chapter are already Web enabled. In order to use them from Apache, you need to modify the PERL5LIB setting in httpd.conf to use our Oracle-enabled Perl interpreter rather than the one that Oracle ships, which doesn't have built-in Oracle functionality. To find the value to use as the replacement, use the output from the following command, make the change to PERL5LIB, and then stop and restart the Web server:

```
perl -e "print join ':',@INC"
```

You can now test one of the scripts to see how it works on the Web. Copy dbcool_db_up.pl into the cgi-bin directory and then run it by entering the following URL into the browser and pressing Return:

```
http://srv1.dbcool.com:7777/cgi-bin/dbcool_db_up.pl?sid=OMFD1&log=n
```

In the previous URL, you identify the end of the script name by ? and separate the arguments with =. When you run a form on the Web and submit it, the URL command string is created, but in this case you're creating the URL by hand without a form. In general, there's nothing to stop you from typing in the URL yourself as in the example. You should receive a message in the browser:

```
DATABASE ORACLE_SID=OMFD1 IS UP
```

Security

Security is a major concern on the Web due to the easy accessibility of sites. A full discussion of Web security is beyond the scope of this book. However, as a minimum, a virtual directory should be password protected to ensure that only the DBA can run DBA-related scripts in it. As a security example, we'll protect the cgi-bin directory with the username oradba and the password guess22. To do this, you need to create a file called .htaccess (don't forget the period on the front) in the cgi-bin directory. Add contents to it as follows:

```
AuthUserFile /u01/app/oracle/.htpassword
AuthGroupfile /dev/null
AuthName "Members Only"
AuthType Basic
<Limit GET>
require user oradba
</Limit>
```

AuthUserFile is the location where the passwords will be stored. We'll create it outside of the cgi-bin directory for security reasons. In reality, the password file contains encrypted values, and the Web server is set up to protect access to .htpassword files, so the file could reside in the cgi-bin directory without too much danger. AuthName is the caption that appears in the password dialog box when a user tries to run a script in the directory. The Limit section contains a list of allowed users, which in this case contains oradba. Now create a password file for the account oradba using the command htpasswd and the password guess22 when prompted:

```
$ export PATH=$PATH:$ORACLE_HOME/Apache/Apache/bin

$ htpasswd -c /u01/app/oracle/.htpassword oradba
```

When you access the dbcool_db_up.pl script, you should be prompted for the username and password that protect the virtual directory. If you find that a dialog box doesn't appear, check the setting of AllowOverride in httpd.conf and make sure the setting for the cgi-bin directory is AuthConfig.

Summary

This chapter has covered the requirements for a standard DBA environment both for interactive commands and batch scripts. Such an environment enhances availability by providing a standard interface for common DBA operations like database shutdown and startup, which can also be easily embedded in other scripts. Through a standard set of scripts written in Perl, the Oracle services can be shut down and started up in a reliable way, synchronized with server boot and shutdown, and even invoked via a Web browser. These scripts are the building blocks for other scripts used in the rest of the book.

Securing Your Database

Oracle security discussions often focus only on logon authentication and data access levels, which isn't enough. Security for your Oracle infrastructure operates at various levels and doesn't apply to your database alone. For example, a malicious user that has the Names Control utility locally installed on his PC can shut down your Names servers. Without your Names servers, client users in your organization can't connect to their Oracle databases. To prevent such a possibility, you can and should protect privileged Names server shutdown operations with an encrypted password.

Consider another situation, where an enterprising business user develops a Microsoft Access application that connects to your database using Open Database Connectivity (ODBC). The subsequent reports executed by the user perform multiple full-table scans of the largest table in the database and cause all other user sessions to perform much more slowly as a result. Some of those other users are taking telephone orders, and orders are lost as potential customers get impatient waiting and hang up. How can you prevent that user from running a Microsoft Access application against your database?

This chapter covers how to secure your end-to-end Oracle infrastructure to ensure that access to your Oracle database is appropriately controlled, including the following topics:

- Logon authentication options
- Password management policies
- How to reduce the cost of user administration
- Application security and how to prevent database access to specific applications

- How to secure Oracle networking software
- How to perform a security audit

Database Logon Authentication Options

Before an Oracle user can connect to a database, the user needs to be authenticated. Oracle provides various ways to do this. The simplest way involves storing the encrypted password in the database itself. More secure alternatives include authentication by external services such as SecurID and Kerberos. These are covered in this section. The more secure options require extra spending on software and also have a higher installation, configuration, and maintenance cost.

Authentication by Database-Encrypted Password

All connections to an Oracle database should be password protected with a password that's not easy to guess and conforms to a set of naming rules that are enforced. The simplest method to administer involves storing the encrypted password in the database itself. In a simple interactive two-tier application, the user typically runs an application on a PC. When the application presents a login dialog box, the user fills in his username and password, and the login request is sent to the database. The password entered by the user is encrypted and compared against the encrypted password stored in the data dictionary before login is permitted.

A lot of debate has taken place in the past about the possibility that Oracle passwords can be transmitted across the network in clear text, both for login requests and for connections resulting from database links. The two settings relevant to this case are the client side environment setting, ORA_ENCRYPT_LOGIN, and the server init.ora parameter DBLINK_ENCRYPT_LOGIN, which both have a default setting of FALSE. The good news is that Oracle passwords have not been transmitted in clear text on the network in either case since Oracle8*i*, and much earlier on some server platforms. It you want to confirm this for yourself, then take a look at Chapter 28 for information on how to do network sniffing both for Oracle Net packets and for general network traffic.

External Authentication by the Operating System

Operating system authentication is an administrative convenience that is frequently used in companies that have a large user base of clients on a secure operating system, such as Microsoft Windows NT or Windows 2000 and UNIX database servers. Such accounts are referred to as being externally identified by the operating system. In this case, Oracle enables logons to proceed without requiring the user to specify a password by assuming that the user's operating system is secure, and the user has already been authenticated by the operating system. To enable this facility, the database administrator (DBA) needs to specify the following in the init.ora file:

```
REMOTE_OS_AUTHENT=true
OS_AUTHENT_PREFIX=""
```

The DBA then creates an account using the operating system account name as the Oracle username:

```
create user smithjoh identified externally;

grant connect, resource to smithjoh;
```

The OS_AUTHENT_PREFIX specifies a string that Oracle prefixes onto the name passed as the Oracle logon account name from the client before checking it against the list of Oracle accounts in the SYS.USER$ table. Traditionally, this string was OPS$, but nowadays the value is usually left empty. Once the OS-authenticated account has been created, the user can connect to Oracle simply by specifying / as the username and password. So a SQL*Plus user could enter the following to connect:

```
$ sqlplus /@remotedb.dbcool.com
```

It needs to be emphasized that just because the DBA has specified to Oracle that the operating system is secure, it doesn't mean that database access is secure. Externally identified accounts actually present a large security hole. All it takes is for a single user anywhere on the corporate PC network to create a local Windows account on a PC, using the same name as an externally identified Oracle account. For example, the DBA may create an Oracle account smithjoh for the Windows domain account TRADERS\ smithjoh, knowing that the user needs to supply a Windows password to log onto the Windows network. At this point, everything is fine. However, an unscrupulous Windows user with access to the local Administrator password on his PC creates a local Windows account named smithjoh and logs onto it, in order to masquerade as the secure domain account. The Oracle UNIX database can't tell the domain account and the local NT account apart and lets both users access the database without supplying a password, on the assumption that the operating system is secure. Any user with unauthorized root access on an Oracle UNIX client can create a UNIX account in the same way.

You can avoid the security issues of externally identified operating system accounts by not using them and instead requiring users to supply a password at connect time. It's certainly more inconvenient for the users and requires extra administration to handle users who forget their passwords, but it's more secure.

External Authentication Using a Token

If you require users to remember passwords, then they are either likely to forget passwords on a regular basis or write passwords down in case they forget them. The first scenario creates an administration overhead due to the need for regular password resets, and the second one creates a security risk if another user gains access to the password.

These problems can be overcome by using a token-based authentication scheme, such as SecurID from RSA Security Inc. SecurID hardware tokens are small devices containing a microprocessor that generates a continually changing code, usually every 60 seconds. In order to gain access to a SecurID-secured system, the user must provide a passcode consisting of a secret personal identification number (PIN) code, typically four digits chosen by the user at the time of activitating the device, along with the continually changing code. The user hardware token is synchronized with a SecurID server that validates the PIN code and generated code combination. Only if a match is obtained is the request authenticated. To gain unauthorized access requires possession of the hardware token device and the PIN code.

A considerable overhead is added to the security infrastructure using such an approach. The Oracle Advanced Security option is required on both the client and server, and this option is only available with the Enterprise edition under a separate license. Proprietary products need to purchased and installed on both the client and server, in this case from RSA Security Inc. Once the SecurID components have been installed, the client specifies that it requires SecurID authentication services through an entry in the sqlnet.ora file:

```
SQLNET.AUTHENTICATION_SERVICES=(SECURID)
```

At connection time, the user supplies the SecurID passcode as the Oracle password. If you choose to implement SecurID, you should be aware that each passcode is a one-time only code. So if your application spawns additional connections internally based on the supplied password, then those other connections will fail. This is a design feature of SecurID and can't be changed.

External Authentication with Single Sign-On

To use single sign-on for Oracle access, an organization deploys authentication servers to provide a one-off single point of authentication for a user within an organization's network environment. All services that subscribe to the single sign-on approach can then be accessed by a user without requiring further authentication. This single sign-on approach is enabled through a ticket passed to the client from the authentication server before the initial Oracle connection request and authenticated by a password. The ticket is then passed to a database server during all subsequent connections, and the database server itself checks the ticket against the authentication server to validate the user. This extra check is important because the ticket may have expired. In order for the database to authenticate a user via a single sign-on service like Kerberos, the following needs to be set in the init.ora file:

```
remote_os_authent=false
os_authent_prefix=""
```

Creation of user accounts needs to be performed in an authentication method-specific way, for example:

```
create user "K5USER@UK.DBCOOL.COM"  identified externally;
grant create session to "K5USER@UK.DBCOOL.COM";
```

Note the use of double quotes to allow nonstandard characters to appear in the username. The username and database both need to be established separately as Kerberos security principals using the Kerberos administration tools. For the authentication to succeed, both Oracle and Kerberos need to agree on the names to be used for the client user and the database instance. Use of a single sign-on service requires several modifications to the sqlnet.ora file, including a setting to identify the authentication method used:

```
SQLNET.AUTHENTICATION_SERVICES=(KERBEROS5)
```

Single sign-on via Kerberos requires the installation of the separately licensed Oracle Advanced Security option and Kerberos components on both client and server. Oracle also provides single sign-on over secure sockets layer (SSL) by integration of the sign-on process with a Lightweight Directory Access Protocol (LDAP) compliant directory such as Oracle Internet Directory (OID). Chapter 3 includes a brief overview of LDAP. As in the Kerberos example, single sign-on enables users to be authenticated once only. Further connections authenticate the user based on the user's X.509v3 compliant digital certificate, which is made available to subsequent connection requests, following initial authentication. Oracle's position on certificate-based security is that it's typically deployed where there is a requirement for end-to-end SSL. For most companies running Oracle behind a firewall, there is no such requirement.

Using Password Management Policies

Most organizations, as part of their technology risk protection procedures, require users to change their passwords on a regular basis and to choose their passwords to meet a complexity requirement to prevent easy guessing. This complexity requirement typically requires a minimum password length and a mixture of alpha and numeric characters. Additional requirements may be specified to prevent the user recycling old passwords within a certain time period or within a certain number of password changes. Oracle enforces password management policies through the use of profiles, an example of which can be installed by running the utlpwdmg.sql script as follows:

```
$ sqlplus "sys as sysdba" @utlpwdmg.sql
```

This script modifies the DEFAULT profile, so under no circumstances should you run the script against a production database without understanding the implications. The modifications to the DEFAULT profile result in the following additional attributes:

```
CREATE PROFILE DEFAULT LIMIT
  .
  .
  .
```

```
FAILED_LOGIN_ATTEMPTS 3,
PASSWORD_LIFE_TIME 60,
PASSWORD_REUSE_TIME 1800,
PASSWORD_REUSE_MAX UNLIMITED,
PASSWORD_VERIFY_FUNCTION VERIFY_FUNCTION,
PASSWORD_LOCK_TIME .0006,
PASSWORD_GRACE_TIME 10
```

The PASSWORD_VERIFY_FUNCTION, in this case a function named VERIFY_ FUNCTION, is a SYS-owned object written in PL/SQL, and it takes the new and the old password as arguments and checks that the new password meets the complexity requirements before enabling it. You can write your own function to meet your organization's naming standards. The requirement to provide the old password when setting the new one is good from a security viewpoint and has long been used for the protection of UNIX system accounts. The downside is that the ALTER USER command can no longer be used to set passwords in Oracle9i if a policy is in use. Attempts to run ALTER USER give:

```
alter user scott identified by lion99#;

ERROR at line 1:
ORA-28003: password verification for the specified password failed
```

The situation in Oracle8i was different but had its own problems. In Oracle8i, you could circumvent the verify function by using ALTER USER. So Oracle8i had password management policies that could be circumvented, and Oracle9i enforces them by stopping the use of ALTER USER. This change has caused a lot of discontent in the DBA community as DBAs are very much in favor of password management policies, but don't want to lose the ability to set passwords with ALTER USER. Oracle has stated that the semantics of ALTER USER won't be changed to enable the old password to be included. As a kind of half-way house, SQL*Plus provides the SET PASSWORD command:

```
SQL> password scott
Changing password for scott
Old password:
New password:
Retype new password:
ERROR:
ORA-28003: password verification for the specified password failed
ORA-20002: Password length less than 4
```

What a DBA needs is the ability to set a password using a SQL statement that can apply the policy and allow the old password to be provided. It's not easy or convenient to embed SQL*Plus into an existing application to facilitate password changes. Oracle's alternative, requiring the DBA to call OCIPasswordChange, means Oracle Call Interface (OCI) programming. That has its own set of problems and has not proved popular either.

Oracle's password management policy features are straightforward to use and include facilities for account locking, password aging and expiration, password history, and password complexity verification. You still need to provide a service for user password resets because these features are more likely to cause users to forget passwords if you choose to enforce complexity. A grace period to warn users of imminent password expiration is a good idea, to avoid support calls.

Simplifying User Management

You might wonder why Kerberos, SecurID, X.509v3, and all the other methods of increasing Oracle security are not more widely used. The available evidence suggests that the cost of the tools and the extra configuration and management overhead are not justified. For most companies that operate their database behind a firewall, the extra benefits of these additional services are not cost effective. As an example, how many sites need data encrypted on the wire? The answer would appear to be not very many. In the real world, there's usually not much advantage to be gained from employees sniffing Oracle data traffic on the wire. So, in general, encryption is an unnecessary additional cost both up front, due to the need for the Advanced Security option and in terms of operational overhead due to the increased network traffic and the increased CPU usage required to encrypt and decrypt data. The exception is the use of infrared rather than wire-based networks, which potentially open up data access in a way that wouldn't previously have been possible.

Before looking at how to simplify user management, it's important to understand the costs of traditional Oracle user management by focusing on the real problems. A typical business user in a large company has access to several Oracle applications that require database password authentication. The user may have several different accounts with different names and possibly different passwords in each database. As a result, the user forgets passwords from time to time and needs to follow a procedure to get the password reset. The cost of this approach is the cost of the time for the DBA to do the reset and the opportunity cost of the user's time wasted while waiting for the reset. When a user joins or leaves the company, or changes departments, there is the extra cost of having to reconfigure the user's privileges in all databases. What's perhaps more irritating than the cost of the password reset is the fact that a business user typically doesn't actually own any objects in the application database. In the most common application configuration, one schema owns all the application tables and objects, and business users are granted access to the schema objects through roles, after logon. So a business user typically owns no objects in any of the databases he or she uses and yet requires a password to be maintained for each one.

Oracle9*i* has a solution to this problem by introducing the concept of Enterprise User Security. This provides password-based authentication for a user through a single, unique user identifier held in an LDAP-compliant directory. You might find it helpful to review the discussion of LDAP in Chapter 3 before continuing with this section. At connect time, the user is validated against the password for their LDAP enterprise account, and this enterprise account is mapped to a real schema in a database at connection time. The database schema, which is usually shared across many enterprise users, is known as a *shared schema*. The directory provides facilities for specifying enterprise users and enterprise roles. The major benefit is that instead of creating a user schema in every database and maintaining a local database password, the user is created as an enterprise user in an LDAP-compliant directory, such as OID, and can use the centrally held password and user for access to all database accounts.

> **NOTE** Before you consider implementing Oracle user administration based on enterprise users, keep in mind that both SSL and Oracle wallets are required to secure authentication between the database and the LDAP directory, and for current user database links. Failure to configure SSL and Oracle wallets will result in database connection attempts failing with an ORA-28030 message. The Oracle Advanced Security Administrator's Guide provides full details of how to perform the configuration. Oracle 9*i* Release 2 includes the User Migration Utility to ease bulk migration of database accounts into a directory where they are known as password authenticated enterprise users.

Each enterprise user using the shared schema can have different roles. This leads to the concept of enterprise roles. Enterprise users in the directory can be granted enterprise roles also held in the directory. Enterprise roles are mapped to real database roles in the target database, known as *global roles*, at connect time, using mapping information held in the directory. It's not as complicated as it sounds. The essence of the concept is that Oracle users and roles can exist as entities outside of an Oracle database and can be mapped to real database roles and account names in different databases at connect time, based on information in the directory.

In this example, we'll create a shared schema called SHARED_SCOTT that will be used by enterprise users to access the standard EMP and DEPT tables in SCOTT's schema. For maximum security, it's best not to assign any local roles or create objects in the shared schema to allow access to the data only via the enterprise roles. The shared schema can be identified from DBA_USERS by a password of GLOBAL, and we create it as follows:

```
create user shared_scott IDENTIFIED GLOBALLY as ''
temporary tablespace temp default tablespace tools;


select username,password
from dba_users where username='SHARED_SCOTT';


USERNAME        PASSWORD
-------------   ----------
SHARED_SCOTT    GLOBAL
```

The use of IDENTIFIED GLOBALLY flags the account as a special type of account that can be connected to using information from the directory. Next we create a global database role that will be used to provide access to the EMP and DEPT tables in SCOTT's schema for enterprise users. The role is created as follows:

```
REM   requires GRANT CREATE ROLE TO SCOTT privilege
create role global_empdept_modify IDENTIFIED GLOBALLY;
```

```
grant all on emp to global_empdept_modify;
grant all on dept to global_empdept_modify;
```

The significance of the IDENTIFIED GLOBALLY clause on the role is that you can't grant it to a local user in the database. If you try GRANT GLOBAL_EMPDEPT_ MODIFY TO SYSTEM for example, you'll get:

```
ORA-28021: cannot grant global roles
```

Now let's turn to the LDAP configuration required to support this shared schema and global role. This section uses a step-by-step approach, including several screen shots to help you get the configuration right the first time. Oracle provides several tools to do this that aren't yet well integrated, so the process is somewhat fragmented, which doesn't make it easy to follow.

Before you can use the OID-based LDAP directory, you need to install OID using the Oracle Installer. OID requires an Oracle database to store the LDAP directory information tree (DIT), which holds directory entries that you create using Oracle Directory Manager. Each entry in the DIT is identified by a unique name referred to as the distinguished name (DN).

During the OID installation, you can choose an existing database to hold the directory or let the installer create a new one. To install the Oracle9*i* version of OID, you first choose Oracle9*i* Management and Integration from the Available Products list in Oracle Installer, and then choose OID from the Installation types. The rest of the installation is straightforward, although you should be aware that the OID schema contains many objects and may take a while to create.

After OID installation is complete, make sure your LDAP server is running by executing the following commands on the UNIX server in the Oracle9*i* environment where OID is installed:

```
$ oidmon start
$ oidctl server=oidldapd instance=1 start
```

The oidctl command requires a connect alias for the database that holds the LDAP directory. In this case it's not supplied, so the connection defaults to the current ORACLE_SID set in the environment. The example in this section demonstrates enterprise user access to a database identified by the GLOBAL_NAME omfd1.uk.dbcool .com. In order to create the directory entry to hold the DN related to this name, you must first create an Oracle Context in the DIT. An Oracle Context is a special entry in the DIT that contains Oracle subentries to support directory naming and enterprise security. Based on the name we want to register (omfd1.uk.dbcool.com), an Oracle Context is required under the DN dc=uk,dc=dbcool,dc=com. Note that the DN of the Oracle Context in the directory (dc=uk,dc=dbcool,dc=com) bears a strong resemblance to the domain component of the Transparent Network Substrate (TNS) alias (uk.dbcool.com). In fact, the DN of the Oracle Context performs an identical function to the NAMES. DEFAULT_DOMAIN value for TNS aliases. Chapter 3 covers NAMES.DEFAULT_ DOMAIN in detail. The difference is that TNS aliases are understood only by Oracle Names and networking software, whereas the format of entries in an LDAP-compliant directory is based on an open standard that can be understood by any client application that is LDAP aware. The structure we have chosen for directory component names (such as dc=uk,dc=dbcool,dc=com) is referred to as the domain component model. In order to maintain entries in the DIT, you use Oracle Directory Manager.

NOTE For best performance, you should run Oracle Directory Manager from a PC where the Oracle management tools have been installed. You run the program from the Integrated Management Tools menu under the Oracle program group. Alternatively, you can use the oidadmin program on a UNIX server, and display the GUI on an X Window display. The default username and password for connection to the directory are orcladmin and welcome. For security reasons, you should change these before production deployment of OID.

It's helpful to go through the LDAP registration process step by step, including the creation of the Oracle Context. To create the part of the tree below on which the Oracle Context will reside, log in as the OID administrator using Oracle Directory Manager and navigate to Entry Management in the tree. Right click the node and choose Create. Then create an entry with a DN of dc=com and an ObjectClass of domain. Next add an entry in the same way, specifying a DN of dc=dbcool,dc=com, and then add a third entry with a DN of dc=uk,dc=dbcool,dc=com. The Create Entry screen for this third entry is shown in Figure 5.1.

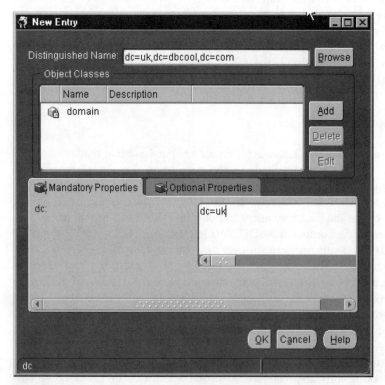

Figure 5.1 Adding dc=uk,dc=dbcool,dc=com to OID.

After adding this entry, an Oracle Context needs to be created below it, under which we'll add information about the databases that require enterprise user support. To add the Oracle Context, start Net Configuration Assistant (a program named netca on UNIX) and choose Directory Usage Configuration. Next, choose the option to create an additional Oracle Context and then specify Oracle Internet Directory as the directory type. Connect to OID and then enter the DN under which to create the Oracle Context as dc=uk,dc=dbcool,dc=com. The final step is to supply the credentials for connecting to OID to add the Oracle Context. If you are using the default credentials set for OID at installation time, enter cn=orcladmin for the user and welcome for the password. If everything worked, you should get a message stating that the DN of your default Oracle Context is:

```
cn=OracleContext,dc=uk,dc=dbcool,dc=com
```

The structure containing the newly created Oracle Context should look like Figure 5.2.

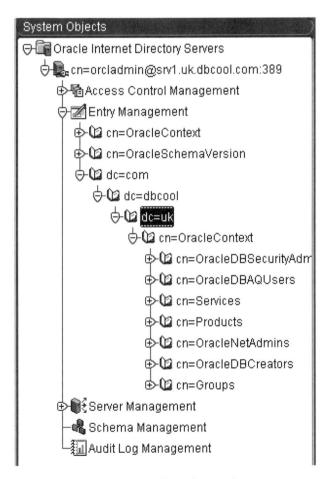

Figure 5.2   The DIT after adding the Oracle Context.

At this point you should check your ldap.ora file in $ORACLE_HOME/network/ admin to ensure that it contains the following:

```
DEFAULT_ADMIN_CONTEXT = "dc=uk,dc=dbcool,dc=com"

DIRECTORY_SERVERS= (srv1.uk.dbcool.com:389:636)

DIRECTORY_SERVER_TYPE = OID
```

The ldap.ora file identifies the LDAP server to use for resolving Oracle database names. The DIRECTORY_SERVERS entry identifies the host where OID is running. The default context DN is important because it determines where the next entries we add are inserted in the DIT. In our case, we want entries inserted under the Oracle Context below dc=uk,dc=dbcool,dc=com, and this is the one we just created. If you recall, when OID is installed, a default Oracle Context is created at the root of the DIT, and we *don't* want to use that one.

Now we'll register our database and a TNS entry for it under the default Oracle Context in the DIT. To perform this operation, we use the Database Configuration Assistant utility (a program named dbca on UNIX). After starting Configuration Assistant, choose the Configure operation. Choose the instance you want to register from the list of available instances, and then choose the option to register the database with the LDAP server. You'll need to supply the credentials for the LDAP server as before, using cn=orcladmin for the user, and welcome for the password. Be warned that your database will be restarted if you want to continue. Assuming that a database System ID (SID) of omfd1 was registered, the init.ora file contains the following modification so that the database and the LDAP server can agree on the DN of the registered database:

```
rdbms_server_dn="cn=omfd1,cn=OracleContext,dc=uk,dc=dbcool,dc=com"
```

You should see an entry in the DIT in Oracle Directory Manager with the DN given previously. If you click on it and look in the right hand panel, you should see that the DN belongs to the object class orclService and the object class orclDBServer, to identify that the database has been registered as an Oracle service for TNS network addressing, and as an Oracle database server for the purpose of enterprise security. However, the TNS information doesn't contain a connect description and so it isn't useable yet. To add this information you need to run yet another tool: Oracle Network Manager. To run Oracle Network Manager on UNIX, execute the program netmgr and connect to the LDAP directory using the usual credentials. Click on the Directory entry in the tree and then Service Naming. An entry should exist for the service that was added by Database Configuration Assistant, which for our example is omfd1. Click the + button, specify the port and server where the database in located, and then choose Apply. If you now refresh the subtree for omfd1 in Oracle Directory Manager, you should see that a DESCRIPTION_0 entry has appeared. Now you can connect to the database from a remote client provided that the client contains an ldap.ora file as previously described, and the sqlnet.ora file specifies that an LDAP server should be used to resolve the database names through an entry:

```
names.directory_path = (LDAP)
```

The following connect strings both work. The first example specifies the full DN of the database, and the second relies on the DEFAULT_ADMIN_CONTEXT value in ldap.ora in a similar way that the NAMES.DEFAULT_DOMAIN value in the sqlnet.ora file can be used for resolving names from an Oracle Names server:

```
$ sqlplus sys/pwd@'cn=omfd1,cn=OracleContext,dc=uk,dc=dbcool,dc=com'
$ sqlplus sys/pwd@omfd1
```

The structure of the DIT containing the full Oracle service information for omfd1 is shown in Figure 5.3.

Now that the LDAP information for the database has been configured, another utility, the Oracle Enterprise Security Manager, can be used to map enterprise users to shared schemas in a given database. On UNIX, Enterprise Security Manager is started by executing:

```
$ oemapp esm
```

First, we need to create an enterprise user, and this is performed by choosing Create Enterprise User . . . from the Operations menu and filling in the form shown in Figure 5.4.

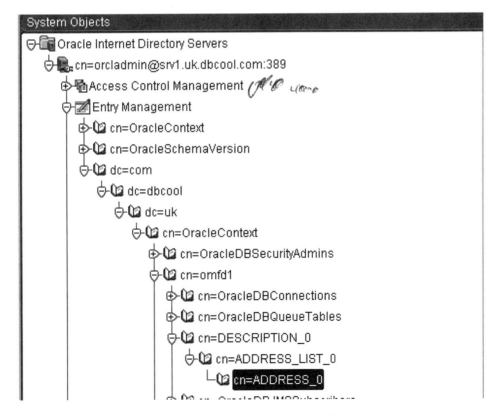

Figure 5.3 The DIT after adding the Oracle service description.

Figure 5.4   Creating an enterprise user.

Next, we need to create an enterprise domain and an enterprise role in that domain, and these operations are both performed via the Operations menu. For the purposes of this example, the domain is left as OracleDefaultDomain, and the enterprise role in that domain is named er_empdept_modify. Be sure to choose the correct Oracle Context when creating the role and domain. This should *not* be the Default Oracle Context. Now add the enterprise user to the enterprise role by displaying the enterprise user in Users, by Search Base, editing the user details, displaying the enterprise roles in the Oracle Context, and adding the user to the chosen role. Figure 5.5 shows the Enterprise Security Manager view of the DIT after assigning the enterprise user to the enterprise role. At this stage, there is no reference to a real database.

Using enterprise security has the potential for reducing user management over-heads by defining users once in an LDAP directory and mapping them to real schemas and roles at connection time. However, the choice of using OID should not be taken lightly and requires considerable design and planning. Oracle doesn't make things easy for you by requiring you to use several different tools to manage the DIT. Hope-fully in the future, Oracle's tools will become more integrated. Oracle's use of Java provides portable management tools across different platforms at the cost of high memory usage. Responsiveness is very poor when running the tools against an X display over a wide area network (WAN), so you should consider installing them locally on a Windows PC to run against a remote LDAP server.

Use of a directory raises questions about 24 × 7 availability, supportability, and scalability that need to be addressed. You might want to consider using Microsoft Active

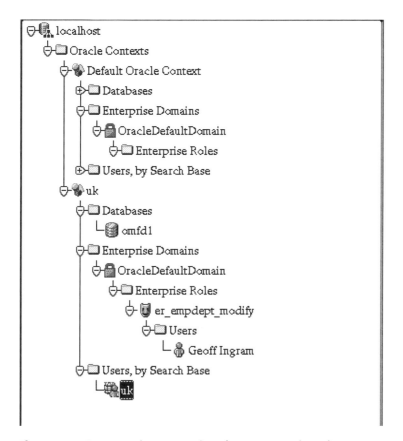

Figure 5.5 An enterprise user assigned to an enterprise role.

Directory as your LDAP directory instead of OID. Oracle supports both. Whatever LDAP directory you use, make sure you have a complete understanding of Oracle and LDAP before you implement it for production systems: You can't afford to get it wrong if your enterprise relies on it.

Using SET ROLE for Application Security

Oracle has long recommended using the SET ROLE command to enforce application security. In this case, a user logon typically has no privileges except the capability to connect, based on the CREATE SESSION privilege. To set up security in this way, the application schema owner first creates a password-protected role and assigns some privileges to it:

```
create role password_protected identified by xxxxxxxxxxxxxxxx;
grant select on EMP to password_protected;
```

Oracle enforces security on the ROLE password by storing the password for the role in the USER$ table in encrypted form. If you try to trace the CREATE ROLE statement, Oracle truncates the SQL to hide the password:

```
PARSING IN CURSOR #8 len=42 dep=0 uid=5 oct=52 lid=5 ...
create role password2 ide
END OF STMT
```

This role is granted to a user in the usual way:

```
grant password_protected to business_user;
```

When BUSINESS_USER logs onto the application, the first action by the application is to run the SQL:

```
set role password_protected identified by xxxxxxxxxxxxxxxx;
```

This has two obvious shortcomings from a security viewpoint: The application needs to have the password embedded in it, and the application developer needs to know the password. Most DBAs keep application passwords secure to avoid developers from making unauthorized changes on production systems. The application programmer can work around the embedding of the password in the application by obfuscating the value, but a determined hacker with a binary file viewer might be able decode it. Oracle protects the password from SQL trace snooping by truncating the SET ROLE statement in the trace:

```
PARSING IN CURSOR #8 len=39 dep=0 uid=5 oct=55 lid=5 tim=...
 set role password_protected identi
END OF STMT
```

Finally, let's look at the network packet sent from the application using the SET ROLE command:

```
 64: 034a 1b01 0101 03ac a218 0001 3a00 0000    .J . . . . . . . .:. . .
 80: 0000 eceb 1200 0101 0000 0000 0000 0000    . . . . . . . . . . . . . . .
 96: 0000 0000 0000 0000 0000 003a 7365 7420    . . . . . . . . . .:set
112: 726f 6c65 2070 6173 7377 6f72 645f 7072    role password_pr
128: 6f74 6563 7465 6420 6964 656e 7469 6669    otected identifi
144: 6564 2062 7920 7878 7878 7878 7878 7878    ed by xxxxxxxxxx
160: 7878 7878 7878 0102                        xxxxxx..
```

It's clear that the SET ROLE command sends the password to the database server in clear text, and the security implications are obvious. For this example, I chose a password with lots of x's so that it would show up clearly in the network trace. In reality, whatever password you choose, it's sent to the database in clear text, and this represents a potential security hazard. Any user obtaining the password could set the role using the tool of their choice, for example SQL*Plus, and gain free access to the data that was only ever intended for access through the role-protected application. Enterprise User Security addresses this requirement to enable access to an application only through roles granted at connection time and does it in a way that avoids hard coding or exposing the role password.

Preventing Application Access

For business-critical applications, you might want to prevent access to your database from ad-hoc query tools such as SQL*Plus or Microsoft Access. If you allow ad-hoc query tools to access your production database, then you allow the possibility that business users will try to develop new reports against your production data, often using very inefficient SQL that can impact the performance of the whole database.

Reports development should be run against your development database first, where the DBA's input can be used to ensure that the SQL is as efficient as possible. This section presents techniques that are guaranteed to prevent access with SQL*Plus and Microsoft Access from any user except the DBA accounts SYS and SYSTEM. Probably the most simple way to prevent access from SQL*Plus and Microsoft Access is through the use of an AFTER LOGON database trigger. AFTER LOGON database triggers are something we'll return to as they have many uses, especially for transparent collection of session statistics. In this case, we check the name of the application program at logon time, and if it's SQL*Plus or Microsoft Access, we raise an exception. As there is no exception handler the logon fails:

```
create or replace TRIGGER SYS.TRG_STOP_APPLICATIONS
AFTER LOGON
ON DATABASE

begin

  FOR REC IN (SELECT USERNAME,PROGRAM
                FROM V$SESSION
                WHERE AUDSID = USERENV('SESSIONID')) LOOP

    if rec.username not in ('SYS','SYSTEM') and
      upper(rec.program) in ('MSACCESS.EXE','SQLPLUSW.EXE') then
      RAISE_APPLICATION_ERROR(-20001,
        'SQL*Plus and Microsoft Access not allowed');
    end if;

  end loop;

end;
/
```

There are two additional points of interest in this code. The first is the use of AUDSID = USERENV('SESSIONID')) to identify the currently connected session within the trigger. The second is the use of the FOR REC IN in the main loop of the code. You might ask why a loop construct is used when we only expect the query to return a single row containing the details of the connected session. The benefit of this approach is that there's no need to declare any local variables or cursors, which reduces the code size considerably and makes coding easier. This trigger should foil most people trying to use SQL*Plus and Microsoft Access. The more enterprising user who discovers that this security is based on the program name can circumvent this by renaming his program as follows:

```
C:\> copy sqlplusw.exe cant_stop_me.exe
```

It is possible to produce a solution that works in all cases. Even if you don't choose to use it, it raises some interesting possibilities for the customization of application access that can be enforced in the database. The solution relies on the fact that SQL*Plus queries its Product User Profile tables whenever you run it, immediately after connection. The SQL*Plus Product User Profile tables are installed as SYSTEM by the pupbld.sql script in the SQL*Plus product installation directory. Failure to run pupbld.sql is the cause of the following message after you log onto SQL*Plus, which you may have seen before:

```
Error accessing PRODUCT_USER_PROFILE
Warning:  Product user profile information not loaded!
You may need to run PUPBLD.SQL as SYSTEM
```

You can insert rows into the Product User Profile tables to restrict SQL*Plus access to individual users. Instead of maintaining information in this table for perhaps hundreds of individual users, you can prevent access to any SQL*Plus session, whatever the name of the program, by dropping one of the Product User Profile views using DROP VIEW SYSTEM.PRODUCT_PRIVS, and then creating a SYS-owned trigger on the Oracle audit trail to detect the reference to this missing table when SQL*Plus starts up:

```
CREATE OR REPLACE TRIGGER SYS.TRG_STOP_SQLPLUS_AND_MSACCESS
AFTER INSERT ON SYSTEM.AUD$
FOR EACH ROW
BEGIN

    -- MSYSCONF means client is Microsoft Access
    -- PRODUCT_PRIVS means client is SQL*Plus
    if :new.returncode=942 and
        :new.obj$name in ('MSYSCONF','PRODUCT_PRIVS')
        and user not in ('SYS','SYSTEM') then
        for rec in (select s.sid,s.serial#
                    from v$session s
                    where s.audsid=userenv('sessionid')) loop

            -- signal other session to kill me
            dbms_alert.signal(
              'KILL SESSION',rec.sid||','||rec.serial#);

        end loop;
```

```
        end if;

EXCEPTION
    WHEN OTHERS THEN
        null;
END TRG_STOP_SQLPLUS_AND_MSACCESS;
/
```

This code works by checking the Oracle audit trail for 942 errors (table or view does not exist), in order to identify users that run queries on nonexistent tables. SQL*Plus queries the PRODUCT_PRIVS table at startup time, and Microsoft Access queries the MSYSCONF table. When an audit record meeting the requirements is detected, a signal is sent to a watcher process running in another session, and the watcher session kills the triggering session. This watcher process is required because it's not possible for a session to kill itself. The watcher process runs a loop that waits to receive session identifiers from the trigger and kills the session given by the details that are passed in:

```
declare
    v_message varchar2(100);
    v_status integer;
begin
  DBMS_ALERT.REGISTER('KILL SESSION');
  loop
    DBMS_ALERT.WAITONE('KILL SESSION', v_message, v_status, 1);

      if v_status = 0 then
        execute immediate
          'alter system kill session '''||v_message||'''';
        exit when v_message = 'END KILL SESSION';
      else
        null;
      end if;

    end loop;
    DBMS_ALERT.REMOVE('KILL SESSION');
end;
/
```

Users whose sessions are killed receive a message, "ORA-00028: your session has been killed." To implement this in a production system, you would need to wrap the trigger call to DBMS_ALERT in another procedure, otherwise you leave open the possibility that anyone with permission to execute DBMS_ALERT can send a signal to the watcher and terminate any session.

If you are familiar with triggers, you'll know that it's not possible to create triggers on SYS-owned objects like the Oracle audit trail, which is installed into SYS.AUD$. This example uses an audit trail relocated in a different tablespace and owned by SYSTEM, and requires that auditing is enabled in the init.ora file and for object access. You can find more information on the audit trail in Chapter 11 on auditing.

Row-Level Access Control

Many applications have a requirement to control access to data at the row level. A traditional way to implement this in Oracle is through the use of views. For example, SCOTT as the owner of the EMP table, might want to allow users to access their own row in the EMP table. This could be done through the following view:

```
REM as SCOTT
create view v_me as
select * from emp where ename=user;

grant select on v_me to public;
```

The user ALLEN can connect and view his own data as follows:

```
select * from scott.v_me;

    EMPNO ENAME    JOB         MGR   HIREDATE    SAL   COMM   DEPTNO
    ------- ------- --------- ----- ---------- ----- ------ --------
     7499 ALLEN    SALESMAN   7698  20-FEB-81  1600   300      30
```

More sophisticated approaches are possible that use a separate security table to map the user access to specific rows. For example, SCOTT decides to allow users to access rows for specific jobs. In this case, ALLEN is allowed to view information for people with the job title CLERK through the use of a security table and view:

```
insert into authorization(ename,job) values ('ALLEN','CLERK');

create view v_others as
select  * from emp where job in
    (select job from authorization
     where ename=user);

grant select on v_others to public;
```

The user ALLEN can connect and view information for people whose jobs he is authorized to see:

```
select * from scott.v_others;

    EMPNO ENAME    JOB         MGR   HIREDATE    SAL   COMM   DEPTNO
    ------- ------- --------- ----- ---------- ----- ------ --------
     7369 SMITH    CLERK      7902  17-DEC-80   800            20
     7876 ADAMS    CLERK      7788  13-JUL-87  1100            20
     7934 MILLER   CLERK      7782  23-JAN-82  1300            10
     7900 JAMES    CLERK      7698  03-DEC-81   950            30
```

Oracle8*i* and later provides virtual private database (VPD) to enforce fine grained access control without the necessity to create the views, and hence dependencies, on the target table. Through the use of a security policy, whenever a user executes the query SELECT * FROM SCOTT.EMP, the query is rewritten transparently as

```
SELECT * FROM SCOTT.EMP
WHERE job in (select job from authorization
             where ename=sys_content('userenv','session_user'))';
```

The predicate is generated by a function associated with a security policy on the EMP table and silently added to every query on EMP. In this case, the function that returns a predicate with equivalent functionality to the V_OTHERS view is

```
create function f_others(p_user varchar2,p_object varchar2)
return varchar2 is
l_where varchar2(2000);
begin
   l_where:= 'job in (select job from authorization '||
             'where ename=sys_context(''userenv'',''session_user''))';
   return l_where;
end;
```

The policy itself can be created either through the Oracle Policy Manager component of Enterprise Manager or by a direct call to the DBMS_RLS.ADD_POLICY package procedure as in this example:

```
begin
dbms_rls.add_policy(object_schema=>'SCOTT',
                    object_name=>'EMP',
                    policy_name=>'POLICY_OTHERS',
                    function_schema=>'SCOTT',
                    policy_function=>'F_OTHERS');
end;
```

ALLEN can now run a query against SCOTT.EMP that returns the same information as the view through the enforcement of the policy:

```
select * from scott.emp;

  EMPNO ENAME   JOB      MGR   HIREDATE    SAL   COMM   DEPTNO
------- ------- ------ ----- ---------- ----- ------ --------
   7369 SMITH   CLERK   7902 17-DEC-80   800             20
   7876 ADAMS   CLERK   7788 13-JUL-87  1100             20
   7934 MILLER  CLERK   7782 23-JAN-82  1300             10
   7900 JAMES   CLERK   7698 03-DEC-81   950             30
```

This overview gives a flavor of the possibilities of VPD, which can be integrated with security information held in an LDAP-compliant directory rather than a database table. Developers can use the CREATE CONTEXT command to set application contexts at run time for individual users, usually in an AFTER LOGON database trigger. Application contexts are used in a similar way to SYS_CONTEXT in the example.

The SYS_CONTEXT contains fixed values that can't be changed, whereas application contexts can be populated at run time according to the security requirements.

Preventing Network Access

Oracle provides a facility to restrict client network access to a database by specifying a list of invited or excluded client names or IP addresses. Before Oracle9*i*, these settings were configured in the protocol.ora file. In Oracle9*i*, the sqlnet.ora file is used instead. In order to enable the feature, you must make the following setting in sqlnet.ora:

```
TCP.VALIDNODE_CHECKING=yes
```

Once the setting is enabled, you can allow or exclude connections from clients using TCP.EXCLUDED_NODES and TCP.INVITED_NODES. The TCP.EXCLUDED_NODES setting prevents access from a named list of clients:

```
TCP.EXCLUDED_NODES=(devsrv1.dbool.com,169.243.27.55)
```

The TCP.INVITED_NODES setting enables connections only from the invited list:

```
TCP.INVITED_NODES=(prodsrv1.dbool.com,169.243.27.53)
```

If a server appears in both lists, the node is excluded. After making a change to sqlnet.ora, you must reload or restart the Oracle network listener for the settings to take effect. The capability to prevent network access from certain clients can enhance your ability to protect production data from accidental access when you have two or more production databases connected by database links, and you periodically restore those databases onto a development server. This scenario represents a potential hazard to your production data because immediately after a physical restore of the production databases onto the development server, the database links in the development database point to the production databases. This situation is shown in Figure 5.6.

In a situation like this, the DBA's first task after restore is to fix the links on the development server and passwords. If this task is delayed or accidentally overlooked, then the production data is at risk. The use of TCP.EXCLUDED_NODES on the production server can protect against accidental access from the development server.

Roles versus GRANT and REVOKE

Most professional DBAs take for granted that Oracle's role-based security is a flexible and easy-to-manage model for enforcing security on objects. One subject that continues to cause confusion is the difference between role-based security and explicit GRANT and REVOKE statements. Roles can be toggled on and off for sessions, whereas grants are stored persistently in the Oracle data dictionary on completion of the GRANT or REVOKE statement that was executed.

All roles are *disabled* during DDL statements that create objects such a packages, stored procedures, stored functions, database triggers, and views. For the case of

**Before Production
Restore to Development**

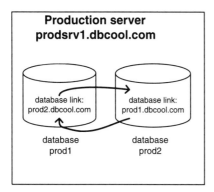
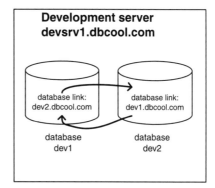

**Immediately after Production
Restore to Development**

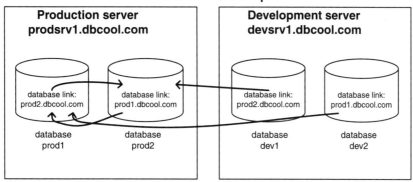

**Production server sqlnet.ora to protect production from
development access:**

```
TCP.VALIDNODE_CHECKING=yes
TCP.EXCLUDED_NODES=(devsrv1.dbcool.com)
```

Figure 5.6   Use of TCP.EXCLUDED_NODES.

named PL/SQL objects, the object exists but remains invalid after creation. The view creation fails. This Oracle behavior is by design, but still catches all Oracle DBAs and developers at some stage in their careers. Here's an example of what can happen based on a scenario where SCOTT has permission to create roles, owns the standard EMP table, and grants privileges on EMP to user JOHN through a role:

```
REM connect as SYSTEM
grant create role to scott;
create user john identified by john;
grant create session to john;
```

```
grant create procedure to john;
grant create view to john;


REM connect as SCOTT
create role role_emp_select;
grant select on emp to role_emp_select;
grant role_emp_select to john;
```

The user JOHN then executes the following SQL with the given results, based on the prerequisite that SCOTT has granted JOHN the role ROLE_EMP_SELECT:

```
REM this works:
select count(*) from scott.emp;

REM this PL/SQL block works:
begin
  for rec in (select count(*) the_count from scott.emp) loop
    dbms_output.put_line(rec.the_count);
  end loop;
end;

REM fails, because view requires role privilege
create view v_scott_emp as select * from scott.emp;

REM function is invalid after creation
create or replace function count_emp return integer as
begin
  for rec in (select count(*) the_count from scott.emp) loop
    return rec.the_count;
  end loop;
end;
```

The view creation fails with an "ORA-01031: insufficient privileges" error because the ROLE_EMP_SELECT privileges are required to create it and are disabled. The procedure creation succeeds, but the function is invalid because the grant on SCOTT.EMP is through a database role, which is turned off. When JOHN investigates the reason for the invalidation, the error "ORA-00942: table or view does not exist" occurs on the line referencing SCOTT.EMP.

JOHN can identify this issue in advance by using SET ROLE NONE, and then running SELECT * FROM SCOTT.EMP. This SELECT gives an ORA-00942 because JOHN can't access SCOTT.EMP without the role. If JOHN can't access an object after SET ROLE NONE, then he won't be able to access it in any named PL/SQL that he creates or any view creation statements.

To fix the invalid function and allow the view creation, SCOTT needs to perform an explicit grant on the EMP table to JOHN using GRANT SELECT ON EMP TO JOHN. However, this explicit grant works against the management benefits of roles, even though it's required to avoid potential ambiguities caused by the dynamic nature of roles. In general, this behavior of roles is not a problem if an application is accessed through a single schema, and all stored application PL/SQL and views reside in the same schema as the tables. If an application contains multiple schemas, and those schemas contain named PL/SQL objects and views that run against tables in a different schema, the issue is likely to manifest itself.

Using a Password File

It's recommended that you use a password file to allow remote SYSDBA and remote SYSOPER connections to your database. Password files are required to access many of the features of Oracle Enterprise Manager (OEM). We'll also be using them to support Legato Networker server initiated backups and for checking the status of standby databases. To create a password file at any time, set the environment to your Oracle SID, and then:

```
$ cd $ORACLE_HOME/dbs
$ orapwd file=orapwd${ORACLE_SID} password=sys-password
```

Next, add the following entry to your init.ora file and restart the database:

```
remote_login_passwordfile=EXCLUSIVE
```

Once you have a password file in place, you can perform remote SYSDBA connections from SQL*Plus (started with the /nolog command-line option) as follows:

```
connect sys/pwd@orad2.standby.dbool.com as SYSDBA
```

Connections using AS SYSDBA are enabled even if the remote database is in a mounted rather than open state, making them essential for checking the status of a standby database. Without using AS SYSDBA, connections against a mounted database will fail.

Protecting the Data Dictionary

Protecting the data dictionary should be high on the list of the DBA's priorities because loss of the data dictionary means loss of the database, and the loss of the dictionary prevents database logins from taking place. By default, Oracle9*i* implements extra data dictionary protection through the init.ora parameter:

```
O7_DICTIONARY_ACCESSIBILITY = FALSE
```

This setting prevents users with ANY privilege from performing ANY privilege operations against the data dictionary. For example, a user with DROP ANY TABLE is prevented from dropping data dictionary tables. Other protection arising from this setting means that any user connecting to the SYS account must connect as SYSDBA or SYSOPER only, or the connection will be refused. Any user with the DBA role, including SYSTEM, by default no longer has access to the dictionary tables such as USER$, LINK$, and so on.

Oracle considers it acceptable to grant the SELECT_ANY_CATALOG role to an account to enable read access to the dictionary tables, but strongly recommends that O7_DICTIONARY_ACCESSIBILITY = FALSE remains in force in all cases. In Oracle9i, FALSE is the default setting. In Oracle8i, the default setting is TRUE, and you are recommended to change it.

If you use database links that are password authenticated, then anyone that can view SYS.LINK$ can view the passwords in clear text. With O7_DICTIONARY_ACCESSIBILITY=FALSE enabled, this access is restricted to users with SYSDBA or SYSOPER privilege. This is another reason you should take advantage of the extra dictionary protection.

Oracle Names Security

Your Oracle Names servers are part of your enterprisewide Oracle infrastructure, and privileged operations should be protected against unauthorized use through an encrypted password. To create an encrypted password, you need to run Oracle Net Manager on the Names host, click the local Names server, and then choose Configure Server. Once you have confirmed the password, choose Exit from the File menu, and save the configuration. You should have an entry in the names.ora containing the encrypted password that looks like the following:

```
NAMES.PASSWORD = 77B9DDF30AF483C9
```

The password takes effect from the next restart of the Names server and applies to all STOP, RESTART, and RELOAD operations, but not START operations. When you need to stop a Names server, you must provide the password in response to the prompt from the SET PASSWORD command, or you'll receive an error:

```
NNL-00013: not performed, permission denied for supplied password
```

You should set a different password on each site to ensure that the DBA shuts down the correct server. For example, if you run two Names servers and the local one is already shut down, NAMESCTL will connect you to the remote one transparently. Any command you run, such as SHUTDOWN, will run against the remote Names server. Use of a site-specific password prevents accidental shutdown of the wrong server. One side effect of using a password is that you need to hardcode the password in a file somewhere so that it's available to the dbcool_ora_startup.pl script at server boot time. That raises security considerations of its own, and you need to protect any file holding a password at the UNIX level so that only the DBA group can view the contents.

Oracle Listener Security

Your Oracle listeners must be up and running at all times to allow client network connections. Oracle's network architecture enables a listener to be shut down remotely. This can happen accidentally if you copy a listener.ora file from an existing server onto a newserver and stop the listener. For example, if you copy this listener.ora file from oldserver onto newserver, forget to modify the host to newserver and run lsnrctl stop, then the listener on oldserver will stop.

```
LISTENER =
  (DESCRIPTION_LIST =
    (DESCRIPTION =
      (ADDRESS_LIST =
        (ADDRESS = (PROTOCOL = TCP)
                   (HOST = oldserver)
                   (PORT = 1521))
      )
    )
  )
```

Using such a technique, all nonpassword-protected listeners could be shut down maliciously, compromising availability. Therefore, privileged operations, like RELOAD and STOP, should be protected against unauthorized use through an encrypted password, which is unique to the listener on each server. To create an encrypted password, you need to run Oracle Net Manager on the listener host, click Local, and then Listeners to display the named listeners, click the required listener, and choose General Parameters from the poplist. Next, choose the Authentication tab and set a password. On exit, save the configuration. If you are using the default listener named LISTENER, you should see an entry in your listener.ora file containing the encrypted password that looks like this:

```
PASSWORDS_LISTENER= (AF7FFD1C595F23FE)
```

You need to restart the listener for the password to take effect. When you need to stop the listener, you must provide the password at the prompt in response to the SET PASSWORD command. You should set a different password on each site to ensure that the DBA always shuts down the correct listener. One side effect of using a password is that you need to hardcode the password in a file somewhere so that it's available to the dbcool_ora_startup.pl script at server boot time. As for the Name server, that raises security considerations of its own: You need to protect any file holding a password at the UNIX level so that only the DBA group can view the contents.

NOTE It's worth mentioning at this point that providing UNIX account access on your database servers to non-DBAs should be considered very carefully. If you allow this and UNIX privilege, settings on the database datafiles enable non-DBAs to read the file contents, any passwords held as clear text can be identified and potentially abused. Remember that database links in the SYS.LINK$ table store passwords in clear text.

Performing a Database Security Audit

Performing a security audit is an important process that provides visibility that your security procedures are working. You can perform a quick security audit of your database by running the dbcool_audit.pl script, which is downloadable from the companion Web site, as follows:

```
$ dbcool_audit.pl userid=system/password tns=omfd1.uk.dbcool.com
```

This searches your database for potential security problems, such as accounts having passwords matching the account name, accounts having the default password, and accounts that have potentially dangerous privileges such as UNLIMITED TABLESPACE, or ANY. As the source code is provided, you can customize the checks. Here's some sample output, where lines that indicate potential problems contain "!".

```
PASSED: userid=SCOTT password different from account name
WARNING!: SCOTT has default password TIGER
      System privs:
            CREATE ROLE NO
          ! UNLIMITED TABLESPACE NO
      Table privs:
      Role privs:
            CONNECT NO
            RESOURCE NO


PASSED: userid=SYS password different from account name
PASSED: SYS has non-default password

PASSED: userid=SYSTEM password different from account name
WARNING!: SYSTEM has default password MANAGER

WARNING!: userid=ODS password same as account name
      System privs:
          ! CREATE ANY SYNONYM NO
            CREATE TABLE NO
          ! DROP ANY SYNONYM NO
          ! UNLIMITED TABLESPACE NO
```

The list of privileges checked by the script is given by the following Perl pattern matches:

```
SWITCH:
    {
        if ($priv =~ m/FORCE/) { $warning='!'; last SWITCH;}
        if ($priv =~ m/RESTRICTED/) { $warning='!'; last SWITCH;}
        if ($priv =~ m/UNLIMITED/) { $warning='!'; last SWITCH;}
        if ($priv =~ m/DROP USER/) { $warning='!'; last SWITCH;}
        if ($priv =~ m/CREATE USER/) { $warning='!'; last SWITCH;}
        if ($priv =~ m/ALTER USER/) { $warning='!'; last SWITCH;}
        if ($priv =~ m/TABLESPACE/) { $warning='!'; last SWITCH;}
        if ($priv =~ m/ADMIN OPTION/) { $warning='!'; last SWITCH;}
        if ($priv =~ m/ANY /) { $warning='!'; last SWITCH;}
```

```
    if ($priv =~ m/PUBLIC /) { $warning='!'; last SWITCH;}
    if ($priv =~ m/DBA /) { $warning='!'; last SWITCH;}
}
```

You can modify the list to add new privileges or change the existing ones. These are the privileges that I look for as a starting point. The UNLIMITED TABLESPACE privilege, which is granted separately as a side effect of granting RESOURCE, is often overlooked. This privilege enables the grantee to potentially fill up the SYSTEM tablespace and halt the database, and should be revoked immediately after RESOURCE has been granted to a user. Finally, the script is also Web enabled, so you can call it from a URL in a browser as follows, after you have copied it to your cgi-bin directory:

```
http://site.com/cgi-bin/dbcool_audit.pl?userid=system/
pwd&tns=omfd1.world
```

Summary

Oracle security has many different aspects, and you need to consider them all in order to deliver the performance and availability that your business users require. Security considerations need to take into account the complete end-to-end infrastructure of your Oracle systems, including user authentication, the network and name resolution, data and dictionary protection, and more. Oracle provides most of the features required to enforce the required degree of protection, but considerable effort and diligence is required to cover all of them.

User security administration has long been an issue in the Oracle world because security requirements used to mean that users had to remember many different passwords for different systems. Such an approach often works against security by causing users to choose memorable (and therefore easy to crack) passwords. Enforcing secure (therefore unmemorable) passwords often leads to a need for expensive administrative procedures to perform password resets for users on demand. Oracle9*i* provides the solution to this longstanding problem through the introduction of enterprise users stored in an LDAP directory. Use of enterprise users requires the separately licensed Advanced Security Option.

PART
Two

Designing Fast and Supportable Applications

Designing Supportable Applications

What exactly does making an application supportable mean? It means that when a running application encounters a problem, the exact location in the code can be located immediately, and the root cause identified as quickly as possible. It means that an application reports back on its status in a format that can be easily assimilated by support staff and automated monitoring processes. It means that an application needs to be written in a way that is robust against various types of failures and takes advantage of available features to mitigate the effects of those failures. Many factors influence supportability, and this chapter covers the following topics to address them:

- Tips for supportable SQL
- How to provide tracing facilities
- How to enable error reporting and logging
- Run-time application configuration
- The importance of restartability
- How to use resumable operations in Oracle9*i*

This chapter is intended for both the database administrator (DBA) and developer. If you're a developer, consider implementing the suggestions to aid supportability. Supportability translates directly to increased availability through reductions in outages and faster problem resolution. If you're a DBA, then you can put forward the information in this chapter as a blueprint for the developers in your organization, with a goal of reducing support costs.

Creating Supportable SQL

This section contains four simple tips for SQL layout and naming that are frequently missing from Oracle code yet can provide significant benefits to supportability with minimal effort.

SQL Layout for Readability

Professional DBAs can spend a significant amount of time inspecting resource-intensive SQL statements and investigating ways to improve them in order to improve application response times for end users. It might surprise developers how much this process can be expedited if SQL is written in a way that makes the SELECT list columns, tables in the FROM clause, and WHERE predicates clear in the statement. This is easily seen with an example. Consider this free formatted SQL statement:

```
SELECT Deal_Type, Deal_Num, Thin_Pack FROM TT_FX_OTC d WHERE
(((DEAL_STATE not in ('DLTD', 'MTRD', 'EXCD','ABND') or
EOD_REALISED_PREMIUM <> 0.0 or EOD_REALISED_PREMIUM_REVERSED <> 0.0) and
ALLOCATION_STATUS<>'ALLOC') or (DEAL_STATE in ('DLTD', 'MTRD','MTDL')
and d.DEAL_NUM in (select dt_vals.DEAL_NUM from DT_VALUES dt_vals where
dt_vals.DEAL_NUM = d.DEAL_NUM and dt_vals.PL_INC_SUR <> 0.0))) and
DEAL_ROLE <> 'BACK'
```

A DBA attempting to make sense of this SQL has a real challenge on his hands. As a contrast, consider the same SQL formatted for readability:

```
SELECT Deal_Type, Deal_Num, Thin_Pack
FROM TT_FX_OTC d
WHERE
(
  (
    (DEAL_STATE not in ('DLTD', 'MTRD', 'EXCD','ABND')
    or EOD_REALISED_PREMIUM <> 0.0
    or EOD_REALISED_PREMIUM_REVERSED <> 0.0
    ) and ALLOCATION_STATUS<>'ALLOC'
  )
  or
  (DEAL_STATE in ('DLTD', 'MTRD','MTDL')
   and d.DEAL_NUM in
     (select dt_vals.DEAL_NUM
     from DT_VALUES dt_vals
     where dt_vals.DEAL_NUM = d.DEAL_NUM
     and dt_vals.PL_INC_SUR <> 0.0
     )
   )
)
and DEAL_ROLE <> 'BACK'
```

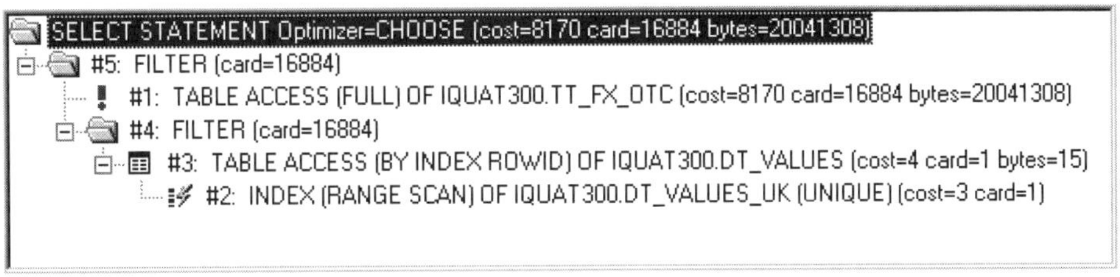

```
SELECT STATEMENT Optimizer=CHOOSE (cost=8170 card=16884 bytes=20041308)
  #5: FILTER (card=16884)
    ! #1: TABLE ACCESS (FULL) OF IQUAT300.TT_FX_OTC (cost=8170 card=16884 bytes=20041308)
    #4: FILTER (card=16884)
        #3: TABLE ACCESS (BY INDEX ROWID) OF IQUAT300.DT_VALUES (cost=4 card=1 bytes=15)
            #2: INDEX (RANGE SCAN) OF IQUAT300.DT_VALUES_UK (UNIQUE) (cost=3 card=1)
```

Figure 6.1   Explain plan structure.

The reformatted version shows the tables involved clearly and more importantly shows that the query result set depends on two OR clauses, where the second has a dependency on another table. The structure of the query often relates directly to the appearance of the query explain plan. The more closely the two match, the easier it is to identify the part of the query on which to concentrate tuning efforts. The query explain plan for the previous query is given in Figure 6.1 and shows that the first part of the query requires a full table scan of the TT_FX_OTC table, identified by the exclamation mark. Tuning efforts could therefore concentrate on that part. Using the unformatted statement, the relationship between the query plan and the SQL is not evident.

Most developers would never consider laying out code—be it Java, C, or PL/SQL—in an unformatted way. The same rule should apply to SQL statements.

Use Table Aliases

Another simple SQL fix that can make tuning efforts easier is to always use table aliases in SQL statements, in order to make explicit the table from which a SELECT list column originates. Identification of the underlying table for each SELECT list column is required during SQL tuning in order to check whether appropriate indexes on the table are being used. The process can be appreciably slower when a query contains one or more joins, and columns in the SELECT list don't identify the table in the join. The following SQL contains a SELECT list column that could originate from any of three underlying tables:

```
SELECT SUM(PREMIUM_REVAL)
FROM TT_FX TT,DT_VALUES DT,SD_LIVE_DEAL_STATES LDS
WHERE DT.DEAL_NUM = TT.DEAL_NUM
AND TT.TRADING_BOOK = :b2 AND TT.DEAL_STATE = LDS.NAME   AND
LDS.LIVE = 'Y'
```

In this case, a simple change to the SELECT list to include the table alias, DT, means the DBA no longer needs to query the Oracle dictionary to identify the underlying table, as shown:

```
SELECT SUM(DT.PREMIUM_REVAL)
FROM TT_FX TT,DT_VALUES DT,SD_LIVE_DEAL_STATES LDS
```

```
WHERE DT.DEAL_NUM = TT.DEAL_NUM
AND TT.TRADING_BOOK = :b2 AND TT.DEAL_STATE = LDS.NAME   AND
LDS.LIVE = 'Y'
```

When used together with the previous tip on layout, the speed with which DBAs can analyze queries can be increased significantly, even for the simple examples shown. The gains are much higher for longer and more complicated SQL.

Use Explicit Constraint Names

Explicit names should be used for Oracle constraints in DDL statements, rather than allowing Oracle to generate them. Oracle-generated names always begin with the prefix SYS_C. Constraint names are used in error messages generated by Oracle when constraints are violated. The more meaningful the name, the quicker the DBA can identify the cause of the underlying problem. The following example shows the Oracle-generated constraint names for a primary key and foreign key on the EMP table:

```
create table emp
        (empno number(4) primary key,
         ename varchar2(10),
         deptno number(2) references dept);

select constraint_name,constraint_type
from user_constraints where table_name='EMP';

CONSTRAINT_NAME    CONSTRAINT_TYPE
----------------   -----------------
SYS_C002402        P
SYS_C002403        R
```

The existence of system-generated constraint names can be avoided by explicit naming of the constraints. The previous example can be rewritten using the following SQL:

```
create table emp
        (empno number(4) constraint pk_emp primary key,
         ename varchar2(10),
         job varchar2(9)
         deptno number(2) constraint fk_deptno references dept);
```

Using explicit names has an extra benefit when the DBA needs to compare schema objects during schema upgrade procedures, such as using Oracle Change Manager. If you allow Oracle to choose the names, the chances are that a constraint with the same purpose will have different names in different databases. Choosing explicit names avoids that possibility and makes change management less complicated. Reduction in complexity for any process generally leads to higher availability.

In Oracle9i, the data dictionary views that display constraint information include an extra column named GENERATED to make it easy to identify constraints that use system-generated (as opposed to user-generated) names, as shown in the following example:

```
select constraint_name,constraint_type,generated
from all_constraints
where table_name like 'EMP%' and constraint_type='P';


CONSTRAINT_NAME    CONSTRAINT_TYPE    GENERATED
----------------   ----------------   ---------------
PK_EMP             P                  USER NAME
SYS_C001898        P                  GENERATED NAME
```

Use Meaningful Object Names

A consistent naming scheme for objects helps the DBA to identify the types of objects used in SQL statements more quickly by enabling the types to be identified from the name. For example, many development teams use a V_ prefix or _V suffix to identify views, an SP_ prefix to identify stored procedures, and _SEQ to identify sequences. The use of IX prefixes or suffixes for indexes also helps to make sense of explain plans.

The ability to directly identify the underlying objects in SQL speeds up the tuning process. Proponents of naming standards fall into two camps, those who use prefixes and those who prefer suffixes. Prefixes are easier to identify in SQL because they appear on the front of names, whereas suffixes make for easier identification of groups of related objects by enabling the use of a wildcard on the end of the base object name during queries of the Oracle data dictionary tables. The exact details of the standard are not as important as having one and adhering to it at a company level.

Trace Facilities

All applications—whether interactive graphical user interface (GUI) or batch—should provide built-in features for enabling and disabling Oracle SQL trace, including standard SQL tracing, tracing with bind variables, and tracing with event waits.

> **NOTE** SQL tracing is used for the performance profiling of SQL statements submitted to the database server and is covered in more detail in Chapters 9 and 28.

The options can be set using the SET_EV procedure, as shown in the following examples for a session identified by SID=8 and SERIAL=149:

```
REM identical to ALTER SESSION SET SQL_TRACE TRUE, level 1
begin SYS.DBMS_SYSTEM.SET_EV(SI=>8,SE=>149,EV=>10046,LE=>1,NM=>'');end;

REM trace SQL with bind variables, level 5
begin SYS.DBMS_SYSTEM.SET_EV(SI=>8,SE=>149,EV=>10046,LE=>5,NM=>'');end;

REM trace SQL with event waits, level 9
begin SYS.DBMS_SYSTEM.SET_EV(SI=>8,SE=>149,EV=>10046,LE=>9,NM=>'');end;
```

```
REM trace SQL with bind variables, event waits, level 13
begin SYS.DBMS_SYSTEM.SET_EV(SI=>8,SE=>149,EV=>10046,LE=>13,NM=>'');end;

REM trace off for one session, level 0
begin SYS.DBMS_SYSTEM.SET_EV(SI=>8,SE=>149,EV=>10046,LE=>0,NM=>'');end;
```

Although the DBA can set SQL trace for any session, it's better for developers to provide facilities to set the trace within applications themselves, as this provides finer granularity over the traced sections of code. For example, it's possible to create a mapping table of procedure names and trace levels in a table, and have the procedure read and set the trace settings at the top of the procedure, and unset them at the end. That enables tracing to be turned on and off for individual procedures. In general, it's better to concentrate tracing efforts on the smallest code section possible because tracing can generate massive amounts of trace information in a short time. In the case of batch applications, tracing may need to be turned on at the start of processing, in which case the DBA will not be able to allow tracing early enough during execution by calling SET_EV from a separate session. Command-line utilities should enable tracing to be set through command-line arguments.

The ability to trace the values of bind variables and values is especially important when diagnosing the causes of obscure Oracle error messages in PL/SQL code, especially triggers. It's surprising how often code fails with incorrect values that, according to the developer, couldn't possibly be passed into subroutines. By building extensive tracing facilities into an application, the causes of such problems can be definitively identified more quickly. The inclusion of tracing facilities in code adds an overhead to the software development process. It usually pays off quickly. Chapter 28 shows more examples.

It's necessary for the application code to have access to the System ID (SID) and SERIAL# values that identify the current session in order to pass the values to the SET_EV procedure parameters SI and SE. One way to facilitate that is for the DBA to provide a wrapper around the SET_EV procedure that has the relevant privileges required to access the session settings. Chapter 25 on auditing shows three different ways for identifying the SID and SERIAL# for the current session.

Error Reporting and Logging

All application error messages should provide sufficient information to identify unambiguously the exact location at which an error occurred in code and the cause. Too often, applications use a single error number as a cover-all for several possible causes, and this makes root cause diagnosis more difficult than it needs to be for support staff. Oracle itself has been guilty of this. If you've ever reported an error message to Oracle worldwide support (WWS) and it has taken a long time to identify the root cause, that's probably because the developer of the underlying code could have provided a more specific cause for the error but chose not to in order to get the code completed quicker. Error-handling code is tedious for the developer to implement, but that's a poor excuse for not implementing in a way that can minimize support requirements. If error handling is not complete, then the onus is on the customer and WWS to try and work out which of the range of possible causes is the real one. In such cases, most of the effort to resolve the problem needs to be made by the customer.

For the developer, incomplete error handling makes application delivery slightly quicker, but it's a completely false economy from a business point of view. For example, an extra couple of minutes spent by a developer adding code to identify the location of an error and to specify the exact cause can translate into savings in terms of hours when an error manifests itself in the code at run time. It's not necessary to report locations in a way that is meaningful to users but to report information in a way that is meaningful to support. The following is a PL/SQL code fragment showing the use of a simple numeric variable whereami and string, the_location, that can be used to identify the precise code location of errors in error messages:

```
...
the_location:='update_procedure';
whereami  := 6;
cursor_name  := dbms_sql.open_cursor;
whereami  := 7;
dbms_sql.parse(cursor_name,update_sql,dbms_sql.v7);
whereami  := 8;
ret  := dbms_sql.execute(cursor_name);
whereami  := 9;
dbms_sql.close_cursor(cursor_name);
whereami  := 10;
cursor_name  := dbms_sql.open_cursor;
whereami  := 11;
dbms_sql.parse(cursor_name,update_last_check_sql,dbms_sql.v7);
whereami  := 12;
ret  := dbms_sql.execute(cursor_name);
whereami  := 13;
dbms_sql.close_cursor(cursor_name);
EXCEPTION
when others then
         dbms_output.put_line(location||':'
                              whereami||':'||
                              sqlerrm||':'||sqlcode);
```

An example of error message reporting in one of Oracle's own products is quite enlightening. If you've set up Oracle Real Application Clusters (RAC), as described in Chapter 22, you'll be aware that Oracle uses the UNIX remote copy (rcp) command to enable the delivery of the Oracle software to each node in the cluster during installation using the Oracle Installer. Chapter 1 covers the basic configuration requirements for rcp. These days, other Oracle products use rcp also.

If you've failed to configure rcp correctly, then the Oracle Installer will report on a failure to connect to the other nodes in the cluster at install time. The developer could have taken the trouble to report that an rcp connection failed but chose not to. If he or she had, you could have addressed the problem in a couple of minutes. Instead, you, as the customer, are left to work out what failure to connect to the other nodes means. Eventually, through a process of trial and error, you'll probably discover that the remote shell (rsh) configuration is incorrect and that resolving this fixes the install problem, but you shouldn't have to. The developer, with a little extra diligence, could have saved you the effort by being more specific on the cause of the problem when reporting the error. Who knows how many other problems will result in that same error message and cause the whole process to be repeated?

The mechanism used to report errors is just as important as the content of the messages themselves. Three main techniques are typically used for reporting errors, in addition to message dialogs typically returned by interactive GUI applications: files, tables, and email. Use of email is covered in Chapter 24 on monitoring and health checks. Files and tables have an advantage in that records of problems and status information are stored persistently to enable historical information to be searched easily.

The format used to log information should be designed to be easy for search tools to scan and follow a standard format. For example, log output might contain a fixed format date as the first field, then a severity indication in the second field, then the database instance in the third, and so on. If logging information has a poorly thought out format, it can add complexity to the processing performed by monitoring tools that need to raise alerts based on the logged information. Oracle's own alert log information does not follow a standard published format. As a result, it's sometimes necessary to join lines together to pull out the times that events occurred. Performing pattern matching on various parts of the message information is less complex if all messages follow a standard, predefined format and fit into a single line.

Error Logging Using Files

Oracle provides the UTL_FILE package to provide developers with a facility to log messages in server side files. In order to use the facilities of the UTL_FILE package, the DBA needs to make sure the UTL_FILE_DIR initialization parameter is set to the directories in which the file creation is to be enabled.

> **NOTE** Sometimes DBAs choose to use the wildcard "*" as the UTL_FILE_DIR parameter. This requires less effort than choosing an explicit list of directories but represents a major security loophole because it enables any file owned by the UNIX oracle account to be accessed by UTL_FILE, including files that are part of the database. As a result, * should never be used for a production system.

Whenever you use UTL_FILE, great care needs to be taken to ensure that exceptions raised during logging via UTL_FILE don't affect the behavior of the application. In general, error and status logging failures should be transparent to the application. For example, you wouldn't expect an Oracle application to stop working if the disk on which the Oracle alert log is located became filled. The following example shows a procedure that can be used to log errors to a file /tmp/logfile.txt:

```
procedure sp_error_log(vtext in varchar2) is
      fhandle utl_file.file_type;
      location varchar2(16) := 'sp_error_log';
```

```
begin

  fhandle := utl_file.fopen('/tmp','logfile.txt','a');
  utl_file.put_line(fhandle,vtext);
  utl_file.fclose(fhandle);

exception
  when utl_file.invalid_path then
    sp_mail_log_error(location||': invalid path');
  when utl_file.invalid_mode then
    sp_mail_log_error(location||': invalid mode');
  when utl_file.invalid_operation then
    sp_mail_log_error(location||': invalid operation');
  when utl_file.invalid_filehandle then
    sp_mail_log_error(location||': invalid filehandle');
  when utl_file.write_error then
    sp_mail_log_error(location||': write error');
  when utl_file.read_error then
    sp_mail_log_error(location||': read error');
  when utl_file.internal_error then
    sp_mail_log_error(location||': internal error');
  when others then
    utl_file.fclose(fhandle);
end;
```

Errors during logging itself still need to be notified because valuable information is potentially lost while logging is failing. In this case, SP_MAIL_LOG_ERROR uses SMTP mail to notify the DBA team of logging failures. Chapter 24 contains a procedure SP_SENDMAIL that could be used as the basis for such a procedure.

It's worth pointing out that the procedure doesn't cache the file handle between calls and instead opens it every time. This means that the log file can be removed or compressed between calls and the logging will continue to work. The Oracle alert log behaves in a similar way. Opening files in append mode, as indicated by "a," creates the named file if it doesn't exist already. The procedure also reports all the possible causes of failures to write to the log file. It would be easier to simply use a single WHEN OTHERS exception to handle all the possible errors, but, as explained earlier, this makes it more difficult to identify the actual cause of the problem if logging fails. So the error handler mails the specific cause of any problem with logging so it can be resolved more quickly.

Error Logging Using Tables

Error logging using tables rather than files makes it significantly easier to report on error and status information because SQL can be used to perform the process and present the information. However, the need to commit error and status information in log tables in order to view it from other sessions can interfere with the transaction units of processing that failed. Oracle provides a feature known as autonomous (or nested) transactions to enable persistent logging to tables to be performed in a way that doesn't have side effects on the transactions from which the log message is generated. Autonomous transactions are enabled using the AUTONOMOUS_TRANSACTION pragma in a PL/SQL procedure as shown in the following example:

```
create table log_table(msg varchar2(10));

create procedure log_record(p_msg in varchar2) is
  pragma autonomous_transaction;
begin
  insert into log_table values(p_msg);
  commit;
end;
```

You can demonstrate the behavior by inserting rows into LOG_TABLE from within the same session both directly via SQL INSERTS and using the autonomous transaction. Subsequent viewing of the contents of LOG_TABLE from another session will confirm that inserts performed via the autonomous transaction will be present, and those performed via INSERTS won't be visible until you commit them. This shows that the autonomous transaction has taken place without side effects on the main transaction in the other session.

Run Time Configuration

Application performance and supportability can benefit from the capability to set session attributes at run time. The attributes might include the optimizer goal for the session, the sort area size, trace settings, and resumable space allocation, among others. The following example shows a database logon trigger, which is an appropriate point at which to configure session-specific parameters:

```
create trigger session_config after logon on database
declare
begin

    configure_session_for_user(user);

exception
  when others then
    null;
end;
```

The session-specific settings might be held in a table containing name value pairs for each username and parameter, and be activated through the configure_session_for_user procedure. Some possible settings are shown in the following:

```
select * from user_parameters;

USERNAME    NAME            VALUE
----------  --------------  ---------
BATCH       optimizer goal  ALL ROWS
```

```
BATCH      resumable       YES
BATCH      sort area       10000000


ONLINE     optimizer goal  FIRST ROWS
ONLINE     sort area       65536
ONLINE     resumable       NO
```

By providing mechanisms for influencing session behavior through data held in tables, the developer makes it possible for code behavior to be enhanced without requiring more risky changes to application code.

Reporting on Application Status

Oracle provides a package, DBMS_APPLICATION_INFO, that contains procedures to enable developers to build facilities into their applications to report on the status of application processing. Each procedure call updates a related column in the V$SESSION table. The three package procedures and the related column in V$SESSION are shown in Table 6.1.

The DBA can then query the columns in V$SESSION using SQL to determine the application status, for example, if users report that the application appears to be stalled. Although the procedures can be used in any way the application developer chooses, the names are intended to suggest the usage. So the SET_CLIENT_INFO might be called once, at application connection time, to identify the application as follows:

```
begin dbms_application_info.set_client_info('DbCool'); end;
```

The SET_MODULE routine is typically used to identify a business process, which itself might map to a single PL/SQL stored procedure in the application. The ACTION_NAME, used to identify the current action within the module, can be set at the time of the call to SET_MODULE or be passed as an empty string at the top of a procedure and set separately using the SET_ACTION procedure as in the following example:

```
procedure sp_process_trades is
begin
  -- identify the module to V$SESSION
  dbms_application_info.set_module(
          module_name=>'Trade Processing',
          action_name=>'');

  for rec in (select trade_id from all_trades where processed='N') loop

      -- identify the current trade to V$SESSION
      dbms_application_info.set_action('Processing Trade '||trade_id);

      -- process the trade..
      sp_process_one_trade(rec.trade_id);

  end loop;
```

Table 6.1 DBMS_APPLICATION_INFO Procedures

PROCEDURE NAME	V$SESSION COLUMN
SET_CLIENT_INFO	CLIENT_INFO
SET_MODULE	MODULE
SET_ACTION	ACTION

```
-- MUST UNSET THE VALUES when processing complete
-- don't forget to unset in exception handlers also
dbms_application_info.set_module(
        module_name=>'',
        action_name=>'');

end;
```

The use of DBMS_APPLICATION_INFO has a very beneficial side effect on performance management as well as supportability. The ability to identify business transactions is a critical success factor for efficient performance management. As you might expect, the best performance management tools can present information based upon time spent in business transactions, rather than individual microscopic SQL statements. The ability to do this relies on the application setting values for MODULE_NAME and ACTION_NAME at appropriate points in the code and unsetting them when processing is complete.

In effect, DBMS_APPLICATION_INFO provides a facility for developers and designers to instrument the performance of business transactions using a few simple procedure calls. If all Oracle applications were designed up front to include calls to DBMS_APPLICATION_INFO, then performance problems would be identified faster and solved faster. Chapter 16 on using performance management tools shows how the power of DBMS_APPLICATION_INFO can be unleashed using a suitable tool that takes advantage of the information.

It's worth noting that an additional procedure present in DBMS_APPLICATION_INFO, SET_SESSION_LOGOPS, can be used to log status information about long-running operations into the V$SESSION_LONGOPS table. Several of Oracle's own tools, such as RMAN, make use of this feature, and Oracle designers can do the same. The specification of the package is shown in the following code:

```
procedure set_session_longops( rindex      in out pls_integer,
                               slno        in out pls_integer,
                               op_name     in varchar2 default null,
                               target      in pls_integer default 0,
                               context     in pls_integer default 0,
                               sofar       in number default 0,
                               totalwork   in number default 0,
                               target_desc in varchar2
                                              default 'unknown target',
                               units       in varchar2 default null);
```

Restartability

Restartability is a term I use to define the behavior of applications that can continue to function when Oracle database management system (DBMS) errors occur during processing. For example, if a tablespace space shortage occurs during a batch insert, an application can either exit and report an error, or report an error and attempt to repeat the failed operation on a timer until the underlying problem is fixed. Programmers using Oracle's precompiler interfaces, such as Pro*C, can take advantage of features in the language to identify the array index at which an array insert fails and restart the insert from that point. In general, making programs robust against database errors of any kind adds complexity to the code, and it can be difficult to balance the cost and complexity of extra coding against the benefits that result.

The consequences of aborting a long-running operation, rather than suspending it, can be very significant in terms of resource usage. For example, if a long-running batch job fails due to a space shortage, then the transaction needs to be rolled back and resubmitted. Both operations cause large amounts of redo generation. Prior to Oracle9*i*, it was the responsibility of the programmer to build features to work around space problems. For some situations like rollback segments filling up during a long transaction, there was often no practical alternative other than to roll back the transaction and restart. By their very nature, transactions that cause space problems tend to be long running and costly to repeat.

Resumable Operations in Oracle9*i*

Oracle9*i* provides resumable space management features that can be used to suspend sessions at the database level when space problems are encountered, until the DBA adds more space. Oracle's own products take advantage of these features. For example, Oracle's import utility includes a resumable=y option. Using features in the database rather than providing similar features at the application is preferable because it reduces application-coding complexity.

Three classes of spaces errors are resumable: those resulting from out-of-space errors on data segments and rollback segments, those resulting from maximum extents-reached conditions, and those resulting from space quota-exceeded errors. Even long-running queries that perform sorts that exceed temporary space availability can be resumed. Be aware that space allocation errors for rollback segments in dictionary managed tablespaces are not resumable. This should not be an issue, as you should be using the automatic undo features of Oracle9*i* in any case (as covered in Chapter 2). In the simplest case, making an operation resumable means adding the following SQL statement to a section of code:

```
alter session enable resumable;
```

Because suspended statements can lock system resources, possibly for an extended period, the RESUMABLE privilege is required in order to execute resumable operations. The following statement disables resumable operations:

```
alter session disable resumable;
```

Resumable operations that are suspended are shown in the DBA_RESUMABLE view, and if resumable operations are in use, it's essential that the DBA group performs monitoring for the early detection of such errors. Here is an example of a transaction that has suspended due to lack of undo space, which could be resolved by extending the undo tablespace datafile:

```
select error_msg from dba_resumable where status <> 'NORMAL';


ERROR_MSG
---------------------------------------------------------------------
ORA-30036: unable to extend segment by 16 in undo tablespace 'UNDOTBS2'
```

After a timeout period, which by default is set to 7,200 seconds and configurable through the ALTER SESSION ENABLE RESUMABLE TIMEOUT *seconds* statement, the suspended statement returns an error to the application. The DBMS_RESUMABLE package contains routines to enable resumable parameters to be set and to read named sessions, and it includes an ABORT procedure to enable a suspended operation to be aborted by a DBA, if necessary.

Constraining Undo Requirements

Long-running batch jobs, such as data load and purge operations, can exhaust the available undo space. Although Oracle9*i* provides resumable operations to provide the potential for space shortages to be fixed, it's not always a good idea to do that. Developers can take steps to constrain undo requirements by performing operations in batches, rather than in a single large transaction. In general, Oracle performs the same bulk DML operation faster when undo requirements are constrained within limits by performing the operation across several transactions. Chapter 19 contains an example showing that a reduction in import time can result from placing an upper limit on transaction size.

For simple purge operations using the DML DELETE operation, the ROWNUM pseudocolumn can be used to constrain transaction size to a fixed number of rows. For example, the following statement has unbounded undo requirements that are determined by the number of rows in the ALL_TRANSACTIONS table in the given state:

```
delete from all_transactions where processed='Y';
```

The following PL/SQL does the same job but commits after each batch of 10,000 rows deleted, which means that the undo requirements are limited to the space required to delete 10,000 rows, independent of the size of the ALL_TRANSACTIONS table:

```
while true loop

  delete from all_transactions where processed='Y'
  and rownum <=10000;
```

```
    exit when SQL%NOTFOUND;

    commit;

end loop;
```

Summary

In some large organizations, the development and DBA teams often work in isolation without a clear understanding of each other's roles. By making the developer and DBA more aware of the requirements of the other, both performance and availability can be enhanced. Apparently mundane development practices, such as adherence to well-thought-out naming standards, code layout, and error reporting, can pay off significantly in production environments. The use of the procedures in the DBMS_APPLI-CATION_INFO package systematically throughout the development cycle for all Oracle applications can pay off significantly in terms of earlier problem diagnosis and an enhanced capability for performance management. The DBA can enhance availability by ensuring that organizations make use of the resumable space operations available in Oracle9i. The potential for reducing outages through these features is a very compelling reason to upgrade to Oracle9i, and the DBA has an important role to play as an evangelist for Oracle9i within the development community.

Choosing Third-Party Software

Every organization needs to purchase software applications to meet their business requirements. The application may be enterprise-wide, such as Oracle Financials, or a simple application that employees use to submit their timesheets. From my experience, all too often companies purchase third-party software based on functional requirements alone. In this case, the requirements are far too narrow in scope to ensure successful deployment of the software.

This chapter is essentially a checklist that you can use when your company asks third-party software developers to develop an Oracle-based application or supply an off-the-shelf product for your company. This will help you avoid situations where purchased software doesn't deliver the benefits that were expected. Although it's easier to blame the software producer, the company purchasing the software needs to have a clear list of requirements in order to ensure that the software meets the requirements for supportability and performance, not just functionality. If things go wrong, the purchaser suffers. The fact that a software producer goes out of business because it didn't deliver what it said it could is no consolation to the purchaser. The degree to which the criteria in this chapter should be applied depends on the product being purchased and how likely it is to affect the purchaser's bottom line.

The following checklist is the basis of the contents of this chapter and is designed to help you purchase or acquire software that meets your requirements:

- Check the vendor's financial health.
- Meet with the vendor to establish a working relationship.
- Request and follow up on reference sites.
- Evaluate the application development environment used by the vendor.

- Request performance benchmarks from the vendor and perform some of your own.

- Evaluate high availability solutions proposed by the vendor.

- Check the quality of the install processes, documentation, and supportability features.

- Perform a formal evaluation of your requirements against the vendor features that are available.

Perform Vendor Health Checks

Before purchasing software, you should start with an analysis of the vendor company's financial health. This is the kind of thing that takes place implicitly when a company chooses to purchase software from Oracle or Microsoft, for example. Everyone knows that these companies make announcements on future directions and that the promises on those announcements are usually fulfilled within the stated timeframes. Research analysts call this the ability to execute. Basically, ask yourself the following: Has the company delivered on its claims in the past and is it likely to continue to do so in the future?

The financial strength of Microsoft and Oracle is considerable, and there is a high probability that they will be around in the future. When buying software from a smaller company, you should never take this for granted. If a company from which software was purchased goes bust, the purchaser must spend funds to find a replacement and face a business risk due to the possible nonavailability of support.

The Web is a good place to start when researching a company's health. For example, stock exchange filings are available for U.S. quoted companies. These provide useful insight into a company's past and future performance. Most company Web sites contain an investor's section, which provides details of past and present revenue streams. If you have access to research information from companies like Gartner Group (www .gartner.com), this can be invaluable for comparing a company with its peers under various categories. A comparison of the vendor's market position and technology strength to their competitors is important for determining whether a company will likely be around in the future.

Meet with the Vendor

You should arrange informal meetings with vendors in order to view their technology. These meetings can reveal many things about a company, particular how seriously they treat you as a potential customer and how they treat customers in general. Do they arrange for senior or junior technical people to meet with you? What is the quality of the presentation? Are they open about the weaknesses as well as the strengths of their technology? Do they ask about your own expertise and take the trouble to really understand your requirements? What are the qualifications and backgrounds of the people involved?

My experience is that some vendors find this kind of questioning impertinent, but because you're a potential customer, possibly with millions of dollars to spend, then you are entitled to ask anything you like. As a potential customer, you should never be afraid to ask questions. Other vendors use such questions as an opportunity to impress. The difference in those attitudes can set a stake in the ground for how you might envisage an ongoing relationship with the vendor.

It's always useful to seek a vendor's view of their strengths and weaknesses compared to their competitors. Too often vendors position functionality gaps in their own products, not as weaknesses, but as features that aren't required, simply because they don't have them.

Ask for Reference Sites

References sites should always be requested. A satisfied customer that is prepared to share its satisfaction on the record is worth its weight in gold, although you need to recognize that any decision to purchase is yours alone. It is always possible that a reference site has some kind of financial inducement for such positive responses. This is a difficult question to ask directly, but it's certainly something that you would like to know. It's interesting how often research documents on various technologies are sponsored by companies that the research shows in the best light. That doesn't mean the company that comes out on top isn't the best, but you should not make a purchase decision based solely on such research.

If you can see a product in action at a customer's site, it's worth much more than any slick demonstration performed by a salesperson who has done it many times before. I've often requested demonstrations at existing customer sites and have sometimes been refused. I've also had salespeople ask me to demonstrate their products. You shouldn't shy away from asking. If you are responsible for the procurement of a product that fails, then you'll probably wish you did more research up front and asked the difficult questions sooner.

Interestingly, I received a personal email from Ken Jacobs, VP of DBMS at Oracle Corporation, during the writing of this book, asking for customer success stories regarding Oracle9i. Although I am quite sure that Ken Jacobs has never heard of me and that the mail-shot was directed to everyone who downloaded the first patch release of Oracle9i, the point is that Oracle and everyone that sells software knows that just about nothing helps sell a product as well as glowing reviews from current customers.

Evaluate the Application Development Environment

The strength of the software-engineering development environment in any company that develops Oracle-based solutions has a significant effect on the quality of the end product. When you purchase software, how do you know that it's fit for its purpose, aside from the vendor's own claims? How can you be sure that claims for performance, scalability, and robustness will be delivered?

If you check the first page in the Oracle documentation, you'll see a paragraph containing a legal disclaimer that states the following: "This software was not developed for use in any nuclear, aviation, mass transit, medical, or other inherently dangerous applications." In other words, Oracle considers its software fit for the purpose of managing data, but not for something like aviation, where a software bug in flight control software could potentially lead to fatalities. However, when you board an aircraft that uses computer software to control movements to the flight control surfaces such as the wing flaps (known as *fly-by-wire*), how do you know that the computer system is fit for its purpose, especially when Oracle keeps out of that market?

The key is to investigate and understand the development process used by the airline to create the flight control software. The knowledge you gain provides the information that leads you to trust that the software is fit for its purpose. In the case of fly-by-wire, the approach used was to create the entire flight control system software multiple times using different development teams working in complete isolation from each other based on the same specification. The independently created systems were deployed on each aircraft. By developing multiple ways of producing the same result, the arbitration software can decide which value to use if the multiplexed systems don't agree on a calculation. The goal is for all of the independent systems to produce the same result and ensure that a bad result from one system (due to a software bug) is overruled by the correct result from one of the other systems based on the premise that the same bugs won't be duplicated in all systems because they were developed independently by different teams.

Based on this knowledge, you probably wouldn't buy flight control software from Oracle as it uses a single code base. In any case, they don't want to sell it to you for that purpose because they are honest about the purpose for which their software should be used. However, you can't be so sure of the credentials of third-party software vendors. This section covers some of the questions you should ask about the development process and software-engineering practices used by any third-party vendor before you purchase their software or services. You can check the vendor's techniques against those used within your organization and those suggested in Chapter 6.

Choosing the Oracle Version and Features

The nature of the development process of the software within a third-party vendor can be very revealing. For example, the version of Oracle used for the current version of the product and a roadmap for future Oracle versions can tell you something about the company's Oracle expertise and the importance placed on the database management system (DBMS) of their product.

If a company proposes to sell you a product that requires Oracle version 8.0.6 when that version is long out of support, then you could rightly question that company's level of Oracle expertise and judgement. Also, a requirement for an old version of Oracle doesn't demonstrate a focus on customer requirements, which definitely includes using a supported version of Oracle.

Older versions of Oracle also fail to take advantage of potential performance and manageability features that could benefit the customer and vendor alike. Some vendor products use Oracle as a relational data store and don't use Oracle-specific features in order to enable their products to run against multiple relational DBMSs (RDBMSs) from the same code base. This is definitely better from the vendor's point of view as it potentially lowers development cost, but it might not be so beneficial for the customer.

Choosing a Development Language

The choice of language that the vendor uses to develop its Oracle software should be considered. For example, a company that chooses Oracle Call Interface (OCI) for its programming interface, as compared to Pro*C, might be harboring potential supportability problems. This is because the difficulty of programming in OCI and the availability of skills in the marketplace may make the company dependent on one or two gurus for development and support. If those people are no longer around, then the support as well as the company's ability to execute in the future might be at risk. In addition, any language that places the responsibility of allocating and freeing memory onto the programmer's shoulders (such as OCI) presents an increased risk of problems such as memory leaks and corruption at run time.

Regression Testing

You should also inquire about the nature of the regression testing performed on the product. Regression testing is the testing performed against a product's feature set using known inputs and outputs in order to confirm that the product is working as intended. For something like a batch process, it might mean running a list of Structured Query Language (SQL) statements against known data, running a report, sending the output to a text file, and comparing the output with a known result. For products based on a graphical user interface (GUI), it's more difficult, but products are available that will do it.

Regression testing is something that you take for granted when purchasing products from successful vendors of software products such as Microsoft and Oracle. When I was a developer at Oracle, it was necessary to instrument product code and certify that regression testing covered a high percentage of the code before the code could be certified as production status. It might seem like overkill to expect this of a third-party software vendor. The vendor might even consider this to be commercially sensitive information. But, as usual, if a company is happy to provide visibility of its development process, it means the company is confident that its software-engineering standards are likely to provide products that work.

Something I read quite a while back sticks in my mind on this subject. In an early release of Microsoft Visual C++, Microsoft produced a small magazine that basically showed off their development process by highlighting the number of people involved in development, quality assurance (QA), and documentation. What was striking was that the number of people involved in each group was approximately the same, which gave visibility to the seriousness with which Microsoft viewed, and still views, QA and documentation compared to development. This kind of information can help when deciding whether to purchase a product.

Naming Standards

Naming standards for Oracle objects in the product application schemas tell you something about whether the vendor uses a standards-based development process. If no consistent naming standard exists, it might imply that developers in the organization are left to get on with their own work without looking at the bigger picture.

Security

How seriously does the vendor treat database and application security? If the vendor requires that the application schema have database administrator (DBA) privileges or other potentially insecure privileges, then that needs to be addressed before a product is purchased. A vendor that doesn't build an appropriate security model into their product immediately demonstrates a lack of customer focus, because security is an important consideration for customers. For certain types of applications, it's a regulatory requirement. Obviously, it's easier (and cheaper) for a vendor to develop an application without including a proper security model, but it certainly reflects poorly on the vendor whichever way you consider it.

Request Application Benchmarks

Never take a vendor's claims for application scalability at face value. Ask for evidence of benchmarks or other metrics. Ask the vendor how performance is built in during the development cycle, and what technologies and techniques the application uses to ensure that performance is maintained during increases in the user base or database size. Best of all, run some benchmark tests in house.

Find out what tools the vendor uses for Oracle performance management. The criteria for choosing a performance management tool are covered in Chapter 16. How did the vendor decide on which tools to use? If the vendor already uses a tool that you use in your own organization, it's a good sign that the vendor has a similar view on performance and places the required emphasis on performance.

My experience of third-party Oracle software is that performance is often an issue after purchase because the vendor didn't really place much emphasis on it during development and the customer didn't ask the right questions before purchase. If the vendor immediately points the finger at the customer and suggests that poor database configuration is the root cause of performance problems on the customer's site, it is a bad omen for at least two reasons. The first is that the vendor doesn't understand Oracle performance management because the configuration of the database is not usually the cause of dramatic performance degradation. The second is that the customer failed to collaborate fully with the vendor to understand the performance requirements before purchase.

Ensure That Space Management Procedures Exist

The subject of database space growth is often ignored during the early days of product rollout and prior to purchase because the size of the database in the early days of deployment is not likely to be an issue. However, it's often extremely difficult to do anything about it once the database reaches a certain size.

Before purchase, the vendor's advice should be sought on how the database size can be constrained during production deployment. The need to purge data for space and performance reasons often conflicts with business requirements to keep data available. As a result, archiving and purging strategies need to be considered and understood up front before purchase and deployment. They can't be bolted on afterwards without a huge effort from both the business and technical staff. For that reason, products that come with built-in data and archiving capabilities should receive extra credit during any evaluation process because the vendor has recognized that space growth is an important consideration for customers and has done the hard work to address it. Oracle provides features such as partitioning and transportable tablespaces to facilitate data archiving and purging, and the vendor should be aware of them.

Review the Vendor's High Availability Solution

The vendor's solution for delivering high availability in their application, possibly 24×7, should be sought, if only to see whether it has been considered, in order to learn the vendor's understanding of customer requirements. Sometimes vendors go as far as building availability features into a product at the application level. This can be a key selling point, provided that the vendor isn't duplicating features at the application level that are provided by the DBMS.

Oracle has many features, including replication, standby databases, and Real Application Clusters (RAC) to provide high availability. These are covered in Part Five of this book (Chapters 20 through 23). It's interesting to find out the vendor's awareness of these features and whether they are appropriate for their application.

Evaluate Product Installation

The installation of application schema objects and data should always take place using SQL scripts. These SQL scripts should contain text headers indicating the version of the script. If the vendor supplies schemas and data using an export dump, there is a danger that the vendor has simply provided you with whatever data was in their development database on the day they shipped the product, including any junk. The use of an export dump is easier, faster, and cheaper for the vendor in the short term, but in the long term, it's a false economy that is likely to lead to support issues. For example, the vendor should allow you to choose the schema and tablespaces into which the application schema tables and indexes are installed. However, this is much more complicated than using an export dump.

PL/SQL package headers and bodies should be supplied as separate scripts to enable the header to be installed before the body. This makes problems relating to the installation order of objects less likely. An installation verification script should be provided so that the installation can be checked after completion. A deinstallation script is useful if you discontinue use of the product in the future. All these suggestions are used in varying degrees by Oracle's own product installations and serve as good models for vendors' as well.

The customer should be able to carry out installation from the supplied installation documentation. If the vendor sees it as a requirement to provide staff to perform the installation, it could be because the installation documentation is of poor quality, and the procedure is complicated and requires manual intervention and customization. It might also be used as an excuse to charge consultancy fees. All of these issues might indicate signs of support problems to come. Oracle has an excellent tool, Oracle Change Manager, for managing schema changes and creating installation scripts as well as a package in Oracle9i for generating Data Definition Language (DDL). There is no excuse for a vendor not to use these or similar tools.

Check Documentation Quality

If you recall the Microsoft Visual C++ example earlier in this chapter, it's clear that Microsoft places a high priority on documentation on a level that is comparable with product development. Oracle takes a similar approach. This is not always the case for all vendors. If product documentation is incomplete, then you'll find yourself involved in extended discussions with the vendor's support staff on how to use the product. Their time would be better spent addressing genuine problems with the use of the software.

Chapter 27 on working effectively with Oracle support shows that requests for technical assistance from Oracle worldwide support (WWS) are often due to requests for information on how to use products. This could be due to the customer's failure to read the documentation, but in my experience, it's more often due to incomplete documentation. A high standard of product documentation saves time for both the vendor and customer.

The other possible downside of poor documentation is that a vendor may interpret customer requests for product information as requests for consultancy on how to use their products, which can cost the customer a considerable expense. Before purchasing any product, the evaluation stage should include a comprehensive evaluation of the available documentation.

Check Supportability

If you're a production Oracle DBA in a large organization, you've probably spent countless hours of your career arguing with developers, system administrators (SAs), networking staff, and end users about the root cause of performance problems involving Oracle databases. To my mind, that's a failure of the application to have built-in supportability. Chapter 6 on designing supportable applications includes many simple tips that developers can follow to make their applications easier to support. This applies especially to providing continual feedback on what processing the application is performing. You can check whether any application that you are considering purchasing uses these techniques or others.

Supportability is even more critical for multitier applications, where it can be difficult to identify the tier at which a problem has occurred. In general, these kinds of problems can only be solved by instrumentation and logging provided by the application itself. If the application doesn't do that, support overheads for everyone involved, at both the customer and vendor end, are likely to be very expensive.

You should determine how the product can be monitored to check if it's working. More sophisticated products might include the ability to generate Simple Network Management Protocol (SNMP) traps in order to interface with standard system management frameworks. If a product can't be monitored easily, and started and stopped via command-line tools that can be run via simple character terminals, supportability might be compromised.

Before you purchase any software, you'll need to have a support agreement in place. You should ensure that service levels are included and that the vendor has sufficient staff to meet the requirements. Support is a potentially thorny issue, as it won't typically be put to the test until something goes wrong. It's useful to preempt support issues by asking the vendor to provide a list of bugs grouped by severity as reported by customers in the last few months. If the vendor can't provide this information, then that should be a warning, as vendors that don't track the occurrence of problems aren't likely to focus on efforts to address them. A list of recent maintenance and patch releases can be useful for determining the frequency with which users experience problems.

The vendor should provide an online support knowledge base via the Web. This can be a useful source of past problems encountered by customers and how well the vendor has addressed them. Both Microsoft and Oracle's Web sites are fine examples of how to provide online support. They make the support process more customer-centric, and save time and effort for both the customer and vendor. Discussion forums are also useful sources of information on how well a product works in practice and the level of support that is actually provided compared to the marketing hype.

Formal Evaluation of Third-Party Software

Before you purchase third-party software, you should perform a formal evaluation. The headings in this chapter can be used as a basis for that. It doesn't need to be a very time-consuming exercise if you make the effort to design a standard template that can be reused. A formal evaluation is important because it gives visibility to the procurement process and makes the requirements explicit. Both business and technology people should be involved. The evaluation should be as quantitative as possible, which means assigning weights to the relative importance of the various criteria and rating the product in each category.

Table 7.1 shows part of a matrix used in the early stages of an evaluation of three products proposed as possible solutions for a business requirement in an organization. It's not uncommon for products with similar functionality to be developed against different DBMS technologies (depending on the vendor's preferences), in which case the DBMS technology can strongly influence the choice of application because the features available in the underlying DBMS can determine the performance and availability of the application as a whole. If you are considering a nonmainstream DBMS technology, such as an object database management system (ODBMS), then you should be aware that performance gains for such technologies often come at the expense of the robust-

Table 7.1 Sample Product Evaluation Matrix

	PRODUCT A	PRODUCT B	PRODUCT C	NOTES
DBMS Technology	JBase	Oracle	Progress	
Performance Considerations				
Scalable to 1,000 users	?	Yes	Yes	
Scalable to terabytes of data	?	Yes	Yes	
Vendor benchmark	?	Yes	Yes	
TPC benchmark available	No	Yes	No	
Tunable and configurable OS resource usage	?	Yes	Yes	
Availability Considerations				
Transaction logging	Yes*	Yes	Yes	*Purchased separately
Online full backup	?	Yes	Yes	
Online incremental backup	?	Yes	Yes	
Network backup to silo	No	Yes	No	No Legato modules available
Automatic crash recovery	?	Yes	Yes	
Fast crash recovery	?	Yes	No	
DBMS vendor HA solution	Yes*	Yes	Yes	*Purchased separately
Wide availability of skills in job market	No	Yes	No	

ness and availability features that you take for granted with Oracle and other mainstream DBMSs. Security, for example, is something that you can't turn off in Oracle, but some ODBMSs consider it to be an application-level issue, which is implemented each time as part of the application.

Summary

To successfully deploy third-party, Oracle-based software in your organization, you must collaborate with the software vendor. Collaboration, through face-to-face meetings and information exchanges, ensures that both the customer and vendor have a clear understanding of the requirements and critical factors for successful deployment. As the potential customer, you shouldn't be afraid to ask difficult questions of the vendor and you must ensure that the answers fully address the issues. Answers to the difficult questions may be the ones on which a project succeeds or fails.

If the evaluation process consists solely of a set of functionality requirements determined by the business people, then deployment is likely to fail. As the customer, you need to be aware of the many factors, which were discussed in this chapter, that can influence successful deployment. If the customer doesn't have a clear set of requirements, failures are as much the customer's responsibility as the vendor's.

Performance Management and Tuning Techniques

## CHAPTER 8

End-to-End Performance Management

Before jumping straight into the Oracle aspects of application performance, it's essential to have a broad understanding of the challenge of end-to-end performance management. End-to-end performance management isn't about tweaking the init.ora parameters of your database, although that's usually part of it at some stage. It's actually about taking a usercentric view of application performance to deliver on the end-user requirements for response times. This chapter covers important concepts that are prerequisites for both tuning Structured Query Language (SQL) (see Chapter 9) and using performance management tools (see Chapter 16). Both those chapters need to be understood within the context of a clear set of requirements for performance management, and this chapter sets out to provide them. The initial sections of this chapter concentrate on the requirements for performance management, and then cover the cost of managing performance, including ways to measure the return on investment from any tools that you purchase.

The list of topics covered is as follows:

- Why a usercentric view of performance management is necessary
- The technology challenges of implementing end-to-end performance management based on end-user requirements
- The cost of identifying and fixing performance issues
- The measurement and collection of transaction times
- Estimating the return on investment from end-to-end performance management

The Usercentric View of Performance

Consider an end-user view of a computer-based application. The end user typically has no interest in the technology used behind the scenes and has no understanding of terminology such as client/server or n-tier applications. The goal of the end user is to service customer requests within a time acceptable to the customer. For Web-based applications, the end user and the customer are one and the same. As far as the end user is concerned, the complex multilayered software, hardware, and network infrastructure behind the scenes and the challenge of managing it is irrelevant. The end user typically fills in a few fields on a form, clicks a button, and results are returned, hopefully within a few seconds.

Sometimes the technologists involved in the development and management of applications lose track of the end-user requirement. The Oracle database administrator (DBA), attempting to ensure that the database buffer cache hit ratio exceeds some arbitrary value based on an alert from a third-party monitoring agent, is on the wrong track. That's doing things the wrong way around. The emphasis on performance management should start with the end-user requirements. The goal should be to ensure that performance requirements for key transactions are defined in terms of simple elapsed times at the outset of a project. Then it naturally follows that monitoring and measurement of performance involves collecting performance information on those key user transactions to ensure they stay within the allowed limits, as well as a collection of associated information that can identify the root cause of performance problems that prevent the key transactions from completing within the agreed limits.

A simple example of an application with clear performance requirements is the TPC-C Online Transaction Processing (OLTP) benchmark covered in Chapter 14. The TPC-C benchmark defines five different transactions, four of which need to complete within five seconds. If the benchmark can't meet these requirements, it doesn't meet the TPC-C requirements. The TPC-C benchmark is designed to model the essential characteristics of an OLTP system. It's not unreasonable to suggest that many applications contain just a handful of time-critical transactions.

In summary, performance management means managing end-to-end performance of the technology stack in order to ensure that response times for key end-user transactions fall within a predefined limit. As is often the case, stating the requirements is not that difficult; ensuring that the requirements are met is often much more challenging.

The Challenge of End-to-End Performance Management

In the early 1990s, the nature of computer-based applications changed from hardwired terminals running character-based applications to graphical user interface (GUI) applications running thin clients against a server, usually on a network based on Transmission Control Protocol/Internet Protocol (TCP/IP). In terms of managing end-to-end performance, client/server applications represented a bigger challenge. Whereas hard-wired "dumb" terminals could be ignored in terms of performance impact, client/server applications meant that performance problems could potentially have a root cause on the client, the server, or even the network. In 2001, Oracle CEO Larry Ellison was announcing the death of client/server computing in the computer press. In a nutshell, he said that only multiple-tier applications using application servers could meet the performance and scalability needs of modern applications at an acceptable cost. The problem with multitier applications in reality seems to be that performance management tools and techniques haven't kept up with the complexity of the architecture that needs to be managed. As a result, the identification of the root cause of a performance management problem in multitiered applications takes on the difficulty of looking for a needle in haystack. It seems to be a rule of multitiered applications that when a performance problem occurs, the most difficult task is often identification of the root cause quickly and with certainty: Fixing the problem, once identified, is often more straightforward. Figure 8.1 actually shows four layers in order to demonstrate that performance issues may be introduced in the network between the database server and the disk storage in a modern infrastructure that uses a storage area network (SAN).

For a single-user transaction, multiple roundtrips are usually required between the middleware layer, the database layer, and the physical storage, as indicated by the bidirectional arrows, before results are returned to the client. The situation is actually more complicated than it appears at first sight because the middleware, database, and storage all provide features to cache data, so that it's never obvious how far down the

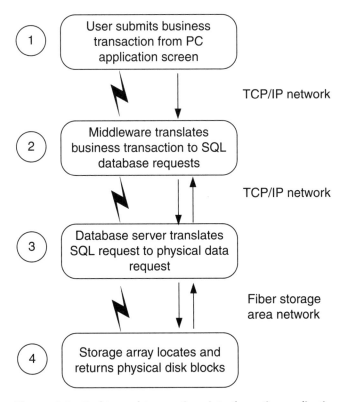

Figure 8.1   End-to-end transactions in a three-tier application.

stack a single end-user transaction reaches. In fact, the same transaction executed at a later time may complete faster because data is cached from the previous invocation.

Although a simple client/server application certainly doesn't provide the scalability and modularity of a multitier application, when viewed from the performance management space, it's a lot simpler to address. On the other hand, when a performance problem occurs in a multitier application, the complexity of the stack typically makes it difficult to identify the root cause of the problem. In theory, the problem can be due to issues with the software or hardware components at any of (1), (2), (3), or (4) in Figure 8.1, or the network paths between them. If performance management isn't designed either through instrumentation in code or through the use of appropriate tools (usually both), then meeting the agreed performance requirements can be a very expensive business. These costs can be exacerbated by company culture. It's not uncommon for the network, development, DBA, and system administration groups in an organization to exist as islands of technology that don't communicate well. This is the worst scenario for implementing a multitier application because when performance is an issue, problems tend to circulate between each group without anyone prepared to take ownership. Even when one group is prepared to take ownership, a lack of quantitative performance metrics to drive the resolution results in blame storming. The end result is that problem resolution is a painful, iterative, slow, and expensive process.

A Sample Three-tier Transaction

The following example shows the end-to-end transaction processing that could take place for an online trading application when the user submits a simple transaction, "Get my portfolio value." Although the transaction is simple from the end user's viewpoint, the underlying processing is quite complex. The indentation shows the order of nested operations as processing passes between the layers shown in Figure 8.1.

- The end user clicks an application button on the screen that says "Get my portfolio value."

- The end-user transaction "Get my portfolio value" is submitted to the middleware, identifying the user who made the request.

    - The middleware translates the end-user request into two low-level transactions: a database transaction, "Get my stocks," and a request, "Get stock prices," that returns stock prices from a network feed provided by an external service.

    - The middleware sends database transaction "Get my stocks" to the database.

        - The database sends a request to the storage to return the stock list from disk.

        - The storage locates the required blocks on disk and returns them to the database.

        - The database returns the list of stocks to the middleware.

- The middleware sends the second request, "Get stock prices," to the external service and collects the results.
- The middleware calculates the portfolio values based on the lists of stocks and prices.
- The middleware returns the portfolio value to the end-user application.
- The end-user application updates the portfolio value item on the screen.

In a real-world application, as mentioned previously, each layer typically caches data in memory from previous transactions. As a result, the same transaction, executed at a different point in time, can pass through all the layers on first execution and be satisfied from a cache in the middle tier on the second execution.

The Cost of Performance Problems

There are two main costs incurred when addressing a performance problem:

- Time spent identifying the root cause
- Time spent deploying a solution to address the root cause

We will examine both of these costs in the following sections.

The Costs of Identifying a Performance Problem

The personnel involved in root cause analysis of a performance problem at each layer of a multitier stack includes:

- End users, client application developers, and network analysts
- Middleware application developers and network analysts
- DBA and UNIX system administrator (SA) and network analysts
- Storage management experts (for SAN environments)

Without the right tools, the process of root cause analysis can take many hours. Potential solutions are often based on guesswork rather than facts, due to a lack of detailed performance information at the time a problem occurred. When the root cause can't be identified with certainty, custom-based monitoring usually needs to be developed to try to identify the cause of the problem the next time it occurs. This cycle might need to be repeated many times to identify the root cause. Solutions based on guesswork often result in the proposal of more than one possible solution for fixing a problem. Guesswork typically means that more than one of the proposed solutions needs to be implemented to actually fix the problem based on a trial and error approach. This is especially bad news for a production application because any change, however small, tends to require a significant effort (and therefore cost) to implement. For a third-party application, the cost tends to be even higher.

The Cost of Fixing a Performance Problem

The cost of deploying a solution to a performance problem is related to the stage in the application lifecycle in which the problem is addressed. For any firm that spends significant amounts on third-party applications, the cost of fixing performance problems can be very high. Table 8.1 shows the states in the process of fixing performance problems, depending on the stage of the lifecycle at which the problem is found and whether the application is developed in house or by a third-party vendor.

The cost of fixing a performance problem is clearly much lower when it takes place at the development stage of the lifecycle because less work is involved. Once an application is deployed in production, much more extensive quality assurance (QA) and testing is required, and change management effort is required to coordinate the work. For a third-party application, QA needs to be performed both by the vendor before the product release and by the customer that uses the application. Often, considerable time and effort is required to convince the vendor that the problem lies with their software. It's not unusual for the vendor to blame performance problems with database configuration issues on the client site. Without quantitative evidence on the root cause of the performance problem, customer-vendor disagreements can waste a lot of time. In the worst case, the vendor may not accept ownership of the problem or choose not to release a new version in the timeframe required by the customer.

Keep in mind that this scenario would never have occurred if performance requirements were specified at the outset and that instrumentation was built into the application by the vendor to measure and monitor the performance of key transactions. On rare occasions, in order to meet business performance requirements and address other problems, the original application might be written off and replaced with a different one. Chapter 7 contains suggestions to avoid this scenario by focusing on the techniques used by a third-party vendor to develop and deliver software. Sometimes contracts with third parties include performance requirements that enable the buyer to withhold payment until requirements are met. Ultimately, these don't have much real value if the vendor can't actually deliver on the promises due to a lack of resources.

Table 8.1   Performance Problem Resolution Process During the Lifecycle

DEVELOPMENT (IN-HOUSE APPLICATION)	PRODUCTION (IN-HOUSE APPLICATION)	PRODUCTION (THIRD-PARTY VENDOR APPLICATION)
Developer code fix, Limited QA and test	Developer code fix, Full QA and test, Change management implementation	Problem notification to vendor, Vendor code fix, Vendor QA and test, Vendor patch release
		Full QA and test, Change management Implementation

Everyone loses in this situation. Whether software is developed in house or by a third party, the same techniques need to be applied to build in end-to-end performance management capabilities.

Instrumenting Middle-tier Code

Instrumentation of code in the middle tier to include performance metrics is the responsibility of developers. In simple terms, instrumentation takes the form of extra code to measure and record the elapsed times for key transactions. The middle tier contains business logic that consists of high-level transactions that are usually a mixture of code that performs both low-level database and nondatabase processing, as shown in the earlier step-by-step example. As another example, in a banking environment, complex financial analytics may be performed in the middle tier based on information read from the database at an earlier point in the transaction. All too often, the processing split between database and nondatabase processing isn't clear. For example, if a particular transaction spends only 5 percent of the total processing time on database processing, then reducing this to near 0 will still lead to only a 5 percent reduction in elapsed times. In this situation, the tuning effort needs to target middle-tier code that doesn't involve database access. If the split in the processing load between the tiers is not known, then the tuning effort starts with guesswork, and this inevitably leads to wasted time and effort. The instrumentation of code is required to measure transaction performance. Instrumentation may be a manual coding task if the middle tier is written using a 3GL (third-generation language) like C or C++, requiring the developer to embed calls that measure elapsed times of business transactions and save the results.

With the use of appropriate performance management software on the database server, the database can be eliminated or confirmed as the root cause of a performance problem with minimal effort. As a result, if it can be shown that the database is not the cause, then by a process of elimination, other processing performed in the middle tier is very likely to be the cause. The existence of high-quality performance management software on the database tier can actually drive performance management resources to where they are most required by rapidly eliminating the database as the root cause. In this case, if the middle tier is not well instrumented, then the database is a good place to start looking for problems. My experience is that when multitiered applications don't perform well, people always look to the database first, not necessarily because the problem exists there, but because it's possible to confirm whether the database is or isn't the cause and thereby direct the next steps of the investigation.

The split between database and nondatabase processing on the middle tier can be inferred from an analysis of the Oracle wait states (as described in Chapter 9) of the middleware client sessions that connect to the database. For example, based on the information described in Chapter 9, when an Oracle session is idle and waiting for client requests from the middle tier, then it's in a state waiting for the event "SQL*Net message from client." Therefore, if an end-user performance problem is experienced and all Oracle sessions are in an idle state, then the database isn't the problem. Either the problem has occurred because the middle tier is overloaded and SQL requests aren't being submitted to the database tier, or a network problem means that middleware requests aren't reaching the database.

The Oracle view V$SESSION_WAIT shows the wait states of all Oracle sessions instantaneously at the present time. This information can change several times a second, as existing SQL statements complete and new ones begin. In order to obtain the required level of detail to identify a performance problem on the database, the view needs to be queried several times a second. This isn't possible without impacting the performance of the database server. In general, monitoring loses much of its value if it's so intrusive that it causes performance problems of its own.

Tools are available to provide high-precision Oracle monitoring alongside low CPU and I/O consumption. For example, Precise/Indepth from Precise Software, which is covered in Chapter 16, is a tool that enables Oracle performance problems to be rapidly identified by highlighting SQL statements that spend the longest time executing in the database based on capture of Oracle wait state information at high sample rates. It needs to be emphasized that statements that spend a long time in a wait state aren't necessarily high consumers of the central processing unit (CPU) or input/output (I/O), so tools based solely on Oracle statistics (rather than wait states) can miss important information.

A classic illustration of this is the "user gone to lunch" syndrome. In this scenario, a data entry operator starts a business transaction that locks an underlying database row and then goes to lunch, leaving the row locked. Other data entry operators that need to change the same row either receive a "transaction locked" message or their session blocks waiting for the first operator to commit or rollback the original transaction. The actual behavior is determined by the application designer. In the latter case, the end user typically sees an hourglass, and the application hangs. The end result is that processing can't proceed. When a user session blocks waiting for a row lock to free, it doesn't actually consume much resources because it's waiting and therefore idle. Viewed from the end user's perspective, this scenario is a disaster, especially if a customer is on the phone waiting for a response. The Oracle wait event that can be seen in V$SESSION_WAIT in this case is an *enqueue*, which is simply the Oracle kernel term for a lock. Only tools based on Oracle events rather than statistics can identify such problems.

In addition to inferring information about the middle-tier performance, a collection of Oracle session wait information can provide useful information on the performance of the storage subsystem. As the database sits above the storage tier, if the database *is* the root cause of performance problems, wait events can indicate whether the problem lies with CPU shortages on the database server or is due to I/O waits from overloading of the underlying storage subsystem. However, for the most complete picture of performance, there is a need to correlate performance metrics provided by an operating system with Oracle statistics, and this is another key requirement for an Oracle performance management tool.

Although monitoring database performance can provide an insight into the performance of the tiers above and below the database, what's really required is a framework that can associate the performance of business transactions in the middle tier with performance information on the tiers below. Products exist to add performance instrumentation to middle-tier code without developer effort. The Quantify product from Rational Software can produce executable images with modified code. The modified code includes embedded instructions that measure the time spent on each line of code. Quantify is a product that Oracle Corporation has used in the past during development. However, the modified code has a significant performance overhead and is typically stripped out before products are shipped: It's intended for development and QA only. If the middle tier runs the J2EE platform, then it's possible to run applications using a special Java class loader that automatically includes special byte codes to instrument the time spent in each Java application component.

This is a similar approach to Quantify but applies to Java rather than native executable programs. Precise/Indepth for the J2EE platform extracts CPU resource usage data from the underlying operating system to provide a correlated view of CPU usage with Java application components and specific end-user requests. When used in conjunction with Precise/Indepth for Oracle on the database server, it then becomes possible to correlate the performance of middle-tier transactions with Oracle database SQL statements. This leads to an interesting question: Should the requirement to provide end-to-end performance management actually drive the development environment for in-house applications and be considered when purchasing third-party applications? Precise/Indepth for J2EE requires that you develop and deploy applications on specific application servers, such as BEA WebLogic or IBM Websphere. If your organization doesn't use these environments today but requires end-to-end performance management, then you might even consider switching in order to gain the benefits of end-to-end performance management that these environments provide. It is clear that performance instrumentation needs to be provided, whether manually or automatically, in order for the root cause of performance problems to be identified quickly.

Instrumenting Database Code

Oracle provides package procedures to enable performance information for a single middle-tier transaction to be collected as a group by tagging the underlying SQL statements that make up the transaction using a specified name. As Figure 8.1 shows, a single end-user transaction can result in the execution of several SQL statements on the database tier. The challenge is to group these together and measure the performance of the collection of SQL statements as a whole. This can be done by embedding code on the middle tier explicitly to measure performance.

A different approach that provides useful information with less effort involves embedding calls to routines in DBMS_APPLICATION_INFO. Chapter 6 includes a complete example of how to use the SET_MODULE and SET_ACTION routines in DBMS_APPLICATION_INFO. Here's a summary of how it works. Consider a middle-tier transaction that processes a stock trade with ID 9503. The complete transaction performs two database SELECT statements followed by an UPDATE based on processing the results of the two SELECT statements. The first action of the middle-tier transaction is to call DBMS_APPLICATION_INFO to set the ACTION column in V$SESSION to identify the trade being processed in the Oracle session as follows:

```
-- identify the current trade to V$SESSION
dbms_application_info.set_action('Trade 9503');
```

After the middle-tier transaction has started, the following SQL can be executed several times to show the events waited for and the action set by SET_ACTION during execution:

```
select /*+ RULE */ s.sid||','||s.serial# o_sid,sq.executions
execs,w.event,s.action,
sql_address||','||sql_hash_value o_sql_address
from v$session_wait w,v$session s,v$process p,v$sqlarea sq,audit_actions
a
where w.sid = s.sid
and s.command = a.action
and sq.address =s.sql_address and sq.hash_value = s.sql_hash_value
and S.PADDR = P.ADDR (+)
and event not in ('rdbms ipc message','smon timer','pmon timer',
'SQL*Net message from client','pipe get');
```

```
O_SID     EXECS EVENT                        ACTION       O_SQL_ADDRESS
-------   ------- ---------------------- ----------- --------------------
28,67         1 direct path write        Trade 9503   90DF6670,772587599
28,67         1 db file sequential read  Trade 9503   70AF6581,992346510
28,67         1 db file scattered read   Trade 9503   81A74391,500247891
```

Running the monitoring SQL three times after the transaction starts shows that the ACTION value hasn't changed. This information indicates that the same business transaction is still executing for Oracle session 28,67 in each case. On the other hand, the O_SQL_ADDRESS column is different in each sample, showing that a different SQL statement is executing at each point in time.

In short, the use of SET_ACTION enables the different statements that run on behalf of Trade 9503 to be grouped together for monitoring purposes. Oracle provides SET_ACTION and SET_MODULE specifically to enable performance-monitoring software to collect the information. Precise/Indepth collects wait information several times a second, including the ACTION and MODULE columns in V$SESSION. As a result, the top SQL in any time interval can be presented in order of the top ACTION or MODULE values to identify the most expensive business transactions rather than just the top individual statements. Figure 8.2 shows the Precise/Indepth chart for some transactions instrumented using SET_ACTION that are ordered by the time spent consuming resources in Oracle.

Once Precise/Indepth has been used to chart to in-Oracle resource consumption by transaction, the next stage is to drill down and analyze the performance of each individual statement within the transaction. More examples can be found in Chapter 16.

Some lower-cost options are available for providing insight into performance on the database. The Diagnostics Pack component of Oracle Enterprise Manager (OEM) includes Performance Overview, which presents an overview of database server performance memory, CPU, I/O, and event waits in chart form that is sampled every few seconds. The presentation is split between overall server metrics and the database. Figure 8.3 shows disk performance information as presented in OEM Performance Overview for the host and the database.

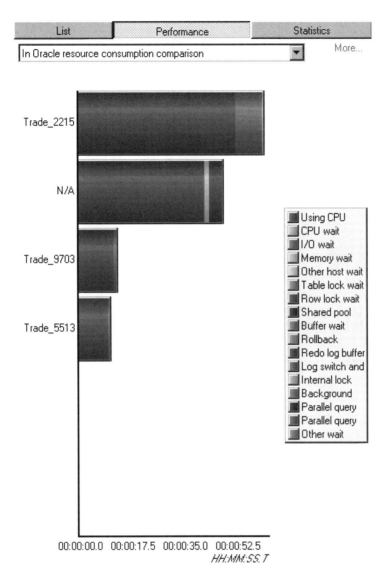

Figure 8.2 Precise/Indepth resource consumption by ACTION.

OEM Performance Manager is a very useful addition to the performance management arsenal of an Oracle DBA. If you use Oracle STATSPACK to collect Oracle performance metrics, as discussed in Chapter 27, then Performance Manager can chart the collected information. In order to identify the top SQL where tuning effort needs to be concentrated, tools are required that can identify those statements with a high degree of accuracy and minimum effort. Ultimately, I/O and CPU statistics and rates, however interesting, guide you toward the SQL you need to investigate. I prefer tools that try to take you straight to the SQL, and these are covered in Chapter 16.

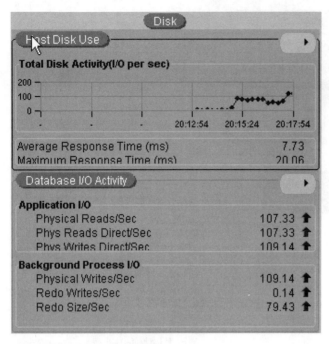

Figure 8.3 EM Performance Overview.

A free option for the Oracle server performance information collection is the DBCOOL_MON package referred to later in Chapter 14. DBCOOL_MON saves statistics and events either for all sessions, the current session, or the system as a whole, and it optionally enables you to provide a name to associate with each collection. I like to use it to save all statistics and event waits for every database session with minimal effort. The package is written to minimize the space required for the sampled data by using event and statistic ID numbers rather than names. It can be downloaded from the companion Web site. This is an example of a trigger that collects all statistics and event waits for every session at logoff time using DBCOOL_MON:

```
create or replace TRIGGER SYS.dbcool_on_logoff before logoff on database
declare
begin

    dbcool_mon.logoff_sample;

exception
  when others then
    null;
end;
/
```

Quantifying the Return on Investment

End-to-end performance management tools are expensive. Given the potential to save your organization money, it's not surprising. Before your organization invests in such a tool, it's essential to try to quantify the benefits. This section uses Precise/Indepth as an example, but the approach is generically applicable to any tool. Traditional Oracle performance management techniques usually don't provide sufficient details on the cause of Oracle performance problems to identify the root cause at any point in time accurately and quickly. This results in the following costs in terms of personnel hours:

- The analysis of traditional performance metrics, often resulting in failure to determine the root cause

- The development of bespoke monitoring targeted at the specific problem in hand

- Information collection, possibly causing performance degradation on the monitored system

- The presentation and reporting of results

Precise/Indepth for Oracle solves these problems through the following features:

- Automated collection of data 24×7

- High accuracy on the determination of the root cause

- Very low impact on the target system

- Automated presentation of results

The end result is that time spent on traditional approaches to root cause analysis of Oracle performance problems can be reduced to almost zero using Precise/Indepth. These savings arise because the process of collection, analysis, and presentation is completely automated. At a high level, the time spent on root cause analysis of Oracle performance problems per database instance per year (based on a requirement to present production and nonproduction costs separately) is as follows:

(Number of production systems) × (average hours per system per year)
    × (cost per hour)

(Number of nonproduction systems) × (average hours spent per system per year)
    × (cost per hour)

Time spent needs to include time for all support and development staff, including time spent liaising with vendors of third-party applications to address performance problems. Keep in mind that performance problems in a multitier application often require analysis from personnel at all levels in the technology stack, not just Oracle. Use of Precise/Indepth means the database can be definitively eliminated or confirmed as the root cause immediately, enabling resources to be directed to where the problem actually resides. Many other potential savings can be demonstrated from the deployment of an end-to-end performance management framework, including the following:

- Reductions in staff due to higher transaction rates, enabling fewer staff to perform the same workload

- Reductions in overtime payments due to processing completion within business hours

- Savings in costs of third-party software due to making the right purchase the first time

- Reductions in performance management consultancy fees

- Savings through performance enhancements via software code changes rather than hardware expansion

Summary

It's easy to lose sight of your primary goal: to deliver an application that meets end-user requirements in terms of functionality, performance, and availability. A typical end-user transaction in a multitier application translates to multiple roundtrips between the middle tier, the database tier, and the storage, with a network dependency between each layer. Due to the complexity of the infrastructure, it's often difficult to identify the root cause of a performance problem unless performance instrumentation is built into code at development time. Lack of instrumentation can cause efforts to identify the root cause of a performance problem to begin at the wrong tier. A product like Precise/Indepth for Oracle can identify performance problems on the database tier with minimal effort. As a result, the database can immediately be eliminated or confirmed as the source, leading to the most cost-effective deployment of resources.

End-to-end performance management can't be solved at the database tier alone. It's a complex subject in its own right. It requires a framework that can correlate end-user transactions with activity at all the other tiers. Today, solutions require a lot of time, effort, and expense, but they are usually cost effective when compared to the extra costs of hardware, software, and people incurred when end-to-end performance is treated as an afterthought.

Fundamentals of SQL Tuning

Application performance issues are common, judging by the volume of postings on the Oracle Metalink forums (metalink.oracle.com) and on the Web concerning Oracle tuning and performance. As you're probably aware, there are many books on Oracle tuning. This chapter won't tell you how to tune every single Structured Query Language (SQL) statement on the planet. However, it does provide techniques for determining why your SQL isn't performing as you would like it to perform. You can't fix SQL performance problems until you understand them. This chapter concentrates on how to understand performance.

The chapter starts with a discussion of how opportunities for tuning change during the application lifecycle. No matter when performance tuning takes place, you need to have an understanding of Oracle's internal performance metrics based on waits and events. Once you understand how to measure the performance of SQL, you need the tools to help you do it. If you don't have the tools that make performance measurement easy and systematic during the development process, then it's unlikely that you will place sufficient emphasis on creating optimal SQL. SQL tuning requires a clear set of goals that includes identifying table scans and the SQL that causes them. After you have tuned your SQL, you can further improve performance by controlling the lifetime of data in the Oracle buffer cache and through parallel operations. Caching and reusing Oracle's internal representation of SQL statements (cursors) can also speed up performance, so you to need to understand how cursors work and how you can control them. Even the network can influence your SQL performance for client-server applications, and you need to understand Oracle's array-processing interface to ensure that network data transfers make the most of available bandwidth.

Performance tuning doesn't stop when a system goes live. During the production lifecycle, it's still necessary to identify the most expensive SQL and provide improvements for the development cycle. Once a system is in production, SQL code changes may not be possible, due to the risks of side effects. As a result, it's important to be aware of techniques that influence SQL performance without changing the SQL.

This chapter covers the following topics:

- Tuning and the application lifecycle
- Oracle statistics and events
- Tools for measuring statistics and events
- Viewing the Oracle buffer cache and controlling its contents
- Detecting full table scans
- Goals for SQL tuning
- SQL execution plans
- Parallel operations
- Identifying which SQL to tune
- Making SQL faster with and without code changes
- Performance and cursors
- Tuning SQL for the network
- Defining server memory requirements

Tuning and the Application Lifecycle

This chapter places an emphasis on tuning during the development stage of the application lifecycle where it's easiest to make changes. Everyone seems to agree on that approach. Nearly every book on Oracle tuning contains a graph showing how the cost of tuning rises during the production stage of the lifecycle. However, there's a huge gap between stating a problem, which is typically easy, and fixing it, which typically isn't.

In order to succeed in SQL tuning during the development stage, the approach of measuring everything all the time needs to be in place. Usually, the goal is to minimize the elapsed time to completion for each and every statement. When this doesn't happen, performance problems manifest themselves during the production stage when it's often too late to address them meaningfully without incurring a delay and additional expense.

For example, if your company purchases a software package from a third party and performance problems show up in the production environment, then fixing the problem becomes orders of magnitude more complex than having the vendor fix it at the development stage before the product's release. First, your in-house database administrators (DBAs) need to convince the vendor that there's a real problem. Often the vendor blames the database configuration on the client site. Once this hurdle has been overcome, the vendor must, but maybe doesn't, regression test the new code. Then change management is required to implement the solution, possibly involving business downtime. Chapter 7 contains ways to avoid this scenario, but doing so is not easy. It would be much better if you knew that the vendor had designed performance into the application.

Consider how this measure-everything-all-the-time approach is put in place. First, the developer or DBA needs information on how to measure performance. Once that's in place, he or she needs the tools to measure SQL performance and compare this with previous results to see if changes have had positive effects. In order to encourage systematic use, these tools should be easy to use.

At the production stage of the lifecycle, when the live application is running, the problem space is somewhat different. Even if you've done everything you can to ensure that SQL was designed for best performance during development, the possibility of contention for limited server hardware resources arises. This is difficult to simulate during development or testing and requires a different approach.

This chapter covers the bottom-up approach to Oracle SQL development. The bottom-up approach is based on the reasonable premise that if you ensure that each and every SQL statement is developed to minimize the elapsed execution time, then any system where you put together all those statements will perform reasonably well.

Chapter 8 on end-to-end performance management takes a systemcentric top-down approach to the subject of performance management. Both approaches are required to deliver scalable systems that perform well from day one and into the future.

Statistics and Events

It is pointless to try tuning SQL statements until you fully understand how to measure performance. To facilitate this measurement, Oracle provides performance metrics that are available through SQL views. These metrics exist in the form of counters (known as *statistics*) and wait times (known as *events*). In Oracle9*i*, there are over 200 different statistics and events. You can see a complete list of names using the following SQL:

```
select * from v$statname;
```

```
select * from v$event_name;
```

The statistics are incremented continually from database startup, beginning at zero, and are provided databasewide in the V$SYSSTAT view and for individual sessions in the V$SESSTAT view. The special view V$MYSTAT can also be used to show the statistics for the currently connected session. The V$SYSSTAT view includes the statistic name from V$STATNAME, whereas the V$SESSTAT view doesn't. Identifying statistics for the current session can be performed using the following SQL:

```
select st.*,n.name
from v$sesstat st,v$statname n,v$session se
where st.statistic# = n.statistic#
and   st.sid=se.sid
and   se.audsid = (select userenv('sessionid') from dual);
```

The wait times behave slightly differently and appear in V$SYSTEM_EVENT and V$SESSION_EVENT. In order for the event times to appear, the parameter TIMED_STATISTICS=TRUE must be in place. This can be set in the init.ora file or for individual sessions using ALTER SESSION SET TIMED_STATISTICS=TRUE. The recommendation is to always enable the setting at the database level. It incurs a small performance overhead—one that is so small I've never been able to isolate it. Information on events includes the number of waits as well as wait times. If an event never incurs a wait, it won't appear in the relevant view, unlike statistics, which are always present, even if the value is zero. This SQL shows the wait information for the current session:

```
select  ev.*
from    v$session_event ev, v$session se
where   ev.sid = se.sid
and     se.audsid = (select userenv('sessionid') from dual);
```

Due to the huge number of metrics that Oracle makes available via SQL, it's not surprising that there is such a large number of Oracle performance management tools on the market. Most tools sample the various statistics over time (and sometimes the wait events), save the values, and plot graphs of the values over time. When the statistics are available, the next stage is to understand what they mean, identify the ones that have the most effect on performance, and take steps to reduce them.

Essential Statistics and Events

Disk input/output (I/O) is typically at least three orders of magnitude slower than memory access no matter what the application. As a general rule, if you can reduce physical disk I/O by caching more of the frequently used data in memory, then performance should improve. How do you determine which of the 200+ statistics to focus on when tuning SQL during development? Oracle's own chosen statistics, as displayed using the SET AUTOTRACE ON STATISTICS feature in SQL*Plus, are a good place to start. SQL*Plus AUTOTRACE is covered in the next section. Some of the statistics it produces are shown in Table 9.1.

Table 9.1   Selected SQL*Plus AUTOTRACE Statistics

NAME	MEANING
db block gets	The number of blocks fetched in current mode
consistent gets	The number of blocks fetched in read-consistent mode
physical reads	The number of physical blocks read
redo size	The redo generated in bytes
sorts (disk)	The disk sorts performed

Table 9.2 Other Useful Statistics

NAME	DESCRIPTION
CPU used by this session	The time in tens of milliseconds of a second
data blocks consistent reads–undo records applied	The blocks fetched from undo to provide a read-consistent view of data
db block changes	The count of blocks changed
physical writes	The count of physical write operations
table fetch by rowid	The rows fetched using a ROWID value (the fastest way to identify a row)
table scan blocks gotten	The blocks fetched via a full table scan
table scan rows gotten	The rows fetched via a full table scan
table scans (long tables)	The count of table scans of long tables

If you do any tuning at all, writing SQL that minimizes or reduces the statistics in Table 9.1 will go a long way toward producing an efficient application that meets end-user performance requirements with the lowest possible central processing unit (CPU) and I/O cost. Note that blocks fetched in current mode are those modified by the current session. For example, during a query, blocks are usually fetched in read-consistent mode. However, if the current session has modified some of the blocks without a commit (via an insert, update, or delete), then those blocks are fetched in current mode for the session that made the changes. This list omits some other statistics that can be useful when analyzing SQL performance. Some additional statistics are shown in Table 9.2.

Ultimately, the only way you won't miss any information is to inspect all the statistics that have changed after the execution of each SQL statement during development. In the same spirit, Table 9.3 shows the most common event waits and their possible causes from a survey of several large production databases of various sizes and application types.

Wait events have parameters that can provide more information on the nature of the wait. For example, "latch-free" events identify the number of the latch waiting to be freed. The related name of the latch can be identified from the V$LATCHNAME view. Enqueue events can contain information about the object and session holding a row-level lock. Oracle ships a script called catblock.sql (located in $ORACLE_HOME/rdbms/admin on UNIX systems) to display a lock dependency tree for the sessions involved. DbCool provides a lock viewer utility that does the same thing graphically. Oracle's script requires the creation of temporary tables to display the tree, and the Data Definition Language (DDL) can cause further lock contention. DbCool's lock viewer uses in-memory information only and isn't subject to the same restrictions. The parameter information for both the "db file scattered read" and "db file sequential read" events contains the Oracle file and block that the read request has waited for.

Table 9.3   Common Event Waits

NAME	CAUSE
buffer busy waits	Wait for a buffer to become available, due to a buffer being read into the cache by another session or a buffer being held in an incompatible mode because another session is changing it.
change write item	Elapsed redo write time for changes made to current-mode blocks, in tens of milliseonds.
db file scattered read	Wait for a multiblock read on a specified Oracle file and block, which is often during a full table scan.
db file sequential read	Wait for a single block read on a specified Oracle file and block, which is often during an index lookup or table access by ROWID.
direct path read	Wait for a read that bypasses the buffer cache to complete, which is often caused by a disk sort or character large object (CLOB) read.
direct path write	Wait for a write that bypasses the buffer cache to complete, which is often caused by a disk sort.
enqueue	Wait for an enqueue (lock) to free, which is sometimes due to a row-level lock held by another session.
latch free	Wait for a latch held by another process to become free based on the given latch number. Latch names "cache buffer lru chain" and "cache buffers chains" indicate a busy buffer cache.
log buffer space	Wait for space in log buffer because log writer process (LGWR) can't write redo to disk fast enough.
log file switch completion	Wait for a log switch to complete.
log file sync	Wait for session redo to flush to the redo log file during a commit.
redo synch writes	Elapsed time of all synchrnous writes that take place during COMMIT operations, in tens of milliseconds.

These file and block values can be decoded into a database object name, as shown in an example later in the chapter in the section *Detecting Full Table Scans*. Some events indicate idle sessions and can generally be ignored. These are shown in Table 9.4.

If a user logs onto a database via SQL*Plus (either locally or via a network connection) and does nothing, the session remains in a "SQL*Net message from client" state. The view V$SESSION_WAIT shows the event that each session is waiting for at the time the view was queried. V$SESSION_WAIT is a good place to start looking for performance problems if users report that the system is running slow. On a system under

Table 9.4 Idle Event Waits

NAME	CAUSE
SQL*Net message from client	Idle user session awaiting SQL request from client
pipe get	Idle session waiting for message on database pipe
rdbms ipc message pmon timer smon timer wakeup time manager	Idle events for background process
dispatcher timer virtual circuit status	Idle events for shared server
PX Idle Wait PX Deq Credit: need buffer PX Deq Credit: send blkd	Idle events for parallel query
ges remote message lock manager wait for remote message	Idle events for a Real Application Clusters (RAC) configuration

stress, you might expect to see several sessions simultaneously in a nonidle wait state. These are usually waiting on one of the events listed in Table 9.3.

Tools for Measuring Events and Statistics

If it was possible to display the event waits and statistics for each SQL statement run during a session, then the developer or DBA would receive immediate feedback and potentially take action at the development stage to address any problems. The ability to provide immediate feedback is essential when using this systematic approach. In order to provide this functionality, it's necessary to sample the statistics and events before running every SQL statement, sample them afterwards, and then present the differences. Features that show the changes in waits and statistics between different statements are also very useful. This section describes three different tools that provide those features to varying degrees.

SQL*Plus

Oracle's SQL*Plus tool, when running with the SET AUTOTRACE ON STATISTICS option enabled, can provide immediate feedback on a few selected statistics after the execution of each SQL statement. Because only a subset of the available statistics is provided, information that could help to identify the root cause of a performance problem may be missing. The PLUSTRACE role is required for non-DBA accounts to use this feature. The SET TIMING ON option can be used to provide elapsed time. The following is sample output for a SELECT statement on a table without a primary key:

```
SQL> /

  COUNT(*)
----------
      5000

Elapsed: 00:00:01.07

Statistics
-------------------------------------------------
          0  recursive calls
        225  db block gets
       5054  consistent gets
          0  physical reads
          0  redo size
        202  bytes sent via SQL*Net to client
         89  bytes received via SQL*Net from client
          2  SQL*Net roundtrips to/from client
          0  sorts (memory)
          0  sorts (disk)
          1  rows processed
```

A short time later, the same SQL runs, producing the same result. The elapsed time hasn't changed, and some of the statistics have increased:

```
Elapsed: 00:00:01.04

Statistics
-------------------------------------------------
          0  recursive calls
        225  db block gets
      20053  consistent gets
          0  physical reads
     260000  redo size
        203  bytes sent via SQL*Net to client
        191  bytes received via SQL*Net from client
          3  SQL*Net roundtrips to/from client
          0  sorts (memory)
          0  sorts (disk)                1  rows processed
```

Something strange is going on due to the amount of redo, but the statistics don't provide many clues. SQL*Plus doesn't show event waits at all, and because the results are presented in a simple text format, inline with the SQL, the number of statistics presented needs to be much less than the total available in order to fit the screen. As a result, some additional information that could give the SQL designer on insight into what's happened is missing.

In particular, it would be useful to perform a side-by-side comparison of the results in each case to identify exactly which statistics have changed between the two statements. If you can identify all the statistics and events that change as a result of your SQL, then you're well on your way to understanding how to fix performance problems. This usually involves nothing more complicated than taking whatever action is necessary to reduce the use of resources identified by the statistics and event waits. At the simplest level, it means doing whatever is necessary to reduce physical I/O caused by physical reads and logical I/O caused by reading blocks from the buffer cache.

A tool is required that can capture all the necessary information and present it in a format that's easy to use. SQL*Plus is a good starting point, but it doesn't go far enough. For example, it doesn't provide statistics for DDL or PL SQL; it only provides statistics for Data Manipulation Language (DML).

DbCool

DbCool was designed partly to provide the functionality that encourages systematic tuning by taking a measure-everything-all-the-time approach. By default, DbCool maintains a history of the elapsed time, the rows fetched, the SQL statement text, and the results grid (for SELECT statements) for every statement executed in a session. The results grid means that query results can be recalled without the expense of rerunning a query.

By selecting the Monitoring menu, Events (Choose Session), and then Statistics (Choose Session), the SQL history additionally stores all statistics and event wait times for every statement executed in the session. By right-clicking any statement in the history, which is accessible from the main toolbar, statistics and event times can be compared with any other statement executed in the session. Figure 9.1 shows the complete set of statistics in DbCool's SQL history in exactly the same scenario as the SQL*Plus example.

Now there is plenty of evidence as to what's going on, as shown in the following statistics:

```
5000 => cleanouts and rollbacks - consistent read gets
5000 => CR blocks created
9999 => data blocks consistent reads - undo records applied
5000 => db block changes
5000 => immediate (CR) block cleanout application
5000 => redo entries
```

The line "data blocks consistent reads - undo records applied" indicates that the SELECT is causing many undo records to be applied from the rollback segments (or automatic undo tablespace in Oracle9*i*). This occurs when a session needs to read changed but uncommitted data from another session in order to create a read-consistent view. The line "immediate (CR) block cleanout application" means that data blocks are being changed during the consistent view generation, and such changes result in the generation of redo information. If you have ever wondered why Oracle can generate

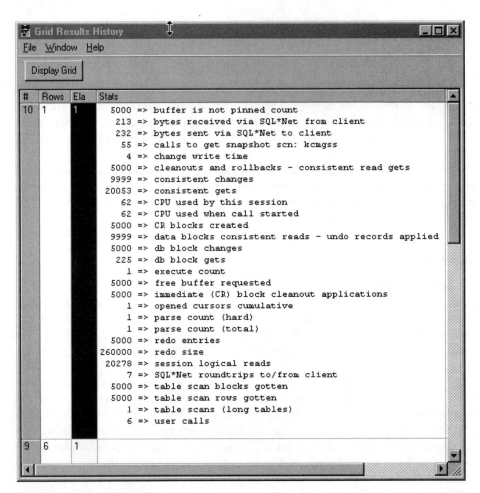

Figure 9.1 DbCool SQL history.

redo during query execution, access to the full statistics provided by an appropriate tool can help you find the answer.

The capability of one session to read preupdate versions of blocks that have been changed in another session but not yet committed is part of Oracle's multiversion read-consistency model. This model, which provides concurrent access to changing data from multiple sessions by maintaining multiple versions of the same block, is a unique and powerful Oracle feature. However, the benefits can come at considerable I/O cost in the wrong circumstances, as shown in the previous example. Even if you don't have the expertise at this stage to determine the cause of the problem from the statistics, collecting all of the relevant statistics is an important first step. For the record, in this example, another session deleted all the rows from MY_OBJECTS and didn't yet commit the changes, causing the results shown.

TKPROF

TKPROF is an Oracle command-line tool that runs on the database server. It processes a trace file created by using ALTER SESSION SET SQL_TRACE=TRUE in the current session or through the execution of the other trace options described in Chapter 28.

TKPROF needs to be an integral part of the tuning process. Unlike EXPLAIN PLAN, which shows a theoretical execution plan for a SQL statement, TKPROF can generate the plan that was actually used to execute a statement after running it, along with logical and physical I/O information as well as CPU and elapsed times for the parse, execute, and fetch phases of the execution. Table 9.5 shows some of the more useful command-line arguments.

Recursive SQL is generated when Oracle needs to perform additional system-level SQL resulting from the user-executed SQL. For example, an insert might generate recursive SQL if extents need to be allocated for the table, resulting in the modification of various dictionary tables—for example, EXT$. As another example, the following recursive SQL might be generated by an INSERT statement that needs more space, leading to a search of the Oracle free space list (fet$) to find an extent of the required size:

```
select length from fet$ where file#=:1 and block#=:2 and ts#=:3
```

During queries, recursive SQL might be required to look up table and column definitions from the data dictionary during the parse phase if the information is not in the object cache. The section in this chapter titled *Cursors and the Shared Pool* contains more information on the object cache and processing performed during the various stages of a SQL statement. Recursive SQL can make a trace file seem exceedingly verbose. You can disable recursive SQL from the trace using SYS=NO. If you do this, be aware that recursive SQL statistics are not included in the user statement that caused them. If you ignore them and they use significant resources, you might miss something important. Care needs to be taken to ensure that the EXPLAIN connect string used is the one that actually ran the trace session, using the correct database; otherwise, misleading results can be generated.

The following example reads the trace file D1_ora_1l.trc (based on the first argument) and creates the profile file D1_ora_11.prf (based on the second argument). The output is sorted by the sum of the CPU time for each statement, and the top five statements appear in the output file:

```
$ tkprof D1_ora_11 D1_ora_11 sort=prscpu,execpu,fchcpu print=5 sys=no
```

Table 9.5 Useful TKPROF Parameters

NAME	PURPOSE
SYS=NO|YES	Include recursive SQL, default YES.
SORT=*options*	Sort output in *various* ways according to *options*.
PRINT=*n*	Show only *n* statements in output.
EXPLAIN=*user/password*	Generate EXPLAIN PLAN .

Table 9.6 Useful TKPROF SORT Parameters

RESOURCE USED	SORT PARAMETER STRING
Longest elapsed time	PRSELA, EXEELA, FCHELA
Most CPU consumed	PRSCPU, EXECPU, FCHCPU
Most physical I/O	PRSDSK, EXEDSK, FCHDSK

Table 9.6 shows some of the most useful combinations of SORT arguments.

Because a trace file needs to be created on the server and the file can be quite large, running TKPROF causes an execution overhead on the session being traced. From my testing, this can be as high as 10 percent of the elapsed time. As a result, TKPROF should be used with care. If necessary, tracing can be turned on databasewide for all sessions by using SQL_TRACE=TRUE in the init.ora file. This option should only be used in extreme circumstances, because it requires a database restart to enable and disable it, among other things. Note that if you enable tracing for wait events as well as SQL, as described in Chapter 28, a new Oracle 9i TKPROF parameter, WAITS=YES, summarizes wait times for each cursor in the profiled output.

TKPROF profile output shows the information for the parse, execute, and fetch (for queries) phases of the execution along with the rows processed at each stage of the execution. The values of DISK (statistic "physical reads"), QUERY (statistic "consistent gets"), and CURRENT (statistic "db block gets") in the profiled output show the physical and logical I/O performed in blocks. The ratio rows/fetches shows the size of any arrays, as discussed later in this chapter in *Tuning SQL for the Network*, and provides evidence of efficient SQL. This is an example of TKPROF output for a simple query:

```
select tx_name,tx_type,count(*)
from tx,tx_hist h
where tx.tx_id = h.tx_id
group by tx_name,tx_type

call     count       cpu    elapsed   disk      query    current        rows
-------  ------  --------  ---------  -----  ---------  ----------  ----------
Parse        1      0.01       0.01      0          0           0           0
Execute      2      0.00       0.00      0          0           0           0
Fetch        7      0.22       0.22     34        191          33          88
-------  ------  --------  ---------  -----  ---------  ----------  ----------
total       10      0.23       0.23     34        191          33          88

Misses in library cache during parse: 1
Optimizer goal: CHOOSE
Parsing user id: 5  (SYSTEM)
```

```
ROWS      ROW SOURCE OPERATION
-------   -------------------------------------------------------
     88   SORT GROUP BY
  14841     HASH JOIN
  20000       TABLE ACCESS FULL TX_HIST
  24680       TABLE ACCESS FULL TX
```

When used with the EXPLAIN command-line argument, an *execution plan* is included, showing the number of rows fetched at each stage of the execution, the optimizer mode, and the processing operation, as shown in the following example:

```
ROWS      EXECUTION PLAN
-------   -------------------------------------------------------
      0   SELECT STATEMENT    GOAL: CHOOSE
     88     SORT (GROUP BY)
  14841       HASH JOIN
  20000         TABLE ACCESS   GOAL: ANALYZED (FULL) OF 'TX_HIST'
  24680         TABLE ACCESS   GOAL: ANALYZED (FULL) OF 'TX'
```

There is a fairly subtle difference between "row source operation" and "execution plan" information in the profiled output. The row source operation shows the order that rows were fetched in during the actual run-time execution of the query. On the other hand, the execution plan shows the plan that was generated at TKPROF execution time based on the available information. Usually, you would expect them to match. However, if database objects or other data relevant to the plan generation change between query execution and TKPROF execution, then the row source operation and execution plan may be different. The following example of TKPROF output shows a situation where the row source operation shows INDEX UNIQUE SCAN while the execution plan shows a full table scan:

```
select count(*) from  my_objects where object_id=234


ROWS      ROW SOURCE OPERATION
-------   -------------------------------------------------------
      1   SORT AGGREGATE
      1     INDEX UNIQUE SCAN (object id 7146)


ROWS      EXECUTION PLAN
-------   -------------------------------------------------------
      0   SELECT STATEMENT    GOAL: CHOOSE
      1     SORT (AGGREGATE)
      1       TABLE ACCESS   GOAL: ANALYZED (FULL) OF 'MY_OBJECTS'
```

In this example, the statement was executed using a primary key during the trace session. The primary key was later dropped. TKPROF was executed after the drop, causing the execution plan to generate an inaccurate plan based on the information that was available at the time TKPROF was run. The row source operation shows actual processing at execution time.

Trace Filename Location

In order to run TKPROF on a trace file, the trace file for a session needs to be located on the database server. You can determine the filename in advance using SQL, as it's based on the value of the user_dump_dest parameter, the Oracle System ID (SID) value from V$INSTANCE, and the dedicated server process ID from V$PROCESS. The following SQL shows an example for a UNIX Oracle SID called ORAD1:

```
select udd.value||'/'||i.instance_name||'_ora_'||p.spid||'.trc'
trace_file
from
(select value from v$parameter where name='user_dump_dest') udd,
(select instance_name from v$instance) i,
v$process p, v$session s
where p.addr = s.paddr
and s.audsid = (select userenv('sessionid') from dual);


TRACE_FILE
-------------------------------------------------------
/u01/app/oracle/admin/ORAD1/udump/ORAD1_ora_29582.trc
```

The following SELECT list can be used to show the location of the trace file for a dedicated server session on Microsoft Windows 2000:

```
select udd.value||'\Ora'||lpad(p.spid,5,'0')||'.trc' trace_file
.
.
.


TRACE_FILE
---------------------------------------------
c:\apps\ora901\admin\prod1\udump\Ora01536.trc
```

If you don't specify an explicit value for user_dump_dest in the init.ora file, the directory as selected from V$PARAMETER contains the character ? in place of the $ORACLE_HOME value.

TKPROF and Shared Server Configurations

The use of TKPROF on shared server configurations (covered in Chapter 3) presents problems because the trace for a particular session can be spread across several different trace files, depending on which shared server executed the SQL. Also, each trace file can contain a trace for several different sessions. The AGGREGATE=NO command-line option can be used to ensure that TKPROF keeps statistics separate for different users executing the same SQL.

The best solution is to ensure that during TKPROF profiling all sessions use dedicated servers to guarantee a unique trace file for each session. This can be enforced by using the (SERVER=DEDICATED) option in the CONNECT_DATA section of the connect alias, as follows:

```
prod1.dbcool.com =
  (DESCRIPTION =
    (ADDRESS_LIST =
      (ADDRESS = (PROTOCOL = TCP)(HOST = srv1.dbcool.com)(PORT = 1521))
    )
    (CONNECT_DATA = (service_name=prod1.dbcool.com)(SERVER = DEDICATED))
  )
```

Running TKPROF from the Client

TKPROF is an essential tool that developers should use throughout the development cycle, and it's present in all Oracle server software installations. In order to encourage developers to use it as much as possible, it needs to be easily accessible and easy to use. Accessibility presents a potential problem because TKPROF needs to run on the database server using trace files from the server user_dump_dest directory. For two security reasons, I prefer not give access to developers on the database server machine. The first reason is that developers running the UNIX ps command have the ability to see passwords that are used to connect to command-line utilities such as SQL*Plus and middleware running on the server. In the case of SQL*Plus, passwords can be hidden by using the /nolog command-line option, but it's difficult to enforce. The second reason is that commands are available to fetch strings out of files, such as the UNIX strings command. If a developer runs this on the SYSTEM tablespace datafile on the server, then it's possible to view passwords in database links held in the SYS.LINK$ table. Usability is also an issue because TKPROF is a command-line tool. As such, it's easy to forget the available options, and you need to identify the trace file name and user_dump_dest before you run it. In any case, non-DBA UNIX accounts don't have the privilege to view the file contents by default.

These drawbacks are likely to prevent the kind of developer buy-in that TKPROF needs in order to become an integral part of the development cycle. To repeat the mantra, it's easy to state that a continual emphasis on performance is required during the development cycle. However, making it happen requires work. If the required tools are not freely available and easy to use, then it won't happen.

To reconcile these conflicting requirements, you can download and install a package DBCOOL_TKPROF from this book's companion Web site. The purpose of DBCOOL_TKPROF is to initiate TKPROF on the server from PL/SQL on any client machine with network access to the database server. For example, the procedures can be called from SQL*Plus or DbCool.

After you've enabled tracing for your session using ALTER SESSION SET SQL_TRACE TRUE or one of the other options discussed in Chapter 28, then the Oracle trace

file should be created on the server. You can use the CHECK_TRACE_FILE_
EXISTS procedure to check this as follows before running the TKPROF procedure to
generate the trace profile output:

```
begin dbcool_tkprof.check_trace_file_exists; end;
/
```

If the trace file doesn't exist, then an exception is raised. You can check the trace filename that the DBCOOL_TKPROF package attempts to open using the GET_TRACE_
FILE_NAME function as follows:

```
select dbcool_tkprof.get_trace_file_name from dual;

GET_TRACE_FILE_NAME
--------------------------------------------------------
/u01/app/oracle/admin/ORAD1/udump/ORAD1_ora_2673.trc
```

After the trace file has been checked to ensure that it exists, the following PL/SQL
block runs TKPROF on the server for the current session and displays the contents of
the profiled trace file using DBMS_OUTPUT.PUT_LINE:

```
set serverout on
declare
r integer;
l_line varchar2(512);
l_end varchar2(512);
begin
   dbms_output.enable(1000000);
   r:=dbcool_tkprof.tkprof; -- run tkprof and create a .prf file

   -- fetch lines from the .prf file on the server until done
   while true loop
      dbcool_tkprof.get_next_line(l_line,l_end); -- fetch next line
      exit when l_end=-1; -- no more lines
      dbms_output.put_line(l_end||':'||l_line);
   end loop;
end;
/
```

The Buffer Cache

Oracle maintains a cache of the most recently used (MRU) data blocks requested by
SQL statements. This cache, referred to as the *database buffer cache*, is held in the System
Global Area (SGA). Given that reading cache data from memory is orders of magnitude faster than physical file reads, understanding the behavior of the cache with
respect to individual statements is likely to benefit SQL performance by ensuring that
the most frequently accessed blocks remain in the cache for the longest time.

In previous versions of Oracle, this buffer cache size was fixed at database startup time using the DB_BLOCK_BUFFERS setting (in blocks), which is specified in the init.ora file. In Oracle9i, this static technique is not recommended and the DB_BLOCK_BUFFERS parameter is deprecated. In Oracle9i, the preferred approach is to use the SGA_MAX_SIZE parameter to specify the maximum SGA size and use the dynamic DB_CACHE_SIZE setting to control the size of the buffer cache for the database default block size. When used with a server parameter file (covered in Chapter 2) rather than an init.ora file, the value can be modified permanently while the database is up, which is limited by SGA_MAX_SIZE. Oracle9i supports the use of different block sizes at tablespace creation time, and each block size requires its own cache. These additional caches must be specified using the following init.ora parameters:

- db_2k_cache_size
- db_4k_cache_size
- db_8k_cache_size
- db_16k_cache_size
- db_32k_cache_size

Viewing the Buffer Cache Contents

The V$BH view can be used to display the contents of the buffer cache at any point in time. The following SQL statements show objects using most cache blocks, including blocks from the data dictionary, and cached blocks for a single table and its index:

```
REM whole cache...
select name,objd,cnt blocks from
(select objd,count(*) cnt from v$bh group by objd) cnt,
(select object_id,owner||'.'||object_name||' ('||object_type||')' name
from dba_objects) obj
where cnt.objd = obj.object_id (+)
union select 'total blocks',to_number(null),count(*) from v$bh
order by 3 desc;


NAME                                            OBJD    BLOCKS
----------------------------------------------- ------- --------
total blocks                                             20000
O.TT_FX_OTC (TABLE)                             28096    7750
SYSTEM.MY_OBJECTS (TABLE)                       28137    4996
SYS.SOURCE$ (TABLE)                                64    3210
SYS.I_SOURCE1 (INDEX)                             109    1339


REM one table and index...
select name,objd,cnt from
   (select objd,count(*) cnt from v$bh group by objd) cnt,
   (select object_id,owner||'.'||object_name||' ('||object_type||')' name
from dba_objects
```

```
      where object_name in ('MY_OBJECTS','PK_MY_OBJECTS')) obj
   where cnt.objd = obj.object_id
   order by cnt;


   NAME                                OBJD   CNT
   ------------------------------      ------ -----
   SYSTEM.PK_MY_OBJECTS (INDEX)        28138    11
   SYSTEM.MY_OBJECTS (TABLE)           28137  4985
```

Many other reports are possible. For example, V$BH contains a STATUS column to indicate how many blocks are free and in use. For the serious DBA or developer, the X$BH view contains information that can be used to identify which cache a block resides in and determine whether multiple buffer pools are in use and whether a block is in the least recently used (LRU) list.

The Buffer Cache Hit Ratio

The cache hit ratio is an often-used Oracle performance metric, derived from other statistics, that shows the percentage of Oracle data block requests that are satisfied from Oracle's buffer cache compared to those that require a physical read from Oracle's datafiles. Keep in mind that physical read requests are requests made to the operating system by Oracle. If the operating system keeps its own file system cache, like Sun Solaris, for example, or your disk storage uses a controller cache, the Oracle physical read may not require a genuine physical read. As a result, identical SQL statements that perform the same number of Oracle physical reads may differ in elapsed time. If you run two of these statements close together, the second is more likely to benefit from file system or disk controller caching.

The cache hit ratio value can be measured systemwide and for specific sessions using statistics in V$SYSSTAT and V$SESSTAT. It can also be derived for queries in the shared SQL cache, V$SQLAREA, by using the DISK_READS and BUFFER_GETS columns. The classical Oracle cache hit ratio, which is based on buffer cache statistics, is given by the following:

```
hit ratio = 1-[physical reads/(db block gets+consistent gets)]
```

The following SQL presents the value as a percentage for the whole system since startup:

```
select sum(decode(name,'db block gets',value,0))    "db block gets",
       sum(decode(name,'consistent gets',value,0)) "consistent gets",
       sum(decode(name,'physical reads',value,0))  "physical reads",
       round(
          100*(1 -(sum(decode(name,'physical reads',value,0)))/
                 ((sum(decode(name,'db block gets',value,0)))+
                  sum(decode(name,'consistent gets',value,0)))))) "hit %"
```

Due to the possibility of direct path reads that bypass the buffer cache in Oracle8i and later (for example, those due to reads of CLOB columns), this figure isn't completely accurate in all cases. The situation is further complicated by the possibility of multiple buffer caches. The following SQL shows the hit ratio expressed as a percentage for all connected user sessions:

```
select s.sid,se.username,
       sum(decode(n.name,'db block gets',value,0))   "db block gets",
       sum(decode(n.name,'consistent gets',value,0)) "consistent gets",
       sum(decode(n.name,'physical reads',value,0))   "physical reads",
       round(
         100*(1-(sum(decode(n.name,'physical reads',value,0))))/
               ((sum(decode(n.name,'db block gets',value,0)))+
                 sum(decode(n.name,'consistent gets',value,0))))) "hit %"
from v$sesstat s,v$statname n,v$session se
where s.statistic# = n.statistic#
and   s.sid = se.sid
and   n.name in ('physical reads','db block gets','consistent gets')
and   s.value > 0
and   se.username is not null
group by s.sid,se.username
order by 6 desc;
```

Although the cache hit ratio is interesting, I rarely find that it's actually useful for tuning purposes. Addressing tuning issues requires statistics for individual statements rather than session or instance cache ratios. In particular, absolute values of statistics and wait information times are much more useful.

The LRU Algorithm and Default Cache Behavior

Oracle uses an LRU algorithm to try keeping the most frequently used blocks in the buffer cache. If a block is not available in the cache, a more expensive physical disk read is required. It's useful to look into the LRU algorithm more closely because correct configuration of the cache and an understanding of the available options can significantly improve performance. The cache can be viewed logically as a list containing a fixed number of blocks with an MRU end and an LRU end.

During a sequential read operation, which reads a single block from the cache, the block is placed at the MRU end of the list. When a block is added, the existing blocks are shifted toward the other LRU end, where the LRU block is removed from the cache. As a result, frequently accessed blocks tend to shift toward the MRU end and stay in the cache. Rarely used blocks tend to age out of the cache.

The LRU Algorithm and Table Scan Cache Behavior

By default, Oracle treats blocks fetched as a result of a full table scan in a different way from the default behavior just explained. It's important to understand why and how Oracle does this. Consider a buffer cache containing 10,000 blocks and a table containing 20,000 blocks. According to the normal caching rules, any SQL on that table requiring a full table scan would flush all those 10,000 blocks from the cache, including those that are frequently used or hot. This would have a disastrous effect on performance because future reads of those hot blocks will require physical I/O.

Oracle does two things to avoid scans from flushing the buffer cache completely. The first is that rows from a scan are placed on the LRU end of the cache. This has no use in our example because 20,000 data blocks will flush 10,000 cache blocks no matter which end of the cache is used. Oracle imposes an additional restriction that states that the number of blocks placed on the LRU end during a scan is limited to the value of the init.ora parameter DB_BLOCK_MULTI_READ_COUNT. This parameter typically has a value from 8 to 32. As a result, the excess flushing of the cache that might result from scans is avoided. The downside is that scans typically need to perform physical I/O on each execution, which harms performance. For some types of scanned data, such as small lookup tables, it would be advantageous to try keeping their blocks in the cache for as long as possible. Oracle provides several options for overriding the default behavior of block caching to enable fine-grained control of the lifetime of blocks in the cache.

Controlling the Cache

Although table scans don't affect the buffer cache unduly because their impact is limited by DB_BLOCK_MULTI_READ_COUNT, segments accessed using large or unbounded index range scans can flush out hot blocks from the cache. In this case, the multiple buffer pools feature can be enabled to more closely control the lifetime of blocks in the cache through the creation of two additional pools: the KEEP and RECYCLE pool. These can exist in addition to the default cache. Both KEEP and RECYCLE need to be specified in blocks in the init.ora file at database startup in a way that's Oracle version dependent:

```
# 8i parameters
db_block_buffers = 20000      # deprecated in 9i
buffer_pool_keep=3000         # deprecated in 9i
buffer_pool_recycle=1500      # deprecated in 9i
db_block_lru_latches=6        # obsolete in 9i


# 9i parameters for multiple buffer pools
db_cache_size=200971520       # bytes
db_keep_cache_size=1000       # blocks
db_recycle_cache_size=2000    # blocks
```

The use of the RECYCLE buffer cache means that blocks resulting from large index range scans can be assigned to a separate pool, so they don't affect hot blocks in the default cache. Alternatively, hot blocks can be moved to the KEEP cache, so they remain unaffected by large flush operations on the default cache. The allocation of segment blocks to a specific buffer cache is controlled by the segment STORAGE clause either at creation time or through the ALTER command. The following is an example of a storage clause that will cache a segment's blocks to the RECYCLE pool:

```
storage (initial 10k buffer_pool recycle)
```

The number of blocks in each pool can be determined using this SQL:

```
select id,name,buffers from v$buffer_pool;

ID   NAME       BUFFERS
---- --------  ---------
   1 KEEP           501
   2 RECYCLE        501
   3 DEFAULT       2505
```

The lifetime of blocks in the cache can also be influenced using the CACHE option for tables and large object (LOB) columns. When you use the ALTER TABLE *tablename* CACHE option, blocks fetched as a result of a table scan are placed on the MRU end of the cache rather than the LRU end. The CACHE option has no effect on blocks in the KEEP pool.

LOB columns present special problems due to their size. For example, a single LOB column of several hundred megabytes read into the buffer cache could flush out many existing hot blocks. As a result, CACHE and NOCACHE can be provided at the column level for LOB columns. By default, LOBs are created using NOCACHE. When NOCACHE is used, requests for LOB column out-of-line blocks are read directly from the database files using direct path reads, thus passing the buffer cache to avoid flushing it. If most LOBs are actually of a fairly small size that is comparable to regular columns, then the CACHE option can be enabled as follows to ensure that the LOB column contents are cached:

```
alter table trade_q modify lob (message_data) ( cache );
```

This option must be used with great care because a fetch of an LOB column, unlike a table scan, can flush the whole buffer cache. This is because LOBs are loaded onto the MRU end of the cache without the DB_BLOCK_MULTI_READ_COUNT block limit imposed on scans.

Full Table Scans and the High Watermark (HWM)

In a full table scan operation, all blocks in the table are read up to the table high watermark (HWM). The HWM marks the last block in the table that has ever had data written to it. Even if all rows in the table have been deleted, those empty blocks will still be processed up to the HWM during a scan. As a result, table scans can result in higher physical I/O requirements than those required based on the actual data available. The TRUNCATE command can be used to reset the HWM back to the start of the table. If this is not possible, Chapter 13 contains instructions on how to rebuild a table to reduce the HWM while maintaining existing data. The following SQL can be used to show allocated and empty (that is, never used) blocks in the table, following an ANALYZE command:

```
select blocks,empty_blocks from dba_tables where
table_name='MY_OBJECTS';
```

The DBMS_SPACE.UNUSED_SPACE procedure can be used to return the HWM for a segment into the parameters LAST_USED_EXTENT_FILE_ID, LAST_USED_EXTENT_BLOCK_ID, and LAST_USED_BLOCK.

Detecting Full Table Scans

When the optimizer decides that there is no appropriate index available to execute a SQL statement to meet the optimizer goal, Oracle performs a full table scan to execute the statement. Typically, table scans involve a lot of physical I/O. Physical I/O is the primary resource that needs to be minimized, or parallelized, if you want your SQL to run faster. For some types of applications, such as data warehouses, table scans take place by design. For index-driven applications, such as Online Transaction Processing (OLTP) applications, table scans should be avoided for best performance. Often, if they do take place, it wasn't intended. During the application development stage of the life-cycle, query execution plans from TKPROF and the EXPLAIN PLAN command can be used to show DML that performs a full table scan. The string TABLE ACCESS (FULL) identifies such queries. DbCool EXPLAIN PLAN output displays full table scans with a red exclamation mark to draw attention to them.

On a running production system, the first step to take when users report a performance problem is to run a few queries on the V$SESSION_WAIT view a few seconds apart to identify any sessions that are waiting for the event "db file scattered read." Those sessions are waiting for data accessed by a multiblock read associated with a full table scan. Although it's not guaranteed that a session performing a scan will experience a wait for a scattered read, it's almost certain, given that scans usually perform a lot of physical I/O. The full process of identifying a scan and the SQL causing it is as follows:

1. Detect sessions from V$SESSION_WAIT waiting on event "db file scattered read."

2. Find the SQL executing in the waiting session using SQL_ADDRESS and SQL_HASH_VALUE columns.

3. Run EXPLAIN PLAN on the SQL to see the query plan and identify the scan.

The following describes the various SQL and information that's required to perform the process. The following SQL returns sessions waiting on a "db file scattered read" event and presents the event parameters in a user-friendly format:

```
select /*+ RULE */ s.username,
decode(p1text,NULL,NULL,p1text||'='||p1)||' '||
decode(p2text,NULL,NULL,p2text||'='||p2)||' '||
decode(p3text,NULL,NULL,p3text||'='||p3) params,
sql_address,sql_hash_value
from v$session_wait w,v$session s,v$process p,v$sqlarea
sq,audit_actions a
where w.sid = s.sid
and s.command = a.action
```

```
and sq.address =s.sql_address and sq.hash_value = s.sql_hash_value
and S.PADDR = P.ADDR (+)
and s.audsid <> userenv('SESSIONID')
and event= 'db file scattered read';


REM.. here's one...
USERNAME PARAMS                                  SQL_ADDRESS SQL_HASH_VALUE
-------- ------------------------------          ----------- --------------
SYSTEM   file#=27 block#=39596 blocks=8 8C84760C              2855390177
```

In order for the output to fit the screen, several other useful columns such as S.PRO-GRAM (program running), P.SPID (server process ID), and SQ.EXECUTIONS (total execution count for the SQL) are not shown in the SELECT list.

The values in the PARAMS column contain a lot of useful information. The BLOCKS value in PARAMS shows the number of database blocks read during the scattered read operation. This equals the DB_BLOCK_MULTI_READ_COUNT init.ora parameter. Oracle uses this parameter as part of the process to determine when to use a full table scan in a plan when other options are available. Larger values are more likely to bias the plan toward performing a scan because the more blocks read during the multiblock read operation, the more efficient the operation. The other event parameters in the PARAMS column display enough information at this stage to identify the object that is being scanned, because the FILE# and BLOCK# parameters identify a database file and block. These values can be transformed to show the scanned object using the following SQL based on the event parameters:

```
select owner||'.'||segment_name segment,segment_type
type,tablespace_name
from dba_extents where
(file_id=27 and 39596 between block_id and (block_id + blocks -1));


SEGMENT      TYPE    TABLESPACE_NAME
------------ ------- -----------------
APP.FX_HIST  TABLE   FX_TABLES
```

Given the address and hash value for the SQL executed by the session at the time of the wait, which was taken from the ADDRESS and HASH_VALUE column in V$SQLAREA, the following SQL can be used to generate the full text of the SQL statement from the Oracle dictionary:

```
select sql_text
from v$sqltext_with_newlines where address='8C84760C' and
hash_value+0=2855390177
order by piece;


SQL_TEXT
----------------------------------------------------------------
select count(*) from app.fx_hist where hist_state='OPEN';
```

The addition of +0 onto HASH_VALUE is deliberate and prevents this SQL from causing a server session spin in some versions of Oracle8i. The EXPLAIN PLAN for the statement can be generated by running something like the following:

```
explain plan set statement_id='s519_1' for
select count(*) from app.fx_hist where hist_state='OPEN'
```

Finally, the plan can be displayed using the following:

```
select lpad(' ', 2*level)||operation||decode(id,0,'cost =
'||position) op,
  options,object_name
from plan_table
where statement_id='s519_1'
connect by prior id = parent_id start with id = 0
order by id;
```

Performing this sequence of operations is a chore, although the results are invaluable. This type of manual operation is tailor-made for a graphical user interface (GUI) application. DbCool provides features that enable you to perform these steps much more easily by using just a few key clicks:

1. Choose Session Waits Detector from the Monitoring menu. This polls V$SESSION_WAIT on a user-selected time interval and stores a full history of each nonidle wait (not just scattered reads) into the grid.

2. When you see a wait you are interested in, press the Stop Autorefresh (square) button on the toolbar.

3. Click the grid row you are interested in.

4. Right-click the grid cell containing the file and block, and choose Show Wait Object Name to see the scanned object. This is optional.

5. Right-click the grid row, choose Grid SQL . . . , and then choose Send Grid Row to Explain Plan to pop up an Explain Plan form to show the SQL that generated the wait.

6. In the Explain Plan form, generate the plan using the Generate Plan button on the toolbar. If the user who executed the SQL, as shown in the wait event, doesn't match your Oracle logon, choose the user who ran the SQL by using the popup list.

If you want to see plans for more than one grid row, change the grid selection mode to List, select multiple grid rows, and choose Send Grid Row to Explain Plan. This creates one Explain Plan form for each grid row selected.

SQL Tuning Goals

Even before you begin tuning, you need to determine the goals for your SQL performance. Oracle provides two fundamentally different approaches to the generation of an execution plan for SQL: cost based and rule based. The cost-based approach uses

Table 9.7 Oracle SQL Optimizer Modes

NAME	PURPOSE
CHOOSE	Choose between rule- and cost-based optimization. If statistics exist for *any* table in the SQL, use cost-based optimization with a goal to minimize total resource consumption. Otherwise, use the rule-based optimizer.
ALL_ROWS	Minimize the total resource consumption using the cost-based optimizer.
FIRST_ROWS(*n*)	Minimize the time to return first *n* rows using the cost-based optimizer.
RULE	Ignore statistics and choose the execution plan according to a set of rules.

table and column statistics that need to be explicitly generated and information based on actual sizes of objects stored in the Oracle dictionary. If the available statistics don't match the actual data, then a nonoptimal plan can be generated. Chapter 10 provides details of the required data, how to collect it, and how often to collect it. Table 9.7 provides a summarized list of the available optimizer modes. To specify the optimizer mode, do the following:

- Use OPTIMIZER_MODE in init.ora to set it databasewide.
- Use ALTER SESSION SET OPTIMIZER_MODE mode at the session level.
- Use /*+ ALL ROWS */, /*+ FIRST_ROWS */, /*+ CHOOSE */, /*+ RULE */ HINTs in SQL.

Note that the ALTER SESSION SET OPTIMIZER MODE statement does not affect SQL within PL/SQL blocks. To modify the optimizer mode for that SQL, you need to use a HINT.

The difference between CHOOSE and FIRST_ROWS or ALL_ROWS is quite subtle and is best seen with an example that demonstrates many of the subtleties of the optimizer at one time. This requires an example table with a primary key that contains a few thousand blocks as follows:

```
create table my_objects tablespace tools pctfree 99 pctused 1
  as select * from all_objects where rownum <=5000;

alter table my_objects add constraint pk_my_objects
  primary key(object_id);


REM sizes...
select segment_name,segment_type, blocks from dba_segments
where segment_name like '%MY_OBJECTS';
```

```
SEGMENT_NAME     SEGMENT_TYPE     BLOCKS
--------------   --------------   --------
MY_OBJECTS       TABLE               5120
PK_MY_OBJECTS    INDEX                 24
```

Consider how the SQL SELECT COUNT(*) FROM MY_OBJECTS runs under each of the optimizer modes. This is shown in Table 9.8.

Based on the presence of the primary key, it seems reasonable that the fastest way for Oracle to return the results for this query is to count the entries in the index rather than in the table by using an optimization known as an index FAST FULL SCAN. The index is much smaller than the table, containing far fewer blocks, so reading the index causes less logical and physical I/O, resulting in a shorter elapsed execution time. In the example, only ALL_ROWS and FIRST_ROWS use FAST FULL SCAN.

CHOOSE fails to use the primary key index because the table hasn't been analyzed yet, so no statistics exist. This causes CHOOSE to fall back to the rule-based optimizer. The rule-based optimizer is provided for historic reasons only and generally shouldn't be used. RULE isn't aware of many of the optimizations available in newer Oracle versions, such as a FAST FULL SCAN, which appeared in Oracle8.

Therefore, both CHOOSE and RULE execute using a full table scan. Even though the table hasn't been analyzed, both ALL_ROWS and FIRST_ROWS can take advantage of information other than analyzed statistics in order to use the cost-based optimizer. As a result, they both perform a much more efficient FAST FULL SCAN of the index.

You need to be aware of the OPTIMIZER_FEATURES_ENABLE init.ora setting that lets you change the behavior of the Oracle optimizer based on an Oracle release number. If you've just performed an upgrade, then leaving this value at its previous setting can mean that newer optimizer features are not available. On the other hand, increasing the value can cause query behavior to change if new optimizer features are incorporated into existing DML and do not necessarily have the best results.

Generating Execution Plans

Before executing a DML statement, Oracle generates a query execution plan that determines how a SQL statement will execute. The plan-generation process uses various information including the following:

Table 9.8 Query Plans Using Different Optimizer Modes

NAME	PLAN USED	ELAPSED (SECONDS)
CHOOSE	FULL TABLE SCAN	3.8
ALL_ROWS	FAST FULL SCAN of index PK_MY_OBJECTS	0.4
FIRST_ROWS	FAST FULL SCAN of index PK_MY_OBJECTS	0.4
RULE	FULL TABLE SCAN	3.8

- The generated statistics
- The object sizes
- The presence of indexes
- The optimizer mode
- The presence of HINTs
- The existence of a stored outline

The execution plan typically consists of several steps. Each step in the plan physically fetches blocks from the datafiles or buffer cache and then processes the table rows or index data in each block in preparation for the next step. The final stage is the creation of the result set. It's helpful to think of an execution plan in terms of a hierarchy, or tree, where the leaf nodes perform physical data access, the intermediate nodes process the physical data, and the raw data eventually passes up to the root node, which represents the result set presented to the user.

Oracle provides the EXPLAIN PLAN command to write the execution plan information for a SQL statement into a table, which can then be queried to produce a hierarchical view of the execution order of the statement. It's important to note that the SQL is *not* executed by EXPLAIN PLAN. As a result, there's always an uncertainty, however small, that the plan generated by EXPLAIN PLAN is not the same as the plan that would actually be used when the SQL runs. The actual plan used to execute SQL can be found in the V$SQL_PLAN view, which is new in Oracle9i.

EXPLAIN PLAN requires the existence of a table named PLAN_TABLE. This can be created using the Oracle utlxplan.sql script, which is part of the server software distribution. EXPLAIN PLAN works best when all users share the same plan table. To share a single table systemwide, the PLAN_TABLE can be created as SYSTEM, for example. The following commands enable all users to access the table using the unqualified name PLAN_TABLE:

```
create public synonym plan_table for plan_table;

grant all on plan_table to public;
```

If a shared plan table is in use, it's essential that plans written to the plan table are identified by a unique STATEMENT_ID so that subsequent queries to fetch the plan don't accidentally fetch rows for other sessions or previous queries for the same session. The following is an example of a plan-generation statement that writes information to PLAN_TABLE using a statement ID of s591_1, followed by a query that fetches the generated plan in an indented format to give the appearance of a tree:

```
explain plan set statement_id='s519_1' for
select count(*) from app.fx_hist where hist_state='OPEN';

REM select the plan, present as a tree...
select lpad(' ',2*level)||operation||decode(id,0,' cost = '||position)
op,
  options,object_name
from plan_table
```

```
where statement_id='s519_1'
connect by prior id = parent_id start with id = 0
order by id;
```

The PLAN_TABLE actually contains many more columns containing information relevant to the plan than the ones shown in this query. The output is constrained by the need to display in a text window. As a result, information is lost on presentation. For plans involving parallel execution or more complex joins, this method of display is not adequate for presenting the plan information. The following shows a plan generated and queried using the technique just outlined:

```
OP                              OPTIONS           OBJECT_NAME
------------------------------  ---------------   ---------------
   SELECT STATEMENT cost = 21444
      FILTER
        NESTED LOOPS
           INDEX                FAST FULL SCAN    ML_I1_TT_FX_OTC
           TABLE ACCESS         BY INDEX ROWID    TT_FX_OTC
              INDEX             UNIQUE SCAN        FX_OTC_PK
        FILTER
           TABLE ACCESS         BY INDEX ROWID    DT_VALUES
              INDEX             RANGE SCAN         DT_VALUES_UK
```

Although this output is useful, lots of available information is missing, such as the cost associated with each stage of processing, the object owner, and the order of execution steps. In addition, the effort required to get the output to fit the page width in SQL*Plus is considerable and varies depending on the SQL. DbCool can display an execution plan with all the missing information as well as the extra information generated for parallel execution. Figure 9.2 shows the same plan in DbCool's Explain Plan form.

The DbCool version includes all the available information in the PLAN_TABLE. The plan can be printed and stepped through in the order of statement execution. Execution order is displayed using the # character followed by a number. Different icons are used to display table and index access operations for easy visual assimilation. Scans, such as full table scans and fast full scans of indexes, are shown with a red exclamation mark.

The status bar contains a statement ID that is automatically generated for each plan. The toolbar also enables the optimizer mode to be changed to any of CHOOSE, RULE, ALL_ROWS, and FIRST_ROWS prior to regenerating the plan. The form maintains a history of the last 50 statements and their plans, so you can review a previous statement and its plan without regenerating the plan using options on the View menu. If you're serious about Oracle SQL tuning, then you need a tool that presents all of the relevant information. DbCool has the added advantage of being free. Just to recap, EXPLAIN PLAN doesn't execute the SQL. For that reason, the number of rows fetched at each stage, as provided by TKPROF, can't be shown.

The SQL*Plus AUTOTRACE facility can be used to automate the plan-generation process in SQL*Plus by generating a plan automatically after the execution of each statement. This requires an existing PLAN_TABLE, which is like that required for a

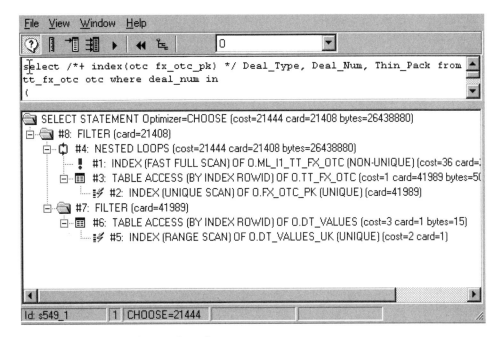

Figure 9.2 A query plan in DbCool.

manual EXPLAIN PLAN. For non-SYSTEM users, AUTOTRACE requires the PLUS-TRACE role. Here's an example:

```
SQL> set autotrace on explain
SQL> select count(*) from my_objects;

  COUNT(*)
----------
      5000


Execution Plan
----------------------------------------------------------
   0      SELECT STATEMENT Optimizer=CHOOSE
   1    0   SORT (AGGREGATE)
   2    1     TABLE ACCESS (FULL) OF 'MY_OBJECTS'
```

Oracle9*i* provides a significant new feature compared to previous releases of Oracle through the V$SQL_PLAN view. This view provides the plan that was actually used to execute a SQL statement present in the shared SQL area, given by the V$SQL view. Other columns in the table have a similar meaning to those in the PLAN_TABLE, with three additional columns that indicate the run-time resources that were used:

```
CPU_COST        NUMBER
IO_COST         NUMBER
TEMP_SPACE      NUMBER
```

The following SQL shows how to generate the execution plan from V$SQL_PLAN for a SQL statement currently in the shared SQL area: V$SQL. Each SQL statement in the shared SQL area is uniquely identified by values in the ADDRESS, HASH_VALUE, and CHILD_NUMBER columns, and these values must be specified in the query against V$SQL, as shown in the following SQL:

```
select lpad(' ',2*level)||operation||decode(id,0,' cost =
'||position) op,
  options,object_name
from v$sql_plan
where address='address'
and    hash_value=hash_value
and    child_number=child_number
connect by prior id = parent_id start with id = 0
order by id;
```

Oracle9*i* Release 2 extends the information available for tuning SQL by significantly extending the level of available performance-related information. The information in presented in V$SQL_PLAN and PLAN_TABLE execution plans is enhanced through two additional columns that show access and filter predicates within the each plan for steps that perform those operations:

```
ACCESS_PREDICATES   VARCHAR2(4000)
FILTER_PREDICATES   VARCHAR2(4000)
```

In order to match this additional predicate information with the operation to which it relates in the SQL statement execution plan you need a tool that can present it, such as DbCool. The following SQL statement results in an execution plan that includes both an access predicate and a filter predicate, but EXPLAIN PLAN output in SQL*Plus doesn't display the access and filter predicates in the execution plan:

```
select count(*) from my_objects where object_id=1
having count(*) > 1;

Execution Plan
----------------------------------------------------------
    0       SELECT STATEMENT Optimizer=CHOOSE
    1   0     FILTER
    2   1       SORT (AGGREGATE)
    3   2         INDEX (UNIQUE SCAN) OF 'PK_MY_OBJECTS' (UNIQUE)
```

In the previous SQL query, the access predicate "MY_OBJECTS". "OBJECT_ID"=1 is associated with the INDEX (UNIQUE SCAN) operation in the execution plan, and the filter predicate COUNT(*)>1 is associated with the FILTER operation. This information is available from the PLAN_TABLE and V$SQL_PLAN.

Further enhanced tuning information available in Oracle9*i* Release 2 includes detailed statistics on physical and logical I/O *at each stage of the execution plan*, through the view V$SQL_PLAN_STATISTICS. For this information to be made available, the dynamic STATISTICS_LEVEL database parameter must be set at either the system level, or at the session level as follows:

```
alter system set statistics_level=all;
```

Finally, Oracle9*i* Release 2 provides I/O statistics for individual objects. This information is made available through a set of "Top Objects" charts in OEM, and also through the V$SEGMENT_STATISTICS view, as shown in the following query:

```
select statistic_name,value
from v$segment_statistics
where object_name='MY_OBJECTS' and value>0
order by 2 desc;


STATISTIC_NAME              VALUE
----------------------     -------
logical reads               6720
physical writes             5160
physical reads              5000
physical writes direct      5000
db block changes             352
```

Using Parallel Operations

Recall that the performance goal of our SQL is to reduce elapsed execution time. In certain circumstances, table scans are unavoidable or even desirable for data-warehouse—type applications. For example, index creation often requires a full table scan in order to identify all the data to the index. Consider a scan that requires 10 seconds of CPU resource to complete on a single CPU. On a server with two (or more) CPUs, the total available CPU resource is wasted during the execution on a single CPU.

Using an Oracle feature known as *parallel query*, the scan can be split into two processes that each scan half of the data concurrently, one per CPU. In the best case, the 10-second CPU load, split concurrently across two processes, each on a single CPU, means the scan can complete in 5 seconds. The original server session in this case is referred to as the *query coordinator*, and the two sessions that perform the scan are referred to as *parallel query slave processes*. The slaves pipe results to the query coordinator, which then processes them by serializing them into a single stream to form a result set to return to the client.

When used carefully, parallel query facilities can demonstrate significant reductions in elapsed time by utilizing the maximum available CPU and disk I/O resource on a multi-CPU server or RAC configuration. In order for Oracle to generate a plan for a parallel operation, the operation must involve a table scan for a SELECT statement, and the optimizer needs to be explicitly directed to use parallelism with a given number of parallel streams. The parallel operations that are supported are shown in Table 9.9.

Table 9.9 Parallel Operations

TYPE	ENABLED USING	EXAMPLE USAGE
Query	Parallel attribute on table or HINT	Any table scan
DLL	PARALLEL clause	CREATE TABLE AS SELECT CREATE INDEX ALTER INDEX REBUILD ALTER TABLE MOVE (partitioned table)
DML	ALTER SESSION ENABLE PARALLEL DML	insert into trades_hist select * from trades;

The maximum and minimum numbers of parallel servers per instance are specified by the PARALLEL_MAX_SERVERS and PARALLEL_MIN_SERVERS parameters in the init.ora file. It's important to emphasize that the number of parallel servers is available per instance, not per query. So although it's possible to specify that all appropriate operations on a given table or index are to be run in parallel by default, it's probably better to use HINTs or stored outlines (which are covered later) to control parallelism on a statement-by-statement basis.

If the optimizer has determined that a query should run in parallel, but at execution time there are insufficient resources available to meet the desired parallel degree, then the query will run in serial mode by default. This silent serialization of execution could cause the operation to take much longer than required. For example, a scan intended to run on eight CPUs could take eight times as long when serialized on a single CPU.

The PARALLEL_MIN_PERCENT init.ora parameter can be used to turn off this default serialization and abort the SQL instead. If PARALLEL_MIN_PERCENT is set and the required minimum resources aren't available at execution time, then an ORA-12827 message is returned to the client application. The following options set a default parallelism on a table or index and correspond to the DEGREE column in DBA_TABLES and DBA_INDEXES, respectively:

```
alter index pk_my_objects parallel 2;
alter table my_objects default parallel 2;
```

You can check to see that parallel query is being used for the queries and DML statements in the current session by using the following SQL:

```
select * from v$pq_sesstat;

STATISTIC            LAST_QUERY   SESSION_TOTAL
-------------------- ------------ ---------------
Queries Parallelized          1              11
DML Parallelized              0               0
```

The CPU resource used for a particular parallelized statement can be calculated by the differences in the CPU_SECS_TOTAL column before and after the statement by using the following SQL:

```
SELECT slave_name,status, cpu_secs_total
FROM v$pq_slave;

SLAVE_NAME   STATUS    CPU_SECS_TOTAL
------------ --------- ----------------
P000         IDLE                    5
P001         IDLE                    5
P002         IDLE                    5
P003         IDLE                    5
```

When the number of slaves significantly exceeds the number of CPUs, contention between the slave processes at the UNIX level for fixed CPU resources can actually cause parallel operations to increase the elapsed times for a given SQL statement compared to single CPU operation. The following SQL statements show an example of an explicit parallel operation requested via a HINT:

```
REM 2 parallel slaves...
select /*+ parallel(x,2) */ count(*) from acctlog_accessed x;

REM 3 parallel slaves...
select /*+ parallel(x,3) */ count(*) from acctlog_accessed x;

REM RAC provides a third value in the HINT (4 in this example) to
REM specify the number of instances to distribute the query over . . .
select /*+ full(x) parallel (x,3,4) */ count(*) from acctlog_accessed x;
```

Extra information is produced in the PLAN_TABLE during EXPLAIN PLAN execution for a parallel operation. In this case, the OTHER_TAG column gives details of the select that is being performed by the query slave referenced in the OBJECT_NODE column. In particular, the existence of PARALLEL_TO_SERIAL tags needs to be investigated. These tags indicate a parallel operation that has been serialized. Of course, at some stage in the execution plan, results do have to be serialized before being returned to the client. For example, results from slaves performing a parallel scan need to be serialized in order to be counted by a COUNT(*) operation. DbCool produces a plan that displays the parallel query information in the plan tree using an Information icon to indicate the operations. Figure 9.3 shows the EXPLAIN PLAN for a parallel query using DbCool.

The same information can be provided by Oracle's SQL Analyze tool, but it's not displayed in a tree, so you could miss it unless you scroll the window to view the extra information. Figure 9.4 shows the same plan using SQL Analyze.

Oracle's parallel features can be hard to manage if you choose to use HINTs or specify the PARALLEL attribute explicitly in segment definitions along with a value for parallelism. In these cases, you need to consider changing the values if you upgrade

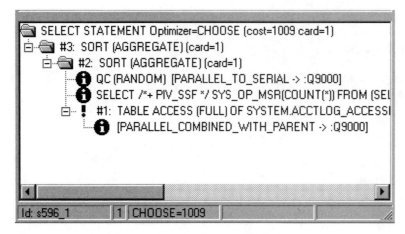

Figure 9.3 DbCool EXPLAIN PLAN for a parallel query.

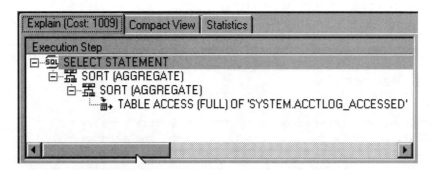

Figure 9.4 Oracle SQL Analyze EXPLAIN PLAN for a parallel query.

your server with additional CPUs. From a usability standpoint, why should the designer need to specify parallelism at all? Shouldn't the database management system (DBMS) decide when to use it automatically based on the operation being performed and the CPU available? Oracle believes this is the case, and since Oracle8*i*, Oracle recommends that you set the initialization parameter parallel_automatic_tuning=true. When set, Oracle determines the default values for parameters that control parallel execution. To take advantage of this feature, you must set the PARALLEL clause on tables for which you require parallel operations. Oracle then tunes all subsequent parallel operations automatically. Closely tied to parallel_automatic_tuning is the parallel_adaptive_multiuser setting, which is set to true automatically when automatic tuning is enabled. This option switches on an adaptive algorithm that automatically reduces the degree of parallelism based on the system load when a query starts. The actual parallelism used is based on the default degree of parallelism, or the value specified as a table attribute or used in a HINT, reduced by an internally computed scale factor.

Identifying Which SQL to Tune

If you have an Oracle system that didn't use the measure-everything-all-the-time approach during the development of the SQL, then you'll need to identify the most expensive SQL after it has executed on a production system. It's a good idea to do this anyway. The good news is that Oracle caches the MRU statements in the shared SQL area of the shared pool along with the physical and logical I/O and execution count. The following SQL can be used to identify the most expensive SQL in the shared pool:

```
select    /*+ RULE */ executions Execs,
       disk_reads reads,
       decode(executions,0,null,round(disk_reads/executions))+0
"R/EXEC",
       buffer_gets gets,
       decode(executions,0,null,round(buffer_gets/executions))+0
"G/EXEC",
       sorts,
       rows_processed rowsproc,
       decode(parsing_schema_id,0,'?',username) parsed_by,
       decode(optimizer_mode,
          'MULTIPLE CHILDREN PRESENT','CHILDREN',optimizer_mode) o_mode,
       sql_text,
       address,hash_value
from v$sqlarea,dba_users
where parsing_schema_id = user_id and lower(sql_text) like '%' and
executions >= 0 and buffer_gets >= 0 and disk_reads >=0
and username like '%';
```

The metric you use to identify the most expensive SQL is a matter of taste and circumstances. For example, you might choose total physical I/O using the PHYSICAL_READS column or logical reads indicated by the BUFFER_GETS column. Both of these values are in blocks. If you consider the most expensive SQL *per execution*, then you can use the PHYSICAL_READS and BUFFER_GETS divided by the EXECUTIONS column. Yet another approach is to use the I/O per row processed because SQL that performs huge amounts of I/O for a few rows processed may be wasting many resources. The V$SQLAREA view only shows the first 1,000 characters of each SQL statement. The ADDRESS and HASH_VALUE columns can be used to identify the full SQL statement from the V$SQLTEXT_WITH_NEWLINES view as follows:

```
select sql_text
from v$sqltext_with_newlines where address='8C84760C' and
hash_value+0=2855390177
order by piece;
```

Once you have the full SQL text, the next step is to look at the execution plan to see if any low-risk ways to improve performance can be identified, such as the creation of indexes to avoid table scans. DbCool has features to automate this process and make it easy. The SQL Statistics option from the Tuning menu of DbCool can query

V$SQLAREA according to the criteria of your choice and send results to the grid. Once in the grid, you can click the grid column headers to sort the data according to your chosen method for identifying expensive SQL. Once you have identified one or more statements of interest from the grid, you can send them straight to the Explain Plan tool by right-clicking on the grid and making the appropriate choice from the Grid SQL menu option. The section *Detecting Full Table Scans* earlier in this chapter shows you how to do it. The SQL Analyze component of the Oracle9*i* Enterprise Manager Tuning Pack provides these features and more as a separately licensable option from Oracle.

The column PARSING_SCHEMA_ID in V$SQLAREA identifies the user who originally parsed the SQL statement. Use of this column is required to guarantee correct results from EXPLAIN PLAN, because the plan for a given statement must be generated in the same schema that parsed the statement. For example, the statement SELECT COUNT(*) FROM EMP could generate any number of different plans if the database contains many different EMP tables in different schemas containing different numbers of rows. Oracle provides a statement (which works in all versions including Oracle9*i*) that enables you to become another user for the purpose of generating a plan or executing a statement. The following is an example:

```
alter session set current_schema=scott;
```

After executing this statement, all subsequent statements in the session resolve object names in SQL statements as if the current user was SCOTT. As a result, the SQL statement SELECT COUNT(*) FROM EMP generates a plan as if the SCOTT.EMP table was used in the query and returns results from the SCOTT.EMP table. This doesn't mean that Oracle security is circumvented because the privileges available remain those of the original user at logon time, not the user in the ALTER SESSION statement. If the logon user didn't have privileges to select from the SCOTT.EMP table, the usual ORA-0942 error would result. This command is invaluable for DBAs who need to generate execution plans for statements in V$SQLAREA that were parsed by other accounts.

Oracle actually provides two views of the shared SQL area. In addition to V$SQLAREA, the view V$SQL can be used. The difference between the two is worth understanding and is best seen by an example. Consider a situation where two different sessions execute the same SQL statement: one using the CHOOSE optimizer goal and the other using ALL_ROWS:

```
select /* XX */ count(*) from system.my_objects;
```

In this example, the comment /* XX */ has no purpose other than to make the SQL easy to identify in the shared SQL area during the rest of the discussion. Even though both sessions execute exactly the same SQL against the same object, a separate cursor, known as a *child cursor*, is required to distinguish that the runtime behavior in each case is different because each session uses a different optimizer goal. In such situations, the V$SQLAREA column VERSION_COUNT contains a value greater than 1 to indicate that multiple child cursors exist, and V$SQL maintains a separate row for each child cursor, as shown by the following two SQL statements:

```
select address,sql_text,version_count
from v$sqlarea where sql_text like '%XX%';


ADDRESS   SQL_TEXT                                          VERSION_COUNT
--------  ------------------------------------------------  -------------
81D06664 select /* XX */ count(*) from system.my_objects              2

REM V$SQL contains one row for each child cursor...
select address,child_address,sql_text
from v$sql where sql_text like '%XX%';


ADDRESS    CHILD_ADDRESS  SQL_TEXT
---------  -------------  ---------------------------------------------
-
81D06664  81D06148       select /* XX */ count(*) from system.my_objects
81D06664  81D05E5C       select /* XX */ count(*) from system.my_objects
```

Note that related child cursors in V$SQL have the same value in the ADDRESS column indicating that they originate from the same parent cursor. Oracle provides an additional view called V$SQL_SHARED_CURSOR, which can be used to identify the reason for the existence of multiple child cursors for a statement. It's usually worth following up on these because they are probably not intended. In this example, the difference results from uniqueness in the optimizer mode for each session, but there are many other possible reasons, such as the use of a stored outline in one session and not in another. The following SQL shows that in this example the child cursors of the parent cursor (identified by the column KGLHDPAR) result from an optimizer mismatch, which is indicated by values in the OPTIMIZER_MISMATCH column:

```
select address,KGLHDPAR,optimizer_mismatch from V$SQL_SHARED_CURSOR
where KGLHDPAR='81D06664';


ADDRESS    KGLHDPAR    OPTIMIZER_MISMATCH
---------  ----------  --------------------
81D06148  81D06664    N
81D05E5C  81D06664    Y
```

Making SQL Faster

This section contains tips for making SQL faster. Severe restrictions are likely to exist on the scope of changes depending on the stage of the application lifecycle where the change needs to be made. The Oracle Enterprise Manager (OEM) has some great tools to help you make SQL faster. Of these, Oracle Expert and SQL Analyze were only available on Windows on the first release of Oracle9*i*, although they can run against Oracle databases on any platform.

Rewriting SQL

SQL is a declarative language. A SQL SELECT statement specifies what results are required rather than how to fetch them, which is left to Oracle to decide during the generation of an execution plan. As a result, a particular result set can usually be obtained by several equivalent SQL statements, each with a potentially different cost and elapsed time. The most significant reductions in elapsed time for SQL statements often involve rewriting SQL statements so that they are semantically identical to the original statement and use fewer memory, CPU, and I/O resources. The earlier parts of this chapter have provided an extensive background on how to measure performance using statistics and event waits.

Rewriting SQL is a low-cost, low-risk option only during the development cycle. That's the basis of the mantra for this chapter, which is to measure everything all the time when writing SQL. Writing a complex SQL statement can take quite a while, and it makes sense to change it while the requirements are fresh in the designer's mind. Rewriting SQL later can be difficult and risky because you need to guarantee that the new SQL is semantically identical to the original. This requires extensive regression testing for a production system. If SQL changes actually requires a client application upgrade, it becomes even more risky due to the challenge of change management.

This chapter strongly recommends the use of REF CURSOR data types to return result sets from the database to your application rather than coding SQL inline. The use of REF CURSORS at least limits the scope of your changes to the database rather than the client application; therefore, it reduces change complexity and risk. The use of REF CURSORS means you can place a HINT in a statement on the server without affecting the client in any way.

Although it's difficult to provide general rules for efficient SQL in a meaningful way, there is one general rule to keep in mind. If you recall the discussion on execution plans earlier in the chapter, you can think of the execution plan for a SELECT statement as a tree where the leaf nodes perform fetches of index and table data blocks, which are passed up the tree for processing by joins, sorts, and filters, eventually producing the result set at the root of the tree. The client receives the result set.

The more you minimize the low-level requirements for data blocks at the leaf node in the plan (whether from logical or physical I/O), the less data is required, and the less data is required for processing as the data passes up the tree. Whenever your SQL requires a scan of a large table, you break the rule of minimizing the data requirements. Indexes can also make a significant difference to performance by reducing the logical and physical I/O required to execute the SQL.

The use of inline views in place of a table in the FROM clause of a query is a useful and often overlooked technique for providing the SQL designer with explicit control of the order of executing a statement. If the execution order can be driven so that the number of rows passed toward the root of the execution plan is reduced early in the execution order, fewer rows need to be processed at later stages, reducing resource requirements and elapsed times. Consider two tables containing trades (TX) and a history of trades (TXHST). Each trade has a name, numeric ID, and type. To save database space, the history contains only the ID. The use of a numeric ID as the foreign key is standard practice. The two statements shown in Table 9.10 show the counts for trades in the history grouped by name and type.

Table 9.10 A Join with and without Using an Inline View

STANDARD JOIN	SAME JOIN USING INLINE VIEW
`select tx_name,tx_type,count(*)`	`select tx_name,tx_type,c.cnt`

`from tx,txhst h`
`where tx.tx_id = h.tx_id`
`group by tx_name,tx_type`
	`from tx,`
	`(select tx_id,count(*) cnt`
	` from txhst group by tx_id) c`
	`where tx.tx_id = c.tx_id`

```
Rows    Row Source Operation          Rows    Row Source Operation
------  -----------------------       ------  ---------------------
    88  SORT GROUP BY                     88  HASH JOIN
 14841   HASH JOIN                        93   VIEW
 20000    TABLE ACCESS FULL TXHST         93    SORT GROUP BY
 24680    TABLE ACCESS FULL TX         20000     TABLE ACCESS FULL TXHST
                                       24680     TABLE ACCESS FULL TX
```

Both queries return identical result sets containing 88 rows. The right-hand version groups trades in the history *before* the join using an inline view named *c*. As a result, only 88 rows need to be joined at the HASH JOIN stage because the inline view has already reduced the rows to process later in the query. The standard join version on the left needs to process 14,841 rows at the HASH JOIN stage and performs the group operation *after* the join. The plan for the inline view is much more likely to produce a plan that runs faster. Another effect of inline views is that they usually make the purpose of queries easier to understand.

In order to write efficient SQL, you need to be familiar with the capabilities of Oracle's SQL implementation. Oracle includes an exceptionally powerful set of functions referred to as the *analytic functions*, which were designed for use in data warehouse applications, but have many general uses. They enable you to perform operations in SQL that in the past would have required procedural processing using PL/SQL or another procedural language. The analytic functions provide the following capabilities:

- Rankings and percentiles
- Sliding window calculations
- Lag/lead analysis
- First/last analysis
- Linear regression statistics

The following example demonstrates the power of the analytic functions by taking a simple list of candy bar sales and presenting the information grouped by type along with a running total:

```
REM the original list of items...
ITEM          QUANTITY
---------- ----------
Mars                 5
Mars                 3
Mars                 1
Snickers             2
Snickers             3
Milky Way            4
Milky Way            6


REM the analytic SQL...
select item ,sum(quantity) item_total,
       sum(sum(quantity)) over
(order by item rows unbounded preceding ) as running_total
from sales group by item;


ITEM          ITEM_TOTAL   RUNNING_TOTAL
---------- ------------ ---------------
Mars                 9               9
Milky Way           10              19
Snickers             5              24
```

SQL Rewrite Tools

Third-party tools exist that claim to rewrite your SQL to make it more efficient. They are usually expensive. My experience with these tools is that they fail to add value to anything but the most basic SQL statements. Often they simply reexecute your statement multiple times in its original form using the various optimizer modes and different HINTs, and then measure the cost in each case. You don't need to spend large amounts of money to do that, although the ability to automate the process can potentially save you a lot of time in processing all the possibilities. Oracle's SQL Analyze tool can also assist you with HINT creation and provides a limited rewrite capability. Ultimately, for the best-performing SQL, there is no substitute for an Oracle designer with the following:

- A clear set of performance requirements
- An awareness of the performance metrics
- Tools to measure and influence performance metrics
- SQL expertise

Adding or Changing Indexes

Sometimes a DML statement can clearly benefit from the use of an index. For example, an OLTP system that executes DML using a table scan can often benefit from the creation of an index on a column used in the WHERE clause. In this example, provided that the OBJECT_ID column contains many distinct values, the following SQL will benefit from an index on OBJECT_ID:

```
select * from my_objects where object_id=22;
```

The addition of the index changes the access path to the data to use the index instead of the full table scan. Don't forget that when running in CHOOSE mode, the optimizer won't detect the index until the ANALYZE command has been executed.

You should remember that indexes slow down inserts, updates, and deletes, and generate extra redo. The benefits of additional indexes for speeding up SELECT statements need to be balanced with the cost of data modifications. An additional consideration is that the existence of a new index may affect the execution plan of other existing statements—and not always beneficially. The addition of an index has a lower risk than a SQL statement change, but it still requires an impact analysis. Chapter 12 contains more information on managing indexes.

Chapter 16 on using performance management tools discusses the use of Oracle Expert for providing a top-down analysis of your whole database performance. Oracle Expert provides an Index Tuning Wizard to recommend and optionally implement additional indexes for performance.

Changing the Optimizer Mode

Changing the optimizer mode can make a massive difference in the performance of SQL by modifying the execution plan. It has the added advantage that no changes to the SQL are needed. Although the optimizer mode can be changed at the database or session level, the changes could have detrimental side effects on the performance of other statements. Changes to the optimizer mode are better made through explicit HINTs. You can place HINTs in the code itself. For example, the following HINT causes the optimizer to generate an execution plan using the ALL_ROWS goal. This results in an appropriate index being used without requiring the table to be analyzed after index creation when compared to CHOOSE, which requires the ANALYZE command:

```
select /*+ ALL_ROWS */ count(*) from my_objects;
```

It's not unheard-of for the rule-based optimizer to produce the lowest elapsed time for a SQL statement. The use of RULE should never be ruled out. Oracle has been threatening to remove it for years. It seems likely that until the Oracle cost-based optimizer is perfect, RULE mode will continue to be available. Changing the optimizer mode at the session level can be performed without requiring an application code change. For example, if you create this trigger on your database, you may find that the RMAN LIST BACKUPSET command runs up to 10 times faster because it avoids table scans of the RMAN.BS table that the Oracle optimizer considers the best way to run the statement:

```
create or replace TRIGGER rman_after_logon after logon on database
  begin
```

```
-- assume RMAN runs as RMAN user
-- if RMAN running, change to RULE...
if user='RMAN' then

    execute immediate 'alter session set optimizer_goal=rule';
end if;

exception
  when others then
    null;
end;
```

Modifying Statistics

The cost-based optimizer uses table and column statistics information during plan generation. The DBMS_STATS package, which is covered in Chapter 10, can be used to modify statistics manually and generate them automatically in order to influence the query execution plan.

Using SQL HINTs

Sometimes Oracle doesn't generate a plan that minimizes the elapsed time for statement execution, assuming that's the requirement. This occurs for a number of reasons. For example, the optimizer mode in use may have the goal of minimizing resource usage, such as ALL_ROWS. Usually, minimizing resource usage (cost) reduces elapsed time—*but not always*. If you use EXPLAIN PLAN to compare the cost of two semantically identical SELECT statements using the cost-based optimizer, you'll see that Oracle chooses one plan over the other based on the calculated cost, even if the query actually executes slower. Sometimes the generated plan may be based on inadequate or out-of-date statistics that don't reflect the actual size and distribution of the data in the tables and indexes. The generation of optimizer statistics is covered in Chapter 10. In rare circumstances, the optimizer may contain a bug. Sometimes a human is superior to a computer because the human has a more complete understanding of the problem. In any of these situations, a HINT can be used to make suggestions to the optimizer on the best plan to generate. The HINT can take many forms, for example

- Specify the optimizer mode: select /*+ ALL_ROWS */ count(*) from my_objects;

- Request the use of an index: SELECT /*+ INDEX(t pk_trades) */ count(*) from trades t;

You must use the string "/*+" to introduce a HINT and "*/" to terminate it. If you make a mistake with the syntax, the optimizer will ignore it. Also, the optimizer may decide to ignore the value in any case because it's only a suggestion. Due to the sheer number of different types of HINTs, it can be difficult to get the syntax right and set in the correct position in the query. The Hint Wizard component of SQL Analyze, which is part of the Oracle9i Enterprise Manager Tuning Pack, contains a GUI to help you add HINTs. SQL Analyze is highly recommended, but remember that the Tuning Pack is a separately licensable component.

Stored Outlines

Oracle introduced plan stability features in Oracle8. Plan stability guarantees that your SQL will always execute using the same plan based on a persistent representation of the plan stored in the database. The persistent representation, known as a *stored outline*, is stored across three tables (OL$, OL$HINTS, and OL$NODES) in the OUTLN schema. The views USER_OUTLINES and DBA_OUTLINES present the information from the underlying tables in a user-friendlier format. The following privilege is required to create outlines, in this case, for the user SCOTT:

```
grant create any outline to scott;
```

Outlines can then be created for all statements in a session in named categories or for individual statements, as shown in the following examples:

```
REM create stored outlines for all session SQL into the DEFAULT category
alter session set created_stored_outlines=true;

REM created stored outlines for all session SQL into the ALLMYSQL
category
alter session set created_stored_outlines=allmysql;

REM create a named outline onesql
create stored outline onesql on
select count(*) from my_objects;
```

The OUTLINE_CATEGORY and OUTLINE_SID column in the V$SQL view indicates whether a stored outline was used at execution time. The use of stored outlines takes place when the cost-based optimizer is used and when the SQL text provided by an application matches *exactly* with the SQL text of a stored outline. As a result, the creation of named outlines requires care to ensure that the statement in the outline matches whatever is provided by the application. Two settings are required to enable the use of existing outlines; these can be set databasewide in the init.ora file or at the session level as follows:

```
alter session set query_rewrite_enabled=TRUE;
alter session set use_stored_outlines=TRUE;
```

Stored outlines were originally designed to provide plan stability. However, it's clear that the appropriate modifications of stored outlines can change the execution plan for statements *without requiring SQL changes*. Here's an example of how to swap stored outlines for two statements that return identical results, where one causes a table scan and the other is fast when using an index provided with a HINT. Following the change, the slow SQL can execute with the fast plan, provided that outlines are in use. The technique is unsupported because it changes the underlying outline tables directly, but it works:

```
REM create outline for slow statement...
create or replace outline slow on
select count(*) from my_objects o;

REM create outline for fast version, using index HINT...
create or replace outline fast
select /*+ index(o pk_my_objects) */ from my_objects o;

REM associate plan for fast version with slow version...
update outln.ol$hints
set ol_name=decode(ol_name,'FAST','SLOW','SLOW','FAST')
where ol_name in ('SLOW','FAST');

REM drop fast version (which now has slow plan)...
drop outline fast;

REM now "select count(*) from my_objects o" can use the index
```

Oracle has officially recognized the usefulness of this technique, and the Tuning Pack option of Oracle9*i* Enterprise Manager includes a GUI to manage and edit stored outlines—for example, by adding HINTs. The Oracle9*i* version also enables the effects of changes to a stored outline to be tested before publishing the plan for global use.

Editing outlines has great potential for improving the performance of some SQL statements when you don't have access to the application code. For example, if a third-party application performs badly, then the stored outline editor is a useful tool for fixing performance without requiring a new application release from the vendor. Figure 9.5 shows the generated outline for the inline view join query earlier in the chapter.

Performance and Cursors

A typical Oracle database application usually executes a limited range of SQL statements many times. For multitier applications, the complete list of SQL ever executed by the application may be completely determined in advance by the designer. Sometimes these statements differ only in the literal values used in the WHERE clause of DML statements. For example, the following statements differ only in the literal values 23 and 24:

```
select * from trades where trade_id=24;
select * from trades where trade_id=34;
```

The performance of SQL statements can be influenced by factors not related to the resource consumption of the SQL statement itself, such as how well Oracle can reuse information from previous executions of the statement. Execution of a SQL statement

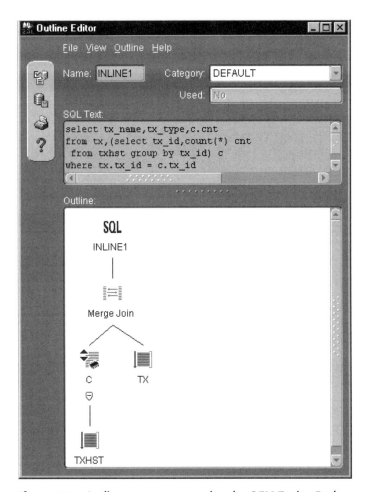

Figure 9.5 Outline management using the OEM Tuning Pack.

actually passes through several distinct stages within the DBMS itself. If you only use a tool like SQL*Plus to execute SQL, these stages are hidden from you. On the other hand, if you use a low-level Oracle programming interface like Oracle Call Interface (OCI) or Pro*C, or submit your SQL statements from PL/SQL, you have a high degree of control over each stage. Whatever Oracle interface you use, information created at some of the execution stages can potentially be reused on subsequent executions. In general, the more information you can reuse, the better the performance. Reuse leads to reduced I/O and CPU requirements, in the same way that caching data blocks in the block buffer cache can reduce resource requirements for subsequent statements that require the same data.

This section considers SQL performance in terms of cursor usage and SQL parsing, and describes how these can be reduced in order to provide more efficient use of hard-

Table 9.11 Query Processing Stages

OPERATION	PURPOSE
OPEN	Allocate memory for data structures.
PARSE	Check syntax, generate parse tree, check privileges, and create execution plan. Allocate private SQL area. Allocate shared SQL area.
DESCRIBE	Return the types and length of query SELECT LIST columns. Only required for queries provided by an application at run time.
DEFINE	Define program memory location, type, and size of variables for SELECT LIST columns.
BIND	Specify the memory location and value of bind variables.
EXECUTE	Execute the statement using all of the information provided so far.
FETCH	Fetch the results into the DEFINE values.
CLOSE	Free up resources and deallocate memory.

ware resources for the Oracle instance as whole, leading to better performance. Table 9.11 shows the stages of processing for a SQL query statement executing for the first time.

> **NOTE** For other DML statements like INSERT, DELETE, and UPDATE, some of the stages in Table 9.11, such as DESCRIBE, DEFINE, and FETCH don't apply.

Cursors and the Shared Pool

A cursor is a name, which is also referred to as a *handle*, for the private SQL area allocated at the parse stage. A private SQL area is an area of memory containing runtime state information for the query, such as SELECT LIST memory locations, bind variable locations and values, and the stage that processing has reached in the session running the query. Although you hear the term *cursor* often in the Oracle world, it's helpful to understand exactly what it means because a comprehensive understanding of cursors can lead to applications that perform better through the choice of appropriate programmatic interfaces and cursor management. The maximum number of cursors that can be opened in a single session at any time is controlled by the OPEN_CURSORS init.ora parameter.

The shared SQL area contains the parse tree for the statement and the execution plan. As the name suggests, it has the potential to be reused by other users executing the same statement against the same objects at a later time. Therefore, if many users execute the same SQL, each invocation has a separate, private SQL area and a *common*, shared SQL area.

You'll notice that the Purpose column in Table 9.11 doesn't state who performs the operation. This is because the choice of programmatic interface determines who performs the operation. For example, if you use PL/SQL or Microsoft's ActiveX Data Objects (ADO), those interfaces perform the memory allocation for the DEFINE and BIND stage. If you use Pro*C or OCI, then the programmer performs those operations. If you use SQL*Plus as the application for processing, then everything is taken care of for you. SQL*Plus is simply an OCI program that Oracle provides to abstract the full complexities of SQL statement execution away from the user. However, SQL*Plus code needs to manage all the intricacies of DESCRIBE, DEFINE, and BIND so that you, as a user, don't have to.

It's important to highlight that the parse stage is relatively expensive. During parsing, the Oracle server needs to lexically scan and parse a SQL statement to make sure that it's syntactically correct. If that SQL is several tens of kilobytes long and contains several objects, then Oracle needs to read information from the Oracle dictionary to check that the tables, views, columns, and possibly stored PL/SQL objects used in the SQL exist and that the caller has appropriate access rights to use them. Once that stage has completed, memory needs to be allocated to hold the SQL text in the SGA. If the client accesses the database over a WAN, then the actual cost of simply transmitting a large SQL statement over the network can be significant.

The next most important point to note is that if the SQL uses bind variables, then repeated execution of the SQL can take place simply by supplying new values for bind variables and re-executing. In this case, all of the preceding processing doesn't need to be repeated. This is one situation where the microscopic control of cursor allocation in OCI can provide benefits. If you are writing a three-tier application, where all the SQL that needs to run is fixed within the middle tier, cursors can be opened only once for the lifetime of the session. All subsequent executions need to provide values for bind variables. In this case, SQL execution becomes a matter of sending bind variables from the middleware to the Oracle server and returning the results using simple remote procedure calls. This approach minimizes the number of cursors required, memory usage on the server, and network traffic.

The shared SQL areas have to be stored in the SGA. The location of private SQL areas depends on the type of connection. If the connection uses a dedicated server connection, the private SQL area is located in the shadow process for the session. If the connection uses a shared server, some of the private SQL area information is located in the SGA.

The resources required to parse SQL include Oracle metadata information held in the Oracle dictionary, which might require physical I/O to fetch. Oracle caches both types of information in the shared pool. The shared pool is the area of the SGA that contains the dictionary cache and library cache. The dictionary cache stores reference data for the Oracle data dictionary, such as object privileges, user privileges, and metadata descriptions of objects including column descriptions. Some of this information is required by Oracle when parsing SQL statements, so it makes sense for Oracle to cache this information in memory to avoid rereading it from the SYSTEM tablespace. The library cache stores parse and compile information about recently executed SQL and PL/SQL statements.

As the amount of memory required to hold all the necessary information may exceed the memory available in the shared pool, Oracle uses a least recently used (LRU) algorithm to age objects out of the shared pool when space is required for current requests. At times of space shortage, dictionary cache information takes precedence over library cache information. The following SQL shows the breakdown of the SGA shared pool memory into some of the categories related to the library cache and dictionary cache:

```
select  /*+ RULE */ * from v$sgastat;


POOL          NAME                        BYTES
-----------   -------------------------   ----------
shared pool   free memory                 16869732
shared pool   trigger source                   848
shared pool   table columns                  18052
shared pool   dictionary cache              221984
shared pool   sql area                     1149416
```

It's very important to emphasize that a large value for free memory in this case is *not* actually a good thing because it implies that too much memory has been allocated to the shared pool and that memory is left unused. Once memory is allocated to the shared pool, it can't be used by anything else, and if it remains unused, it's wasted. The goal should be for the shared pool to be sized appropriately to cache as much information as possible without needing to age objects out of the cache too frequently. If an application makes an execute call for a SQL statement whose execute-state information has been aged out of the library cache to make room for another statement, then Oracle implicitly needs to reparse and create a new shared SQL area for the statement before execution. As shown earlier, parsing should be kept to a minimum for performance reasons.

It's important to emphasize the difference between a soft parse and hard parse. A hard parse occurs when the parsing stage of a statement needs to start from scratch, including checking the syntax and privileges. The failure to find a parsed representation of a statement in the library cache during the parse stage (which results in the hard parse) is referred to as a *library cache miss*. Library cache misses can occur at both the parse and execute stage of SQL processing. If information for a statement exists in the library cache in a shared SQL area, the existing parse tree and execution plan can be reused. This is a soft parse. The following SQL statements show how to identify the number of total parse requests and hard parse requests from the system and session statistics:

```
REM system parse statistics...
select name,value
from v$sysstat
where name in ('parse count (total)','parse count (hard)');


NAME                  VALUE
-------------------   ---------
parse count (total)   42976921
parse count (hard)    11145360
```

```
REM session parse statistics...
select s.sid,n.name,s.value
from v$sesstat s,v$statname n
where n.name in ('parse count (total)','parse count (hard)')
and s.statistic# = n.statistic#;
```

The precise memory allocation and execution count for all objects in the shared pool can be shown using the following SQL:

```
select  owner, sharable_mem shr_mem, type, kept, executions exec, name
from v$db_object_cache;

OWNER     SHMEM TYPE       KEPT   EXEC NAME
-------  ------- --------- ------ ------ --------------------------
SYS        7516 LIBRARY    NO        0 DBMS_SPACE_ADMIN_LIB
           9900 CURSOR     NO        2 SELECT PL FROM HD WHERE TX=12356
           8345 CURSOR     NO        2 SELECT PL FROM HD WHERE TX=94567
SYS        2484 TABLE      YES       0 OBJ$
```

For cases where the shared pool is sized too small to meet the current space requirements, an ORA-04031 error results. The SQL statement ALTER SYSTEM FLUSH SHARED_POOL can be used by the database administrator (DBA) at any time in order to flush objects that aren't currently used from the shared pool. This should only be used in an emergency because statements that were cached previously will require a hard parse upon the next execution, possibly causing a noticeable degradation in response time. To avoid the fragmentation caused when frequently used objects are aged out of and reloaded into the shared pool, the DBMS_SHARED_POOL.KEEP procedure can be used to pin objects into the shared pool, as shown in the following example. Note that cursors can also be pinned if required. Cursor pinning is useful if the same statement is being executed very frequently, and reduces CPU usage. The following trigger pins the SP_INDEX_REBUILD package into the shared pool at database startup time, and the SQL that follows shows all of the pinned objects in the SGA object cache:

```
create or replace trigger tr_pin_plsql
after startup on database
begin
     sys.dbms_shared_pool.keep('SYS.SP_INDEX_REBUILD','P');
end;
/


REM This SQL shows objects pinned in the shared pool...

select  /*+ RULE */ owner, sharable_mem shr_mem, type, kept , loads,
executions exec, name
from v$db_object_cache where kept='YES';


OWNER     SHR_MEM TYPE       KEPT   LOADS   EXEC NAME
-------  --------- ---------- ------ ------- ------ ----------------
SYS        23192 PROCEDURE   YES        4      4 SP_INDEX_REBUILD
```

It's possible for memory used in the shared pool to be close to the limit without resulting in an ORA-04031 error. This is manifested by large numbers of objects being aged out of the cache in a short period of time. The following SQL, run as SYS, can be used to show the size of requests and the number of objects aged out of the cache in order to satisfy current requests:

```
select  KSMLRCOM,KSMLRSIZ,KSMLRNUM,KSMLRHON from x$ksmlru;

KSMLRCOM              KSMLRSIZ KSMLRNUM KSMLRHON
-----------------    -------- -------- --------------------------------
kafco : qkacol           4116        8 SELECT /*+NESTED_TABLE_GET_R . . .
BAMIMA: Bam Buffer       4132     1592 SELECT "A1"."OWNER"||'.'||"A . . .
ckydef : kkdlcky          236        8 SELECT Transaction_Num, XTR_ . . .
qsmksol : qsmg_all        244        8 SELECT Transaction_Num, XTR_ . . .
frodef : prstnm           444        8 SELECT Transaction_Num, XTR_ . . .
```

Results are displayed only once and don't persist. So, for a system where an insignificant aging-out activity is occurring, you would expect the output to be empty on the second execution a few seconds after the first. For a system where shared pool memory thrashing is taking place due to the need to continually find space for large-sized requests, you would expect to see new entries appearing every few seconds with large values for the KSMLRSIZ and KSMLRNUM columns.

Reducing Parse Calls by SQL Sharing on the Server

Based on the information in the previous sections, the optimal approach for the best performance of any programmatic interface is to share as much information as possible between all sessions to avoid hard parsing and make the best use of available memory in the SGA. These two requirements are very closely related and can be controlled in different ways. One way to reduce hard parsing is to write code so that the SQL can be shared in the Oracle server.

When a session submits a SQL statement to the server for execution, Oracle first checks whether a shared SQL representation of the statement already exists in the shared pool so that the parse tree and execution plan can be reused. This sharing takes place independently of the programmatic interface being used, but requires statements to be written in a way that takes advantage of it. Statements must be identical (including whitespace) to enable sharing. The previous output from v$db_object_cache contains the following two statements, which have the potential to be shared:

```
OWNER SHMEM TYPE         KEPT   EXEC NAME
----- ----- ----------   ------ ------ --------------------------------
      9900  CURSOR        NO       2 SELECT PL FROM HD WHERE TX=12356
      8345  CURSOR        NO       2 SELECT PL FROM HD WHERE TX=94567
```

Various Oracle data dictionary tables contain information that can be used to identify statements that could potentially be shared by replacing hard-coded values in the WHERE clause with bind variables. These include V$SQLAREA and V$OPEN_

CURSOR. Queries on these tables can be quite expensive. DbCool enables you to query these tables and then sort the results afterwards on the client as required. This avoids the need to repeat queries on the dictionary in order to sort the output in a different order. Both of the previous statements can be replaced with a single statement using a bind variable, although it should be emphasized that the application needs to be recoded to provide the TX value at run time:

```
SELECT PL FROM HD WHERE TX=:transaction_id
```

Keep in mind that there is a risk and effort required to make any kind of application change, so the cost and benefits of changes need to be carefully considered. The best approach is to build awareness of such issues into standard programming practices so that developers take the best approach at design time when it's less expensive.

You should also be aware that Oracle generates a query plan at parse time before bind values are known. In order for the Oracle cost-based optimizer to choose the lowest-cost execution plan for tables where data distributions are skewed in some of the columns, the actual column values are required at parse time. Using bind variables instead loses this information, which might result in a degradation of performance for some SQL due to the generation of an execution plan that is nonoptimal.

For statements that are identical except for the values used in the WHERE clause, Oracle provides cursor-sharing features within the Oracle server to allow you to share SQL without requiring application changes. You should consider cursor sharing exclusively in situations where many statements differ only in the values of literals in the WHERE clause, many library cache misses are evident, and those misses are degrading performance. Cursor sharing has no effect on SQL statements in PL/SQL.

The use of cursor sharing has a slight overhead compared to a regular soft parse because Oracle needs to transform the original statement containing the literal values into one containing bind variables. Cursor sharing can be set systemwide using CURSOR_SHARING=SIMILAR or CURSOR_SHARING=FORCE in the init.ora file. It's probably safer to set the value on a per-session basis as required in order to avoid unwanted side effects, for example, using the following:

```
ALTER SESSION SET CURSOR_SHARING=SIMILAR;
```

The FORCE option forces similar SQL to share an existing plan, even if it involves the generation of a suboptimal plan, and should be used with the greatest care. In Oracle8*i*, only the FORCE option is available. The result of executing similar statements in Oracle9*i* using SIMILAR cursor sharing is shown in the following example:

```
REM run two statements differing in literal values...
select * from emp where empno=7521;
select * from emp where empno=7369;

REM check the object cache to show the shared cursor which
REM contains the literal values replaced with a generated bind value
select name,executions
from v$db_object_cache
where name like 'select * from emp%';
```

```
NAME                                              EXECUTIONS
----------------------------------------- ------------
select * from emp where empno=:"SYS_B_0"          2
```

The shared SQL area is invalidated after any change to any object in the SQL statement or after the ANALYZE command has been used to modify the statistics of any object used in the SQL. In both cases, the statement will be reparsed on the next execution. The use of ALTER SYSTEM FLUSH SHARED_POOL has the same effect. Modifying a database's global name causes the shared pool to be flushed. Even shared SQL areas related to open cursors could be flushed if the LRU algorithm determines that the cursor hasn't been used for some time. Once again, the reparse and creation of a new shared SQL area takes place on the next execution.

Using Cursor Variables

One of the many benefits of PL/SQL is that it enables the developer to encapsulate DML statements in packages so that the implementation is hidden from the client application. In addition to providing benefits in terms of reducing network traffic, this enables the server implementation to change without affecting the client, provided that the external interface of the package remains unchanged. This clear separation of the client and server code enables much easier development.

Although most client applications take advantage of server-side PL/SQL packages, they often contain embedded SQL statements. As a result, changes to the SQL require application changes along with all the hard work and risk that this process entails. Oracle provides cursor variables through the REF CURSOR type to allow server-side procedures to return result sets in order to enable SQL statements to be encapsulated on the server. Executing SELECT statements through cursor references can have several potential benefits for your client application:

- The details of the SQL are hidden from the caller.
- The SQL is already parsed on the server and ready to run.
- Network traffic is minimized.
- Hints can be added to SELECT without changing the calling code.
- Statements can be parameterized.

In programming terms, the client application needs to perform an extra execute operation in order to open the cursor reference returned before results can be fetched. This is performed in similar ways, regardless of the client language. This section contains an example using ADO to show how easy it is to use cursor references. For a long time, it wasn't possible to return Oracle result sets into a Visual Basic application and this was a major drawback for Oracle compared to Microsoft SQL Server. Thankfully, that hasn't applied for quite a while now.

Once you start using cursor references in your code, you should find that performance improves and that the application is easier to maintain. All queries become a result set rather than a SQL statement as far as the client is concerned. In order to return a result set, a package needs to contain a procedure with an OUT variable of type REF CURSOR, as shown in the following example:

```
create or replace package mycursor as

   type t_cursor is ref cursor;

   procedure myobjects(p_cursor out t_cursor,
                        p_name in varchar2);

end mycursor;


create or replace package body mycursor as

procedure myobjects(p_cursor out t_cursor,
                     p_name in varchar2) is

   begin

      OPEN p_cursor FOR
      select object_name,created from all_objects
      where object_name like p_name and rownum <=3;

   end myobjects;

end mycursor;
```

There's no reason why a package can't return more than one cursor variable and therefore execute multiple SQL statements within the server from a single call from the client. This is actually more efficient in terms of reducing network traffic. In order to return the result set in the example, the programmatic interface needs to open the returned reference and fetch the results. Depending on the interface, the open operation is either explicitly performed by the programmer or managed by the interface. At the OCI level, once the cursor is opened, fetching takes place in exactly the same way as it does for a regular SQL SELECT statement.

Displaying a Result Set with SQL*Plus

It's possible to display the result set for a cursor variable in SQL*Plus. The following example uses the MYCURSOR package created previously and passes in a parameter to return the first three user objects beginning with the letter *E*:

```
SQL> variable c1 refcursor
SQL> exec mycursor.myobjects(p_name=>'E%',p_cursor=>:c1);
SQL> print c1

OBJECT_NAME                     CREATED
------------------------------- ---------
ERROR$                          14-AUG-01
ERROR_SIZE                      14-AUG-01
EXISTSNODE                      14-AUG-01
```

In this case, SQL*Plus knows that C1 is a cursor variable because it is explicitly stated in the VARIABLE C1 statement. The PRINT command can be used to open the cursor and return the results. In SQL*Plus, the actions required to return a result set from a stored procedure are very different from those required to execute a SELECT statement, although both have the same end result.

Displaying a Result Set with ADO

By using ADO and Oracle's OLE DB provider for ODBC, result sets can be returned more easily. With ADO, the provider detects that the package procedure returns a variable of type REF CURSOR by querying the Oracle data dictionary first and opens the returned cursor automatically. The following Visual Basic subroutine includes a complete, self-contained example of how to populate an Oracle result set into a Microsoft grid control:

```
Sub ResultSetToGrid()

    Dim conOra As New ADODB.Connection
    Dim rsOra As New ADODB.Recordset
    Dim cmdOra As New ADODB.Command
    Dim prmObject As New ADODB.Parameter

    conOra.ConnectionString = "DSN=prod1;UID=system;PWD=manager;"
    conOra.Open
    cmdOra.ActiveConnection = conOra

    cmdOra.CommandText = "{ CALL mycursor.myobjects(?) }"

    ' create a parameter to hold the object_name value...
    Set prmObject = cmdOra.CreateParameter(Type:=adVarChar, _
                                    Direction:=adParamInput, _
                                    Size:=30, _
                                    Value:="E%")
    cmdOra.Parameters.Append prmObject

    Set rsOra = cmdOra.Execute  ' execute the stored procedure

    ' send result set to the grid
    Set Me.MSHFlexGrid1.DataSource = rsOra


End Sub
```

There are several points to note in this code. The call to the package procedure uses the escape syntax {} for specifying database vendor-specific functionality. This is required because ODBC doesn't recognize Oracle's PACKAGE.PROCEDURE notation. ODBC assumes that names of the form X.Y refer to OWNER.OBJECT. To circumvent this, many ODBC drivers require that you create a procedural wrapper around a package procedure. This means that you should choose an ODBC driver at the outset of a project because different drivers handle Oracle-specific functionality differently, and if you try to change a driver midway through a project, your application will probably break. Not surprisingly, Oracle's driver is the best for interfacing with an Oracle database.

The next point to note is that only one parameter is supplied, even though the procedure requires a REF CURSOR variable as well. ADO simplifies the process because Oracle's OLE DB provider detects that the other variable is a cursor variable and processes it for you under the covers. This is a nice improvement compared to SQL*Plus and other interfaces, which require you to process the cursor explicitly. A server trace of the session shows that the following SQL is actually parsed by the server, clearly showing the existence of the cursor variable, even though it wasn't set in the client code:

```
BEGIN MYCURSOR.MYOBJECTS( :P_CURSOR,:1 ); END;
```

Populating the grid is as simple as assigning the ADO result set to the grid Data-Source. If you actually run this example, you'll find that the column data overflows the grid columns, so you need to resize the columns manually to see the complete contents.

Tuning SQL for the Network

For the majority of GUI applications based on an Oracle server and connected over a local area network (LAN), most of the time for any SQL statement is spent on processing within the DBMS server. However, in some cases the performance of components in your GUI application can affect response time. For example, if your application needs to display thousands of rows in a grid on the client, then the time to render the grid can be significant compared to the time spent processing a query on the server. In this case, a GUI application designer might question the usability of an application that needs to display thousands of rows. The exact version of the ODBC driver that you choose to access the server usually doesn't matter. If your client and server components are connected across a wide area network (WAN), then the network latency can become a factor in client application responsiveness. In this case, it's necessary for the client application to try to batch up requests in order to minimize the number of roundtrips to the server.

Using Bulk Operations in PL/SQL

Oracle8*i* introduced the BULK COLLECT feature to enable array operations to be performed in PL/SQL for the first time. Although PL/SQL runs in the database server, when PL/SQL code contains references to a database link, the code block acts as a client application for the remote database referenced in the link. This is a suitable environment to demonstrate the potential for many more performance improvements due to a reduction in network roundtrips for applications that are constrained by network performance. Table 9.12 shows a complete code example that is used to test the BULK

Table 9.12 PL/SQL BULK COLLECT Benchmark Code

BULK COLLECT CODE	STANDARD CODE

```
declare                              declare
type t_oo is table
  of dba_objects.owner%type;
type t_on is table
  of all_objects.object_name%type;

l_oo t_oo;                           l_oo dba_objects.owner%type;
l_on t_on;                           l_on dba_objects.object_name%type;

cursor c1 is select                  cursor c1 is select
owner,object_name                    owner,object_name
from dba_objects@d1.jp.dbcool.com    from dba_objects@d1.jp.dbcool.com
where rownum <=1000;                 where rownum <=1000;

rows natural :=1000;
begin                                begin
   open c1;                             open c1;
   loop                                 loop
       fetch c1 bulk collect                fetch c1
       into l_oo,l_on limit rows;           into l_oo,l_on;
       exit when c1%notfound;               exit when c1%notfound;
   end loop;                            end loop;

   close c1;                            close c1;

end;                                 end;
/                                    /
```

COLLECT performance compared to standard code across an international WAN link with a 400-millisecond latency.

In each case, 1,000 rows are selected from the DBA_OBJECTS table at the remote database. In the BULK COLLECT code, the LIMIT ROWS qualifier on the FETCH is used to request that rows be returned in batches of 1,000 into the table variables based on the ROWS variable setting. This ensures that the network packets passed from the remote server are completely filled with rows. In the standard case, each row is sent from the remote server in a separate network packet because standard scalar variables rather than tables are used to request the results. You can see this by comparing the definitions of L_OO and L_ON in each case. If necessary, you can view the network packets using the techniques in Chapter 28.

Table 9.13 shows session statistics for the categories of interest in each case. The Statistics (Choose Session) option from the Monitoring menu of DbCool was used to collect the statistics.

It's interesting to compare the amount of network traffic sent back to the client from the database link compared to the actual size of the data in the result set. The result set consists of the OWNER and OBJECT_NAME columns in the DBA_TABLES view. The

Table 9.13 PL/SQL BULK COLLECT versus Scalar Performance

STATISTICS	BULK COLLECT	STANDARD
bytes received via SQL*Net from dblink	25115	226562
bytes sent via SQL*Net to dblink	792	177330
SQL*Net roundtrips to/from dblink	9	2013
Elapsed Seconds	4	750

raw length of column data that needs to be transferred over the link can be obtained using the following SQL:

```
select sum(length(owner)),sum(length(object_name))
from dba_objects@d1.jp.dbcool.com
where rownum <=1000;


  SUM(LENGTH(OWNER))    SUM(LENGTH(OBJECT_NAME))
------------------- -------------------------
              3000                    14485
```

In this example, the raw data in the result set is approximately 17KB. You would expect the data returned via the database link to be larger than this because of the various headers on the network packets, but the scale of the overhead can be compared in each case. The results table shows the massive network overhead resulting from fetching rows one at a time across the network compared to performing the same operation using bulk arrays. What's perhaps most striking is the amount of data that needs to be sent via the database link to the remote server in order to request the next row for the standard case. The elapsed time to complete the operation shows a very close correlation with the number of network roundtrips. Therefore, any techniques that can be used to batch up requests and reduce network roundtrips are likely to improve performance.

As a general rule, Oracle operations work faster when arrays are used to process multiple rows together in bulk rather than a single row at a time. For DML operations, PL/SQL includes the FORALL operation to enable arrays rather than scalar values to be used for inserts.

Defining Server Memory Requirements

It should be clear from the preceding discussions in this chapter that the availability of Oracle data blocks in the Oracle block buffer cache and cursors in the shared pool can improve SQL performance. The existence of previously accessed data and metadata from cache memory avoids the overhead of data and metadata access from disk. A key DBA design decision is therefore the sizing of these caches. The goal is to set the cache sizes sufficiently large so that the effects of data reuse will provide maximum benefit without oversizing them so that memory is wasted. The caches include:

- The block buffer cache (including the KEEP pool and RECYCLE pool)
- The shared pool
- The java pool (for systems using Oracle's Java virtual machine)

For some applications where initial memory requirements were undersized, increasing the cache sizes will continue to increase performance up to a point. However, because physical memory is a finite server resource, excessive memory paging will cause performance of all processes on the server to degrade at the point where the total memory required approaches the physical memory available. Excessive paging can be identified using the UNIX vmstat command, as shown in Chapter 28.

While Oracle9*i* provides increased flexibility to allow the cache settings to be changed dynamically, the DBA continues to have responsibility for setting the total maximum size available to the various caches through the SGA_MAX_SIZE initialization parameter.

As well as the caches, Oracle needs to allocate private session memory for work areas that are used to perform sorting, hashing, bitmap creation and merging, and other operations for a user session. For dedicated server environments, this memory is allocated from the Program Global Area (PGA), which is a private memory region containing data and control information for each server process. For shared server environments, this memory is allocated from another pool in the SGA controlled by the setting of the LARGE_POOL_SIZE initialization parameter. The large pool is also used by shared server systems for allocation of message buffers for parallel execution when PARALLEL_AUTOMATIC_TUNING is set to TRUE. Dedicated and shared server configurations are covered in Chapter 3.

The choice of appropriate cache sizes and memory allocation for PGAs to make best use of the available server memory is an iterative process. Oracle has recognized this through the provision of *Advisories* for sizing the block buffer cache, shared pool, and the aggregate target memory size of all PGAs for dedicated server sessions. The Advisories for the buffer cache and shared cache are intended to answer questions like "how many more cache hits would be achieved if the cache was twice as big" or "would reducing the cache size by 30 percent cause a significant reduction in cache hits?" The effects on performance predicted by the Advisories are contained in the following views, and the information can be used to iteratively modify the values:

```
REM new for Oracle9i
select * from v$db_cache_advice;

REM these two are new for Oracle9i Release 2
select * from v$pga_target_advice;
select * from v$shared_pool_advice;
```

The population of V$DB_CACHE_ADVICE requires that the DB_CACHE_ADVICE parameter is enabled as follows:

```
alter system set db_cache_advice = on;
```

Memory allocation in the PGA prior to Oracle9*i* was controlled through the use of database initialization parameters such as SORT_AREA_SIZE. To enable automatic management of PGA memory in Oracle9*i*, you need to set the initialization parameter PGA_AGGREGATE_TARGET to a target value for the total amount of PGA memory available to all dedicated server sessions in the instance. Once enabled, Oracle takes over management of all parameters named *type*_AREA_SIZE (such as SORT_AREA_SIZE) for each user session that connects via a dedicated server connection, and the original parameter settings are ignored. The views V$SQL_WORKAREA and V$PGA_STATS contain detailed information to help determine the aggregate size required to ensure that work areas for cursors make best use of available memory.

> **NOTE** Through integration with OEM in Oracle9*i* Release 2, it's possible to modify database initialization parameters directly from information provided by the Advisories.

Summary

Tuning SQL requires a continuous emphasis on the measurement of Oracle statistics and events for each statement executed beginning at the start of the development cycle. This measurement can be performed using SQL Analyze in the OEM Tuning Pack, which is a separately licensable option. DbCool is a free tool that provides several of the same functions.

In general, reductions in logical and physical I/O lead to reductions in elapsed time for SQL execution. Physical I/O takes orders of magnitude longer than logical I/O, and it's important to be able to detect full table scans, which can cause excessive I/O. The Oracle buffer cache can be tuned to reduce physical I/O by caching hot data in memory for as long as possible.

In cases where table scans are unavoidable, the use of parallel query options can be used to execute a DML statement across multiple CPUs simultaneously to reduce elapsed time. Parallel query must be used with care because SQL statements intended for parallel execution may be serialized transparently if insufficient CPU resource is available at execution time. The alternative option, to abort parallel SQL when the required CPU resource is not available, is not especially attractive either. The solution is to use Oracle's automatic parallel tuning capabilities.

During development, several techniques are available for tuning SQL including rewriting the SQL embedding HINTs. Rewriting SQL usually shows the most dramatic improvements in performance. For production systems, the scope of SQL tuning is usually limited to changes that don't involve changing the SQL. The use of stored outlines and the Stored Outline Manager and Editor in Oracle9*i* Enterprise Manager make it possible to modify DML statement execution plans (for example, to include HINTs) without changing the SQL.

Identification of resource-intensive SQL is made easier than ever before in Oracle9*i*. For the first time, it's possible to view the actual plan that was used to execute any SQL statement that's present in the shared pool, and view detailed information on the performance of cursors. Oracle9*i* Release 2 takes tuning capabilities to a new level by including features to present detailed performance information at each stage in a DML execution plan, and I/O access statistics for individual segments.

Memory sizing for database caches and PGAs is critical for optimal SQL performance. Oracle9*i* provides Advisories to help predict the effects of different cache sizes on performance, and Oracle9*i* Release 2 takes things a step further by allowing information produced by the Advisories to modify database cache sizes directly, through integration with OEM.

## CHAPTER 10

Collecting and Using Optimizer Statistics

The Oracle optimizer determines the most efficient way to execute a Structured Query Language (SQL) statement and generates a query execution plan during the early stages of Data Manipulation Language (DML) processing. The query execution plan determines which data is accessed, the order it is accessed, and how it is processed. Because SQL is a declarative language, there are many ways that Oracle could process the underlying data to produce the same results. Chapter 9 gave an overview of how the designer can specify the Oracle optimizer mode, which the optimizer uses when generating an execution plan.

Assuming that the cost-based optimizer is used, and this is strongly recommended by Oracle, then the plan chosen relies heavily on the availability of accurate statistics on the tables, columns, and indexes used in the query. In order to make best use of statistics, it's important to understand the statistics available and where to find their values in the data dictionary. For column statistics, an appreciation of data skew—and how to identify it—is required to avoid generation of nonoptimal plans.

The collection of statistics can be performed in two different ways. Traditionally, the ANALYZE method has been used for statistics collection. The DBMS_STATS package represents a different approach, and it's important to understand how the two differ and to be aware of the extensive enhancements to DBMS_STATS in Oracle9i. As well as enhancements to DBMS_STATS, a new approach to optimization is introduced in Oracle9i based on the system central processing unit (CPU) and input/output (I/O) statistics collected during execution to enable plans to adapt dynamically to resource usage patterns. Whatever approach for collection is used, considerable host resources are usually required, and it pays to be aware of techniques for migrating and restoring previously captured statistics to ensure that previous efforts can be reused.

This chapter covers the following topics:

- Basic table and index statistics
- Column statistics and skewed data
- The ANALYZE command
- Statistics collection with DBMS_STATS
- System statistics in Oracle9*i*
- Statistics tables

Basic Table and Index Statistics

The cost-based optimizer uses any available table and index statistics during the generation of an execution plan for a DML statement. Basic table and index statistics can be viewed through DBA_TABLES and DBA_INDEXES. Other views are used to hold information at the partition level and column statistics. Table 10.1 shows columns in DBA_TABLES that hold statistical information collected by either the ANALYZE command or the DBMS_STATS package.

Standard indexes are stored in a data structure called a B*tree. A B*tree index has two different types of blocks: data blocks and leaf blocks. Leaf blocks contain ROWID values that indicate real table rows that the index points to. Data blocks hold index structure information on ranges of key values that are searched by index lookups to identify leaf blocks that hold ROWID values. Table 10.2 shows columns in DBA_INDEXES that hold statistical information on indexes.

Note that for indexes that are used to implement UNIQUE and PRIMARY KEY constraints, AVG_LEAF_BLOCKS_PER_KEY is always 1, and the DISTINCT_KEYS value is equal to the NUM_ROWS value in DBA_TABLES. Higher values of CLUSTERING_FACTOR mean the optimizer is less likely to choose to use that index when generating a plan. When the ANALYZE command is used to collect statistics, the BLOCKS and EMPTY_BLOCKS table statistics and the BLEVEL index statistic are always calculated exactly.

Table 10.1   Columns in DBA_TABLES Holding Statistics

COLUMN NAME	MEANING
NUM_ROWS	Number of table rows, often referred to as *cardinality*
BLOCKS	Number of used data blocks in the table (blocks that ever held data)
EMPTY_BLOCKS	Number of empty blocks (blocks that never held data)
AVG_ROW_LEN	Average length of a row in bytes

Table 10.2 Columns in DBA_INDEXES Holding Statistics

COLUMN NAME	MEANING
BLEVEL	Number of blocks traversed from the root node of the B*tree to a leaf node
LEAF_BLOCKS	Number of leaf blocks in the tree
DISTINCT_KEYS	Number of distinct combinations of the index columns
AVG_LEAF_BLOCKS_PER_KEY	Average number of leaf blocks in which each distinct value in the index appears
AVG_DATA_BLOCKS_PER_KEY	Rounded average number of data blocks in the table that are pointed to by a distinct value in the index
CLUSTERING_FACTOR	A measure of the likelihood that rows in the same leaf block point to rows in the same table block

Column Statistics and Data Skew

In order to determine whether to use an index lookup in the query plan for a DML statement containing a WHERE clause, the cost-based optimizer can use any available statistics on columns referenced in the predicate. The column needs to be referenced using an equality, range, or like operator. The statistics are collected during a standard table ANALYZE command. Available columns statistics can be displayed as follows:

```
select column_name,num_distinct,density
from dba_tab_columns where table_name='table';
```

The availability of additional column value information related to frequency distributions is likely to lead to better execution plans, especially when the distribution of values is skewed. This extra frequency information is held in a histogram. A simple example can be used to demonstrate skewed data and how it can lead to nonoptimal execution plans unless column histogram statistics are present. This example requires a table, MY_OBJECTS, with an index, I0_MY_OBJECTS, created as follows:

```
REM use PCTFREE 99 to spread the table across a few thousand blocks
create table my_objects tablespace tools pctfree 99 pctused 1
as select * from dba_objects where rownum <=5000;

create index i0_my_objects on my_objects(object_id) tablespace tools;

analyze table my_objects compute statistics;
```

In the table MY_OBJECTS, the average number of rows per key in the index can be shown using the following SQL:

```
select avg(rows_per_key),stddev(rows_per_key) from
(
select count(*) rows_per_key from my_objects
group by object_id
);
```

```
AVG(ROWS_PER_KEY)    STDDEV(ROWS_PER_KEY)
-----------------    --------------------
                1                       0
```

In this example, the average number of rows per key is 1. The standard deviation function STDDEV is a measure of fluctuations in the average value of rows per key and is a mathematical measure of data skew. Every key value occurs once in this case because there is no data skew. As a result, the standard deviation is 0 because every key value occurs the same number of times. Data skew can be introduced into MY_OBJECTS as follows, by setting 4,500 of the 5,000 rows in the table to have the same value:

```
update my_objects set object_id=0 where rownum <=4500;
```

Rerunning the previous SQL to display the distribution of the OBJECT_ID values now gives different results:

```
AVG(ROWS_PER_KEY)    STDDEV(ROWS_PER_KEY)
-----------------    --------------------
            34.7                   404.7
```

The average number of rows per key is now 34.7. However, the standard deviation of rows per key has a high value relative to the average number of rows per key. This is clear evidence of skewed data because the average value of rows per key contains signification fluctuations, caused in this case because one key value (0) occurs 4,500 times. Without the standard deviation (that is, without a measure of the distribution of the key values), there's no evidence of a problem. Note that the previous query using STDDEV can be modified to show the skew in any set of columns by replacing GROUP BY OBJECT_ID with the list of columns to investigate. The effect of data skew on a query execution plan can be disastrous. The following SQL statements both generate the same query execution plan (shown after the SQL) because the optimizer has no knowledge that the data is skewed at this stage:

```
select count(object_type) from my_objects where object_id=100;
select count(object_type) from my_objects where object_id=0;

REM... plan for both queries:
Execution Plan
--------------
```

```
SELECT STATEMENT Optimizer=CHOOSE (Cost=3 Card=1 Bytes=8)
  SORT (AGGREGATE)
    TABLE ACCESS (BY INDEX ROWID) OF 'MY_OBJECTS'
      INDEX (RANGE SCAN) OF 'I0_MY_OBJECTS' (NON-UNIQUE)
```

Based on the available statistics, the optimizer decides that on average, each key will return around 35 rows. As a result, the most efficient way to execute both queries is to look up the OBJECT_ID in the index, and then use the ROWID values in the index blocks to locate the rows for that OBJECT_ID in the table. Of course, that's fine when OBJECT_ID is 100. In this case, only three block reads are required to execute the query.

When OBJECT_ID is 0, that's definitely not the case. It's actually considerably more efficient to execute the query by a scan of MY_OBJECTS because the index-based plan actually requires nearly all the table blocks and index blocks to be read. This results in a higher cost and a longer elapsed execution time compared to a table scan, which needs to read the table blocks only. The optimizer can only make decisions based on the available information, and as things stand, there is no evidence of data skew available in the statistics held in the data dictionary.

The solution to this problem is to create a histogram of the distribution of occurrences of OBJECT_ID values so the optimizer can determine whether the OBJECT_ID provided in the SQL has a skewed distribution. Information on histograms can be found in DBA_HISTOGRAMS. In this case, the following ANALYZE commands can be used to create the histogram:

```
analyze table my_objects compute statistics for columns object_id;
analyze table my_objects compute statistics for all indexed columns;
```

The ALL INDEXED COLUMNS option generates distribution information for all indexed columns in a table, based on the reasonable assumption that columns used in a simple WHERE clause are likely to be indexed in order to provide faster access paths to the data. As a result, the availability of histograms on those columns is likely to lead to the generation of more suitable execution plans. One of the problems when creating histograms is to determine when they are appropriate. Oracle9*i* provides additional features to enable the database management system (DBMS) rather than the user to determine columns that would benefit from histograms, through DBMS_STATS using the AUTO and SKEWONLY options discussed later in the chapter. These new options represent a major step forward in the design of the optimizer and another reason to use DBMS_STATS in preference to ANALYZE.

It must be emphasized that the use of bind variables rather than literal values in the WHERE clause of a DML statement prevents histograms from being used. With a literal value, the optimizer can compare the supplied value with the data distribution in the histogram at parse time and generate a plan based on the value. With a bind variable, the actual value is supplied at execution time after the plan has already been generated. This issue is covered in more detail in Chapter 9, including a discussion of the CURSOR_SHARING initialization parameter, which enables the Oracle DBMS to transform end-user SQL containing literals into queries using bind variables automatically. In general, the use of bind variables increases the possibilities for sharing cursors in the shared SQL area and is a good idea. If this results in suboptimal plans being generated because the optimizer requires literal values to take advantage of histograms when data is skewed, then bind variables are a bad idea.

The ANALYZE Command

In the past, the ANALYZE command was used to generate statistics for cost-based optimization. However, Oracle no longer recommends the use of ANALYZE and instead recommends the use of the DBMS_STATS package. From a performance perspective, a major drawback of ANALYZE is that it always runs serially. DBMS_STATS, on the other hand, has the capability to run a parallel query to gather statistics on a table using a specified degree of parallelism. If parallelism isn't available, a serial query of the ANALYZE statement is used instead. Parallel ANALYZE only applies to tables and not indexes. This is an example of a simple analyze command that generates statistics on a table, FX_TRADES, based on a sample of 10 percent of the data:

```
analyze table fx_trades estimate statistics sample 10 percent;
```

ANALYZE has particular limitations when it's run against partitioned objects. Partitioned objects can contain multiple sets of statistics because statistics can be generated at the object, partition, or subpartition level. Global statistics are those that refer to the entire object. For partitioned tables and indexes, ANALYZE gathers statistics for the individual partitions and then calculates the global statistics from the partition statistics. For composite partitioning, ANALYZE gathers statistics for the subpartitions and then calculates the partition statistics and global statistics from the subpartition statistics. The optimizer uses the global statistics unless the WHERE clause in a query restricts the result to a particular partition. As a result, the accuracy of global statistics is paramount when Oracle needs to generate a plan for DML involving a partitioned object. The technique that ANALYZE uses to generate global statistics from partition-level statistics can lead to inaccuracies in global statistics. For example, if a particular column value exists in multiple partitions, it's not possible to calculate the number of distinct values of the column globally with any certainty based on deriving it from the number of distinct values for the column in each partition. For partitioned objects, DBMS_STATS is highly recommended because it can calculate statistics at each level separately. A value of YES in the GLOBAL_STATS column for a partitioned table in DBA_TABLES indicates that statistics were collected for the object as a whole and not derived from the partitions.

Note that the ANALYZE command does not overwrite or delete some of the values of statistics that were gathered by DBMS_STATS. For those statistics, DBMS_STATS is the only way to modify them. Most importantly, ANALYZE will not collect statistics needed by the cost-based optimizer in the future. For that reason, you should start to use DBMS_STATS today, even if you are not yet running Oracle9i.

There is a subset of ANALYZE functionality that is not provided by DBMS_STATS. For example, the number of chained rows, average free space, and number of unused data blocks returned by ANALYZE are not set by DBMS_STATS. Strictly speaking, these are not statistics used by the optimizer, but it seems likely that Oracle will provide a procedural interface for collecting the values in the future.

From a performance perspective, any statistics generation can potentially have a detrimental effect on the whole system. That's not surprising when you consider that huge numbers of blocks need to be read for large tables and indexes, and that sorting (potentially to disk) may be required to calculate data distributions and distinct values. These operations may be I/O, memory, and CPU intensive.

Statistics Collection with DBMS_STATS

In the past, a brute-force approach to collecting statistics was often taken through use of the ANALYZE_SCHEMA procedure to gather statistics for the cost-based optimizer. As the name suggests, ANALYZE_SCHEMA analyzes all objects in a schema. The following example shows an example that analyzes all tables and indexes in SCOTT's schema based on a sample of 10 percent of the existing data:

```
begin
dbms_utility.analyze_schema(schema=>'SCOTT',
                            method=>'ESTIMATE',
                            estimate_percent=>10)
end;
/
```

The ANALYZE_SCHEMA procedure generates statistics for all tables and indexes in the schema, including those that haven't changed since the last execution. Therefore, ANALYZE_SCHEMA potentially wastes resources by recalculating statistics for data that hasn't changed since the last calculation. Prior to Oracle 8i, no method was available at the database level to identify tables that had changed in order to identify candidates for statistics recalculation. It was necessary to store change history information by adding triggers to tables in order to maintain a reference count of updates, deletes, and inserts in a separate table. Oracle8i took the first step toward automatic identification of DML changes to tables through the MONITORING attribute. This can be specified at table creation time or through ALTER TABLE. The following PL/SQL block enables monitoring on all tables except those owned by SYS and SYSTEM, and you are strongly recommended to use it in order to allow table monitoring on all application schemas in your Oracle8i databases:

```
declare
l_mon varchar2(128);
begin
  for r in (select 'alter table '||owner||'.'||table_name||
            'monitoring' s
            from dba_tables where owner not in ('SYS','SYSTEM') loop
    l_mon := r.s;
    execute immediate l_mon;
  end loop;
end;
/
```

The MONITORING column in DBA_TABLES and USER_TABLES shows a value YES for all tables that have monitoring enabled. Oracle9*i* provides new procedure calls in DBMS_STATS to provide shortcuts for enabling monitoring on all existing tables in a schema and for all existing non-SYS-owned tables in the database as whole, as shown in the following example:

```
REM enable monitoring for all SCOTT's tables
begin
sys.dbms_stats.alter_schema_tab_monitoring(ownname=>'SCOTT',
                                         monitoring=>true);
end;
/

REM enable monitoring for all non-SYS tables
begin dbms_stats.ALTER_DATABASE_TAB_MONITORING; end;
/
```

These new procedures are especially useful to enable monitoring for all tables in an application purchased from a third-party vendor. Based on experience, the requirement to collect accurate statistics is often not a priority for such applications. It needs to be emphasized that tables added after the procedure execution don't have monitoring enabled automatically: The procedure needs to be repeated. Once monitoring is enabled, changes to tables can be viewed through the DBA_TAB_MODIFICATIONS view and the equivalent user view. The following SQL shows changes to the SCOTT table immediately after an INSERT statement:

```
insert into scott.emp select * from scott.emp;
commit;

select table_name,inserts,updates,deletes from sys.dba_tab_modifications
where  table_owner='SCOTT';


TABLE_NAME      INSERTS   UPDATES   DELETES
------------ --------- --------- ---------
EMP               14        0         0

delete * from scott.emp where rownum <=5;
commit;


select table_name,inserts,updates,deletes from sys.dba_tab_modifications
where  table_owner='SCOTT';

TABLE_NAME      INSERTS   UPDATES   DELETES
------------ --------- --------- ---------
EMP               14        0         0
```

In the previous example, the results of the DELETE statement are not available immediately. Prior to Oracle9*i*, it wasn't possible to predict with any certainty when table modifications were actually flushed out to DBA_TAB_MODIFICATIONS. Oracle simply flushed out the information according to its own internal rules. Oracle9i addresses this issue through a new procedure in DBMS_STATS, which makes all change information available immediately after execution, as shown in the following example:

```
REM flush out all monitoring statistics now
begin sys.dbms_stats.flush_database_monitoring_info; end;
/
```

An equivalent function for flushing schema-monitoring information was docu-mented in Oracle9i Release 1, but the procedure itself was not supplied. Once table monitoring is in place, statistics can be collected using the GATHER_SCHEMA_STATS procedure in DBMS_STATS rather than the ANALYZE_SCHEMA procedure in DBMS_UTILITY. The GATHER_SCHEMA_STATS has a significant advantage over ANALYZE_SCHEMA because it can use information on monitored table changes in order to determine which tables need to have their statistics refreshed, as shown in the following example:

```
begin
sys.dbms_stats.gather_schema_stats(
     ownname=>'SCOTT'
    ,estimate_percent=>dbms_stats.auto_sample_size
    ,method_opt=>'FOR COLUMNS SIZE (SKEWONLY)'
    ,cascade=>TRUE
    ,degree=> dbms_stats.default_degree
    ,options=>'GATHER STALE');
end;
/
```

As well as the GATHER STALE option, which causes Oracle to query table modifi-cations to identify tables to analyze, Oracle9i provides the GATHER AUTO option, which gathers all necessary statistics automatically. Using GATHER AUTO, Oracle implicitly determines which objects need new statistics and how to gather those statis-tics. How it does this isn't explained, but as it exists as a separate option to GATHER STALE, it seems reasonable that it will be the choice to use in the future. Other options include GATHER, which unconditionally gathers all statistics in a way similar to ANALYZE and GATHER EMPTY; they collect statistics for objects that don't have any. It's possible to show objects that would be analyzed without actually performing the collection using the LIST STALE and LIST AUTO options as shown in the following PL/SQL block for a schema MDS (Multipoint Distribution Service):

```
set serverout on
declare
  objlist dbms_stats.objectab;
  begin
  dbms_stats.gather_schema_stats(
     ownname=>'MDS',options=>'LIST STALE',objlist=>objlist);

  dbms_output.put_line('stale count='||objlist.count);
```

```
   for i in 1..objlist.count loop
     dbms_output.put_line(objlist(i).objname);
   end loop;

   dbms_stats.gather_schema_stats(
       ownname=> 'MDS',options=>'LIST AUTO',objlist=>objlist);

   for i in 1..objlist.count loop
     dbms_output.put_line(objlist(i).objname);
   end loop;
end;
/
```

Both the GATHER STALE and GATHER AUTO options can take an optional argument that returns a list of analyzed objects. You may find that GATHER STALE and GATHER AUTO (and the corresponding LIST STALE and LIST AUTO) options don't identify any objects to analyze even when changes exist in DBA_TAB_MODIFICATIONS. In this case, a SQL TRACE created during execution of the GATHER_SCHEMA_STATS procedure call shows why. The GATHER STALE option runs the following test to identify a stale object that requires statistics regeneration:

```
(INSERTS + UPDATES  + DELETES ) > 0.1 * ROWCOUNT
```

In other words, if the sum of changes to the table doesn't exceed 10 percent of the rows in the table, GATHER STALE doesn't regenerate the statistics because the statistics aren't considered to be stale. Initial releases of Oracle9i used the identical calculation for GATHER AUTO, although this is likely to be enhanced in future. From the observed behavior, GATHER AUTO appears to detect changes to tables immediately, even before change details are flushed from the SGA to appear in DBA_TAB_MODIFICATIONS. Based on that evidence, GATHER AUTO should be used in preference to GATHER STALE. The LAST_ANALYZED column in DBA_TABLES can be checked to determine if an analyze actually took place.

The METHOD_OPT argument provides two new SIZE options for Oracle9i: SKEWONLY and AUTO. These enable the DBMS to generate column histograms based on usage. This is a major step forward, especially if you ever wondered why the database administrator (DBA) should be responsible for detecting skewed data and column usage. The SKEWONLY setting means that Oracle only stores histograms persistently in the dictionary for skewed data distributions, having first collected and analyzed the data in memory. With the SIZE option set to AUTO, the DBMS collects histogram data in memory and persists them in the dictionary only for those columns referenced at parse time in statements involving an equality, range, or like operator.

In the interest of simpler administration, GATHER_SCHEMA_STATS can be called without arguments, in which case statistics are collected for the current schema using the COMPUTE option. The use of AUTO_SAMPLE_SIZE, as shown in the example, is a new feature for Oracle9i that enables Oracle to decide on the sample size required to generate statistically significant results. The sample size starts at approximately 5,000 rows and is increased as required to provide the required level of confidence. As a result, the sample size can differ for each table and column, and for different partitions in a partitioned object. The distinct value in a column is one statistic that tends to require a higher number of samples, especially when each distinct value repeats a relatively small number of times. Collection is executed in parallel through the DEGREE parameter. The DEFAULT_DEGREE uses the default parallelism specified in the init.ora file. A NULL value uses the degree specified for the table currently being processed.

Three other parameters are of interest. The GRANULARITY parameter (not used in the example) determines the level of information collected for partitioned tables. By default, information is collected at the global and partition level but not the subpartition level. The CASCADE option is set to FALSE by DEFAULT, and a value of TRUE causes statistics collection on indexes. Index statistics collection always runs serially. The NO_INVALIDATE argument (not used in the example) is set to FALSE by default. This setting determines whether cursors in the shared SQL area are invalidated by the statistics generation. By default, invalidation takes place, which results in a hard parse on the next use of the statement. Setting NO_INVALIDATE to TRUE avoids the invalidation. Chapter 9 contains a detailed discussion of cursors. In addition to gathering statistics at the schema level, DBMS_STATS provides similar procedures for gathering statistics for individual tables and indexes, as well as for the entire database through the following procedures:

- GATHER_INDEX_STATS
- GATHER_TABLE_STATS
- GATHER_DATABASE_STATS

System Statistics in Oracle9*i*

Oracle9*i* includes a significant new method of collecting statistics. For the first time, Oracle provides features for the collection of both system CPU and I/O information for use in query execution plans. The new routines that provide this functionality in DBMS_STATS are listed in the following:

- GATHER_SYSTEM_STATS
- DELETE_SYSTEM_STATS
- EXPORT_SYSTEM_STATS
- IMPORT_SYSTEM_STATS
- GET_SYSTEM_STATS
- SET_SYSTEM_STATS

Note that the plan table used by EXPLAIN PLAN in Oracle9*i* Release 1 contains three additional columns compared to the Oracle8*i* version. Two of these are used by EXPLAIN PLAN to show an estimate of the I/O cost and CPU cost of the statement based on information collected by GATHER_SYSTEM_STATS. The plan table is created through the utlxplan.sql script on UNIX Oracle installations. The new-for-9*i* columns are shown here:

```
cpu_cost   numeric
io_cost    numeric
temp_space numeric
```

The presence of system statistics enables the optimizer to consider both the system's I/O and CPU resource availability and utilization when considering candidate execution plans. As a result, it's crucial that this information is as accurate as possible at the time the execution plan is generated. The collected information includes the following:

- Single-block read time in milliseconds for sequential reads
- Multiblock read time in milliseconds for scattered reads
- Average number of blocks read in a scattered read
- CPU speed in MHz

The server statistics information must be present in the SYS.AUX_STAT$ table in order for the cost-based optimizer to use it. An example of the stored information that corresponds to the values listed previously can be displayed by the following SQL:

```
select pname,pval1
from sys.aux_stats$ where sname='SYSSTATS_MAIN';


PNAME       PVAL1
---------   -------
CPUSPEED      220
MBRC            5
MREADTIM    5.143
SREADTIM    2.003
```

Recall from the discussion in Chapter 9 that waits for single-block reads result from index block access and table block access by ROWID. The event "db file sequential read" is evident when contention for single-block reads takes place. When table scans take place, blocks are read using scattered reads up to the value of DB_FILE_MULTI-BLOCK_READ_COUNT blocks each time. The event wait "db file scattered read" is evidence of contention for these requests. One of the benefits of making accurate system statistics available to the optimizer is that high values for the init.ora parameter DB_FILE_MULTIBLOCK_READ_COUNT no longer cause the optimizer to bias execution plans in favor of full table scans. Instead, based on the statistics available for both single-block and multiblock reads and the average number of blocks read in a multiblock read, the optimizer can make a better decision based on the requirement to minimize the elapsed time according to the actual resource usage.

The system statistics management routines in the DBMS_STATS package enable DBAs to capture statistics over a specified period of time and store them as a named set in a specified database table. Typically, the name is chosen to associate it with the workload that took place during a monitored interval. For example, a named OLTP might be chosen for the system statistics collected during the OLTP workload in business hours and BATCH for the overnight batch jobs.

Once statistics have been collected that are representative of the workloads in the chosen periods, the IMPORT_SYSTEM_STATS procedure is used to copy the collected statistics into the dictionary table SYS.AUX_STATS$ where they are available to the optimizer. The decision regarding which statistics to import and when to do it is under the control of the DBA. Typically, a database job would be used to automatically schedule the import of different sets of statistics at different times of day, depending on the workload.

Note that the availability of server statistics does not invalidate existing statements in the shared SQL area. This is different than the behavior of the optimizer when table, index, or column statistics are modified, in which case statements using those objects are reparsed at next use. Instead, the optimizer uses system statistics only for statements newly parsed after the statistics are made available. The following is a step-by-step example of how to generate and activate system statistics. First, a table is required to hold the collected statistics:

```
begin
dbms_stats.create_stat_table(ownname=>'SYSTEM',stattab=>'APPST');
end;
```

Next, the collection of statistics needs to be performed, and this requires the Oracle job queue system to be enabled:

```
REM ensure that at least one job queue is started...
REM GATHER_SYSTEM_STATS will fail if it's not
alter system set job_queue_processes = 1;

/*
gather statistics using DBMS_STATS.GATHER_SYSTEM_STATS
this should be a one-off run started at the beginning of the OLTP
workload period for INTERVAL minutes, then during the BATCH. The times
should not overlap.
*/

begin
dbms_stats.gather_system_stats(
    interval =>720,
    statown =>'SYSTEM',stattab=>'APPST',statid=>'OLTP');
end;
/

begin
dbms_stats.gather_system_stats(
    interval =>720,
    statown =>'SYSTEM',stattab=>'APPST',statid=>'BATCH');
end;
/
```

While collection is in progress, the C1 column in APPST has the value AUTOGATH-ERING. After the collection completes successfully, the APPST table contains information about system statistics that were collected successfully during the monitored period:

```
select STATID,C1,C2,C3 from appst;



STATID   C1          C2                 C3
-------- ----------- ------------------ ------------------
OLTP     COMPLETED   01-26-2002 07:30   01-26-2002 19:30
BATCH    COMPLETED   01-26-2002 19:30   01-26-2002 07:30
```

The final step is to copy the appropriate statistics collection into the Oracle data dictionary table SYS.AUX_STATS$, where the information can be used by the cost-based optimizer. The best approach is to take the following two routines and schedule them using the DBMS_JOB procedure so that the correct statistics are in place at the appropriate periods:

```
REM schedule this to set OLTP stats at 07:30...
begin
dbms_stats.import_system_stats(
    statown =>'SYSTEM',stattab=>'APPST',statid=>'OLTP');
end;
/

REM schedule this to set BATCH stats at 19:30...
begin
dbms_stats.import_system_stats(
    statown =>'SYSTEM',stattab=>'APPST',statid=>'BATCH');
end;
/
```

Changing Statistics Manually

Given that the cost-based optimizer uses statistics in the generation of a query execution plan, it follows that by modifying the statistics manually using DBMS_STATS, you potentially modify the execution plan of a DML statement without changing the SQL. This can be useful when you know that a statement would execute faster with a different plan than the one that the optimizer generates. The following is a simple example of how table statistics can be changed manually to modify the execution plan. The example requires a table to be created as follows:

```
REM use PCTFREE 99 to spread the table across a few thousand blocks
create table my_objects tablespace tools pctfree 99 pctused 1
as select * from dba_objects where rownum <=5000;

alter table my_objects add constraint pk_mo primary key(object_id)
using index tablespace tools;
```

```
alter session set optimizer_goal=ALL_ROWS;

select count(*) from my_objects;
```

In this case, the optimizer mode is set to ALL_ROWS to enable the COUNT(*) query to use an optimization known as an index FAST FULL SCAN. You can use EXPLAIN PLAN, as described in Chapter 9, to demonstrate this. Note that the same optimization would not take place using COST mode unless table statistics were generated first. Even without statistics available, the ALL_ROWS optimizer mode can use the size of objects referenced in the query to calculate that a scan of the index has a lower cost than a scan on the table based on the actual size of each object held in DBA_SEGMENTS, as shown in the following code:

```
select segment_name,blocks from dba_segments
where segment_name in ('MY_OBJECTS','PK_MO');



SEGMENT_NAME      BLOCKS
--------------    --------
MY_OBJECTS          5120
PK_MO                 16
```

At this stage, the BLOCKS column in DBA_TABLES is still set to NULL because no statistics have been generated yet. It's interesting to investigate the effects on the query execution plan if the statistic holding the number of blocks is modified manually using the SET_TABLE_STATS procedure in DBMS_STATS as follows:

```
begin
sys.dbms_stats.set_table_stats(
    ownname=>'SYSTEM',numblks=>5,tabname=>'MY_OBJECTS');
end;
/
```

The Oracle cost-based optimizer will now use the available statistics during plan generation. As a result of the manual change, the optimizer now calculates that a scan of MY_OBJECTS has a lower cost than a FAST FULL SCAN of the index, based on the statistic that MY_OBJECTS contains five blocks. Physically, it still comprises 5,120 blocks, but the statistic now states 5, and this is the value used by the optimizer to generate the cost. The execution plan confirms the effect of changing BLOCKS by indicating a full table scan:

```
Execution Plan
----------------------------------------------------------
    0       SELECT STATEMENT Optimizer=ALL_ROWS (Cost=1 Card=1)
    1    0    SORT (AGGREGATE)
    2    1      TABLE ACCESS (FULL) OF 'MY_OBJECTS' (Cost=1 Card=2000)
```

The cardinality (or number of rows) in the table is set to 2,000 by default because whenever you set one of the table statistics using SET_TABLE_STATS, any others not supplied are assigned default values. The default number of rows is set to 2,000, and the default average row length is set to 100. The following SQL shows the statistics from DBA_TABLES resulting from the call to SET_TABLE_STATS, including the USER_STATS column that is used to indicate whether Oracle or the user (as in this case) is generating the values:

```
select blocks,num_rows,avg_row_len,user_stats
from dba_tables where table_name='MY_OBJECTS';


  BLOCKS    NUM_ROWS    AVG_ROW_LEN USER_STATS
-------- ----------- ------------- ------------
       5        2000           100 YES
```

Using Dynamic Statistics

Oracle9i Release 2 includes a new feature called dynamic sampling, which is enabled through the dynamic database parameter OPTIMIZER_DYNAMIC_SAMPLING. The parameter takes a range of values from 0 to 10. By default, the parameter is set to 0 (disabled) unless the OPTIMIZER_FEATURES_ENABLE parameter is set to 9.2.0 or higher, in which the value defaults to 1. Dynamic sampling is designed to reduce resource costs for DML statements by determining more accurate selectivity and cardinality estimates than those available. For example, existing statistics may be out of date, inaccurate, or simply nonexistent. On-the-fly generation of dynamic statistics in these situations may lead to the generation of more resource-efficient execution plans for DML that would otherwise result in resource-intensive full table scans of large tables.

Dynamic sampling works by generating recursive SQL to scan a small random sample of a table's blocks at query compile time. Higher values of OPTIMIZER_DYNAMIC_SAMPLING lead to more extensive sampling. Due to the I/O overhead introduced, dynamic sampling produces maximum benefits for SQL statements that have a significant elapsed time compared to the sampling time and are executed frequently.

Statistics Tables

The Oracle optimizer only uses statistics present in the data dictionary. The DBMS_STATS package lets you store collections of statistics in a statistics table, and then transfer statistics between the table and the data dictionary, and vice versa. This is useful, for example, when you want to take statistics from your production system onto your development system to ensure that query execution plans match on both, even if the volumes of data on development are significantly smaller than production. Oracle's Import and Export command-line tools can be used to transfer the contents of statistics tables between databases. A single statistics table can store multiple named collections of statistics, or alternatively, multiple tables can be used. Statistics can be imported and exported at the column, index, table, schema, database, and system levels. The following procedures in DBMS_STATS are used to create and drop statistics tables:

- CREATE_STAT_TABLE
- DROP_STAT_TABLE

The following procedures are used to export statistics from the dictionary into user tables and import them from user tables into the data dictionary:

- EXPORT_COLUMN_STATS
- EXPORT_INDEX_STATS
- EXPORT_TABLE_STATS
- EXPORT_SCHEMA_STATS
- EXPORT_DATABASE_STATS
- EXPORT_SYSTEM_STATS
- IMPORT_COLUMN_STATS
- IMPORT_INDEX_STATS
- IMPORT_TABLE_STATS
- IMPORT_SCHEMA_STATS
- IMPORT_DATABASE_STATS
- IMPORT_SYSTEM_STATS

Summary

Accurate statistics on table, index, and column information are required by the Oracle optimizer to generate query execution plans that meet the designer's requirements. In the past, statistics were generated by the ANALYZE command. Today, Oracle recommends that all statistics collections use the DBMS_STATS package. DBMS_STATS has many advantages over ANALYZE, including parallel execution and the capability to automatically regenerate only those statistics that are out of date.

Enhancements to DBMS_STATS in Oracle9i include features to collect system CPU and I/O statistics for use in plan generation. The new SKEWONLY and AUTO options enable the Oracle DBMS rather than the DBA to make decisions on when column histograms are required, and system-generated sample sizes are available to produce statistically significant results automatically. Oracle has stated that in the future, the optimizer will generate plans based only on information generated by DBMS_STATS.

The increasing power and complexity of DBMS_STATS makes using it a challenge. Oracle has addressed this in part through the Analyze Wizard component of Oracle Enterprise Manager (OEM), which exposed only a small subset of DBMS_STATS functionality in early releases of Oracle9i but promises to be the interface of choice in the future.

Partitioning

Oracle introduced partitioning in Oracle8 to address performance and availability issues associated with large tables and indexes. By splitting large tables and indexes into smaller pieces (called *partitions*), finite bounds can be placed on resource requirements for operations that would otherwise grow in step with the size of the table or index.

A good example to illustrate this point is an index rebuild. When a table grows over time, the sort space required to create or rebuild the index grows along with it. When partitioning is used to split the index into smaller pieces of a finite size, the maximum sort space required for the rebuild is constrained to the size of the largest partition instead. In this case, availability is enhanced because rebuilds can be done partition by partition and in parallel, reducing the time that the index is not available. However, if partitions are implemented without careful consideration, then availability can actually be compromised. This chapter covers the following topics:

- An overview of partitioning performance and availability features
- Partition creation examples using range, list, hash, and composite methods
- Partition indexing techniques
- Availability and global indexes

Partitioning Overview

It's quite easy to become overwhelmed by the sheer number of partitioning options. This is not helped by the complex syntax that often appears when creating partitioned objects. It's important to keep in mind a few key features of partitioning:

- All partitions in a table or index must have the same column names, data types, and constraints.
- All partitions may optionally have different physical storage attributes, such as PCTFREE and PCTUSED, and reside in different tablespaces.
- Partitioning is transparent to Data Manipulation Language (DML) statements.
- DML statements can continue to run against a partitioned table even when a subset of partitions is unavailable due to maintenance, provided that the DML doesn't refer to data in the unavailable partitions.

Because Oracle backup and recovery can be performed at the tablespace level, it's worth emphasizing that a decision to store each partition (or subpartition) in its own tablespace means that backup and recovery become possible at the partition level. As a result, the impact of restores resulting from logical data corruption or physical media failure can be limited to the partition level. Availability is enhanced as a result. For backups, the use of separate tablespaces enables backups to take place in smaller chunks and minimizes the performance impact of a full database backup. In this case, the performance hit resulting from the input/output (I/O) resource demands of the backup impacts performance for a much shorter time. For systems that maintain historical data in a fixed time window (for example, the last 12 months), the ability to purge or archive data through a simple partition-level operation can reduce archiving or purge times by several orders of magnitude as compared to a DELETE statement that performs the same function. A massive reduction in redo generation occurs with the partition-based approach. Partitioning can cause dramatic reductions in elapsed time for DML statements in the right circumstances through the following features:

- Partition elimination
- Partition-wise joins
- Parallel DML

For example, when the optimizer generates a query execution plan that accesses a small subset of available partitions (referred to as *partition elimination*), the reduction in I/O that results can reduce elapsed times by orders of magnitude. When tables are partitioned on the join column used in a query predicate, an optimization referred to as a *partition-wise join* is available to the query optimizer. Partition-wise joins enable the join to be decomposed into smaller joins that can be performed sequentially or in parallel. When the operations are performed in parallel, elapsed times for queries are typically reduced by decreases in I/O from the partition-wise join. DML such as bulk inserts can be performed at the partition level, leading to the possibility of multiple concurrent, parallel insert streams and associated reductions in data load times for data-warehousing applications.

Table-Partitioning Methods

Oracle provides four different methods for partitioning tables:

- Range partitioning
- List partitioning (new for Oracle9*i*)
- Hash partitioning
- Composite partitioning

The different behavior of each partitioning option is most easily understood by using examples, which are provided in this chapter. Indexes can also be partitioned in the form of global and local indexes. Global indexes can only use the range-partitioning method, whereas local index partitions are determined by the table-partitioning method. It's difficult to have a discussion on table partitioning that avoids all references to index partitioning since the two are related. As a result, partitioned indexes are covered in the section after this one, *Partitioned Indexes*, where you will find full descriptions of index-partitioning terminology.

Range Partitioning

Consider a scenario where a database holds a sales table that needs to be updated in real time in an Online Transaction Processing (OLTP) application. After 12 months, sales data is no longer required in the production database and can be removed. In this situation, range partitioning on the SALES_DATE column is appropriate because it enables the old data to be removed with a simple partition drop operation rather than a much more expensive DELETE operation. Provided that any indexes are partitioned (using the LOCAL option) on the same column as the table, the index partition is automatically dropped along with the table partition. As a result, the removal of old data benefits from the lower cost of both the table and index maintenance on the partitioned objects when compared to the same operations on a standard table using DELETE. The following Structured Query Language (SQL) creates the SALES table partitioned on the SALES_DATE column for the first 6 months of 2002:

```
create table sales (sale_id number,
                    item integer,
                    qty integer,
                    store varchar(30),
                    dept number,
                    empno number,
                    sale_date date)
partition by range (sale_date)(
partition p200201 values less than(to_date('01/02/2002','dd/mm/yyyy')),
partition p200202 values less than(to_date('01/03/2002','dd/mm/yyyy')),
partition p200203 values less than(to_date('01/04/2002','dd/mm/yyyy')),
partition p200204 values less than(to_date('01/05/2002','dd/mm/yyyy')),
```

```
partition p200205 values less than(to_date('01/06/2002','dd/mm/yyyy')),
partition p200206 values less than(to_date('01/07/2002','dd/mm/yyyy'))) ;
```

In this example, the partition names have been chosen so that sorting on the partition name shows the date-of-creation order for each partition. This can be useful when the list of partitions for a table needs to be displayed:

```
select partition_name
from dba_segments where segment_name='SALES'
order by 1 desc;
```

Even though the SALES_DATE column is specified to allow NULL values, an attempt to insert a row with a NULL SALES_DATE value will fail with an ORA-01440 error because Oracle can't determine which partition to store the row in. To allow NULL values to be inserted as part of the partition key, a special range value called MAXVALUE must be used. When MAXVALUE is used, NULL values in the partition key sort greater than all other range values except MAXVALUE. The following SQL adds a partition to SALES that allows NULL values for SALES_DATE to be inserted:

```
alter table sales add partition p999999 values less than (maxvalue);

REM... now this works:
insert into sales store('LEEDS');
```

The ALL_TAB_PARTITIONS view can be used to show the number of rows in each partition after the table has been analyzed. The following example demonstrates that the previous insert has added a row to the P999999 partition that holds all rows that include NULL as part of the partition key:

```
select partition_name,num_rows from all_tab_partitions
where table_name='SALES';
```

PARTITION_NAME	NUM_ROWS
P200201	0
P200202	0
P200203	0
P200204	0
P200205	0
P200206	0
P999999	1

Although partitioning is designed to be transparent to application DML, it's possible to select rows from partitions explicitly if required by using a PARTITION clause to qualify the table. Oracle's Import and Export tools also support partition-level operations. The following SQL shows how to use a PARTITION clause in a SELECT statement:

```
select count(*) from sales partition(p999999);


   COUNT(*)
----------
         1
```

Rather than simply dropping the partition, data can be also be moved from the table with a simple near-instantaneous Data Definition Language (DDL) operation on the partition. For example, if the sales data needs to be kept for the long term, then the oldest monthly partition can be exchanged with a table or exported using a transportable tablespace (provided that each partition is located in its own tablespace) rather than simply dropped. Chapter 19 contains an example that shows how to move data between systems using transportable tablespaces. Partition exchange operations do not involve any movement of the rows and have a very low cost.

If the SALES table is used in a Decision Support System (DSS)—rather than an OLTP—application, partition exchange is also useful for bulk loading sales data one month at a time. For a DSS application, bulk loading monthly sales data would typically take place on a table using SQL*Loader with the direct path option for maximum speed. Next, indexes would be created on the table, and the table and index would be exchanged with a precreated partition to move the monthly data and index into the SALES table instantaneously. The following SQL shows how to add the partition for July 2002 to the SALES table created earlier and how to exchange data in a preloaded table into it:

```
REM add partition for next month...
alter table sales add partition p200207
values less than(to_date('01/08/2002','dd/mm/yyyy'));


REM table rows ready to exchange into partition...
select count(*) from tab_200207;


   COUNT(*)
----------
     28161


/*
 * assume table tab_200207 exists loaded with data for July 2002
 * and with an index on SALE_DATE
 */
alter table sales exchange partition p200207
with table tab_200207 including indexes with validation;

REM confirm rows in tab_200207 moved out...
select count(*) from tab_200207;
```

```
COUNT(*)
----------
         0
```

The EXCHANGE PARTITION command adds the contents of table TAB_200207 as the new partition, P200207. Keep in mind that EXCHANGE PARTITION is a logical operation that doesn't physically move any data; it operates by remapping extents associated with the table to become part of the partition. As a result, EXCHANGE PARTITION completes almost instantaneously. If the SALES table has a local partitioned index defined on the SALE_DATE column, an existing index on the same column on TAB_200207 can be exchanged along with the table as part of EXCHANGE PARTITION. Partitioned indexes and terminology are covered in the following section. The index on SALES, when partitioned on the same key as the table, is said to be *equipartitioned* with the table. The INCLUDING INDEXES option causes the table index to become the partition index for the new table partition. The WITH VALIDATION option ensures that rows in the table meet the range limits for the partition with which the table is exchanged. The following SQL can be used to ensure that the added index is in a USABLE state after the exchange:

```
select partition_name,status
from user_ind_partitions where index_name='I0_SALES';
```

```
PARTITION_NAME    STATUS
----------------  --------
P200201           USABLE
P200202           USABLE
P200203           USABLE
P200204           USABLE
P200205           USABLE
P200206           USABLE
P200207           USABLE
```

List Partitioning

Oracle9*i* provides a new partitioning model called *list partitioning*. List partitioning enables the designer to provide complete control of the mapping between rows and partition keys by specifying a list of values for the partitioning key. This is useful for situations where there is a requirement to partition data on values that are not related to the collating sequence of the key values. Based on the SALES table, list partitioning could be used to partition data based on explicit lists of STORE names in order to distribute data equally across each partition. A few restrictions exist with the use of list partitions: A single column must be used as the partition key, each key value must be used in a single partition list only, and partitions can't be empty. Partition elimination, partition-wise joins, and parallel DML are all supported by list partitions. The following SQL shows an example of list partitioning using the values in the STORE column:

```
create table sales (sale_id number,
                    item integer,
                    qty integer,
                    store varchar(30),
                    dept number,
                    empno number,
                    sale_date date)
partition by list (store)(
partition range1 values ('BRISTOL','GLASGOW','LEEDS'),
partition range2 values ('LONDON'));
```

NOTE In Oracle9*i* Release 2, list partitioning now supports the concept of a default partition, into which rows that don't match the list values can be stored. In Oracle9*i* Release 1, attempts to insert such values resulted in an error, and required special handling in applications. Oracle9*i* Release 2 also provides composite range-list partitioning for the first time.

Hash Partitioning

Hash partitioning enables data to be distributed evenly between different partitions based on the results of a built-in hashing function provided by Oracle. If you choose to deploy hash partitioning, you're implicitly making the following assumptions:

- Associating each partition with a separate tablespace is the best way to distribute Oracle I/O.

- Even distribution of data across partitions is required for the best performance.

It's important for you to make sure those assumptions are correct, in order to benefit from hash partitioning. If you intend to follow the recommendations put forward in this book for Oracle layout (as covered in Chapter 2), then the first assumption probably doesn't apply; therefore, a decision to deploy hash partitioning based on that assumption should be reconsidered. Setting aside performance considerations for a moment, the use of many different tablespaces across many file systems fragments disk space and leads to labor-intensive and complex Oracle database management. Complex database management usually leads to reduced availability. Although this approach *may* also result in better performance, this book proposes a different approach to deliver performance and availability *at the same time* for the Oracle physical layout through the following practices:

- Database layout across large file systems so that all databases on a server can use all available space

- AUTOEXTEND and LOCAL UNIFORM space allocation for 100 percent usage of available disk space and database growth on demand

- High I/O throughput due to the performance of the storage underlying the filesystems rather than database administrator (DBA) placement of many tablespaces across many file systems

It's fair to say that hash partitioning does enable parallel index scans across all partitions, in which case the use of hash partitioning to ensure the even distribution of data across partitions is worth considering. For a system with many central processing units (CPUs) that is not I/O bound, the even distribution of data across many partitions may lead to a reduction in elapsed time when hash partitioning is used and parallel index scans take place, because the DBMS can reduce processing time by making use of multiple CPUs at the same time.

The hash-partitioning method requires the number of partitions allocated to be a power of 2 in order to ensure a uniform distribution of data in the different partitions. It's not possible to provide different storage attributes for each partition explicitly. However, each partition inherits storage attributes from the tablespace in which it resides. As a result, storage attributes for each partition can be specified individually by ensuring that each partition is located in its own tablespace. The original SALES table in this chapter was partitioned by SALE_DATE in order to enable historical data to be removed at very low cost. However, as sales are typically higher in January, the data in each partition may not be evenly distributed, as shown by the following SQL:

```
select partition_name,num_rows
from user_tab_partitions where table_name='SALES';
```

```
PARTITION_NAME      NUM_ROWS
----------------  ----------
P200201              44379
P200202              10222
P200203              11005
P200204              10979
P200205              11217
P200206              10910
```

The table can be created using hash partitioning to evenly distribute the same data across eight partitions as follows:

```
create table sales (sale_id number,
                    item integer,
                    qty integer,
                    store varchar(30),
                    dept number,
                    empno number,
                    sale_date date)
partition by hash (sale_id)
partitions 8
store in (ts01, ts02, ts03, ts04, ts05, ts06, ts07, ts08);
```

In this example, partition names are not specified explicitly (although they can be) and Oracle generates them automatically. The distribution of rows across partitions is shown in the following code, demonstrating how data is evenly distributed across partitions with names generated by the system:

```
PARTITION_NAME     NUM_ROWS
----------------   ----------
SYS_P1                12444
SYS_P2                12410
SYS_P3                12404
SYS_P4                12351
SYS_P5                12169
SYS_P6                12220
SYS_P7                12472
SYS_P8                12224
```

Although hash partitioning enables data to be evenly distributed across partitions, the benefits of historical data management from range partitioning are not available.

Composite Partitioning

Oracle introduced composite partitioning in Oracle8*i* in order to provide the historical data management features of range partitioning alongside the parallel DML and data placement features of hash partitioning in the same table. When using composite partitioning, data is partitioned using the range method, and then subpartitioned within each partition using the hash method. Range partitioning is a logical division of data that supports the use of partition-level operations using range values. The physical distribution of data is determined by the subpartitions that provide enhanced performance through parallel DML and the fine control of data placement at the tablespace level. The following SQL shows the SALES table partitioned by range on SALE_DATE, and then subpartitioned by STORE, with rows distributed across four tablespaces:

```
create table sales
partition by range (sale_date)
subpartition by hash(store)
subpartitions 4
store in (ts01, ts02, ts03, ts04)(
partition p200201 values less than(to_date('01/02/2002','dd/mm/yyyy')),
partition p200202 values less than(to_date('01/03/2002','dd/mm/yyyy')),
partition p200203 values less than(to_date('01/04/2002','dd/mm/yyyy')),
partition p200204 values less than(to_date('01/05/2002','dd/mm/yyyy')),
partition p200205 values less than(to_date('01/06/2002','dd/mm/yyyy')),
partition p200206 values less than(to_date('01/07/2002','dd/mm/yyyy')));


REM show row distribution per tablespace for first three partitions . . .
select partition_name,subpartition_name,num_rows,tablespace_name
from user_tab_subpartitions where table_name='SALES';


PARTITION_NAME    SUBPARTITION_NAME     NUM_ROWS TABLESPACE_NAME
----------------  --------------------  -------- -----------------
P200201           SYS_SUBP63              13652 TS01
P200201           SYS_SUBP64              15373 TS02
```

```
P200201          SYS_SUBP65              8523 TS03
P200201          SYS_SUBP66              6831 TS04

P200202          SYS_SUBP67              3186 TS01
P200202          SYS_SUBP68              3580 TS02
P200202          SYS_SUBP69              1924 TS03
P200202          SYS_SUBP70              1532 TS04

P200203          SYS_SUBP71              3328 TS01
P200203          SYS_SUBP72              3808 TS02
P200203          SYS_SUBP73              2173 TS03
P200203          SYS_SUBP74              1696 TS04
```

In this example, where four STORE values exist, the subpartitions identify the distribution of sales across the stores for each month. Each subpartition can take part in parallel DML and enables partition elimination. Equality, range, and IN predicates are considered by the optimizer for partition elimination with range partitioning, and equality and IN predicates are considered for partition elimination with hash partitioning. Note that although range partitioning has a logical meaning when combined with subpartitions, Oracle is able to map the logical range partition to the underlying subpartitions so that the following operation works in the same way as the original range-partitioned example and avoids unusable indexes, provided that indexes on SALES are local:

```
REM drop partitions (and sub-partitions) for Jan 2002...
alter table sales drop partition p200201;
```

Partitioned Indexes

Some of the most challenging aspects of partition management involve the choice and use of partitioned indexes. Partitioned indexes can be created as either local or global. A local index is partitioned using the same range values as the underlying table. The local index is said to be equipartitioned with the table. The best way to think of a local index is to first consider the partitioned table as a collection of independent tables. The local index is a collection of indexes created on each individual table. As a result of the equipartitioning, an operation on a table partition affects only the associated index partition. For example, when a partition is dropped, the index partition is dropped automatically. Before considering which columns to index in the SALES table, it's worth restating that in the original example, the overriding requirement was to maintain the contents of the SALES table on a sliding window so that the previous 12 months of data were available. Any indexing strategy must be considered with that in mind.

Indexes are created for either performance reasons (to speed up access paths to data) or integrity reasons (to enforce primary key and unique key constraints). The same rules apply to indexes on the partitioned SALES table. When running reports on the SALES table, it's likely that grouping on the SALE_DATE column will be required. Therefore, an index on SALE_DATE is appropriate in order to provide a fast access path to SALES data by sale date. The equipartitioned local index on SALE_DATE is created using the following SQL:

```
create index i0_sales on sales(sale_date) local;

REM show that index partition names are the same as the table
partitions . . .
select partition_name from all_ind_partitions where
index_name='I0_SALES';

PARTITION_NAME
----------------
P200201
P200202
P200203
P200204
P200205
P200206
P999999
```

When an index partition key matches the leftmost columns in the index, the index is said to be *prefixed*. In this case, the index column is SALE_DATE and the index partition key is also SALE_DATE because local indexes use same the partition key as the table on which the index exists. Therefore, our I0_SALES index is prefixed. Figure 11.1 shows a representation of the SALES table and the equipartitioned index I0_SALES. For each table partition, there is an identically named index partition (as shown in the previous SQL output), which is indicated by the arrows in Figure 11.1. Each indexed SALE_DATE value in a given table partition has an entry in the associated index partition, as shown by the matching date and part of the ROWID value.

Consider the benefits of a local partitioned index on the SALE_DATE column. When a query such as SELECT COUNT(*) FROM SALES WHERE SALE_DATE BETWEEN '01-JAN-2002' AND '31-JAN-2002' is executed, the table partitioning on SALES_DATE means that Oracle optimizer can eliminate all partitions except P200201 from processing immediately. As the index is equipartitioned with the table, a range scan of the index partition P200201 associated with the table will be sufficient to produce the query results. If the table contained millions of rows representing 12 months' worth of data, a nonpartitioned table and index would require an index 12 times as big to be scanned (assuming that each month has an equal number of sales). If it was later decided to keep data for 24 months online, then the index would be around 24 times as big as the single index partition for 1 month. By using partitions, the I/O requirement to satisfy the query is bounded by the size of a single partition compared to the nonpartitioned case where the I/O grows with the size of the table. By placing finite bounds on processing requirements, partitions enable scalability. Figure 11.2 shows the DbCool EXPLAIN PLAN for the previous statement, where steps #2 and #3 in the plan indicate the use of the partition key on SALES_DATE, and step #3 indicates the use of the equipartitioned I0_SALES column.

At this point, it's worth considering the processing that would take place for the same SQL if the index I0_SALES did not exist. In this case, a full scan of the partition

SALES Table Partitions

P200201 (Jan 2002)				P200202 (Feb 2002)				P200203 (Mar 2002)		
SALE_DATE	STORE	EMPNO		SALE_DATE	STORE	EMPNO		SALE_DATE	STORE	EMPNO
14-JAN-02	BRISTOL	4		04-FEB-02	LONDON	11		03-MAR-02	LEEDS	2
14-JAN-02	LONDON	12		05-FEB-02	LEEDS	2		11-MAR-02	LONDON	8
18-JAN-02	BRISTOL	10		07-FEB-02	LEEDS	2		19-MAR-02	GLASGOW	13
19-JAN-02	GLASGOW	13		10-FEB-02	GLASGOW	3		22-MAR-02	GLASGOW	3
22-JAN-02	LONDON	9		22-FEB-02	LONDON	8		27-MAR-02	LEEDS	2
22-JAN-02	LONDON	9		28-FEB-02	GLASGOW	14		28-MAR-02	LONDON	8

LOCAL Index I0_SALES(SALE_DATE) Partitions

SALE_DATE	ROWID		SALE_DATE	ROWID		SALE_DATE	ROWID
14-JAN-02	E6KAAD		04-FEB-02	E6MAAD		03-MAR-02	E6OAAE
14-JAN-02	E6KAAE		05-FEB-02	E6MAAA		11-MAR-02	E6OAAF
18-JAN-02	E6KAAB		07-FEB-02	E6MAAC		19-MAR-02	E6OAAB
19-JAN-02	E6KAAC		10-FEB-02	E6MAAF		22-MAR-02	E6OAAD
22-JAN-02	E6KAAA		22-FEB-02	E6MAAB		27-MAR-02	E6OAAC
22-JAN-02	E6KAAF		28-FEB-02	E6MAAE		28-MAR-02	E6OAAA

Figure 11.1 Equipartitioned index I0_SALES.

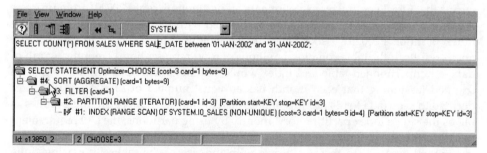

Figure 11.2 EXPLAIN PLAN with a partitioned index.

P200201 alone would produce the results because partition elimination is still available. On the other hand, a nonpartitioned table would require a full table scan of all the data for every month. Therefore, scalability is still improved even without the existence of the index. Figure 11.3 shows the DbCool EXPLAIN PLAN for the previous

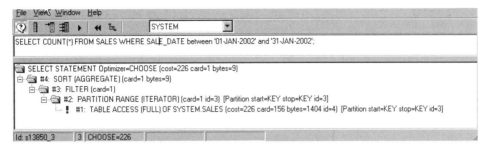

Figure 11.3 EXPLAIN PLAN without a partitioned index.

statement without an index. The plan indicates that without the index, a full scan of SALES is required, but that partition elimination restricts the scan to a single partition.

Now consider another requirement. In this case, it's required to group output by the name of the store using a query like SELECT COUNT(*) FROM SALES WHERE STORE='GLASGOW'. Leaving aside partitioning for the moment, it would be reasonable to create an additional index on the STORE column. It's possible to create another local index on the STORE column. The use of LOCAL means that the index is partitioned on the partition key of the table as before, which is SALE_DATE. In this case, the index partition key is no longer a leftmost match with the index columns, so the index is said to be *nonprefixed*. The following SQL creates the I1_SALES index on column STORE, partitioned by SALE_DATE (based on the underlying table partitioning):

```
create index i1_sales on sales(store) local;
```

Figure 11.4 shows the index entries for the local index I1_SALES table showing only the store value GLASGOW in order make the behavior of queries that use the index easier to understand.

It's clear from Figure 11.4 that if the index I1_SALES is to be used in a query execution plan such as the COUNT(*) example used previously, each partition of the index will need to be searched in order to identify rows where the STORE='GLASGOW'. This is because the index key (STORE) doesn't match the partition key (SALE_DATE). The operation of searching each index partition in this scenario is referred to as an *index probe*. The more partitions that exist, the more probes are required. The use of a local index on STORE means that the availability advantages of equipartitioning apply to I1_SALES. For example, if the table partition P200201 is dropped, then both index partitions on SALE_DATE and STORE for that date range are dropped automatically and the index remains in a useable state.

If LOCAL is not specified for an index, then the index is a global index. A global index doesn't have to be partitioned and can be created on a nonpartitioned table. The following two statements create the same nonpartitioned global index on SALES(STORE):

```
create index i2_sales on sales(store) global;

REM GLOBAL is the default so this is the same...
create index i2_sales on sales(store);
```

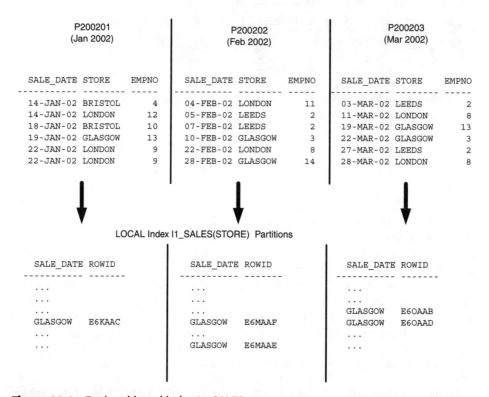

Figure 11.4 Equipartitioned index I1_SALES.

The major difference between a local and global index is that the global index can use a different partition key from the table partition key. So in order to gain the maximum performance from SELECT COUNT(*) FROM SALES WHERE STORE= 'GLASGOW', it makes sense to create a global index on SALES and partition on the STORE column to enable partition elimination in the query execution plan. The definition of a global index partitioned on STORE looks like this:

```
create index i2_sales on sales(store)
global
partition by range (store)(
partition store_d values less than('D'),
partition store_i values less than('I'),
partition store_n values less than('N'),
partition store_s values less than('S'),
partition store_max values less than(maxvalue));
```

Figure 11.5 shows the index partitions and how they map to data in the partitioned table. The dashed lines indicate that all table rows matching STORE='GLASGOW' are

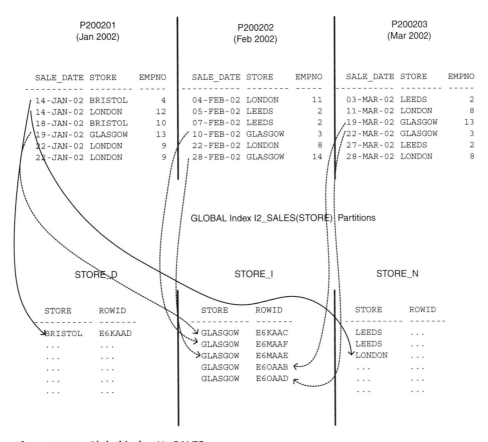

Figure 11.5 Global index I2_SALES.

located in the same index partition for the global index. This contrasts with Figure 11.4, which shows that for a local index on the same column (STORE), rows for STORE='GLASGOW' can be located in different index partitions. For the global index scenario, when the query SELECT COUNT(*) FROM SALES STORE='GLASGOW' executes, the optimizer can determine that a partitioned global index exists on the STORE column and can use partition elimination to generate the query results from a FAST FULL SCAN operation on the STORE_I partition of the I2_SALES index.

Clearly, global indexes provide performance benefits. However, the drawback of global indexes stems from the fact that the table and index are not partitioned on the same key. As a result, maintenance dependencies are introduced that don't exist when local indexes are used. Consider what happens in Figure 11.5 when table partition P200201 is dropped. The existence of the global index on STORE means that index entries exist in all index partitions for rows in P200201, as shown by the lines from the rows in P200201 to the index partitions that hold the index entries. As a result, when the partition is dropped, one or more index partitions contain entries for rows that no longer exist. To ensure that this index can't be used, Oracle marks the global index as UNUSABLE:

```
alter table sales drop partition p200201;

REM now check the state of I2_SALES partitions...
select partition_name,status
from user_ind_partitions where index_name='I2_SALES';



PARTITION_NAME    STATUS
----------------  ---------
STORE_I           UNUSABLE
STORE_D           UNUSABLE
STORE_N           UNUSABLE
STORE_S           UNUSABLE
STORE_MAX         UNUSABLE
```

During the time that the index is in an unusable state, DML that requires the use of the index produces errors. Therefore, if partition maintenance operations are carried out without careful consideration, availability can be compromised. For example, the previous query using the predicate STORE='GLASGOW' produces the following error:

```
ORA-01502: index 'SYSTEM.I2_SALES' or partition of such index is in
unusable
```

The solution to this problem is to rebuild the index. Rebuilding a partitioned index requires rebuilding each partition separately, as shown in the following example, which rebuilds the index partitions rendered unusable by the previous partition drop command:

```
begin
  for rec in (select partition_name p from
                 user_ind_partitions where index_name='I2_SALES'
                 and status='UNUSABLE')
  loop
    execute immediate
      ' alter index I2_SALES rebuild partition '||rec.p;
  end loop;
end;
```

Using the unusable index can be skipped by enabling ALTER SESSION SET SKIP_UNUSABLE_INDEXES=TRUE in the session before executing a query that would require the index. This approach just works around the problem and enables the query to complete by using a full scan of the table, typically with a large increase in elapsed time as compared to the execution when the index is usable. The use of global indexes can therefore reduce both performance and availability.

Oracle9*i* introduces the UPDATE GLOBAL INDEXES option for various partition maintenance functions, such as DROP PARTITION. The use of UPDATE GLOBAL

INDEXES means that global indexes are updated in step with the DDL operation on the partition in order to prevent the index from becoming unusable. The following DROP PARTITION statement enables the global index I2_SALES to remain usable at all times and doesn't require an explicit rebuild of the index:

```
alter table sales drop partition p200202
update global indexes;
```

The use of UPDATE GLOBAL INDEXES increases availability at the cost of slower partition maintenance operations. For example, partition operations such as DROP and EXCHANGE now require partition scans to identify the affected rows, and the index changes for the affected rows generate redo and rollback. For large indexes, consideration should be given to the use of the index rebuilds if a maintenance window is available, due to the increased efficiency of an index rebuild compared to an index update.

In general, global indexes are required for performance, and they introduce the possibility of reduced availability. The use of local indexes enables partition maintenance operations to be carried out without resulting in unusable indexes. The requirement for unique indexes of type LOCAL places additional constraints on how the index must be created. In this case, the index key *must* contain the partitioning key. In other words, the index must be prefixed. This requirement guarantees that a unique index key is unambiguously located in a single partition. If this is not the case, then the following error message is returned when trying to create an index that fails to meet the requirement:

```
ORA-14039: partitioning columns must form a subset of key columns of a
UNIQUE index
```

In general, it's desirable to create local indexes because they support partition administration operations without producing unusable indexes. However, sometimes the requirements for a unique index take precedence and a local unique index isn't possible. In this scenario, it's necessary to create a global index and manage the possibility of unusable indexes. For example, the creation of a primary key on a table partitioned on a date range (such as SALES) presents problems that can only be solved using global indexes. In the SALES table example, the SALE_ID column is a value that uniquely identifies each sale. Therefore, SALE_ID is the primary key. In general, a primary key constraint can be based on an existing index, if the index was created on the same columns as the primary key. Here's a simple example for a nonpartitioned table:

```
create table junk(x number, y number);
create index i0_junk on junk(y,x);
alter table junk add constraint pk_junk primary key (x,y);
```

It's important to note that the index IO_JUNK is not UNIQUE, and the order of columns in the index doesn't match the order of columns in the primary key. However, the ALTER TABLE ... ADD CONSTRAINT operation still works. The operation succeeds because Oracle checks to see if the values in the index are unique before enabling the index to be used in the primary key. Oracle also changes the column attributes for the table to NOT NULL. The same processing is possible whether the index is a global or local partitioned index. For the SALES table example, the equivalent statements would be as follows:

```
create index i3_sales on sales(sales_id) local;
alter table sales add constraint pk_sales primary key(sales_id);
```

In this case, the ALTER TABLE . . . ADD CONSTRAINT operation fails with ORA-01408: such column list already indexed, whereas it succeeded for the simple nonpartitioned example on the JUNK table. In order for the ADD CONSTRAINT to succeed, the underlying index must be unique. If this index is a local partition index, the partitioning imposes the additional requirement that the index key *must* contain the partition key, as explained previously. In this case, it doesn't.

Even though the I3_SALES index is not specified using UNIQUE, it must be checked for uniqueness in order to be used as a primary key. When the ALTER TABLE . . . ADD CONSTRAINT operation is specified, Oracle attempts to use the I3_SALES index to enforce the primary key because the primary key column matches the index column. The uniqueness constraint can't be satisfied for the local index, and the operation fails. The only way to create the primary key for the partitioned SALES table is to create the underlying index as a global index, leading to the possibility of reduced availability or performance when partitions are dropped. The following SQL statements create the primary key based on a global index:

```
create index i3_sales on sales(sales_id) global;
alter table sales add constraint pk_sales primary key(sales_id);
```

Summary

Partitioning can provide significant performance and availability benefits for large databases by dividing large tables and indexes into smaller pieces that can be managed independently and processed in parallel. Applications that need to keep a fixed window of historical data online benefit significantly from partitioning. The ability to manage data at the partition level means that data can be removed by simple partition-level operations rather than the much more expensive DELETE statements. To experience the benefits of low-cost administrative operations in this case, tables need to be partitioned on date columns by using the range method, and indexes need to be equipartitioned on the same columns by using the LOCAL option. In many cases, the use of LOCAL is not compatible with best performance or primary key integrity requirements. This leads to the requirement for global indexes.

Although they often enhance performance, using global indexes can lead to availability issues. Many partition maintenance operations, such as DROP, cause global indexes to become unusable. Oracle9i provides a new option called UPDATE GLOBAL INDEXES to prevent global indexes from being rendered unusable by partition maintenance operations. However, this operation can cause significant performance degradation because global indexes need to be updated in synch with the table data and should be used with care.

Oracle provides the hash-partitioning method in order to distribute data evenly across partitions. However, the hash method loses the advantages of the range method when historical data needs to be managed. The composite-partitioning method, whereby data is logically partitioned by range and then physically subpartitioned by hash, is available to provide the advantages of both methods.

## CHAPTER 12

Managing Indexes

Oracle uses indexes for two main purposes. The first is to enforce integrity through primary key and unique constraints. The second is to provide faster access paths to table data during Data Manipulation Language (DML) statements. The downside of indexes is that they can incur considerable input/output (I/O) and central processing unit (CPU) resources to maintain.

This chapter will help you manage indexes to provide maximum benefit at minimum cost. It covers the following subjects:

- The cost of index management
- Understanding index types
- Identifying which columns to index
- Identifying unused indexes
- Determining when to rebuild indexes
- Building function-based indexes

The Cost of Index Management

You should ensure that you index the minimum number of columns in any table in order to meet integrity and performance goals. Indexes typically provide faster access paths to data, at the cost of more expensive DELETE, INSERT, and UPDATE statements. The extra expense consists of additional overhead from the following:

- The extra disk space needed to store the indexes
- The extra processing needed to maintain the index data structure in synch with the table data
- The extra redo that needs to be generated to store changes to the index data structure

A simple example can be used to demonstrate the overhead needed to maintain indexes during an INSERT statement, by inserting 5,000 rows into a table without indexes, and then comparing performance with the same insert when indexes are in place. The following SQL runs the test:

```
REM create empty table...
create table my_obj tablespace tools as
select * from dba_objects where 1=2;

REM - INSERT 5000 rows without index...
insert /*#1*/ into my_obj select * from dba_objects where rownum <=5000;

truncate table my_obj;

REM - repeat INSERT with 2 indexes in place...
alter table my_obj add constraint pk_mo primary key(object_id)
     using index tablespace tools;
create index i0_mo on my_obj(owner,object_name) tablespace tools;

insert /*#2*/ into my_obj select * from dba_objects where rownum <=5000;
```

A comment /*...*/ is used in each INSERT statement to more easily identify the statement in V$SQL. The Oracle9i version of V$SQL contains CPU_TIME and ELAPSED _TIME columns to provide high-level metrics about the performance of each statement. The following SQL displays information from V$SQL for each insert:

```
select substr(sql_text,1,12) sql ,executions execs,elapsed_time,cpu_time
from v$sql where sql_text like 'insert /*%';
```

More detailed information about the statistics and event waits for each insert can be displayed using DbCool (as shown in Chapter 9) by sampling the V$SESSTAT and V$SESSION_EVENT views before and after each insert. In this example, the elapsed time for the insert is more than doubled when the indexes are in place. The following list shows the output from the DbCool History display, where the values shown indicate the *increase* in statistics from the insert performed with the indexes in place:

```
1328244 => redo size
   3183 => session logical reads
   3030 => db block changes
   2948 => db block gets
   1557 => redo entries
   1128 => enqueue releases
   1128 => enqueue requests
    235 => consistent gets
    135 => consistent gets - examination
    129 => change write time
     46 => leaf node splits
```

It's clear that the presence of the indexes causes a large increase in redo along with large increases in the number of block changes and enqueue requests and releases. In a real application, it's not unusual for a table with many columns to have several indexes. Each index contributes extra cost to inserts, updates, and deletes, especially through increases in redo generation. In order to reduce the cost of changes, index columns should be chosen so that they are used to speed up access paths to table data. If indexes are required to enforce data integrity through primary key and unique constraints, they can't be avoided.

Understanding Index Types

The purpose of an index is to store pointers to the rows in a table that contain a given key value. Recall that every row in a database can be uniquely identified by its ROWID value, which comprises the following components:

- The database file where it resides
- The block offset in the file
- The record offset in the block

These ROWID values can be stored in an index in two fundamentally different ways, using either B*trees or bitmaps. As well as indexes, Oracle provides index organized tables (IOTs), which provide table-like data access with less maintenance overhead than a traditional table.

B*tree Indexes

In a B*tree index, the ROWID values are stored as a binary encoding of the file, block, and record values. A B*tree index, fundamentally, is very similar to the index at the back of a book. When you need to find the page where a word is located in a book, you typically scan the list of alphabetic headings until you find the one your word begins with. Then you look down the list and find the word. Associated with the word are the pages where the word can be found. An Oracle B*tree index contains two types of blocks: branch blocks and leaf blocks. The branch blocks are like the alphabetic headings in a back-of-book index: They help you to quickly narrow down the scope of your search. The leaf blocks are like the word entries in a back-of-book index: They point to blocks that hold the data that was indexed. B*tree indexes are designed to stay balanced so that the number of branch blocks that need to be checked before locating the leaf block is kept to a minimum. For a unique index, each leaf entry contains a single key value and ROWID. For nonunique indexes, the key value may be repeated several times. In this case, the ROWID value itself is used as part of the key to ensure uniqueness of the key value.

Bitmap Indexes

In a bitmap index, a bitmap is maintained for each key value. Bit offsets in the bitmap correspond to ROWID values in the table. A bit value of 1 in the bitmap means that the key exists at the ROWID value represented by that particular bit in the bitmap. During the execution of a query plan, Oracle uses an internal function to convert a given bit offset in a bitmap to a real ROWID value. A simple example demonstrates that bitmap indexes have the potential for massive space savings compared to B*tree indexes in the right circumstances. The following SQL creates a table called gender where 10,000 rows contain the value MALE and 10,000 contain the value FEMALE:

```
create table gender as
select decode(mod(rownum,2),1,'MALE','FEMALE') mf
from all_tab_columns where rownum <=20000;
```

Using this simple example, a B*tree index on GENDER, created using the following SQL, is more than 20 times as large as a bitmap index (57 blocks compared to 2 blocks) because the bitmap index only needs to maintain 2 bitmaps for the values MALE and FEMALE, whereas the B*tree index needs to store a ROWID value for all 20,000 instances of MALE and FEMALE:

```
create bitmap index i0_gender on gender(mf);
```

In terms of space savings, the previous example presents a bitmap index in the best possible light compared to a B*tree index. When key values in a B*tree index repeat so frequently, then space can be saved by using the COMPRESS option at index creation time. The COMPRESS option results in the repeated key values being stored separately as a prefix that needs to be applied to the index entries when they are required during a DML execution. This requirement to regenerate the key using the prefix adds an overhead during query processing. The following SQL creates a compressed B*tree index, resulting in an index 37 blocks in size, compared to 2 blocks for the bitmap index and 57 blocks for the uncompressed B*tree index:

```
create index i0_gender on gender(mf) compress;
```

Bitmap indexes are most suitable for query-intensive applications, where queries use combinations of low cardinality columns in predicates containing equality, AND, OR, and NOT operations. Data warehouse applications are a good fit with these requirements. Queries that use range operations can't take advantage of bitmap indexes on columns. The cardinality of a column is a measure of the number of distinct values in the column compared to the total number of rows in the table. Low cardinality columns are candidates for a bitmap index where Oracle defines low cardinality as follows:

- The number of distinct values of a column is less than 1 percent of the number of rows in the table.
- The values in a column are repeated more than 100 times.

When bitmap indexes are present, AND, OR, NOT, and equality predicates can be implemented during completion of the execution plan through simple binary arithmetic on the bitmaps. This can lead to stunning improvements in response times.

Bitmap indexes have another benefit compared to B*tree indexes because NULL values are indexed. In a B*tree index, they aren't. Parallel query and parallel DML work with bitmap indexes in exactly the same way as B*tree indexes. Bitmap indexes on partitioned tables are enabled, but they *must* be local indexes. Partitioning is covered in Chapter 11. Parallel create index generation and concatenated indexes are also supported for bitmap indexes.

There's always a strong caveat that bitmap indexes shouldn't be used with Online Transaction Processing (OLTP) type applications. Based on the earlier example, the bitmap index is only two blocks in size. This suggests that the index blocks could become a source of contention if bitmaps need to be updated simultaneously by different sessions. As there are only two blocks, any concurrent updates on the bitmap index columns are likely to lead to contention. It's interesting to investigate this more closely. The techniques in Chapter 14 can be used as the basis for a benchmark to study the effects. Before the benchmark runs, a column needs to be added to identify each row uniquely, as would be the case for a table in an OLTP-type application. The following SQL adds a primary key ID column to GENDER:

```
alter table gender add (id number);

update gender set id=rownum;

alter table gender add constraint pk_g0 primary key(id);
```

The procedure SP_TEST_INDEX used to test the bitmap versus B*tree index performance is shown in the following:

```
create or replace procedure sp_test_index as
cursor c1 (p_in number) is
select mf,rowid from gender where id=p_id;
l_gender varchar2(6);
l_rowid rowid;
l_id number;
i number;
begin

    for i in 1..1000 loop
        l_id := round(dbms_random.value(1,20000));
```

```
        open c1(l_id);
        fetch c1 into l_gender,l_rowid;

        -- change the gender
        if l_gender='MALE' then
            l_gender:='FEMALE';
        else
            l_gender:='MALE';
        end if;

        close c1;

        update gender set id=l_id where rowid=l_rowid;

        commit;

    end loop;

end;
```

The procedure generates a random number between 1 and 20,000 and uses this value to select a row from GENDER, which contains 20,000 rows identified by a unique value from 1 to 20,000 in the ID column. The query is typical of an index-driven row selection from a table in an OLTP application. Next, the gender value in the MF column is switched from MALE to FEMALE or vice versa and is written back to the same row. This transaction is repeated 1,000 times. A comparison of the performance of the same routine executed in two concurrent sessions on a 2-CPU Sun Solaris server (using DbCool StressTester) shows evidence of nonscaleable behavior when the GENDER table uses a bitmap index compared to a B*tree index. In a simple test, elapsed time to complete the test with a bitmap index in place increases by 100 percent for two sessions compared to one. In effect, the bitmap index results in changes to the table being serialized rather than concurrent. With a B*tree index, the elapsed time increased by 10 percent for two sessions compared to one.

Due to contention on the two bitmap index blocks as a result of frequent changes to the blocks caused by the index update, events such as *buffer busy waits, enqueues,* and *latch free* are evident. These are described in Chapter 9. The bitmap index generates large amounts of redo (70 percent more than the B*tree index), which results in waits for the *log buffer space* event. This evidence confirms that bitmap indexes are not suitable for OLTP applications due to the increased possibly of multiple sessions contending for the bitmaps in the blocks at the same time.

Bitmap Join Indexes (BJIs)

Oracle9*i* introduces a new type of index called a BJI that enables a table index to include values from a column in another table that previously required a join operation to fetch. The goal is to avoid potentially expensive join operations, leading to reduced I/O during query processing and reduced elapsed times for DML execution.

BJIs are designed for use in data warehouse applications to eliminate join operations between that fact and dimension tables typically used in a data warehouse schema. Consider a data warehouse containing a fact table, SALES, and a dimension table, PRODUCTS, which are related by a primary key and foreign key relationship on the PRODUCT_ID column. Ignoring the presence of other dimension tables that would be expected (such as CUSTOMERS), the two tables might look like the following:

```
create table products
(product_id number primary key,
 product_name varchar2(30),
 category varchar2(30));

create table sales
(amount number,
 product_id number references products);
```

A query to identify the amount of sales for a particular category requires a join between SALES and PRODUCTS that looks like this:

```
select  sum(s.amount)
from    sales s, products p
where   s.product_id = p.product_id
and     p.category = 'Sporting Goods';
```

If the category information for the product were stored in an index on the SALES table, there would be no need for the join because the required information would be available from the index. In Oracle9i, you can create a BJI for this purpose:

```
create bitmap index i1bj_product_sales
on      sales (p.category)
from    sales s, products p
where   s.product_id = p.product_id;
```

Figure 12.1 shows a query execution plan for the previous SQL, which confirms that no access to the PRODUCT table is taking place.

Index-Organized Tables (IOTs)

Consider a scenario where you need to store a lookup table containing millions of name/value pairs and access the value by a query on the name. Oracle's own V$PARAMETER table is an example of a lookup table. The obvious way to implement the requirement is to create a table, along with a primary key value based on the name. For performance reasons, you might create an additional unique index on the name and value columns. The unique index means that queries of the form SELECT VALUE FROM LOOKUP WHERE NAME='*key*' can be satisfied from the index alone. This approach has some inefficiencies because the NAME is stored three times: in the table, in the primary key, and in the unique index.

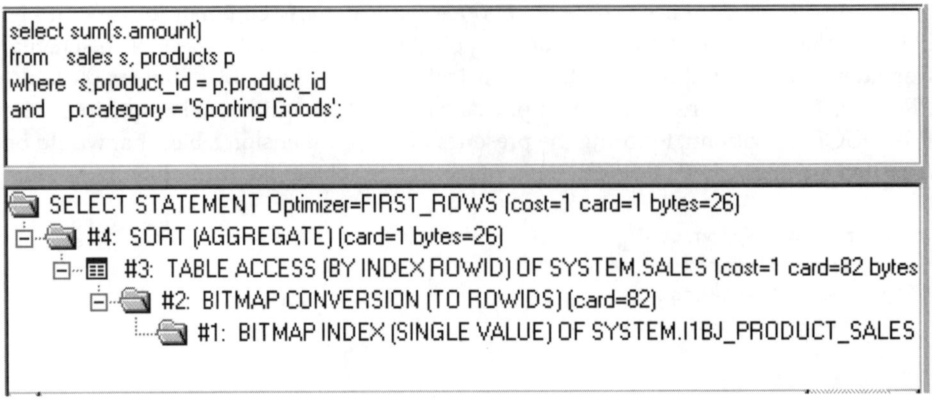

```
select sum(s.amount)
from   sales s, products p
where  s.product_id = p.product_id
and    p.category = 'Sporting Goods';
```

SELECT STATEMENT Optimizer=FIRST_ROWS (cost=1 card=1 bytes=26)
  #4: SORT (AGGREGATE) (card=1 bytes=26)
    #3: TABLE ACCESS (BY INDEX ROWID) OF SYSTEM.SALES (cost=1 card=82 bytes
      #2: BITMAP CONVERSION (TO ROWIDS) (card=82)
        #1: BITMAP INDEX (SINGLE VALUE) OF SYSTEM.I1BJ_PRODUCT_SALES

Figure 12.1   EXPLAIN PLAN for BJI.

An IOT provides the solution to this problem by storing the table data itself in a B*tree index structure rather than using separate table and index structures. As a result, the primary key value is physically stored once only. This leads to more efficient access with reduced I/O for an IOT compared to a standard table and index approach, which in turn can reduce the elapsed time for DML execution. The key to the usability of an IOT is that it behaves like a regular table in terms of DML operations because the underlying storage implementation as a B*tree is hidden.

The data in a regular table is stored as an unordered collection, known as *heap ordered*. Unlike heap-ordered tables (where ROWID is used to physically identify rows), IOTs *must* have a primary key to enable unique row identification. Primary keys on heap-ordered tables are optional. Whereas a primary key on a heap-ordered table stores ROWID values in the index entries, the B*tree entries in an IOT store the primary key value along with nonkey column values. Because rows in an IOT are stored in primary key order, the use of key compression (as described previously) can lead to significant space savings.

Just like heap-ordered tables, IOTs have an associated ROWID pseudocolumn. For an IOT, the ROWID represents a *logical* row identifier. The presence of the ROWID in an IOT enables additional indexes (referred to as *secondary indexes*) to be created on nonkey columns in the table, for performance. As well as enabling secondary indexes, the presence of logical ROWIDs, rather than physical ROWIDs, means that IOTs can be relocated using the ALTER TABLE MOVE command without causing the IOT B*tree index to become unusable. This can lead to higher data availability compared to using a table and primary key to hold the same data. Using a table and primary key, the physical relocation of the MOVE command on the table renders all the ROWID values in the primary key invalid, requiring a rebuild of the primary key.

In a B*tree index on a heap-ordered table, as many index entries as will fit are stored in each index block. This leads to index lookups that require the minimum I/O. On the other hand, with an IOT potential performance issues arise when the IOT contains many columns that aren't part of the primary key. Because these columns need to be stored in each index entry, they increase the space used in each B*tree block, and the resulting index lookups in the B*tree are less efficient. In effect, the nonkey columns work against the requirement to store as many keys as possible in each B*tree block. To solve this problem, you can create an IOT using the optional OVERFLOW clause to store infrequently accessed columns that are not part of the key in a separate overflow area with a heap-organized structure.

Associated with the OVERFLOW clause are options to specify a physical or logical threshold (or both) for splitting the contents of a row into two parts that are stored in the B*tree section of the IOT and the heap-organized overflow area:

- The PCTTHRESHOLD clause is a physical threshold, where the part of a row that exceeds a percentage of the block size is placed in the overflow heap.

- The INCLUDING clause specifies a column name, such that any nonkey columns that appear in the CREATE TABLE statement after that specified column will be stored in the overflow heap.

The PCTTHRESHOLD value may cause additional columns other than those following INCLUDING to be stored in the overflow heap. The following SQL shows how to create an IOT using both overflow thresholds, where the B*tree part is stored in tablespace TS_DATA, and the overflow is stored in TS_OVERFLOW:

```
create table lookup
   (name      varchar2(30) primary key,
    value     varchar(30),
    comment$ varchar(128))
  organization index
  including value
  pctthreshold 30
tablespace ts_data
overflow tablespace ts_overflow;
```

Identifying Columns to Index

In the simplest case, DML statements involving an equality, range, or like operator can use an index to provide faster access to table data. Here are some simple examples based on the MY_OBJ table created previously:

```
REM these two can use an index on OBJECT_ID
select /* equality */ * from my_obj where object_id=42;
select /* range */    * from my_obj where object_id between 1 and 100;

REM this can use an index on OWNER
select /* like */     * from my_obj where owner like 'SYS%';
```

In reality, application DML statements are usually nowhere near this simple. The Index Tuning Wizard component of the Oracle Enterprise Manager Tuning Pack is designed to address the challenge of deciding on the optimal indexes and index types for best performance. The Index Tuning Wizard uses the same technology as Oracle Expert to identify the best indexes. Chapter 16 contains examples of how to use Oracle Expert.

A less automated approach, but a perfectly acceptable one, is to identify expensive SQL (using the techniques in Chapter 9), create the candidate index to improve performance based on a visual inspection of the query, and then analyze it and check whether the query now results in a plan that uses the index and has a lower cost than the original. DbCool and the SQL Analyze component of Oracle Enterprise Manager both provide features to facilitate the comparison of execution plans before and after a new index is available.

Indexing SELECT List Columns

A very useful technique to reduce I/O for DML statements is to index the columns in the SELECT list such that query results can be satisfied from the index alone, without requiring a table lookup. This technique is especially useful for tables with only a few rows per block. When tables have only a few rows per block (often because the table has long rows), then a requirement to fetch just a few rows can result in significant block I/O. This technique can be demonstrated with a simple example based on the MY_OBJ table shown earlier. The following SQL counts the number of object types for objects in the range of 1 to 100:

```
select count(object_type) from my_obj where object_id between 1 and 100;
```

```
Execution Plan
-----------------------
Order   SELECT STATEMENT
3         SORT (AGGREGATE)
2           TABLE ACCESS (BY INDEX ROWID) OF 'MY_OBJ'
1             INDEX (RANGE SCAN) OF 'PK_MO' (UNIQUE)
```

The query execution plan shows the order of processing when the query is executed. First, the primary key index is scanned to identify ROWID values in the MY_OBJ table for rows having an OBJECT_ID between 1 and 100. This action is identified by the INDEX (RANGE SCAN) operation. Next, for each ROWID value in the index, the related MY_OBJ table block holding the row is located using the ROWID value. The ROWID value identifies the datafile, block, and row in the block where the row can be located, as indicated by the TABLE ACCESS operation. The OBJECT_TYPE in the row is then read from the table block. Finally, the list of OBJECT_TYPE values is sorted to identify unique values, and the count of the unique values is returned. Each ROWID identified in the index requires a table block lookup. This query execution plan can be improved by creating an index to avoid the TABLE ACCESS operation on MY_OBJ. Consider the plan for the original SELECT statement when a new index is added on the OBJECT_ID and OBJECT_TYPE columns as shown in the following example:

```
create index i1_mo on my_obj(object_id,object_type) tablespace tools;
```

```
Execution Plan
-----------------------
Order   SELECT STATEMENT
```

```
2        SORT (AGGREGATE)
1           INDEX (RANGE SCAN) OF 'I1_MO' (NON-UNIQUE)
```

When the I1_MO index exists, the execution plan no longer requires the TABLE ACCESS operation because the OBJECT_TYPE used in the select list is available from the index block containing the OBJECT_ID. Using this approach, it's possible to end up with several indexes containing the same columns but in a different order. That's fine if the goal is to speed up queries, at the cost of more expensive inserts, updates, and deletes. For applications that are read intensive, query response times are of paramount importance. As a result, the overhead of inserting each row is counted once, whereas the benefits of the extra index are obtained each time the query runs. When OLTP applications run queries that require full table scans of large tables, this technique can sometimes be used to avoid the full table scan by ensuring that all select list columns can be satisfied from the index using an index scan. If the index is smaller than the table on which it is based, a scan of the index is usually faster than a scan of the table because fewer blocks need to be processed.

Using Index Scans

The Oracle optimizer sometimes chooses index scans in execution plans for DML that would otherwise result in a full table scan. An index scan is usually chosen in preference to a full table scan if the index is much smaller than the table it indexes. In this case, a scan of all keys in the index will cost much less in terms of I/O than a table scan, and complete faster. Three types of index scans are available:

- Full scans
- Fast full scans
- Skip scans (Oracle9*i* only)

In order for an index scan to be chosen during the generation of an execution plan for a DML statement, at least one index column of the index table must have the NOT NULL constraint. However, it's *not* required that the WHERE clause reference the leading index column using an equality, range, or like operator. This is in contrast to a standard B*tree index search. In fact, some DML can take advantage of index scans when there is no WHERE clause. To understand the benefits of index scans, consider a SALES table containing millions of rows, and an index on two NOT NULL columns as follows:

```
create index i0_sales on sales(region_id,product_id);
```

The execution of the query SELECT COUNT(*) FROM SALES can take advantage of an index fast full scan on I0_SALES. An index fast full scan is similar to an traditional index scan with two important differences: The fast full scan performs multi-block rather than single block reads, and can execute in parallel. The EXPLAIN PLAN output for the query identifies that a fast full scan took place:

```
Execution Plan
------------------------------------------------------------
    0        SELECT STATEMENT Optimizer=CHOOSE (Cost=4 Card=1)
```

```
1    0    SORT (AGGREGATE)
2    1       INDEX (FAST FULL SCAN) OF 'I0_SALES' (NON-UNIQUE)
```

Because at least one of the index columns refers to a NOT NULL table column, all rows are guaranteed to have entries in the index. As a result, Oracle can compute the number of rows in the table by scanning all the index blocks, and counting the index entries. The index used in this example is around 60 times smaller than the table, so an index scan results in less I/O than a full table scan of SALES and returns the result quicker.

When a query such as SELECT SUM(AMOUNT) FROM SALES WHERE PRODUCT_ID=1567 executes, it's not possible for Oracle to identify rows that match the query using a standard B*tree search because the WHERE clause doesn't contain the leading index column (REGION_ID). One way to identify the matching rows is via a full table scan. However, due to the fact that the REGION_ID column is NOT NULL, all PRODUCT_ID values will be present in the index as the second part of a two-part composite key, with REGION_ID as the first part. Given a complete list of all index keys resulting from an index fast full scan, Oracle can determine the PRODUCT_ID component of each key, and then use it to determine ROWID values that match PRODUCT_ID=1567. The ROWID values are then used to fetch table rows from which the AMOUNT column is read, leading to the SUM(AMOUNT).

Rather than executing the previous SQL using an index fast full scan, Oracle9*i* can provide a more optimal execution plan by using an index skip scan instead, as shown by the following EXPLAIN PLAN:

```
0         SELECT STATEMENT Optimizer=CHOOSE (Cost=14 Card=1 Bytes=6)
1    0    SORT (AGGREGATE)
2    1       TABLE ACCESS (BY INDEX ROWID) OF 'SALES'
3    2          INDEX (SKIP SCAN) OF 'I0_SALES' (NON-UNIQUE)
```

The index skip scan reduces I/O during execution by eliminating the need to read all index blocks, as compared to a fast full scan that always reads all blocks. For tables where the leading column has a few distinct values and the nonleading column has many distinct values, the optimizer is more likely to choose an index skip scan. All three scan types can be requested by using SQL HINTs in the SELECT list as shown in the following examples, based on the SALES table and I0_SALES index:

```
/*+ index(sales i0_sales) */
/*+ index_ffs(sales i0_sales) */
/*+ index_ss(sales i0_sales) */
```

NOTE Always keep in mind that the optimizer may choose to ignore a HINT.

Identifying Unused Indexes

If indexes aren't being used, then the database takes all of the cost of maintaining the indexes without any of the benefits of faster DML statements through faster access paths. Such indexes are candidates for removal. The capability to detect indexes that are being used (and by implication those that aren't) has improved very significantly in Oracle9*i* compared to Oracle8*i*. This section provides step-by-step details on how to detect index usage in both versions.

Indexes and Foreign Keys

It should be noted that indexes sometimes have uses that can't be identified from statement execution plans alone. In particular, Oracle8*i* uses nontransactional locks (often referred to as *pins*) on foreign key indexes to avoid the need for share locks on the child table when enforcing foreign key constraints. The standard DEPT and EMP tables are examples of a parent and child related by a foreign key. The existence of referential integrity without an index on the foreign key column means that:

- Attempts to delete rows in the parent table result in a table-level share lock on the child.

- Attempts to update rows in the parent result in a table-level share lock on the child, if the update affects any columns referenced by the child.

The share lock means that no insert, update, or delete statements are permitted on the child until the parent transaction executes COMMIT or ROLLBACK. Some DBAs create indexes on all foreign keys as standard procedure to avoid the possibility of such locks occurring. This is generally accepted as best practice for all versions of Oracle including Oracle9*i*. As a result, it's not unusual for these foreign key indexes to remain unused by query execution paths. In this situation, removal could have disastrous side effects on application response times. Therefore, all decisions to remove indexes must take a broad view of how indexes are used.

Oracle9*i* no longer requires a share lock on unindexed foreign keys when doing an update or delete on the parent. It still obtains the table-level share lock, but then releases it immediately after obtaining it. If multiple primary keys are updated or deleted, the lock is obtained and released once for each row. Oracle9*i* also provides the ALTER *table* DISABLE TABLE LOCK statement to disable table locking. This can be used on the child table. In this case, no share lock is taken on the child table even if the child table has no index on the foreign key. If this approach is used, it's important to reenable locking afterwards, or Data Definition Language (DDL) against the table will fail. DbCool contains a built-in script accessible via Script Manager to display all unindexed foreign keys in the current schema.

Determining Index Usage in Oracle8*i*

The Oracle8*i* approach to determining which indexes are used means running EXPLAIN PLAN (see Chapter 10) on all statements in the shared SQL area, and then querying the OPERATION column in the plan table to identify index access on the index identified by the OBJECT_OWNER and OBJECT_NAME columns. Consider the EXPLAIN PLAN for the simple index-driven statement used previously:

```
explain plan set statement_id='!!' for
select count(object_type) from my_obj
```

```
where object_id between 1 and 100;


select object_owner,object_name,operation,options
from plan_table where operation='INDEX'
and statement_id='!!';


OBJECT_OWNER   OBJECT_NAME   OPERATION    OPTIONS
-------------- ------------- ----------- -----------
SYSTEM         I1_MO         INDEX        RANGE SCAN
```

The PLAN_TABLE output shows the index access. Whenever an index would be used during execution, the plan contains a value INDEX in the OPERATION column, and the values in the OBJECT_OWNER and OBJECT_NAME columns identify the index. This approach can be extended to the cover all the statements in the shared SQL area. A complete solution involves fetching the ADDRESS and HASH_VALUE of each statement, fetching the associated full SQL text of the statement, and then generating a plan for the statement. On completion, a query on the plan table, similar to the previous one, can be used to identify all the indexes used by all statements current in the shared SQL area. Because the shared SQL area is dynamic, the procedure needs to be repeated sufficiently often that all SQL is explained before it is aged out of the cache. The following PL/SQL block implements the procedure:

```
declare
l_sql varchar2(32000);
l_id number;
begin

  -- run this as SYSTEM, with a single system-wide PLAN_TABLE
  execute immediate 'truncate table system.plan_table';

  l_id := 1;

  -- for each statement in shared SQL area except those owned by SYS
  for rec1 in (
    select s.address,s.hash_value,u.username usr
    from v$sql s,dba_users u
    where s.parsing_schema_id=u.user_id and username <> 'SYS'
    and lower(sql_text) not like '%explain plan%') loop

    l_sql:='';

    -- fetch the full SQL statement text into l_sql  . . .
    for rec_sql_text in (select sql_text from v$sqltext_with_newlines
                        where address=rec1.address and
                        hash_value=rec1.hash_value
                        order by piece) loop
      l_sql:=l_sql||rec_sql_text.sql_text;
    end loop;
```

```
    if length(l_sql) > 0 then
      -- set the schema to the user that parsed it originally . . .
      execute immediate 'alter session set current_schema='||rec1.usr;
      l_id := l_id + 1;
      -- generate the plan...
      l_sql := 'explain plan set statement_id=''s'||l_id||
               ''' for '||l_sql;
      begin
        execute immediate l_sql;
      exception
        when others then
            null;
      end;
  end if;

end loop;
exception
    when others then
    dbms_output.put_line(sqlerrm);
    dbms_output.put_line('sql='||l_sql);
end;
/
```

There are some important points to note about the routine, which can impose a significant performance overhead, so it should be run on a busy production system only after careful consideration. The EXPLAIN PLAN statement is executed in its own nested block, which ignores errors. That's because the shared SQL area may contain PL/SQL blocks and DDL statements that EXPLAIN PLAN does not understand, as well as DML statements that are of interest for identifying index usage. Statements to which EXPLAIN PLAN can't be applied cause an ORA-00905 error (missing keyword) if EXPLAIN PLAN is executed against them, and these can be silently ignored.

The use of ALTER SESSION SET CURRENT SCHEMA just before the execution of EXPLAIN PLAN is critical to the success of the routine. For example, if two schemas contain a table with the same name and columns and identical SQL is executed against each, then EXPLAIN PLAN needs to resolve the table names in the schema that was used when the SQL was executed. The PARSING_SCHEMA_ID in V$SQL contains the schema used to resolve the name when the statement executed, and ALTER SESSION SET CURRENT SCHEMA enables a DBA to effectively become that user for the purpose of generating a plan. A PL/SQL restriction limits the length of the explained statement to 32,000 bytes. That's definitely not large enough for all systems, and any requirement to explain longer statements needs a 3GL solution using Pro*C, for example. Once execution is complete, the indexes used by all statements in the shared SQL area can be found in the plan table. This example shows indexes, the number of statements that use them, and the type of index operation used:

```
select object_owner,object_name,options,count(*)
from plan_table where operation='INDEX'
and object_owner<>'SYS'
```

```
group by object_owner,object_name,operation,options
order by count(*) desc
```

OBJECT_OWNER	OBJECT_NAME	OPTIONS	COUNT(*)
FXTRADER	REP_HUB_QUEUE_UK2	UNIQUE SCAN	76
FXTRADER	REP_HUB_DATA_PK	UNIQUE SCAN	38
FXTRADER	FX_PK	UNIQUE SCAN	14
FXTRADER	SETTLEMENTS_PK	UNIQUE SCAN	10
FXTRADER	FX_HOLDING_PK	UNIQUE SCAN	7
FXTRADER	DT_VALUES_UK	RANGE SCAN	6
FXTRADER	FXDLT_LN1	RANGE SCAN	5
FXTRADER	FXDLT_LN1	RANGE SCAN (MIN/MAX)	5

Determining Index Usage in Oracle9*i*

The situation is much more straightforward in Oracle9*i* because a new dictionary view V$SQL_PLAN stores the actual plan used to execute the statement in the shared SQL area. The V$SQL_PLAN view has a very close resemblance to the plan table, but uses ADDRESS and HASH_VALUE columns to identify statements, rather than the user-supplied STATEMENT_ID column used by the plan table. The following SQL shows all the indexes used by statements present in the shared SQL area in an Oracle9*i* database:

```
select object_owner,object_name,options,count(*)
from v$sql_plan where operation='INDEX'
and object_owner<>'SYS'
group by object_owner,object_name,operation,options
order by count(*) desc
```

All approaches to identifying index usage based on information in the shared SQL area leave open the possibility that collected information is incomplete. The shared SQL area is a dynamic structure, and unless it can be sampled with sufficient frequency, then SQL statements may be aged from the cache before information on index usage has been collected. Oracle9*i* provides the solution to this problem by providing a MONITORING USAGE clause for ALTER INDEX. When MONITORING USAGE is enabled, Oracle records a simple YES or NO value to indicate whether an index was used during the monitored interval. The subsequent sequence of SQL statements performs the following actions:

- Enables index usage monitoring for a single index
- Runs a query that uses the indexes
- Runs a query to show that the index has been used
- Disables the monitoring
- Runs a query to display usage in the monitored interval

```
REM enable monitoring for one index...
alter index SYSTEM.I1_MO monitoring usage;


REM execute SQL that uses the index...
select count(object_type) from my_obj
where object_id between 1 and 100;


  COUNT(OBJECT_TYPE)
-------------------
               99

REM check that monitoring has detected use of the index...
select index_name,monitoring,used,start_monitoring,end_monitoring
from v$object_usage;


INDEX_NAME  MONITORING  USED  START_MONITORING     END_MONITORING
----------- ----------- ----- -------------------- ----------------

I1_MO       YES         YES   01/29/2002 19:43:07


REM now disable monitoring, and display the monitored interval
alter index SYSTEM.I1_MO nomonitoring usage;

select index_name,monitoring,used,start_monitoring,end_monitoring
   from v$object_usage;


INDEX_NAME  MONITORING  USED  START_MONITORING     END_MONITORING
----------- ----------- ----- -------------------- --------------------

I1_MO       NO          YES   01/29/2002 19:43:07  01/29/2002
19:43:38
```

The following PL/SQL block enables monitoring for all indexes in the database except those owned by SYS and SYSTEM:

```
declare
l_sql varchar2(128);
begin

  for rec in
    (select 'alter index '||owner||'.'||index_name||
           ' monitoring usage' mon from dba_indexes
     where owner not in ('SYS','SYSTEM') and index_type='NORMAL') loop
     l_sql:= rec.mon;
     execute immediate l_sql;
  end loop;
end;
/
```

One anomaly of the V$OBJECT_USAGE view is that it only enables information to be displayed for indexes owned by the connected user. Oracle is likely to address this in the future. If your database only shows object usage information for the connected user, the following view (which must be created as SYS) can be used to provide information on all monitored indexes from any account:

```
create or replace view
V$ALL_OBJECT_USAGE (INDEX_NAME, TABLE_NAME, MONITORING, USED,
START_MONITORING, END_MONITORING) as
select io.name, t.name, decode(bitand(i.flags, 65536), 0, 'NO', 'YES'),
decode(bitand(ou.flags, 1), 0, 'NO', 'YES'), ou.start_monitoring,
ou.end_monitoring
from sys.obj$ io, sys.obj$ t, sys.ind$ i, sys.object_usage ou
where i.obj# = ou.obj# and io.obj# = ou.obj# and t.obj# = i.bo#;

grant select on v$all_object_usage to public;


create public synonym  v$all_object_usage for  v$all_object_usage;
```

When to Rebuild Indexes

When tables are subject to large volumes of deletes or inserts, the indexes on those tables can become disorganized. Disorganization manifests itself as empty space in the index. The existence of empty space means that scans of the index are less efficient because the empty space leads to wasted I/O operations during index lookups. The empty space can be eliminated by rebuilding the index. Due to the overhead imposed by index rebuilds, only indexes that would be benefit from a rebuild should be rebuilt. The ANALYZE command can be used to identify indexes with a large proportion of wasted space. The following SQL shows the results of ANALYZE on an index:

```
analyze index I0_MY_OBJ validate structure;

select lf_rows,del_lf_rows,btree_space,used_space,pct_used
from index_stats;
```

LF_ROWS	DEL_LF_ROWS	BTREE_SPACE	USED_SPACE	PCT_USED
4686	0	263900	223271	85

Statistics on the index are available through the INDEX_STATS view immediately after the ANAYLZE . . . VALIDATE STRUCTURE completes. The values in it are overwritten by the next ANALYZE INDEX command executed by any session. The output in the example shows that 4,686 rows are represented in the leaf blocks of the index and that no entries represent deleted rows (because DEL_LF_ROWS is 0). The amount of space used to hold index data relative to the total space allocated for the B*tree structure is quite high at 85 percent. Together, the information suggests that this index isn't wasting much space. The picture changes when all rows are deleted from the indexed table. After deletion and ANALYZE, the statistics show that all index entries referred to deleted rows:

```
select lf_rows,del_lf_rows,btree_space,used_space,pct_used
from index_stats;
```

LF_ROWS	DEL_LF_ROWS	BTREE_SPACE	USED_SPACE	PCT_USED
4686	4686	263900	223271	85

Although the data in the index is held quite efficiently because PCT_USED remains at 85 percent, the data in the index is effectively wasted because it refers to deleted rows. The index can be rebuilt to free up the wasted space as follows:

```
alter index I0_MY_OBJ rebuild;
```

One major advantage of a rebuild, compared to an index drop and re-create, is that the original index data can be used in the rebuild, which leads to faster completion of the operation. The ANALYZE command following the rebuild shows that the 260KB space used to hold the B*tree is now reduced to a mere 8KB as a result of the rebuild:

LF_ROWS	DEL_LF_ROWS	BTREE_SPACE	USED_SPACE	PCT_USED
0	0	7996		

If you enable table monitoring on all your tables, as recommended in Chapter 10, then tables subject to deletes and inserts can be identified in ALL_TAB_MODIFICATIONS. The indexes on these tables are candidates for a rebuild because they are likely to contain wasted space. The following SQL and output show the index statistics for an index on a table subject to both deletes and inserts:

```
select inserts,updates,deletes from all_tab_modifications;
where table_name='REP_TRANSACTIONS';
```

INSERTS	UPDATES	DELETES
147559	0	310372

LF_ROWS	DEL_LF_ROWS	BTREE_SPACE	USED_SPACE	PCT_USED
159238	3461	50646276	12743204	26

The number of entries representing deleted leaf rows is quite small as a percentage of the total leaf rows. However, due to the combination of repeated inserts and deletes, the index structure has become inefficient in its use of space: Only 26 percent of the total B*tree space is used. This index is a strong candidate for a rebuild. Note that when rebuilding, the PCTUSED storage parameter can't be specified for an index. The PCTFREE parameter can be used to specify the percentage of free space to leave for inserts and updates to index blocks. Keep in mind that the location of index key values inserted after the index creation is determined by the key value of the row being inserted. As a result, PCTFREE for an index doesn't provide the same level of control of space usage as it does for a table.

The following stored procedure, SP_INDEX_REBUILD, automates the process of rebuilding indexes for a schema APP, whose PCTUSED value is less than a threshold value passed as an argument. If no argument is passed, all indexes are checked. A further test is made to ensure that only indexes with more than one extent are considered, to avoid rebuilding small indexes. The extent test assumes that you are using fixed size extents of a few megabytes at the most, as recommended throughout this book:

```
Procedure SP_INDEX_REBUILD (p_in_rebuild_threshold_pct integer default
0) AS
   l_sql varchar2(32000);
BEGIN
   execute immediate 'alter session set sort_area_size=10000000';

   -- consider rebuild of all indexes owned by APP with > 1 extent
   for rec in (
      select 'alter index '||owner||'.'||index_name||
             ' rebuild unrecoverable' rebuild_sql,
             'analyze index '||owner||'.'||index_name||
             ' validate structure' validate_sql
      from dba_indexes where owner='APP'
      and index_type='NORMAL'
      and (owner,index_name) in
          (select owner,segment_name from dba_segments where extents >
1)
      ) loop

      -- create the index stats...
      l_sql := rec.validate_sql;
      execute immediate l_sql;

      -- only rebuild indexes where pct_used < threshold
      for rec2 in (select pct_used from index_stats) loop
         if (100-rec2.pct_used) < p_in_rebuild_threshold_pct then
            l_sql := rec.rebuild_sql;
            execute immediate l_sql;
         end if;
      end loop;
   end loop;

END SP_INDEX_REBUILD;
```

The SP_ INDEX_REBUILD procedure uses a large sort area to ensure that as much sorting as possible takes place in memory during the index creation. As shown in the analysis of Import performance in Chapter 19, avoiding disk sorts is a key requirement for ensuring that index builds take place as quickly as possible. To ensure that an index build for a large index succeeds the first time, sufficient sort space must also be available on disk. This can be guaranteed by enabling AUTOEXTEND on the temporary tablespace datafiles or creating another large temporary tablespace specifically for the purpose of the rebuild. You should aim to extend the size of the temporary tablespace in advance to avoid possible performance degradation caused by dynamic growth of the file. Two other techniques are available to speed up index builds. These involve using parallel operations and the NOLOGGING option to avoid the generation of redo, as shown in the following examples:

```
alter index i0_my_source rebuild parallel 2;
alter index i0_my_source rebuild nologging;
alter index i0_my_source rebuild parallel 2 nologging;
```

If you increase the SORT_AREA_SIZE for a session before an index rebuild, keep in mind that the same sort area will be allocated for each parallel stream if PARALLEL is used. The PARALLEL option should only be used when multiple CPUs are available. Using a large sort space and PARALLEL should lead to significant reductions in index rebuild time. The NOLOGGING option can also reduce the elapsed time and needs to be used with care if you are running a standby database. Indexes rebuilt using NOLOGGING will be in the UNUSABLE state when a standby is activated. By default, these indexes need to be rebuilt in order for DML (including queries that use the index in an execution plan) on the table to succeed. The V$DATAFILE view provides the UNRECOVERABLE_CHANGE# and UNRECOVERABLE_TIME columns to indicate datafiles with unrecoverable changes in the primary database. Standby databases are covered in Chapter 23. Don't forget that you can continue to execute DDL statements when UNUSABLE indexes exist by setting SKIP_UNUSABLE_INDEXES to TRUE at the session level as follows:

```
alter session set skip_unusable_indexes=true
```

Remember that after a rebuild, statistics on the index should be regenerated. This can be done inline with the rebuild, if required:

```
alter index i0_my_source rebuild compute statistics;
```

For situations where availability rather than performance is the driver, indexes can be rebuilt online using the ONLINE option. In this case, changes can be made to the indexed table while the index build takes place, but DDL operations are not permitted, and parallel support is not available. Bulk inserts should be avoided during an index build if possible, due to the increased likelihood of lock contention between the rebuild process and regular end-user block changes caused by DML. Online rebuilds are supported for more types of indexes in Oracle9i compared to Oracle8i, which is consistent with Oracle's philosophy of providing features in Oracle9i to enhance availability.

Building Function-Based Indexes

Function-based indexes enable the creation of indexes on values returned from a function. The function must be created using the pragma DETERMINISTIC. The use of DETERMINISTIC indicates that the function return value for a given input value must always be the same. There are many possible situations where a function-based index can reduce the cost of a SELECT statement.

One of the most useful situations for a function-based index involves date handling, using an index on the truncated part of a date value. For a given date like 04-JUN-2001 15:44:57, the truncated part identifies only the date with the time set to 0, for example, 04-JUN-2001 00:00:00. Often, applications require dates to be stored in the full format to identify the exact time an event occurred, whereas reports against the same data often need to group activities by day. That involves stripping off the time part. The following SQL reports all the stocks in a trading system where the settlement date was 04-JUN-2001. Because the SETT_TIMESTAMP column holds the exact time that settlement occurred, the TRUNC function needs to be used to strip off the time part:

```
select count(*) from settlements
where trunc(sett_timestamp)=to_date('04-JUN-2001','DD-MON-YYYY');
```

In this example, the SETT_TIMESTAMP column is indexed, but the existence of the function TRUNC on the column means that the index on the column can't be used. In general, the use of a function on a column value used in a predicate prevents an index on that value from being used in a query execution plan. This can lead to some obscure performance problems. For example, if you store numbers in a VARCHAR2 column by accident, the use of a predicate like WHERE TRADEID=99 causes Oracle to convert the number to a string, using an internal function call. This function prevents an index on TRADEID from being used because the index contains strings and not numbers. In this example, you would have to use '99' to force the number to be treated as a string value.

One approach to this problem on the SETT_TIMESTAMP column is to store the date twice in the row (as both the exact and truncated version), index the truncated version, and use the truncated version in the WHERE clause. This duplicates data. Another approach is to rewrite the SQL to use BETWEEN instead of TRUNC to identify all the hours in the day. This makes the SQL less readable. The most appropriate solution in this case is to create a function-based index on the TRUNC value of the SETT_TIMESTAMP column. That way, an index can be used to identify rows processed on a particular day. The required function and the index on it are created as follows:

```
create or replace function trunc_date(d date) return date deterministic
as
begin
    return trunc(d);
end trunc_date;
/

create index i1_settlements on settlements(trunc_date(sett_timestamp));
```

Once the index is in place, session settings need to be enabled in order for the function-based index to be used, as follows:

```
alter session set query_rewrite_enabled=true;
alter session set query_rewrite_integrity=trusted;


select count(*) from settlements
where trunc_date(sett_timestamp)=to_date('04-JUN-2001','DD-MON-YYYY');
```

The EXPLAIN PLAN command can be employed to confirm that the index is used in the plan for the new query, although a massive reduction in elapsed time is usually enough evidence. Care must be taken not to change the stored function on which the index is based. If that occurs, DML, attempting to use the index (for example, in a query execution plan), will fail. If the change to the function did affect return values, the index needs to be rebuilt, as shown in the previous section. The index can be reenabled if the change made to the function did not affect return values, as follows:

```
alter index i1_settlements enable;
```

If it is not appropriate to either rebuild or enable the disabled index, then it can be marked unusable as follows, to allow DML against the table to continue by ignoring the index:

```
alter index i1_settlements unusable;
alter session set skip_unusable_indexes=true;
```

Summary

Indexes can provide performance benefits for queries by enabling lower-cost access paths to data. However, this comes at an increased cost for INSERT, UPDATE, and DELETE performance. Much of the additional cost results from extra redo generation related to the index. The Index Tuning Wizard component of the Oracle Enterprise Manager Tuning Pack can help automate the process of choosing appropriate columns to index, but the tried and tested method of identifying expensive queries and trying out additional indexes for cost reductions is perfectly valid. The technique of adding select-list columns to indexes can avoid expensive table data lookups in cases where table data can be located from the index.

B*tree indexes (including IOTs) are most suitable for OLTP-type applications and the use of the COMPRESS option can save significant amounts of space for nonunique indexes that contain key values that repeat many times. Bitmap indexes can produce orders-of-magnitude savings in index space. For OLTP-type applications, they aren't appropriate, due to the increased likelihood of contention on blocks in the index. Bitmap indexes work best for data-warehouse–type applications that use equality, AND, OR, and NOT operations in predicates, especially for combinations of low cardinality columns.

Unused indexes lead to overheads without any benefits and should be removed. Oracle9*i*, through the existence of the V$SQL_PLAN view and the MONITORING USAGE option, provides vastly superior facilities for identifying unused indexes compared to previous versions. Indexes that waste space are likely to increase the cost of the DML that uses them in execution plans. These indexes can be identified by the ANALYZE command and rebuilt. The SORT_AREA_SIZE parameter and the PARALLEL and NOLOGGING options on REBUILD can be used to speed up index builds. The NOLOGGING option needs to be used with care, due to side effects on standby databases.

Managing Space Growth

The appropriate management of space growth results in the most cost-effective use of disk space for Oracle databases. If disk space in your organization is provided as a managed service from a third party via a storage area network (SAN), then you can directly reduce the financial cost of the databases you manage by ensuring that no space is wasted and that databases use space on demand. In order to manage space growth efficiently, it's necessary to measure it first and identify where it's being wasted.

This chapter discusses how to manage space growth for tables; indexes are covered in Chapter 12. This chapter covers the following subjects:

- Collecting space growth information
- Presenting space growth information
- Identifying space waste
- Minimizing space waste
- The effects of row migration and chaining
- Correcting space waste

Collecting Space Growth Information

This section describes a simple approach to the collection of space growth information for all Oracle databases in an organization. The approach involves the following:

- The creation of a schema and tables to hold space information for all databases in a centralized warehouse
- The installation of stored procedures in the warehouse to collect the data
- The creation of database links in the warehouse to each monitored database
- The execution of the stored procedures using scheduled database jobs to pull information for each monitored database into the centralized warehouse across a database link
- The recording of when the last collection took place

This enables you to present information on Oracle database space usage at the following levels:

- The total Oracle used and free space for the whole organization, which is split between production and nonproduction instances
- The total used and free space for each database and tablespace
- The space growth for individual tables and indexes in each instance

Presentation involves plotting graphs based on the collected information using Microsoft Excel. Of course, you can use any charting package you like. Excel provides a low-cost solution based on Visual Basic. It produces great-looking charts, using easy-to-follow code, and you can deploy charts for Web publication with minimal effort. You can also use this technique to plot session and instance statistics and events. The collection of information alone has minimal value unless the information can be published so that everyone can see it. All too often, the presentation of information is left as an afterthought. By publishing Oracle space growth information on the company intranet using charts, anyone who is interested can see how much database space is managed by the Oracle database administrator (DBA) group and how efficiently it is managed in terms of used and free space in each database. The visibility of such information makes the estimation of future disk requirements for each application trivial for situations where database growth is linear. If growth is nonlinear, then the tablespace- and object-level information can help identify which objects are growing most rapidly, and these can be matched to business requirements to see if the nonlinear growth has a sound business basis. Perhaps most important of all, the presentation of information split between used and free space highlights those systems where disk space is overallocated.

In the past, it was traditional to overallocate space for Oracle databases to avoid the dynamic growth of the database datafiles during inserts. My personal experience is that the performance overhead of dynamic growth is very much overstated on modern disk architectures when the EXTENT MANAGEMENT LOCAL option is used for tablespaces. The use of the EXTENT MANAGEMENT LOCAL option means that extent information is held in bitmaps within the tablespace rather than the data dictionary in the SYSTEM tablespace. This typically reduces contention on the SYSTEM tablespace during dynamic extension. A simple exercise tests this theory: Perform a CREATE TABLE AS on a large table into a new one using preallocated space in the tablespace to avoid dynamic extension. Next, repeat the test into a small tablespace that extends dynamically during the insert and compare the elapsed time in each case.

> **NOTE** Oracle9*i* Release 2 allows EXTENT MANAGEMENT LOCAL to be used for the SYSTEM tablespace, which was not possible in earlier releases.

A much more efficient use of disk space, especially when space is rented from a disk farm and made available via a SAN, is to run databases in AUTOEXTEND mode on large file systems. This leads to the allocation of space automatically on demand, exactly where and when it is needed, and enables all the available space to be used. This is fundamentally different from the traditional approach of overallocation, based on multiple smaller file systems. The AUTOEXTEND approach leads to systems that grow into the available space on demand and require less day-to-day management.

Mapping Oracle Segments to Disk Storage Locations

According to Chapter 2, modern storage architectures such as SAN insulate the DBA from details of the exact location of database objects on physical disk. Oracle has recognized that microscopic details on disk storage layout for objects can still be useful for DBAs, by providing a file mapping feature in Oracle9*i* Release 2. The file mapping feature provides a framework to enable Oracle to map the locations of database objects in the file system down through the I/O stack to locations in logical volumes, storage arrays and physical disks.

Responsibility for providing Oracle with mapping information lies with the storage and volume manager vendors, who provide mapping libraries for their products. At the time of the initial announcement of Oracle9*i* Release 2, mapping was available for directly attached EMC storage arrays. Once a mapping library is available and installed for your storage stack, you need to enable mapping through the database initialization parameter file_mapping=true. The DBMS_STORAGE_MAP package includes procedures for generating mapping information, which can then be presented through views such as V$MAP_FILE and V$MAP_FILE_EXTENT.

Tablespace Space Collection

This approach to space collection involves pulling data from remote databases accessed via database links into a centralized Oracle warehouse database. The advantage of this approach is that no change is required on the monitored databases. As a result, it can be implemented on all databases in an organization with minimum risk and effort. The table that holds the database instance and tablespace-level space information for each instance in the warehouse can be created with the following Structured Query Language (SQL):

```
create table ora_instances
(global_name         varchar2(30)
          constraint pk_ora_instances primary key
          using index tablespace tools,
 system_pw           varchar2(30),
 db_status           varchar2(15)
          constraint status check
          (db_status in ('Production','Non-Production')),
 link_status         varchar2(128),
 last_ts_collection  date,
 last_seg_collection date
 ) tablespace tools;


create table ora_ts_space
(global_name     varchar2(30)
    constraint fk_ts_space references ora_instances,
 timestamp date  not null,
 tablespace_name varchar2(30),
 bytes_alloc number not null,
 bytes_free      number not null
 ) tablespace tools;
```

NOTE The examples use the TOOLS tablespace to store collected information, which you can change. You might also consider creating additional indexes to speed up queries. All the tables can be created using the DBCOOL_SPACE_ TABLES.SQL script downloadable from this book's companion Web site.

The DBA needs to populate the GLOBAL_NAME, SYSTEM_PWD and DB_STATUS columns in ORA_INSTANCES for each database that needs to be monitored. The ORA_INSTANCES table uses the database GLOBAL_NAME value to uniquely identify each database in the organization. GLOBAL_NAME is designed for this purpose. However, it's up to the DBA to enforce correct use of the value and ensure that the GLOBAL_NAME value is actually unique in all databases. Chapter 3 recommended strict naming standards for both the internal and network names of Oracle databases. To recap, the naming standard dictates the following:

- The database GLOBAL_NAME matches the external Transparent Network Substrate (TNS) alias.

- The database GLOBAL_NAME is a concatenation of DB_NAME and DB_DOMAIN init.ora parameters.

- The GLOBAL_NAME value in init.ora is set to TRUE.

These naming standards pay off many times in various situations, including space collection. Some methods of information collection (for example, Oracle STATSPACK) use the DBID column from V$DATABASE to identify each database uniquely. You might choose to use DBID instead of GLOBAL_NAME because it takes up less storage space. If you do, keep in mind that if you copy a database to another server, it will have the same DBID as the original, even if you rename the database. As a result, information from two different databases may be collected and presented as if it belongs to the same database. I prefer to use GLOBAL_NAME. It requires more space than DBID, but it's the true primary key of the database (or should be if used as intended), and it's usually self-evident when it's set incorrectly.

In order to collect the growth information into the warehouse for each monitored database in ORA_INSTANCES, a database link needs to be created in the warehouse database. The database link definition uses the following information:

- The SYSTEM password held in the SYSTEM_PW column

- The GLOBAL_NAME value

Provided that the naming standard in Chapter 3 has been followed, the TNS alias for the remote database matches the GLOBAL_NAME, and the database link can be created using the GLOBAL_NAME value. The DB_STATUS column identifies whether the database is a production database in order to enable collected information to be presented in terms of production and nonproduction database space.

Before collection can take place, the database links need to be created and validated. The SP_CREATE_LINKS procedure in the DBCOOL_SPACE package (which is downloadable from this book's companion Web site) is provided to automate the link creation and test process. After SP_CREATE_LINKS has run, the LINK_STATUS column in ORA_INSTANCES holds the status of the database link used to reference the monitored database. The SP_CREATE_LINKS procedure is as follows:

```
procedure sp_create_links as
  l_global_name varchar2(128);
  l_err varchar2(256);
  l_sql varchar2(256);
begin

-- set NULL for status to indicate test not run yet . . .
execute immediate 'update ora_instances set link_status=null';

 -- create link and test, for each instance in ORA_INSTANCES
for rec in (select * from ora_instances) loop
  if rec.system_pw is null then
    update ora_instances set link_status='null: SYSTEM password'
    where global_name=rec.global_name;
    goto next;
  end if;

  -- drop existing link, ignore error if it doesn't exist
  begin
```

```
        execute immediate 'drop database link '||rec.global_name;
    exception
      when others then null;
    end;

    -- create database link
    begin
      l_sql:='create database link '||rec.global_name||
               ' connect to system identified by '||rec.system_pw||
               ' using '''||rec.global_name||'''';
      execute immediate l_sql;
    exception
      when others then
        l_err := sqlerrm;
        update ora_instances set link_status='create: '||l_err
        where global_name=rec.global_name;
        goto next;
    end;

    -- test link by SELECT on it
    begin
      execute immediate 'select 1 from global_name@'||rec.global_name
      into l_global_name;

      update ora_instances set link_status='ok'
      where global_name=rec.global_name;
    exception
      when others then
        l_err := sqlerrm;
        update ora_instances set link_status='test: '||l_err
        where global_name=rec.global_name;
    end;

    <<next>>
    null;

  end loop;

  commit;

end sp_create_links;
```

NOTE The privilege CREATE DATABASE LINK needs to be explicitly granted to the account that owns the links and table in order for link creation to work within the procedure.

On execution, the SP_CREATE_LINKS procedure attempts to create a database link using values previously inserted into the GLOBAL_NAME and SYSTEM_PW columns. The following is an example of a statement generated to create a link:

```
create database link ORAD1.DBCOOL.COM
connect to system identified by manager using 'ORAD1.DBCOOL.COM'
```

After execution, an ok value in the LINK_STATUS column means that the link was created and tested successfully. A non-NULL value indicates that an error occurred for one of three reasons:

- The SYSTEM password that needed to create the link is NULL.
- The CREATE DATABASE LINK command failed.
- The link test failed.

The following output shows an example of the contents of ORA_INSTANCES after the execution of SP_CREATE_LINKS, indicating that two links failed to be created because of a missing SYSTEM password and a failure to resolve the TNS alias (based on the value of GLOBAL_NAME) while testing the link:

```
GLOBAL_NAME          SYSTEM_PW    DB_STATUS       LINK_STATUS
------------------   -----------  --------------  ----------------------
NOSUCHDB.COM         XXX          Production      test: ORA-12154: TNS:
ORAD1.DBCOOL.COM     MANAGER      Non-Production  ok
ORAP1.DBCOOL.COM     TEST1T       Production      ok
TEST1.DBCOOL.COM                  Non-Production  null: SYSTEM password
```

To save space, the sample output doesn't show the LAST_TS_COLLECTION and LAST_SEG_COLLECTION columns, which show the time when the last data collection executed successfully. Once the database links have been created and tested successfully, the procedure SP_COLLECT_ONE_DB_SPACE can be executed from the data warehouse against each remote database via its database link to collect used and free space information into ORA_TS_SPACE from each database in ORA_INSTANCES. The procedure uses a SELECT statement like the following to collect the used and free space for each database:

```
select gn.global_name,sysdate timestamp,
alloc.tablespace_name,alloc.bytes alloc,free.bytes free from
(
select tablespace_name,sum(bytes) bytes
  from dba_data_files
  group by tablespace_name
 union all
  select tablespace_name,sum(bytes)
  from dba_temp_files
  group by tablespace_name
) alloc,
(
select t.tablespace_name,nvl(sum(bytes),0) bytes
  from dba_free_space f,dba_tablespaces t
  where t.tablespace_name = f.tablespace_name (+)
  group by t.tablespace_name
) free,
```

```
(select global_name from global_name) gn
where alloc.tablespace_name=free.tablespace_name;

REM a sample of output from the SELECT list for one database . . .
GLOBAL_NAME          TIMESTAMP TABLESPACE_NAME          ALLOC        FREE
----------------     --------- ---------------     ----------  ----------

ORAP1.DBCOOL.COM     31-JAN-02 RBS                 524288000   419422208
ORAP1.DBCOOL.COM     31-JAN-02 SYSTEM              419430400    70909952
ORAP1.DBCOOL.COM     31-JAN-02 TEMP                209715200           0
ORAP1.DBCOOL.COM     31-JAN-02 TOOLS               264437760    48529408
ORAP1.DBCOOL.COM     31-JAN-02 USERS               261095424   260825088
```

The actual SQL used is slightly more complex than the previous example because it runs from the warehouse against each remote database. This requires the use of dynamic SQL to append the database link name to each object in the SQL statement, followed by EXECUTE IMMEDIATE to execute it. Full details can be found in the DBCOOL_SPACE package, which is downloadable from this book's companion Web site. Collection takes place through two routines. SP_COLLECT_ONE_DB_SPACE collects data from one database, where the GLOBAL_NAME of the database is passed as a parameter. SP_COLLECT_ALL_DB_SPACE collects data from each database in ORA_INSTANCES that has a validated database link by calling SP_COLLECT_ ONE_DB_SPACE:

```
procedure sp_collect_all_db_space as
begin

  for rec in (select global_name from ora_instances
              where link_status='ok' and
              trunc(last_ts_collection)<> trunc(sysdate)) loop
    sp_collect_one_db_space(rec.global_name);
  end loop;

end sp_collect_all_db_space;
```

The use of TRUNC(LAST_TS_COLLECTION)<> TRUNC(SYSDATE) in the main loop means that the procedure only collects statistics once each day for a particular database, no matter how many times the procedure is executed. This is useful if you discover that some of your databases are down during the collection, and you want to collect space information from only those databases without re-collecting from databases where the collection has already succeeded. As a result, you can execute the procedure as many times as required on a particular day in order to build up a complete view of the space usage on that day. Complete information is required in order for the overall split of used and free space between production and nonproduction databases to be accurate each day. The procedure SP_COLLECT_ONE_DB_SPACE uses the following code at the end to save the time of a successful collection into ORA_ INSTANCES for a single database:

```
-- save time if collection successful
update ora_instances set last_ts_collection=sysdate
```

```
    where global_name=p_link;

    commit;
```

If the collection fails for any reason, no exception is raised in order to allow the process to continue for other databases. However, you can test to see if the procedure worked for a given database by checking the LAST_TS_COLLECTION time in ORA_INSTANCES after the collection process completes.

Segment Space Collection

The collection of segment (that is, table and index) space takes a similar, but more sophisticated approach. Information is gathered into the following table:

```
create table ora_seg_space
(global_name     varchar2(30)
    constraint fk_seg_space references ora_instances,
 timestamp date   not null,
 tablespace_name varchar2(30),
 owner           varchar2(30),
 segment_name    varchar2(30),
 segment_type    varchar2(30),
 partition_name  varchar2(30),
 bytes           number not null,
 extents         number not null
);
```

You might choose to collect additional information on NEXT_EXTENT, MAX_EXTENTS, and PCT_INCREASE if these values are likely to change for segments in your databases. However, if you use UNIFORM extent allocation, as recommended, then these values will never change; therefore, collecting them is pointless. For databases that contain many thousands of objects, most of which don't change in size on a day-to-day basis, it makes sense for information to be collected only for objects that have changed from the previous sample. This approach saves collection time and space in the warehouse into which information is collected and means that growth charts can be plotted faster because fewer points need to be displayed.

Oracle Financials is an example of an application that contains many thousands of objects, of which only a few change daily. Both SAP and Siebel are similar. One important feature of this approach is that when collection runs against an instance for the first time, all segment information is collected because none exists in the warehouse yet. On subsequent invocations, only changes are collected. The changes comprise either new objects that appeared since the last collection or objects for which the BYTES or EXTENTS value has changed. The collection procedure uses the V_ORA_SEG_GROWTH_LAST view to identify the objects in the most recent collection of segment statistics for each instance. The view definition is as follows:

```
create view v_ora_seg_growth_last
(global_name,timestamp,owner,segment_name,segment_type,partition_name)
```

```
as
select global_name,max(timestamp)
timestamp,owner,segment_name,segment_type,partition_name
from ora_seg_space
group by global_name,owner,segment_name,segment_type,partition_name;
```

The SQL to collect segment space information for each instance can be described in pseudocode as follows:

```
select all segment information for the remote database
minus
select information in the most recent sample in the warehouse
```

The following statement shows an example of the SQL that runs against a remote database ORAD1.DBCOOL.COM to determine the changes from the previous sample. Although it may look complicated at first sight, it does nothing more than implement the previous pseudocode:

```
select global_name,sysdate,owner,
segment_name,segment_type,partition_name,tablespace_name,bytes,extents
from
(
  select global_name,owner,segment_name,
  segment_type,partition_name,tablespace_name,bytes,extents
  from dba_segments@ORAD1.DBCOOL.COM,global_name@ORAD1.DBCOOL.COM db
  where segment_type not in ('ROLLBACK','TEMPORARY','CACHE') and
  lower(db.global_name)=lower('ORAD1.DBCOOL.COM')
minus
  select db.global_name,g.owner,g.segment_name,
  g.segment_type,g.partition_name,tablespace_name,bytes,extents
  from ora_seg_space g,
       v_ora_seg_space_last gl,global_name@ORAD1.DBCOOL.COM db
  where lower(db.global_name)=lower('ORAD1.DBCOOL.COM')
  and g.global_name=gl.global_name
  and g.global_name=db.global_name
  and g.owner=gl.owner
  and g.segment_name=gl.segment_name
  and g.segment_type=gl.segment_type
  and nvl(g.partition_name,' ')=nvl(gl.partition_name,' ')
  group by db.global_name,g.owner,g.segment_name,
  g.segment_type,g.partition_name,tablespace_name,bytes,extents);
```

Like the tablespace space data collection methodology, the SQL in the DBCOOL _SPACE package is parameterized to run against a single database or all databases in ORA_INSTANCES through two stored procedures:

- SP_COLLECT_ONE_DB_SEG_SPACE
- SP_COLLECT_ALL_DB_SEG_SPACE

To recap, only new segments or those that have changed size are collected on each execution. If none has changed, then no information is collected, even if the procedures are run several times each day. The following SQL shows the last time that segment information was collected for each instance and the number of segments that have changed from the previous collection:

```
select global_name,timestamp,count(*) segments
from v_ora_seg_space_last
group by global_name,timestamp;
```

After multiple samples have been taken, ANALYTIC functions such as LEAD and LAG can be used to display changes between consecutive samples. The following output from the SQL*Plus script DBCOOL_SPACE_CHANGES.SQL (which can be downloaded from this book's companion Web site) shows a segment that has changed today and the differences compared to the last time the segment changed, which was three days earlier:

```
SINCE_LAST SEG      BYTES_K   PREV_K DELTA_K DELTA_PCT     EXT DELTA_EXT
---------- ------- -------- -------- ------- --------- ------- ---------
         3 EQ_SETT  164880   164760     120         0    1374         1
```

NOTE The DBCOOL_SPACE_CHANGES.SQL script requires that you pass the database GLOBAL_NAME as a parameter, for example ORAD1.DBCOOL.COM.

Sampling should typically take place on a daily basis, and the list of changes can be incorporated into your daily database health checks to show the segments responsible for the most space growth. The output shows both the percentage change in the size of the object (0 percent in this case), the absolute increase in size (120KB), and the change in the number of extents (1). Both the absolute and percentage change values are useful in order to display objects that have grown by the largest amount of space and those that have grown at the largest rate.

Presenting Space-Growth Information

Simple Excel macros can be used to display Oracle space-usage information in an organization based on the collected data. This section describes macros for different levels of space usage along with sample charts that are suitable for display on the intranet site of the Oracle DBA group.

Production and Nonproduction Space

The stored procedure SP_COLLECT_ONE_DB_SPACE collects information for each database in ORA_INSTANCES at the tablespace level, possibly multiple times per day. Although SP_COLLECT_ALL_DB_SPACE is designed to collect information once per day for each database, nothing stops a DBA from running a collection multiple times for a single database on the same day by calling SP_COLLECT_ONE_DB_SPACE directly.

In order to present the free and used space totals for all databases daily (split between production and nonproduction), it's necessary to ensure that information for each database is counted only once each day, although it may have been sampled multiple times. The following SQL can be used to show the latest collection time daily for each database, even when multiple collections have taken place in a day:

```
select global_name,max(timestamp)
from ora_ts_space
group by global_name,trunc(timestamp)
```

The daily total of Oracle allocated, used, and free space at the organization level can be displayed using information from the following view, which groups and presents information in a format that is suitable for display with a stacked chart in Microsoft Excel, using megabytes as the unit of space:

```
create view v_ora_db_space as
select timestamp,db_status,
round(bytes_alloc/(1024*1024)) mb_alloc,
round((bytes_alloc-bytes_free)/(1024*1024)) mb_used,
round(bytes_free/(1024*1024)) mb_free
from
(
  select trunc(space.timestamp)timestamp,db_info.db_status,
   sum(bytes_alloc) bytes_alloc,
   sum(bytes_free) bytes_free
  from ora_ts_space space,
( select global_name,max(timestamp) timestamp
  from ora_ts_space
  group by global_name,trunc(timestamp)) last,
( select global_name,db_status from ora_instances) db_info
where space.timestamp=last.timestamp
and    space.global_name=last.global_name
and    space.global_name=db_info.global_name
group by trunc(space.timestamp),db_status);


REM display some output from the view...
select * from v_ora_db_space
order by timestamp desc;
```

TIMESTAMP	DB_STATUS	MB_ALLOC	MB_USED	MB_FREE
03-FEB-2002 00:00:00	Non-Production	12007	8585	3423
03-FEB-2002 00:00:00	Production	3041	2049	991
02-FEB-2002 00:00:00	Non-Production	12007	8585	3423
02-FEB-2002 00:00:00	Production	3041	2049	991
01-FEB-2002 00:00:00	Non-Production	12007	8597	3411
01-FEB-2002 00:00:00	Production	3041	2049	991

Charting Space Usage with Excel

A simple Excel macro (or subroutine) can be used to generate charts for production and nonproduction space usage over time based on the V_ORA_DB_SPACE view. The source code for this macro is contained in a spreadsheet: DBCOOL_SPACE.XLS, which is available for download from this book's companion Web site. The sheet contains subroutines that create space charts at the organization, database, and segment level. This section shows a complete step-by-step example of displaying the total Oracle space in an organization. The following prerequisites are required in order for the macro to run successfully:

- An Open Database Connectivity (ODBC) Data Source Name (DSN) to identify the connection to the database containing V_ORA_DB_SPACE. The example uses a DSN called Oracle Warehouse.

- Oracle Net software installed on the PC running Excel.

- An Excel spreadsheet containing two worksheets named Production and Non-Production.

A top-level macro, Generate_Db_Space_By_Status, is defined to create charts for both production and nonproduction databases:

```
Sub Generate_Db_Space_By_Status()
    Generate_Space_Chart "Production"
    Generate_Space_Chart "Non-Production"
End Sub
```

The macro Generate_Space_Chart fetches rows from V_ORA_DB_SPACE via ODBC. Fetched rows are stored in cells in the worksheet, and a chart is plotted based on the cell contents. Finally, the chart is saved in Graphics Interchange Format (GIF) (which is suitable for display on the Web) in the same directory as the workbook holding the macro. The strDbConnection variable in Generate_Space_Chart holds the ODBC connection string of the database that contains the collected space information. You need to modify this to identify your database. The full source code for Generate_Space_Chart is as follows:

```
Sub Generate_Space_Chart(strDbStatus As String)

    Dim strDbConnection As String
    strDbConnection = "ODBC;DSN=Oracle Warehouse;UID=SYSTEM;PWD=MANAGER"

    ' Requires two worksheets named Production and Non-Production
    ' Clear worksheets from previous execution first...
    Application.DisplayAlerts = False
    For Each w In Worksheets
        If w.Name = strDbStatus Then
            w.Activate
            w.Cells.Select
```

```
            Selection.Clear
            Dim mychart As ChartObject
            For Each mychart In w.ChartObjects
                w.ChartObjects(1).Delete
            Next
        End If
Next

Application.DisplayAlerts = True

For Each w In Worksheets
    If w.Name = strDbStatus Then
        w.Activate

        strSql = "select timestamp,mb_used,mb_free " & _
                 "from v_ora_db_space " & _
                 "where db_status='" & strDbStatus & "' order by 1"

        ' return query results into current sheet, at cell A1 . . .
        With ActiveSheet.QueryTables.Add(_
                    Connection:=strDbConnection, _
                    Destination:=Range("A1"), Sql:=strSql)
            ActiveSheet.QueryTables(1).BackgroundQuery = False
            .Refresh ' run the query
        End With

          ' Create a chart based
        Set ch = ActiveSheet.ChartObjects.Add(10, 10, 400, 300).Chart
        ch.ChartType = xlAreaStacked
        ch.SetSourceData ActiveSheet.QueryTables(1).ResultRange, _
                        PlotBy:=xlColumns

        ch.Location Where:=xlLocationAsObject, Name:=w.Name
        ch.HasTitle = True

        ActiveChart.ChartArea.Select
        ActiveChart.ChartTitle.Select
        Selection.AutoScaleFont = True
        With Selection.Font
          .Name = "Arial"
          .Size = 10
        End With

        ch.ChartTitle.Characters.Text = _
         "Oracle " & w.Name & " Space " & Format(Date, "Short Date")

        ' Set Y axis title
        ch.Axes(xlValue, xlPrimary).HasTitle = True
        With ch.Axes(xlValue, xlPrimary).AxisTitle
            .Characters.Text = "Space (Mb)"
            .HorizontalAlignment = xlCenter
```

```
                        .VerticalAlignment = xlCenter
                        .Orientation = xlUpward
                  End With

                  ch.Legend.Position = xlBottom
            End If

      Next

      ' create a GIF from chart in spreadsheet directory
      For Each w In Worksheets
            If w.Name = strDbStatus Then
                  w.Activate
                  FilePath = ActiveWorkbook.Path & _
                        "\Oracle_" & w.Name & "_Space.gif"
                  ' save the chart as a GIF
                  w.ChartObjects(1).Chart.Export FilePath,
FilterName:="GIF"
            End If
      Next

End Sub
```

The use of Visual Basic in Excel produces code that is easy to understand and customize. Figure 13.1 shows the chart of used and free space resulting from the execution of the subroutine Generate_Space_Chart "Production".

The spikes in the chart result from incomplete collections that took place on days when one or more databases were not available. This information can be cleared by deleting the rows collected on those days from the underlying table ORA_TS_SPACE and reexecuting Generate_Db_Space_By_Status() to generate the charts without the spikes. Alternatively, monitoring can be used to detect the number of instances available for collection on a given day using the LAST_TS_COLLECTION time in ORA_INSTANCES to enable the DBA to investigate which databases were unavailable and provide the opportunity to reexecute SP_COLLECT_ALL_DB_SPACE on the same day. The DBCOOL_SPACE.XLS spreadsheet contains other macros that display used and free space for the following:

- A single database

- Individual tablespaces within each database

- Individual segments within each database

The following subroutine call in the spreadsheet generates a space chart for the segment APPUSER.TRADE_HIST in the database ORAP1.DBCOOL.COM based on the SQL that follows:

```
Generate_Segment_Chart "ORAP1.DBCOOL.COM","APPUSER","TRADE_HIST"
      .
      .
      .
```

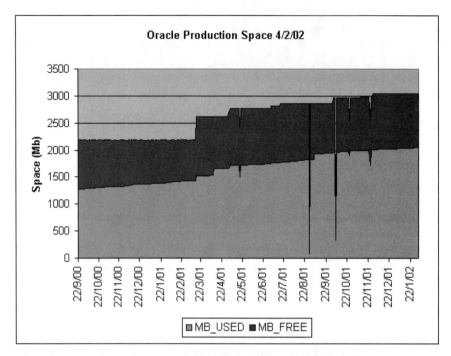

Figure 13.1 Oracle used and free space charted with Excel.

```
select timestamp,round(bytes/(1024*1024))bytes_mb
from ora_seg_space
where global_name='ORAP1.DBCOOL.COM'
and owner='APPUSER' and segment_name='TRADE_HIST'
order by 1;
```

Figure 13.2 shows the resulting chart of the table growth for a 10-month period, demonstrating that the table is growing in a linear fashion.

Identifying Excessive Free Space

Space wastage manifests itself in two ways: an excess of free space in DBA_FREE_SPACE and an excess of free space in table blocks, which is often due to inappropriate use of the PCTFREE and PCTUSED segment attributes at segment creation time. Space can appear in DBA_FREE_SPACE for two reasons:

■ Datafiles were oversized at creation time. This can be addressed by using the ALTER DATABASE DATAFILE *'file'* RESIZE command to reduce the physical size of the file. If the RESIZE command fails, it means that some of the blocks above the specified resize value have contained data at some stage.

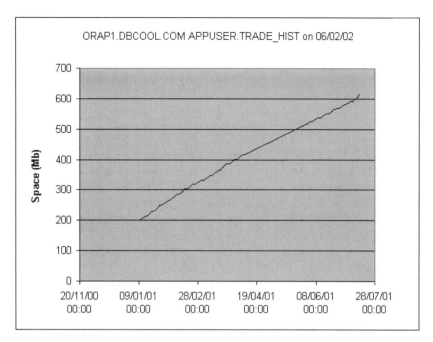

Figure 13.2 Space growth for a table charted with Excel.

■ A mixture of segments with different extent sizes in the same tablespace. Over time this usually results in *holes* in the free space that are too small to hold extents for some of the segments stored in the tablespace. As a result, when one of those segments needs to extend, additional space with the required extent size needs to be allocated in the tablespace so that the segment can grow.

The space collection procedures described previously can identify excessive free space in DBA_FREE_SPACE. Based on the information in the chart in Figure 13.1, it's evident that the production databases are running with 30 percent free space because 3GB are allocated and only 2GB are used based on the most recent sample. This free space could waste money if it is never used. This also prevents other databases on the same server from using it. The following SQL can be used to identify which databases and tablespaces have the largest allocation of free space based on the most recent sample:

```
select sp.global_name,sp.tablespace_name,bytes_free
from ora_ts_space sp,
( select global_name,max(timestamp) timestamp
  from ora_ts_space
  group by global_name) last
where sp.global_name=last.global_name
and    sp.timestamp=last.timestamp
order by bytes_free desc;
```

```
GLOBAL_NAME          TABLESPACE_NAME      BYTES_FREE
-----------------    -----------------    -----------
ORAD1.DBCOOL.COM     ROLLBACK               943714304
ORAD1.DBCOOL.COM     APP_INDEXES            655126528
ORAD1.DBCOOL.COM     SYSTEM                 190167040
ORAD1.DBCOOL.COM     APP_TABLES             153923584
ORAP3.DBCOOL.COM     SYSTEM                 118845440
```

The output indicates that ORAD1.DBCOOL.COM has several tablespaces with a lot of free space. The name ROLLBACK suggests that the tablespace probably holds rollback segments. Rollback segments often result in transient requirements for significant amounts of space when large transactions are underway. After these large operations are completed, the space is freed when the rollback segments shrink back to the optimal value. Therefore, it's possible that the large amount of free space in the ROLLBACK tablespace is justified based on further investigations. For APP_INDEXES and APP_TABLES, space can possibly be freed up by resizing the database files belonging to those tablespaces.

Identifying Wasted Space in Tables

In order to identify wasted space in tables, it's necessary to understand the concept of the high watermark (HWM) for a table. A table may contain empty blocks for two reasons. The first is that data was inserted into the blocks and then deleted. In this case, the resulting blocks are effectively empty, but they don't show up in the EMPTY_ BLOCKS column in DBA_TABLES after an ANALYZE TABLE command. This is because they lie below the table HWM. Only blocks that *never* had data in them are included in the EMPTY_BLOCKS statistic. These blocks lie above the HWM. Space in empty blocks above the HWM can be returned to the pool of free space using SQL like the following:

```
alter table system.my_objects deallocate unused;
```

Previously used blocks that no longer contain rows aren't affected by DEALLOCATE UNUSED because they lie below the HWM. One side effect of this behavior is that a full scan of a table that once contained millions of rows but now contains zero rows (due to deletes) requires blocks to be read up to the HWM of the table. As a result, the existence of many empty blocks can cause an increase in elapsed time for Data Manipulation Language (DML) that needs to process the blocks. The DELETE command has no effect on the HWM. The TRUNCATE command needs to be used to reset the HWM of a segment to 0 and returns the space back into the pool of free space.

If many table blocks below the HWM contain no rows, you can potentially reduce the space used by a segment. It's possible to find the number of table blocks that contain row data by counting the number of distinct block ID values from the ROWID of each row in the table. Blocks that no longer contain rows (due to deletes) won't contain any ROWID values. The following SQL counts all blocks in the table SYSTEM.MY_ OBJECTS that contain at least one row:

```
select count(distinct substr(rowid,1,15)) "Blocks with 1 or more
rows . . . "
from system.my_objects;
```

The difference between this value and the BLOCKS statistic from DBA_TABLES (following ANALYZE on the same table) is that it shows the number of blocks below the HWM that do not contain rows. Another situation that can result in wasted space at the table level is the use of inappropriate PCTFREE and PCTUSED values at table creation time. The PCTFREE value sets aside free space in each block in the table for updates. When block fullness falls below the PTCUSED threshold, the block becomes a candidate for new row inserts. If PCTUSED is never reached, inserts will require new extents to be allocated. Based on information about optimizer statistics in Chapter 10, it's possible to enable table monitoring in order to identify tables that never experience updates or deletes. In an ideal world, these tables would be identified in advance by the application designer. If they aren't, then the default PCTFREE value of 10 percent means that 10 percent of space can be wasted in every block. If you use DBCOOL_SPACE.XLS to create used and free space charts and notice tablespaces where free space is running at around 10 percent of the total allocated, then you might be experiencing this problem. The solution required to free up the space is to use the ALTER TABLE . . . MOVE command to re-create the table with a PTCFREE value of 0. The following SQL re-creates the insert-only table MY_OBJECTS with a PCTFREE value of 0, in its original tablespace:

```
REM table...
alter table my_objects move pctfree 0;

REM note that LOB columns need to be handled explicitly...
alter table my_tab move
   pctfree 0
   lob (my_lob_col) store as lobsegment (pctfree 0);
```

Keep in mind that the table MOVE command physically moves data between blocks. As a result, indexes based on the table become unusable until they are rebuilt after the move. Chapter 12 contains the code to rebuild unusable indexes in batch. In addition to the MOVE command, Oracle9*i* introduces the DBMS_REDEFINITION package to enable tables to be reorganized while online. This operation requires a primary key on the table in order to proceed, and the precreation of a table with the required modified storage parameters to hold the reorganized data. The table that holds the reorganized data is referred to as the *interim table*, which is required for the duration of the reorganization only. It can be dropped when the operation is complete. The three procedures listed need to be called in order:

1. **CAN_REDEF_TABLE.** Checks that the source table has a primary key or raises an exception.
2. **START_REDEF_TABLE.** Copies the source table to the interim table.
3. **FINISH_REDEF_TABLE.** Swaps the interim table with the original table.

Before the final stage of redefinition using FINISH_REDEF_TABLE, any triggers, indexes, and constraints must be created on the interim table first. Also, any grants on the interim table should be defined as they replace the grants on the original table when the procedure call is complete.

With regard to PCTUSED, for a given table, the DBMS_SPACE.FREE_BLOCKS procedure can be used to show the number of blocks below the table HWM with a fullness threshold below PCTUSED. These blocks are candidates for new row inserts. If PCTUSED is set too low, then it's possible for blocks to become relatively empty, yet never be made available for inserts. Table MOVE or reorganization can be used to address the problem.

Given the possibility of empty blocks above the HWM and empty or sparsely filled blocks below the HWM due to deletes or inappropriate use of PCTFREE and PCTUSED, it can be a challenge to quickly identify tables that potentially waste space. My preferred approach is to try identifying tables that don't use space efficiently using a single SQL statement that takes all the previous factors into account. A prerequisite for running this SQL is the use of ANALYZE on tables under consideration to ensure accurate values for the AVG_ROW_LEN and NUM_ROWS values in DBA_TABLES. The SQL is based on the comparison between two values for each table:

- BLOCKS from DBA_SEGMENTS

- AVG_ROW_LEN*NUM_ROWS/DB_BLOCK_SIZE from DBA_TABLES

The first value shows the actual space allocated to the table. The second value shows the number of blocks that would be required based on the actual size of existing row data, if each block could be packed 100 percent full with data. Of course, the difference between the two values might be large deliberately due to design decisions such as large PCTFREE values or low PCTUSED values. Then again, large differences might be due to accidental space wastage that results from the overallocation of extents for a small table or accidental use of a nonzero PCTFREE attribute for insert-only tables. The SQL presents a list of tables for further investigation based on the difference between the actual number of allocated blocks and the theoretical minimum number of blocks required calculated from ACG_ROW_LEN*NUM_ROWS/DB_BLOCK_SIZE:

```
select wasted.*,act_blocks-th_blocks blocks_wasted
from
(
select tab.owner,tab.table_name,
       seg.blocks act_blocks,
       round(tab.avg_row_len*tab.num_rows/bs.value) th_blocks
from
  ( select owner,table_name,avg_row_len,num_rows
    from dba_tables) tab,
  (select owner,segment_name,blocks
    from dba_segments where segment_type='TABLE') seg,
  ( select value
    from v$parameter where name='db_block_size') bs
where seg.owner=tab.owner
and   seg.segment_name=tab.table_name
and seg.owner not in ('SYS','SYSTEM')
```

```
and avg_row_len is not null
) wasted
order by 5 desc;
```

Be aware that this SQL requires slight modification if multiple block sizes are in use as supported by Oracle9*i*. Negative numbers for BLOCKS_WASTED indicate an inaccurate value for TH_BLOCKS caused by incorrect row statistics. This problem can be addressed by analyzing the data with a larger sample size.

> **NOTE** Oracle Enterprise Manager (OEM) Tuning Pack provides the Tablespace Reorg Wizard to help automate the process of efficient space management. The Reorg Wizard also analyzes data for excessive row chaining and migration, which are covered in the following section.

The Effects of Row Chaining and Migration

Row chaining and migration are common subjects for this discussion with respect to both performance and space. Row chaining occurs when a row is too large to fit into a single block during an insert. Typically, this occurs in large rows associated with large object (LOB) or LONG columns and is unavoidable. To reduce row chaining, the database block size can be enlarged to increase the likelihood that a row will fit in a single block. However, the same amount of data needs to be fetched irrespective of the block size. As a result, the time spent on eliminating row chaining doesn't always result in significant reductions in elapsed times for DML.

Row migration occurs when a row is updated and grows in size in such a way that the row can't fit in the original block. In this case, Oracle migrates the *entire row* into a new block and stores a reference to the new block from the original block. The ROWID of the row does not change. After migration, when the row contents are required during DML, two blocks rather than one are now required to satisfy input/output (I/O). This leads to higher resource requirements for I/O on migrated rows. Once again, the time spent eliminating row migration needs to be balanced with the performance benefits anticipated. If necessary, the PCTFREE value can be increased to provide sufficient space for updates to fit the existing block.

Row chaining and migration can be identified using ANALYZE TABLE *tablename* LIST CHAINED ROWS. This writes the ROWID values of chained and migrated rows into a table (by default, this is named CHAINED_ROWS). Oracle provides the UTLCHAIN.SQL script to create the table. Note that Oracle does not distinguish between row chaining and migration in CHAINED_ROWS. The ALTER TABLE ... MOVE command can be used to rebuild tables to avoid chaining and migration. If you are considering table rebuilds, make sure you measure the benefits they have on DML performance afterwards. You may find that a lot of time is being wasted solving a problem that doesn't actually manifest itself in terms of performance degradation.

Index-organized tables (IOTs) present special challenges for space management due to the need to balance the size of the B*tree with the size of overflow data. More information on IOTs can be found in Chapter 12. The following procedure can be used to identify row chaining in an IOT:

```
begin sys.dbms_iot.build_chain_rows_table('owner','iot tab'); end;
/

analyze table iot_tab list chained rows into iot_chained_rows;

select * from iot_chained_rows;
```

Avoiding Wasted Space

The fragmentation of free space due to holes caused by different extent sizes can be avoided by ensuring that all segments in the same tablespace use the same sized extents. As a result, no space is wasted, and little free space needs to be allocated up front. Instead, datafiles can start small and grow according to demand. The following SQL can be used as a template for all tablespace creation in Oracle9i databases based on the recommendations made in Chapter 2:

```
create tablespace users
datafile
  '/u02/oradata/linuxd1/users01.dbf' size 100m
 autoextend on next 1280k maxsize unlimited
 online permanent extent management local uniform size 128k
 segment space management auto;
```

Using AUTOEXTEND enables datafiles to grow on demand up to the maximum Oracle file size allowed. The maximum file size is a fixed number of blocks and is therefore related to the block size of the tablespace to which the datafile belongs. For example, the maximum file size for an 8KB block size is 32GB. Using LOCAL UNIFORM extent management ensures that all segments have extents of the fixed size 128KB. It's worth restating the basis for the use of uniform extents based on Oracle's recommendations, as described in Chapter 2:

- The performance of DML is largely independent of the number of extents in the segment.
- Segments smaller than 128MB should be placed in 128KB extent tablespaces.
- Segments between 128MB and 4GB should be placed in 4MB extent tablespaces.
- Segments larger than 4GB should be placed in 128MB extent tablespaces.

When autoextension is required due to a space shortage, the extension is set to 10 times the extent size in the example through the NEXT 1,280KB setting to avoid excessive dynamic extension in small chunks. To enable easier segment space management, Oracle9i introduces the concept of automatic segment space management for locally managed tablespaces as indicated by the SEGMENT SPACE MANAGEMENT AUTO

A NOTE ON ARCHIVING AND PURGING

If your application runs DML that requires table scans, then you can expect performance to degrade as the database size increases. In order to guarantee the performance of DML requiring scans, data archiving and purging operations are required to constrain the database to a limited size. On the other hand, the need to keep data available online is usually driven by business requirements. For financial systems, regulatory requirements may be the driver that determines when data can be removed.

It should not be overlooked that archiving and purging facilities need to be built in at the design stage of a project because the need to maintain performance and data availability can result in conflicting requirements that can't be met at the same time. It can be an extremely risky and time-consuming process to add archiving and purging facilities after go-live, when it's difficult to test whether business data integrity is compromised after data removal. Oracle partitioning (as covered in Chapter 11) provides simple techniques for rapid purging and archiving by enabling partitions to be dropped and optionally transported to another database. In the real world, the complex relationships between data in different tables mean that such simplistic solutions are usually not workable. Consideration also needs to be given to the requirement to reinstate archived data back into the production database at a later date.

clause. This feature removes the need for the DBA to specify the FREELIST, FREELIST GROUPS, and PCTUSED settings for tablespace objects. Instead, through information stored in a bitmap, Oracle maintains the free space available in blocks. The bitmap determines the blocks that are available for insert. As a result, Oracle can manage the space efficiently without DBA assistance.

NOTE If you witness a lot of recursive SQL on the Oracle free extent list (FET$) at times when the database is slow, you may have a problem that can be fixed by changing your tablespace to use local extent management alongside automatic segment space management.

If you are considering migrating from a dictionary-managed tablespace to a locally managed one, you need to be aware that the MIGRATE_TO_LOCAL procedure in DBMS_SPACE_ADMIN used to perform the migration does *not* result in a tablespace with the same behavior as a locally managed tablespace created from scratch. Migrated tablespaces are not subject to the UNIFORM or SYSTEM policy of newly created locally managed tablespaces, although the benefits from reduced contention are available. For tablespaces migrated to locally managed tablespaces, the ALLOCATION_TYPE in DBA_TABLESPACES is displayed as USER rather than UNIFORM or SYSTEM. The best approach for migrating to locally managed tablespaces with uniform extents is to:

1. Create a scratch tablespace with the required locally managed and uniform properties.

2. Use ALTER TABLE . . . MOVE to move all tables out of the original tablespace.

3. Drop and re-create the original tablespace using locally managed and uniform properties.

4. Use ALTER TABLE . . . MOVE to move the tables back into the original tablespace.

If you are prepared to use new tablespace names, you can choose to perform steps 1 and 2 only. Afterwards, all indexes related to the moved tables need to be rebuilt. Chapter 12 explains the options for the index rebuild. Although this migration and rebuild is a time-consuming process, it's worth the effort in the long term for low-cost management and better performance. The best approach of all is to use locally managed tablespaces with uniform extents and automatic segment management from the outset. For the end result, you should see the free space in all your databases practically disappear as datafiles grow to meet space demands as they occur.

> **NOTE**   Oracle9*i* Release 2 provides the COMPRESS table attribute, which is a brute force way to make your tables take up less space. Using COMPRESS, Oracle compresses data before storing on disk. The space savings come at a considerable cost in extra CPU needed to compress data before writing, and decompress before reading. Therefore, COMPRESS should be used with care for tables with significant insert, update, and delete activity, but can benefit read-only applications very significantly.

Summary

In order to manage space effectively, information on space growth needs to be collected on a regular basis and presented in a form that's easy to understand. This can be achieved with a few simple stored procedure calls followed by the generation of charts. Microsoft Excel provides a low-cost, sophisticated, and easy-to-program charting solution. The collected information can be used to identify databases with large amounts of free space.

In most cases, there is no need to allocate large amounts of free space in advance. For existing databases with large amounts of free space, datafiles can be downsized to return the space to the file system for use elsewhere. If free space is fragmented, the ALTER TABLE . . . MOVE command can be used to pack existing data more efficiently into a different tablespace and ensure that no space is wasted. At the table level, appropriate values for PCTFREE and PCTUSED should be set and be consistent with the use of the data. For example, for tables that are insert only, PCTFREE can be set to 0 because no space overhead needs to be allocated for updates.

An easy-to-administer, low-waste approach to space management means using AUTOEXTEND, local extent management, uniform space allocation, and automatic segment space management. When such an approach is taken, databases typically run with minimal free space overhead. The result is that space is allocated on demand, exactly where and when it's required. When used in combination with the RESUMABLE space allocation features in Oracle9*i* (as described in Chapter 6), application outages from space shortages should become a thing of the past.

## CHAPTER 14

Stress Testing and Benchmarks

Chapter 9 covered the fundamentals of Structured Query Language (SQL) tuning and recommended a measure-everything-all-the-time approach to SQL development. The premise here is that if you ensure—from the bottom up—that each and every SQL statement is written to minimize memory, input/output (I/O), central processing unit (CPU), and network resources, then when you put those statements together in a complete system, your system will have a reasonable chance of performing well.

This chapter introduces the basics of stress testing and discusses some benchmarking techniques. The purpose of stress testing is to understand how the system behaves when the workload imposed on the system exceeds the available hardware resources. Benchmarking plays several possible roles in an organization. It might be used to compare one version of Oracle with another, Oracle on one operating system with Oracle on another, or even Oracle with another database management system (DBMS) such as Microsoft SQL Server. Benchmarks are useful when an organization needs to make key technology decisions based on factors such as the benefits that can be gained from upgrading to Oracle9*i* from a previous version, and the potential costs and benefits of extending the organization's strategic range of hardware platforms to include new architectures. This chapter covers the following topics:

- How to run a basic stress test
- An overview of the Transaction Processing Council (TPC-C) benchmark
- Using a simple benchmark to compare Oracle on two operating systems

Basic Stress Testing

Consider a situation where a developer has written some SQL for the middleware component of an application. The SQL has been optimally written to minimize resource usage. The business analysts have decided that the SQL might need to execute concurrently in four sessions to service the likely demand. A simple stress test can be created by running the SQL four times concurrently in different sessions, followed by an investigation of the CPU used by each session and the Oracle events waited for by each session, as shown in Chapter 9.

In the best case, if the statement took 10 seconds for a single execution, then it would continue to take 10 seconds for four concurrent executions. Such a result depends on the available hardware resources and the nature of the resource usage of the statement. For example, in this scenario, if the SQL statement in question is CPU intensive (requiring I/O from the buffer cache rather than physical disk reads) and the server has four CPUs, then it's theoretically possible for the four concurrent streams to complete in 10 seconds. On other hand, if the SQL results in intensive physical I/O, then the elapsed time depends more on how fast the I/O subsystem can service the concurrent I/O requests.

What happens if the peak system load indicates that, in the worst case, eight sessions might actually execute the query concurrently? Some simple arithmetic can estimate the expected elapsed time based on the fact that for each second of wallclock time, 4 seconds of CPU resource are available (1 second per available CPU).

For the CPU bound example, the total CPU requirement is now 80 CPU seconds, which is calculated from eight sessions each requiring 10 seconds of CPU. Because 4 seconds of CPU are available per elapsed second, the elapsed time for each session might be estimated as $^{80}/_4 = 20$ seconds. In other words, by adding twice the load for a fixed CPU resource, the elapsed time for each session has doubled compared to the four-session example.

The trouble with real-world systems is that they don't always degrade in a linear fashion like this because of factors such as how efficiently the operating system can schedule eight running processes on four available CPUs. One of the benefits of an industrial-strength operating system, such as Sun Solaris, is that it can demonstrate linear increases in elapsed times in these kinds of scenarios. On the other hand, an operating system such as Linux—due to its less-widespread deployment for enterprise-wide commercial applications—may be more likely to hit the wall when stressed and demonstrate a stepwise rather than graceful linear degradation.

Like SQL tuning, easy-to-use tools are needed to try out some stress testing during the development phase of the lifecycle in order to encourage everyone to do it. This doesn't require a full-blown benchmarking suite. It simply requires you to run multiple SQL statements (possibly different ones) across multiple sessions at the same time and present the results. Some useful information to present would include the CPU used by each session and the event wait times for Oracle events. Event waits indicate sessions waiting for a resource to become available and provide strong evidence of contention for resources. As shown in Chapter 9, Oracle provides this information for each session in the V$SESSTAT and V$SESSION_EVENT tables.

A tool like SQL*Plus is quite difficult to use for basic stress testing because it wasn't designed for that purpose. A shell script that spawns multiple SQL*Plus sessions and waits for them to complete could possibly be created. An alternative to this approach is DbCool's Stress Tester. Stress Tester provides a user interface that enables simple stress testing to be performed with minimal effort. Stress Tester is launched from the File menu on the main window of DbCool. After launching Stress Tester, the Connect tab is used to create the desired number of concurrent sessions. The next step is to execute a simple statement in those sessions at the same time. Figure 14.1 shows the Execute tab after running the statement SELECT SUM(LENGTH(LINE)) FROM SYS .SOURCE$ in eight sessions concurrently.

Stress Tester provides the following features at execution time to enable a simple stress test:

- Multiple iterations of a statement to provide an average value
- The capability to run statements in selected sessions only using Windows multiple selection keys
- The capability to cancel all or selected executing statements
- Separate elapsed times for the execute and fetch phases of a statement
- A count of the rows fetched in each session

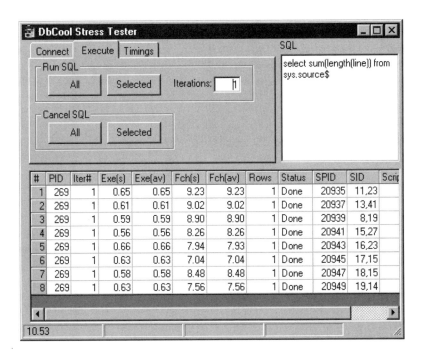

Figure 14.1 DbCool Stress Tester Execute tab.

- The overall elapsed time for all sessions (displayed in the status bar)
- The UNIX server process ID (SPID) of the server session doing the work

All times and row counts are updated in real time while the statements are executing. In Figure 14.1, the server in question contains two CPUs and the SQL statement takes approximately 2.25 seconds on a single CPU. Based on the previous calculations, the total CPU requirement for eight sessions is 18 CPU seconds (8 × 2.25). Given that 2 seconds of CPU are available for each second of wallclock time, an estimate of the elapsed time for eight sessions would be approximately $\frac{18}{2} = 9$ seconds. The results in Figure 14.1 correspond quite closely with this estimate. After the test is complete, the Timings tab in Stress Tester presents Oracle event waits and CPU that are used for each session during execution, either in a grid or chart format. Figure 14.2 shows the times in chart format for each Oracle session on the server (not just those user sessions shown in Figure 14.1). The ability to show information for all sessions is useful because it includes Oracle background sessions that perform work on behalf of the client sessions running the stress tests.

As expected, Figure 14.2 shows that each session requires approximately 2.25 seconds of CPU. The value of 2.25 CPU seconds is fixed for each execution. The elapsed time is longer because only two CPUs are available and the operating system needs to

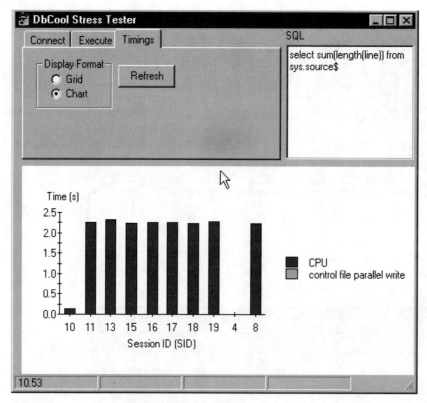

Figure 14.2 DbCool Stress Tester timing chart.

schedule the processes to share the available CPU between all the sessions. In this example, the operating system is Sun Solaris, and Figure 14.1 shows how the elapsed time is fairly constant across each session, demonstrating that the operating system scheduler is doing a good job of allocating available resources fairly to each session. The control file parallel write event shown actually occurred for a very small time during one session, but it is too small to show in the chart. The system ID (SID) values on the X axis in Figure 14.2 correspond to the Oracle session ID values in the SID column in Figure 14.1 to enable the performance of individual sessions to be related to the SQL being executed. This example runs the same SQL in each session. By modifying the value of the Script column for each session in the Execute tab shown in Figure 14.1, each session can run a different statement. The statement can be any valid SQL, including an anonymous Procedure Language/Structured Query Language (PL/SQL) block or a call to a stored procedure. Figure 14.3 shows a more interesting chart for a statement that performs SELECT COUNT(*) on a 2-million-row table in eight sessions concurrently. In addition to CPU usage, this SQL results in I/O waits caused by a full table scan (as shown by the db file scattered read event) and buffer cache contention (as shown by the buffer busy waits event) due to multiple sessions attempting to access the same blocks at the same time.

In order to introduce some random aspects of testing (for example, to simulate a system where transactions are split between five different transaction types in different ratios), the DBMS_RANDOM package can be used. This is shown in an example in the section *A CPU Performance Comparison* at the end of the chapter.

The TPC-C Benchmark

Every database administrator (DBA), developer, and IT manager responsible for application procurement should have a basic familiarity with the TPC, its aims, and its benchmarks. The TPC is a not-for-profit organization that was founded in 1988 and included eight vendors from the outset. Nowadays, all of the major software and hardware players are members. This section discusses the TPC-C benchmark, which is one

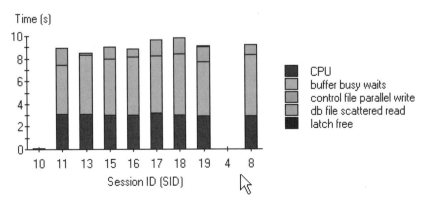

Figure 14.3 DbCool Stress Tester charting a stressed system.

of several made available by the TPC. The TPC-C benchmark models a moderately complex Online Transaction Processing (OLTP) system, comprising nine tables. It took around 2 years to develop, and the specification was approved in 1992.

The TPC's stated goal for its benchmarks is to define a set of functional requirements that can be run on any transaction-processing system. These requirements are independent of hardware, operating systems, and database software. As a result, benchmark results allow a like-for-like comparison between throughput on different hardware platforms, operating systems, processor architectures, and DBMS software vendors.

The benchmark test sponsor is required to submit proof (in the form of a full disclosure report) that all TPC requirements have been met. In the past, the test sponsor was typically a hardware vendor (such as IBM or HP) that would run a TPC benchmark to present their latest go-faster hardware in the best light. Interestingly, Oracle mounted a major advertising campaign in 2001 against IBM based on the fact that IBM had used Oracle rather than DB2 in a benchmark. Over time, Microsoft SQL Server has come to dominate the TPC-C benchmark both in terms of absolute performance on clustered architectures and price performance.

Oracle maintains a strong showing in nonclustered configurations. In January 2002, Oracle had a single entry in the top-10 TPC-C clustered performance list, 6 in the non-clustered list, and no entries in the top-10 price performance list. It's worth pointing out that Oracle TPC benchmarks (and other DBMS vendor benchmarks) typically execute in an environment that uses a transaction-processing monitor such as BEA Tuxedo from BEA Systems Inc. A straw poll of experienced Oracle DBAs suggests that real-world Oracle systems running on transaction-processing monitors are relatively rare. That's not surprising because supportability and ease of development are very important requirements to take into account when considering the business benefits of an Oracle system. On the other hand, a TPC benchmark aims to achieve best performance at the cost of practically everything else because the hardware vendor (as the sponsor) is looking to sell hardware units based on publicity from the benchmark. In the real world, best performance is never the only goal of any end-user application.

This doesn't mean that the TPC-C benchmark has no relevance to a real-world Oracle system. The TPC-C benchmark was designed, as far as possible, to model a company in the real world. Although all benchmarks cost a considerable amount of money to run and this will likely prevent you from running a full TPC-C benchmark in house, the design goals of TPC-C can be applied to varying degrees in any benchmark that you decide to run yourself. TPC-C is the OLTP benchmark of the TPC and measures the throughput of a system in terms of maximum sustained performance. TPC-C runs five different transactions as defined in the following list:

New-Order.   A new order entry at a terminal.

Payment.   An update of a customer order on payment.

Delivery.   A batch transaction of delivered orders.

Order-Status.   The retrieval of a customer's most recent order.

Stock-Level.   The monitoring of warehouse inventory.

Throughput in TPC-C is defined as the maximum sustained number of New-Order transactions per minute that the system can generate while the system is currently executing the other four transaction types. All of these transactions have a minimum response time, which is set at less than or equal to 5 seconds for everything except for the Stock-Level warehouse query, which has a limit of 20 seconds. The TPC-C unit of throughput is tpmC, which represents the number of New-Order transactions per minute. The price performance metric is in dollars per tpmC. In order to provide maximum real-world relevance, the price performance figure attempts to take into account the total cost of ownership, which includes things like software cost (including the DBMS), terminals, communications equipment, and three years of maintenance. The total cost divided by the tpmC figure gives the price performance in dollars per tpmC. The following list contains some of the most desirable attributes that an internal benchmark has over a TPC-C benchmark:

- Is relevant and meaningful to the problem domain

- Produces understandable results

- Doesn't oversimplify the target environment

The first two attributes conflict to some degree with the TPC-C benchmark. By its very nature, the TPC-C benchmark needs to be organization independent and utilizes a generic order entry system. This doesn't mean that it's not relevant to your organization; it just means that a different approach might be more relevant. For an internal benchmark, if possible, it's preferable to use transactions that run against a real business application using real business data. This provides results that business users within an organization can relate to better. However, such an approach makes the benchmark more domain specific, which is something the TPC-C benchmark tries to avoid in order to provide generic results.

One of the most important aspects of the TPC-C benchmark, which is applicable to any benchmark, is that it sets clearly defined goals based on measurable and repeatable objectives. The TPC-C benchmark is careful not to oversimplify an OLTP system by performing all of the processing on the server. Instead, TPC-C recognizes that a typical OLTP system has user terminals and real human users who select menu choices based on the list of five TPC-C transactions, key in requests, and then inspect and assimilate the results before repeating the process. In other words, the end-to-end time taken by a transaction is not simply the database response time: It also includes human factors that need to be incorporated into the model. The workflow of a TPC-C transaction passes through the following states, which can be modeled on a computer system using random number generation to provide a distribution of responses or response times in each state:

- The choice of transaction type (A New-Order transaction is 45 percent, a Payment transaction is 43 percent, and Order-Status, Delivery, and Stock-Level transactions are each 4 percent.)

- The menu response time

- The input screen keystroke entry time

- The database transaction response time

- The time for a visual inspection of database output

In the past, both Oracle and Microsoft have been accused of technical stunts in order to produce better TPC benchmark results. Oracle's original delivery of materialized views led to accusations that the effective precalculation of results rendered TPC results less meaningful. On the other hand, the real-world value of materialized views is beyond question. Microsoft's federated clustering approach, which now dominates all high-end tpmC results, led to accusations of trophy hunting; however, if the technology provides benefits to genuine business applications, then such accusations lose meaning. TPC-C states that data partitioning must be transparent to application code, and if DBMS software meets those requirements, it's allowed. More generally, TPC requires Data Manipulation Language (DML) to have the capability to execute against any data, regardless of its physical location.

In the final analysis, using TPC-C benchmarks for marketing purposes is not the fault of the TPC organization. The TPC has developed a rigorous set of requirements to help customers of hardware and software make meaningful comparisons between different systems. Those requirements are invaluable as a starting point for any benchmark, TPC or otherwise, and an awareness of them can help organizations develop their own.

If you are considering a TPC-C-style benchmark in house, then you need to invest in a tool that can manage such a comprehensive requirement and have the capability to simulate client terminals. The clear market leader for some years in this area is LoadRunner from Mercury Interactive. The effort required to set up a fully fledged TPC-C-style benchmark is considerable, and LoadRunner is relatively expensive. LoadRunner is typically not available as a trial download for prepurchase evaluation, so you need to have a well-defined set of requirements before you go ahead with it. In many cases, the rigor of a TPC-C-style benchmark is not actually required. Often, within an organization, the requirement is simply to compare what you already have with something new in a way that's meaningful to your organization.

Comparing Two Hardware Platforms

From time to time, this book has supported Linux as an appropriate platform for consideration when choosing the hardware environment for running Oracle technology. On the plus side, Linux on Intel processors appears to provide some attractive price/performance possibilities. The preconception regarding Linux is that it won't perform as well as Solaris on a comparable platform. In a real-world comparison like the one in this section, the goal is to get a stake in the ground regarding performance. It's not necessarily designed to show that one hardware platform is better than the other. In any case, the definition of "better" needs to take a broader range of requirements into account, not just performance. In terms of reliability, and hence availability, Solaris is an excellent platform for running Oracle. It has been shown that Solaris can do the job many times. The same applies to other mainstream platforms on which Oracle runs, such as HP-UX and others. Linux, on the other hand, is unproven. This doesn't mean that Linux can't do the job. It just means that Linux requires further evaluation. It's interesting that Oracle CEO Larry Ellison announced the death of large server computing in the computer press in February 2002 along with a statement claiming that Oracle was moving to Real Application Clusters (RACs) for internal systems, although he subsequently claimed that the statements were taken out of context.

In this case, the goal is to obtain some data points to see how the claims of enterprise readiness for Linux match the reality. This is not a very quantitative goal, but if you are designing an internal benchmark, then it needs to meet your own requirements and not necessarily those of the TPC. When performing such a benchmark, a good approach is to ensure as a baseline that the Oracle configuration matches on both systems. This means checking that the init.ora parameters such as SORT_AREA_SIZE and DB_BLOCK_BUFFERS (or DB_CACHE_SIZE in Oracle9*i*) match on both systems. It's not necessary to ensure that both platforms use the same storage at the same Redundant Array of Independent Disks (RAID) level. What's probably more relevant is that both platforms are configured in a way that is typical in your organization. As a result, the Solaris storage may be configured using RAID 5 on an A1000, and the Linux server may be configured using a Compaq RAID array configured with RAID 0+1. If these configurations represent the way you would deploy these platforms in a production environment, then the comparison has meaning within your organization, which is the main goal of the benchmark. Compare this approach with the TPC-C results. If your organization standardizes on Sun Solaris, for example, the fact that an HP-UX solution produces unprecedented TPC-C performance has nothing more than academic interest. You'll probably never deploy that because your hardware and support infrastructure are based on Sun, and your primary motivation is improved price/performance.

A Baseline Performance Comparison Using Import

I like to perform a data import—using Oracle's Import utility—of a production schema of a reasonable size (say, a few gigabytes) to get a feeling for system performance. Oracle Import and Export are covered in Chapter 19. In this situation, I run Import in a single stream for the maximum likelihood of success the first time, based on the same technique that would probably be used for a database migration of a production database over a weekend. As Chapter 19 demonstrates, Import can be run in multiple stages with the goal of increasing performance at the cost of increasing the complexity of the process. In this case, the requirement is to run Import in a typical configuration that would be used to produce success the first time without the benefits of multiple runs in advance to fine tune performance.

Import actually runs a good mix of Oracle DML and Data Definition Language (DDL), which in turn are I/O and CPU intensive. As such, it's an excellent test driver for a simple Oracle benchmark of a batch Oracle operation running on a single CPU. For a given table, during the batch insert phase, the Import process is I/O intensive as it reads the dump file and writes data to the tables. After the table insert, Import is CPU and I/O intensive as table indexes are created. Indexing requires full table scans of the table, which provides I/O loading and sorting, which is CPU intensive provided that the sort can take place in memory. At the end of the schema import, foreign keys need to be enabled. This operation is typically both CPU and I/O intensive at various times as the DML used to check the foreign key constraints executes. Once you have a set of statistics for a sizeable import containing many different tables of varying row lengths, you can use that as a baseline to compare performance with a different system in the future. After Import completes, the following SQL can be used to show the elapsed time for each imported table and index:

```
select ao.object_name,ao.object_type,
round((ao.next_created-ao.created)*24*60,1) ela
from
(
select object_name,object_type,created, lead(created,1) over
(order by object_id) next_created
from dba_objects o where owner='APP' and object_type in
('TABLE','INDEX')
order by object_id asc) ao;
```

The SQL uses the LEAD analytical function and relies on the fact that a table's indexes are created immediately after the table and that the difference between the CREATED value for two consecutive objects ordered by OBJECT_ID provides the elapsed time to create that object during Import. By comparing this information side by side for two different systems running the same fixed Oracle workload (based on the same Oracle dump file with the same database and Import parameters), significant differences in time can be identified for closer analysis. Assuming that the previous information is written into the table SOLARIS for the Solaris run and the table LINUX for the Linux run, the following SQL shows the side-by-side differences in elapsed times in each case, which is ordered by the largest absolute difference:

```
select s.object_name,s.object_type,s.ela solaris,l.ela linux,s.ela-l.ela
delta
from (select * from solaris) s,
     (select * from linux) l
where l.object_name = s.object_name
and   l.object_type = s.object_type
order by 5 desc;
```

OBJECT_NAME	OBJECT_TYPE	SOLARIS	LINUX	DELTA
I1_TRADING_BOOK	INDEX	96.8	67.6	29.2
I1_VALUE_DATE	INDEX	92.6	66.7	25.9

The source of significant differences in this example is worthy of further study. The DBCOOL_MON package discussed in Chapter 8 provides some simple ways to collect Oracle statistics and event wait information (as covered in Chapter 9) for every session all the time to identify the underlying reasons for differences in performance. The reasons for differences in elapsed time for a fixed workload on two different systems can often be determined by comparing event and statistic differences for the two sessions, side by side, and seeing which values differ most significantly between them. This is similar to determining the reasons for the previous Import times.

A CPU Performance Comparison

In any discussion on the relative merits of Intel versus Reduced Instruction Set Computer (RISC) processors, a performance test is required that's CPU intensive. The Import test is interesting, but differences in elapsed times may be due to I/O considerations as well as CPU because in this example, the storage used is different in each case. If the goal is to try comparing CPU alone, I/O must be taken out of the equation. A simple test in this case involves identifying some real business transactions that require I/O from the buffer cache memory rather than physical I/O from disk. The technique for identifying such SQL in the shared SQL area is covered in Chapter 9. In this case, rather than measuring transaction rates, it's easier to choose a fixed workload based on a fixed predetermined list of transactions, and then see how fast the total workload can be completed, depending on the number of concurrent sessions used to process the fixed workload and the number of available CPUs. Chapter 9 shows how to query the buffer cache to check that the blocks cached for various objects remain constant. It's important that workload is run through a single time before running the benchmark in order to ensure that all table and index blocks accessed by the test are present in the block buffer cache memory, having already been read from the physical disk. A simple benchmark can be created quite easily based on PL/SQL, SQL*Plus, and the Korn shell (ksh) (or bash under Linux). The goal is to compare performance for the same CPU-intensive workload between a workgroup-sized Solaris SPARC and Linux Intel system.

In the following example, the fixed workload comprises 35,000 executions of a business query transaction taken from a production system. Each execution of the statement takes place using a different value for the bind variable that is used to identify the transaction ID in the query. An Oracle sequence is used to serialize access to the bind variable values between multiple sessions that execute concurrently to process the workload. A separate table, referred to as the *transaction list* throughout the rest of this discussion, holds 35,000 rows where each row contains:

- A sequence number between 1 and 35,000

- A transaction ID to use as the bind variable value

- The number of rows fetched by each transaction after it completes

The value in the third column is summed at the end of each benchmark run to make sure that the benchmark carries out the same processing in each run. The following pseudocode describes the sequence of flow during the benchmark:

```
reset sequence to 1
reset row count to NULL in transaction list

spawn n concurrent SQL*Plus sessions
in each session, execute procedure SP_BENCHMARK which does the
following:

  -- SP_BENCHMARK
  loop
```

```
      get next value from sequence.
      if no more values in sequence exit procedure
      lookup transaction ID in transaction list for the sequence
      execute the transaction based on the transaction ID
      count the rows returned and write back to transaction list
   end loop
   -- end SP_BENCHMARK

wait until all sessions complete
save elapsed time
sum the rowcount in the transaction list and check against known value
```

The following shell script runs the benchmark described previously for 1 session, 2 concurrent sessions, and up to 20 concurrent sessions. It additionally saves the Oracle system statistics and events before and after each run using the DBCOOL_MON package:

```
(

for sessions in 1 2 3 4 5 6 7 8 9 10 15 20 ; do

    # reset the sequence and rowcount in the transaction list table
    sqlplus -s "/ as SYSDBA" @benchmark_reset

    # sample system events and stats before...
    sqlplus -s "/ as SYSDBA" @benchmark_stats "$sessions begin"

    # run benchmark for number of sessions shown, time it
    time do_benchmark.sh $sessions

    # sample system events and stats after...
    sqlplus -s "/ as SYSDBA" @benchmark_stats "$sessions end"

    # check results are correct
    sqlplus "/ as SYSDBA" @benchmark_status

done

) | tee -a benchmark.log
```

The do_benchmark.sh script spawns the required number of concurrent sessions that run SP_BENCHMARK and waits for them to complete:

```
:
# do_benchmark.sh

sessions=$1
session=1
while : ; do
   sqlplus -s "/ as SYSDBA" @benchmark_run &
   session='expr $session + 1'
```

```
    if [ $session -gt $sessions ] ; then
      break
    fi
done

echo "*********** " 'date'
echo "running $sessions..."

wait # wait for all spawned sessions to complete
```

The body of the SP_BENCHMARK procedure is shown in the following code without the actual business transaction (which is represented by the cursor c1) in order to save space:

```
create or replace procedure sp_benchmark is
  cursor c1 (p_transaction_id number) is
     your SQL here;

  c1_rec c1%rowtype;
  l_seq number;

  cursor c2(p_seq number) is
    select transaction_id
    from transaction_list where seq=p_seq;

  c2_rec c2%rowtype;
  l_rows number:=0;
begin

  while true loop
     -- loop exits with exception when sequence exhausted
     -- sequence maxval is 35000 (number of deals to process)
     select benchmark_seq.nextval into l_seq from dual;

     open c2(l_seq); -- c2: get transaction ID for sequence
     fetch c2 into c2_rec;
     open c1(c2_rec.transaction_id); -- run the business transaction
     close c2;
     l_rows :=0;

     -- fetch transaction results, count rows fetched
     while true loop
       fetch c1 into c1_rec;
       exit when c1%notfound;
       l_rows := l_rows+1;
     end loop;

     close c1;

     -- save rows fetched, to check benchmark worked
```

```
        update transaction_list set rowcount=l_rows where seq=l_seq;

end loop;

end;
/
```

Figure 14.4 shows benchmark results when running the previous example on a two-processor Sun E450 running Solaris as compared to a four-processor Compaq DL580 running Linux. For a CPU-intensive Oracle workload, you would expect the elapsed time for a fixed workload to decrease until all of the processing power was used. In this case, the E450 bottoms out at two sessions (using both processors at 100 percent) and the DL580 bottoms out at four sessions (using all four processors at 100 percent). As the servers are overloaded by running more sessions than available CPUs, performance degrades slightly and even more significantly in the Linux case. Based on hardware and maintenance list prices, which are available from the Sun and Compaq Web sites, for a two-processor configuration with the same amount of memory, disk, and network cards, the Sun server was twice as expensive as the Compaq.

In the previous example, the processing order was determined in advance. The DBMS_RANDOM package can be used to choose transaction IDs at random or branch between different paths in the benchmark code based on the likelihood of such a split in the workload of the real system. This is similar to the way in which the TPC-C benchmark simulates the operator choice from among the five TPC-C transactions based on the relative percentage of each transaction type in a typical OLTP system.

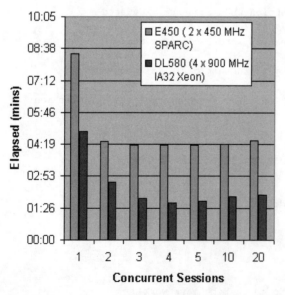

Figure 14.4 Elapsed time comparison chart.

Keep in mind that DBMS_RANDOM operates in the database server, whereas the choice is made by an operator on the client in the TPC-C benchmark.

The following example uses DBMS_RANDOM to return a random number between 1 and 100. The random number is assigned to a TPC-C transaction according to the following rules:

- Values in the of range 1 to 45 (representing 45 percent of the returned values) execute a New-Order transaction.

- Values in the range of 46 to 88 (representing 43 percent of the returned values) execute a Payment transaction.

- Values in the range of 89 to 92 (representing 4 percent of the returned values) execute an Order-Status transaction.

- Values in the range of 93 to 96 (representing 4 percent of the returned values) execute a Delivery transaction.

- Values in the range of 97 to 100 (representing 4 percent of the returned values) execute a Stock-Level transaction.

```
declare
-- TPC-C workload split
-- New-Order 45%, Payment 43%, Order-Status/Delivery/Stock-Level 4%
l_random number;
l_sleep number;
begin

  while true loop -- infinite loop...
    l_random :=DBMS_RANDOM.VALUE(LOW=>1,HIGH=>100);
    if l_random between 1 and 45 then
      -- do New-Order transaction
    end if;
    if l_random between 46 and 88 then
      -- do Payment transaction
    end if;
    if l_random between 89 and 92 then
       -- do Order-Status transaction
    end if;
    if l_random between 93 and 96 then
       -- do Delivery transaction
    end if;
    if l_random between 97 and 100 then
       -- do Stock-Level transaction
    end if;

    -- now wait for a random time from 5 to 11 secs
    -- to simulate user think time
    l_sleep :=DBMS_RANDOM.VALUE(LOW=>5,HIGH=>11);
    dbms_lock.sleep(l_sleep);
  end loop;
end;
/
```

Summary

The effects of stress on a system need to be understood as early as possible in the development cycle in order to address any possible problems before production. A simple stress test can be performed by submitting multiple SQL statements to concurrent sessions at the same time and analyzing the Oracle event waits for each session afterward as the loading exceeds the available hardware resources. The DbCool Stress Tester utility provides a simple and free way to do this.

For a more extensive performance test, a benchmark is required. The TPC-C benchmark is an excellent model for any benchmark as it sets down all of the important requirements for a benchmark. However, TPC-style benchmarks are expensive to perform, take a long time, and require expensive tools such as LoadRunner. One of the major challenges for any benchmark is to decide the exact goal of the benchmark. Unlike a TPC-C benchmark, which sets out to be domain independent, an internal benchmark needs to have a goal that has value within your organization. As such, you should run it on typical hardware and Oracle configurations that you would deploy in your production systems.

An Oracle Import of real business data can provide a meaningful baseline of the single-threaded performance of an Oracle system as it provides a good mixture of Oracle DML and both CPU- and I/O-intensive operations. A simple and low-cost benchmark can be created fairly easily using a mixture of SQL*Plus and UNIX shell scripts.

## CHAPTER 15

Server Consolidation and Resource Management

During the 1990s, many companies experienced an explosive growth in the number of servers in their organizations. Each server usually had its own locally allocated storage. It became clear that this was an inefficient way to manage storage, which needs to be available on demand and used to full capacity. This led to the deployment of disk farms, in which storage is made available over a storage area network (SAN) or network attached storage (NAS). Compared to locally attached storage—where the addition of storage space on a host typically requires purchase orders for disks, rack space in a machine room, and downtime for installation—SAN storage creates extra disk space easily from a centralized pool via a network. SAN storage also avoids the waste of disk space that occurs when an application doesn't use as much local storage as planned.

In theory, the same inefficiencies apply to the central processing unit (CPU) and memory. The result of deploying these locally on each server means that resources are wasted because servers that experience CPU and memory shortages can't take advantage of CPU and memory from a centralized pool or other servers with spare capacity. One solution to this problem is to consolidate servers and run many applications on the same server, although it's worth mentioning that Intel's emerging Infiniband bus technology takes a different approach by enabling all resources to be shared across a network. Server consolidation can cause availability issues unless it is implemented in the appropriate environment.

The right server consolidation environment requires the resource management of CPU and the input/output (I/O), memory, and network resources on the consolidated server in such a way that

- A single badly behaved application doesn't affect the availability of other applications on the server.
- Full use is made of available resources.

This chapter discusses resource management solutions, keeping in mind that the goal is to deliver the benefits of cost savings from server consolidation without compromising availability or performance. The solutions range from resource control at the Oracle session level and instance level to resource management across the entire server. The following subjects are covered in this chapter:

- An overview of server consolidation
- Oracle profiles for the resource limiting of a single Oracle session
- Oracle Resource Manager for the resource control of an Oracle instance
- Solaris Resource Manager (SRM) for the resource control of a Sun server
- Server consolidation using IBM zSeries mainframes

Server Consolidation Overview

In its simplest form, server consolidation for Oracle databases involves taking your existing Oracle instances from several servers and placing them on a single larger server. In theory, there's no reason why the scope of consolidation should be restricted to Oracle databases. For example, there's no technical reason why Oracle and Sybase databases can't coexist. You might expect the total cost of ownership to reduce for several reasons in a consolidated server environment:

- Fewer system administrators are required to manage the system.
- Floor space requirements are lower, due to the reduced footprint of the consolidated server.
- Power requirements are lower.
- CPU, memory, and I/O resources can be used nearer to capacity (more efficiently).

However, unlike disk farms (which are universally accepted as good things), business groups within an organization often view server consolidation with trepidation. Most business groups want their own applications to run on their own servers. This is actually not unreasonable because the best way to protect an application from the resource demands and side effects of other applications is to run it on its own server.

One example of the challenge presented by server consolidation is the use of virtual memory on a server. On a standard UNIX server, disk utilization can be controlled through UNIX privileges on file systems. However, virtual memory is a shared resource for all applications. If one application decides to overload the system with many processes running concurrently, then virtual memory can be exhausted. This can lead to situations where processes can't be created for other applications (in the worst case). Excessive paging due to a memory shortage can also lead to performance degradation for all applications on the server. In this case, server consolidation impacts both performance and availability.

Another possible problem is the allocation of CPU resources. Standard UNIX allows processes to be prioritized in an unsophisticated way to enable some processes to run with a higher priority than others. Oracle doesn't recommend the use of such techniques for Oracle databases. As a result, the operating system doesn't distinguish between an Oracle batch process that needs to complete before the start of the next business day and an Online Transaction Processing (OLTP) transaction that needs to complete within a few seconds.

Solutions to the resource management challenge are provided by Oracle at the database session level and instance level, and at the operating system level by systems that originated in the mainframe world. Resource management is a feature that is built into most mainframe operating systems to ensure availability through the fine-grained control of resource usage.

Oracle provides profiles to throttle resources at the Oracle session level and Oracle Database Resource Manager at the database instance level. Using Oracle Database Resource Manager—rather than an operating system resource manager—is typically an either-or choice because Oracle doesn't support running both at the same time on the database. If both are in use and neither is aware of the other's existence, then the competing behavior of both can lead to unpredictable behavior and database instability. Oracle recommends using Resource Manager to control resource usage within a single instance and an operating system resource manager for the resource management of multiple instances on the same server.

Oracle Profiles

Before Oracle8*i*, Oracle only provided login profiles to control resource usage. *Profiles* are named collections of basic hardware resource limits that can be associated with sessions. The following list shows the configurable resource settings associated with the DEFAULT profile that Oracle installs at database creation time:

- CPU_PER_SESSION
- CPU_PER_CALL
- LOGICAL_READS_PER_SESSION
- LOGICAL_READS_PER_CALL

In order for resource limits in profiles to be enabled, the RESOURCE_LIMIT=TRUE parameter needs to be enabled in the init.ora file (or spfile) or while the database is up by using the following:

```
alter system set resource_limit = true;
```

The following Structured Query Language (SQL) shows how to create a profile with a CPU limit in order to set bounds on the CPU usage for individual SQL statements:

```
create profile cpu_limit limit cpu_per_call 100;

alter user scott profile cpu_limit;
```

After the CPU_LIMIT profile has been set for SCOTT, the SQL that exceeds the limit fails with an error:

```
select sum(length(text)) from all_source;

ORA-02393: exceeded call limit on CPU usage
```

Using profiles to limit end-user workloads is very user-unfriendly and probably has no place in a usercentric application. In most cases, users execute SQL because they need the results to carry out their jobs. The act of aborting statements means that those statements typically need to be reexecuted some other way until they complete. As a result, the use of profile settings to abort SQL simply wastes resources. Overall, profiles are not sophisticated enough solutions to meet the requirements of resource management, which in turn enables server consolidation.

Using Oracle Database Resource Manager

Oracle Database Resource Manager provides a more sophisticated approach to Oracle resource management by providing the database administrator (DBA) with facilities to allocate resources to sessions or groups of sessions (consumer groups) based on business performance requirements. For example, OLTP users can be allocated more CPU resources than batch sessions because response times for OLTP transactions must complete in a predictable time, allowing small variations.

It's important to emphasize that Resource Manager controls resource usage within a single instance when the CPU load runs close to 100 percent. As such, it's not practical to use it for resource management across multiple instances on the same server. However, it's useful to understand its behavior for two reasons. The first is that Resource Manager features can be contrasted with operating system resource managers, which are discussed later in the chapter in the sections on SRM and IBM zSeries. The second reason is that it seems like a small step for Oracle to extend the concept of a resource consumer group to groups of users across multiple databases and therefore manage resources across multiple instances at the same time. The concept of an enterprise user (held in a directory) that isn't tied to an instance already exists. The same approach can easily be applied to consumer groups.

Database Resource Manager is designed to manage system throughput in a such a way that business performance requirements are met when CPU is loaded at 100 percent and all available CPU resources can be made available where needed when the CPU is not fully loaded. Specifically, Database Resource Manager addresses the following problems stemming from operating system behavior:

- The overhead of the operating system context switching between many Oracle server processes when the number of server processes is high

- Descheduling the Oracle server processes that hold time-critical database resource (such as latches), leading to longer-than-necessary latch waits

- The inability of the operating system to prioritize database tasks according to business requirements

- Operating system nonawareness of the parallel processing capabilities of the database

It's important to understand that Resource Manager is not designed to keep CPU usage within fixed bounds at all times for particular groups of users. Resource Manager enables available CPU resources to be overallocated to a group of users if no other group requires it.

Users are assigned an initial resource consumer group at logon time, as shown by the DBA_USERS view. Resource consumer groups are named collections of sessions that the DBA wants to group together based on resource requirements. Users are assigned a default group at logon time, although this can be changed dynamically during processing. The following SQL shows that DBA accounts are assigned to SYS_GROUP and regular user accounts are assigned to DEFAULT_CONSUMER_GROUP:

```
select username,initial_rsrc_consumer_group from dba_users
where username in ('SCOTT','SYSTEM');


USERNAME    INITIAL_RSRC_CONSUMER_GROUP
----------  ----------------------------
SYSTEM      SYS_GROUP
SCOTT       DEFAULT_CONSUMER_GROUP
```

Users who are not assigned explicitly to a group are assigned to DEFAULT_CONSUMER_GROUP. The DBA_RSRC_CONSUMER_GROUPS view lists all resource consumer groups in the database, including the CPU resource allocation method for the consumer group, as shown by the following SQL:

```
select consumer_group,cpu_method from DBA_RSRC_CONSUMER_GROUPS;


CONSUMER_GROUP          CPU_METHOD
----------------------- ------------
OTHER_GROUPS            ROUND-ROBIN
DEFAULT_CONSUMER_GROUP  ROUND-ROBIN
SYS_GROUP               ROUND-ROBIN
LOW_GROUP               ROUND-ROBIN
```

A resource plan contains information that specifies the method used to allocate resources to resource consumer groups that use the plan. The DBA_RSRC_PLAN view lists all of the resource plans in the database. As installed, Oracle contains a plan named SYSTEM_PLAN in both Oracle8*i* and Oracle9*i*. Additional resource plans can be created using the DBMS_RESOURCE_MANAGER package. The V$RSRC_PLAN view can show the systemwide active resource plans at any time. Keep in mind that, by default, Resource Manager is disabled. An active plan can be enabled through the init.ora parameter RESOURCE_MANAGER_PLAN or it can be set using ALTER SYSTEM when the database is up, as follows:

```
REM set the active resource plan to SYSTEM_PLAN...
alter system set resource_manager_plan=SYSTEM_PLAN;

REM this disables Resource Manager...
alter system set resource_manager_plan='';
```

The association between resource consumer groups and resource plans is shown through the DBA_RSRC_PLAN_DIRECTIVES view:

```
select plan,group_or_subplan,cpu_p1,cpu_p2,cpu_p3
from dba_rsrc_plan_directives;
```

PLAN	GROUP_OR_SUBPLAN	CPU_P1	CPU_P2	CPU_P3
SYSTEM_PLAN	SYS_GROUP	100	0	0
SYSTEM_PLAN	OTHER_GROUPS	0	100	0
SYSTEM_PLAN	LOW_GROUP	0	0	100

This SQL shows a subset of the columns in DBA_RSRC_PLAN_DIRECTIVES related to levels associated with the CPU resource allocation method. This method enables the administrator to specify how CPU resources are to be allocated among consumer groups or subplans and the priority of allocations. Eight levels of CPU allocation are available, and three are shown. Levels provide a way to prioritize CPU allocation across consumer groups. The total at each level cannot exceed 100 percent. Level 2 gets resources only after level 1 is unable to use all its resources. Level 3 gets resources only after level 2 is unable to use all its resources.

The values for CPU_P1, CPU_P2, and CPU_P3 for SYSTEM_PLAN in the example represent the levels that determine the allocation of CPU resources to consumer groups on a system where the CPU is fully loaded. In this case, users in resource consumer group SYS_GROUP take 100 percent of the CPU resources, as determined by the value 100 for CPU_P1. As a result, sessions for the SYS and SYSTEM accounts, which reside in SYS_GROUP, take priority when the system is heavily loaded to ensure that DBA tasks have priority. Of course, if the CPU usage is not loaded 100 percent, then the remaining CPU resources fall through to the next level (CPU_P2) where they can be used by OTHER_GROUPS. Finally, unused CPU is available to LOW_GROUP. This allocation of CPU resources means that in a fully CPU-loaded system, sessions in OTHER_GROUPS or LOW_GROUP could wait forever because 100 percent of the CPU resources is made available to SYS_GROUP.

Usually, the procedures in DBMS_RESOURCE_MANAGER are used by the DBA to create additional resource consumer groups and resource plans that enable CPU resources to be split between different groups. This process requires the following steps:

1. Create a resource plan using the CREATE_PLAN procedure in DBMS_RESOURCE_MANAGER.

2. Create resource consumer groups using the CREATE_CONSUMER_GROUP procedure in DBMS_RESOURCE_MANAGER.

3. Create resource plan directives using the CREATE_PLAN_DIRECTIVE procedure in DBMS_RESOURCE_MANAGER.

4. Grant privileges to allow the use of resource groups using the GRANT_SWITCH_CONSUMER_GROUP procedure in DBMS_RESOURCE_MANAGER_PRIVS.

5. Enable the resource plan to be used by the instance using ALTER SYSTEM SET RESOURCE_MANAGER_PLAN.

For example, the following information from DBA_RSRC_PLAN_DIRECTIVES indicates that CPU resources should be allocated 80 percent to the OLTP group when OLTP_PLAN is active and 90 percent to BATCH when BATCH_PLAN is active:

```
PLAN           GROUP_OR_SUBPLAN     CPU_P1    CPU_P2    CPU_P3
------------   ------------------   --------  --------  --------
OLTP_PLAN      OLTP                     80         0         0
OLTP_PLAN      BATCH                    20         0         0

BATCH_PLAN     BATCH                    90         0         0
BATCH_PLAN     OLTP                     10         0         0
```

The ALTER SYSTEM SET RESOURCE_MANAGER_PLAN command can be used to enable different resource manager plans at different times of day. This simplistic approach is somewhat inflexible if the allocation of CPU to OLTP for OLTP_PLAN needs to be increased. Because percentages at each level can't exceed 100 percent, it follows that any increase in CPU for OLTP requires a reduction in the value for BATCH in OLTP_PLAN.

A multilevel approach, which is similar to that used by SYSTEM_PLAN, enables resource allocation to be changed at the first level for a single group without requiring other changes at the same level for other groups. The following example passes at least 20 percent of the available CPU to BATCH (which will use all [100 percent] that remains) while enabling the overall percentage of CPU used by OLTP to be increased independently, if required:

```
PLAN           GROUP_OR_SUBPLAN     CPU_P1    CPU_P2    CPU_P3
------------   ------------------   --------  --------  --------
OLTP_PLAN      OLTP                     80         0         0
OLTP_PLAN      BATCH                     0       100         0
```

Resource Manager also enables the use of subplans (plans within plans) to provide more fine-grained control of resource allocation between consumer groups. Subplans allow the further subdivision of resources among different users of an application. In addition to controlling CPU resource allocation, Resource Manager enables a parallel degree limit to be associated with a consumer group to control the maximum degree of parallelism for any operation within the group. Oracle9*i* extends the functionality of Resource Manager in the following areas:

- An active session pool can be created to control the number of concurrent sessions allowed within a consumer group. Above the limit, sessions queue until existing sessions in the group complete.

- Users can be switched automatically between groups based on rules provided by the DBA.

- An UNDO pool can be created to control the undo space used by a consumer group.

- The MAX_EST_EXEC_TIME directive is available to limit the execution time of a session.

To summarize, Oracle Database Resource Manager provides extensive features for managing Oracle resource usage within a single instance. The Oracle Enterprise Manager (OEM) provides additional features in Oracle9*i* to make resource management easier to use, including a Resource Manager Wizard to automate the creation of resource plans and consumer groups and enable the setting of resource plans to be scheduled. The features are available under the Instances node for each database registered with the OEM repository, as shown in Figure 15.1.

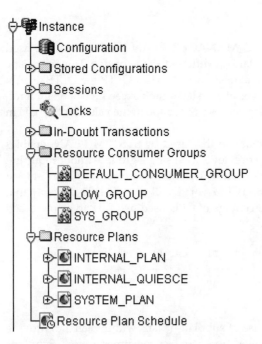

Figure 15.1 Resource Manager features in OEM Oracle9*i*.

DbCool's Stress Test (which is covered in Chapter 14) is a tool that can be used to demonstrate resource management for consumer groups. A simple CPU-intensive PL/SQL procedure can be run in two sessions at the same time. Provided that the sessions are logged on as two different users and each user is in a different consumer group, the elapsed time to complete the same task should be split according to the CPU levels specified in the resource plan directives.

Using SRM

SRM is a software product from Sun Microsystems that enables the control of various server resources between applications. It's a component of the Solaris 8 Operating Environment. The facilities provided by SRM are based on methods that have existed on mainframes for a long time. SRM aims to provide mainframe levels of resource management and control without the expense of a fully fledged mainframe server. SRM is a key enabling technology for facilitating the server consolidation of Oracle database instances on Sun Solaris.

SRM enables the administrator to control server resources so that multiple users, groups, and applications can be guaranteed a consistent level of service on a single server. When CPU resources are in short supply, policies guarantee that the allocation of resources is based on predefined business requirements. At the same time, unused CPU capacity can be allocated dynamically to active applications to ensure that resource utilization is maximized. By dynamically allocating unused CPU capacity to active users and applications, resource utilization is increased. The use of policies to control resource usage leads to simpler and easier systems management. The following lists the resources that SRM can manage:

- CPU
- Virtual memory per process
- Virtual memory for the whole system
- The number of processes
- The number of logins
- Connection time

Based on the list of resources that SRM can manage, the next step is to decide which of those are relevant to the management of Oracle instances. The goal of SRM in the Oracle domain is to manage resource allocation across multiple Oracle instances running on a single server. The final three resources in the list can be controlled directly by Oracle at the instance level, so there's no requirement for SRM to manage them.

Sun only recommends the use of SRM to manage CPU allocation across Oracle instances. However, it's not uncommon for badly behaved code to exhaust virtual memory on an Oracle database server. This can easily be achieved by writing a PL/SQL procedure that accidentally calls itself using infinite recursion. In this case, a virtual memory per-process limit would ring fence the effects of the fault and prevent virtual memory on the server as a whole from being exhausted. It's important to remember that when virtual memory is in short supply, excessive paging takes place, and this usually causes a degradation of performance on the entire system. This is still better than running out of virtual memory completely. The exhaustion of virtual memory at the server level causes more serious problems, such as preventing new processes from spawning and UNIX administration commands from working.

Under SRM, resources are allocated to a UNIX lnode (or process group). By default, each UNIX user account, including the Oracle account, has an associated lnode. As SRM resources are allocated to lnodes, it's clear that each Oracle database instance needs to be associated with a different lnode, if resources are to be allocated specific to each instance. At first sight, it appears that each Oracle instance therefore needs to run under a different UNIX account in order to be associated with a different lnode. This would be a disaster in terms of manageability because it's standard practice to run all Oracle instances on a single server under the same UNIX account, which is typically named oracle. Fortunately, multiple UNIX accounts are not required under SRM. The UNIX account and the lnode are actually loosely coupled. This means that two different Oracle instances can have file access privileges associated with the UNIX oracle account and resource allocation associated with different lnodes, such as oracle1 and oracle2. In this way, multiple Oracle instances can be assigned different CPU allocations according to their lnode, yet still be owned by the same UNIX account (oracle). SRM includes an administration tool to link lnodes to UNIX accounts. As a result, each instance can start under user ID (UID) oracle by using a different linked lnode that is specific to the instance.

It's important to understand the behavior of the Oracle listener with respect to lnodes. Once a process is started within an lnode, all of its children inherit the same lnode. On a multiple instance Oracle server *without* SRM, a single listener process is typically used to service remote client connect requests for all instances. When a connection request is received, the listener spawns an Oracle process under the $ORACLE_HOME of the instance specified in the connection request. However, when SRM resource management is required, the spawned process must be spawned under the lnode associated with the instance. This is required to ensure that all shadow processes for each instance can be identified by SRM and treated as a group for resource management purposes.

Therefore, each instance in an SRM configuration must have a separate listener started under the lnode associated with the instance. This is a considerable management overhead compared to a non-SRM configuration. Recall from Chapter 3 that dynamic listener registration means that from Oracle8*i* on, it's possible to run an Oracle network listener without a listener.ora file at all. Dynamic registration relies on the use of a standard Transmission Control Protocol/Internet Protocol (TCP/IP) port (1521) for servicing Oracle connection requests. On the other hand, each listener in an SRM configuration needs to listen on a different TCP/IP port, and each listener requires an explicit name if each one is required to be stopped and started independently of the others. So, the benefits of resource management through SRM add considerable complexity to the startup and shutdown of Oracle instances and network listeners.

To allocate CPU resources to lnodes, SRM introduces the concept of CPU shares. The most significant difference between CPU allocation in SRM and Oracle Database Resource Manager is that the use of shares means that shares do not have to add up to 100 percent. For example, if the Equities instance is allocated 10 CPU shares and the

Foreign Exchange instance is allocated 10 CPU shares, then both are entitled to 50 percent of the resources. If you decide to increase the allocation of shares for Equities to 15, then Equities now has a 15/(10+15) share of the total CPU. It's not necessary to modify the Foreign Exchange allocation in any way. It's possible to subdivide an lnode into other lnodes to provide multilevel resource allocation in a similar way to the CPU-level approach of Resource Manager. Using CPU shares, it's trivial to add a new Oracle instance to the list of resources managed by SRM. Virtual memory can be limited at the lnode level. For individual processes, it can be used to prevent a runaway process from grabbing all virtual memory on a server. SRM provides command-line tools to manage applications and lnodes. The most frequently used tools are as follows:

- srmuser *lnode_name command* is used to start the named command from the same UNIX account (for example, oracle) under a specified lnode. This command is used to ensure that Oracle instances and network listeners are started under different lnodes.

- limit -p pid returns the lnode ID of the specified process and can be checked to ensure that processes are started under the right lnode.

- lminfo -v *lnode_name* shows the resource allocation settings (for example, CPU shares) associated with a specific lnode.

Security in an SRM environment needs to be considered carefully because the capability to start an application under a different lnode (as required by the oracle account) requires additional SRM privileges that must be granted explicitly. It's helpful to consider lnode dependencies as a tree representation to understand what's possible. For example, the oracle account and its two lnodes—oracle1 and oracle2 (to manage two different instances)—can be represented as a tree with the oracle UID as the root and the oracle1 and oracle2 lnodes as children. This representation is appropriate for a single-level approach to resource allocation. In its simplest form, SRM security can be configured to enable a user to start applications under the lnodes of any of its children. A single-level resource allocation approach fits in well with this security model. If multilevel lnodes are required, then SRM security needs to be configured to enable a user to start applications under any lnode in the tree, whether or not it's related to Oracle databases. This scenario is open to abuse. As a result, a single-level representation is recommended for security reasons, and in most cases, it provides acceptable resource management capabilities between multiple Oracle instances on the same server.

Using IBM zSeries

SRM is designed to bring the benefits of mainframe-style resource management to nonmainframe (and therefore less expensive) environments. IBM zSeries is a mainframe computing environment designed to deliver the benefits of a mainframe running many (perhaps hundreds) virtual instances of popular operating system environments, such as Linux, on a single mainframe. This book has already recommended that you consider the price performance benefits of Linux on Intel as a suitable environment for running Oracle in an organization. In this context, it is interesting to report that at the end of January 2002, Oracle CEO Larry Ellison predicted the "inevitable" demise of large server systems and a move to clustered Real Application Cluster (RAC) environments on Intel within Oracle Corp.

Although the zSeries environment is fairly new, the ability to run many virtual Linux kernels on the same mainframe, with each potentially running a different Oracle instance, leads to some exciting possibilities. The zSeries mainframe can run Linux in two different ways. The first involves running standard 32-bit versions of Linux, such as those from Red Hat or SuSE on a zSeries in 32-bit emulation mode. Oracle is certified on those versions of Linux. The zSeries hardware can be logically partitioned into a maximum of 15 separate partitions. Each logical partition (LPAR) can run Linux or one of the other operating systems that IBM provides. Resources can be controlled at the LPAR level.

IBM also produces a 64-bit version of Linux based on a Linux kernel modified specifically for zSeries. Using the z/VM Guest Support option, Linux can run as a virtual machine using z/VM. The advantage of z/VM is that it provides the virtualization of CPU processors, I/O subsystems, and memory. While running in z/VM Guest Support mode, potentially hundreds of Linux virtual machines can run concurrently on the same server, each with an Oracle instance. A single server could potentially support most (possibly all) production and development Oracle instances on a server, with each ring fenced in its own Linux virtual machine.

As a modern mainframe operating system, the resource management capabilities of z/VM provide very sophisticated CPU, I/O, and memory usage control. In addition, the support for multiple Oracle instances, each in its own Linux virtual machine, leads to the possibility of Real Application Clusters (RAC) between the virtual machines. Although certification of Oracle on zSeries Linux needs to be confirmed, the potential lowered cost of ownership and resource sharing of Oracle on zSeries along with the mainframe levels of reliability definitely merit further investigation. This configuration looks to have genuine possibilities in the enterprise after Oracle announced its commitment to delivering a production release in mid 2002.

It's worth restating that mainframes provide potential reductions in total cost of ownership (TCO) due to lower floor space and power consumption requirements. In the Linux-on-Intel world, new architectures such as Egenera's BladeFrame (www.egenera.com) set out to provide similar benefits as mainframes, based on widely used hardware such as Intel CPUs. These blade architectures provide significant potential for Oracle server consolidation.

Summary

The availability of a resource manager is a critical success factor for server consolidation, leading to the ability to run many Oracle instances on the same server. Without the presence of a resource manager, it is possible that a single badly behaved application can affect the performance and availability of all the applications on the server. For example, a single process can theoretically use all of the available virtual memory, effectively shutting down the entire server and applications on it.

Oracle Resource Manager is not designed to manage multiple instances of Oracle on a single server. It's designed to ensure that CPU resources can be allocated fairly between groups of users on a single instance when CPU usage runs at 100 percent. The model used to implement Resource Manager based on resource consumer groups leads naturally to a situation where consumer groups could be defined in a directory outside of a specific database. Should Oracle choose to take this approach in the future, it would appear to be a small leap to implement resource management across multiple instances.

SRM has the capability to share CPU and virtual memory resources on a single Sun server across multiple Oracle instances on the server. This capability comes with an increased cost and complexity of Oracle instance and network listener management on the server, due to the need to run each Oracle instance and listener in its own process group (lnode).

IBM zSeries is a mainframe solution that offers potential price-performance and high-availability features by running each Oracle database on the mainframe in its own virtual Linux environment. The zSeries includes the very sophisticated resource management capabilities typically associated with mainframes, leading to the potential for the full use of all CPU, memory, and I/O resources on the server between virtual environments without compromising availability.

Selecting and Using Performance Management Tools

Choosing the right performance management tools is a critical part of meeting performance and availability requirements. One thing that enterprisewide Oracle performance management tools have in common is that they are expensive, so the choice of tools is one that you want to get right the first time. You should keep in mind that an ever-increasing range of freeware (including DbCool) can provide some of the functionality that you need. The term management emphasizes that performance is something you should manage, rather than something that manages you.

It's important to separate the requirements from the evaluation stage because database administrators (DBAs) tend to have a fixed view of what's in scope when discussing Oracle performance management tools. As a result, key requirements might be overlooked at the outset because they are considered technically impossible to meet. The premise of this chapter is that you should focus on the requirements of an ideal Oracle performance management tool first, and then perform an evaluation of real-world tools against these requirements in a separate exercise. The flow of the topics is designed to take you from the requirements' definition stage to an evaluation of candidate tools, and on to making comparisons. The flow of topics for this chapter is presented in the following list:

- Roles and responsibilities for those involved in performance management

- Setting performance goals

- Standardization of approach

- Tool requirements

- Using Oracle Expert

- Using Precise/Indepth
- A comparison of Oracle Expert with Precise/Indepth

NOTE Before purchasing Oracle performance management software, you should also consider the recommendations in Chapter 7. Although those recommendations are intended for the prospective purchaser of Oracle-based end-user business applications, the requirements apply equally to Oracle performance management software purchased for internal use within the DBA team.

Performance Management Roles

During the design stage, the business analyst, DBA, and developer all need to be involved in performance management. The business analyst should set down the performance requirement goals of critical parts of the system, and the DBA and developer should work together to ensure that the appropriate Oracle features and technologies are used to meet these goals. Steps should also be taken to ensure that appropriate instrumentation is included in the application to measure performance.

Hardware is often purchased at the early stages of a project, without requiring much input from the DBA or developer. Often, the limiting factor is the availability of funds for the project. This isn't such bad news in reality because Oracle application performance is chiefly determined by application design and, in many cases, poor database performance results from poor performance of a few Structured Query Language (SQL) statements. The DBA and developer can save the effort needed for a time-consuming, capacity-planning exercise and instead work together to design a system that meets the performance goals within the known constraints of the hardware.

In an ideal world, the server platform would be chosen based on the capacity requirements of a model of the production system. In reality, it's difficult to predict the likely performance of the system when information on load requirements is incomplete, which it usually is. Even if information on database size, projected growth, and the user base is available, it's extremely difficult to model the performance of a system up front with any certainty, due to the complexity of the interacting parts, and it can take a lot of effort to produce results that turn out to have limited value.

During development, the DBA and developer both have a responsibility for managing performance. The developer needs to be able to view the cost and understand the resource consumption of each and every SQL statement written during development so that they can be minimized. Suitable tools are required to make it as easy as possible for the developer to do this. The DBA should be monitoring performance on a regular basis through performance-related information collection and cross-checking with the developers on any performance issues.

During production, the responsibility for performance management lies with the DBA. Effort spent preventing performance issues early in the lifecycle pays off because business applications stand or fail by their production performance. However, a production system typically has different load profiles and usage patterns that can't be simulated earlier in the lifecycle, so you can expect performance issues to occur. During production, the DBA needs to identify the root cause of each and every performance problem reported by business users as soon as possible, and work with the developers to provide solutions. In addition to this reactive performance management, the DBA needs to identify long-term trends in performance to proactively address them before they impact business users. Reactive performance management should not be taken as a sign that the performance management process has failed: It's a fact of life.

Who Is Responsible for Performance Management?

Let's consider who is responsible for Oracle performance management. In some organizations, performance is not considered until production rollout. After production rollout, performance usually becomes an issue and the DBAs become involved in fire-fighting performance issues. The end result is overworked DBAs and dissatisfied users. To address this situation, it's clear that performance management must be built into the development lifecycle and not simply left until production. At this point, it's traditional to produce some graphs to express the cost and benefit of tuning during the application lifecycle and I'll do the same. Figure 16.1 shows the cost and benefits of performance tuning during the application lifecycle.

What's important is the general form of the two curves, rather than the lack of any units on the Y axes. The information presented by such graphs is best regarded in a qualitative sense only. You can summarize the information in the graphs by saying that performance management should begin as early as possible during the application lifecycle, and that the earlier you do it, the more likely you are to deliver an application that meets performance requirements. DBAs and developers have the major responsibility for ensuring that requirements are met.

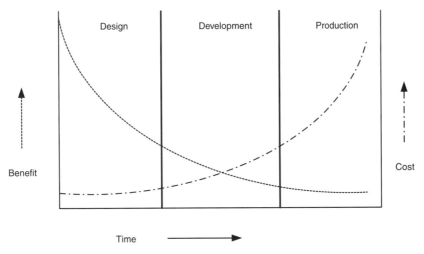

Figure 16.1   Cost and benefits of performance tuning.

Setting Performance Goals

Any performance management that you carry out should be done with a clear understanding of the performance you are trying to achieve. That means the application performance requirements should be set down and agreed upon with the business analysts at the time of the project requirements definition, or close to it.

The terminology used to specify performance goals needs be in a form that everyone can understand. Low-level metrics such as database cache hit ratios are meaningless in this context because the relationship between such low-level metrics and the users' experience of performance is not always closely related. In any case, business users have no interest in such jargon. Goals are usually best expressed in terms of the response times of application screens for interactive applications, or elapsed times for batch completion. Developers can build performance instrumentation into their applications without much extra coding effort if the requirement is raised early enough in the development cycle. If there are no performance goals, you never know whether the application is meeting them. Without clear goals, you're likely to be notified of performance problems by users when performance has become business critical rather than just irritatingly slow.

Standardization of Approach

Every DBA and developer recognizes the importance of performance management. However, in the real world, the quality of Oracle performance management is often determined by the skill level of an individual DBA or developer on a project. The lack of a consistent approach leads to failures when determining the root cause of performance problems. Often, the delay in addressing Oracle performance problems is caused by the failure to understand the true cause, rather than difficulties in implementing a solution. The key to overcoming this problem is the standardized use of tools and techniques that work.

By standardizing, all DBAs have a common understanding of what's involved in performance management and can apply those techniques to all databases in the same way. The result is that the performance profile of a production application is no longer determined by the luck of the draw. If you run databases as part of a global organization, standardization is essential to provide a consistently high level of service across all your sites.

Tool Requirements

This section lists the requirements for a performance management tool, against which candidate tools can be evaluated. The requirements are grouped into mandatory requirements and optional requirements.

Mandatory Requirements

These mandatory requirements are the bottom line for identifying the real cause of performance problems in your Oracle database.

Monitor Performance in Near-Real Time

Production problems often need a fine-grained view of performance over a short time period to identify the root cause. This requires the sampling of performance metrics on a subsecond time interval. Some performance methodologies take a view that because it's not considered practical or even possible to do such high sampling rates, it's not a requirement. That seems to be the wrong way around. The Oracle performance information is changing on a subsecond basis, and if you want to truly understand performance issues, you need a tool that can sample on a subsecond interval. Whether it's possible or not is another question. As a requirement, it's valid.

Monitor Performance with Low Impact

It's not possible to monitor a database without impacting performance. Traditional Oracle performance monitoring involves running SQL queries against the various Oracle performance counters in the X$ or V$ tables. This traditional approach is both a strength and a weakness. It's a strength because the openness of Oracle's performance counters means that information can be collected via SQL queries. As a result, many tools on the market can carry out this kind of monitoring, some commercial and some free. DbCool is one such free tool. (Also, it's quite straightforward to develop your own.) The weakness of these tools stems from the performance hit involved in running the collection SQL statements at very small time intervals. These statements have all the parsing and execution overhead of regular SQL statements. In a very busy system, these statements are subject to waits like any regular statement and can cause waits for business-related SQL. Storage of the low-level sampled information in Oracle database tables is likely to be incompatible with a requirement for high sampling rates and low impact: If the SQL queries themselves have a significant impact, inserts are likely to have an even higher impact.

To summarize, we want to monitor performance at subsecond intervals *and* with a sufficiently low impact that it doesn't cause a noticeable performance degradation on the whole database. Maybe this sounds like the Holy Grail of Oracle performance, but it's still a valid requirement.

Correlate Oracle and Operating System (OS) Statistics

According to Chapter 9, Oracle provides many internal counters that provide performance information through wait events and statistics. One of the key statistics is "CPU used by this session." Because Oracle only updates this statistic at the end of a SQL statement, a long-running statement (such as CREATE INDEX on a large table) might appear not to be using the central processing unit (CPU). The CPU usage is then reported by Oracle as a huge CPU spike when the statement completes. As a result, using Oracle's statistics to measure CPU use over time can be misleading. To address this, CPU can be measured accurately in near-real time from the UNIX process statistics for the Oracle session. This requires the performance management tool to collect and correlate both Oracle and OS statistics for accurate results.

Identify Top SQL

This appears to be a very obvious requirement. When you have an Oracle performance problem, you know that it's caused either by a single SQL statement with excessive resource requirements, or possibly many SQL statements running at the same time and contending for resources—causing other user sessions to wait for service. By my definition, the top SQL is the application SQL that spends the most time executing in the Oracle database management system (DBMS).

At this point, you might be expecting a discussion of buffer cache hit ratios, latch miss rates, data and rollback segment input/output (I/O) rates, and other low-level Oracle performance metrics. If so, you'll be disappointed. It's not very straightforward to find the top SQL using traditional Oracle performance-monitoring techniques. As a result, there's an understandable obsession with the collection of I/O statistics on tablespaces, I/O statistics on datafiles, and measurements of various ratios and rates. Let's take the buffer cache hit ratio as an example: Some experts say that the buffer cache hit ratio (a measure of the percentage of data block reads satisfied from the Oracle System Global Area [SGA] buffer cache in memory rather than physical disk) must be greater than 95 percent; otherwise, you have a de facto performance problem. Other experts say that a hit ratio as high as 99 percent might actually be a bad thing, and that a ratio in the 60s is perfectly acceptable. I haven't found such rules to be helpful in solving performance problems. All these numbers do is direct you toward your top SQL. It would be better to end the discussion and instead identify the top SQL directly and reduce its resource usage. That's a nice, simple, easy-to-understand requirement.

It's important to recognize that some performance problems are not caused by contention for OS resources, but by application design. The classic scenario is *user gone to lunch*. In this case, a user locks a row and updates it, and then goes to lunch. All users who need to update the same row have to wait. If they're lucky, the application is designed so that they can cancel the wait. If not, the end user experiences increased response times.

Traditional Oracle performance metrics, such as cache hit ratios or I/O rates, give no insight into such problems because the waiting session is actually idle and consuming little I/O, CPU, or memory. Based on traditional methods, the SQL experiencing the lock doesn't show up in any list of top SQL. However, an approach based on wait times clearly shows the SQL waiting for the lock. If you can see that a SQL statement spent a long time executing in Oracle, and that it waited on a row lock, you can probably work out what caused the lock, and how to fix it.

It's important to have the ability to display top SQL over time intervals of various sizes, say, from 5 minutes up to an hour, and to display the database sessions, programs, and OS accounts that ran the SQL. After you have identified the SQL, you need to understand its significance to the application. Knowing the program that ran it, and the user, is a fast track for getting that information without having to consult the developer or business analyst.

Collect Performance Information All the Time

Any tool that collects performance information needs to be able to collect it all the time, 24×7 if necessary, without requiring human intervention or management, apart from the initial startup. If the database goes down for any reason, the collection should restart automatically as soon as the database is up. You don't want to find that you have no performance information available for a time window when users were experiencing performance problems. Any information not collected at the time is lost forever. By collecting all the time, with a high sampling rate, you can check for performance problems that occurred at any hour of the day or night on your 24×7 global application. You don't need to be there at the time to find out what caused the performance problem. You don't need to wake up at 3:00 A.M. to manually enable the bespoke monitoring you've written specially to analyze that batch job that has started to overrun its window.

Optional Requirements

The facilities in this section are nice to have. Some of them might actually belong in the mandatory section, but I've deliberately kept that section as small as possible to give some focus to the requirements.

Provide Comparison with Baselines

Performance can degrade in a gradual and imperceptible way over time. Performance can also degrade in a sudden stepwise fashion. The ability to store performance baselines enables you to answer queries like "Show me which SQL has changed in execution time most significantly between this month and last month."

Provide Oracle Statistics for SQL Statements

The Oracle statistics referred to are those held for individual user sessions in the V$SESSTAT table. This requirement to provide statistics is subtly different from the requirement to show top SQL. During the development stage, developers need to check the cost of their SQL as soon as they execute it, so they can minimize resource usage. This checking needs to be carried out systematically for all SQL whether or not it eventually shows up in the top SQL list in the production system. The availability of statistics can provide additional insight into the performance of an SQL statement in the top SQL list in production.

Show Oracle Execution Time versus Idle Time

It's not unusual for a perceived database problem to actually have nothing to do with database performance. An example would be a middleware server that spent some of its time processing data feeds from the network, and some of its time storing the data in an Oracle database. In this case, the database could be eliminated as the source of the performance problem if it can be shown that the time spent executing code in the database is actually a small percentage of the elapsed time in a given interval. If you start with an assumption that an application performance problem is database related, and it's actually not, you're heading for a lot of wasted effort.

Aggregate Data Permanently into an SQL Database

Although frequent sampling of performance metrics (many times a second) is required for accurate identification of performance problems, it's not practical to store the results directly in a SQL database because attempts to do this affect the performance of the database being monitored.

It can be useful to aggregate the frequently sampled data into longer time periods for trend analysis. This also allows the large amounts of disk space required to hold the frequently sampled data to be reused in a circular fashion. In this case, a SQL database is the best solution for maintaining a warehouse of all performance statistics. Using this approach, for example, hourly statistics can be rolled up into days, days into weeks, and weeks into months. As a result, the most detailed information is kept for the most recent time periods.

Provide Open Access to Performance Data

Access of raw performance data through standard interfaces such as Open Database Connectivity (ODBC) and Java Database Connectivity (JDBC) enables the presentation of data through reporting tools of the user's choice. This is especially important if the tool's built-in presentation capabilities are weak. The ability to leverage this data requires that the tool vendor publish information on the database entity model used to store performance metrics.

Provide a Query Rewrite Facility

In database utopia, a performance management tool would not only identify the top SQL, but rewrite it in a semantically identical form to produce the same query result set at a much lower resource cost.

Provide Database Growth Trend Analysis

In some cases, performance problems can result from unanticipated growth of the database. The collection of space metrics for the database at the tablespace and object level can be used to cross-check performance trends against database size.

Provide Schema Change Tracking

Schema changes without a full change impact analysis can result in unexpected performance degradation. This applies especially to the inclusion or removal of new indexes. If schema changes are tracked by the performance management tool, it's possible to relate schema changes to performance degradation—enabling such changes to be identified quickly and backed out, restoring performance.

Perform an Impact Analysis of Index Changes

Indexes can have a severely detrimental impact on insert and update performance. Any modification or dropping of an index needs to come with a guarantee that it won't have side effects that impact the performance of existing queries.

Present Results in Charts Using Popular Formats

The tool should be able to present information in the form of charts using popular formats such as GIF and JPEG, and for use in reports and publications on the Web. The ability to report and present the results of performance management information to all levels of the business is essential for the DBA group, mainly for the purpose of increasing visibility of the proactive nature of performance management and the resulting benefits to the users.

Demonstrate Alliance with Database Vendor

The tool vendor must have a technology alliance with the database vendor and provide a roadmap for future releases of its own tools and synchronization with database vendor releases. This requirement is designed to avoid a situation where Oracle provides a new release and you can't roll it out because your performance management tool won't be available for several more months on your chosen platform.

Demonstrate a Clear Upgrade/Migration Path

Captured information must either be compatible with future releases of the product, or a migration tool for collected data must be provided. The situation to be avoided is the one where existing performance data needs to be thrown away due to incompatibilities with the new version of the tool.

Summary of Requirements for a Performance Management Tool

This section has set out requirements for choosing an Oracle performance management tool and discussed the roles and responsibilities of DBAs and developers in the performance management process. A performance management tool should at least analyze

Oracle performance information over both very short and long time periods, with low impact, and present the top SQL. The importance of setting performance goals for applications in simple terms can't be overemphasized. Without these goals, it's hard to know where to start performance tuning and when to stop.

The following sections in this chapter provide an analysis of two different tools (Oracle Expert and Precise/Indepth from Precise Software Solutions) against some of the criteria defined earlier. Oracle Expert is part of the separately licensed Tuning Pack component of Oracle Enterprise Manager (OEM) and is a popular choice for Oracle performance management in the DBA community. The version covered in this chapter is the one bundled with Oracle9i. Precise/Indepth is the Oracle component of an end-to-end performance management framework from Precise Software Solutions and contains some unique features that make for a better match with the requirements.

Using Oracle Expert

Oracle Expert is an Oracle-supplied graphical user interface (GUI) tool that facilitates the Oracle Expert tuning methodology. The goal of the tuning methodology is to present the DBA with a list of suggestions for improving instance performance, based on data collected during a tuning session and analyzed afterward. The scope of potential changes is limited to instance parameters, indexes, and database structures. Within that scope, the DBA can selectively narrow the scope of the data collection. For example, data can be collected for particular schema objects or for the most poorly performing SQL statements. When collection and analysis is complete, Oracle Expert generates tuning recommendations and reports that identify the rationale behind the suggestions. The tuning recommendations take the form of scripts that can be executed to implement the suggestions. The basic flow of processing for an Oracle Expert tuning session proceeds through the following stages:

- Scope
- Collection
- Review
- Recommendations
- Scripts

Setting the Scope

To begin a tuning session, the DBA first needs to provide some information on the type of application to be analyzed, and the scope of the tuning session. Figure 16.2 shows the information that the DBA needs to provide after creating a new tuning session and before starting the analysis.

Oracle Expert uses the DBA-specified tuning session characteristics to help drive the post-collection analysis of the data. For example, the database application type determines the post-analysis recommendation of appropriate init.ora settings. Some of the information requested might seem unusual. For example, you might expect a perfor-

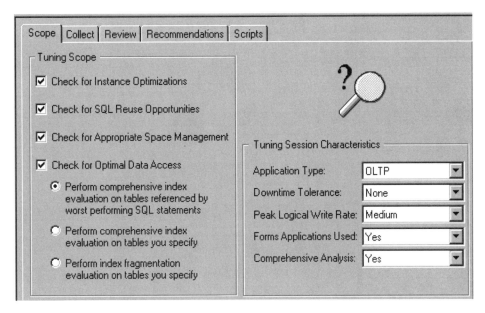

Figure 16.2 Oracle Expert tuning session scope definition.

mance analysis tool to identify the database application type by the workload it finds on a running database during information collection. Instead, Oracle Expert requires that you provide information such as the application type and peak logical write rate yourself, in advance.

Given that you might choose an inappropriate value, and this might affect Oracle Expert's recommendations, you need to do some work up front to ensure that your choice is correct. Even then, it's still difficult to know for sure that you provided accurate information. If your database has a mixed workload, such as OLTP-type transactions during the day and batch runs at night, you need to perform multiple tuning sessions, each with a different scope to identify the type of workload at the time the collection was performed. Oracle Expert also requires you to specify whether Oracle Forms Applications are used against the database. This information could be identified automatically for existing database sessions using information in the PROGRAM column from V$SESSION as shown by the following SQL, which lists all current database sessions along with some other useful information (such as the server process ID of the session):

```
SELECT /*+ RULE */ s.username,s.osuser,s.sid||','||s.serial# o_sid,
to_char(logon_time,'DD-MON-YY HH24:MI:SS') logon,
s.terminal,s.machine,s.process client_pid,p.spid server_pid,
s.program client_prog,p.program server_prog,
s.sql_address||','||s.sql_hash_value o_sql_address
from v$session s, v$process p, audit_actions a
where s.command = a.action and s.paddr = p.addr (+)
order by s.username ,s.sid;
```

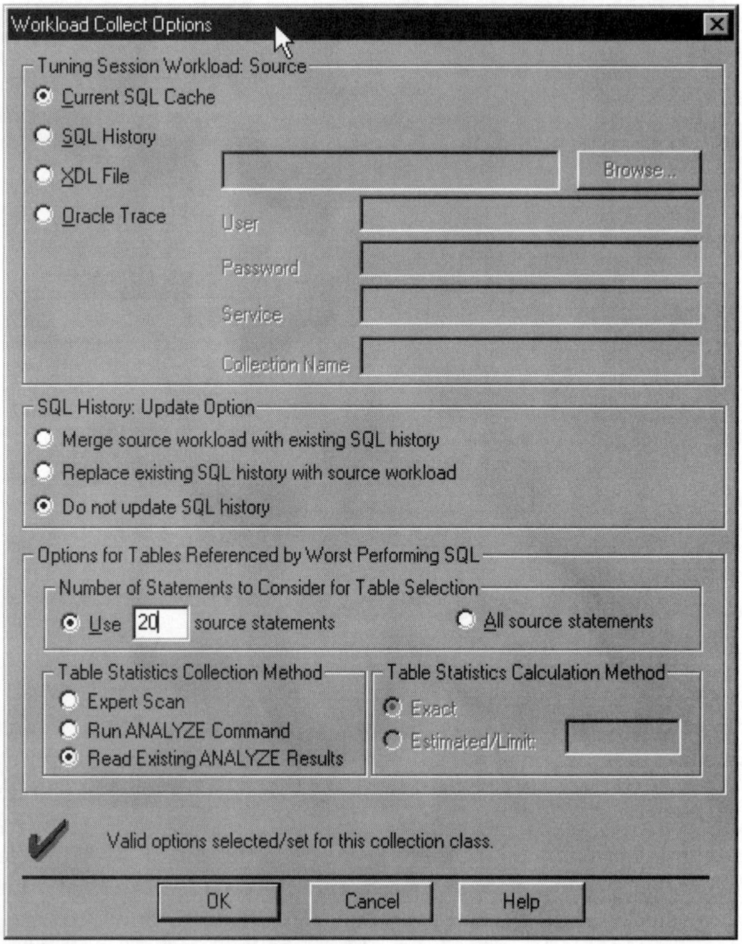

Figure 16.3 Workload collection options.

Figure 16.3 shows the workload collection options that the DBA can specify before starting collection.

The table statistics collection option needs to be considered carefully. By default, Oracle Expert bases its recommendations on existing database statistics collected from the most recent ANALYZE command. These need to be correct; otherwise, the recommendations might be invalid. Additionally, options to let Oracle Expert run ANALYZE to regenerate statistics before collection, or to gather statistics based on existing data, need to be used with care because running these options on a production system can increase business-user response times. If you delete statistics on any table to modify the query execution plan, it presents the problem of how to make the correct statistics available for that table when Oracle Expert requires it. The number of worst performing SQL statements to analyze can be modified from the default of 20 at this stage. The techniques used by Oracle Expert to identify the worst-performing SQL statements are similar to those presented in Chapter 9.

Collection

Before starting collection, the DBA needs to provide the following system parameters, as Oracle Expert uses this information when making its recommendations:

- Total physical memory (RAM)
- Total RAM available for instance (%)
- Average memory utilization (%)
- Maximum memory utilization (%)
- CPU use over time (%)
- Maximum CPU utilization (%)
- OS page size (bytes)

It needs to be emphasized that for Oracle Expert to generate appropriate results, these numbers must be accurate. Information on memory and CPU utilization needs to be collected via an external tool. You might find it surprising that the DBA is required to provide memory size information when that information is available for the database instance via the V$SGA view and for the database server via an OS-specific routine. On Sun Solaris 2.6, the memory page size and total server RAM are returned by the following OS-dependent commands:

```
$ /usr/bin/pagesize
$ prtconf|grep Memory
```

Recommendations

After collection is completed, recommendations can be generated and viewed under the Recommendations tab. It's important that you are aware of the disclaimer on the recommendations:

```
Both collected and user-provided data significantly impact index tuning
analysis.  If the data is incomplete or inaccurate, Oracle Expert may
recommend changes that reduce rather than increase database performance.
```

Two Oracle Expert recommendations, based on Oracle Expert analysis, for the init.ora file of a production system are provided in the following code, along with some comments on likely improvements to be gained from the suggestions:

```
Oracle Expert recommends changing the parallel_automatic_tuning instance
parameter from :

      FALSE --> TRUE

Significant usability improvements were made in the Oracle8i parallel
execution system, formerly know as Parallel Query.  It can now perform
fully automatic self tuning and management with the instance parameter
PARALLEL_AUTOMATIC_TUNING set to TRUE.  The tremendous benefits of
```

```
parallel execution can be realized without a significant investment of
time by a DBA, or knowledge on the part of the user.  Implementing this
recommendation will enable parallel execution on this database instance.
```

This suggestion looks promising, but it should be kept in mind that the suggestion is based on CPU average utilization figures that you need to provide. If you don't provide any, the value defaults to 0, which is likely to result in recommendations for operations that utilize more CPU, such as parallel operations. This recommendation doesn't need a running database. It can be provided from a static analysis of init.ora parameters. It would be helpful if Oracle Expert could provide recommendations separately for settings that don't actually require any data collection on a running database. That would save time. The "tremendous benefits of parallel execution" need to be considered in the light of the discussion of parallel operations in Chapter 9. This might be overstating the case, although the ability to provide parallelism without significant time spent by the DBA or user is important to make the best use of available CPU and disk resources all the time. The second recommendation concerns the DB_BLOCK_LRU_LATCHES parameter:

```
Oracle Expert recommends increasing the db_block_lru_latches instance
parameter from :

    2 latches --> 4 latches

The current number of buffer cache LRU latches is below the minimum
recommended value for the database instance.  The recommended value is
based on the number of CPUs in the host system.  When there are fewer
LRU latches than CPUs, a condition may arise where processes are waiting
for LRU latches held by other processes.

    Implementing this recommendation will increase the number of
database buffer cache LRU latches on this instance.  This will allow a
higher degree of transaction concurrency among processes/CPUs.
```

Once again, this recommendation is based on a static analysis of init.ora parameters that don't require a running database. In this case, the database instance is version Oracle8*i*. It's certainly worth investigating the change. Although there is no quantitative measure of the expected benefits, you wouldn't expect changing the setting to be harmful. If you're wondering why Oracle doesn't choose latches automatically, based on the available CPUs on the server, you'll be pleased to know that Oracle9*i* addresses this, and that the parameter is obsolete. Based on the existing SQL analyzed during workload data collection, Oracle Expert can recommend the addition of extra indexes or the removal of unused indexes, both for performance reasons. Here's an example:

```
Table name:  APP.FXOTC
     Index type:   B*-tree
     Status:       Existing, Unused
     Cardinality:  Table: 44565 Index: 368
     Workload:     oltp

     Columns
```

```
      BOOK
      DTYPE
      DSTATE
      DDATE
```

```
Oracle Expert could find no evidence of necessity, and therefore,
recommended removal. Either the collected workload is incomplete or the
represented applications no longer execute SQL that would benefit from
this index.
```

The crucial point to note in this recommendation (once again on an Oracle8*i* instance) is that the index is determined to be unused by any SQL discovered in the collected workload. In general, before you remove an index, you need to be absolutely sure it's never used at any time, and that means collecting information on every statement executed during a complete business cycle. One way to achieve that more quickly is to make sure all the SQL in the shared SQL area is chosen for analysis by Oracle Expert, rather than the limited number actually chosen earlier (as shown in Figure 16.3). Chapter 12 shows the pre-Oracle9*i* and Oracle9*i* methods of identifying which indexes are being used. Oracle Expert also recommends a new index where information on collected SQL indicates that a statement could benefit from one, as shown in the following example:

```
Due to its calculated high relative importance, this change
recommendation is considered a high impact adjustment.  High impact
refers to the relative performance enhancement that may be achieved by
implementing the suggested change.

      Table name:   APP.SETTLEMENTS
      Index type:   B*-tree
      Status:       New
      Cardinality:  Table: 437391 Index: 526
      Workload:     oltp


      Recommended columns
      -------------------


      ENTITY_ID
            There was at least one reference by an equality operator.
```

In this case, the recommended change is noted as having a high impact, where high impact is defined in the recommendation itself. Additional indexes can cause a significant increase in insert, update, and delete elapsed times, as shown in Chapter 12, and the cost/benefit of such changes needs to be factored into any final decision. Oracle Expert does this analysis automatically, as shown in its recommendations:

```
The following requests are used to calculate the threshold by which
index solutions are formed.  Because table update performance is
directly influenced by the index maintenance, Oracle Expert limits the
number of indexes by comparing the relative access method gain to the
cost of updating index keys.
```

As usual, it's most important that the collected workload reflects all the relevant statements that could be impacted by the index, both positively and negatively. Collections can be added to over time by storing collection results persistently in the OEM Repository, using the SQL History option in the Workload Collect Options dialog box (displayed in Figure 16.3). A different approach, which gives a more complete collection than the one created in this example, would be to collect information for all source statements at several different times during the business lifecycle of the database, and use "Merge source workload with existing SQL history" to build up a complete picture.

Oracle Expert can optionally produce SQL scripts to implement changes. In addition, Oracle Expert Analysis reports can be used to track changes in resource usage for a database over time. By comparing a current Oracle Expert Analysis report to analysis reports produced during earlier tuning sessions, changes in resource usage can be identified, and then trend analysis can be used to determine when shortages might cause performance problems in the future.

Using Precise/Indepth

Before considering how Precise/Indepth works, a brief review of Chapter 9 on the fundamentals of SQL tuning is useful. At any given point in time, an Oracle session is either idle, executing on CPU, or waiting for an event to complete. The following statement shows sessions that are active at any time, including the ADDRESS and HASH value of the statement that identifies the full SQL text of the statement in V$SQL_TEXT_WITH_NEWLINES:

```
select * from v$session where status='ACTIVE';
```

Consider an Oracle session, for example, running SQL*Plus that is waiting for a user to submit some SQL. A query on V$SESSION_WAIT shows that the session is idle, waiting on the following event:

```
SQL*Net message from client
```

After the request is received on the network, the SQL statement needs to be checked for existence in the shared SQL area. The session needs to obtain the library cache latch for a short time to perform this action, causing a wait for an event:

```
latch free
```

Next, the statement is parsed (only if it's not found in the shared SQL area), and then executed. Results are returned to the client during execution or after execution is complete, depending on the type of SQL statement. Statement processing requires CPU. Oracle maintains CPU used by the session in the V$SESSTAT table. If, during execution, the SQL needs to wait for I/O to complete or to read blocks from the buffer cache, the following waits take place (with some example event parameters shown):

```
db file scattered read      file#=5 block#=3749761 blocks=8
db file sequential read     file#=5 block#=3735560 blocks=1
buffer busy waits           file#=5 block#=3729185 id=130
```

Recall from Chapter 9 that event waits include parameters that in some cases identify the object whose blocks were waited for. In these examples, FILE# and BLOCK# information identifies the object required by the SQL during execution. To summarize, Oracle provides microscopic detail on the state of each session, whether it's idle or doing work, along with the resources and events for any executing SQL at any point in time. This information can provide details down to the individual datafile that is busy. Additional information such as the Oracle account, client program, and OS account is also available from V$SESSION.

If the relevant V$ tables could be sampled at a high enough rate, a complete profile of every executing statement could be produced to provide the time that each and every statement spent executing within the DBMS, what resources it waited for, how long it waited, the user and program that executed the statement, and the CPU used. This approach is exactly what's required to provide a top-down view of overall Oracle instance performance, based on the most expensive SQL. It's important to remember that even when the bottom-up approach of Chapter 9 has been followed during development to ensure that each and every SQL statement performs as well as possible, performance issues still occur in production systems due to contention between many Oracle sessions for finite CPU, I/O, memory, and network resources. Contention manifests itself within Oracle and the OS through queuing and waiting, which increases elapsed times for the completion of SQL execution.

The major drawback to monitoring the V$ tables at very high sample rates is the database overhead that results. One of the most important requirements for an Oracle performance management tool is for any monitoring to be nonintrusive. Queries on the V$ tables are treated by Oracle just like any other and can cause a noticeable increase in response times for the whole system if executed too frequently.

Precise/Indepth takes a different approach to this problem by reading V$ information directly from the SGA rather than via a SQL interface. Keep in mind that the V$ tables are actually memory structures that exist in the SGA only while an instance is running. They actually require very little space (probably a few tens of kilobytes at the most), so any tool that can scan their contents directly from memory without using SQL can also do it at a high frequency (for example, 10 times per second) and just as important, do it with very low impact on the database or system as a whole. This is what Precise/Indepth does. In addition, the Precise/Indepth architecture includes an agent that runs with root privileges on UNIX so that OS performance metrics can be collated with Oracle performance metrics to provide a true picture of SQL performance, with a fine level of time granularity. To avoid the overhead of inserting rows into tables to store the sampled information, Precise/Indepth first stores the information in its own shared memory segments, and then writes it to its own proprietary file format. As you can imagine, large volumes of data can be generated quite quickly. To address this, Precise/Indepth includes a Performance Warehouse component. The Performance Warehouse enables detailed performance information to be rolled up over time in an automated manner, such that more detailed information is available for more recently executed SQL, while keeping all the most important data for the long term to support performance trend analysis.

Time Intervals

Precise/Indepth includes three configurable time intervals. The sample interval determines how often Oracle and OS statistics are sampled by the Precise collector agent. Five or ten times per second usually provides accurate results with low impact. Within the Precise/Indepth GUI, sampled performance information is rolled up into an interval that is referred to as a time slice. This is the lowest level of granularity over which performance information can be presented. A value of 5 minutes is usually adequate. If you know in advance that a performance problem occurred at a certain time, you can view exactly what was the most expensive SQL (in terms of time spent executing in the DBMS) down to a 5-minute interval. Finally, for a top-down analysis of performance, information can be rolled up and presented over an interval that is referred to as a historical time unit. A value of 1 hour gives good results. The historical time unit is useful if you want to perform a proactive tuning study. In this case, you view historical time units first and inspect performance over hourly time intervals. The most expensive hourly intervals stand out clearly. When a relatively expensive interval has been identified, you can drill down to 5-minute intervals using the time slice. Then, within a 5-minute interval, you can see a list of the most expensive SQL statements.

From my experience, the main challenge of Oracle performance management is the identification of the root cause of performance problems. Any performance management tool needs to do that, with high precision and low impact. Precise/Indepth is a tool that provides an excellent match with those requirements. Figure 16.4 shows historical time units for an Oracle instance based on a historical unit of 1 hour.

The X-axis scale is in hours, minutes, and seconds. The legend shows the proportion of time spent consuming CPU, or waiting for Oracle or OS resources (as displayed by the color-coded bars). Clearly, most time spent executing in the DBMS occurred in the hours beginning 06:35 and 21:35. In a proactive top-down performance study, these two time units might be a good place to start looking for SQL to improve. Figure 16.5 presents information on the programs that spent the most time-consuming Oracle resources in that hour beginning 06:35.

The SNP0 database background process indicates a database job in progress, and the presence of rman (Oracle's Recovery Manager program) indicates that a database backup is running within this interval. Figure 16.6 presents performance over 5-minute time slices for this hour using an alternative display format, showing the busiest intervals to be 06:40 and 06:45.

Finally, Figure 16.7 shows the most expensive SQL statements in the 5-minute interval beginning at 06:40. On the evidence, one or two statements are the cause of most of the resource consumption. This is typical of many, if not most, database applications. If you focus performance-tuning efforts on the top few most resource-intensive SQL statements and reduce their resource consumption, overall response times improve. Usually, the challenge is to identify what those statements are. Precise/Indepth makes identification trivial, so effort can instead be spent on finding solutions. Note that the

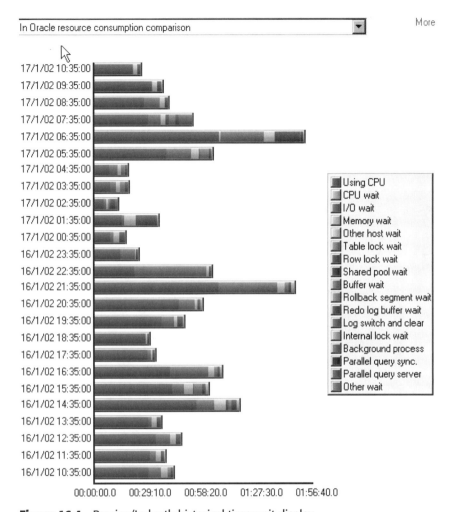

Figure 16.4   Precise/Indepth historical time unit display.

actual text of each SQL statement (identified by a unique string in Figure 16.7) is available in an alternative Precise/Indepth view and is not shown in this example.

Comparing Oracle Expert and Precise/Indepth

Oracle Expert collections need to be initiated explicitly. The precision of recommendations made by Oracle Expert needs to be treated with care because there is a considerable burden on the DBA to describe the system parameters accurately in advance so

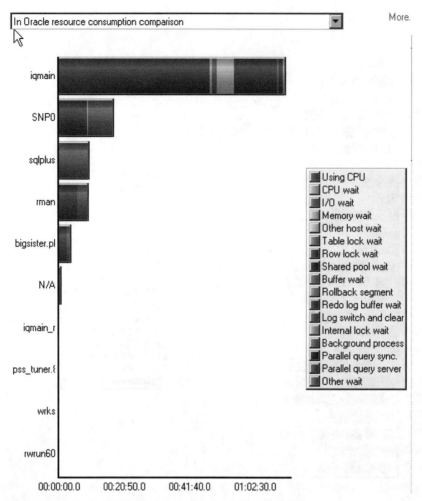

Figure 16.5 Precise/Indepth's most expensive programs.

that recommendations are valid. In particular, information on OS memory and CPU utilization is required. Oracle Expert has a potentially high impact on the performance of the target system being managed. As this is difficult to determine in advance, a decision to run Oracle Expert on a production system requires careful consideration. For Oracle Expert recommendations to be valid, extensive information collection is required. The more extensive the collection information, the higher the likelihood of performance impact on the managed instance. Oracle Expert can generate scripts to implement recommended changes related to instance parameters and data access methods, stemming from the addition and removal of indexes. Oracle Expert can identify significant performance changes over time to enable proactive analysis.

Precise/Indepth can provide information on the most expensive SQL statements in any Oracle system with very high precision and low impact on the target system. Col-

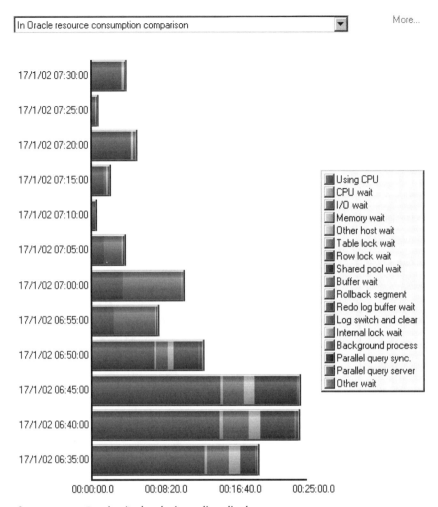

Figure 16.6 Precise/Indepth time slice display.

lection takes place automatically all the time, without requiring hands-on day-to-day management. Both Oracle and OS information is collated to provide an accurate picture. As a result, performance issues in Oracle client applications that are related to non-Oracle aspects of the application can be distinguished from database-related aspects by considering the percentage of time the application spends performing Oracle processing. All too often, performance issues in Oracle middleware applications stem from nondatabase processing. Information in Precise/Indepth can be presented in many different dimensions (such as time, program, and user). This enables the exact source of problematic SQL to be identified rapidly, right down to file I/O waits on individual database files. Precise/Indepth can proactively identify SQL statements that significantly increase in expense over time through historical information stored in its Performance Warehouse.

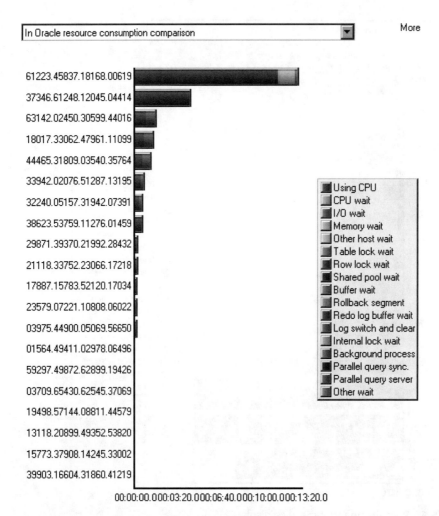

Figure 16.7 Precise/Indepth's most expensive SQL.

Summary

The most fundamental requirements for an Oracle performance management tool are:

- Low impact of collection
- 24×7 collection of information
- Precision of results
- Ability to identify trends in performance over long periods
- Powerful user interface for the presentation of results
- Ease of installation, configuration, and management

Although you might not agree with these requirements, it is critically important that you have a defined set of your own before you invest in such a tool, which is likely to be very expensive. After you have defined a set of criteria, you should perform a comparative analysis of several tools from different companies to ensure that you select the one that best meets your needs. Based on the study of Oracle Expert and Precise/Indepth in this chapter, it's quite likely that you might need more than one performance management tool to meet all the requirements.

Many tools on the market take the traditional approach to Oracle performance management, which is based on the collection of Oracle performance metrics from the V$ and X$ views using SQL. In general, traditional Oracle performance management tools are still useful, but they don't meet the requirements as comprehensively as a more modern tool like Precise/Indepth does and, as a result, it can be difficult to identify the top SQL quickly when using them.

PART

Four

Backup, Restore, and Recovery

## CHAPTER 17

Fundamentals of Oracle Recovery

Over the years I've seen various descriptions of how Oracle performs recovery. The Web site of a very high-profile company comes to mind, where their description stated that during an online backup, no changes were made to the database datafiles. This description is not correct. However, I don't believe that Oracle's recovery process is complex or difficult to understand. On the contrary, the simplicity of the process is one reason for its robustness and reliability.

This chapter takes you through the concepts and terminology you need to be familiar with in order to understand Oracle recovery and it covers some associated areas of interest, including how to view the data that Oracle requires to perform recovery. A step-by-step example of how to use Oracle9*i* to view data at an earlier point in time without incurring the overhead of a restore and recovery operation is also included. The following topics are covered:

- Understanding the Oracle System Change Number (SCN)
- Recovering from an instance crash
- Recovering from a media failure
- Using and viewing Oracle redo with LogMiner
- Using Oracle9*i* Flashback Query to recover without a restore

Understanding the SCN

In order to understand how Oracle performs recovery, it's first necessary to understand Oracle's SCN in terms of the various places where it can be stored and how it's used for instance and media recovery.

The SCN is an internal number maintained by the database management system (DBMS) to log changes made to a database. The SCN increases over time as changes are made to the database by Structured Query Language (SQL). By understanding how the SCN is used, you can understand how Oracle recovery works. Oracle9*i* enables you to examine the current SCN using the following SQL:

```
select dbms_flashback.get_system_change_number from dual;
```

Whenever an application commits a transaction, the log writer process (LGWR) writes records from the redo log buffers in the System Global Area (SGA) to the online redo logs on disk. LGWR also writes the transaction's SCN to the online redo log file. The success of this atomic write event determines whether your transaction succeeds, and it requires a synchronous (wait-until-completed) write to disk.

NOTE The need for a synchronous write upon commit is one of the reasons why the online redo log can become a bottleneck for applications and why you should commit as infrequently as is practical. In general, Oracle writes asynchronously to the database datafiles for performance reasons, but commits require a synchronous write because they must be guaranteed at the time they occur.

SCN and Checkpoints

A checkpoint occurs when all modified database buffers in the Oracle SGA are written out to datafiles by the database writer (DBW*n*) process. The checkpoint process (CKPT) updates all datafiles and control files with the SCN at the time of the checkpoint and signals DBW*n* to write out the blocks. A successful checkpoint guarantees that all database changes up to the checkpoint SCN have been recorded in the datafiles. As a result, only those changes made after the checkpoint need to be applied during recovery. Checkpoints occur automatically as follows:

- Whenever a redo log switch takes place
- Whenever the time set by the LOG_CHECKPOINT_TIMEOUT initialization parameter is reached
- Whenever the amount of redo written reaches the number of bytes associated with the LOG_CHECKPOINT_INTERVAL

Typically, LOG_CHECKPOINT_INTERVAL is chosen so that checkpoints only occur on log switches. Oracle stores the SCN associated with the checkpoint in four places: three of them in the control file and one in the datafile header for each datafile.

The System Checkpoint SCN

After a checkpoint completes, Oracle stores the system checkpoint SCN in the control file. You can access the checkpoint SCN using the following SQL:

```
select checkpoint_change# from v$database;



  CHECKPOINT_CHANGE#
-------------------
            292767
```

The Datafile Checkpoint SCN

After a checkpoint completes, Oracle stores the SCN individually in the control file for each datafile. The following SQL shows the datafile checkpoint SCN for a single datafile in the control file:

```
select name,checkpoint_change#
from v$datafile where name like '%users01%';



NAME                                CHECKPOINT_CHANGE#
----------------------------------- --------------------
/u02/oradata/OMFD1/users01.dbf                  292767
```

The Start SCN

Oracle stores the checkpoint SCN value in the header of each datafile. This is referred to as the *start SCN* because it is used at instance startup time to check if recovery is required. The following SQL shows the checkpoint SCN in the datafile header for a single datafile:

```
select name,checkpoint_change#
from v$datafile_header where name like '%users01%';



NAME                                CHECKPOINT_CHANGE#
----------------------------------- --------------------
/u02/oradata/OMFD1/users01.dbf                  292767
```

The Stop SCN

The stop SCN is held in the control file for each datafile. The following SQL shows the stop SCN for a single datafile when the database is open for normal use:

```
select name,last_change#
from v$datafile where name like '%users01%';
```

```
NAME                                  LAST_CHANGE#
------------------------------------- ------------
/u02/oradata/OMFD1/users01.dbf
```

During normal database operation, the stop SCN is NULL for all datafiles that are online in read-write mode.

SCN Values while the Database Is Up

Following a checkpoint while the database is up and open for use, the system checkpoint in the control file, the datafile checkpoint SCN in the control file, and the start SCN in each datafile header all match. The stop SCN for each datafile in the control file is NULL.

SCN after a Clean Shutdown

After a clean database shutdown resulting from a SHUTDOWN IMMEDIATE or SHUTDOWN NORMAL of the database, followed by STARTUP MOUNT, the previous queries on v$database and v$datafile return the following:

```
select checkpoint_change# from v$database;


  CHECKPOINT_CHANGE#
 -------------------
              293184

select name,checkpoint_change#,last_change#
from v$datafile where name like '%user%';


NAME                                  CHECKPOINT_CHANGE#    LAST_CHANGE#
------------------------------------- -------------------- --------------
/u02/oradata/OMFD1/users01.dbf                     293184          293184


select name,checkpoint_change#
from v$datafile_header where name like '%users01%';


NAME                                  CHECKPOINT_CHANGE#
------------------------------------- --------------------
/u02/oradata/OMFD1/users01.dbf                     293184
```

During a clean shutdown, a checkpoint is performed and the stop SCN for each datafile is set to the start SCN from the datafile header. Upon startup, Oracle checks the start SCN in the file header with the datafile checkpoint SCN. If they match, Oracle checks the start SCN in the datafile header with the datafile stop SCN in the control file. If they match, the database can be opened because all block changes have been applied, no changes were lost on shutdown, and therefore no recovery is required on startup. After the database is opened, the datafile stop SCN in the control file once again changes to NULL to indicate that the datafile is open for normal use.

SCN after an Instance Crash

The previous example showed the behavior of the SCN after a clean shutdown. To demonstrate the behavior of the checkpoints after an instance crash, the following SQL creates a table (which performs an implicit commit) and inserts a row of data into it without a commit:

```
create table x(x number) tablespace users;

insert into x values(100);
```

If the instance is crashed by using SHUTDOWN ABORT, the previous queries on v$database and v$datafile return the following after the database is started up in mount mode:

```
select checkpoint_change# from v$database;

  CHECKPOINT_CHANGE#
--------------------
            293185


select name,checkpoint_change#,last_change#
from v$datafile where name like '%users01%';

NAME                                 CHECKPOINT_CHANGE#   LAST_CHANGE#
------------------------------------ -------------------- --------------
/u02/oradata/OMFD1/users01.dbf              293185


select name,checkpoint_change#
from v$datafile_header where name like '%users01%';

NAME                                 CHECKPOINT_CHANGE#
------------------------------------ --------------------
/u02/oradata/OMFD1/users01.dbf              293185
```

In this case, the stop SCN is *not* set, which is indicated by the NULL value in the LAST_CHANGE# column. This information enables Oracle, at the time of the next startup, to determine that the instance crashed because the checkpoint on shutdown was not performed. If it had been performed, the LAST_CHANGE# and CHECK-POINT_CHANGE# values would match for each datafile as they did during a clean shutdown. If an instance crashes at shutdown, then instance crash recovery is required the next time the instance starts up.

Recovery from an Instance Crash

Upon the next instance startup that takes place after SHUTDOWN ABORT or a DBMS crash, the Oracle DBMS detects that the stop SCN for datafiles is not set in the control file during startup. Oracle then performs crash recovery. During crash recovery, Oracle applies redo log records from the online redo logs in a process referred to as *roll forward* to ensure that all transactions committed before the crash are applied to the datafiles. Following roll forward, active transactions that did not commit are identified from the rollback segments and are undone before the blocks involved in the active transactions can be accessed. This process is referred to as *roll back*. In our example, the following transaction was active but not committed at the time of the SHUTDOWN ABORT, so it needs to be rolled back:

```
insert into x values(100);
```

After instance startup, the X table exists, but remains empty. Instance recovery happens automatically at database startup without database administrator (DBA) intervention. It may take a while because of the need to apply large amounts of outstanding redo changes to data blocks for transactions that completed and those that didn't complete and require roll back.

Recovery from a Media Failure

Up until this point, the checkpoint start SCN in the datafile header has always matched the datafile checkpoint SCN number held in the control file. This is reasonable because during a checkpoint, the datafile checkpoint SCN in the control file and the start SCN in the datafile header are both updated, along with the system checkpoint SCN. The following SQL shows the start SCN from the datafile header and datafile checkpoint SCN from the control file for the same file:

```
select 'controlfile' "SCN location",name,checkpoint_change#
from v$datafile where name like '%users01%'
union
select 'file header',name,checkpoint_change#
from v$datafile_header where name like '%users01%';


SCN location    NAME                                        CHECKPOINT_CHANGE#
-------------   -----------------------------------------   ------------------
controlfile     /u02/oradata/OMFD1/users01.dbf                          293188
file header     /u02/oradata/OMFD1/users01.dbf                          293188
```

Unlike the v$datafile view, there is no stop SCN column in the v$datafile_header view because v$datafile_header is not used at instance startup time to indicate that an instance crash occurred. However, the v$datafile_header does provide the Oracle DBMS with the information it requires to perform media recovery. At instance startup, the datafile checkpoint SCN in the control file and the start SCN in the datafile header are checked for equality. If they don't match, it is a signal that media recovery is required. For example, media recovery is required if a media failure has occurred and the original datafile has been replaced with a backup copy. In this case, the start SCN in the backup copy is less than the checkpoint SCN value in the control file, and Oracle requests archived redo logs—generated at the time of previous log switches—in order to reapply the changes required to bring the datafile up to the current point in time.

> **NOTE** In order to recover the database from a media failure, you must run the database in ARCHIVELOG mode to ensure that all database changes from the online redo logs are stored permanently in archived redo log files. In order to enable ARCHIVELOG mode, you must run the command ALTER DATABASE ARCHIVELOG when the database is in a mounted state.

You can identify files that need recovery after you have replaced a datafile with an older version by starting the instance in mount mode and running the following SQL:

```
select file#,change# from v$recover_file;


    FILE#     CHANGE#
---------- ----------
        4     313401
```

In this example, file 4 is the datafile in the USERS tablespace. By reexecuting the previous SQL to display the datafile checkpoint SCN in the control file and the start SCN in the datafile header, you can see that the start SCN is older due to the restore of the backup datafile that has taken place:

```
select 'controlfile' "SCN location",name,checkpoint_change#
from v$datafile where name like '%users01%'
union
select 'file header',name,checkpoint_change#
from v$datafile_header where name like '%users01%';


SCN location    NAME                                            CHECKPOINT_CHANGE#
-------------   --------------------------------------------    --------------------
controlfile     /u02/oradata/OMFD1/users01.dbf                             313551
file header     /u02/oradata/OMFD1/users01.dbf                             313401
```

If you were to attempt to open the database, you would receive errors like the following:

```
ORA-01113: file 4 needs media recovery
ORA-01110: datafile 4: '/u02/oradata/OMFD1/users01.dbf'
```

You can recover the database by issuing RECOVER DATABASE from SQL*Plus while the database is in a mounted state. If the changes needed to recover the database to the point in time before the crash are in an archived redo log, then you will be prompted to accept the suggested name:

```
ORA-00279: change 313401 generated at 11/10/2001 18:50:23 needed for
thread
ORA-00289: suggestion : /u02/oradata/OMFD1/arch/T0001S0000000072.ARC
ORA-00280: change 313401 for thread 1 is in sequence #72

Specify log: {<RET>=suggested | filename | AUTO | CANCEL}
```

If you respond to the prompt using AUTO, Oracle applies any archived redo logs it needs, followed by any necessary changes in the online redo logs, to bring the database right up to the last committed transaction before the media failure that caused the requirement for the restore.

So far, we've considered recovery scenarios where the goal is to recover the database to the most recent transaction. This is known as *complete recovery*. The RECOVER DATABASE command has several other options that enable you to recover from a backup to a point in time before the most recent transaction by rolling forward and then stopping the application of the redo log changes at a specified point. This is known as *incomplete recovery*. You can specify a time or an SCN as the recovery point. For example,

```
recover database until time '2001-11-10:18:52:00';
recover database until change 313459;
```

Before you perform incomplete recovery, it's recommended that you restore a complete database backup first. After incomplete recovery, you must open the mounted database with ALTER DATABASE OPEN RESETLOGS. This creates a new incarnation of the database and clears the contents of the existing redo logs to make sure they can't be applied.

Recovery from a Media Failure Using a Backup Control File

In the previous example, we had access to a current control file at the time of the media failure. This means that none of the start SCN values in the datafile headers exceeded the system checkpoint SCN number in the control file. To recap, the system checkpoint number is given by the following:

```
select checkpoint_change# from v$database;
```

You might be wondering why Oracle needs to maintain the last system checkpoint value in the control file as well as checkpoint SCNs in the control file for each datafile (as used in the previous example). There are two reasons for this. The first is that you might have read-only tablespaces in your database. In this case, the database checkpoint SCN increases, and the checkpoint SCN for the datafiles in the read-only tablespace remains frozen in the control file. The following SQL report output shows a database with a read-write tablespace (USERS) and read-only tablespace (TEST). The start SCN in the file header and the checkpoint SCN in the control file for TEST are less than the system checkpoint value. Once a tablespace is read only, checkpoints have no effect on the files in it. The other read-write tablespace has checkpoint values that match the system checkpoint:

```
SCN location          NAME                              CHECKPOINT_CHANGE#
------------------    --------------------------------  ----------------
controlfile           SYSTEM checkpoint                             355390

file header           /u02/oradata/OD2/users01.dbf                 355390
file in controlfile   /u02/oradata/OD2/users01.dbf                 355390

file header           /u02/oradata/OD2/test01.dbf                  355383
file in controlfile   /u02/oradata/OD2/test01.dbf                  355383
```

The second reason for the maintenance of multiple checkpoint SCNs in the control file is that you might not have a current control file available at recovery time. In this case, you need to restore an earlier control file before you can perform a recovery. The system checkpoint in the control file may indicate an earlier change than the start SCN in the datafile headers. The following SQL shows an example where the system checkpoint SCN and datafile checkpoint SCN indicate an earlier change than the start SCN in the datafile header:

```
select 'controlfile' "SCN location",'SYSTEM checkpoint'
name,checkpoint_change#
from v$database
union
select 'file in controlfile',name,checkpoint_change#
from v$datafile where name like 'users01%'
union
select 'file header',name,checkpoint_change#
from v$datafile_header where name like '%users01%';
```

```
SCN location         NAME                            CHECKPOINT_CHANGE#
------------------   ----------------------------    ------------------
controlfile          SYSTEM checkpoint                           333765
file header          /u02/oradata/OD2/users01.dbf               355253
file in controlfile  /u02/oradata/OD2/users01.dbf               333765
```

If try you to recover a database in the usual way in this situation, Oracle detects that the control file is older than some of the datafiles, as indicated by the checkpoint SCN values in the datafile headers, and reports the following message:

```
SQL> recover database
ORA-00283: recovery session canceled due to errors
ORA-01610: recovery using the BACKUP CONTROLFILE option must be done
```

If you want to proceed with recovery in this situation, you need to indicate to Oracle that a noncurrent control file—possibly containing mismatches in the SCN values identified by the previous error messages—is about to be specified for recovery by using the following command:

```
recover database using BACKUP CONTROLFILE;
```

How Oracle Applies Changes during Recovery

During recovery, data and redo blocks are read and compared. In order for Oracle to identify which blocks of redo to apply during recovery, each redo block and database block is versioned. A higher version number indicates a more recent change. If the block version in the datafile is less than the block version in the redo, then the redo block is applied to the datafile. This process continues during the application of the archived redo logs until the required SCN is set in the datafile (you'll recall that the SCN of each transaction is stored in the redo so Oracle knows when to stop applying it).

Setting Bounds on Instance Recovery Time

If your instance uses very large online redo logs, sized at 100MB, for example, then in the worst case the instance could crash just before a log switch, which means that a large amount of redo needs to be applied at instance recovery time if you have configured checkpoints to take place only at a log switch. As checkpoints are expensive, fewer checkpoints are good for online performance, but they increase instance recovery time. Rather than configuring your database service to meet online performance requirements alone, you might instead have a requirement to return the database to service within a guaranteed time, such as in the case of an instance crash. If you need to meet a service requirement like this, you should consider using the FAST_START_IO_TARGET parameter in Oracle8*i*, which was replaced by FAST_START_MTTR_TARGET in Oracle9*i*.

The purpose of these parameters, which are available only in the Oracle Enterprise Edition, is to set an upper bound on the number of inputs/outputs (I/Os) that will be performed during instance crash recovery. Smaller values cause DBW*n* to write dirtied blocks from the SGA more frequently. As a result, faster instance recovery comes at the cost of higher I/O during normal operation.

In addition to these new parameters, the more traditional LOG_CHECKPOINT_INTERVAL and LOG_CHECKPOINT_TIMEOUT can influence recovery performance because they influence the frequency of checkpoints, which also cause dirty buffers to be written to disk. You can query the TARGET_REDO_BLOCKS parameter in the V$INSTANCE_RECOVERY view to see which of the parameters that influence recovery time is actually in effect. The TARGET_REDO_BLOCKS column is the minimum value of the columns that affect recovery time.

Fast-Start On-Demand Rollback

If a database crashes during a very large transaction, the rollback phase of recovery can take a very long time. From Oracle8*i* on, Oracle has enabled the database to open immediately after the rollforward phase using the *fast-start on-demand rollback* feature, which is enabled automatically. The rollback operation is performed in the background, and Oracle rolls back on demand for any transactions that would lock new transactions. This fast-start recovery feature is only available in the Enterprise Edition. You can monitor the progress of recovery through the following SQL:

```
select * from v$session_longops where time_remaining > 0;
```

SCN Values during Online Backup

How does this discussion of SCN relate to an online backup? If you perform a user-managed online backup, you need to use the Oracle7-style ALTER TABLESPACE *tablespace_name* BEGIN BACKUP command on each tablespace before you use an external operating system utility to back up the files in the tablespace. After you run this command, Oracle no longer updates the SCN on the datafile headers during a checkpoint. Any SQL Data Manipulation Language (DML) statements on objects in that datafile continue to cause block changes just as before. By freezing the SCN during the backup, Oracle is simply recognizing that any process that backs up data in the file may or may not find blocks in the state they were in before the backup. Some blocks may not change, some may be backed up before being changed, and some may change before being backed up, depending on the order in which the backup process scans the file. This uncertainty in the data means that during the recovery of such a "fuzzy" file, Oracle will assume nothing about the state of blocks, except that the data has been known to be changed up to the last checkpoint SCN stored in the header. It's possible, and even likely, that some of the blocks were changed while the backup was executing and have higher versions than those associated with the SCN. During the recovery process for such a file, Oracle checks each block to see if its version has changed. The only guarantee is that all blocks will at least have the version associated with the last checkpoint SCN before the backup started. The ALTER TABLESPACE *tablespace_name* END BACKUP command simply unfreezes the SCN in the datafile header after the file backup is completed so that checkpoints can update the SCNs as usual.

Using and Viewing Oracle Redo

Oracle change logging, which is referred to as *redo*, is fundamental to Oracle's recovery behavior. An understanding of redo and how it is used is essential for a complete understanding of recovery behavior. For example, consider a transaction, such as a bulk update, that generates sufficient redo that causes several log switches but is never committed. The redo is generated by changes to the datafiles *and* changes to the undo tablespace or rollback segment for each update to each row. In this case, redo generation takes places as follows for each row:

1. The rollback segment transaction table is updated to create an undo entry. This is a datafile block change and generates redo.

2. The prechange value of the updated row is written to the rollback segment. This is a datafile block change and generates redo.

3. The datafile block is changed to hold the updated values identified by SQL. This is a datafile block change and generates redo.

By now, you should be gaining insight into why Oracle can generate so much redo. Redo information is generated by all changes to data blocks. These blocks include:

- Changes to database datafiles caused by end-user SQL statements
- Changes made to rollback segments by the Oracle DBMS as a result of end-user SQL statements

DBAs and developers sometimes overlook the fact that changes to rollback segments themselves generate redo. In this case, if the database crashes before a bulk data update operation is committed, the recovery process needs to undo the large transaction that was active at the time of the crash. This involves applying the rollback information to the datafile blocks—a process that generates redo. This is why it's possible to generate many archived redo logs during instance startup after a crash in the middle of a large transaction.

Using LogMiner to View Redo

In Oracle8*i*, Oracle introduced LogMiner to enable you to view the contents of archived redo log files. Oracle9*i* takes the usability of LogMiner a step further by providing a graphical user interface (GUI) to make the interrogation of redo information even easier, including the capability to view the online redo logs. Prior to Oracle8*i*, you needed expensive third-party products to view redo information. LogMiner is useful if you need to understand what is causing the apparent excessive amounts of redo. If you understand the cause, then you can probably take steps to reduce the generation. LogMiner is also useful as a teaching aid for understanding how redo works. This is how it will be used in this section. In this example, Data Definition Language (DDL) and DML changes are made to an Oracle9*i* database, and the redo is investigated to see how it relates to the changes. The following SQL is required to set up the example:

```
alter system switch logfile;

create table emp_redo
       (empno number(4),ename varchar2(10),job varchar2(9),
        mgr number(4),sal number(7,2),comm number(7,2));

insert into emp_redo values(7369,'SMITH','CLERK',7902,800,NULL);
```

```
create index i0_emp_redo on emp_redo(ename)

insert into emp_redo values(7499,'ALLEN','SALESMAN',7698,1600,300);

update emp_redo set ename='JONES' where ename='SMITH';

delete from emp_redo where ename='ALLEN';

commit;

alter system switch logfile;
```

Table 17.1 shows the redo generated by each SQL statement. You can use the AUTO-TRACE STATISTICS feature in SQL*Plus to find the redo size for the DML statement. I use the Session Statistics facility in DbCool because SQL*Plus only shows the redo size for DML statements, whereas DbCool shows the redo size for all statements, including DDL.

What immediately stands out in Table 17.1 is the amount of redo generated by DDL commands such as CREATE TABLE and CREATE INDEX. The next step is to take a detailed look at the redo log contents using LogMiner.

Running LogMiner Manually

Before you run LogMiner, you need to make a decision about which database you are going to use to view the redo. Redo data contains Oracle identification numbers for objects (such as tables and columns) and the users that own them, rather than the names themselves. In order to resolve the numeric information into meaningful names, it's necessary to have Oracle data dictionary information available to map the ID numbers to the names. If you use the same database to view the redo log information as the one in which the redo information was generated, then the Oracle data dictionary for that database can be used in place.

You can optionally view redo log contents in a *different* database than the one in which the redo was generated. This is a good idea if you intend to inspect a large

Table 17.1 Redo Size Generated for SQL

SQL STATEMENT	REDO SIZE (BYTES)

create table emp_redo
    (empno number(4),ename varchar2(10),
     job varchar2(9),mgr number(4),
     sal number(7,2),comm number(7,2));
	14264

insert into emp_redo values(7369,'SMITH','CLERK',7902,800,NULL);	624
create index i0_emp_redo on emp_redo(ename);	7592
insert into emp_redo values(7499,'ALLEN','SALESMAN',7698,1600,300);	648
update emp_redo set ename='JONES' where ename='SMITH';	728
delete from emp_redo where ename='ALLEN';	484
commit;	84

amount of redo log information because it avoids loading on the source database. If you take this option, you need to create a dictionary file containing mappings of the ID numbers to names in the source database where the logs were generated and transfer this across to the database you intend to use to mine the logs, along with the redo logs. The following PL/SQL block creates a dictionary file /tmp/dic.lgmr, where the directory /tmp is in the UTL_FILE_DIR list in the init.ora file:

```
begin

sys.dbms_logmnr_d.build(
    dictionary_filename=>'dic.lgmr',
    dictionary_location=>'/tmp');

end;
/
```

For an Oracle9i data dictionary, the file can be several megabytes in size. The dic.lgmr file is actually a SQL script containing INSERT statements to create dictionary information in the LogMiner tables in the destination database where LogMiner runs. This example views the redo logs in place in the source Oracle9i database where they were generated without a dictionary file—a feature that is not available in Oracle8i. The next step is to build up a list of the redo log files to mine. This example uses only one, but you can call the procedure repeatedly before beginning searches:

```
begin

sys.dbms_logmnr.add_logfile(
logfilename=>'/u02/oradata/OMFD1/arch/T0001S0000000080.ARC');

end;
/
```

The final step is to start LogMiner on the list of redo log files that were added. In this example, the procedure is executed without any parameters except OPTIONS :

```
begin

sys.dbms_logmnr.start_logmnr(
        options=>sys.dbms_logmnr.dict_from_online_catalog);

end;
/
```

The START_LOGMNR procedure takes several other optional parameters that aren't used in this example. One of the parameters, DICTFILENAME, can be used to specify the name of the dictionary file that was created in the source database in situations where LogMiner runs on a different database or Oracle8i is being used. As we're mining the logs in the Oracle9i source database, the Oracle data dictionary can be used as indicated by the OPTIONS parameter, and no separate dictionary file is needed. This represents a major enhancement of LogMiner in Oracle9*i*. If you're using Oracle8*i*, you always need to create and load a dictionary file. Other parameters allow a time or SCN range to be supplied in order to restrict the range of the log information to mine. The following SQL shows some useful information about the redo that was generated:

```
select scn,cscn,commit_timestamp,sql_redo,sql_undo
from v$logmnr_contents;
```

This is the undo generated for the SQL DELETE statement for the employee ALLEN:

```
insert into
"SYSTEM"."EMP_REDO"("EMPNO","ENAME","JOB","MGR","SAL","COMM")
values ('7499','ALLEN','SALESMAN','7698','1600','300');
```

Because the generated undo needs to undo the delete, the undo is actually an INSERT statement. Some of the SQL contained in the undo for the EMP_REDO table creation statement is as follows:

```
Update "SYS"."OBJ$" set "OBJ#" = '1', "DATAOBJ#" = '27933', "TYPE#" =
Insert into "SYS"."OBJ$"("OBJ#","DATAOBJ#","OWNER#","NAME","NAMESPACE"
Insert into "SYS"."FET$"("TS#","FILE#","BLOCK#","LENGTH") values ('0',
Update "SYS"."FET$" set "LENGTH" = '2' where "TS#" = '0' and "LENGTH"
Insert into "SYS"."SEG$"("TS#","FILE#","BLOCK#","TYPE#","BLOCKS","EXTE
Insert into "SYS"."UET$"("TS#","SEGFILE#","SEGBLOCK#","EXT#","FILE#","
Update "SYS"."TSQ$" set "GRANTOR#" = '0', "BLOCKS" = '613', "MAXBLOCKS
Delete from "SYS"."FET$" where "TS#" = '0' and "FILE#" = '1' and "BLOC
Insert into "SYS"."TAB$"("OBJ#","DATAOBJ#","TS#","FILE#","BLOCK#","BOB
Insert into "SYS"."COL$"("OBJ#","COL#","SEGCOL#","SEGCOLLENGTH","OFFSE
```

During table creation, and within DDL in general, SQL is generated internally by the database to store the following information in the Oracle dictionary:

- Object name and owner details
- Segment name and owner details
- Details of the extents allocated
- Column information

This recursive SQL is what causes the several thousand bytes of redo to be generated from the CREATE TABLE statement. When you've finished, the following procedure call should be used to end the LogMiner session:

```
begin

sys.dbms_logmnr.end_logmnr;

end;
/
```

Running the LogMiner GUI

Oracle Enterprise Manager (OEM) provides the LogMiner Viewer to take the monotony out of viewing the redo log contents. By using the viewer, you request the redo logs you want to interrogate and specify values to limit the search, all within the GUI. There is no need to call the procedures in the manual example. The cost of using the viewer is the one-off cost of setting up OEM with a Management Server and an OEM repository database. To start the viewer on the database server, you must set your X Windows DISPLAY environment variable to a valid X screen and enter the following:

```
$ oemapp lmviewer
```

The connection you use requires SYSDBA privileges, whereas the manual process requires less restrictive DBA privileges. Figure 17.1 shows the redo information for the CREATE TABLE statement in the LogMiner Viewer.

One nice usability feature of the viewer is the capability to specify a file on the server containing a list of redo logs to load. This is much easier compared to the effort required to add redo logs individually using the ADD_FILE procedure in the manual process. To load up a redo log from a file, you need to choose the Redo Log Files tab, press the Change Redo Log File . . . button, and enter information into the form, as shown in Figure 17.2.

In this example, the file /tmp/logs.list on the database server would contain a list of log names as follows:

SCN	Operation	Table	SQL Redo	SQL Undo
415156035...	INSERT	COL$	insert into "SYS"."CO...	delete from "S...
415156035...	INTERNAL	COL$,I_C...		
415156035...	INTERNAL	COL$,I_C...		
415156035...	INTERNAL	COL$,I_C...		
415156035...	INSERT	COL$	insert into "SYS"."CO...	delete from "S...
415156035...	INTERNAL	COL$,I_C...		
415156035...	INTERNAL	COL$,I_C...		
415156035...	INTERNAL	COL$,I_C...		
415156035...	DDL	EMP_REDO	create table emp_redo	
415156035...	UPDATE	SEG$	update "SYS"."SEG$"...	update "SYS"."...
415156035...	COMMIT		commit;	
415156035...	START		set transaction read ...	

Figure 17.1 Redo displayed in the LogMiner Viewer.

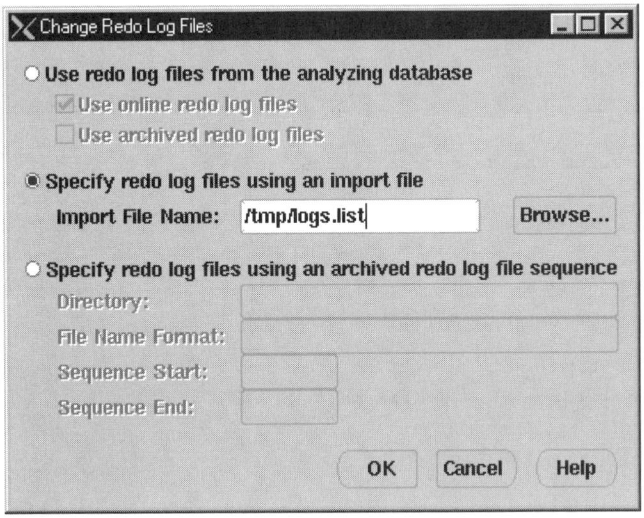

Figure 17.2   Addling a log list in the LogMiner Viewer.

```
/u02/oradata/OMFD1/arch/T0001S0000000082.ARC
/u02/oradata/OMFD1/arch/T0001S0000000083.ARC
/u02/oradata/OMFD1/arch/T0001S0000000084.ARC
/u02/oradata/OMFD1/arch/T0001S0000000085.ARC
/u02/oradata/OMFD1/arch/T0001S0000000086.ARC
```

Using Flashback Query to Recover without a Restore

Flashback Query is a fantastic feature of Oracle9*i* that enables you to see data as it was at an earlier point in time in an open database without doing any recovery. For example, you can view data as it was before a user made an error that modified data incorrectly or recover data to the point in time before a known business transaction, provided that you stored the current system SCN in a table just before the business transaction started along with a string that you can use to identify the transaction. The Flashback Query features are accessed through procedures in the DBMS_FLASHBACK package. For example, to find the current SCN, you would run the following SQL statement:

```
select dbms_flashback.get_system_change_number from dual;

GET_SYSTEM_CHANGE_NUMBER
------------------------
                  417153
```

Once you have the SCN, you can reset it back to this saved value at a later time—after changes have been made to the data—in order to see the data as it was before. The previous point to which the data is displayed can be specified by SCN or time, as in the following examples:

```
begin

dbms_flashback.enable_system_change_number (417153);

end;
/

begin

dbms_flashback.enable_at_time(
to_date('10-NOV-2001 13:15:00','DD-MON-YYYY HH24:MI:SS'));

end;
/
```

You need to be aware that the time you specify in ENABLE_AT_TIME is mapped to an SCN value through data recorded in the SYS.SMON_SCN_TIME table. These times are recorded every 5 minutes, so you may see unexpected results in your queries as a result of the time apparently being rounded down by up to 5 minutes. The following query shows the information held in SMON_SCN_TIME:

```
select * from sys.smon_scn_time where trunc(time_dp)=trunc(sysdate);


    THREAD    TIME_MP               TIME_DP             SCN_WRP    SCN_BAS
   --------  -----------  ---------------------  ---------  ---------
         1   1005613204   10-NOV-2001 00:00:06          0     355525
         1   1005613512   10-NOV-2001 00:05:13          0     355528
         1   1005613820   10-NOV-2001 00:10:20          0     355531
```

If you receive the error "ORA-01466: unable to read data—table definition has changed" during a Flashback Query, this is a result of the time-to-SCN mapping. The error can be avoided by using SCNs rather than times as the flashback point, although the restriction also applies if you perform a Flashback Query to an SCN just after a DDL operation such as CREATE TABLE. As an example of Flashback Query, consider a situation where the EMP table contains zero rows at the SCN identified by 417153, and a user inserts and commits a row:

```
select count(*) from EMP;

  COUNT(*)
----------
         0


insert into emp(ename,empno) values ('ALLEN',2000);
```

```
 COUNT(*)
----------
        1
```

```
commit;
```

The following SQL can be used to view the data at the earlier point in time associated with SCN 417153:

```
select count(*) from EMP;

  COUNT(*)
----------
        1
```

```
begin
dbms_flashback.enable_at_system_change_number(417153);
end;
/
```

```
select count(*) from EMP;

  COUNT(*)
----------
        0
```

If you want to convince yourself that the feature works, be sure to leave at least 5 minutes after any DDL you run to set up the demonstration—such as CREATE TABLE —before you make DML changes to data. If you don't, you'll probably get the ORA-01466 error. Oracle9*i* maintains 5 days of SCN mappings in the mapping table, where the number of days corresponds to database uptime rather than wallclock time. To run Flashback Queries against earlier transactions, you need to use SCNs rather than times.

> **NOTE** Oracle 9*i* Release 2 significantly extends the scenarios in which you can use Flashback Query to include generation of flashback information within a single SQL statement rather than just within a session. It's also possible to select data differences between two points in time and to restore deleted rows and previous table versions.

Summary

Understanding Oracle's use of an internal SCN is the key to understanding the Oracle recovery process. By using checkpoint SCNs stored in datafile headers and the control file, Oracle is able to identify which redo blocks need to be applied to datafiles during recovery and where to find the changed blocks. Depending on the point in time at which recovery is required, the changed blocks may exist in the online redo log files or archived redo log files.

The redo generated to protect the database from failures can be a source of considerable space and performance overhead. Oracle provides the LogMiner tool through both a procedural interface and a GUI in OEM to provide a fine-grained presentation of redo information. This enables the DBA to determine the exact cause of redo generation, leading to the possibility for reducing it.

Guaranteed recovery times may be a requirement for some Oracle applications. In these cases, it becomes business critical to reduce the time it takes to make the database available after an instance crash in the middle of a long transaction. Oracle Enterprise Edition can use fast-start features to enable the database to open before all active transactions are rolled back to make the instance available for use sooner than previous versions of Oracle. The time required for a recovery resulting from an application coding error—or DBA mistake such as an accidental DROP TABLE command—can be considerable when database and archived redo log restores from tape are needed. Through the use of a Flashback Query, Oracle enables data to be viewed at previous points in time in an open database without requiring any recovery. This feature alone and the potential for higher availability are compelling reasons for upgrading to Oracle9i.

## CHAPTER 18

Backup and Recovery Using Recovery Manager (RMAN)

You need to perform regular backups of your Oracle databases to provide protection from storage media failures and human errors that require database recovery to a previous point in time. Human errors include database administrator (DBA) mistakes such as accidental DROP TABLE commands and logical errors in applications. Before you decide on a backup strategy, it's important to understand the requirement that lies behind the need for backups. *You create backups because you might need to perform restore and recovery.* If you are not using Oracle's Recovery Manager (RMAN) tool to perform the backup and recovery of your Oracle database management system (DBMS), this chapter sets out to convince you to start using it. For the systematic backup and recovery of databases, no other tool will do.

This might seem obvious to you, but that's not the case everywhere. I like RMAN because I can create a command script as a one-off operation, run the command script on demand, and check the RMAN return code. No programming is involved. If the RMAN command returns 0, I know that the entire database and archived redo logs (if any exist) were backed up and stored offsite to tape on a remote server, and the details of the backup were cataloged in the control file of my database, and, optionally, in another Oracle database. As a result, I can sleep easily because I know that if I need to restore that database to any point in time from within its agreed retention period, I can get it back on any other machine on the network—no ifs or buts. I can monitor those database backups daily for failures. Other considerations, such as backup performance, are important, but the ability to recover the database in an emergency is paramount. Too many backup and restore procedures place all the emphasis on the backup part of the process. If you do that, you're likely to identify flaws in your backup procedures at restore and recovery time. By then, it's too late—you have lost your database.

This chapter takes you step by step through the process of performing RMAN backups and restores. The Perl scripts in Chapter 4 are instrumental in making the implementation as simple as possible. You don't need to use them, but if you do, everything falls into place much more quickly. In its most powerful configuration, RMAN can interface to a tape library at a remote site through third-party media management software. This chapter covers such a configuration using Legato's NetWorker for Oracle as an example.

RMAN is a specialist DBA subject in its own right these days, as you can tell from the size of the manuals. To restrict the scope of the discussion, I'll assume that you buy into the approach that RMAN should manage your backups and restores for you. You can still continue performing so-called user-managed backups via RMAN (those based on synchronizing ALTER DATABASE BEGIN BACKUP and ALTER DATABASE END BACKUP commands with operating system file backup utilities), but this chapter assumes that you want to give that up for something more powerful, flexible, robust, and easy to manage. The chapter starts with an overview of backup and recovery requirements—including the risks of scripts developed in house—and then moves on to basic RMAN backup and recovery techniques, followed by an enterprisewide RMAN backup and recovery solution based on Legato NetWorker. The following topics are covered:

- Backup and recovery requirements: how RMAN addresses the risks of in-house scripts
- A simple backup using RMAN
- Checking that a backup succeeded
- A backup using a backup catalog
- Using Oracle Net to connect to the target database
- Cloning a database with the RMAN DUPLICATE command
- Managing archived redo logs on disk
- Interfacing to Legato NetWorker
- Performing an RMAN restore
- Disaster recovery restore with Legato
- Backup and restore troubleshooting

Oracle Backup and Recovery Requirements

As a DBA, you need the ability to back up and recover Oracle databases as quickly as possible with the maximum reliability. At restore time, you need the ability to restore a backup taken from one server onto a different server to cope with disaster recovery scenarios. This section explains some of the problems of in-house-developed Oracle backup and recovery solutions that can be identified when a clear set of backup and recovery requirements are put in place. A solution based on RMAN overcomes all these problems.

It's worth keeping in mind that if you use RMAN you get a database block corruption check free because RMAN checks blocks for corruption as a matter of routine during backups. If you already use the DBVERIFY command-line utility or a full database export to perform this function, they are no longer necessary.

> **NOTE** The database itself can perform block corruption checking when the dynamic db_block_checksum initialization parameter is set to true. In Oracle8*i* the default value is set to false, and in Oracle9*i* the default value is set to true.

The Risks of In-House Scripts

Some people still use in-house-crafted backup solutions, which represent a risk to your business compared to using RMAN solutions. I can't quantify the risk for you, but it depends on things like a programmer's ability to detect all possible errors in a script and handle them appropriately. A single failure to handle an error correctly in the code in any situation could result in a failed backup being marked as successful. When do you find out the backup problem? If you're unlucky, you discover the problem too late when the restore and recovery of a production system fails. Let me give you three real-world examples of problems that result from these types of Oracle backup solutions.

In the first example, an Oracle DBA wrote a script to back up an Oracle 8.0.5 database online using the BEGIN BACKUP and END BACKUP commands. The Oracle documentation stated that the SYSTEM tablespace could not be taken offline to perform an offline backup while the database was up, which was unlike regular tablespaces. Somehow the DBA misinterpreted this to mean that the SYSTEM tablespace could not be backed up online. As a result, the SYSTEM tablespace was not backed up for several months. If a media failure had occurred, the entire database would have been lost, costing the company millions of dollars. The backup code was never validated, and the success of the backup was fundamentally untestable without performing a full-scale restore of the very large database. The resources weren't available to do this.

In the second example, an Oracle DBA wrote an online backup for an Oracle 8.1.7 database that read the list of database files for each tablespace to a single record in a separate file, with one record per tablespace. In theory, this meant that the backup script didn't need to change when datafiles were added to a tablespace. In this scenario, there was a limit on the operating system file record length, and the backup program code wrote all datafiles in a tablespace to a single record. The database grew over time and eventually a datafile was added that caused the record containing the list of datafiles for a tablespace to overflow. The program didn't detect the overflow, and for a time, the new datafile was never backed up.

In the third example, a UNIX system administrator (SA) wrote a script that shut down an Oracle database, copied all of the files to tape, and then restarted the database. On one occasion, the database shutdown operation failed, but the files were copied to tape anyway while the database was up. The database SHUTDOWN command was never checked. When the backup was restored, it was unusable because the datafiles were in use at the time of the backup.

Of course, Oracle can back up a database while it's open, which leads to another important point: If you use Oracle's RMAN tool, you can back up your database while it's open with no additional effort because you can use an RMAN backup command script that is identical to the one you used for your closed backup. You don't need to shut down. This immediately removes the risk of a shutdown failing and being undetected. Some DBAs have an unreasonable paranoia about open database backups: They are somehow deemed to be less robust than closed backups. Oracle has provided them for many years and they have been proven to work. If you understand the basic operation of Oracle redo and undo (which are covered in Chapter 17), you can see that it's not really a big deal to back up a database while it's open. Finally, the old Oracle7 technique of BEGIN BACKUP and END BACKUP is no longer required for open database backups with Oracle8 and later, although it is still useful for creating standby databases. Standby databases are covered in Chapter 23, which discusses Oracle Data Guard.

Years ago, you could have made the excuse that there was no other option than writing these Oracle backup scripts, but that hasn't been the case for many years. I found myself in a similar position when I decided give up writing backup code (it was too scary!) and decided to try Oracle's Enterprise Backup Utility (EBU) tool for Oracle7. EBU is the Oracle7 predecessor to RMAN. My expectations were low, as I had tried an earlier incarnation of EBU without much success. That particular version (EBU v2.2) worked great and still does, without writing any code. RMAN replaces EBU for Oracle8 and Oracle9, and is a huge leap forward in terms of functionality.

Don't rely on a programmer's ability and diligence for your Oracle backups. Backup and restore procedures are definitely not a game of chance. Switch to RMAN. Oracle's position on RMAN has changed since Oracle8, and the product has a much higher profile, which augurs well for the future. For some Oracle configurations, such as Real Application Clusters (RAC), which are covered in Chapter 22, the complexity is such that RMAN represents the only practical solution.

You still need to check your backup and recovery procedure from time to time and at least before go-live. However, there's a much lower chance of things going wrong at recovery time if you use RMAN, and you can check your backups as part of your database healthchecks.

Less-Than-Optimal Performance

In general, the reasons for the less-than-optimal backup and restore performance include the inability to stream to multiple physical devices simultaneously and utilize high-performance devices to maximum capacity.

Also, due to the typical DBA technique of sizing databases for future growth, the use of disk image backups indicates that physical files are frequently backed up for databases that may contain a few hundred megabytes of actual data. Such empty space consisting of initialized but empty Oracle data blocks is highly compressible, but few backup tools take advantage of this.

It is always possible to identify the exact set of files required for an Oracle backup using SQL queries against the Oracle data dictionary. However, due to the difficulty of writing robust scripts to perform this function, a brute-force approach of backing up all disks is sometimes taken, resulting in more backup space requirements and longer backup and restore times than necessary.

Lack of Automation

Backups sometimes rely on the explicit issuance of instructions by operations personnel. Even when scheduling tools are used to automate the initiation of backup procedures, human intervention may be required for tape labeling, changing, and tracking, due to the lack of a tape autochanger.

As a result of this lack of automation, backup runs may be omitted by accident, and those problems during backups are not identified as early as possible and sometimes are not identified at all. The identification of problems may be difficult for operators, especially when the management console in the operations center contains a lot of other information. Problems with labeling and tracking often only come to light when a restore is required.

High Maintenance

It may be possible to write a custom-built Oracle backup script that is robust, detects changes to the physical structure of the database automatically, and is portable across different operating systems rather than using RMAN. However, this is an exercise that is best left to the database vendor, and there's no reason to duplicate it. Solutions that were developed in house may leave the business at risk if the original developer leaves. In any case, there are likely to be long-term maintenance issues with in-house code.

Writing in-house restore procedures and tools is even more problematic than backups. Complex and time-consuming restore procedures make it more difficult to organize the periodic testing of the end-to-end backup and restore process that should be performed for any production system. If you use RMAN, you restore using information in a command script. The script contains the system change number (SCN) or date and time you want to restore to, and RMAN works out the details of which files are required and where they are stored. In reality, it's not even necessary to provide the SCN or time because RMAN assumes that you wish to restore the most recent backup by default.

Lack of Standards

To provide a uniformly high level of service in an organization, standards need to be put in place to develop a consistent approach to Oracle backups. This standard should, as much as possible, be independent of the host location and database platform in use. A global application might require support from personnel in different countries depending on the time of day. Standards are paramount in making such a requirement workable, and RMAN is a good tool on which to base standardization efforts.

A Simple Backup Using RMAN

RMAN can be configured in many different ways. It's an extremely flexible tool that can be used for performing an on-demand backup to disk or a scheduled backup to the corporate Legato backup server at a remote site. Oracle catalogs all successful backups in one or two places. Information always appears in the control file of the database being backed up and optionally appears in a backup catalog database. If you need guaranteed accessibility to your Oracle backups, perhaps going back several months or even years, you must use a catalog database.

The init.ora parameter CONTROL_FILE_RECORD_KEEP_TIME, which has a default of 7 (days), determines how long backup information is kept in the control file. If backup records (including the records of archived redo log backups) are newer than this retention period, then the control file expands to retain the information. This explains why control files can grow to be quite large from Oracle8 on.

In this example, we back up the database OMFD1 to disk while it's up and running without using a backup catalog. The purpose of this script is to show you how easy it is to run an RMAN backup even if you have never run one before. The RMAN documentation is very comprehensive and long, which can intimidate new users. It's not necessary to understand the full potential of RMAN before using it. In many ways, it's a typical Oracle tool: It provides a fantastic amount of flexibility that in most cases you don't need to use at all, and the apparent complexity may put you off from using it in the first place.

NOTE The keywords in the RMAN command language are case insensitive like SQL keywords and database initialization parameter names. Within script code examples, I prefer to use lowercase for readability.

In the most simple case, a backup script allocates a disk channel (to indicate that a backup to disk is required), and then specifies a full database backup. This disk channel is associated with a database server session that streams data to disk. To perform an open backup, the database (OMFD1 in the example) must be running in ARCHIVELOG mode. Various RMAN parameters can be used to determine the name of the backup file on disk, which contains data in Oracle RMAN proprietary format. Backing up a database using RMAN format means that RMAN must be used to perform any subsequent restores. The script OMFD1.open.disk.rman looks like the following:

```
run {
allocate channel c1 type disk;
backup full (database format '/u02/OMFD1/ORA_O_%d_%t%s%p%u');
}
```

NOTE The script can be made even simpler by using the BACKUP FULL DATABASE command without the FORMAT option, which creates the backup file in $ORACLE_HOME/dbs using an Oracle-generated file name. This is probably too inflexible for most organizations. Also, the Oracle9*i* version of RMAN allocates a disk channel by default, so you don't need to specify one. If you do specify one, your scripts will work unchanged with Oracle8*i* and Oracle9*i*.

To perform the backup, a SYSDBA connection is required. In this case, we connect as SYSDBA using the target=/ command-line option to connect to the Oracle instance identified by $ORACLE_SID, using the set_env alias from Chapter 4 to set the Oracle environment first:

```
$ set_env OMFD1
$ rman nocatalog target=/ cmdfile=OMFD1.open.disk.rman log=backup.log
```

After the backup has completed successfully, you can see information about the backup held in the control file by querying the v$backup_piece view:

```
select  device_type,handle from v$backup_piece;


DEVICE_TYPE    HANDLE
------------   --------------------------------------------------
DISK           /u02/OMFD1/backup/ORA_O_OMFD1_4359431202102cvntmg
```

The v$backup_piece view holds a lot of other useful information such as the elapsed time of the backup and the start time. Only the backups that succeeded will be present. You can use this information to track the performance of your backups over time and compare the actual backups with the scheduled backups to identify failures. The DEVICE_TYPE column holds either DISK or SBT_TAPE, and is useful if you are running both disk and tape backups and need to distinguish between them.

It's very helpful to define a naming standard for the backup pieces. The convention used in the example is ORA_ followed by the type of backup (*O* for open database, *C* for closed database, and *A* for archived redo log), followed by the name of the database, followed by other information guaranteed to make the name of the piece unique. Structuring the names of your backup pieces might not seem so important now, but it becomes much more significant when you send your backups to a Legato server and you need to distinguish between the different types of backups held on the corporate server, such as NT and UNIX file backups, and Microsoft SQL Server database backups. The chosen naming convention immediately identifies the backup piece as belonging to an Oracle database named OMFD1 that is backed up using RMAN.

NOTE RMAN in Oracle9*i* includes a new command to back up archived redo logs and the database in the same command: BACKUP DATABASE PLUS ARCHIVELOG. Keeping the command separate provides more flexibility on the backup piece names.

Performing a closed database backup isn't much more difficult. In fact, we could use the previous OMFD1.open.disk.rman script, but instead we will create a different one to identify that the backup piece was created by a closed backup rather than an open one. In this case, the OMFD1.closed.disk.rman script contains the following, where the only difference from the open backup script is that ORA_O changes to ORA_C to identify the type of backup in the name of the piece:

```
run {
allocate channel c1 type disk;
backup full (database format '/u02/OMFD1/ORA_C_%d_%t%s%p%u');
}
```

The major difference between an open and closed backup is that the database must be in a mounted rather than open state before the closed backup script begins. This could be done manually using SQL*Plus, but it's not necessary because we already have a script that can do that, as shown in Chapter 4. The dbcool_ora_shut.pl script can perform a clean SHUTDOWN and then a STARTUP MOUNT to prepare for the closed backup:

```
$ dbcool_ora_shut.pl sid=OMFD1 startup=mount
```

At this stage, the benefits of a standard set of scripts should be evident. The dbcool_ora_shut.pl script returns 0 if it succeeds and 1 if it fails, and logs its actions. This behavior will become useful when we eventually run our script scheduled from a Legato server. Legato enables you to specify a prebackup command before executing an RMAN backup and expects it to return 0 or 1. So if we want to perform a closed backup via Legato, we simply specify the previous command as the Legato prebackup command: It meets the Legato requirements exactly. Once the database is in a mounted state, we can execute the closed backup using the following:

```
$ set_env OMFD1
$ rman nocatalog target=/ cmdfile=OMFD1.closed.disk.rman log=backup.log
```

At this stage, we haven't backed up any archived redo log files. This draws attention to an important feature of RMAN: You need to tell it exactly what you want to back up. You actually get a control file backup free without requesting it explicitly, but if you want to back up archived redo log files, you must place a command in the backup script. In our case, we indicate that the backup piece contains archived redo log files by prefixing ORA_A on the name:

```
run {
allocate channel c1 type disk;
backup full (database format '/u02/OMFD1/ORA_O_%d_%t%s%p%u');

# backup archivelogs as well...
backup (archivelog all format '/u02/OMFD1/ORA_A_%d_%t%s%p%u');
}
```

The ARCHIVELOG ALL command backs up all archivelogs found in the log destination. Other options are possible such as backing up only the most recently created logs based on a specified time limit and removing archived redo logs from disk as soon as they are backed up. We'll be taking a different approach to managing archived redo logs on disk.

Checking That a Backup Was Successful

Various techniques are available to check that an RMAN backup was successful. You can query the v$backup_piece view at any time, as shown in the previous section. Only backups that completed successfully will cause output to appear in this view. The existence of naming standards for the pieces makes it easy to identify the backup that was performed, but doesn't provide visibility of exactly which datafiles or archived redo logs are present in each piece.

As an alternative, you can check the return code from the RMAN command immediately after it completes. If the code is 0, then the backup was successful and other values represent failure. Keep in mind that UNIX provides the return code of the last command executed in the environment symbol $?. This approach has the drawback that it doesn't contain any information on exactly what was backed up.

A third technique can be used to check how many days of archived redo logs would be required to recover the database from the most recent backup. For example, if you perform a daily RMAN full database backup, then you would expect no datafiles to need 2 or more days of archived redo logs for recovery from the most recent backup, assuming that all backups have worked. On the other hand, if yesterday's backup failed, then you would expect the datafiles to require more than 1 day of archived redo logs to be applied during recovery. RMAN provides the REPORT NEED BACKUP COMMAND to display datafiles that need more than a specified number of days of archived redo logs for recovery:

```
$ rman target=/
RMAN> report need backup days=2 database;

using target database controlfile instead of recovery catalog
Report of files whose recovery needs more than 2 days of archived logs
File Days  Name
---- -----  -------------------------------------------------------
1    24     /u02/oradata/ORAD1/system01.dbf
2    24     /u02/oradata/ORAD1/undotbs01.dbf
3    24     /u02/oradata/ORAD1/tools01.dbf
```

In this example, the ORAD1 database was created 24 days ago and has never been backed up using RMAN. On the other hand, if the most successful backup had taken place today, the list of output files would be empty. This approach is the most reliable for checking that backups have been successful.

Using a Backup Catalog

So far, we've kept backup information only in the control file of the database being backed up. If you want to keep information on your Oracle RMAN backups all the time, then you should use a backup catalog database. Using a backup catalog is recommended by Oracle. Some features of RMAN are only available by using a backup catalog, and a backup catalog can track incarnations of your database. New incarnations of your database are created whenever you open a database with the RESETLOGS option. If you might need to restore to a point in time before a RESETLOGS operation, then you must use a catalog database.

You should choose a database with high availability to hold the catalog because if you choose to use a backup catalog and it's not available, then the backup will fail. The use of a backup catalog database can be specified in your RMAN command script. The default option is nocatalog. You should keep a single backup catalog for all your Oracle databases. If you need to perform backups of Oracle8*i* and Oracle9*i* databases, create the catalog in an Oracle9*i* database using the Oracle9*i* catalog format. This discussion assumes that you need to back up Oracle8*i* and Oracle9*i* databases, so you create the catalog in an Oracle9*i* database.

When you choose to use a catalog database, naturally you want to back up that database as well. Although Oracle EBU for Oracle7 contained a backup catalog command, RMAN doesn't. To back up the backup catalog database itself, you can:

- Perform regular exports of the backup catalog using the Oracle Export utility and back up the dump files using a file backup utility.

- Back up the catalog database using RMAN, and use another database to act as the catalog for the catalog database backup. This can get complicated because then you need to decide how to back up the second catalog database.

- Perform nocatalog backups of the catalog database, and rely on information held in control file backups to restore the catalog.

The third option becomes more attractive in Oracle9*i* because RMAN includes a new feature to automate the backup of the control file, described in the section *Using the CONTROLFILE AUTOBACKUP Command* later in this chapter.

Keep in mind that should you lose the catalog database and can't restore the original contents, all is not lost. In this case, you can create a new catalog database from scratch, reregister all your Oracle databases back into the catalog, and synchronize their control file contents back into the catalog. Because each database control file keeps seven days' worth of backup details by default, you still have access to information for the most recent backups, which can potentially be used to perform a restore. However, you have lost information on all backups prior to the previous week, and these can't be restored.

Creating the Catalog

After you have chosen the database that will hold the catalog, create a tablespace to hold the RMAN catalog schema and create a user to own the tables. In our example, the catalog database is RMANP1, the tablespace is RMAN_DATA, and the schema owner is RMAN. These operations must be performed from a SYSDBA connection:

```
REM requires tablespace rman_data to exist
create user rman identified by xyz123
temporary tablespace temp
default tablespace rman_data
quota unlimited on rman_data;

REM grant privileges to rman
grant recovery_catalog_owner to rman;
grant connect, resource to rman;
revoke unlimited tablespace from rman;
```

You might consider not granting CONNECT to the RMAN user for security reasons. It's not actually required in order to run backups that use a catalog. Once you've created the RMAN account, you need to create the backup catalog itself. To do this, set the environment to that of the catalog database, connect to the RMAN account using the RMAN command utility, and then run the CREATE CATALOG command:

```
$ set_env RMANP1

$ srv1.dbcool.com:RMANP1 >rman catalog=rman/xyz123

Recovery Manager: Release 9.0.1.1.0 - Production

(c) Copyright 2001 Oracle Corporation.  All rights reserved.

connected to recovery catalog database
recovery catalog is not installed

RMAN> create catalog

recovery catalog created
```

Specifying the Catalog for Backups

If you want to store database backup information in a catalog, then you need to register it in the backup catalog. The database that you want to back up is referred to as the *target database*. In order to register the target database, you need to run RMAN and connect to the target database and the catalog at the same time, and then run the REGISTER DATABASE command. The REGISTER command stores the physical structure of the database into the backup catalog.

In this example, we'll register the database OMFD1. You can specify connections to the catalog and target database using any valid Transparent Network Substrate (TNS) connect strings. These will be required when we run Legato backups. For now, we set the environment to that of the target database and connect to the target using a local, non-TNS connection. The catalog database, which usually resides on a remote machine, uses a TNS connect string. The target database account must have SYSDBA privileges. The complete sequence looks like this:

```
$ set_env OMFD1
srv2.dbcool.com:OMFD1 >rman target=/
catalog=rman/xyz123@rmanp1.dbcool.com

Recovery Manager: Release 9.0.1.1.0 - Production

(c) Copyright 2001 Oracle Corporation.  All rights reserved.

connected to target database: OMFD1 (DBID=3159171023)
connected to recovery catalog database
```

```
RMAN> register database;

database registered in recovery catalog
starting full resync of recovery catalog
full resync complete
```

Now that OMFD1 is registered in the catalog database, we can make a small change to the original script and rerun the backup from the OMFD1 environment to store information about the backup into the backup catalog as well as the OMFD1 control file. In addition to adding a reference to the catalog connection, we can move the target connection details into the script, which enables the script to be run from a very simple command line:

```
$ rman @OMFD1.disk.open.rman
```

In this case, OMFD1.disk.open.rman contains the following:

```
connect target /
connect catalog rman/xyz123@rmanp1.dbcool.com
run {
allocate channel c1 type disk;
backup full (database format '/u02/OMFD1/ORA_O_%d_%t%s%p%u');
backup (archivelog all format '/u02/OMFD1/ORA_A_%d_%t%s%p%u');
}
```

> **NOTE** The RMAN commands CONNECT CATALOG and CONNECT RCVCAT can be used interchangeably to connect to a backup catalog. Some third-party backup libraries mandate the use of CONNECT RCVCAT.

Connecting to the Target Using Oracle Net

Up until this stage, all of the examples have connected to the target database using a local database connection. RMAN is not so restrictive. Using RMAN, you can specify both the catalog connection and the target database connection at backup time using TNS connect strings. Legato backups rely on this functionality, so the next step is to configure the target database to allow remote connections as SYSDBA. In order to do this, you need to create a password file for your database, as described in Chapter 5 in the section *Using a Password File*. Once the target database is up and running with a password file, create an account called RMAN in the target database and grant SYSDBA privileges to it:

```
GRANT SYSDBA to RMAN;
```

It's not necessary to grant CONNECT to the account. To see if the remote SYSDBA connection is working, set the Oracle environment to one that doesn't include the System ID (SID) of the target database, and then use RMAN to test to make sure you can connect to the target database and catalog at the same time using TNS connect strings:

```
$ srv2.dbcool.com:OMFD1 >set_env 9.0.1

$ srv2.dbcool.com:9.0.1 >rman

rman> connect target rman/abc123@omfd1.dbcool.com

rman> connect catalog rman/xyz123@rmanp1.dbcool.com
```

If you have configured the password file correctly, both commands should work. Now the configuration is suitable for use with a Legato server.

Duplicating a Database

As a DBA, you've almost certainly been in a situation where you need to set up a new database and the easiest way to accomplish the task is to clone the database files from an existing database. You might do this simply by shutting down the source database, making a tar image, and unpacking it on the new machine. If you're likely to require RMAN backups for the cloned database, then you first need to understand how RMAN uniquely identifies databases in the backup catalog; if you don't understand this, you're likely to run into problems with RMAN backups of your cloned database.

Understanding DBID and Catalog Uniqueness

When you use the REGISTER DATABASE command to register your database in the backup catalog, RMAN uses the database ID (DBID) column from V$DATABASE as a unique identifier for your database. The DBID column is set for your database at creation time and is guaranteed to be unique. Historically, it hasn't been possible to change it. If you are an Oracle7 EBU user, this is fundamentally different. EBU uses a combination of the hostname and SID to uniquely identify a database in the EBU catalog, whereas RMAN uses no external identifiers; it simply uses the DBID in the database. If you clone an Oracle8 or later database onto another server, change the SID, and even rename the database by recreating the control file, the DBID remains the same. If you try to register the cloned database, you're likely to receive the following error:

```
RMAN-20002: target database already registered in recovery catalog
```

Of much greater concern is the potential for confusion if you use OPEN RESETLOGS for your cloned database before attempting to register it with REGISTER DATABASE. In this case, RMAN thinks your cloned database is actually a new incarnation of the original database! There *are* situations where you use OPEN RESETLOGS for a database (for example, after incomplete recovery following a media failure), but this isn't one of them.

RMAN registers your cloned copy quite happily, and then your original database backups fail because RMAN detects that a later incarnation of the database exists.

Here's an example of how you can get into this situation and how you can fix it. Say you have a database called OMFD1 that you have been backing up for some time using RMAN with a backup catalog. You decide to take a copy to a different server, rename the database to OMFD2, and register it with the backup catalog after opening it with OPEN RESETLOGS. At this point, you actually have two databases. RMAN thinks you have one database, with the OMFD2 version being a later incarnation of OMFD1. If you connect to the RMAN catalog as the RMAN account, you can identify what's happened using the following SQL:

```
select db_key,dbid,dbinc_key,name,resetlogs_time,
       current_incarnation current
from   rc_database_incarnation where name in ('OMFD1','OMFD2');


  DB_KEY       DBID   DBINC_KEY NAME    RESETLOGS_TIME           CURRENT
  --------  ----------  ----------- -------  --------------------  ----------
  1326013  849152607     1544963 OMFD1   18-JUN-2001 17:45:03  NO
  1326013  849152607     2212174 OMFD2   11-OCT-2001 14:02:12  YES
```

The output of the query clearly shows that there are two incarnations for the database with DBID 849152607, and the later one that is dated 11-OCT-2001 is the current one. The fact that the database has been renamed might appear to be significant, but as far as RMAN is concerned, it's incidental. The information available shows two incarnations of the same database. Attempts to back up the incarnation corresponding to OMFD1 will fail. This problem can be addressed by resetting the incarnation of the database back to the previous one, which is indicated by the DBINC_KEY given by 1544963. To do this, you need to connect to the target database and the backup catalog using RMAN, and then run the following RMAN command:

```
reset database to incarnation 1544963;

RMAN-03022: compiling command: reset
RMAN-03023: executing command: reset
RMAN-08066: database reset to incarnation 1544963 in recovery catalog
```

Reexecuting the previous query confirms that the previous incarnation is now current and backups of OMFD1 can continue as before. However, this doesn't solve the issue of how to back up OMFD2 using a backup catalog:

```
  DB_KEY       DBID   DBINC_KEY NAME    RESETLOGS_TIME           CURRENT
  --------  ----------  ----------- -------  --------------------  ----------
  1326013  849152607     1544963 OMFD1   18-JUN-2001 17:45:03  YES
  1326013  849152607     2212174 OMFD2   11-OCT-2001 14:02:12  NO
```

This problem has two solutions. One uses the RMAN DUPLICATE command and the other uses a command-line utility to reset the DBID, which is available in Oracle9*i* Release 2. The utility is called DBNEWID and Chapter 23 contains an example of how to use it.

Using the RMAN DUPLICATE Command

You can use the RMAN DUPLICATE command to clone a database. This does two useful things compared to cloning a database yourself using operating system commands like rcp or tar. First, the database is renamed as an integral part of the process, and second, a new DBID is created automatically for the cloned database, so it can be backed up using an RMAN catalog.

The RMAN DUPLICATE command has the capability to clone a database with almost no effort. The DUPLICATE command restores and recovers a backup of one database to a database with a different name through a single RMAN command script. You can clone a database onto the same machine or a different machine. You can use a tape or disk backup as the basis for your restore and recovery, but it should be emphasized that you need to have a backup of the source database available, otherwise the duplication will fail. The source database needs to be in ARCHIVELOG mode, which means that you can clone the source database while it's up and running.

In this example, for simplicity, we'll duplicate a database onto another database with a different name on the same server. Oracle refers to the cloned database as the *auxiliary database*. We will use this terminology from this point on.

RMAN provides the flexibility to restore backup files from one name to a different name using the SET NEWNAME command. If possible, we want to avoid the overhead of having to specify the restored file name for each file in the source database when we create the duplicate database. If you've followed the earlier recommendations of this book for Oracle physical layout using a large file system, then RMAN DUPLICATE can be performed with the maximum simplicity by specifying the names for the restored files in the init.ora file of the cloned database using a simple rule. In this case, the only difference between the file names in the source database and the auxiliary database is the SID in the file name, which in this example is OD1 for the source database and OD2 for the auxiliary database, as shown in Table 18.1.

Before running the DUPLICATE command, you need to make sure that the Optimal Flexible Architecture (OFA) structure for the OD2 database (cdump, udump, bdump,

Table 18.1   Source and Auxiliary Files for Database Duplication

SOURCE FILE	AUXILIARY FILE
/u02/oradata/OD1/cntrl01.ctl	/u02/oradata/OD2/cntrl01.ctl
/u02/oradata/OD1/cntrl02.ctl	/u02/oradata/OD2/cntrl02.ctl
/u02/oradata/OD1/redog1m1.log	/u02/oradata/OD2/redog1m1.log
/u02/oradata/OD1/redog1m2.log	/u02/oradata/OD2/redog1m2.log
/u02/oradata/OD1/redog2m1.log	/u02/oradata/OD2/redog2m1.log
/u02/oradata/OD1/redog2m2.log	/u02/oradata/OD2/redog2m2.log
/u02/oradata/OD1/rbs01.dbf	/u02/oradata/OD2/rbs01.dbf
/u02/oradata/OD1/system01.dbf	/u02/oradata/OD2/system01.dbf
/u02/oradata/OD1/temp01.dbf	/u02/oradata/OD2/temp01.dbf
/u02/oradata/OD1/users01.dbf	/u02/oradata/OD2/users01.dbf

Table 18.2   Source and Auxiliary init.ora Differences

SOURCE FILE	AUXILIARY FILE
db_name=od1	db_name=od2
instance_name=od1	instance_name=od2
service_names=od1.dbcool.com	service_names=od2.dbcool.com
control_files= ("/u02/oradata/OD1/cntrl01.ctl", "/u02/oradata/OD1/cntrl02.ctl")	control_files= ("/u02/oradata/OD2/cntrl01.ctl", "/u02/oradata/OD2/cntrl02.ctl")
background_dump_dest = /u01/app/oracle/admin/OD1/bdump	background_dump_dest = /u01/app/oracle/admin/OD2/bdump
Core_dump_dest = /u01/app/oracle/admin/OD1/cdump	core_dump_dest = /u01/app/oracle/admin/OD2/cdump
User_dump_dest = /u01/app/oracle/admin/OD1/udump	user_dump_dest = /u01/app/oracle/admin/OD2/udump
log_archive_dest =/u03/oradata/OD1/arch	log_archive_dest =/u03/oradata/OD2/arch

and so on) and all database file directories and archived redo log directories are created in advance. If you don't, the duplication will fail. It would be nice if RMAN had an option to create directories for you as needed, but as of today it doesn't. You also need to make sure that an init.ora file and password file exist for the auxiliary database. The differences between parameters that exist in both the auxiliary and source database init.ora files are shown in Table 18.2.

Perl is a great language for automating processes that modify strings in scripts, and it would be fairly straightforward to write a Perl script to create the directories and init.ora file for the auxiliary database. The init.ora file for the auxiliary database has two very important *additional* parameters that are not present in the init.ora file of the source database. These parameters (DB_FILE_NAME_CONVERT and LOG_FILE_NAME_CONVERT) are used by the DUPLICATE command to determine how the source database backup files are to be restored from backup to create the database files and redo logs for the auxiliary database:

```
DB_FILE_NAME_CONVERT=(/OD1/,/OD2/)
LOG_FILE_NAME_CONVERT=(/OD1/,/OD2/)
```

As Table 18.1 shows, the only difference between the file names for each database is the SID in the paths. The CONVERT parameters provide the information that RMAN needs to change OD1 to OD2 for both database file names and redo logs on restore. You also need to create a password file for the auxiliary database, as shown in Chapter 5, and ensure that the TNS alias for the auxiliary database exists in your Oracle Names server (or your tnsnames.ora file, which hopefully you're no longer using). The following is a checklist you should use before running the RMAN DUPLICATE command:

- Perform an RMAN backup of source database.
- Make sure a backup is available.

- Create the OFA structure for auxiliary.

- Create an oratab entry for auxiliary.

- Create init.ora for auxiliary with CONVERT parameters.

- Create a password file for auxiliary.

- Create TNS alias for auxiliary.

- STARTUP NOMOUNT the auxiliary database.

After the prerequisites are in place, you need a script to create the auxiliary, for example, create_od2.rman:

```
run {
sql "alter system archive log current";  # flush out the most recent log
allocate auxiliary channel c1 type disk;
duplicate target database to od2;
}
```

To create the auxiliary, set the Oracle environment to that of the source database and run the create_od2.rman script while connected to the auxiliary database (which must be running in the NOMOUNT state) as follows:

```
$ set_env OD1

$ rman nocatalog target=/ auxiliary=od2.dbcool.com
cmdfile=create_od2.rman
```

With only three commands, this script restores your source database to SID OD2 and recovers it to the change in the most recent archivelog from OD1 without any DBA intervention. It couldn't get much simpler. In this example, the auxiliary has been restored to the change in the most recent archived redo log from the source database, and this log was flushed out by the first line of the create_od2.rman script. This highlights that the duplication process applies the actual archived redo logs from the source database: There is no need to have backups of archived redo log files available in this case. RMAN DUPLICATE is much more flexible than this simple example shows. For example, rather than applying all the archived redo log files from the primary during the recovery, you can restore the auxiliary to an earlier point in time by specifying a date or SCN before the DUPLICATE command in the script. For example,

```
set until scn 40120815949;
```

If your physical layout is fragmented and you can't restore the auxiliary by changing the SID in each file name in the source database, you can still run the DUPLICATE command. In this case, the process becomes more manual because you can't use a simple rule to map the source files to the auxiliary file on restore, as performed by the CONVERT parameters in the init.ora file of the auxiliary database. Instead, you need to remove the CONVERT parameters and specify the restore file names in the create_od2.rman script file by file using SET NEWNAME. If you use large file systems for your Oracle databases, you can do this easily using CONVERT.

The DBNEWID Utility

The Oracle DBNEWID command-line utility solves the problem of the duplicated DBID following a manual database copy operation by enabling you to change the DBNAME, the DBID, or both. The utility is shipped with Oracle9*i* Release 2 and runs against all database versions from Oracle8 and later.

Generating Backup Scripts

Several types of backups require the following options:

- Backup to tape or disk
- Backup with or without a backup catalog
- Backup of the database open or closed
- Backup of the database with and without an integral archived redo log backup
- Backup of archived redo logs only

There are minor differences between the scripts in each case. This is a situation that can benefit from the excellent text-processing capabilities of Perl. To automate the creation of RMAN backup command scripts compatible with Oracle8*i* and Oracle9*i* databases, a Perl script is available on this book's companion Web site to generate a selection of RMAN scripts for the previous cases. The script is dbcool_rman_generate.pl and it has the following command line:

```
dbcool_rman_gen.pl sid=sid target=targ [catalog=cat] {dir=dir|tape=srv}
[pool=poolname] [overwrite=y|n]

sid:       ORACLE_SID of target database to be backed up
target:    user/pwd@tns for the target database SYSDBA connection
cat:       user/pwd@tns for the catalog database connection
dir:       path for disk backups
srv:    name of Legato server
pool:      optional Legato tape Pool name
overwrite: force overwrite of existing scripts
```

Both dir= and tape= can be specified if you have to perform both disk and tape backups. This is an example of command-line arguments for the Oracle SID OMFD1 that lead to generation of scripts for both disk and Legato server backups:

```
sid=OMFD1
target=rman/abc123@omfd1.dbcool.com
catalog=rman/xyz123@rmanp1.dbcool.com
dir=/u03/backups
tape=lg1.dbcool.com
pool=Ora
```

The script produces 21 RMAN scripts in $ORACLE_BASE/admin/OMFD1/scripts to cover all the possible combinations. The names of the scripts are structured to clearly identify the type of backup performed. Here are two examples:

```
OMFD1.tape.catalog.archlogs.open.rman
OMFD1.disk.nocatalog.noarchlogs.closed.rman
```

The first script performs an open database backup to tape, using a backup catalog and including archived redo logs. The second performs a closed database backup to disk without a backup catalog and without including archived redo logs. It needs to be emphasized that RMAN *doesn't* include commands to modify the database state. Therefore, if a closed backup is required, the DBA is responsible for ensuring that the database is in a mounted state before the script executes. To place the database in a mounted state, suitable for a closed backup, you run the following SQL*Plus commands:

```
REM run these before a closed backup
shutdown immediate;
startup mount;

REM run this to open database after backup completes
alter database open;
```

It's helpful to compare the contents of two of the scripts to see the effect of the command-line arguments on the generated output. The OMFD1.tape.catalog.archlogs. open.rman script performs an open database backup (including archived redo logs) to a Legato server using a backup catalog with the following commands:

```
connect target rman/abc123@omfd1.dbcool.com
connect rcvcat rman/xyz123@rmanp1.dbcool.com
run {

set command id to 'OMFD1.tape.catalog.archlogs.open.rman';

allocate channel c1 type 'SBT_TAPE'
    parms 'ENV=(NSR_SERVER=lg1.dbcool.com,NSR_DATA_VOLUME_POOL=Ora)';
backup full (database format 'ORA_O_%d_%t%s%p%u');
sql "alter system archive log current";
resync catalog;
change archivelog all crosscheck;
backup (archivelog all format 'ORA_A_%d_%t%s%p%u');
}
```

NOTE RMAN in Oracle9*i* automatically performs ALTER SYSTEM ARCHIVE LOG CURRENT to flush the current online redo log to disk whenever an archived redo log backup command is executed. Leaving the command in the script enables it to work unchanged for both Oracle8*i* and Oracle9*i* databases.

The OMFD1.disk.nocatalog.noarchlogs.closed.rman script performs a closed backup to disk without using a backup catalog and without archived redo log backup by using the following commands:

```
connect target rman/abc123@omfd1.dbcool.com
run {

set command id to 'OMFD1.disk.nocatalog.noarchlogs.closed.rman';
allocate channel c1 type disk;
backup full (database format '=/u03/backups/ORA_O_%d_%t%s%p%u');
}
```

The OMFD1.disk.nocatalog.noarchlogs.closed.rman script has the capability to perform a backup without requiring the database to be in ARCHIVELOG mode. This is useful for development databases that need to be backed up from time to time, but don't run in ARCHIVELOG mode. If such a script included archived redo log backup commands, like those from the previous script, the backup would fail.

For a production system, you're likely to use only three of the scripts on a regular basis. These scripts all back up to tape on a remote Legato server using a backup catalog for robustness:

```
OMFD1.tape.catalog.arch.rman
OMFD1.tape.catalog.archlogs.closed.rman
OMFD1.tape.catalog.archlogs.open.rman
```

In all scripts, the initial SET COMMAND ID command causes the client_info column of v$session to be populated with the supplied string. This enables the Oracle session performing the backup to be identified easily by a DBA using a SQL query, which can be useful if you need to kill a backup, as shown in the section *Backup and Restore Troubleshooting* later in this chapter. Keep in mind that there is nothing to prevent you from running a closed backup script while the database is open. In this case, the backup will still work, but the value reported in the client_info column will be misleading.

As an alternative to running command-line scripts explicitly, you can use the RMAN integration provided with Oracle Enterprise Manager (OEM) to run backups. I prefer to run backups from scripts on disk because it provides immediate visibility on exactly what commands the scripts execute without having to depend on a graphical user interface (GUI) tool.

NOTE RMAN in Oracle9*i* includes new options for storing persistent values for backup channels using the CONFIGURE CHANNEL command rather than the ALLOCATE CHANNEL command. I still prefer to use ALLOCATE CHANNEL as it enables each script to stand alone without requiring previous configuration.

Managing Archived Redo Logs on Disk

Archived redo logs are required to recover a database to a point in time. If any one of those logs is removed without a backup, then you cannot recover to that point in time. So archived redo log backups are mission critical and the management of archived redo log removal needs to be integrated with the backup procedures. Although RMAN can optionally remove archivelogs that have been backed up during script execution and can back up a given archived redo log more than once in a single script, I prefer to manage the removal of archivelogs from disk with a separate process and allow RMAN to deal only with backups. If you wish to delete archived redo logs immediately after backup, you can add the DELETE INPUT option to the archived redo log backup command:

```
backup (archivelog all format 'formatstring' delete input);
```

My requirement for archived redo log backups is to only remove an archived redo log from disk when it has been backed up twice to different tapes on a backup server. As result, there is no dependency on a single tape in order to recover the database to a particular point in time. This can be implemented in different ways.

One way is to back up the archived redo logs through RMAN once a day through a scheduled backup and ensure that your Legato administrator allocates a new tape for Oracle backups on a daily basis. This way, you can check the RMAN backup catalog for a given number of backups, and if the number is 2 or more, you know you can safely remove the archived redo log because it's on different tapes.

Checking Archivelog Backups

RMAN provides a reporting facility that enables you to check how many times an archived redo log has been backed up, among many other features, which is useful if you wish to manage the removal of archived redo logs from disk yourself rather than let RMAN do it for you. For example, if you wanted to check how many times the archived redo log with sequence number 17 had been backed up, you would run an RMAN command like the following after connecting to the target and catalog database:

```
rman> list backupset of archivelog low logseq = 17 high logseq = 17;

List of Backup Sets
===================

BS Key  Device Type Elapsed Time Completion Time
-------  ----------- ------------ ---------------
35      DISK        00:00:10     03-NOV-01
        BP Key: 36   Status: AVAILABLE   Tag:
        Piece Name: /u02/omfd1/ORA_A_OMFD1_4448356603103d879qc

  List of Archived Logs in backup set 35
  Thrd Seq     Low SCN    Low Time  Next SCN   Next Time
  ---- ------- ---------- --------- ---------- ---------
```

```
    1    17     285873    28-OCT-01 291407    03-NOV-01

BS Key  Device Type Elapsed Time Completion Time
-------  ----------- ------------ ---------------
42      DISK           00:00:02     03-NOV-01
        BP Key: 43   Status: AVAILABLE   Tag:
        Piece Name: /u02/omfd1/ORA_A_OMFD1_4448361304104d87a92

    List of Archived Logs in backup set 42
    Thrd Seq     Low SCN    Low Time   Next SCN   Next Time
    ---- ------- ---------- ---------- ---------- ---------
    1    17      285873     28-OCT-01  291407     03-NOV-01
```

By searching the output for instances of backup pieces specific to the instance (in this case, ORA_A_OMFD1) and counting the pieces (in this case, 2), you can confirm that the requisite number of backups exists before removing the archived redo log. The ability to perform this check is made easier by the choice of a standard format for backup pieces, enabling you to search the output more easily. In general, if you use a naming standard for anything having to do with Oracle, then writing scripts to manage the database becomes easier.

Synchronizing Archived Redo Log Backup Information

All the generated backup scripts assume that removal of archived redo logs from disk is managed externally to RMAN, rather than allowing RMAN itself to remove them immediately after backup through a script command. As a result, it's necessary to include commands in the backup script to inform RMAN that archived redo logs on disk may no longer be present due to removal by the external process as follows:

```
sql "alter system archive log current";
resync catalog;
change archivelog all crosscheck;
backup (archivelog all format 'ORA_A_%d_%t%s%p%u');
```

The CHANGE ARCHIVELOG ALL CROSSCHECK command causes RMAN to check the archived redo log files present on disk with those it expects to find and resynchronizes the control file to update the status of any files that have been removed by the external archived redo log management process. RMAN is notoriously strict about what it expects to find on disk. This is one reason its backups are so reliable.

If you simply remove archived redo log files from disk without notifying RMAN in this way, your backups will fail. After you remove an archived redo log file you must use the DELETE EXPIRED ARCHIVELOG COMMAND as shown in the following example, or you will receive "validation failed for archived log" messages when the CHANGE ARCHIVELOG ALL CROSSCHECK is executed during a backup:

```
delete noprompt expired archivelog
  '/u02/oradata/ORAD1/arch/T0001S0000000611.ARC';
```

Archived Redo Log Naming Standards

Using a well-thought-out naming scheme and location for your archived redo log files on disk can make it easier to write scripts to manage them: If you do that, your script will be able to locate the logs without needing to look up the location from the database, and you'll be able to use pattern matching to identify the individual file names easily. You should always be able to locate your archived redo log files on disk in the OFA-compliant location, which for an instance named OMFD1 is:

```
$ORACLE_BASE/admin/OMFD1/arch
```

This doesn't mean that you need to use this location in the init.ora file. It's better to be explicit about the real location of the archived redo log files in the init.ora file, which might specify the real archived redo log destination as:

```
log_archive_dest_1= "location=/u05/oradata/OMFD1/arch MANDATORY"
```

You can have the best of both worlds by creating a symbolic link from the OFA directory to the real location:

```
$ cd $ORACLE_BASE/admin/OMFD1
$ ln -s /u05/oradata/OMFD1/arch arch
```

After you've done this, you can take advantage of the UNIX CDPATH implemented by the set_env (as described in Chapter 4) alias to locate your archived redo log directory for a given instance simply by entering:

```
$ cd arch
```

In terms of a naming standard for individual archived redo log names, the following file specification in the init.ora file is recommended:

```
log_archive_format = "T%TS%S.ARC"
```

This results in names like T0001S0000000017.ARC for individual files, where the name contains both the log thread and sequence number in the thread. The advantage of using the log thread in the file name (identified by the %T) is that exactly the same format can be used for multiple instances in an Oracle Parallel Server or RAC configuration. Some DBAs like to include the instance name in the format, and this can be achieved in a non-instance-specific way, resulting in names like OMFD1_T0001S0000000017.ARC, by using the following:

```
log_archive_format = "@_T%TS%S.ARC"
```

Interfacing to Legato

Legato has a long established relationship with Oracle for providing interfaces from RMAN to an autochanger tape library storage device attached to a Legato server. The autochanger device is sometimes referred to as a *tape library*. Oracle ships Legato Storage Manager (LSM) with the Oracle DBMS product set. This is a cut-down version of Legato that only allows backups to a locally attached tape drive on the same server as the database. This section describes the fully fledged Legato product that you use if you want enterprisewide Oracle backups of your Oracle database directly to tape on a remote server. The examples in this section use Legato NetWorker for Oracle 3.0 on Sun Solaris (32-bit SPARC). The configuration on other UNIX platforms, including Linux, is very similar.

If you use Legato NetWorker Module for Oracle with a tape library on a remote site, your database data is streamed by RMAN directly to tape, giving a guaranteed offsite backup of your data, all from a single RMAN command script. Depending on the configuration of the Legato server, a single database backup can stream to multiple tape devices permitting database backup throughput of hundreds of gigabytes per hour. It's also possible to run several different database backups and restores at the same time. It should be emphasized that when you use Legato NetWorker for RMAN backups, Oracle streams *data*—not operating system files—from the database to the Legato server. This is different from a UNIX file system backup, which explicitly backs up UNIX files. If you use Legato NetWorker for Oracle for your Oracle backups, then you should prevent your regular Legato file system backups from backing up the database files. If you continue to back up these files, you're just wasting space on the server. This section explains how to do that.

Installing Legato NetWorker 3 for Oracle

Legato NetWorker 3 for Oracle on Solaris is delivered as a Solaris package that must be installed by the SA as the root account on the Oracle database server that requires Legato backups. For example, using the tar file downloaded from Legato's Web site, installation proceeds as follows, assuming that the tar file has been unpacked into the /tmp directory and the SA is logged on as root:

```
$ cd /tmp
$ pkgadd -d /tmp LGTOnmo
```

The key components that are installed are

```
/usr/lib/libnwora.so.1
/usr/lib/libnwora.so
/usr/sbin/nsrnmostart
```

The nsrnmostart executable is required to run RMAN backups scheduled by the Legato server, as described later in this section. The shared library libnwora.so.1 is the glue that directs the Oracle server to stream backup data to a Legato server, and libnwora.so is a symbolic link to it. In order to link the Legato shared library into the Oracle DBMS, you need to change the default libobk.so shared library shipped by Oracle and replace it with libnwora.so. You can see which libobk.so is linked into the Oracle8i DBMS executable on Solaris as follows:

```
$ cd $ORACLE_HOME/bin
$ ldd oracle|grep libobk.so
        libobk.so =>      /u01/app/oracle/product/8.1.7/lib/libobk.so
```

The previous output shows that the Oracle executable is using the default libobk.so that was shipped with Oracle. This isn't Legato aware. You need to replace it with the Legato-aware version as follows:

```
$ cd $ORACLE_HOME/lib
$ mv libobk.so libobk.so.default
$ ln -s /usr/lib/libnwora.so libobk.so
```

Legato Client Resource Definitions

After you've Legato-enabled your Oracle executable, you need to have a Legato Client resource definition configured in the Legato server in order to permit Oracle backups to the server. The Client resource identifies the Oracle server as the NetWorker backup client and specifies the policies that the NetWorker server uses for backup data management. Client definitions are saved persistently through the Legato NetWorker server administration tool, nwadmin. The ability to add and modify Client definitions through nwadmin requires Legato server administrator rights.

Most organizations are likely to have a dedicated team for managing an enterprise-wide resource such as a Legato server. Legato actually states in its documentation that the Oracle UNIX account (usually oracle) needs to be in the Legato server administrator list in order to have access to the full Legato Oracle functionality for backups and restores. This raises potential security concerns as your Legato administrators may not want Oracle DBAs to have Legato administrator rights. In this case, you should refer them to the Legato documentation. Having Legato administrator rights means that Oracle DBAs can potentially modify any backup on any client machine, including non-Oracle backups. My experience has been that professional Oracle DBAs can be trusted to manage their own Oracle backups on a Legato server without impacting other backups. In any case, the configuration of Oracle-backup-specific Client resource definitions requires information that is specific to Oracle, which is beyond the scope of what a Legato administrator deals with. For that reason, the Oracle DBA can reasonably expect to have Legato administrator rights.

There are two distinct types of Client resources as far as we are concerned. If your company uses Legato for standard UNIX file system backups on your Oracle server, then a Client resource definition already exists. This Client resource doesn't contain information about Oracle databases, but it does enable the DBA to initiate Oracle backups from the client to the Legato server using RMAN. For example, if the Oracle database server srv1.dbcool.com already has a Client definition on the Legato server lg1.dbcool.com through the use of UNIX file system backups, then it enables the DBA to initiate an Oracle backup from the client, for example, using a script like the following:

```
connect target rman/abc123@omfd1.dbcool.com
connect catalog rman/xyz123@rmanp1.dbcool.com
run {
set command id to 'OMFD1.tape.catalog.archlogs.open.rman';
```

```
allocate channel c1 type 'SBT_TAPE'
        parms 'ENV=(NSR_SERVER=lg1.dbcool.com)';
backup full (database format 'ORA_O_%d_%t%s%p%u');
sql "alter system archive log current";
resync catalog;
change archivelog all crosscheck;
backup (archivelog all format 'ORA_A_%d_%t%s%p%u');
}
```

The channel definition in the script specifies that a backup to tape on the Legato server lg1.dbcool.com is needed. In addition to client-initiated backups, we need to run backups scheduled and initiated from the Legato server. This leads to a requirement for Oracle-specific Client resource definitions.

As we'll configure it, each database backup and backup type on a particular Oracle server will have its own Client resource definition. For example, if there are two instances—OD1 and OD2—on an Oracle server, the following backups will all have a separate Client resource definition:

- OD1 open backup
- OD1 closed backup
- OD1 archivelog-only backup
- OD2 open backup
- OD2 closed backup
- OD3 archivelog-only backup

The Client resource definitions all have the same name (the hostname of the Oracle server) and typically differ only in the contents of two of the Client properties, which are used to identify the type of backup:

- Saveset field
- Backup command

The Saveset field in the Client resource identifies the name of the RMAN script to run. As we've already generated the required scripts using dbcool_gen_rman.pl, we can enter the script name right away. For example, for the OD1 open backup, we specify the following as the value for Saveset:

```
\u01\app\oracle\admin\OD1\scripts\OD1.tape.catalog.open.rman
```

The Backup command in the Client resource is the name of a script run by the Legato client daemon (nsrexecd) on the client machine during a scheduled backup. The client daemon is contacted by the Legato scheduler on the server, passing it information about the Saveset and the name of the Backup command script to run. The Backup command script in the Client resource is used to set up the environment for running the Saveset script. The Backup command script must be in the same directory as the Legato executables (/usr/sbin for Solaris), and it must start with the string nsr. It's clear that for each RMAN script, we need an equivalent nsr script to call it. For that purpose, you can download dbcool_legato_gen.pl from this book's companion Web site and run it as follows:

```
$ dbcool_legato_gen.pl sid=SID
```

To save on the number of scripts generated, it is assumed that all backups to your Legato server will use a backup catalog and the database being backed up is in ARCHIVELOG mode. This results in the creation of three Legato backup scripts in the scripts directory for the SID. For example, the OD1 database has three files generated in $ORACLE_BASE/admin/OD1/scripts:

- nsr_ora_closed_OD1
- nsr_ora_open_OD1
- nsr_ora_arch_OD1

The dbcool_legato_gen.pl script can't write directly into /usr/sbin because it requires root privileges that the Oracle DBA should not have. The best way to get the scripts into /usr/sbin is to ask your SA to create symbolic links from /usr/sbin to the script directory.

Creating a Save Group

Save Group is the name of a Legato resource that you create using nwadmin to initiate a Legato scheduled backup from the backup server. It's simply a text string that you create, and then associate with a Client resource definition. You create the named Save Group and then modify the related Client resource definition by checking a box with the name of the group in the Client resource. As usual, it's best to use a standard format for the names of groups related to Oracle backups so that they stand out clearly in the list. One way is to use the Legato server script name without the nsr prefix leading to group names like the following:

ora_closed_OD1

ora_open_OD1

ora_arch_OD1

By specifying a separate group for each type of Oracle backup for each database, you can run the scheduled backup of each type independently. After you have created the group name, you need to select the time at which to start backups of the associated Client resource each day, and then click Enable in the Save Group definition screen.

It's conceivable that you might not want your scheduled backup to run every day. This is fine because the Save Group start time doesn't determine whether the associated Client resource actually runs the backup. The start time determines when the backup process begins. This is a fairly subtle point. The named schedule in the Client resource determines whether the backup in the Client resource actually runs.

For example, you might configure the group ora_open_OD1 to start at 03:00 each day. This means at 03:00 each day, the Legato scheduler checks the backup schedule for the Client resource associated with the group ora_open_OD1. Legato only runs the backup if the schedule requires it. If the schedule specifies that backups run Monday through Friday only, the scheduler still attempts to initiate the backup at 03:00 on Saturday and Sunday. Once the Client resource schedule is checked, Legato determines that the backup runs only Monday through Friday. As a result, the backup returns immediately with a success code without actually running the RMAN backup.

Legato-Scheduled Backup Scripts

So far, we've created a Client resource using nwadmin to support a scheduled open backup of our database instance OD1 by specifying the following in the Client resource definition:

Saveset.   \u01\app\oracle\admin\OD1\scripts\
OMFD1.tape.catalog.open.rman

Backup command.   nsr_ora_open_OD1

In addition to these settings, it's necessary to check a Group and choose a Schedule from the list in the Client resource definition. This is an appropriate point at which to consider the contents of the nsr script set as the property of the Backup command. All of the generated nsr scripts are based on the Legato-supplied template in /usr/sbin/ nsrnmo. The purpose of the nsr_ora_open_OD1 script is to set up an appropriate UNIX environment before running RMAN with the Saveset command script. As a minimum, the nsr script must set the following environment variables:

ORACLE_HOME.   The $ORACLE_HOME of the database to be backed up.

PATH.   This must include the location of the nsrnmostart executable (for example, /usr/sbin).

Optionally, the following environment symbols can be set:

- LD_LIBRARY_PATH
- NSR_RMAN_ARGUMENTS
- NSR_SB_DEBUG_FILE
- PRECMD
- POSTCMD
- TNS_ADMIN

The POSTCMD and PRECMD symbols can be used to specify scripts to be executed before and after the backup. For an open backup, the PRECMD simply checks to make sure the database is up:

```
PRECMD="su oracle -c \"/u01/app/oracle/perl/dbcool_db_up.pl sid=OD1\""
```

For a closed backup, the database must be in STARTUP MOUNT mode, so the nsr_ora_closed_OD1 script contains the following as the PRECMD:

```
PRECMD="su oracle -c \"/u01/app/oracle/perl/dbcool_ora_shut.pl \
        sid=OD1 startup=mount\""
```

If the PRECMD fails (that is, if it doesn't return the value 0), then the RMAN backup doesn't take place. The NSR_RMAN_ARGUMENTS symbol can be used to pass additional command-line arguments to RMAN. In our case, we want to log the RMAN actions to a $ORACLE_SID-specific directory, which is consistent with our usual standard for logging SID-specific script information. We can do this by setting the value as follows:

```
NSR_RMAN_ARGUMENTS="msglog \
 /u01/app/oracle/admin/OD1/log/OMFD1.tape.catalog.open.rman.log \
append"
```

To actually execute the RMAN command script, the nsr_ora_open_OD1 script calls the nsrnmostart executable (which locates the RMAN executable), passes the Saveset value from the Client resource as the name of the RMAN script to execute (along with any other RMAN command-line arguments), and runs RMAN (as shown by the following lines):

```
#
# Export all necessary environment variables
#
export_environment_variables

#
# Call nsrnmostart to do the backups.
#

#print $BACKUP_COMMAND_LINE
${BACKUP_COMMAND_LINE} &
 Pid=$!
 wait $Pid
 nsrnmostart_status=$?
 if [ $nsrnmostart_status != 0 ] ; then
   echo "nsrnmostart returned status of "$nsrnmostart_status
   echo  $0 "exiting."
   exit 1
 fi

exit 0
```

NOTE Legato's scheduler only provides scheduling for Legato backups. If your organization uses an enterprisewide cross-platform scheduler such as Autosys from Computer Associates, an add-on module is available to enable Legato Save Groups to be scheduled from Autosys instead.

Full Sequence of Operations for a Scheduled Backup

It is useful to list the sequence of operations for a scheduled Legato backup as it may seem confusing at first:

1. The Legato server periodically checks the UNIX server clock for Save Groups that start now.

2. The Legato server runs any Save Group set to start at the current time.

3. The group identifies a Client resource definition.

4. The Client resource specifies a backup schedule.

5. If the backup is not scheduled to run, exit now; otherwise, continue.

6. The Client resource BACKUP command specifies an nsr script to run on the client.

7. The Client resource Saveset identifies an RMAN script to run on the client.

8. The Client resource BACKUP command and Saveset are passed to the nsrexecd daemon on the client.

9. nsrexecd runs the BACKUP command nsr script located in /usr/sbin.10. The nsr script identifies the RMAN executable to run.

10. The RMAN script identified by the Saveset value is passed to RMAN, which executes it.

11. The RMAN script streams data back to the RMAN server.

Miscellaneous Legato Environment Symbols

The example backup scripts have used a single environment symbol in the Legato tape channel allocation command to identify the backup server:

```
parms 'ENV=(NSR_SERVER=lg1.dbcool.com)'
```

The following are some other settings that you can enable through the ENV variable:

```
NSR_CHECKSUM=TRUE
NSR_DATA_VOLUME_POOL=Oracle
NSR_COMPRESSION=TRUE
NSR_DEBUG_FILE=/tmp/nsr.debug
```

The NSR_CHECKSUM is used to perform a checksum on backup data to give the highest degree of confidence that what is stored on tape is exactly what was streamed from RMAN. It has a slight performance cost, but is recommended. NSR_DATA_VOLUME_POOL requires the Legato administrator to configure a volume pool named Oracle explicitly for the purpose of holding Oracle-related backups. The use of a volume pool enables tape devices on the backup server to be associated with the named pool and enables a group of tape devices allocated solely for Oracle backups. If you want the best possible service guaranteed for your Oracle backups and restores, you need to be able to guarantee that one or more tape devices will be available at all times. If a nonexistent pool name is supplied, the default pool is used. The NSR_COMPRES-SION setting causes the RMAN data stream to be compressed on the backup client before it transmits across the network to the backup server. This saves network bandwidth, but may slow the writes to tape on the server, if the tape devices use hardware compression and attempt to compress data that is already compressed. The NSR_DEBUG_FILE setting is described in the section *Backup and Restore Troubleshooting*.

Querying the Media Manager

Legato provides the mminfo command-line utility to enable you to see exactly what's been stored on the backup server. This is another situation where a naming standard pays off. Because the Oracle backup pieces all contain the string ORA_, it's easy to find them. This enables the actual storage space on tape for all your Oracle backups to be identified easily. This simple example shows all Oracle backup pieces for the backup client srv1 on the backup server lg1 in the last 24 hours:

```
$ mminfo -s lg1 -c srv1 |grep ORA_
6023          srv1 11/06/01  224 MB full ORA_A_OMFD1_44506804644491b1d
6023        srv1 11/06/01 2000 MB full ORA_O_OMFD1_44506804719921u8d
```

Increasing Backup Throughput

If you have multiple devices allocated to your Oracle pool, you can reduce the time it takes for a large database backup to complete by streaming the backup to multiple tape devices at the same time. You need to do this very carefully because you don't want to tie up all of the tape devices at once. That would prevent other backups and restores from running at the same time. A setting for each tape device in the Legato server controls the number of target sessions allowed per device at the same time. Each channel allocation command in the backup script requires a target session on the device. As an example, if your tape devices are configured to allow a maximum of two target sessions and you have four devices available, then allocating five channels in the backup script results in three devices being streamed simultaneously:

```
allocate channel c1 type 'SBT_TAPE' parms 'ENV=(NSR_SERVER=lg1);
allocate channel c2 type 'SBT_TAPE' parms 'ENV=(NSR_SERVER=lg1);
allocate channel c3 type 'SBT_TAPE' parms 'ENV=(NSR_SERVER=lg1);
allocate channel c4 type 'SBT_TAPE' parms 'ENV=(NSR_SERVER=lg1);
allocate channel c5 type 'SBT_TAPE' parms 'ENV=(NSR_SERVER=lg1);
```

RMAN provides cumulative and differential backups to reduce the amount of backup data and conserve backup tape space and minimize the network bandwidth requirements during backup. If restore performance is the most important consideration, cumulative backups are preferable to differential backups because fewer incremental backups need to be applied during recovery. The introduction to this chapter emphasized that you back up data because you might need to perform restores. Options to reduce backup times, such as Legato parallel streaming and RMAN cumulative and differential backups, make backup and restore more complex. Consider making sufficient capacity available to perform full backups all the time. This is likely to provide the simplest and, therefore, most reliable backups and restores. Keep in mind that your end users are interested in end-to-end recovery time (which is the sum of tape restore time plus archived redo log application time) and this is what should drive the frequency of your backups and the techniques you use.

Saving Backup Space

If you run Legato NetWorker in your organization for file system backups and you also use Legato NetWorker for Oracle for your database backups, then you should avoid backing up Oracle database files through Legato file system backups. Such backups represent wasted space: You would never use them for an Oracle restore because you couldn't guarantee that they weren't being modified at the time of the backup. You can place a .nsr file in any directory to inform Legato file system backups that some files can be skipped recursively in the current directory and subdirectories. The following command ignores database files, control files, and online redo logs:

    +skip: *.dbf   *control   *.ctl *redo*.log

You could also include archived redo logs, although some DBAs like to have file backups of those files (which are perfectly fine) to give additional robustness to backups.

> **NOTE** Another approach to save space is to selectively back up named tablespaces and database files rather than the entire database, using the BACKUP command in the RMAN script. Although this saves space, it adds complexity to the backup procedure because you need to manage which files and tablespaces are backed up and when to do it.

Performing RMAN Restore

This section covers the basics of the RMAN restore and recover functionality. It's just as simple to perform RMAN restores as it is to perform RMAN backups. In this case, you create an RMAN command script, specify whether your original backup was to tape or disk, along with any datafiles, control files, and archived redo logs you want to restore, and RMAN does the hard work of locating and restoring the files, and, optionally, recovering the database. By default, RMAN restores the most recent versions of all files required.

A Simple Restore and Recovery

For the sake of example, let's say that you have just created a database in ARCHIVE LOG mode, backed it up, and done some processing that has caused a few archived redo logs to be generated. Next, you back up the archivelogs and remove them from disk. Now you want to test the restore and recovery of your database and archived redo logs to ensure that the backups worked. For the test, you keep the current control file and online redo logs, shut down the database, and physically remove datafiles belonging to all tablespaces except for your TEMPORARY tablespace named TEMP.

> **NOTE** Oracle never backs up TEMPORARY tablespaces that use tempfiles because by definition they contain transient data that never needs to be restored. However, the definition of the TEMPORARY tablespace and its datafile still exists in the Oracle data dictionary after a restore. If the tempfile is not present on disk, you can simply add a new one or drop and recreate the tablespace.

Before you recover the database, run STARTUP MOUNT. The following is an example of a restore and recover script that can get the database back to the current point in time based on the described scenario:

```
connect target /
connect catalog rman/xyz123@rmanp1.dbcool.com
run {
allocate channel c1 type disk;
restore database;
recover database;
}
```

Not only does the restore fetch the missing database files from the most recent backup, but it also restores any archived redo log files needed to recover the database to the current point in time without you requesting them. When RMAN is complete, you open the database in the usual way, for example, in SQL*Plus:

```
alter database open;
```

Now everything is back exactly the way it was. The previous example specified the use of the backup catalog during the restore and recovery. Using a backup catalog is highly recommended in general, but you need to have a fallback position for situations where the backup catalog is not available or where the use of a backup catalog can cause some undesired side effects after a restore. In these cases, rather than using a backup catalog, you can use backup information in the control file to restore your database.

Using the CONTROLFILE AUTOBACKUP Command

The previous example used the backup catalog to identify the files to restore. What happens if you lose your backup catalog and the disk with your control files crashes? In this case, you need to perform a restore and recovery, but you don't have a backup catalog or control file with a complete list of recent backups. Oracle9i has a new RMAN feature referred to as *control file autobackup* to help resolve this problem. By default, the feature is turned off. To turn it on, connect to the target database and the backup catalog using RMAN, and run the following command:

```
configure controlfile autobackup on;
```

You only need to do this once and the setting persists for all future backups. After you've turned autobackup on, whenever a run block in an RMAN backup script contains a backup command as the last command in the block, RMAN automatically backs up the control file, which contains the most recent backup information, to either disk or tape, depending on what type of backup is running. If you lose your current control file and your backup catalog database, you can restore the control file autobackup using a simple command:

```
restore controlfile from autobackup;
```

After you restore and mount the control file, you can use it to restore the rest of the database files from backup. How does the RESTORE CONTROLFILE know where to find the autobackup control file in the first place? At first sight, it seems like magic. The reason that the autobackup control file can be found is that it has a fixed name and location that Oracle chooses. For example:

```
/u01/app/oracle/product/9.0.1/dbs/c-3159171023-20011105-01
```

You can change the location and format of the control file autobackup name, but that defeats the purpose. The purpose of the autobackup control file name is that RMAN can find it for you without requiring you to provide the path of the file. The previous example shows the autobackup control file name and location for a disk backup. RMAN also chooses an appropriate name for tape backups that enables the control file to be restored without a name. Incidentally, if you happen to know the backup piece name (for example, by querying the media manager or because the piece is on disk), then you can specify the piece name explicitly using the following command instead:

```
restore controlfile from 'filename';
```

The autobackup file name actually comprises the DBID of the database, and a timestamp and sequence number. The DBID is crucial in enabling the control file backup to be identified. To see a test of how the control file backup can be used, SHUTDOWN IMMEDIATE the target database, and then remove the datafiles as before and the control files used by the database. Then STARTUP NOMOUNT the target database: It's not possible to mount it because there is no control file. Now run RMAN without any arguments and use the SET DBID command to set the DBID of the target database, which we know from the autobackup has the file name 315917102:

```
set DBID 3159171023

connect target

restore controlfile from autobackup;
```

The RESTORE CONTROLFILE command restores the control file to all the names specified in the init.ora file. Now that we have a control file, we can mount the target database and gain access to the list of database backups in it, and then restore and recover them. At no stage has the backup catalog been referenced because this example assumes it's not available. The RMAN log of the operation looks like the following, where the database has a single OMF control file:

```
channel ORA_DISK_1, looking for controlfile autobackup on day: 20011105
channel ORA_DISK_1, controlfile autobackup found: c-3159171023-20011105-02
channel ORA_DISK_1, controlfile autobackup restore complete
replicating controlfile
input filename=/u02/oradata/OMFD1/ora_xwrk4zgp.ctl
```

The following commands can be used to complete the restore and recovery by using exactly the same run block as before:

```
sql "alter database mount";
run {
allocate channel c1 type disk;
restore database;
recover database;
}
```

As a noncurrent control file has been used for the recovery, the database needs to be opened using:

```
alter database open resetlogs;
```

The use of CONTROLFILE AUTOBACKUP should be the default for all your database backups.

Restoring Noncurrent Files

You can restore and recover files to noncurrent versions by providing commands in the restore script to identify the point in time required before running the restore command. For example:

```
set until time 'OCT 15 2001 09:00:00'; # use a specific time . . .
set until scn 123749;                   # or an scn...
set until sequence 21;                  # ...or a log sequence

restore database;
```

If you use UNTIL TIME to specify the point in time without an explicit TO_DATE conversion, then you must set NLS_DATE_FORMAT in the UNIX environment before running RMAN to ensure that dates and times are matched correctly in the backup catalog or control file as follows:

```
$ export NLS_DATE_FORMAT='MON DD YYYY HH24:MI:SS'
```

Although RMAN automatically restores all of the archived redo logs required by your restore, you might need additional logs in some situations. You can restore specific archived redo logs in several different ways. For example, you can specify an explicit sequence of archived redo logs to restore as follows:

```
restore archivelog from logseq=10983 until logseq=11012 thread=1;
```

Restoring Files to Different Names and Locations

RMAN provides the SET NEWNAME FOR DATAFILE command for restoring backup files to a different location. After restoring the datafiles but before recovering them, you must run a SWITCH command in the control file to permanently change the names of the datafiles renamed. The SWITCH command is equivalent to the SQL statement ALTER DATABASE RENAME FILE. The SWITCH DATAFILE ALL is shorthand that you can use to switch all files for which SET NEWNAME was issued in a single operation:

```
run
{
# restore the datafiles to a new location
set newname for datafile '/u02/oradata/OMFD1/system01.dbf' to
'/emergency/system01.dbf';
set newname for datafile '/u02/oradata/OMFD1/users01.dbf' to
'/emergency/users01.dbf';
set newname for datafile '/u02/oradata/OMFD1/rbs01.dbf' to
'/emergency/rbs01.dbf';
set newname for datafile '/u02/oradata/OMFD1/temp01.dbf' to
'/emergency/temp01.dbf';

restore database;
switch datafile all; # updated control file with new filenames
recover database;
}
```

There are several possible reasons you might be restoring files to a different location. For example, you might have an emergency where you have lost a file system and need to get your production database back as soon as possible onto any file system with space. In this case, your restored and recovered database continues to operate as the production database. On the other hand, you might be restoring the database to a different server to test your restore procedures. In this case, *avoid* using a backup catalog during the restore and use a control file instead. If you use a backup catalog and SET NEWNAME during the restore, the catalog will assume that the changes to the file locations are permanent for your production database on the other server. This is due to the behavior of DBID and the fact that the production database has the same DBID as the test restore database. In addition to relocating database files on restore, you can relocate archivelogs, as shown in the following example:

```
run
{
# set a new location for logs 1 through 10.
set archivelog destination to '/tmp/arch';
restore archivelog from sequence 100 until sequence 110;
}
```

Managing Disk Backups

You shouldn't remove backups from disk without notifying RMAN. If RMAN expects to find a disk backup and it's not present, then the restore will fail: RMAN won't ignore a missing file and simply look for an earlier one. You can notify Oracle of the removal of a backup piece on disk using the CROSSCHECK command as follows:

```
allocate channel for maintenance type disk;
change backuppiece '/u02/OMFD1/backup/ORA_O_OMFD1_4450296051510fd8d775'
crosscheck;
```

You can check Oracle's view of what is currently on disk through the following SQL, where a value of A in the status column means that the backup piece should be present on disk and a value of X means that it has been removed and Oracle is aware of it:

```
select handle,status from v$backup_piece
where handle like '%ora02%' order by handle;
```

Running the CROSSCHECK command changes the status of a backup piece from A to X if the piece has been removed. When the file has a state of X, it will be searched for during restores. If you have problems with archived redo logs on disk that have been removed out of sequence, your backups will fail with the following message:

```
RMAN-06089: archived log 'log name' not found or out of sync with
catalog
```

In this case, as a last resort you can use the CHANGE ARCHIVELOG . . . DELETE command, which removes references from the control file and recovery catalog, and physically deletes the file from the operating system if it exists:

```
change archivelog '/u02/oradata/OMFD1/arch/T0001S0000004451.ARC' delete;
```

Disaster Recovery Restore with Legato

If you use Legato NetWorker for Oracle for your backups and take your backups straight to tape on a remote site, you're in a great position for getting your databases restored as quickly as possible in a disaster recovery situation. You can prepare for this scenario before it happens by ensuring that your disaster recovery server has the same file system layout as your production server. If you use large file systems as recommended, then you can restore all the files to their original locations without having to remap them, thus reducing the complexity of the restore process and making it faster.

> **NOTE** Part Five of this book contains other Oracle disaster recovery options, such as Oracle Data Guard, which is discussed in Chapter 23.

Prerequisites

Before you begin the restore on the disaster recovery server, you need to have an init.ora file and password file created in advance, along with all the directories where the restored database will be located. RMAN does not back up the init.ora file or the password file. You can recreate the password file, and if you're using Legato, you should have a regular file system backup from which you can restore the init.ora file.

> **NOTE** Oracle9i Release 2 provides new RMAN features to back up a server parameter file via the command BACKUP (SPFILE), and implicitly through the CONTROLFILE AUTOBACKUP command described previously. The ability to back up a server parameter file using RMAN is yet another reason you should start using server parameter files in preference to init.ora files.

If your production server is srvr1.dbcool.com and your disaster recovery server is dr1.dbcool.com, a Legato Client resource needs to exist for dr1 before you can restore srv1 data to it. If dr1 UNIX files are backed up using Legato, this will already exist. Legato provides a simple authentication facility, which means you need to explicitly register dr1 as an allowed restore client for srv1 backups. To do this, modify the Legato Client resource for srv1 and add the following to the Remote Access property:

```
Remote access: oracle@dr1.dbcool.com
```

Setting the Environment

You need to indicate to Legato before you begin the restore that although you are on the server dr1.dbcool.com, you want to restore backup data from srv1.dbcool.com: This is done through the NSR_CLIENT environment variable, which indicates the original server on which the backup was taken:

```
$ export NSR_CLIENT=srv1
```

Other environment variables are required to indicate the Legato backup server, the timestamp format if you are restoring to a point in time, and the NLS_LANG setting for the target database:

```
export NSR_SERVER=lg1.dbcool.com
export NLS_LANG=AMERICAN_AMERICA.WE8ISO8859P1
export NLS_DATE_FORMAT='Mon DD YYYY HH24:MI:SS'
```

Running the Restore Script

The RESTORE.RMAN command script, shown in the following code, can be used as a template for any Oracle restore. It restores control files, archived redo logs, and the database to a point in time. If you want the most recent versions, leave out the SET UNTIL command:

```
connect target
connect catalog rman/xyz123@rmanp1.dbcool.com
run {

allocate channel c1 type disk;
allocate channel c2 type 'SBT_TAPE';

set until time 'Nov 11 2001 19:00:00';

restore controlfile;

restore archivelog from time 'Nov 11 2001 14:00:00';

restore database;

sql "alter database mount";

recover database;
}
```

To perform the restore and recovery, STARTUP NOMOUNT the database first, set the environment for the target database using set_env, and then run the following script:

```
$ rman @restore.rman
```

After you have completed the restore and opened the database using ALTER DATABASE OPEN RESETLOGS, the database is ready for use. However, before you open it for use, you should make a backup immediately. Before you make the backup, you must connect to the target and catalog with RMAN and run the RESET DATABASE command to indicate to RMAN that this is a new incarnation of the database. If you don't do that, any backups after the OPEN RESETLOGS will fail with the following error:

```
RMAN-20003: target database incarnation not found in recovery catalog
```

Backup and Restore Troubleshooting

This section contains hints and tips for troubleshooting your backups and restores:

- Monitoring the backup progress
- Stopping a backup

- Testing RMAN backups and restores
- Debugging a Legato backup

Monitoring the Backup Progress

Use the following SQL to monitor the progress of your backups for both Oracle8*i* and Oracle9*i*:

```
select totalwork,elapsed_seconds,time_remaining,opname
from v$session_longops where time_remaining > 0
and opname like '%RMAN%';
```

```
  TOTALWORK   ELAPSED_SECONDS   TIME_REMAINING OPNAME
----------- ----------------- ---------------- -------------------------
    110876                66             4027 RMAN: full datafile
backup
```

Stopping a Backup

If your Oracle RMAN backup hangs, you can stop it by identifying the Oracle processes corresponding to your RMAN backup channels and killing them. We've already allowed for this possibility by using the SET COMMAND ID command in all of the backup scripts to enable easy identification of the Oracle server processes. For example, the following SET COMMAND ID command causes the supplied string to show up in the client_info column in v$session:

```
set command id to 'rman_noarchivelog_closed_OMFD1';
```

You can run the following SQL to identify the operating system processes corresponding to your RMAN backup channels as follows:

```
select spid, client_info
from v$process p, v$session s
where p.addr=s.paddr and client_info like 'id=rman%';
```

When you have a list of processes, you can kill them as follows using the UNIX kill command:

```
$ kill -9 pid1 pid2 pid3 ...
```

> **NOTE** You could try UNIX kill without -9 first, but it doesn't usually terminate a process waiting on an RMAN command.

Testing RMAN Backups and Restores

You can run your backup and restore commands with the VALIDATE option to test backup and restore operations without running them. For backup, VALIDATE causes RMAN to check files for physical and logical corruption, and confirms that all files exist in the correct locations without producing backup sets. For restore, RMAN checks that all the files for the requested restore are available without running the restore. Both options are recommended to ensure that backups and restores work the first time, especially for situations like business-critical disaster recovery. This example validates the database files and archived redo logs without backing them up:

```
run {
allocate channel c1 type disk;
backup full validate (database format '/u02/OMFD1/ORA_O_%d_%t%s%p%u');
backup validate (archivelog all format '/u02/omfd1/ORA_A_%d_%t%s%p%u');
}
```

Debugging a Legato Backup

By default, Legato creates a log on the client called dmo.messages. This should always be checked first if any Legato backup problems are experienced. On Solaris, it is located in /nsr/applogs. It's recommended that DBAs also have a read-only UNIX log on the Legato server itself. This can be useful in diagnosing Oracle backup problems. On the Legato server, logs are located in /nsr/logs. You can obtain detailed debug information from the Legato media management software layer through use of the NSR_DEBUG_FILE command in the tape channel allocation command, as shown in the following example:

```
allocate channel c1 type 'SBT_TAPE'
        parms 'ENV=(NSR_SERVER=lg1.dbcool.com,
                NSR_DEBUG_FILE=/tmp/nsrdebug.log)';
```

The debug information in the file should be sufficient to diagnose any Legato issues.

Summary

If you're not using RMAN to perform Oracle backups, you should start using it. RMAN is simply the most reliable and flexible tool for performing mission-critical Oracle backups to guarantee restore success. RMAN provides a wide range of commands for backing up and restoring individual components of the database to both disk and tape, and has the capability to test backups and restores without running them. It also provides corrupt block checking as an integral part of the backup process.

You can keep a permanent record of all backups and restores in a backup catalog. Should you lose the catalog, or should it become unavailable, you can still perform restores through information held in the control file. If you use the CONTROLFILE AUTOBACKUP feature of Oracle9i, RMAN can even restore control file backups for you without requiring you to provide the name and location. Be aware of the requirements imposed on database cloning by the database unique identifier DBID. Oracle has addressed this issue by providing the DBNEWID command-line utility in Oracle9i Release 2 to enable you to change the DBID manually.

If you are prepared to invest in the extra expense of media management software, then a solution like Legato can increase your RMAN throughput with parallel tape streaming and provide you with instant offsite tape backups, which represent an excellent disaster recovery facility for your Oracle databases.

Before you choose RMAN, you may need to be convinced that Oracle is committed to the long-term future of the product. Evidence of Oracle's commitment to RMAN is provided by the new features in Oracle9i. This chapter has covered the control file autobackup feature, but there are several others worthy of mention. For example, Oracle9i RMAN has the capability to perform media recovery on individual blocks in a datafile while the datafile remains online. The block media recovery feature is *only* available with RMAN. Oracle9i RMAN also includes the new NOT BACKED UP SINCE TIME option on the backup command to enable a partially completed backup (that failed) to be restarted without repeating previous work. Although any book on Oracle should always be read alongside the Oracle documentation because Oracle is continually changing, it's fair to say that RMAN is evolving more rapidly than some other products. Although that might not be such good news for this book, it's good news for Oracle customers.

## CHAPTER 19

Backup and Restore Using Export and Import

Every database administrator (DBA) uses Oracle export and import command-line utilities. The goal of this chapter is to provide best practices for running export and import in order to get the best out of both tools in terms of functionality and performance. Export and import both have some exciting new features for Oracle9*i* that make the tools much more powerful. For example, export to a point in time is supported through Oracle9*i* Flashback Query (covered in Chapter 17) and the resumable space allocation features of Oracle9*i* (refer to Chapter 6) enable import to suspend, rather than abort, when a space shortage exists. Best performance has always been a key requirement for both import and export. In the past there's been a shortage of information on which factors affect import performance, and this chapter aims to remedy that, based on a quantitative analysis.

This chapter covers the following topics:

- Using pre-export checks to reduce the chance of import errors
- Using parameter files for export
- National Language Considerations for export and import
- Exporting to a point in time using Oracle9*i* Flashback Query
- Maximizing export performance using direct path
- Limitations and security considerations for direct path
- Controlling the size of export files using UNIX file compression
- Using transportable tablespaces to speed up restore
- Running import for maximum performance

Running Pre-Export Checks

Before you carry out an export, make sure that all objects, triggers, and constraints that you intend to export have a status of VALID. You can check the STATUS column in DBA_OBJECTS, DBA_TRIGGERS, and DBA_CONSTRAINTS to confirm this. The check avoids a situation where the subsequent import fails because of problems originating with the objects in the database that were exported. My personal preference before running export is to create copies of dictionary tables to identify the objects to be exported and export those copies along with the rest of the data. This is useful for post-import checks to confirm that all the required objects were actually imported. Here are some examples:

```
create table exp_triggers as
select owner,trigger_name,status
from dba_triggers;

create table exp_constraints as
select owner,constraint_name,constraint_type,table_name
from dba_constraints;

create table exp_objects as
select *
from dba_objects;
```

Using Parameter Files for Export

I find myself frequently consulting the export documentation due to the sheer number of command-line options that export provides and the need to understand which are compatible and how they relate to each other. Here's a selection of some export error messages, and due to the number of arguments and possibility of conflicts, you've probably seen many more:

```
EXP-00044: must be connected 'AS SYSDBA' to do Point-in-time Recovery
. . .
EXP-00035: QUERY parameter valid only for table mode exports
EXP-00026: conflicting modes specified
EXP-00048: Tablespace mode not supported for normal export
ORA-29341: The transportable set is not self-contained
```

The first tip for getting the best out of export is to always use parameter files for running exports, rather than passing parameters on the command line. This has two main advantages. First, the parameter files serve as a record of what you did and are available for reuse in future exports when you have difficulty in remembering the exact combination of parameters to use. Second, the arcane and operating-system-specific translation of single quotes in the command-line argument list can be avoided by using a parameter file. The following examples compare the specification of the USERID and

QUERY parameter arguments on the command line with a parameter file, indicating how much easier it is to specify parameters using a file:

```
Command line:    userid=\'sys/syspass as sysdba\'
Parameter file: userid="sys/syspass as sysdba"

Command line:    query=\"where ENAME=\'SCOTT\'\"
Parameter file: query="where ename='SCOTT'"
```

Export Modes

Export can dump data based on the following different modes that are not compatible with each other. The top-level command-line options that distinguish the main features are in the following list:

- FULL=Y dumps a full export of all users and objects.
- USERS dumps a named list of users.
- TABLES dumps a named list of tables or table partitions.
- TABLESPACES dumps a list of tablespace metadata, used with TRANSPORT_TABLESPACE=Y.

You can run both the import and export command-line utilities with the HELP=Y option to list all the available options. The TABLES parameter supports the use of the SQL wildcard % and can be combined with the QUERY parameter to restrict both the number of tables dumped and the subsets of rows dumped. For example, the following export parameter restricts the objects dumped to those in the schema of SCOTT and ALLEN matching the supplied patterns:

```
tables=scott.%N%,allen.E%
```

You apply a WHERE clause to all the tables in the export list through the QUERY parameter. The parameter is applied to all tables in the list, and export fails for any tables where the QUERY column would raise an error, such as those tables without an ENAME column in the following example:

```
tables=scott.%N%,allen.E%
query="WHERE ENAME='SCOTT'"
```

Using the Compress Option

The default setting, COMPRESS=Y, causes the table creation statements in the export dump file to specify a single, large extent for use at import time, based on the total size of allocated extents in the export database. Compress is a somewhat misleading term because no actual compression of data takes place. Coalesce would probably be a better choice.

The use of COMPRESS=Y stems from the days when DBAs spent a lot of time exporting and importing data to defragment extents. This practice is no longer necessary provided that you use the UNIFORM extent allocation in your tablespace creation statements, as recommended in Chapter 2 and throughout this book. If you do need to defragment, consider using the MOVE command covered in Chapter 13 instead.

One side effect of using COMPRESS=Y is that you increase the chances of import failing if there isn't sufficient space available to allocate the large extent resulting from the use of COMPRESS=Y at export time. A better approach is to use uniform extent allocation for object storage allocation as shown in the following tablespace creation statement:

```
create tablespace ind
datafile  '/u02/app/oracle/oradata/OMFD1/ind01.dbf' size 1m
extent management local uniform size 128k;
```

Provided that you use COMPRESS=N at export time, and the import database uses the same uniform extent allocation and has the same physical file space as the export database, then your exported data is guaranteed to fit the destination database without a time-consuming pre-import analysis of available space. This is the recommended approach if you want to ensure that your exported data will fit into your import database the first time.

Exporting to a Point in Time

By default, Oracle provides read-consistency at the SQL statement level only. So if you were to SELECT * FROM DEPT and then later perform SELECT * FROM EMP, the possibility exists for the employees in the EMP table to refer to departments that were added after the SELECT * FROM DEPT took place. If an export dump were based on such inconsistent data, the import would fail because the integrity constraint on EMP would cause a constraint violation at import time, due to missing departments in DEPT.

Oracle provides transaction-level, rather than statement-level, read-consistency through the use of the SET TRANSACTION READ ONLY statement. When you run export with CONSISTENT=Y, export runs SET TRANSACTION READ ONLY as the first statement of the session to guarantee that all data exported is consistent to the point in time at the start of the export. The CONSISTENT=Y setting is the default, and there aren't many cases when you'll want to turn it off.

Oracle9*i* provides a major leap forward in export functionality by enabling you to specify that you want to export data consistent with any point in time in the past, not simply the current point in time, through the use of two new parameters related to Flashback Query:

```
FLASHBACK_SCN       SCN used to set session snapshot back to
FLASHBACK_TIME      time used to get the SCN closest to specified time
```

In the past it was necessary to carefully synchronize exports with business processing when there was a requirement to export business data to a particular point in time. For example, if a bank required an export of data at the close of business, it would be necessary to run the export at exactly the right time to ensure the correctness of the data. Using 9*i* and Flashback Query, the business can run a process to create a transaction marker to save the system change number (SCN) at the time of close of business, and the export can run any time afterwards using the SCN in the transaction marker. The export and the business process no longer need to be so tightly coupled, which is much more flexible and easier to manage.

One side effect of the new approach is that the undo needed to regenerate the data at the earlier point in time needs to remain available in exactly the same way it's required for a CONSISTENT=Y export. The difference is that undo requirements may increase, because undo is required for an earlier point in time, instead of just the current point in time. Through the use of automatic undo management and ALTER SYSTEM SET UNDO_RETENTION, undo can be kept for a guaranteed period of time in Oracle9*i* to ensure that it's available to meet the export requirements. This extra undo requirement is the cost of the increased flexibility.

Here's an example to demonstrate the functionality, based on the existence of the standard 14-row EMP table in the SCOTT schema. The first step is to determine the current system SCN through the following SQL:

```
select dbms_flashback.get_system_change_number from dual;


  GET_SYSTEM_CHANGE_NUMBER
  -------------------------
                41515551378
```

The dbms_flashback.get_system_change_number function is used to fetch the current system SCN to use as a transaction marker. An application could store this value in a table, along with a timestamp and a string to identify a key transaction-processing event such as "End-of-day batch complete." For simplicity, we simply fetch the value. The next step is to remove some rows from EMP and commit. The following SQL removes five rows from EMP:

```
select count(*) from emp;


  COUNT(*)
  ----------
          14

delete from emp where rownum <=5;

commit;

select count(*) from emp;


  COUNT(*)
  ----------
           9
```

The final step is to export the table SCOTT.EMP using the prechange SCN to specify that we wish to export the data consistent with the predelete state using the following parameter file:

```
userid=system/manager
tables=scott/tiger
file=emp.dmp
direct=y
flashback_scn=41515551378
```

Flashback Query requires the EXECUTE privilege on the DBMS_FLASHBACK procedure, which isn't granted to SCOTT, so SYSTEM is used to perform the export in this example. The export log confirms that the data exported is the predelete version containing 14 rows, rather than the current 9 rows, based on the predelete SCN value of 41515551378 used in the parameter file:

```
Connected to: Oracle9i Enterprise Edition Release 9.0.1.1.0 - Production
With the Partitioning option
JServer Release 9.0.1.0.0 - Production
Export done in US7ASCII character set and AL16UTF16 NCHAR character set

About to export specified tables via Direct Path ...
Current user changed to SCOTT
. . exporting table                           EMP          14 rows exported
Export terminated successfully without warnings.
```

Maximizing Export Performance Using Direct Path

The best way to speed up exports is to use the following parameter:

```
direct=y
```

The use of direct=y causes Oracle to bypass the Oracle SQL processing engine to read data directly from the database files before writing them to your export dump file. Tables containing certain data types, such as large objects (LOBs) and objects, can only be exported using the conventional path exports. Oracle export using direct path automatically switches into conventional path mode for such objects, which are clearly indicated in the export log output, for example:

```
EXP-00067: Table DEF$_AQCALL will be exported in conventional path.
```

If you choose to use conventional path exports instead of direct path you should ensure that the BUFFER parameter (in bytes) is set to a high value, such as 1,000,000, to ensure that the SQL SELECT operations performed during export to fetch rows take maximum advantage of the Oracle Call Interface (OCI) array-processing interface. A larger buffer reduces the number of OCI execute calls required to fetch the same number of rows. The default buffer size is 64K.

It's not unusual to see a 30 to 50 percent reduction in export time through the use of direct path export compared to a conventional path export of the same data. The RECORDLENGTH parameter can be used to tune the performance of direct path export. The maximum value is 64K. Experiments indicate that changing the setting doesn't make a very significant difference to export performance, maybe giving an extra 5 to 10 percent reduction in elapsed time.

Some parameters are not compatible with the use of direct=y. For example, you can't do direct path exports for transportable tablespaces or use the QUERY parameters to export subsets of row data.

> **NOTE** When using direct=y, you need to ensure that the RECORDLENGTH parameter is set to the same value on import and export when the databases involved run on different operating systems. If you still experience import problems in this case, avoiding direct=y for export should fix the problem.

Security Considerations for Direct Path

If you use direct=y to export data protected by Virtual Private Database (VPD), as covered in Chapter 5, then the security provided by VPD is *not* enforced, because the Oracle SQL interface is bypassed in this case, and the SQL interface is required to apply the VPD security function. Oracle label security implemented through fine-grained access control (covered in Chapter 25) is also not enforced. When these options are used with conventional path export, then protected data is not exported and export completes with the following warning message:

```
EXP-79 "Data in table %s is protected. Conventional
    path may only be exporting partial table."
```

> **NOTE** The SYS user and other Oracle9*i* users granted the EXEMPT ACCESS POLICY privilege (either through a role or directly) are exempt from VPD and Oracle label security enforcement in both direct and conventional path exports.

Controlling the Size of Export Files

You can control the size of your export dumps by splitting the output into files of fixed size using the FILESIZE argument or by using a UNIX pipe in place of the real file and compressing off the pipe. You can use these two techniques together. In order to create dump files larger than 2GB, your operating system may require large file support. Your operating system documentation will provide this information. This parameter file splits the export into four files.

```
userid=sys/pass
direct=y
recordlength=65535
full=y
filesize=1M
file=/u02/full1.dmp,/u03/full2.dmp,/u04/full3.dmp,/u04/full4.dmp
volsize=0
```

This splits the export across files of 1MB in size. You can specify the size in units of bytes K, M, or G. Unfortunately, if your export data requirement is larger than the total size of the files you specify, import will prompt you for the name of the next file. This is very inconvenient, as a large export is definitely the type of job that you want to run in unattended mode and have work the first time. You can protect yourself against this possibility by ensuring you provide sufficient files and space to cope with the total space requirements. The following SQL will give you an overestimate of the space requirements of your export file:

```
select sum(bytes)
from dba_segments
where segment_type <> 'INDEX'
and owner <> 'SYS';
```

There's no need to include the index data size, because the export file contains the SQL needed to recreate the indexes rather than the index data. Many of the SYS-owned objects are not exported so you can ignore them. The space is overestimated because the SQL includes space *allocated* to segments other than indexes, whereas export actually writes out the row data, which is typically less (sometimes a lot less) than the allocated space. Alternatively, you could ANALYZE the main schemas being exported and get a better estimate based on the row data actually present using the following:

```
SELECT SUM(NUM_ROWS*AVG_ROW_LEN)
FROM DBA_TABLES;
```

You can get a pretty exact estimate of the space requirements if you're prepared to take the time to export the data to a UNIX pipe and read the pipe to get the size of the data streamed through it. To accomplish this, you need to do the following:

1. Create a pipe.

2. Export to the pipe.

3. Read data from the pipe and measure the size of it.

Here's an example:

```
$ mknod /tmp/pipe p
$ wc -c </tmp/pipe >/tmp/size.log &
$ imp parfile=size.par
```

This relies on the existence of the UNIX word count (wc) utility to count the bytes read from the UNIX pipe /tmp/pipe that must also be specified in the export parameter file size.par as the FILE parameter as follows:

```
userid=sys/pass
direct=y
recordlength=65535
full=y
file=/tmp/pipe
volsize=0
log=full.log
```

After the export is complete, the file /tmp/size.log contains the size of the export in bytes. Given that a full export is likely to be a long and time-critical task, you need it to work the first time. This pipe-based method is recommended for ensuring that you can correctly size your dump file requirements in advance.

Having demonstrated the use of a pipe to measure the likely dump file size, it's straightforward to write to the pipe and use a UNIX command-line utility to compress the export data stream instead of counting the bytes. This is recommended if the first thing you typically do after creating an export dump is to compress it. You can eliminate the separate compression stage and compress the data on-the-fly instead, which means you don't need to have sufficient disk space to hold the dump file, just the compressed dump file. Given that a typical export dump is highly compressible, especially if it contains many unused blocks, you can easily save 50 percent or more of your uncompressed space requirements.

You have two main options for compression of your export data. You can use the UNIX compress utility or, better still, the Free Software Foundation gzip utility. The gzip utility typically provides greater compression for the same elapsed time compared to UNIX compress. You can also tune gzip minimize space or completion time requirements. UNIX compress requires a parameter file specifying a precreated pipe, such as compress.par:

```
userid=system/manager
direct=y
recordlength=65535
full=y
file=/tmp/pipe.compress
volsize=0
```

To create the pipe and execute export using the pipe, the following commands are required:

```
$ mknod /tmp/pipe.compress p
$ compress -c </tmp/pipe.compress >full.dmp.Z &
$ exp parfile=compress.par
```

The gzip utility can be used in a similar way to UNIX compress. This method also requires a parameter file, such as gzip.par, specifying a precreated pipe:

```
userid=system/manager
direct=y
```

Table 19.1 Export Compression Performance

COMPRESSION METHOD	SPACE (BYTES)	SAVING PERCENTAGE	TIME (SECONDS)
None	3473355	0	177
Compress	992987	72	193
Gzip	508350	85	183

```
recordlength=65535
full=y
file=/tmp/pipe.gzip
volsize=0
```

To create the compressed dump file using gzip, a pipe followed by export is required, as follows:

```
$ mknod /tmp/pipe.gzip p
$ gzip -c </tmp/pipe.gzip >full.dmp.gz &
```

Table 19.1 contains some figures showing space savings using compression, based on a small export and a single-processor Solaris server. It shows that gzip gives a higher-compression ratio than compress, and that both save a lot of space, compared to the noncompressed case.

Compression can provide a significant space savings for your export dumps. Because compression is a highly central processing unit (CPU)-intensive activity, it's possible that the elapsed time may increase compared to a standard file export, depending on the power of your processors and the speed of your disks. In order to import using a pipe, you specify a pipe in the parameter file, reverse the direction of data flow into the pipe, and use decompression instead of compression. Here is an example:

```
$ mknod /tmp/pipe.uncompress p
$ uncompress -c >/tmp/pipe.uncompress <full.dmp.Z &
$ exp parfile=compress.par
```

National Language Considerations for Export and Import

Consider a situation where your database was created with an 8-bit character set, such as WE8ISO8859P1, and the data you intend to export actually contains 8-bit characters such as those found in French or Spanish. Chapter 2 contains more information on database character sets. If you don't set the NLS_LANG symbol appropriately in the UNIX environment before the export, it's possible that some of your 8-bit characters will be exported as 7-bit characters, which means that data is actually modified and won't match the original database when you import it. If you see the warning message "possible charset conversion" at either export or import time, that's a clear indication that character set conversion may be taking place. Here are the export messages you receive in the previous example:

```
Export done in US7ASCII character set and AL16UTF16 NCHAR character set
server uses WE8ISO8859P1 character set (possible charset conversion)
```

You can avoid the conversion by making sure the national language support (NLS) environment is set correctly before you run export and before you import the same data into another database. If the environment is set correctly, you won't receive a warning message. This sets the correct environment for the previous example in the Bourne or Bash shell:

```
$ NLS_LANG=AMERICAN_AMERICA.WE8ISO8859P1; export NLS_LANG
```

Keep in mind that export doesn't actually store the character set name used at export time in the dump file. Instead a numeric ID is used to represent the character set. You can use a UNIX utility like "od" to dump out the header of an export dump in hexadecimal format to determine the character set if you aren't sure which NLS settings were used at the time of the export. The third byte value in the dump contains the numeric character set ID. In the following example, us7ascii.dmp was exported using character set ID 1 (US7ASCII) and we8iso8859p1.dmp was exported using character set ID 1f (WE8ISO8859P1), as shown in a hexadecimal dump of the first few bytes of each file:

```
$ od -x us7asii.dmp  | head -1
0000000 0300 0145 5850 4f52 543a 5630 392e 3032
$ od -x we8iso8859p1.dmp  | head -1
0000000 0300 1f45 5850 4f52 543a 5630 392e 3032
```

The Oracle8 functions NLS_CHARSET_NAME and NLS_CHARSET_ID can be used to map character set IDs to character set names.

Using Transportable Tablespaces

Before using import to restore exported data into a database, you should first consider transportable tablespaces as a much faster way to achieve the same thing. Transportable tablespaces are a feature of Oracle8*i* and later that enable you to move data physically between different databases running on the same operating system by transferring tablespace data in the form of datafiles. Prior to 8*i*, such an operation required a conventional export and import of row data. The operation would typically incur large input/output (I/O) and CPU overheads due to the redo generation from data insertion and index creation on the destination database during import, as well as constraint validation. The export on the source database would itself incur considerable I/O and CPU overhead. Transportable tablespaces address these problems.

Transportable tablespaces are particularly well suited to the migration of historical partitioned data from a production database into a data warehouse. Previously, the movement of data to the warehouse would have required a purge operation in the production database using a SQL DELETE, with all the attendant redo generation from data and index block changes. With suitable partitioning in place, the production tablespace can be unplugged from the production database and plugged in to the data warehouse with minimal overhead on both databases.

To use this feature, you simply export the tablespace metadata (rather than the row data of a traditional export) and use an operating system utility to copy the datafiles in the tablespace to the destination database. Then you plug in the source datafiles into the destination database by importing the metadata. You should be aware of some restrictions, however. The tablespaces being exported must be read only for the export to succeed, and the destination database must not have an existing tablespace of the same name. For transportation between databases of version 8*i*, the database block sizes must match. In Oracle9*i*, this restriction is lifted and 9*i* destinations can plug in tablespaces with any block size from another 9*i* database or even an 8*i* database. The source and target database must use the same character set and national character set. The final restriction is that the data in the exported tablespaces must be self-contained. This last restriction is easiest to understand with a simple example.

A Simple Example

This section describes the configuration for a simple transportable tablespace example. It assumes you already have a schema SCOTT containing the regular EMP table. Next, create two tablespaces, which are required to demonstrate the requirement for the data to be self-contained, and grant SCOTT a quota on them, as SYSTEM:

```
create tablespace ind
datafile  '/u02/app/oracle/oradata/OMFD1/ind01.dbf' size 1m
extent management local uniform size 128k;

create tablespace tab
datafile  '/u02/app/oracle/oradata/OMFD1/tab01.dbf' size 1m
extent management local uniform size 128k;

alter user scott quota unlimited on tab;
alter user scott quota unlimited on ind;
```

Next, create a copy of EMP, EMP_TRANS, to be used in the example, and create a primary key constraint and an index on EMP_TRANS in the IND tablespace:

```
create table emp_trans tablespace tab as select * from emp;

alter table scott.emp_trans
add constraint pk_emp_trans primary key
(
empno
) using index tablespace ind;

create index i0_emp_trans on emp_trans(ename) tablespace ind;
```

Understanding the Self-Contained Data Requirement

Before you attempt to perform a transportable tablespace export, you can perform an analysis in advance to check that your export data is self-contained. In our case, we have a table, EMP_TRANS, in the TAB tablespace that has dependencies on two objects in the IND tablespace, the index I0_EMP_TRANS and the primary key constraint index PK_EMP_TRANS. That means the data in the TAB tablespace that we want to export is *not* self-contained. You can see issues that affect the self-contained data requirement by querying the SYS.PLUGGABLE_SET_CHECK view:

```
select reason from sys.pluggable_set_check
where ts1_name='TAB';


REASON
----------------------------------------------------------------------
Tables and associated indexes not fully contained in the pluggable set
Table and Index enforcing primary key/Unique constraint not in same
tablespace
```

In fact, only the existence of the constraint (the second REASON) will prevent the export of the TAB tablespace from running. The statement about the index is a warning that if you export TAB only, then an index, which is probably present to increase performance, will not exist in the destination tablespace after TAB is plugged in. You can distinguish between self-contained data warnings and violations by executing the transport_set_check procedure in the dbms_tts package to find violations:

```
begin sys.dbms_tts.transport_set_check('TAB',true);  end;
/

select violations from sys.transport_set_violations;


VIOLATIONS
----------------------------------------------------------------------
-------------------------------------------------
Index SCOTT.PK_EMP_TRANS in tablespace IND enforces primary constraints
of table SCOTT.EMP_TRANS in tablespace TAB
```

The result of the query shows that the table TAB tablespace has a dependency on the IND tablespace through the existence of the PK_EMP_TRANS primary key index on EMP_TRANS. In order for your transportable tablespace export to succeed, you must either export both TAB and IND tablespaces to meet the self-contained data requirement or specify the parameter constraints=n at export time, which works around the problem by not exporting the constraint. If you decide to use constraints=n, you should be fully aware of the impact of not having integrity constraints in place on the destination database. For the purpose of this example, we decide to transport both TAB and IND to keep the index and primary key in the destination database, resulting in an export parameter file, trans_exp.par, that looks like this:

```
userid="sys/syspass as sysdba"
tablespaces=tab,ind
transport_tablespace=y
log=trans_exp.log
file=trans.dmp
```

Before the export, performed in this example using "exp parfile=trans_exp.par," be aware that a SYSDBA connection is mandatory for transportable tablespace exports, and that all tablespaces exported must be in read-only mode as follows:

```
alter tablespace TAB read only;

alter tablespace IND read only;
```

Once the export dump, trans.dmp, has been created, everything is now in place to copy the TAB and IND tablespace datafiles to the destination database, which is ready to plug in the TAB and IND tablespaces. It's your responsibility to copy the source database datafiles to the appropriate names and locations for the destination database, using whatever tools you choose. In this example, we copy to the following names, using a destination database with a system ID (SID) of OMFD2:

```
Source:      /u02/oradata/OMFD1/ind01.dbf
Destination: /u02/oradata/OMFD2/ind01.dbf

Source:      /u02/oradata/OMFD1/tab01.dbf
Destination: /u02/oradata/OMFD2/tab01.dbf
```

To import the tablespaces, set the environment to OMFD2 and use a parameter file, trans_imp.par, which contains the destination datafiles copied from the source database:

```
userid="sys/sysomfd2 as sysdba"
tablespaces=tab,ind
transport_tablespace=y
datafiles=(/u02/oradata/OMFD2/ind01.dbf,
/u02/oradata/OMFD2/tab01.dbf)
log=trans_imp.log
file=trans.dmp
```

You can use any order for the database files in the DATAFILES parameter, because import works out the correct order in the destination database by using metadata in the export file and information in the file header. After running the import into OMFD2, you can check which tablespaces are plugged in using the following SQL:

```
select tablespace_name,plugged_in
from dba_tablespaces where plugged_in='YES';
```

```
TABLESPACE_NAME    PLUGGED_IN
----------------- -----------
TAB                YES
IND                YES
```

Running Import for Maximum Performance

This section contains tips and techniques for getting the best import performance. The import example is based on a production database schema export with 200MB of index data and 400MB of table data. Importing a production database schema into a test database is a typical DBA task, which gives the example some real-world relevance. The schema used has the following object types, constraint types, and counts:

```
Tables          50
Indexes        137
Check          134
Primary Key     50
Foreign Key     50
Unique           2
```

The import parameter file uses the following settings to import from the production schema PROD to the development schema DEV:

```
userid=system/manager
fromuser=prod
touser=dev
file=prod.dmp
grants=n
log=prod.log
```

The GRANTS=N parameter is set to prevent the production database grants from being imported. In this case, the development database has a different set of usernames from the production database, and GRANTS=N prevents lots of warning messages that would occur from attempts by import to assign privileges to nonexistent users.

Untuned Import Performance

Although the performance statistics reported are interesting, the purpose of this section is not to set rules in stone for getting the best import performance. Instead, the goal is to demonstrate how to relate the statistics to the causes of performance problems and demonstrate how to make changes to the database and import configuration to speed things up. The first import takes 22 minutes, and the test database is configured with the DBCOOL_MON package (downloadable from the companion web site) to collect all events and statistics for the session. To identify the session, it's necessary to search the DBCOOL_SESSION_LOGOFF table that contains the program name and session identifier of the import session in the AUDSID column. An analysis of the wait event times for this session shows the following waits:

```
select time_waited,event from
DBCOOL_SESSION_EVENT_V
where audsid=10 order by 1 desc;


   TIME_WAITED EVENT
   ------------ ----------------------------------------
        31545 direct path read
        17883 direct path write
         9131 log file switch (checkpoint incomplete)
         8274 log file switch completion
         5066 db file sequential read
         3008 db file scattered read
         2598 log buffer space
```

As an experienced DBA, familiar with the contents of Chapter 9, you should be aware that the cause of direct path read and write events is disk sorts, due to the bulk index creation performed by import after the row data has been inserted. To confirm your suspicions, you can check the sort statistics for the session in DBCOOL_SES-STAT_V:

```
select name,value from DBCOOL_SESSTAT_V
where audsid=10
and name ='sorts (disk)';


NAME            VALUE
--------------- --------
sorts (disk)       15
```

Avoiding Disk Sorts

Sure enough, the presence of disk sorts is evident. To avoid disk sorts, you need to increase the sort area size database parameter to a large enough value to ensure that all sorts take place in memory. Memory speed is much faster than disk speed. Check the database parameter sort_area_size and you'll find that it's set to 65K. That's fine for the production database, but no good for the test database import. However, you only want to change the setting for the import session, not for all database sessions, because that could potentially waste a lot of memory. To meet this requirement, you create an AFTER LOGON database trigger, which sets the sort_area_size to a large value for import sessions only. You can determine the approximate sort_area_size by checking the maximum index size in the import schema using the following SQL:

```
SELECT MAX(BYTES)
FROM DBA_SEGMENTS
WHERE SEGMENT_TYPE='INDEX'
WHERE OWNER='DEV';
```

Having determined the sort_area_size, a trigger is created as SYSTEM that looks for sessions running import and sets the sort_area_size to a large value for those sessions. In this example, the largest index is 80MB, so the sort_area_size is set to that value, plus an extra 50 percent, to ensure that the sort takes place in memory using the following trigger:

```
create trigger trg_sort_area_size after logon on database
declare
begin

    for rec in (select program from v$session
                where audsid=userenv('sessionid')
                and program like 'imp%') loop
       execute immediate 'alter session set sort_area_size=120000000';
    end loop;

exception
  when others then
    null;
end;
/
```

It's important that the trigger uses an exception handler to ignore errors. It's a bad idea in this case for a SQL error in the trigger to raise an unhandled exception, as that will prevent any session from connecting to the database whether or not it's running import. A rerun of the import after first dropping all the objects in the DEV schema reduces the elapsed time to 13 minutes and 15 seconds, a 40 percent reduction from the original. An inspection of the wait events shows that no direct path reads or writes have taken place:

```
select time_waited,event from
DBCOOL_SESSION_EVENT_V
where audsid=20 order by 1 desc;


TIME_WAITED    EVENT
------------   ------------------------------------------
      11112    log file switch completion
      10491    log file switch (checkpoint incomplete)
       5101    db file sequential read
       2415    log buffer space
       2318    db file scattered read
```

Avoiding Log Switch Waits

There is more potential room for reducing the log switch wait times, because the "log file switch (checkpoint incomplete)" event indicates that we don't have sufficient redo log groups, causing log switches to wait while the next log in the sequence is in use. The total redo size generated by the import is given by:

```
select name,value from DBCOOL_SESSTAT_V
where audsid=20
and name like 'redo size';
```

```
NAME            VALUE
----------  ----------
redo size   624535100
```

An inspection of the redo logs shows two groups, each with a single 5MB log. We add another 8 log groups of the same size to make 10 total, using SQL like this:

```
ALTER DATABASE ADD LOGFILE GROUP 3 ('/u02/oradata/ORAD1/redo03.log')
SIZE 5M;
```

Another rerun of the import, after dropping all the objects in the DEV schema, reduces the time elapsed time to 11 minutes, nearly half of the original 21 minutes. An inspection of the wait events shows that events related to log file switch completion have been much reduced:

```
select TIME_WAITED,EVENT
from DBCOOL_SESSION_EVENT_V
where audsid=32 order by 1 desc;
```

```
  TIME_WAITED EVENT
------------- ----------------------------------------
         6564 log buffer space
         4955 db file sequential read
         2271 log file switch (checkpoint incomplete)
         2124 db file scattered read
         1153 log file switch completion
```

It's worth noting at this point that the traditional SQL tracing often used for Oracle performance management and enabled using ALTER SESSION SET SQL_TRACE TRUE has not been required. We are simply looking at the events that the import session spends the most time waiting for and taking steps to reduce the time. It's now worth considering increasing the size of the log buffer from which data is flushed into the online redo log files as a result of data block changes during import. However, at this point, you should be considering stopping your tuning, based on your original goals. Even eliminating the log buffer space wait is only going to gain another 10 percent of savings. It useful to include the CPU used by the session along with the event wait times, and this can be done using the following SQL:

```
select TIME_WAITED,EVENT
from DBCOOL_SESSION_EVENT_V
```

```
where audsid=32
union
select VALUE,NAME
from DBCOOL_SESSTAT_V
where audsid=32
and name = 'CPU used by this session'
order by 1 desc;


  TIME_WAITED EVENT
------------- ----------------------------------------
        39889 CPU used by this session
         6564 log buffer space
         4955 db file sequential read
         2271 log file switch (checkpoint incomplete)
         2124 db file scattered read
         1153 log file switch completion
```

Tuning the Log Buffer

It's clear that use of the CPU is the main cause of elapsed time, and this is where efforts to further reduce the elapsed time should be directed. It's worth trying to reduce the log buffer space wait by increasing the log buffer size by a factor of 10 from 163840 to 1638400. This requires a database restart. Rerunning import now eliminates the log buffer space wait, and reduces the elapsed time to 10 minutes and 10 seconds, down from 11 minutes, with the event list now containing the following:

```
TIME_WAITED    EVENT
------------- ----------------------------------------
        38895 CPU used by this session
         5219 db file sequential read
         3608 log file switch (checkpoint incomplete)
         1903 db file scattered read
         1503 log file switch completion
```

Using Array Inserts and Commits

So far, we haven't taken full advantage of Oracle's array-processing features. During imports, Oracle fills up a buffer of a size specified by the BUFFER parameter with rows before insert. The default size of this buffer is operating system dependent. A large buffer reduces the number of OCI execute operations that need to be performed. By increasing the buffer size and using commit=y to specify that a commit should take place after each buffer insert, we can speed up import by making the process more efficient.

By default, commit=n is used, and Oracle commits after each table has been populated. Using commit=y means more commits are executed, but it places a limit on rollback requirements, because each commit is guaranteed never to insert more than a buffer-size amount of data. This improves import performance if your dump file contains any large tables. Keep in mind that array inserts are not performed for tables containing certain data types such as LOB and LONG. In these cases, the use of commit=y causes a commit after each row. Commit is a relatively expensive operation, so the import of tables containing LONG and LOB columns needs special care where commit=y is concerned. In our example, we don't have any LONG or LOB columns, and the following parameters can be added to the existing import parameter file:

```
buffer=5000000
commit=y
```

The import now completes in 9 minutes and 14 seconds, another 10 percent improvement on the previous results. Table 19.2 shows some of the most significant differences in session statistics between this run and the previous one.

Table 19.3 shows the stepwise improvements made at each stage of the import process.

Table 19.2 Import Statistics Using commit=y

STATISTIC	DEFAULT BUFFER COMMIT = N	BUFFER = 5000000 COMMIT = Y
SQL*Net roundtrips to/from client	39708	1110
bytes sent via SQL*Net to client	4176748	61963
execute count	53645	14493
immediate (CR) block cleanout applications	44529	1
user calls	39708	1110

Table 19.3 Import Performance Improvements

CHANGE	ELAPSED TIME (SECONDS)	PERCENT OF ORIGINAL
None (untuned)	1,322	100
Increase sort_area_size	795	60
Increase redo log groups	659	50
Increase log buffer size	610	46
Increase import buffer and use COMMIT=Y	554	42

Using NOLOGGING to Reduce Redo Size

If your redo write performance is having a detrimental effect on your import performance, you can reduce the amount of redo generated by performing import with indexes=n and creating the indexes afterwards from a SQL script that specifies the NOLOGGING option on all the index creation statements. This adds complexity to the import process but may be worth considering if the reduction in import time can be justified. First, you need to create the index creation script by running import using the INDEXFILE parameter. In this case, import actually inserts no data, but it instead creates a script containing index creation SQL for all the indexes in the dump file. This script *doesn't* include indexes used to implement primary and unique constraints. These constraint-related indexes are still created by the import process. To create an index script, add the following parameter to the parameter file and run import:

```
indexfile=indexes.sql
```

The index file contains index creation statements like the following one:

```
CREATE INDEX "SCOTT"."I0_EMP" ON "EMP" ("ENAME")
TABLESPACE "IND" LOGGING ;
```

You can modify the indexes.sql script and change TABLESPACE "IND" LOGGING to TABLESPACE "IND" NOLOGGING globally. Next, replace the indexfile=indexes .sql parameter in the parameter file with indexes=n and rerun the import to import the data without the indexes. After the import has completed, run the indexes.sql script to create all the indexes. This avoids redo generation from the index creation statements in the export dump file.

You can actually create *all* the indexes, including those generated from primary key and unique constraints, without generating redo. If you want to consider this option, then another level of complexity is added to the import process. The capability to perform this operation relies on the behavior of Oracle and import. Oracle enables you to turn an existing index into a primary or unique key constraint, and import enables you to import constraints in a separate operation using the CONSTRAINTS parameter, which by default is set to Y. This can be seen using an example based on a primary key on the EMP table. In this case, the export dump file actually contains two statements, one to create the index on which the primary key is based, and another run afterwards to create the primary key constraint based on the index, as follows:

```
CREATE UNIQUE INDEX "PK_EMP" ON "EMP" ("EMPNO") TABLESPACE "IND"
LOGGING;

ALTER TABLE "EMP" ADD CONSTRAINT "PK_EMP" PRIMARY KEY ("EMPNO")
USING INDEX TABLESPACE "IND" ENABLE;
```

If you generate a script, cons_indexes.sql, to precreate the constraint indexes using NOLOGGING, then you can run import in the following order to create all indexes, including those belonging to constraints, with NOLOGGING. In the final import run, you import no data or indexes, but import constraints to turn the existing indexes into constraints:

```
1. imp indexfile=indexes.sql # generate index SQL
2. imp indexes=n constraints=n # data without indexes/constraints
3. sqlplus @indexes.sql # use NOLOGGING
4. sqlplus @cons_indexes.sql # use NOLOGGING
5. imp rows=n indexes=n constraints=y ignore=y
```

The fifth step executes the ADD CONSTRAINT command like the one shown for the EMP table. This step converts existing indexes, created at step four, into constraints. Our original import had a single step. Now we need to use five steps. Each extra step introduces the possibility of an error that may require a complete rerun of the whole process. If you intend to increase the performance of import at the cost of process complexity, make sure that you perform a dry run first. One additional challenge of this approach is the requirement to generate the index creation statements for the constraints in advance. A document on the companion Web site titled "Using Oracle Change Manager" shows you how to reverse engineer the SQL required to do this.

NOTE Unrecoverable data resulting from NOLOGGING has implications for standby databases that you should be aware of. Standby databases are covered in Chapter 23.

Importing when Objects Exist

Sometimes you need to refresh the data contents in a schema by truncating the existing table data and leaving all the schema objects in place, rather than recreating all the object definitions from scratch from the dump file. Never import data into a database where the indexes are already in place unless you fully understand the performance implications. The performance degradation, compared to creating the indexes in bulk after all table data is inserted, can make the import take many times longer. Chapter 12 quantifies the overhead of making bulk changes to data when indexes exist on the data being modified.

It's usually quicker in this case to set all the schema indexes to be unusable, import the data using the parameter SKIP_UNUSABLE_INDEXES=Y, and then rebuild the indexes afterwards using a large sort_area_size and the NOLOGGING option. This shows an example for one index, which would need to be applied to all the schema indexes in a real situation:

```
REM ...works for all indexes including primary key and unique
constraints
alter index i0_trades unusable;

REM imports the data in another session using SKIP_UNUSABLE_INDEXES=Y

REM now rebuilds using a large sort area, without redo generation
alter session set sort_area_size=10000000;
alter index i0_trades rebuild nologging;
```

If you need to import data into an existing schema after truncating all the tables in the schema, you need to disable all referential integrity first before the TRUNCATE can succeed. After disabling all foreign keys, you need to use the ignore=y import parameter to cause import to ignore errors from table and index creation statements due to the existence of those objects. Without ignore=y in this case, import would terminate. Finally, you need to remember to enable all the foreign keys after the completion of the data import.

Handling Import Space Errors

In the early days of Oracle, if you experienced a space shortage for one of the import tables during an import, the process terminated with an error, and you were left in the difficult position of having to decide to rerun from the start or having to understand the implications of trying to restart the import from the failure point. Because a large import of a production schema can take several hours, it's worth making an effort to ensure that a space shortage can't occur and that the import works first time. With the advent of Oracle8*i*, you can use the same EXTENT MANAGEMENT LOCAL UNIFORM option for your import data tablespaces on both the source and destination to guarantee that if the data fits in the source database, and the destination database is physically the same size, then the data will also fit in the destination.

Oracle9*i* takes import space management to another level of robustness by allowing import to suspend, rather than terminate, whenever a space error is encountered, and then resume when the problem has been fixed. For example, consider a situation where you perform an import, which exits because it reaches the maximum extents on the imported object:

```
IMP-00058: ORACLE error 1631 encountered
ORA-01631: max # extents (1) reached in table SCOTT.TRADES
IMP-00028: partial import of previous table rolled back...
```

To ensure that import doesn't terminate when space errors occur, you add the additional import parameter:

```
resumable=y
```

When you run import with resumable=y, space errors appear in a database view to warn you of the problem. Provided that you fix the problem before a user-configurable timeout occurs, import will suspend rather than terminate. You can change the default timeout (two hours) using the resumable_timeout parameter and optionally specify a name to identify the problem through the resumable_name parameter. The ability to specify a name is useful if you want to poll the database and send an alert that identifies the business process that is experiencing the problem. In this example, no name is specified, and the following error appears in the Oracle dictionary:

```
select error_msg from dba_resumable;
```

```
ERROR_MSG
```

```
-----------------------------------------------------------------
ORA-01631: max # extents (1) reached in table SCOTT.TRADES
```

The DBA, once alerted about the problem, can run some SQL to fix the problem and enable the import to complete without errors. In this example, the following SQL fixes the problem:

```
alter table scott.trades storage (maxextents unlimited);
```

ANALYZE Considerations

You have the option to import the statistics from the source database using various options for the STATISTICS parameter, which by default has a value of ALWAYS. Other options are NONE, SAFE, and RECALCULATE. If you used the compress=y option on your export, you should consider using the RECALCULATE option to ensure that the statistics in the destination database reflect the data storage layout after import. Be aware that this recalculation of statistics at import time may cause the elapsed time for your import to increase considerably.

Post-Import Checks

After you have completed an import, always check that all the objects and constraints that were exported are present in the imported database. In theory, you shouldn't have to do this, but it protects you from possible bugs in Oracle's import and export utilities that might result in missing objects after import. If you followed the suggestions in the Pre-Export Check section, you have some tables available that you can use to check the imported objects against those that were exported. Always check that objects are valid post-import with the following SQL, and fix any that aren't before using the imported data:

```
select * from dba_objects where status <> 'VALID';
```

Summary

Oracle import and export utilities are standard parts of the core DBA skill set. Both tools include an enormous number of parameters than can make them difficult to use. By using parameter files rather than command-line arguments, the DBA can store the most frequently used combinations of parameters for future reuse. Parameter files also avoid issues associated with escape sequences for quote characters that are required in some of the arguments.

Export performance can be considerably enhanced using the direct path option, and there aren't many compelling reasons for not using it. Direct path export exposes a security loophole if VPD is used to provide application security, and DBAs should be aware of this. The use of compress=y is no longer recommended due to the improvements in space management afforded by UNIFORM space allocation. The use of UNIX compression utilities should be considered for saving export dump file space. These can provide very significant space savings at the cost of increased complexity in the export process due to the use of UNIX pipes.

Understanding the factors that affect import performance and how to manage them is essential in order to reduce elapsed times for import. The recommended approach is to measure statistics and event waits for the import session and act on the results. This can result in dramatic reductions in import elapsed time with minimal DBA effort. Import provides a lot of flexibility for importing data, and it's possible to import data in stages to reduce factors that influence performance, such as redo generation. However, additional complexity in the import process may introduce errors, and dry runs of complex, multistage import processes are essential for procedures that need to complete in a fixed, business-critical time window. The use of Oracle's resumable features for handling space errors, introduced in Oracle9i, is strongly recommended. These features in themselves are a compelling reason for upgrading to Oracle9i, due to the potential for the increased system availability that they deliver.

High Availability (HA) Solutions

## CHAPTER 20

VERITAS High Availability (HA) for Oracle

VERITAS Software Corporation is the leading provider of storage management software for data protection, application availability, and disaster recovery. The VERITAS product set includes offerings specifically to provide HA facilities for Oracle databases. The Oracle suite of products from VERITAS is based on core components such as VERITAS File System (VxFS) and Volume Manager, and an overview of these is provided in this chapter. Offerings specifically for the Oracle database management system (DBMS) are layered on top of the core components. These include VERITAS Storage Rollback, which can provide lightning-fast Oracle restores, and FlashSnap, which provides similar performance for backups. In addition to these Oracle-specific products, VERITAS Cluster Server (VCS) enables a standby facility to minimize application outages in the case of server loss. Using VCS, Oracle databases can be failed over to a standby server in a short time.

If you are considering purchasing software from VERITAS, you might like to revisit the criteria in Chapter 7 that can help you choose third-party software that is likely to meet your requirements. One factor in favor of any third-party software vendor is evidence of a strong corporate partnership between the vendor and Oracle. VERITAS and Oracle enjoy a very close relationship, both at the corporate and technical level, that makes VERITAS worth investigating as a software solution.

This chapter discusses various VERITAS technologies that can provide Oracle HA and the way in which they interoperate with Oracle technology. The technologies covered include:

- Oracle Disk Manager (ODM), an Oracle-specified application programming interface (API) that storage vendors can implement, enabling Oracle to take best advantage of their storage features
- VxFS and VERITAS Volume Manager
- VERITAS Storage Rollback
- VCS
- VERITAS FlashSnap
- VERITAS Volume Replication Facility (VVRF)

VERITAS and ODM

At a technical level, probably the best evidence to date of the collaboration between Oracle and VERITAS is the announcement of ODM. ODM is a disk management API defined by Oracle and designed to provide enhanced file management and disk input/output (I/O) throughput by enabling vendors of storage management software to manage Oracle I/O, by leveraging detailed storage information available only to the storage management software.

VERITAS is the first company to implement the ODM API, which is delivered through a dynamic load library and kernel driver as part of the VERITAS Extension for ODM. ODM support is provided by VERITAS for Oracle9*i* only. It's helpful to understand what types of I/O Oracle DBMS needs to support, and how ODM helps storage management software to control it. Oracle I/O requirements typically include concurrent requests for single and scattered block reads on tables, indexes, and TEMPORARY tablespaces. Asynchronous I/O—where Oracle DBMS performs write operations without waiting for a success or fail code—is used during writes to database datafiles to increase throughput. However, redo log I/O is performed using sequential writes when the next read takes place where the last one finished. During a commit, the write operation of the commit record to the redo needs to be performed synchronously.

In the past, it was traditional for the Oracle database administrator (DBA) to micromanage database space across multiple file systems with different underlying storage attributes to provide the best physical layout to meet the performance requirements of different types of Oracle I/O. To insulate the DBA from the need to address low-level storage performance issues, and at the same time enable Oracle I/O to take best advantage of the underlying storage, ODM provides a single API call: odm_io(). This replaces the many system calls traditionally required to perform different types of I/O on the various kinds of Oracle database files. The existence of odm_io() enables a storage management vendor, such as VERITAS, to provide suitable storage to meet the I/O requirements specified in the call to odm_io(). Using ODM, all types of I/O are enhanced on *both* filesystem files and raw partitions because the underlying storage management software can control it. For example, ODM enables the underlying storage management software to choose blocks on disk that are actually contiguous when allocating an Oracle file using the Oracle-Managed File (OMF) facilities in Oracle9i, and also when increasing the size of a file using the AUTOEXTEND option. Contiguous blocks can reduce the elapsed time for full table scans.

It's important to understand the roles and responsibilities of both Oracle and the vendor with respect to the certification of storage and sophisticated value-added storage facilities discussed in the rest of this chapter. Oracle has created the Oracle Storage Compatibility Program (OSCP) to address storage certification considerations through an audited testing program, designed to ensure interoperability between the database and the storage features. The OSCP facilitates the development of storage solutions for Oracle. Through the OSCP, third-party vendors (such as VERITAS) receive the tools and resources they need to build Oracle-compatible storage solutions. Certification is the responsibility of the vendor based on requirements defined by Oracle. VERITAS certifies all its Oracle-compatible storage products based on the requirements of the OSCP. Detailed information can found in the OSCP area of Oracle's corporate Web site.

VxFS and VERITAS Volume Manager

VxFS is one of the basic building blocks of the VERITAS HA edition for Oracle. The key features of VxFS are raw device performance and the ease of management associated with traditional UNIX filesystems (UFSs). VxFS provides storage virtualization capabilities. These capabilities enable the administrator to manage logical pools of space (volumes) rather than physical devices, providing very large filesystems. This is one of the critical success factors for the low-cost, flexible, and automated administration of Oracle databases.

Management of virtualized storage is performed through a graphical user interface (GUI) called VERITAS Volume Manager. VERITAS Volume Manager runs as an operating system (OS) layer between I/O drivers and the file system or DBMS. As such, it provides features to enhance storage availability, performance, and manageability by presenting parts of disks, entire disks, or groups of disks as logical volumes. The ability to present physical disks as logical volumes leads to storage virtualization. Storage virtualization means that VxFS file systems can be expanded online. The presence of online maintenance operations in general leads to higher availability through avoiding the downtime that is traditionally required to expand UFS when the underlying storage device can't be expanded online. By using VxFS and Volume Manager, database file systems aren't limited to the size of underlying physical devices. VERITAS Volume Manager provides the following basic features:

- Protection of data against loss or loss of access due to disk media or channel hardware failures, typically through mirroring and Redundant Array of Independent Disks (RAID)

- Mapping of volume block address spaces to disk blocks for optimal data access performance, typically using data striping

Volume Manager also provides additional features, such as three-way (or more) mirroring of volumes. By breaking off the third mirror (typically based on low-cost network attached storage [NAS]) for backup, testing, or reporting, higher performance on production systems can be maintained without compromising failure tolerance, which continues to be provided by the first mirror. Volume Manager also facilitates local on-disk snapshots to provide rapid rollback to prefailure states through VERITAS Storage Checkpoint and Storage Rollback.

VxFS provides other features that enhance the performance and availability of Oracle databases. For example, Quick I/O provides levels of performance comparable with raw partitions for write-intensive applications by avoiding the file system locking that causes I/O for traditional UFS to be serialized. VxFS is a journaling file system and provides fast recovery after a server crash to reduce downtime, unlike a default UFS that often requires a time-consuming full file system check (fsck) operation. Due to the presence of journaling, post-crash integrity checks on VxFS typically require just a few seconds.

VERITAS Storage Rollback

VERITAS Storage Rollback enables a quick restore from an on-disk backup and enables a DBA to recover an Oracle database from logical database failures rapidly. Logical errors can occur, for example, as a result of the accidental dropping of a table, removal of a database datafile, or a batch processing error. It's important to keep in mind that protection from media failures still requires backups to secondary storage (usually tape), or the use of disaster recovery techniques that ensure data is copied off site as soon as it's changed. Of course, the use of Recovery Manager (RMAN) tape backups can provide point-in-time recovery of Oracle, and RMAN disk backups provide the same capabilities more quickly because restores from disk are nearly always faster than restores from tape. Use of RMAN, therefore, provides protection from logical errors. You need to judge whether VERITAS products provide the required benefit when compared to cost.

The key benefit of VERITAS Storage Rollback is the ability to restore Oracle database filesystems to the preerror state in the fastest possible time, thereby increasing availability by minimizing the outage caused by the logical error. After the file systems have been restored to the required state, regular Oracle commands are needed to roll the database forward to a transactionally consistent state by performing recovery to a specific point in time or system change number (SCN). VERITAS Storage Rollback can be used in tandem with standard Oracle techniques for identifying the state of the database. For example, by embedding calls to the GET_SYSTEM_CHANGE_NUMBER procedure in the DBMS_FLASHBACK package in Oracle9*i* (which is covered in Chapter 17), key stages in the transaction processing stream can be identified. Recovery can then be performed to return the database to the exact state required to reexecute transactions from that point, based on a restore provided by VERITAS Storage Rollback. VERITAS Storage Rollback technology relies on the existence of a VERITAS Storage Checkpoint. The VERITAS Storage Checkpoint capability is the key to speeding the restoration of the file system to the preerror state.

Storage Checkpoints

The ability to perform a Storage Checkpoint requires the use of a VERITAS filesystem (type VxFS) for physical layout of the Oracle database. A Storage Checkpoint provides an instant, complete, and exact image of a file system. During a checkpoint, the primary file system to which the checkpoint relates is frozen. The freeze operation enables pending and current I/O operations to complete while temporarily suspending new I/O operations. The ability to control the I/O behavior in this way requires features available through VxFS. While I/O is suspended, a block map of all the blocks in the original file system is created. The block map is initially empty and typically requires around 1 percent of the space in the original file system. Each block in the block map contains a link to a block in the filesystem. Because the Storage Checkpoint performs only the I/O necessary to create the empty block map, it usually completes within a few seconds. When the block map of the file system is complete, regular I/O to the file system can begin again. The write order of I/O requests submitted during the freeze operation is maintained.

For write operations that take place after the checkpoint, VERITAS stores a prechange image of the changed block and records the change in the block map created at the time of the checkpoint. As a result, the operation of reinstating the file system data to the state at the time of the checkpoint simply means applying only those blocks that have changed. These are stored in the block map. The operation of reinstating changes is referred to as Storage Rollback. If a block has changed since the Storage Checkpoint, it's not necessary to store subsequent prechange images. Therefore, the overhead of the prechange block copy is triggered after the first post-checkpoint block change only. The Storage Checkpoint accumulates the capture of prechange data block images either until it is removed, or until the next Storage Checkpoint is taken. It's even possible to create multiple Storage Checkpoints. Each checkpoint requires a complete empty block map to be created. Before-image blocks are saved to the most recent block map only, relating to the current checkpoint. In this way, VERITAS can restore an on-disk image to any required checkpoint using the smallest possible disk I/O, resulting in the fastest performance.

If a Storage Checkpoint is required while an Oracle database is open for normal use, it's necessary for the tablespaces that contain the checkpointed file system to first be placed into online backup mode using ALTER TABLESPACE *tspace* BEGIN BACKUP. After the Storage Checkpoint is completed, the tablespaces must be taken out of backup mode using ALTER TABLESPACE *tspace* END BACKUP. If the database is in a cold state (resulting from a SHUTDOWN IMMEDIATE operation), all file systems holding the Oracle control files, online redo logs, and datafiles can be checkpointed. This collection of checkpointed file systems is equivalent to a full offline backup. Unlike UFS snapshot facilities, Storage Checkpoints are persistent across a system reboot.

VxDBA

To lower the administration cost of creating Storage Checkpoints and performing Storage Rollback, VERITAS provides the VxDBA utility. This tool can be used to ensure that the database is in the appropriate state before performing a Storage Checkpoint, and to automate the process of performing Storage Rollback. When a Storage Checkpoint representing a cold backup image is requested, VxDBA performs a clean shutdown before the checkpoint, performs the checkpoint, and then restarts the database. When a Storage Checkpoint is required without shutting the database down, VxDBA ensures that database integrity on rollback is guaranteed by placing tablespaces into backup mode before the checkpoint, and taking them out of backup mode afterward. VxDBA automatically saves a backup copy of the control file during a Storage Checkpoint.

VxDBA also automates the process of a Storage Rollback. This requires the database to be shut down. Storage Rollback restores all datafiles in the chosen checkpoint (not including online redo logs or control files) and can restore the whole database, specific tablespaces, or individual datafiles. The DBA then needs to perform recovery manually to the required point in time or SCN, using the techniques covered in Chapter 17.

VCS

VCS is a HA cluster solution. In its simplest form, a cluster consists of two servers that share a set of mount points and that are both running a single application. At any point in time, the application runs on one server or the other. Only the server currently running the application has the file systems mounted and online. It's critical that the file systems are mounted *only* on the server running the application. This is in contrast to cluster-aware applications like Oracle RAC (which is covered in Chapter 22 that have built-in locking and synchronization facilities to enable two or more database instances on different servers to concurrently access the shared disk at the same time. In a VERITAS cluster, simultaneous access to the disk by two non–cluster-aware applications leads to application data corruption and behavior referred to as *split brain*. Not surprisingly, the cluster software does everything it can to prevent this from occurring.

When a server failure occurs in a two-node VCS configuration, agents running on the cluster detect the failure, mount the file systems on the other server, and restart the application. The application might be an Oracle database. In the VERITAS Database Edition/HA for Oracle, VERITAS provides additional Oracle-aware agents that can restart an Oracle database instance and listener on the other node in a cluster automatically, providing high Oracle availability in the case of server loss. VCS minimizes the outage through two facilities provided as part of the cluster configuration: a private interconnect between the nodes in the cluster and a virtual (floating) IP address to provide a single address that client applications use to connect to the application. The floating IP address is independent of the actual server where the application is currently online. Figure 20.1 shows the components of a two-node cluster running an application on VCS.

In Figure 20.1, the server eq2.dbcool.com is currently hosting the Oracle database application. The file systems containing the Oracle software and database are mounted only on that server, which is said to be active. The server eq1.dbcool.com is currently idle (or passive). To enable the client applications to use the same Oracle Net alias to locate the database, regardless of which node in the cluster is current hosting it, the Net

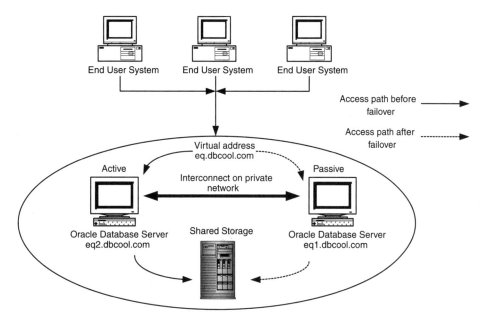

Figure 20.1 A two-node VCS cluster.

alias makes use of the virtual (floating) address of the machine (eq.dbcool.com), as shown in the following alias description:

```
eq.dbcool.com =
  (DESCRIPTION =
    (ADDRESS_LIST =
      (ADDRESS = (PROTOCOL = TCP)(HOST = eq.dbcool.com)(PORT = 1521))
    )
    (CONNECT_DATA =(service_name=eq.dbcool.com))
  )
```

The interconnect is a low-latency private network connecting the nodes in the cluster. The interconnect runs the VCS Low-Latency Transport (LLT) mechanism, which carries the heartbeat that the VCS Global Broadcast (GAB) mechanism uses to communicate information about servers that are members of the cluster and about which servers are active. It's important to be aware that LLT replaces the functions in TCP/IP with low-latency equivalents to identify failures more quickly and reliably. GAB is responsible for ensuring that information about the state of nodes in the cluster is transmitted atomically between nodes. Failure to do this could result in two active nodes at the same time, causing split brain.

When eq2.dbcool.com fails, the eq1.dbcool.com takes on the role of hosting the database application. Typically, end-user applications experience only a small outage while file systems are mounted and recovered on the new active node, and while the database and listener are started. Part of the failover process involves the transfer of the

Table 20.1 Sample Network Configuration for a VCS Cluster

SERVER NAME	ADDRESS	PURPOSE
eq1.dbcool.com	169.243.210.114	Physical network address
eq2.dbcool.com	169.243.210.115	Physical network address
eq.dbcool.com	169.243.210.120	Virtual (floating) network address

floating IP address associated with the name eq.dbcool.com onto eq1.dbcool.com. After the virtual address associated with the cluster is assigned to eq1.dbcool.com, the file systems can be mounted. After the file systems are mounted, the database and listener can be started on eq1.dbcool.com, and end-user access can continue as before. Table 20.1 shows the server names and addresses in the cluster, and their purpose.

The UNIX netstat -rn command can be used to display the network routing table on UNIX, which identifies real and virtual network interfaces. Based on the example shown in Figure 20.1 and Table 20.1, the output of the command shows that the virtual address of the cluster (hostname eq.dbcool.com) is currently active on node eq2.dbcool.com:

```
Destination          Gateway              Flags  Ref   Use    Interface
-------------------  -------------------  -----  ----- ------ ---------
169.243.210.0        169.243.210.115      U      4       312  hme0
169.243.210.0        169.243.210.120      U      4         0  hme0:1
127.0.0.1            127.0.0.1            UH     0    159246  lo0
```

The failover process is conceptually simple to understand. It requires a collection of resources, such as disks, network interface cards (NICs), applications, and databases to be restarted on a different server. However, implementation is more complex because the order of resource failover is critical to the success of the operation. For example, disks must be mounted before Oracle databases can be restarted. In VCS terminology, the collection of resources that needs to be automically restarted in the correct order on another node during failover is referred to as a service group. VERITAS provides a GUI, VCS Manager, for the purpose of creating service groups and dependencies on the resources within those groups. Figure 20.2 shows a complete service group based on an Oracle database application, as represented in VCS Manager.

In Figure 20.2, the application is comprised of an end-user application with a back-end Oracle database. The application depends on programs located on a mount point resource named ibk_apps_mount. The Oracle database depends on three mount points: The ibk_ora01_mount holds the Oracle software distribution, and the ibk_ora02_mount and ibk_ora03_mount resources hold the database files. Each mount point requires a VERITAS volume, and all volumes depend on the disk group ibk_oradg.

The Oracle Net listener resource ibk_listener_sql depends on the existence of the database instance (resource ibk_db_ora), which itself depends on the mount points listed previously. When failover occurs, resources are started in order from the bottom to the top of the dependency network. A service can't start until all its dependents are

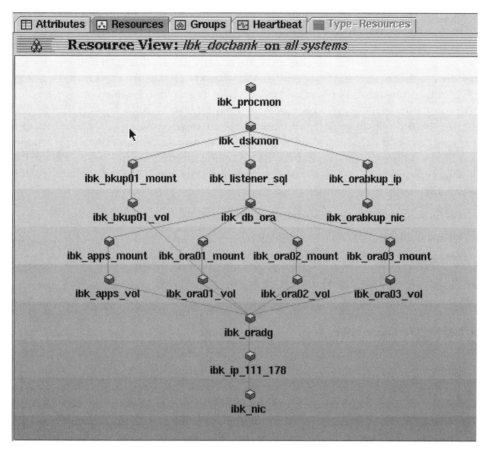

Figure 20.2   A VCS service group.

present. The NIC resource is started first. In Figure 20.2, a second physical NIC is present on the server because RMAN backups are used to back up the database to a centralized Legato server across a private backup–data-only network. Through the GUI, the complex process of configuration and the management of service groups is made as user-friendly as possible.

VCS protects against network failures (usually referred to as network partitions) by requiring that all systems be connected by two or more communication channels. If only a single path is available, and two nodes exist in the cluster, it's not possible to tell whether the failure to contact the other server is due to server loss or network loss. In a VCS cluster, all systems send heartbeats to each other across the available communication channels. If a system's heartbeats are not received across one channel, VCS detects that the channel has failed. If a system's heartbeats are not received across *any* channels, VCS detects that the system has failed. The services running on that system are then failed over to another node. The heartbeats use a broadcast mechanism, which can create significant unwanted traffic across a public network. To address this, it's possible to configure heartbeats to use the public network only when the heartbeats fail across the private interconnect.

VCS includes a collection of command-line utilities to stop and start Oracle database services. It's critical that these cluster-aware utilities are used to start and stop Oracle services, rather than using SQL*Plus STARTUP and SHUTDOWN commands. Use of SQL*Plus commands is likely to lead to VCS detecting an unscheduled outage, leading to the initiation of failover. To provide a consistent interface for Oracle service stop and start operations in both VCS and nonclustered environments, it's fairly straightforward to take the Perl-based tools in Chapter 4 and reimplement them as wrappers around the cluster-aware commands. Based on the information in Figure 20.2, the following commands would be required to stop and start the Oracle services in a cluster-aware manner:

- hactl ibk_db_ora online (start Oracle)

- hactl ibk_db_ora offline (stop Oracle)

- hactl ibk_listener_sql online (start Oracle Net listener)

- hactl ibk_listener_sql offline (stop Oracle Net listener)

VERITAS FlashSnap

VERITAS Database Edition for Oracle integrates with another VERITAS technology called FlashSnap. FlashSnap provides features that enable administrators to create point-in-time copies of data with a minimal impact on applications or users through the use of a VERITAS volume snapshot. If you are familiar with third-mirror break-off techniques, FlashSnap provides a similar but more easily managed and flexible facility at the VERITAS volume level.

The volume snapshot created with FlashSnap can be accessed from the same server or be imported to a different server. The snapshot has several useful purposes. For example, it can form the basis of an Oracle backup or enable the resource-intensive reporting requirements of a typical DSS system to be redirected to a separate server, enhancing performance on the production server. VERITAS provides FastResync technology, enabling split volume snapshots to be synchronized with the original volume, if required, by applying changes made to the original volume since the split. For organizations that are migrating away from locally attached storage, NAS servers can be configured to provide a low-cost option for making good use of the old disk through FlashSnap.

VVRF

VCS is designed to protect applications from prolonged outages due to loss of a single server. Typically, all servers in the cluster are located in the same computer room on the same subnet. Disaster recovery, however, sets out to provide data protection in the face of natural or man-made disasters such as flooding or terrorist attacks. Disaster recovery requires taking copies of production data and data changes to remote sites so that the data is available for disaster recovery procedures on the remote site. This book covers disaster recovery solutions based on the following technologies:

- VVRF

- Oracle multimaster replication (see Chapter 21)

- Oracle standby database functionality in Oracle9*i* Data Guard (see Chapter 23)

One theme common to all approaches is the requirement to trade performance for availability. To maintain the availability of data at the remote site, it's necessary to perform remote writes of replicated data synchronously with local writes. It's useful to understand the data protection capabilities of replication compared to data protection provided by RAID at the storage hardware level. Data protection via hardware RAID mirroring replicates data across a disk and its mirror using I/O channels to both the disk and mirror that are local, reliable, and fast. In this case, both writes typically take the same amount of time. For disaster recovery purposes, the write operation used to replicate data to the remote site typically takes place over a link that is less reliable and has lower throughput than disk I/O channels. The use of synchronous writes in this case can significantly throttle performance on the local site, due to the reduced throughput available, and potentially cause outages on the local server due to transient (though recoverable) network delivery failures.

Data replication based on VVRF (and Oracle standby in 9*i*) can be configured to perform remote replication synchronously if possible, or to buffer data for asynchronous transfers if the link becomes overloaded or unavailable. The ability to switch into asynchronous mode improves performance on the local database by avoiding the need to wait for the remote site to confirm that a write operation has completed. Whenever an outage is experienced by a local site while the transfer is in asynchronous mode, the possibility exists for loss of data at the replicated site if the local site is permanently lost. Asynchronous replication is often a requirement purely for performance reasons. Although it does not guarantee absolute data currency, asynchronous replication might work in situations where a synchronous replication solution would not be feasible. The behavior of VVRF in synchronous mode can be tailored for different data availability requirements at both the remote and local sites. The following options are available for cases when synchronous writes to the remote site fail, leading to the possible divergence of data between the local and remote site in the last two cases:

- Write failure can be signalled to the application, preventing changes to the local site when the remote site is not available.

- Replication can be abandoned, leading to permanent data divergence between the local and remote sites.

- Replication can switch temporarily to asynchronous mode, leading to temporary data divergence between the local and remote sites.

VVRF can be used to replicate Oracle databases to remote sites by placing all Oracle database datafiles, control files, and online redo logs into a VERITAS-replicated volume. If asynchronous mode is used, instance recovery might be required at the remote site to bring the database to a transactionally consistent state before opening it for regular use. If synchronous mode is used, no recovery is necessary. For the case where an unrecoverable disaster occurs at the local site, the database at the remote site can be brought online through the following operations:

- Termination of the replication process
- Change of mode for replication volumes from secondary mode to primary, followed by mount
- Oracle crash recovery to roll forward committed changes from redo and rollback uncommitted changes from undo

Summary

VERITAS provides several HA software solutions for Oracle that rely on the underlying functionality of the VxFS and VERITAS Volume Manager. VCS can provide failover capabilities in the face of server loss, through VCS, which includes Oracle-aware agents. VVRF provides remote data replication services to protect against site disasters.

VERITAS solutions for Oracle HA don't come cheap. As a result, you might want to consider the merits of Oracle solutions such as multimaster replication (see Chapter 21), RAC (see Chapter 22), and Data Guard (see Chapter 23) before making any decision to purchase. It's also possible to use the solutions in combination. What is clear is that Oracle and VERITAS enjoy a close corporate relationship, and that VERITAS is a market leader in its field. As a result, a decision to purchase VERITAS is likely to deliver significant availability benefits for Oracle in both the short and long term.

## CHAPTER 21

Oracle Replication

Oracle provides different types of replication to meet different requirements. For example, materialized views are often used to provide read-only copies of remote data in a local database. In this case, the existence of materialized views is designed to improve performance by avoiding expensive remote Structured Query Language (SQL) operations that would be required if the local database referenced the remote data in place, via a database link. For databases that need access to data from several sites connected via a wide area network (WAN), materialized views against remote data can significantly improve performance. Oracle multimaster replication can be used for similar purposes, resulting in data being found in close physical proximity to where it's used.

As well as enhancing performance, replication provides the possibility of enhanced availability. However, before you consider implementing a high availability solution, you need to be clear on the types of failures your chosen solution protects against. For example, to protect an application against the loss of a single host, you might choose to deploy Oracle Real Application Clusters (RACs), which are covered in Chapter 22. RAC doesn't provide protection against site disasters because it requires storage to be shared between all nodes and a high-speed interconnect between them. These requirements typically mean that all nodes in a RAC configuration need to be located on the same site. If you require protection against a site disaster, a different approach is required.

The configuration in this chapter uses Oracle multimaster replication to maintain database availability in the face of a site disaster on the primary site. Under normal operation, the replicated site isn't accessible to clients. It only becomes accessible when the primary site is lost in a disaster.

Topics covered in this chapter include:

- Comparison of multimaster replication and a standby database for disaster recovery
- Comparison of synchronous and asynchronous propagation
- Conflict resolution and notification
- Issues associated with sequences in a replicated environment
- Prerequisites for a multimaster configuration
- Setting up a multimaster configuration
- Running a multimaster configuration

Multimaster versus Standby Databases

When choosing between multimaster replication and standby databases to implement an Oracle disaster recover solution, several differences should be considered.

Like standby databases, multimaster replication enables a replica of a database to be maintained at a geographically remote location. Because data is transferred via SQL, the replicated sites can be running different releases of Oracle or even different operating systems. This is in contrast to physical standby databases provided as part of Oracle Data Guard. Physical standby databases require the primary and standby sites to match exactly, both in terms of the Oracle version and operating system. Using a physical standby, redo is applied to the standby such that the data in the primary and standby is binary identical. As a result, standby databases require tighter control of the Oracle runtime environments on the servers involved. However, once the standby configuration is up and running, standby databases require less management than multimaster replication, and failover requires a few commands. Data Guard is covered in detail in Chapter 23. Using multimaster replication, some administrative procedures may be necessary to recover transactions at the failed site and to prevent data inconsistencies if a decision is made to fail over back to the original site.

Whereas physical standby databases require the whole of the primary to be physically copied and maintained on the standby site, multimaster replication enables database administrator (DBA)-controlled subsets of data to replicated. For example, a single schema only can be replicated, or even a few tables in a schema.

Synchronous and Asynchronous Data Propagation

Changes between multimaster replicated sites can be propagated in fundamentally different ways, known as synchronous and asynchronous propagation. Synchronous propagation occurs when a change to a local database is made to the remote replica in the same transaction, using Oracle's two-phase commit mechanism. When two (or more) Oracle sites take part in a transaction involving changes on all sites, this is referred to as a distributed transaction. This contrasts with a local transaction, which involves changes only on the local node, and a remote transaction where all changed objects are limited to the same remote node.

The use of synchronous propagation requires distributed transactions. Synchronous propagation requires that all sites involved in the distributed transaction are available at all times, or the transaction (including the part on the local node) will fail and roll back. For example, the loss of the network connection to a remote site will cause local transactions to fail. When sites in a synchronous configuration change the same data at the same time, there is a possibility that deadlocks can occur because Oracle locks the local row first, and then locks the remote row on an AFTER ROW trigger. As usual, locks aren't released until a commit or rollback takes place.

Oracle multimaster propagation actually propagates changes to remote sites using Remote Procedure Calls (RPCs) rather than changing the remote tables directly using SQL statements. When changes are made to a local replicated table, internal database triggers create the RPCs that replicate the changes. Usually, each row change generates an RPC. In synchronous mode, multimaster replication executes the RPC call that changes the remote data within the same transaction as the local data change made by the client application. As this represents a distributed transaction, changes must be made to all sites or none. Failures result in a rollback, which loses the local part of the transaction. Using synchronous replication, all sites contain identical replicated data at all times.

When multimaster replication is configured to use asynchronous propagation, the same RPCs are generated as in synchronous mode. The difference is that the RPCs are recorded in a local queue (actually implemented using database tables) within the same local transaction. Therefore, asynchronous changes require sufficient space in the local queue for the transaction to succeed. Once the local transaction commits, the local queue table records the remote sites against which the RPC needs to run, along with the RPC parameters that identify the values to change. At a later time, and typically using scheduled database jobs, the changes are propagated from the local queue to each remote site, using a distributed transaction. If the remote site is unavailable, then the transaction fails and can be retried later. Asynchronous propagation may be performed serially or in parallel. During serial transmission, transactions are propagated one at a time in the commit order of the originating site. During parallel propagation, replicated transactions are transmitted in concurrent parallel streams leading to higher throughput. Oracle orders the execution automatically in a way that ensures the global integrity of data. Parallel propagation uses the same underlying mechanism used by all parallel operations in Oracle.

Keep in mind that all sites in a multimaster configuration are peers. Therefore, they can all make local changes to the same data at the same time, and these changes need to be propagated to all other sites. Asynchronous propagation leads to the possibility that data on different sites can diverge. For example, if two sites change the same row at the same time and specify different values, a fundamental conflict arises when each site needs to propagate changes to the other.

Conflict Resolution and Notification

This chapter covers an Oracle disaster recovery solution based on multimaster replication. As such, the possibility for data conflicts is minimal because clients don't access the standby multimaster-replicated database until the primary is unavailable.

However, as an aside, conflict resolution is worth discussing, as it presents one of the biggest challenges for running Oracle multimaster replication when all sites are peers that can be updated at the same time. Oracle provides two methods for resolving conflicts automatically. For example, consider a situation where each table contains a column that identifies the last time a change was made to each row. If a conflict occurs, Oracle can apply a rule whereby the values in the row that changed most recently take precedence. Any such automatic resolution needs to take into account possible time zone differences between sites so that the conflict resolution rule is applied correctly. The solution to this time problem is to ensure that each table contains a trigger that updates the time column with a universal time (such as GMT) each time a change is made on the local site. Obtaining a universal time value on each site is not straightforward, and care must be taken to ensure that clocks on all servers are synchronized, for example through the use of the xntpcl service on UNIX. An external C procedure can be used to obtain the local server time in GMT. An easier method is to create a Java stored procedure for use within the trigger, where the procedure returns the local time in GMT through the Java class java.util.Date. An example of Java source code to accomplish this task is shown here:

```java
import java.text.*;
import java.io.*;
import java.util.*;
import java.util.Date ;

public class DbCoolGmt
{
  public static String GmtTime()
  {
    DateFormat df = new SimpleDateFormat( "dd-MMM-yyyy HH:mm:ss" );
    Date currentDate= new Date();
    System.out.println( "GMT is " + df.format(currentDate));
    df.setTimeZone(TimeZone.getDefault());
    System.out.println( "LOCAL time is " + df.format(currentDate));
    df.setTimeZone(TimeZone.getTimeZone("GMT") );
    return ((new String(df.format(currentDate))).toUpperCase());
  }
}
```

Once the class has been compiled, the following SQL script can be used to create a binding to the Java class to enable the function to be called from PL/SQL within a trigger:

```sql
CREATE OR REPLACE FUNCTION DBCOOL_GMT_TIME RETURN VARCHAR2
AS LANGUAGE JAVA
NAME 'DbCoolTime.GmtTime() return java.lang.string';
/
```

Another automatic conflict resolution approach involves the creation of a column in every table to store the site name where the change was made. Using this approach, each replicated table contains a trigger that updates a site column upon each row change. The site column can be populated from the database GLOBAL_NAME value, which should uniquely identify each site. The conflict resolution routine needs to be configured with the order of site precedence. Then, if a conflict occurs, Oracle can apply the values from the site with the highest priority in order to resolve the conflict.

The biggest problem with automatic conflict resolution is that it applies a technology solution to a business problem. My personal preference is never to implement automatic conflict resolution routines. I prefer to notify end users regarding conflicts and let them decide how to resolve them. It's feasible to implement extensive conflict notification routines without implementing automatic conflict resolution routines.

Whatever the approach to conflict resolution, all the solutions require intrusive changes to the replicated schema (through extra columns and tables) or extra effort from business users to ensure that procedures are in place to deal with conflicts that occur. However unlikely the possibility of a conflict appears, procedures need to be tested before production. These issues all have a common root cause, due to the underlying asynchronous propagation of changes. The best approach is to avoid conflicts in the first place, and that's difficult to guarantee. Synchronous operation avoids these requirements but imposes high availability requirements for all networks and servers in the replicated configuration.

Replication Prerequisites

A replication configuration can be created and managed using either the replication application programming interface (API), which is a collection of packages or the Replication Manager component of Oracle Enterprise Manager (OEM). Replication Manager is a graphical user interface (GUI) that manages the interface to the API. In order to run a replicated configuration in a production environment, you'll probably use the GUI, as it provides day-to-day administration at a much lower cost. However, when things go wrong, you may need to resort to the API. If a GUI doesn't expose all the functionality in the underlying API, then this is the case. The downside of using the API is that it requires an advanced level of DBA skills. Therefore, to run a production multimaster configuration, you need sufficient DBAs with advanced-level DBA skills to provide 24×7 coverage for the application. This is a cost you need to keep in mind before you deploy a multimaster configuration.

At the technical level, in order to implement multimaster replication, rows in all tables to be replicated need to be uniquely identifiable. This guarantees that changes on one site can be propagated correctly to all other sites during RPCs. The best way to guarantee this is to ensure that all tables have primary key constraints or unique constraints where all columns are NOT NULL. If a table doesn't have such a constraint, then a set of columns that can be used to guarantee uniqueness must be nominated during the initial replication configuration. If such a set of columns exists, another approach is to add a primary key to the table in a RELY DISABLE state, such as:

```
alter table no_pk add primary key (keycol1, keycol2) rely disable;
```

Table 21.1 Initialization Parameters for Multimaster Replication

PARAMETER NAME	VALUE
compatible	9.0.0
distributed_transactions	5
global_names	TRUE
job_queue_processes	3
open_links	4
parallel_automatic_tuning	TRUE
parallel_min_servers	2
processes	Add 12 to existing value
replication_dependency_tracking	TRUE
shared_pool_size	Add 50MB to existing value

This statement identifies a set of columns that could be used as a primary key, without requiring the overhead of maintaining the underlying index, which is not created. It's important to understand that a primary key in DISABLE state *doesn't* prevent the insertion of duplicate keys. Therefore, you need to be sure that any columns supplied form a genuine primary key and that NULL values aren't inserted if the columns enable NULL values.

Initialization parameters need to be set with care in order to ensure that the replicated configuration will operate correctly. Table 21.1 shows initialization parameters to be set on both sites to support replication. These are used later in an example to demonstrate a multimaster replication configuration based on two Oracle9*i* databases.

The use of parallelism is required to ensure the parallel propagation of changes for replication configurations with high change volumes. By setting PARALLEL_AUTOMATIC_TUNING to TRUE, Oracle can dynamically adjust the degree of parallelism according to the current workload. Note also that the JOB_QUEUE_INTERVAL parameter is missing. This is obsolete in Oracle9*i*, where the job queue has been redesigned to start jobs on demand and to support a dynamic number of jobs up to the value of JOB_QUEUE_PROCESSES.

Replication and Sequences

Before you decide to use multimaster replication, you need to be aware that replicating sequences is not supported. Sequences are typically used in the generation of primary key values. Most often, a BEFORE INSERT trigger is defined on a table, and the trigger selects the next value from the sequence to use as the primary key. Using this technique, primary keys can be generated automatically, transparently to the end user. This simple approach using numeric primary keys won't work in a replicated environment when multiple sites can potentially generate the same key value based on a local sequence. This will lead to replication conflicts.

Two solutions to this problem are possible. One uses a different value for the INCREMENT BY sequence property for the same sequence on different sites to ensure that no overlap in sequence values can occur across sites. The other approach involves changing an existing primary key to include an extra column that uses a unique property of each database (for example, GLOBAL_NAME, DBID, or STANDARD.SYS_ GUID) as a tiebreaker to guarantee a unique value when used in combination with the value generated by the local sequence.

Keep in mind also that the BEFORE INSERT trigger used to generate the primary key value can be fired in two ways. The first is through a local insert by an end-user application. The second is through an insert propagated by a replication RPC from a remote site where the end-user insert was originally performed. In this second case, where the key has been generated at the remote site, the trigger must *not* change the value. The following PL/SQL test can be used in any trigger to identify only those changes resulting from an end-user action on the local site:

```
if (dbms_reputil.from_remote = false and
    dbms_snapshot.i_am_a_refresh = false) then
  -- this is end-user application change...
```

The use of INCREMENT BY is shown in the following code (based on the SCOTT.EMP table) where the trigger is identical on both sites, but the generated sequences can't overlap:

```
REM site 1 trigger, values 1,3,5,7...
create sequence seq_pk_emp
increment by 2 start with 1 nocache;

REM site 2 trigger, values 2,4,6,8...
create sequence seq_pk_emp
increment by 2 start with 2 nocache;

REM Site 1 and 2:
create or replace trigger trg_pk_emp
before insert on emp
for each row
begin
  if (dbms_reputil.from_remote = false and
      dbms_snapshot.i_am_a_refresh = false) then
    select seq_pk_emp.nextval into :new.empno from dual;
  end if;
end;
/
```

The second approach means that the same sequence definition can be used on each site. However, an extra column is required to store the site-unique value that must be used as a tiebreaker along with the sequence value to form the primary key. The following example shows the second approach, where the EMPNO column is used in combination with a GUID column to form the primary key, where GUID is the value returned from STANDARD.SYS_GUID:

```
alter table emp add (guid raw(2000));

alter table emp add constraint pk_emp primary key(empno,guid);

create or replace trigger trg_pk_emp
before insert on emp
for each row
  begin
  if (dbms_reputil.from_remote = false and
      dbms_snapshot.i_am_a_refresh = false) then
      select seq_pk_emp.nextval into :new.empno from dual;
      :new.guid := sys.standard.sys_guid;
  end if;
end;
/
```

Creating a Replication Configuration

This section describes a mixed mode multimaster configuration where changes between the primary and standby are performed using synchronous propagation, and changes between the standby and primary are performed using asynchronous propagation. The assumption is made that the primary and standby sites are geographically remote such that the loss of both sites at the same time, due to disaster, is very unlikely.

The system designed is such that during normal operation of the primary, the standby is not available for end-user activity, although it's up and running normally. The standby exists simply to provide a failover if the primary site is lost due a site disaster. Keep in mind that the use of synchronous propagation relies on the fact that both the network between the sites and the servers on which the primary and standby databases run deliver high availability. If not, the possibility exists that standby server problems or network outages can reduce the availability of the primary. This is definitely a situation that must be avoided, as it defeats the whole purpose of the configuration, which is to increase the availability of the primary.

Creating the Standby Database

During initial setup of replication between the primary and standby sites, the DBA creates a named group of objects to be replicated between sites. This is known as a *master group*. During the creation of the master group, data can optionally be copied between sites to ensure that all tables on all sites contain the same rows as an initial starting point before replication begins. In order to create the standby more quickly for cases where large numbers of rows are involved, the standby can be copied from a cold backup of the primary. Chapter 23 contains instructions for setting up a standby database that can be followed to clone the multimaster standby from the primary. After the standby is opened, the GLOBAL_NAME value must be changed to a unique value different from the primary. If the primary uses TEMPORARY tablespaces that include tempfile files, these need to be created on the standby if they don't exist already.

Network Configuration

Based on a server name, "primary" for the primary database and "standby" for the standby database, three Oracle Net aliases need to be created. Note that both databases must use the initialization setting service_names=orad2.dbcool.com in order to dynamically register with the local database listener on the local server. The use of dynamic registration means that no listener.ora file is required on either server. Chapter 3 provides full details. If a listener.ora file is used, then GLOBAL_DBNAME values must *not* be used to statically register a database with a listener. The use of GLOBAL_DBNAME disables the transparent application failover capabilities of Oracle Net.

The first alias, orad2.dbcool.com, is the one used by end-user applications. This uses the transparent application failover capabilities of Oracle Net to attempt a connection to the primary database first, and then connect to the standby if the primary is not available. Therefore, if the primary is lost, connections will be transparently redirected to the standby. As a result, the standby is never used by end-user connections while the primary is available. The alias definition for end-user connections is provided in the following code:

```
orad2.dbcool.com  =
  (description =
    (address_list =
      (address = (protocol = tcp)(host = primary)(port = 1521))
      (address = (protocol = tcp)(host = standby)(port = 1521))
      (failover = true)
      (load_balance = false)
    )
    (connect_data =
      (service_name = orad2.dbcool.com)
    )
  )
```

The other two aliases are used explicitly to identify each database for the purpose of replication and should be registered as the names of each database in OEM. These are shown in the following code:

```
orad2.primary.dbcool.com  =
  (description =
    (address_list =
      (address = (protocol = tcp)(host = primary)(port = 1521))
    )
    (connect_data =
      (service_name = orad2.dbcool.com)
    )
  )
```

```
orad2.standby.dbcool.com  =
  (description =
    (address_list =
      (address = (protocol = tcp)(host = standby)(port = 1521))
    )
    (connect_data =
      (service_name = orad2.dbcool.com)
    )
  )
```

The GLOBAL_NAME of each database must be set to the Oracle Net alias in order to ensure that Replication Manager can differentiate between them and to ensure the names meet the requirements for naming enforced by the use of GLOBAL_NAMES= TRUE in the initialization files on each site. The GLOBAL_NAME can be set using the following commands:

```
REM run this on primary database...
alter database rename global_name to orad2.primary.dbcool.com;

REM run this on standby database...
alter database rename global_name to orad2.standby.dbcool.com;
```

Using Replication Manager

Replication Manager is a component of OEM. To manage a replicated configuration using OEM, the following prerequisites are necessary:

- An OEM Management Server must be running. This requires an OEM Repository Database. Chapter 24 contains more information on installing and running OEM.

- The Oracle Intelligent Agent must be running on each site.

- The primary and standby databases must be discovered by the agent and registered in the OEM repository. In this example, the names are orad2.primary.dbcool.com and orad2.standby.dbcool.com.

- Operating system and Oracle-preferred credentials must be registered in the OEM repository for the primary and standby server machines and the primary and standby databases. Oracle credentials require SYSDBA privileges, which in turn require the use of a password file on the primary and standby database.

- The Oracle listeners on each site must be configured to enable connections to the local database.

Database links between all sites are required and are authenticated using a DBA account. The Replication Management tool can create the required links. Replication requires named database accounts to perform administration. Although it's possible to use separate Oracle accounts for the administrator, change propagator, and change receiver functions on each site, administration is considerably easier if the same Oracle account is used to perform all roles, and this is strongly recommended.

Traditionally, the username REPADMIN is used, and there's no reason to change it. The easiest way to create the required administration accounts and links on each replication master site is to use the Setup Wizard. The Setup Wizard can be started by right clicking the Multimaster Replication node under the Database node for one of the candidate replication master sites and choosing Setup Master Sites. Figure 21.1 shows the node in the OEM object tree for the primary database.

Before setting up the master sites in Setup Wizard, the chosen sites need to be added to the list of master sites. Figure 21.2 shows the Add Site screen after the two sites in the example have been added.

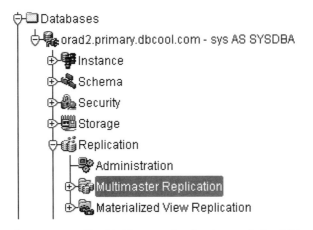

Figure 21.1   The Multimaster Replication node in OEM.

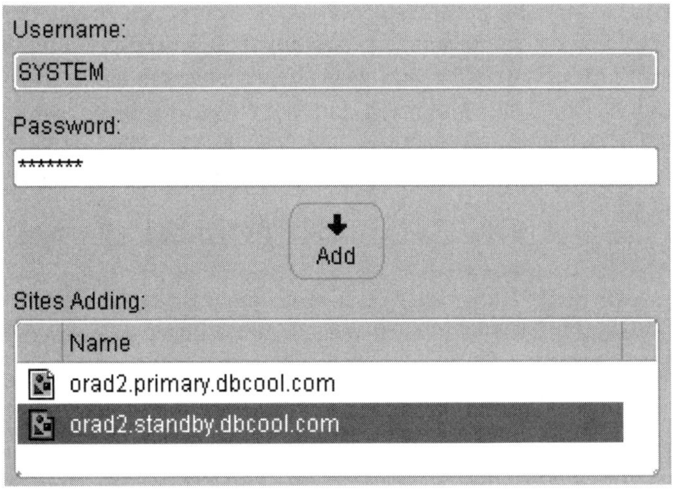

Figure 21.2   The Add Sites screen.

Once the master sites have been added, Setup Wizard performs the following tasks on each master site to create the configuration:

- Creates a database account to serve as a replication administrator, propagator, and receiver. By default, the REPADMIN can be used for all three functions.

- Grants the necessary privileges to the replication administrator account.

- Creates database links to correspond to new replication administrator accounts at each replication site.

- Schedules a job to push changes from the master site to each other master site.

- Schedules a job to purge the deferred transaction queue of completed transactions for all sites in the system.

After the master site configuration is complete, each master site should contain a database link that refers to the other site. For example, the primary site has a link to the standby site that can be tested as follows:

```
select * from global_name@orad2.standby.dbcool.com;
```

The next step is to create a master group that contains a group of objects to replicate between sites. Before this can be performed in Replication Manager, it's necessary to disconnect from the database and reconnect as REPADMIN. This can be performed by right-clicking the database node, and then choosing Disconnect followed by Connect. A master group is created by right-clicking the Master Groups node and choosing Create. Tables, indexes, views, synonyms, and PL/SQL can all be replicated by adding them to a master group. Figure 21.3 shows the Add Objects screen, where all SCOTT's objects have been added to the group.

Next, the master sites to replicate to must be added under the Master Sites tab. In this example, the other master site is orad2.standby.dbcool.com. Figure 21.4 shows the options for replication to the standby site, indicating that synchronous propagation is to be used for replication to the standby from the primary and that existing rows in the primary objects don't need to be copied because the standby in this example is based on a cold backup of the primary, and therefore the rows already exist in the standby.

Immediately after creation, the master group is in a quiesced state until replication support has been added to all objects in the group. That means the replication is not yet active between objects in the group. The group name and contents are displayed in the object tree in OEM as shown in Figure 21.5.

The status of a master group can be viewed in the DBA_REPGROUP view. In this example, the group SCOTT1 is in a quiesced state:

```
select gname,status from dba_repgroup;


GNAME     STATUS
-------   ---------
SCOTT1    QUIESCED
```

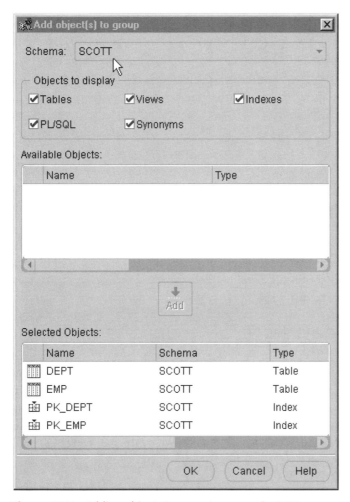

Figure 21.3   Adding objects to a master group in OEM.

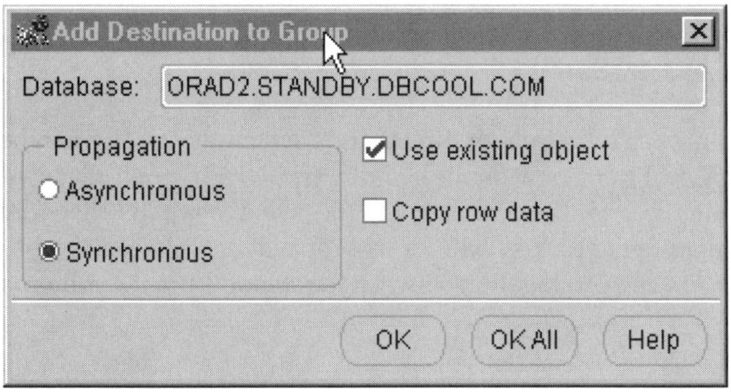

Figure 21.4   Adding a destination to a master group in OEM.

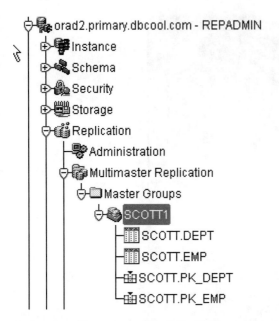

Figure 21.5 A master group defined in OEM.

One of the master sites in a master group is designated as the master definition site. The master definition site must be used to perform administration functions. By default, the master definition site is the site from which the master group was created. In this example, it is ORAD2.PRIMARY.DBCOOL.COM, as shown by the following SQL:

```
select gname,dblink,masterdef,master
from dba_repsites
where gname='SCOTT1';
```

```
GNAME    DBLINK                     MASTERDEF   MASTER
-------  -------------------------  ----------  --------
SCOTT1   ORAD2.STANDBY.DBCOOL.COM   N           Y
SCOTT1   ORAD2.PRIMARY.DBCOOL.COM   Y           Y
```

At this stage, replication propagation in both directions is synchronous. This can be shown by querying the DBA_REPROP view on the standby site, which shows that synchronous propagation is configured for the connection to the primary site and therefore doesn't meet our original requirement for synchronous propagation between the primary and standby, and *asynchronous* propagation between the standby and the primary:

```
REM on the standby...
select * from dba_repprop
where dblink='ORAD2.PRIMARY.DBCOOL.COM';
```

```
SNAME    ONAME   TYPE    DBLINK                   HOW
-------  ------- ------  ------------------------ -----------
SCOTT    DEPT    TABLE   ORAD2.PRIMARY.DBCOOL.COM SYNCHRONOUS
SCOTT    EMP     TABLE   ORAD2.PRIMARY.DBCOOL.COM SYNCHRONOUS
```

The replication propagation mode between the standby and the primary can be modified by a call to the Replication API using the ALTER_MASTER_PROPAGATION procedure in DBMS_REPCAT once the master group is an quiesced state. Many replication administration operations require the group to be quiesced first. The following PL/SQL block quiesces the group before making the change, which must be run under the REPADMIN account on the master definition site:

```
REM !! run as REPADMIN from masterdef site

begin
   dbms_repcat.suspend_master_activity(gname=>'SCOTT1');
end;
/

REM wait for the STATUS in DBA_REPGROUP to say QUIESCED then . . .

begin
dbms_repcat.alter_master_propagation(
                  gname=>'SCOTT1',
                master=>'ORAD2.STANDBY.DBCOOL.COM',
          dblink_list=>'ORAD2.PRIMARY.DBCOOL.COM',
       propagation_mode=>'ASYNCHRONOUS';
end;
/
```

One side effect of configuration changes, such as these, is the need to regenerate replication support for objects in the master group affected by the change. In this case, the EMP and DEPT tables need to have replication support regenerated so that asynchronous propagation is performed between the standby and primary. The contents of the ALL_REPOBJECT view show objects that need regeneration of replication support, including the status of the internal packages generated by Oracle to perform RPC calls, as shown by the following SQL:

```
select sname,oname,type,status,generation_status
from all_repobject where gname='SCOTT1';
```

```
SNAME    ONAME    TYPE           STATUS    GENERATION_STATUS
-------  -------- -------------- --------  -------------------
SCOTT    DEPT     TABLE          VALID     NEEDSGEN
SCOTT    DEPT$RP  PACKAGE        VALID
SCOTT    DEPT$RP  PACKAGE BODY   VALID
SCOTT    EMP      TABLE          VALID     NEEDSGEN
SCOTT    EMP$RP   PACKAGE        VALID
```

```
SCOTT    EMP$RP    PACKAGE BODY   VALID
SCOTT    PK_DEPT   INDEX          VALID
SCOTT    PK_EMP    INDEX          VALID
```

The regeneration of replication support requires repeated calls to the GENERATE_
REPLICATION_SUPPORT procedure in DBMS_REPCAT for each object in the group.
This can be somewhat tedious. It's easier to perform in Replication Manager: The
objects can be selected from a list and pressing the Generate Replication Support button does the rest. Don't forget that you must be connected as REPADMIN to manage a
master group in Replication Manager. Replication administration requests are queued
for execution and can be viewed in the DBA_REPCATLOG view. The following SQL
shows pending requests during regeneration or replication support:

```
select status,request from dba_repcatlog;

STATUS          REQUEST
--------------  -----------------------------
AWAIT_CALLBACK  GENERATE_INTERNAL_PKG_SUPPORT
READY           GENERATE_INTERNAL_PKG_SUPPORT
READY           END_GEN_INTERNAL_PKG_SUPPORT

REM manually push outstanding admin queue requests if you can't wait
begin
dbms_repcat.do_deferred_repcat_admin(gname=>'SCOTT1',all_sites=>TRUE)
end;
/
```

The replication properties from the standby to the primary should now show that
asynchronous propagation is active and that synchronous propagation is active
between the primary and the standby. This can be shown using the following SQL on
either site:

```
select oname,global_name from_, dblink to_,how
from dba_repprop@orad2.standby.dbcool.com,
     global_name@orad2.standby.dbcool.com
where dblink='ORAD2.PRIMARY.DBCOOL.COM'
union
select oname,global_name from_, dblink to_,how
from dba_repprop@orad2.primary.dbcool.com,
     global_name@orad2.primary.dbcool.com
where dblink='ORAD2.STANDBY.DBCOOL.COM'
order by 2;

ONAME FROM_                      TO_                        HOW
----- -------------------------  -------------------------  ------------
DEPT  ORAD2.PRIMARY.DBCOOL.COM   ORAD2.STANDBY.DBCOOL.COM   SYNCHRONOUS
EMP   ORAD2.PRIMARY.DBCOOL.COM   ORAD2.STANDBY.DBCOOL.COM   SYNCHRONOUS
DEPT  ORAD2.STANDBY.DBCOOL.COM   ORAD2.PRIMARY.DBCOOL.COM   ASYNCHRONOUS
EMP   ORAD2.STANDBY.DBCOOL.COM   ORAD2.PRIMARY.DBCOOL.COM   ASYNCHRONOUS
```

Once replication support has been regenerated successfully, replication between sites can proceed using the Submit Start Request from the GUI or the following SQL in the API:

```
begin
  dbms_repcat.resume_master_activity(gname=>'SCOTT1');
end;
/
```

Scheduled Link and Scheduled Purge Operations

A scheduled link determines how a master site propagates its deferred transaction queue to another master site. Scheduled links are created during the initial replication configuration using the Setup Wizard. When a scheduled link is created, Oracle creates a job in the local job queue to push the deferred transaction queue to another site in the system. When Oracle propagates deferred transactions to a remote master site, it does so within the security context of the replication propagator, which is REPADMIN by default. This is the purge job created on the standby site in the example described previously:

```
REM push local deferred transactions to the primary...
declare
rc binary_integer;
begin
  rc := sys.dbms_defer_sys.push(
          destination=>'ORAD2.PRIMARY.DBCOOL.COM',
          stop_on_error=>FALSE, delay_seconds=>0, parallelism=>0);
end;
/
```

A scheduled purge determines how a master site purges applied transactions from its deferred transaction queue. The Replication Manager tool's Setup Wizard creates a job in each master site's local job queue when a master site is defined. It's a good idea to purge the local deferred transaction queue on a regular basis to stop it filling up the database. This is the default purge job created by Setup Wizard:

```
REM purge applied transactions from the queue...
declare
  rc binary_integer;
  begin rc := sys.dbms_defer_sys.purge( delay_seconds=>0);
end;
/
```

Because the primary in the example propagates synchronously to the standby site, the deferred transaction queue is always empty; that is, synchronous propagation doesn't queue transactions. As a result, the database jobs that are created on the primary to perform the purge and push operations never have any work to process. On the standby end, asynchronous propagation is operating, which means that the deferred transaction queue *could* contain transactions. However, because the standby should be closed to end-user access during normal operation, the deferred transaction queue should be empty at the standby end also. To protect the primary, the purge and push jobs can be set to BROKEN on the standby to prevent changes made by end users on the standby from accidentally propagating to the primary while the primary is running. Keep in mind that end-user connections to the standby database should *never* occur while the primary database is running, provided that the Oracle networking configuration is set up correctly.

If the primary server is lost, then the standby database takes over the role of the primary database automatically as a result of the Oracle network configuration. In this case, changes made on the standby are queued until the primary becomes available due to the use of asynchronous propagation. In order for changes made on the standby to propagate back to the primary after it's fixed, the BROKEN purge and push jobs on the standby need to have their state changed so that they can run. The following shows how to change a BROKEN job so that it can run:

```
begin
   sys.dbms_ijob.broken(job=>:jobid,broken=>FALSE);
end;
/
```

Change Management for Replication

Database change management presents some special challenges in a replicated environment. For example, if you make a change to a table by adding a column, this DDL change must be propagated to all other sites. In the past it was necessary to quiesce the replication master group in order to stop replication activity during administration tasks. The quiesce operation itself requires all deferred transactions to complete first. As a result, administration changes in a replicated environment introduce the possibility of reduced availability by requiring scheduled outages. Oracle9*i* makes it possible to carry out more administration operations than previously without requiring a quiesce operation.

Summary

Multimaster replication provides a potentially powerful Oracle disaster recovery facility by propagating changes to a standby site synchronously. Because data changes between sites are propagated using RPCs, it's not required for sites to be running the same operating system or the same version of Oracle. The use of the Replication Manager GUI in OEM makes replicated groups easier to manage than ever before. However, the GUI doesn't expose all the features of the underlying replication API, which is implemented in the DBMS_REPCAT package. As a result, management of a fully fledged production replication configuration requires advanced-level DBA skills. Before you choose to implement multimaster replication for a disaster recovery solution, it's essential to ensure that sufficient DBAs with advanced skills are available to provide 24×7 support. Before choosing multimaster replication for disaster recovery, it's a good idea to first consider using standby databases instead. Standby databases can provide no-data-loss disaster recovery using the features in Oracle9*i* Data Guard with a lower administration cost. Data Guard is covered in Chapter 23.

Oracle Real
Application Clusters

Oracle has long supported the idea of clustered databases. In an Oracle clustered database configuration, a single set of database files resides on a disk that is shared in read-write mode between several servers at the same time. Each server contains an Oracle instance, which consists of background processes that access the database files on the shared disk at the same time, and shared memory holding the Oracle System Global Area (SGA). The goal of clustered Oracle databases is to provide:

- Higher availability
- Better performance
- Scalability

Higher availability is enabled through the existence of other instances should one fail. Sharing the database workload across multiple instances enhances performance, and scalability is enabled by allowing additional servers to be added to the cluster (known as scale-out) to handle increased workloads.

Compared to a single-instance configuration, a cluster database requires additional components. For example, in order to ensure integrity between the Oracle caches, such as the database block buffer cache, in each instance additional distributed lock management services are required compared to a nonclustered configuration.

The original implementation of Oracle clustered databases was Oracle Parallel Server (OPS). OPS first appeared on the VMS operating system, which is often regarded as a legacy operating system today. OPS never really took off on UNIX due to the additional complexities of managing the clustered configuration that are listed in the next section.

In Oracle9*i*, OPS is replaced by Oracle Real Application Clusters (RACs). This chapter explains how RAC addresses the issues associated with OPS while continuing to provide the performance, availability, and scalability for which Oracle clustered databases were originally designed. Oracle's networking capabilities to enable both connection- and statement-level failover are covered in detail, as RAC is the only environment that can make full use of all the available facilities.

This chapter begins with a discussion of the gaps in OPS, followed by a comparison of the fundamental differences in the Oracle configuration for a clustered environment compared to a traditional single-instance configuration. At the highest level, these differences apply to both RAC and OPS. The improvements in RAC, as compared to OPS, are analyzed, and Linux is considered as a suitable operating system for RAC deployment. The high profile of RAC on Linux is food for thought as it's impossible to consider it without also considering the key factors that determine the hardware platform on which any organization chooses to deploy Oracle today. Given the evidence available, it's quite possible that Linux may be the platform of choice for deploying Oracle in the not too distant future. The following topics are covered:

- Functionality gaps in OPS that RAC solves
- Components of an RAC configuration
- Description of cache fusion and improvements
- Installation improvements and manageability enhancements of RAC
- Interconnect configuration
- Parameter differences between RAC and single-instance configurations
- A complete set of initialization parameters for a two-node cluster
- Client network configuration for load balancing and failover
- Considerations for choosing your Oracle operating system
- Choosing to run RAC on Linux

Missing Features in OPS

Oracle OPS on UNIX never really entered the mainstream due to the additional complexities of managing the clustered configuration in order to justify the performance, availability, and scalability benefits that clustered databases were intended to deliver. These additional complexities include the following:

- Manual configuration of the locking configuration parameters.
- The requirement to use raw partitions for the database datafiles.
- The need to maintain a separate parameter file for each instance.
- The need to manage resource affinity manually. Resource affinity is the ability to move database resources around the cluster into the SGA of the instance where they are most frequently used in order to improve performance.

■ The requirement to install Oracle software on each node and perform patches separately to each.

■ The lack of cluster-aware management tools to start and stop Oracle services.

Oracle RAC sets out to address all these gaps. As a result, it's reasonable for Oracle to state that RAC isn't simply a rebadged OPS. The rest of this chapter explains how these deficiencies have been addressed.

Components of an RAC Configuration

An Oracle database consists of a set of files and a set of background processes and shared memory called the *database instance*. In a traditional Oracle configuration, there is a one-to-one correspondence between the instance and the database files. In an Oracle clustered environment, the database is deployed on disks that are shared between multiple nodes in the cluster, and each node runs its own Oracle instance.

NOTE Disk sharing based on Small Computer Systems Interface (SCSI) is usually not suitable. You need to use fiber-connected storage based on Oracle-certified configurations. More information is available at www.oracle.com.

The capability to share processing between nodes in the cluster means that processing capacity in the configuration can be increased simply by adding additional nodes to the cluster, each containing an additional Oracle instance. This is referred to as scale-out, as compared to the more traditional ways to increase capacity by adding hardware resources to an existing server or buying a larger one, which is referred to as scale-up.

Database Components in an RAC Configuration

Figure 22.1 shows the components of an Oracle RAC configuration, including those parts that are present on the shared disks and those that reside on local disks based on a Linux installation of RAC.

Cache Fusion Described

In order to present each Oracle SGA cache on each instance as a single clusterwide global entity, Oracle needs to synchronize data between the database block buffer cache of each instance. This happens through cache fusion, which works by transferring data between the nodes over the interconnect, on demand. The interconnect is simply a high-bandwidth, low-latency connection between the nodes used for interprocess communication, based on asynchronous messaging and queuing.

Enhancements to cache fusion are one of the main improvements in RAC compared to older versions of OPS. In older versions, if a second database instance required a

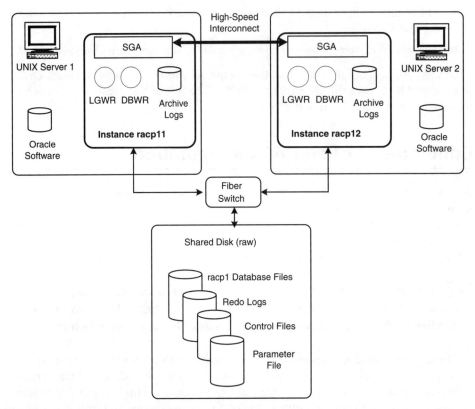

Figure 22.1   An RAC configuration on Linux.

block that was held in the buffer cache of another, the block had to be written to disk by the first instance, a process known as *pinging*. This requirement for block writes to synchronize caches often lead to performance degradation. The solution to this problem was typically to partition workloads between instances to avoid the issue, along with a careful manual configuration of an initialization parameter called gc_files _to_locks. This parameter was used to control the allocation of distributed lock manager resources to database blocks. RAC solves these problems, leading to a configuration where Oracle can decide how to balance client sessions across nodes automatically without requiring pinging, database administrator (DBA) workload balancing, or lock manager configuration.

NOTE Oracle refers to the RAC enhancements that void the need for manual lock management configuration as *resource affinity*.

It's worth mentioning that pinging behavior could be mitigated in OPS to some extent by associating groups of database blocks in a given table with a specific instance through the FREELIST GROUPS parameter set at table creation time. This is followed by the careful distribution of processing between the nodes in the cluster specifically to avoid pinging. So OPS in some cases requires the physical partitioning of data at the instance level.

As a side effect, this situation makes it possible for a table insert to fail when performed by one instance, because there are no free blocks in the FREELIST group associated with that instance, while the insert can succeed from another instance. As soon as you use such features, your application becomes tied to specific nodes in the cluster. This negates the potential for scale-out simply by adding extra nodes to the cluster.

The physical partitioning of data, and the micromanagement of databases that it requires, is totally opposite to the ethos of this book, which places the emphasis on deploying Oracle using features that provide manageability. Manageability translates to availability. Oracle9*i* provides LOCAL extent management and the AUTO setting for segment space management to provide ease of space management. Used together, these two options cause the FREELIST GROUPS setting to be ignored. Although Oracle asks you to consider the use of FREELIST GROUPS for data partitioning in RAC environments to avoid block contention associated with contention for cache fusion resources, I think that's a bad idea. It's much easier and more flexible to manage space in an Oracle database based on LOCAL extent management and AUTO segment space management.

If you can't get acceptable performance in a RAC environment, it might be better to consider other approaches to meeting your performance and availability requirements. However, with the upcoming increased bandwidth for the interconnect through technologies such as Intel's InfiniBand , you're likely to get the performance you require from RAC without resorting to the data partitioning provided by FREELIST GROUPS.

Configuring the Interconnect

The requirement for the interconnect is one of the key features that distinguishes an Oracle RAC configuration from a standard configuration. During Oracle RAC installation using the Oracle Installer, you must provide the interconnect names as the node names, rather than the regular host names.

It's important to set up the interconnect so RAC cache fusion traffic alone is carried over it. The volumes of traffic can be quite high, so it's essential to involve your networking group in order to ensure that the network interfaces are set up properly. The interconnect for a two-node cluster can comprise two standard Ethernet cards connected by a simple crossover cable. For a four-node cluster, Oracle has demonstrated a configuration with a low-cost, high-performance Myrinet switch (www.myrinet.com). In the future, Intel's InfiniBand bus technology promises massively increased bandwidth availability on the interconnect. The bandwidth of the interconnect can act as a throttle on the performance of the cluster as a whole, so it's important to make sufficient bandwidth available. Oracle can't enforce the requirement to place the interconnect on a separate network, but if you don't, performance is likely to suffer. The UNIX netstat command can be used to show the data traffic on the interconnect, as shown in a following example.

To recap, during RAC installation using the Oracle Installer, you need to provide the node names as they are referenced on the interconnect, rather than the names by which the nodes are known on the corporate data network. It's a good idea to include the string "interconnect" or an abbreviation of it, such as "ic," in the names of the nodes as they appear on the interconnect. For example, if you have two servers in the cluster that are known as rac1 and rac2 on the regular corporate network, then the names rac1-ic and rac2-ic would be suitable names to identify the network names on the interconnect. In most flavors of UNIX, you can use the ifconfig command to view the existing network interfaces. The following output shows the sort of network configuration that needs to be in place to support RAC, showing two network interfaces, eth0 and eth1, on a single node in the cluster:

```
$ ifconfig -a
eth0: flags=863<UP,BROADCAST,NOTRAILERS,RUNNING,MULTICAST> mtu 1500
        inet 169.243.69.107 netmask ffffff00 broadcast 169.243.69.255
eth1: flags=863<UP,BROADCAST,NOTRAILERS,RUNNING,MULTICAST> mtu 1500
        inet 172.21.17.29 netmask ffff0000 broadcast 172.21.255.255
```

In this example, eth0 and eth1 are on separate physical network interfaces, where eth0 is the regular corporate network (associated with hostname rac1) and eth1 is the interconnect interface (associated with hostname rac1-ic). The netstat command can be used to show the packet volumes on each interface and is a good way to confirm that networking is configured correctly for RAC, because only interconnect traffic should travel on the eth1 interface identified by hostname rac1-ic:

```
$ netstat -i
Name  Mtu   Net/Dest  Address   Ipkts      Ierrs  Opkts      Oerrs  Collis
Queue
eth0  1500  rac1      srv1      18092533   0      10569475   0      0
eth1  1500  rac1-ic   rac1-ic   5626199    0      1184462    0      0
```

Installation Notes

This section assumes you are installing RAC into a two-node cluster on Linux using raw partitions. In order to install Oracle on Linux, the raw partitions need to be configured by the system administrator (SA) in advance. This section assumes that this has already taken place. Oracle provides facilities to simplify the mapping of database datafiles to raw partitions in order to make this process as simple as possible. However, it's still not simple enough for my liking and is much more complicated than configuring Oracle to run on a UNIX file system. If you use raw partitions for an Oracle database, great care needs to be taken so that a given partition is not used twice, which would result in a corrupt database. That's another reason why I prefer not to use raw partitions for a production Oracle system.

The raw partitions for the RAC database need to be located on a shared disk available to all nodes in the cluster. This disk is likely to be attached using fiber channel connectivity. Manufacturers such as Compaq and Dell provide certified RAC configurations that come with the Oracle software preinstalled and shared storage to bypass this setup stage, which is probably the most difficult part of installation and the most likely to go wrong. Installing RAC requires that you run a regular installation session from the Oracle Installer using runInstaller and you select the Custom option, which presents an option to install Oracle RAC.

Oracle RAC installation is easier to manage than Oracle OPS configuration, because Oracle installs the Oracle software on all nodes on the cluster as part of the RAC installation process. This relies on rcp connectivity being in place between the nodes. Before you begin, you must ensure that the node names of the servers in the cluster, as they appear on the *interconnect* network interface, can be accessed via rsh. Chapter 2 contains information on rsh configuration. In order to test rsh, you can run rsh *interconnect-hostname* from the installation node to check connectivity to other nodes in the cluster. If rsh connects to the remote server without prompting for a password, then it's set up correctly. If not, then you need to configure the .rhosts file in the $HOME directory of the remote node. Be sure to test rsh connectivity to each node in the cluster before you begin installation.

Parameter File Configuration

The database initialization parameters for each instance in an RAC configuration typically differ only in the following values:

- instance_name
- instance_number
- undo_tablespace
- thread

The thread parameter identifies the thread of redo, which is unique to each instance. The db_name is the same for each instance, and the instance_name is simply the db_name name suffixed with a numeric value, instance_number, that Oracle generates in order to identify the instance on each node of the cluster at install time. When you install Oracle for RAC using the Oracle Installer, Oracle requires that you enter a prefix for the instance name. The db_name value is recommended. For example, if you enter racp1 as the prefix, Oracle generates the instance names racp11 and racp12 for each instance in a two-node cluster. It needs to be emphasized that this differs from a standard single-instance, non-RAC installation, where you enter the actual instance name, rather than a prefix for the instance name. Table 22.1 shows the relevant parts of the init.ora configuration related to instance names for a two-node cluster.

If you've installed OPS in the past, you've probably configured it so that each instance in the cluster has the same name and differs only by instance_number. As each instance resides on a physically separate server, that's perfectly reasonable. In fact, it gives the cluster configuration a pleasing symmetry. For RAC, Oracle requires that each instance has a *different* name to allow the cluster management software to identify each instance in the cluster independently of the host name. That's a design decision taken by Oracle that you have no control over.

Each instance requires its own thread of redo. If you've followed the earlier recommendations for naming archived redo logs, then you can use the same log_archive_format parameter for each instance. This is because the presence of %T in the name means that Oracle provides the thread number in each archived log name based on the value of instance_number. It's important to be aware that if you are not using a shared disk to enable archived redo logs for each instance to reside in a shared directory (such as

Table 22.1   init.ora Files for a Two-Node RAC Configuration

INITRACP11.ORA ON RAC1.DBCOOL.COM	INITRACP12.ORA ON RAC2.DBCOOL.COM

<pre># instance specific settings 	
instance_number=1
instance_name=racp11
 	
# some common settings... 	
db_name=racp1
service_names=racp1.dbcool.com
db_domain=dbcool.com
log_archive_format = "T%TS%S.ARC"</pre>
	<pre># instance specific settings
	instance_number=2
	instance_name=racp12
	
	# some common settings...
	db_name=racp1
	service_names=racp1.dbcool.com
	db_domain=dbcool.com
	log_archive_format = "T%TS%S.ARC"</pre>

using Network File System [NFS] or a clustered file system), then you must choose a different directory name for each redo thread.

Each instance also requires its own undo space. The automatic undo features in Oracle9*i* make this easy to configure. The initialization parameters in the following example show how to set a different tablespace for two instances:

```
*.undo_management='AUTO'
racp11.undo_tablespace='UNDOTBS'
racp12.undo_tablespace='UNDOTBS2'
```

As well as the differences, it's worth highlighting the init.ora settings that are common between the instances. For example, the service_names parameter, db_name, and db_domain are identical for each instance. The DBA needs to decide if each node in the cluster should be considered identical for processing purposes or whether instance-specific configuration differences should be introduced. For example, you might allocate one node on a four-node cluster specifically for data warehousing and three for Online Transaction Processing (OLTP) processing. In this case, you might specify that the database block caches are allocated differently on the data warehouse instance in order to better match the processing requirements. I prefer to configure the instances on each node the same, because that allows maximum advantage from the Oracle-provided load balancing and failover features of the cluster. If you need to configure clients to connect to a specific node and instance, then you take away the node transparency of the configuration by associating specific processing with specific instances.

In an RAC configuration, the use of a server parameter file (spfile), rather than an init.ora file is recommended to hold values that are common between the instances of the cluster. This can be achieved by locating the shared settings, such as the size of the shared pool and buffer cache, in an spfile on a raw partition on the shared disk and including a reference to the spfile in the init.ora file of each instance, such as through an init.ora entry like the following:

```
spfile=/dev/raw_racp1_spfile
```

Oracle also enables instance-specific settings to be held in the same parameter file on a shared disk and to be shared by all instances in the cluster by prefixing each parameter with the instance number to which it relates. For example, the following section of a server parameter file shows an instance-specific setting for the sort_area_size parameter. Here the 1 prefix refers to the value used by instance number 1, 2 refers to the value used by instance number 2, and * refers to a generic value used by all instances that don't have an explicit instance-specific value set:

```
1.sort_area_size=200000000
2.sort_area_size=50000000
*.sort_area_size=65536
```

To serve as a reference, the contents of a complete server parameter file for a two-node cluster are as follows, where instance names rather than numbers are used to refer to instance-specific parameters:

```
*.background_dump_dest='/u01/app/oracle/admin/racp1/bdump'
*.cluster_database_instances=2
*.cluster_database=true
*.compatible='9.0.0'
*.control_files='/dev/oracle/racp1/control01_110m'
*.core_dump_dest='/u01/app/oracle/admin/racp1/cdump'
*.db_block_size=8192
*.db_cache_size=52428800
*.db_domain='dbcool.com'
*.db_name='racp1'
*.fast_start_mttr_target=300
racp11.instance_name='racp11'
racp12.instance_name='racp12'
racp11.instance_number=1
racp12.instance_number=2
*.java_pool_size='52428800'
*.job_queue_processes=2
*.large_pool_size='1048576'
racp11.log_archive_dest_1='LOCATION=/u02/oradata/racp1/arch/1'
racp12.log_archive_dest_1='LOCATION=/u02/oradata/racp1/arch/2'
*.log_archive_format='T%TS%S.ARC'
*.log_archive_start=true
*.open_cursors=300
*.processes=150
*.remote_login_passwordfile='exclusive'
*.resource_manager_plan='SYSTEM_PLAN'
*.service_names='racp1'
*.shared_pool_size=52428800
*.sort_area_size=524288
racp11.thread=1
racp12.thread=2
*.timed_statistics=TRUE
*.undo_management='AUTO'
```

```
racp11.undo_tablespace='UNDOTBS'
racp12.undo_tablespace='UNDOTBS2'
*.user_dump_dest='/u01/app/oracle/admin/racp1/udump'
```

Note that the following parameters identify the configuration as that of a clustered database:

```
*.cluster_database_instances=2
*.cluster_database=true
```

The Cluster Manager

The Cluster Manager (CM) software provides a clusterwide view of the nodes in the cluster and cluster membership. It includes a Node Monitor (NM) component that continually polls nodes, interconnect hardware and software, shared disks, and Oracle instances in the cluster to ensure that the cluster as a whole is working as intended. The Global Services Daemon (GSD) works in conjunction with CM to service srvctl requests to start and stop Oracle database and listener services in the cluster.

The CM terminates all processes on a node if it determines that the node is not functioning correctly. For example, aborting GSD or NM will cause a server reboot on Linux by default. On a Linux RAC cluster node, the CM and related software must be started in the following order at machine boot time:

```
$ watchdogd -g dba

$ oranm &

$ oracm &

$ gsd
```

> **NOTE** Oracle provides a script, ocmstart.sh, to start all but GSD. This example refers to Oracle 9*i* Release 1. In Release 2, fewer daemons need to be managed and they need to run as the UNIX root account; further manageability improvements are likely to follow.

Starting and Stopping Instances

After installation, the oratab file contains an entry for the RAC database, *not* the instance name on the node. This is a very significant difference in the configuration compared to a single instance. For the previous example, oratab would contain the following:

```
racp1:/u01/app/oracle/product/9.0.1:N
```

The racp1 value identifies the cluster database name and not the instance name on the node. The presence of the N at the end of the entry is important, because it prevents

Oracle's dbstart and dbshut scripts from attempting to startup and shutdown an instance named racp1. To reiterate, racp1 is not the name of an instance; it's the name of the RAC *database*. In order to start and stop instances and network listeners, RAC instead provides the srvctl utility to perform the operations clusterwide where the -p parameter is the name of the database and -i is the name of an instance. Here are some examples of usage:

```
# start listeners and instances on all nodes
$ srvctl start -p racp1

# stop the instance racp11 only
$ srvctl stop -p racp1 -i racp11

# show the status of instances and listeners on all nodes
$ srvctl status -p racp1
```

Before you start and stop the databases and listeners, the CM software needs to be up and running on each node. One significant advantage of choosing to run Oracle RAC on Linux is that the CM software is provided by Oracle and bundled with the Database Management System (DBMS) software. Due to the open source requirements for Linux, Oracle can provide all the required software components for RAC themselves. On other operating systems for which RAC is available, the operating system vendor provides the CM software.

It's important to use the srvctl command-line utility for stopping and starting Oracle database instances in an RAC configuration to avoid the CM software interpreting the disappearance of the database processes as a node failure. Although you can still use the STARTUP command to start an instance manually and use SHUTDOWN or SHUTDOWN IMMEDIATE to stop an instance, using the SHUTDOWN ABORT command to close your instance on Linux causes a node reboot by default. Although you can disable this behavior, Oracle recommends that you don't unless you are running on a certified RAC configuration.

The srvctl utility has many other functions, including features to add and remove instances from the cluster. Also, Oracle Enterprise Manager (OEM) auto-discovery uses output from the srvctl config command to determine the database configuration for registration into the OEM repository.

Networking Configuration for RAC

Oracle Net is a key technology for leveraging the performance and availability features of RAC. Provided that the behavior of applications is transparent to the node on which the application runs, RAC clustering makes it possible for sessions to failover to other nodes if the local session or node fails. RAC provides the capability to perform session failover during a SELECT statement and enables the SELECT to complete on another node without returning a failure message to the application. Oracle refers to this functionality as Transparent Application Failover (TAF). You might want to review the information in Chapter 3 at this point for more information on Oracle networking.

Listener.ora Configuration

In terms of network listeners, dynamic registration of the database with the listener is required in order to make available the full range of TAF features. Dynamic registration takes place through the services_names setting in the database initialization parameter file. This should be a common value for each instance in the node. Here's an example:

```
service_names=racp1.dbcool.com
```

If the instance is started after the network listener, then PMON will register the instance with the listener after approximately 60 seconds. If you can't wait that long, the SQL command ALTER SYSTEM REGISTER DATABASE can be used to register the instance with the listener on demand. OEM can discover and manage RAC cluster instances. You should be aware that the use of GLOBAL_DBNAME to statically register a database with a listener disables the TAF features of RAC, so you shouldn't use GLOBAL_DBNAME in a listener.ora file in an RAC configuration.

Because a node in RAC typically contains two physical network interfaces, you need to ensure that the listener listens on the interface on the corporate data network, and not the private interconnect between the nodes. In the latter case, you'll probably find that all connections from external client applications fail with a "host unreachable" message. To provide an example, if a server is known as rac1 on the corporate network, and rac1-ic on the interconnect, you need to ensure that the listener listens for connections on rac1. Assuming that rac1 is the name of the host as returned by the UNIX hostname command, the easiest-to-manage approach is to remove any listener.ora file on each node and allow the Oracle defaults to take effect. So when a listener starts on the local node, it listens for Oracle network connections on TCP/IP port 1521 on the network associated with the hostname, in this case rac1.

Client Configuration

There are typically two main requirements for client connectivity using an RAC configuration. The first is the requirement for a client to connect to the least heavily used node in a cluster, as determined by the load-balancing monitoring provided by the CM software. The second is for a client to connect to a specific instance in the cluster. To facilitate load balancing, a generic, noninstance-specific alias is used to provide connectivity to the instance with the lowest utilization. Based on the earlier example, the alias might look like this:

```
racp1.dbcool.com=
  (description=
  (load_balance=on)
  (failover=on)
  (address_list=
   (address=(protocol=tcp)(host=rac1.dbcool.com)(port=1521))
   (address=(protocol=tcp)(host=rac2.dbcool.com)(port=1521))
  )
  (connect_data=
```

Table 22.2 TNS Aliases for Instance-Specific RAC Connections

CONNECTION TO INSTANCE ON RAC1.DBCOOL.COM	CONNECTION TO INSTANCE ON RAC2.DBCOOL.COM
| ```
racp11.dbcool.com=
  (description=
   (address=
     (protocol=tcp)
     (host=rac1.dbcool.com)
     (port=1521)
   )
   (connect_data=
    (service_name=rac1.dbcool.com)
    (instance_name=racp11)
   )
  )
``` | ```
racp12.dbcool.com=
  (description=
   (address=
     (protocol=tcp)
     (host=rac2.dbcool.com)
     (port=1521)
   )
   (connect_data=
    (service_name=rac1.dbcool.com)
    (instance_name=racp12)
   )
  )
``` |

```
    (service_name=racp1.dbcool.com)
   )
  )
```

The presence of the address_list and the load_balance and failover settings provide Oracle with a list of potential instances to connect the client to, depending on the load and availability of each instance. Note that the service_name matches the services_ names parameter used by each instance to register with the local Oracle listener on each node and that there is no reference to a specific instance in the description. Table 22.2 shows the aliases that would be used to provide connectivity to a specific instance.

In this case, the service_name is qualified with a specific instance name on the node, and the host used in the address description identifies the node.

Transparent Application Failover Configuration

It should be emphasized that not all Oracle applications and programmatic interfaces could take advantage of TAF features in early releases of 9i. For example, in the initial release, TAF was restricted to applications using SQL*Plus, Oracle Call Interface (OCI), or the OCI-based Java Database Connectivity (JDBC) interface. Prior to 9i, the Multi-threaded Server option was required, but 9i provides TAF for both dedicated server and shared server connections.

Having specified the network aliases for the generic database service name and specific instance connectivity, both can be used to provide failover in different ways through the addition of a failover_mode section within the connect_data section of the connect description. It's important to be aware that when referring to TAF, the failover takes place *after* a connection is established, as opposed to failover provided at connect time by failover=on in the address list; post-connection TAF failover is a separate feature from connection time failover. To provide failover for SELECT statements in progress at the time of instance failure, the connect_data section for the racp1.-dbcool.com example given previously can be modified as follows to include the highlighted failover_mode section:

```
racp1.dbcool.com=
  (description=
   (load_balance=on)
   (failover=on)
   (address_list=
    (address=(protocol=tcp)(host=rac1.dbcool.com)(port=1521))
    (address=(protocol=tcp)(host=rac2.dbcool.com)(port=1521))
   )
   (connect_data=
    (service_name=racp1.dbcool.com)
    (failover_mode=(type=select)(method=basic))
   )
  )
```

Alternatively, the second instance can be specified as a fallback for the first, and vice versa, by specifying the preconnect method in the failover_mode section, as opposed to the basic method used in the first example. In this second case, failover is faster because the session on the failover instance is already in place at the time of any failure. However, preconnect has a runtime overhead for the regular session before failover takes place. It also introduces a requirement to name specific instances on the cluster for connections (which breaks instance transparency for applications) and doesn't provide automatic failover back to the original instance if and when it becomes available again. The following example extends the racp11.dbcool.com entry that connects to the first instance in the cluster to provide a preconnect failover to the second instance through the highlighted failover_mode section:

```
racp11.dbcool.com=
  (description=
   (address=
     (protocol=tcp)
     (host=rac1.dbcool.com)
     (port=1521)
   )
   (connect_data=
    (service_name=rac1.dbcool.com)
    (instance_name=racp11)
    (failover_mode=
    (backup=racp12.dbcool.com)
    (type=select)
    (method=preconnect))
   )
  )
```

The following SQL can be used to show the failover options in use by all current database connections:

```
select username,failover_type,failover_method,failed_over
from v$session
where failover_method <> 'NONE';
```

Identifying Active Instances

The view V$ACTIVE_INSTANCES can be queried from any node in the cluster to display all the currently active instances as follows, where the interconnect host name prefixes the instance name in the INST_NAME column:

```
select * from v$active_instances;


  INST_NUMBER INST_NAME
------------- -----------
            1 rac1:racp11
            2 rac2:racp12
```

In a RAC configuration, Oracle provides a duplicated set of the V$ views, prefixed with a G (for global) to enable such things as dynamic performance information to be viewed clusterwide from a single instance. The global views are identical to the single-instance views, with the addition of an INST_ID column to specify the instance number to which the information applies. This is shown here for V$SYSSTAT and GV$SYSSTAT:

```
REM single instance view...
desc v$sysstat

STATISTIC#    NUMBER
NAME          VARCHAR2(64)
CLASS         NUMBER
VALUE         NUMBER


REM RAC equivalent, including instance number...
desc gv$sysstat

INST_ID       NUMBER
STATISTIC#    NUMBER
NAME          VARCHAR2(64)
CLASS         NUMBER
VALUE         NUMBER
```

Choosing an Oracle Operating System

The following are some factors that influence which operating system you may choose to deploy Oracle on:

- Robustness and reliability
- Standardization
- Performance
- Price
- Support

It's interesting to consider OPS in light of these requirements. OPS was first available on VMS at Oracle release 6.2. This was because VMS had the most advanced clustering technology for many years and Oracle developed OPS to take advantage of that. In many ways, VMS still has the most advanced clustering technology. For example, UNIX vendors have struggled to make both OPS and RAC available on a clustered UNIX file system, and typically raw partitions are required. From a manageability perspective, raw partitions are diametrically opposite file systems. I never implement Oracle on raw partitions because the drawbacks outweigh the benefits, which means that I wouldn't deploy OPS or RAC in a production environment without careful consideration. A common theme running through this book is a requirement to deploy Oracle in a way that minimizes day-to-day management to reduce support costs and make the best use of people and hardware resources: you simply can't do that with raw partitions.

VMS has supported OPS on standard files since the early days. That means you can allow your Oracle database files to auto-extend on demand wherever space is required. Does that mean VMS is a suitable platform to deploy Oracle? To answer that, you need to consider the whole equation. If you choose to deploy Oracle on VMS, how does that fit in with your organization's strategic IT hardware platform? How does VMS integrate with your backup technology, with your storage technology, and with other infrastructure components? What standard of support can you expect from Oracle when you encounter problems? How likely are you to encounter problems in the first place? If the user base is small, you are much more likely to encounter problems before other customers, which in turn makes problem resolution slower, representing a potential risk to your business from outages. What is the cost of support staff? What is the cost of licenses for the operating system? Is the operating system being developed to take advantage of new processor and other hardware technologies in the future? Does the operating system vendor actively market it? What is the view of research analysts on its long-term viability? What is the cost of the hardware, and how will it change in the future?

Taking all these factors into account, I would guess that your organization is unlikely to deploy OPS on VMS simply because VMS has superior clustering technology. The clustering technology is part of the equation, but the bigger picture is more important. In any discussion on the suitability of an operating system for deploying your Oracle technology, the fact is that RAC represents huge potential for high availability and scalability. In that case, it's impossible to ignore the claims of Linux for delivering the price performance benefits of Oracle RAC because most if not all of the factors that influence your choice are likely to be covered.

Why Linux?

Linus Torvalds developed Linux in 1991 while a student at the University of Helsinki in order to make UNIX available on PCs based on the Intel architecture. A key factor in the popularity and growth of Linux was Torvald's decision to make the source code available for free. It needs to be emphasized: *Linux is free.* Of course, you can purchase Linux CDs from commercial organizations such as Red Hat and SuSE, along with support. You can also purchase commercial products to run on Linux, but the bottom line is that the operating system itself is free, and the source is available. That's a rule of open source.

   Although open source is sometimes positioned as a strength because it allows any programmer to tinker with operating system code and customize it, personally I don't find that compelling as a selling point. What's more compelling is the fact the operating system is under the scrutiny of hundreds of thousands of potential developers, all with the capability to improve it and fix problems. Research analysts Gartner Group made a recommendation in late 2001 for Microsoft Windows users to consider replacing Microsoft's IIS web server with Apache, the most popular open source version, after yet another security hole in IIS was discovered. Although Microsoft can afford the best software engineers in the world, even Microsoft can't compete with the sheer mass of talent available in the open source world. It's also interesting that since Oracle8*i*, Oracle bundles Apache Web Server with the DBMS.

Oracle And Linux

Oracle's commitment to Linux is absolutely clear. Oracle was one of the first vendors to embrace the grass-roots phenomenon of the open source movement and Linux operating system. In the summer of 1999, Oracle announced Oracle8*i* for Linux. Linux is now a strategic operating system for the company, treated on par with Sun Solaris, HP-UX, and Microsoft Windows in terms of release availability.

   Since 1999, Oracle has reported well over 500,000 downloads of Oracle8*i* on Linux. Oracle has released their complete Oracle9*i* product set on at least two implementations of Linux, including Red Hat and SuSE. In December of 2001, Oracle released a 64-bit developer release of Oracle for Intel IA64 processors during Oracle OpenWorld. Speaking from hands-on experience, I can say that the Oracle developer release, running on a 64-bit developer release of SuSE Linux, performed flawlessly for two weeks during a benchmarking exercise in late 2001. The robustness of such an experimental configuration is worth highlighting. The direct involvement of Oracle Corporation in the world of open source is likely to result in beneficial spin-offs for Linux itself. For example, Linux releases based on the 2.5 kernel can leverage asynchronous input/output (I/O) facilities in the same way as operating systems like Solaris. Oracle is likely to help address this and other performance issues in Linux in the near term, and the improvements will be available as open source, because Linux is open source. The announcement by Red Hat of Linux Advanced Server, positioned as the first enterprise-ready version of Linux, is the first evidence of Oracle's influence on the future direction of Linux.

As Linux runs on Intel processors, the volume discounts in pricing that home PC users experience over time manifest themselves in the commercial world also for applications running on Intel processors. Intel is the world leader in processor design, with a clear roadmap for processor architecture improvements in the future, which is difficult for other processor designers to match. As a result, Oracle is likely to leverage Linux increasingly in the future to take advantage of the price and performance benefits of Intel processors. The large-scale takeup of early releases of Linux by developers also means that new versions of the operating system, based on new processor architectures, are likely to be in a production-ready state sooner, allowing Oracle to release their products on them earlier.

At this point you might be wondering why I haven't mentioned Oracle on Windows as a solution for taking advantage of Intel processors. The first is that Linux is free and will remain so, whereas Windows isn't. Secondly, and more importantly, my experience is that Oracle on UNIX is fundamentally more supportable than Oracle on Windows. For example, UNIX comes bundled with tools for performance management. These days all UNIX variants have much in common, particularly those that are POSIX compliant. So one UNIX system administrator (SA) can pretty much adopt to any UNIX in a short time. UNIX also enables you to trace the behavior of the system yourself. You might want to look at Chapter 28 for some examples. My experience of Oracle on Windows is that when something doesn't work, you have no option but to call support. Even support basics that you take for granted on UNIX, such as the ability to log in remotely via telnet to check out a system via command-line utilities, can't be taken for granted on Windows. It's true that in the open-source world it's not uncommon for people to be anti-Microsoft on ethical grounds. I try to steer clear of such discussions. However, if you are considering deploying a database on Windows, I would recommend Microsoft SQL Server most of the time. If you want to deploy Oracle on Intel, choose Linux.

For technologies like clustering, Linux seems to be very much on the leading edge from Oracle's perspective. For example, the open source nature of the operating system enables Oracle to bundle the cluster management tools with the Oracle DBMS on Linux and own the development of the tools. Both factors are likely to make for a better support experience if and when problems are found. This compares favorably with other operating systems when the vendor needs to supply the tools. The support of the Intel world for Oracle RAC is shown by the availability of certified RAC configuration on Linux from Compaq and the emphasis placed on RAC by big names in the industry. For example, Craig Barrett, CEO of Intel, provided a keynote speech at Oracle OpenWorld in December 2001 on the benefits of macroprocessing. This was no coincidence, because Oracle RAC on Linux represents macroprocessing in action.

Oracle on Linux is not perfect. For example, Oracle RAC on Linux still required raw partitions as of late 2001. With the commitment of major players like VERITAS (covered in Chapter 20), the ability to run Oracle RAC on Linux over a file system will be resolved and open up RAC to a whole new world of potential customers. Once again, the open source nature of Linux proves to be an advantage, as it enables smaller companies to engineer file systems on which to run RAC clusters. For example, PolyServe Inc. (www.polyserve.com) demonstrated Oracle9i RAC on Linux over a clustered file system at Oracle OpenWorld in December 2001, for production release in 2002. One thing you can bank on is that technology issues such as clustered file systems will be solved in the Linux community due to the sheer numbers and talent of the engineers available to work on problems, which itself results from open source. It's worth noting that one way you can mitigate some of the problems of raw partitions is to use a volume manager. Both SuSE and Red Hat Linux come bundled with a free commercial-quality volume manager. In addition, Linux provides logging file systems (reiserfs and ext3) for fast startup after a machine crashes. These kinds of features are usually extra cost options for commercial operating systems.

NOTE Oracle announced support for clustered file systems on Windows and Linux in Oracle9*i* Release 2.

Robustness and reliability are ultimately the operating system and hardware attributes required above all others when you choose a platform to run Oracle. If you run Oracle on Sun Solaris, for example, the database can run for months without a problem. In fact, you take that for granted. However, it would be a mistake to think that because something is free, as Linux is, then it's flawed in some way. Perl, for example, is free software and has a huge community of users and developers in the open source world.

My personal experience with Linux is that it is ready to run commercial applications such as Oracle. Over time, the complete set of tools that you need to run your complete Oracle infrastructure on Linux will be available. In reality, you may find that some third-party software you need has already been released on Linux. Legato's Networker Module for Oracle backups is one example. As Linux really takes off for commercial applications, then this trend for Linux to be at the leading edge of release strategies for software vendors looks set to continue.

Summary

RAC, combined with Oracle9*i* manageability features, has the potential to provide almost unlimited scalability with high availability. High availability results from improved session and query failover facilities. Unlike OPS, RAC provides the DBA with the tools needed to manage all Oracle services in the cluster from any node. One major drawback of OPS is the requirement to physically partition data across nodes using FREELIST GROUPS. This is still possible but is not recommended for RAC. RAC provides scalability transparently to applications: if you need more performance, or need to support a large user base, it's as simple as adding a node to the cluster.

Linux is at the forefront of Oracle RAC technology and some big industry names such as Intel and Compaq are raising the profile of RAC. Linux is a key-enabling technology for providing high performance at low cost, based on Intel processors, including 64-bit architectures. On Linux, raw partitions are still a requirement until clustered file systems become widely available and mature enough for use in the enterprise. A careful consideration of the cost and benefits is always required before deploying Oracle on raw partitions, with or without RAC. However, clustered file systems for Linux will be available in a short timeframe. Once the manageability benefits of clustered file systems are available on Linux, Oracle RAC on Linux will likely become the Oracle architecture of the future.

Protecting Data Using Standby Databases

Probably the most effective Oracle disaster recovery solution is the standby database. All Oracle standby databases work by applying changes contained in redo, generated at the primary database, to one or more databases known as standby databases. Typically, the primary and standby databases are on different sites to provide recovery from a site disaster on the primary. Oracle9*i* provides two types of standby: physical and logical. Prior to Oracle9*i*, only physical standby was available and it was based on the transfer and application of archived redo logs from the primary database onto the standby. The transfer and application process needed to be managed by the database administrator (DBA). Oracle9*i* Data Guard enhances disaster recovery capabilities through:

- Automation of the creation, monitoring, and management of a standby database configuration.

- Increased options for transport and application of redo, including the ability to allow redo generated on the primary to be applied synchronously on the standby, leading to no-data-loss operation.

This additional functionality results in a more complex configuration to be managed by the DBA. To provide ease of management alongside the new features, Oracle9*i* provides Data Guard broker. This component enables you to configure your primary and standby databases into a single, managed entity either via a command-line interface or the Data Guard Manager graphical user interface (GUI). The standby database features in Oracle9*i* Data Guard provide a complete and comprehensive disaster recovery capability far more advanced than that in earlier versions. This chapter covers a subset of the available options. There are many more. For example, a standby server can operate as an off-site store for archived redo logs on the primary, without requiring the existence of a full database on the standby.

This chapter covers the following topics:

- An overview of physical and logical standby databases
- Creating and running a physical standby database in Oracle8*i*
- Creating and running a physical standby database using Oracle9*i* Data Guard
- Creating and running a logical standby database using Oracle9*i* Data Guard
- Improving standby management using Oracle9*i* Data Guard Manager and broker

Running a Physical Standby Database

Prior to Oracle9*i*, only the physical standby option was available. When physical standby is operational, data changes are applied to the standby in such a way that its binary is identical to the primary. In fact, it's even possible to run Recovery Manager (RMAN) backups on the standby because it's identical to the primary. If you run your RMAN backups on the standby, you avoid a backup on the primary database server that can impact the performance of the primary database. Using physical standby, the standby database is in a continual state of recovery and changes are applied to the standby through redo blocks, exactly as if a database recovery was in progress on the primary. Recovery is covered in Chapter 17. The database's physical layout on the standby must be identical to the primary in terms of the number of datafiles and their sizes. A physical standby database can be opened in read-only mode for reporting purposes. Redo can't be applied when in the read-only state. If both the primary and standby databases are available, it's possible for the primary and standby to switch roles. If the primary is lost, the standby can be activated in read-write mode, but it can't be switched back to a standby state.

The transfer of redo log information to the standby server in Oracle8*i* required the transport of complete archived redo log files from the primary database, leading to possible loss of transactions on the standby after a disaster on the primary. Oracle9*i* makes it possible to run standby databases with lower levels of data loss, by transferring redo log information to standby redo logs on the standby immediately after generation on the primary, without waiting for a log switch on the primary. In no-data-loss mode, the redo from the primary can be kept in exact synchronization with the primary.

Prerequisites for Running a Physical Standby Database

Before you create a physical standby database, you should configure the primary so that it's suitable for running as a standby, both in manual mode using Oracle8*i* and in Oracle-managed mode using Oracle9*i* Data Guard. If you set up all your databases according to the following rules, they will be in a suitable state for running in standby mode at a later time, should you choose to do that. In fact, the rules are generic for configuring all your Oracle databases, whether or not you run them in standby mode.

TEMPORARY Tablespaces

If you choose to run a standby database and subsequently need to open the standby database in read-only mode (possibly for reporting purposes), the standby must operate without generating redo for sort operations. Keep in mind that sort operations potentially generate redo unless any TEMPORARY tablespaces are created using tempfile files. Therefore, you should make sure that any TEMPORARY tablespaces in the primary database use tempfile files before setting up that database in standby mode. This is an example of a TEMPORARY tablespace created using a tempfile:

```
create temporary tablespace temp
tempfile
  '/u02/oradata/ORAD2/temp01.dbf' size 41943040
autoextend on next 655360 maxsize 33554416k
extent management local uniform size 1048576
/
```

Oracle Password Files

To check whether a standby database is in synch with its primary, you can check the current archived redo log sequence in both and compare the values. To do that from the primary server, it's necessary to create a remote Oracle connection to the standby. As the standby is not running in regular open mode, a remote connection to the standby requires a SYSDBA connection, which is only possible if the standby uses an Oracle password file. Both the primary and standby databases should be configured to use an Oracle password file, which requires the following setting in the database parameter file:

```
remote_login_passwordfile=EXCLUSIVE
```

The following command can be used to create an Oracle password file for the specified Oracle System ID (SID), where the SYS password, *SYSpassword*, is required to authenticate SYSDBA connections:

```
$ cd $ORACLE_HOME/dbs
$ orapwd file=orapwSID password=SYSpassword
```

NOTE The use of password files is also required to take advantage of the standby management automation features of Data Guard Manager.

Format for Archived Redo Log Locations

If you choose to let Oracle manage the redo log transfer to the standby (as shown later in the chapter), you need to specify the archived redo log destinations using the Oracle8 format. The following example shows the archivelog location in Oracle8 format, compared to the archive log location in the older format, which is still widely used:

```
# Oracle8 format
log_archive_dest_1 = "location=/u02/oradata/ORAD2/arch MANDATORY"

# pre Oracle8 format
log_archive_dest      =/u02/oradata/ORAD2/arch
```

Oracle8 (and later versions) provides features to specify multiple archived redo log locations, and to indicate whether the archiving operation must complete (for example, MANDATORY) before processing can continue. These additional options are required to enable the full range of features for Oracle Data Guard.

Oracle Net Aliases for the Primary and Standby

You should ensure that Oracle Net aliases exist for the primary and standby databases in advance, and that these can be resolved from both primary and standby servers. If you are using Oracle Names, as strongly recommended in Chapter 3, you need to add entries to the Names server only once, and the names will be available across your whole network. In terms of naming conventions, it's helpful to choose Oracle Net aliases for the standby and primary that identify the relationship between them. For example, given a primary database with the alias orad2.primary.dbcool.com, you might choose the alias for the standby to be orad2.standby.dbcool.com.

If you're running a physical standby, the design goal is usually to ensure that the database is available on either the primary or standby site at any time, but not on both sites simultaneously. In this case, clients can connect to the database using an Oracle Net alias that directs them to whichever database is available at the time, using the Oracle Net failover capabilities. The following Oracle Net alias (orad2.dbcool.com) directs clients to the database service orad2.dbcool.com located on the server "primary," or to the server "standby," whichever is currently available:

```
orad2.dbcool.com   =
  (DESCRIPTION =
    (ADDRESS_LIST =
      (ADDRESS = (PROTOCOL = TCP)(HOST = primary)(PORT = 1521))
      (ADDRESS = (PROTOCOL = TCP)(HOST = standby)(PORT = 1521))
      (FAILOVER = true)
      (LOAD_BALANCE = false)
    )
    (CONNECT_DATA =
      (SERVICE_NAME = orad2.dbcool.com)
    )
  )
```

Using this approach, clients don't need to know which server the database actually runs on. The SERVICE_NAME value used in the alias also needs to be used as the initialization parameter SERVICE_NAMES, in both the primary and standby database initialization parameter files. This is the name each database uses to dynamically register with the Oracle network listener on each server. Chapter 3 provides full details.

After the standby database has been mounted, and before it runs in standby mode, the following commands should be executed on both the standby and primary servers from SQL*Plus (using the /NOLOG command-line option) to ensure that remote SYSDBA connections are operational against both databases from both servers:

```
connect sys/change_on_install@orad2.standby.dbcool.com as SYSDBA
connect sys/change_on_install@orad2.primary.dbcool.com as SYSDBA
connect sys/change_on_install@orad2.dbool.com as SYSDBA
```

rcp Requirements

You can create the initial copy of the primary on which the standby is based either automatically using Data Guard broker, or manually using the procedure described in this chapter. Both approaches require that rcp is configured to allow remote file copy between the primary and standby servers. You can test that rcp works by using the rsh command on the primary to test that the correct authentication is in place, as follows:

```
$ rsh standby_host
```

If the login takes place without requesting a password, rcp works as well. If not, you should consult Chapter 1 for rsh configuration details.

NOLOGGING Considerations

If you perform Data Definition Language (DDL) statements using the NOLOGGING option, redo is not generated for those operations. As a result, objects in the standby database might be unusable or missing when the standby database needs to be opened in read-write mode following a disaster on the primary site, or read-only mode. These are examples of commands that don't generate redo:

```
create table EMP_NOLOG as select * from EMP nologging;
alter index PK_EMP rebuild nologging;
alter table EMP move tablespace tools nologging;
```

The V$DATAFILE view contains two columns, UNRECOVERABLE_CHANGE# and UNRECOVERABLE_TIME, which can be used on the primary to identify datafiles with unrecoverable changes that might impact the standby. It's possible to transfer new backup copies of files that contain unrecoverable changes to make sure that those objects are present and complete in the standby. Information on NOLOGGING changes is not available in V$DATAFILE on the standby, and the following errors related to such changes might be reported while running Data Manipulation Language

(DML) on the standby after activating it in read-write mode, or opening it in read-only mode:

- ORA-1578: "ORACLE data block corrupted (file # %s, block # %s)"
- ORA-1110: "datafile %s: '%s'"
- ORA-26040: "Data block was loaded using the NOLOGGING option\n"

To keep problems due to NOLOGGING from manifesting themselves during business operation, the ANALYZE TABLE ... VALIDATE STRUCTURE CASCADE command needs to run on all tables, to check for bad objects resulting from NOLOGGING operations. Any unusable indexes can be rebuilt, and tables need to be regenerated either from a backup file, or from some other source. The lowest-risk approach is to avoid all unrecoverable operations on the primary. All NOLOGGING operations increase the elapsed time before the standby can be activated with a complete set of valid database objects.

> **NOTE** In later versions of Oracle9*i*, the ALTER DATABASE FORCE LOGGING command can be used to force generation of redo log information required by a standby database at all times.

Creating a Physical Standby Database

This section takes you through the process of creating a standby database from scratch, manually. As an alternative, Oracle Data Guard Manager in Oracle9*i* provides features for setting up a standby database automatically, using a GUI. However, the principles are the same, and it's useful to understand the fundamentals of standby databases by setting one up by hand the first time. In addition, the manual approach copies files between the primary and standby in parallel, and can therefore reduce the time needed to get the standby up and running, as compared to early releases of Oracle Data Guard in Oracle9*i*.

The following assumptions are made to create a real-world standby configuration:

- The primary and standby databases are on different servers.
- The databases aren't clustered using Oracle Parallel Server (OPS) or Real Application Clusters (RACs).
- The primary and standby conform to Oracle's Optimal Flexible Architecture (OFA) standard for database and software layout.
- The primary and standby servers have the same file systems and sizes.
- The primary and standby use the same log archive directory and run in ARCHIVELOG mode.
- The primary and standby servers have the same version of Oracle and the operating system installed.

It is often the case that when you enforce a standard file system layout for all your Oracle servers, unanticipated benefits result. In this case, the decision to standardize servers makes the process of creating a standby database much easier because the same physical layout can be used on the primary and standby servers for the Oracle software and for the databases. Of course, Oracle provides facilities enabling a file on the primary to be relocated in a different directory on the standby, in case the physical layouts don't match on each server. However, if you standardize your database layout and distribute your databases across a few large file systems, the added complexity of relocating files on the standby is not necessary.

Creating the Oracle Environment on the Standby

To run a standby database, the Oracle environment must exist on the standby server. That means that a database parameter file, password file, OFA directory structure, and archivelog directory must be in place (as well as the Oracle software). The following commands, when run from the Oracle environment of the primary database on the primary server, copy the relevant files to the standby host named sb1 (in locations identical to those on the primary):

```
$ rcp -pr $ORACLE_BASE/admin/$ORACLE_SID sb1:$ORACLE_BASE/admin
$ rcp -p  $ORACLE_HOME/dbs/*$ORACLE_SID* sb1:$ORACLE_HOME/dbs
```

Keep in mind that the rcp -p command doesn't copy symbolic links, so you might need to re-create links for your parameter file and OFA arch directory on the standby server. If the standby database is likely to be opened in read-only mode, use of a database-located audit trail for the standby prevents that. The following error message is reported when an attempt is made to start the standby database in read-only mode:

```
ORA-16006: audit_trail destination incompatible with database open mode
```

Using a database-located audit trail requires database changes, and these changes are incompatible with running the standby database in read-only mode. To permit the standby database to run in read-only mode, the AUDIT_TRAIL parameter for the standby database needs to be set to either NONE or OS.

Creating the Standby Database

Creating the standby database means transporting a backup copy of the primary database to the standby site. It's not necessary to shut down the primary to perform this copy. After the transport is complete, the standby database needs to be mounted using a special type of control file, known as a standby control file. The standby control file is created on the primary site, after the backup of the primary is taken. When the standby has been mounted, the redo application process can begin.

There are two ways to take a backup copy of the primary and transport it to the standby. The first involves taking an RMAN backup (either to tape or disk) followed by a restore on the standby. RMAN is covered in Chapter 18. The second method uses Oracle7-style online backup commands. This second method doesn't require a backup to tape or disk in advance. Instead, after the primary files are in backup mode, they can be copied to the standby using the UNIX rcp command or ftp. As a result, the backup implicitly becomes the restore on the standby end, and is ready to use immediately. Using the second method, it's possible to compress the database files through a UNIX pipe before sending them on the network, and decompress them at the standby. The use of compression means that network transfer times are reduced, especially in WAN environments, allowing the standby to be up and running sooner. The Data Guard Manager GUI (covered at the end of the chapter) provides both methods for creating a standby. Data Guard Manager refers to the rcp-based technique as the OS method. However, Data Guard Manager only sends one database file at a time in early releases of Oracle9i, which doesn't take advantage of all the available network bandwidth or I/O capacity on the standby or primary server.

As an alternative, the dbcool_gen_standby.pl script (downloadable from the companion Web site) can be used to generate a shell script containing the sequence of commands needed to create a backup copy of the primary on the standby, ready for use as the standby database. The dbcool_gen_standby.pl script is run from the Oracle environment of the primary database, and writes the sequence of instructions to UNIX stdout, where it can be redirected to a file. The file can then be executed immediately to create the standby database, or it can be customized by hand first, if required. The following commands show how to create a script that copies a primary database with Oracle SID ORAD2 to a standby server where *pwd* is the SYSTEM password of the ORAD2 instance, and sb1 is the hostname of the standby server:

```
$ export ORACLE_SID=ORAD2
$ export ORACLE_HOME=/u01/app/oracle/product/9.2.0
$ dbcool_gen_standby.pl system_pwd=pwd mode=physical standby_host=sb1
```

The dbcool_gen_standby.pl checks that the server specified as the standby_host parameter doesn't match the name of the local server where the primary runs, by comparing the IP addresses of both machines. If the addresses match, the script exits. This check protects the script from accidentally generating commands that would overwrite the ORAD2 database on the local server, in case the local server name was accidentally used as the value of the standby_host command-line option.

In the following example, the instance ORAD2 contains five tablespaces: SYSTEM, UNDOTBS, TOOLS, USERS, and TEMP. The TEMP tablespace uses a tempfile (as recommended in the prerequisites) and can't be placed in backup mode. As a result, it isn't transferred to the standby site. That's not a problem because it doesn't prevent the standby from running in standby mode. However, if an attempt is made later to run the standby in read-only mode, or run it as the primary after opening it in read-write mode, any DML that needs to perform a sort operation fails with the error "ORA-25153: Temporary Tablespace is Empty." That message indicates that a TEMPORARY tablespace definition exists in the Oracle data dictionary, but the tablespace has no tempfile files associated with it. Before attempting a sort, a new tempfile must be added to the tablespace, based on the following SQL:

```
alter tablespace temp
add tempfile '/u02/oradata/ORAD2/temp01.dbf' size 100m;
```

For the sake of example, assume that the output of dbcool_gen_script.pl has been redirected to a file (to_sb1.sh). The output in to_sb1.sh includes the following commands in the following order, which when executed on the primary create a standby database on the remote standby server. The script doesn't check whether the files on the standby server are already in use by another database. The DBA who runs the script should check this in advance, as a matter of due diligence. This is an example of the contents of to_sb1.sh:

```
#### place datafiles into backup mode...
sqlplus "/ as SYSDBA" <<!
whenever sqlerror exit 1

alter tablespace SYSTEM BEGIN BACKUP;
alter tablespace UNDOTBS BEGIN BACKUP;
alter tablespace TOOLS BEGIN BACKUP;
alter tablespace USERS BEGIN BACKUP;
!

#### transfer all primary datafiles to the standby server in parallel
#### and wait until all complete
(compress -c /u02/oradata/ORAD2/system01.dbf \
 | rsh sb1 "uncompress -c >/u02/oradata/ORAD2/system01.dbf") &
(compress -c /u02/oradata/ORAD2/undotbs01.dbf \
 | rsh sb1 "uncompress -c >/u02/oradata/ORAD2/undotbs01.dbf") &
(compress -c /u02/oradata/ORAD2/tools01.dbf \
 | rsh sb1 "uncompress -c >/u02/oradata/ORAD2/tools01.dbf") &
(compress -c /u02/oradata/ORAD2/users01.dbf \
 | rsh sb1 "uncompress -c >/u02/oradata/ORAD2/users01.dbf") &
wait

#### take datafiles out of backup mode...
sqlplus "/ as SYSDBA" <<!
whenever sqlerror exit 1

alter tablespace SYSTEM END BACKUP;
alter tablespace UNDOTBS END BACKUP;
alter tablespace TOOLS END BACKUP;
alter tablespace USERS END BACKUP;
!

#### create standby control file
sqlplus "/ as SYSDBA" <<!
whenever sqlerror exit 1

alter database create standby controlfile
  as '/tmp/to_standby.ctl' reuse;
!


#### transfer standby control file from primary to standby server . . .
rcp -p /tmp/to_standby.ctl sb1:/u02/oradata/ORAD2/control01.ctl
rcp -p /tmp/to_standby.ctl sb1:/u03/oradata/ORAD2/control02.ctl
```

The generated to_sb1.sh script performs the transfer of datafiles to the standby across the network in parallel. Like Data Guard Manager, the data is compressed before it is sent, and uncompressed at the standby server. The control files at the standby server are copied from the standby control file created at the primary server. The names of the control files to create on the standby are read from the data dictionary of the primary instance. Not shown are the additional commands in to_sb1.sh that create directories for the redo logs, control files, and datafiles at the standby server, based on the file paths of those files on the primary server. Now, the standby server is ready to run in standby mode, and apply redo logs from the primary server.

Running an Oracle8*i* Physical Standby Database

At this stage, the standby server contains an image of the primary database instance, with the same parameter file and password file as the primary. If you were running Oracle9*i*, at this stage you could let Data Guard take over the complete operation of the standby you have just created. Data Guard can manage redo log transfer and apply, and propagate primary database structure changes onto the standby all without manual DBA intervention.

This section assumes that you are running Oracle8*i*, in which case the redo log transfer-and-apply process is managed by the DBA, and changes to the database structure on the primary require DBA manual intervention for the standby operation to continue.

The standby control files are based on a standby control file created on the primary. The standby is now ready to run. The following commands are required to start the standby database:

```
startup nomount;
alter database mount standby database;
```

The following commands, which check network connectivity to the primary and standby databases using network connections, should now work from both the primary and standby server using SQL*Plus, started with the /NOLOG command-line argument:

```
connect sys/pwd@orad2.standby.dbcool.com as SYSDBA
connect sys/pwd@orad2.primary.dbcool.com as SYSDBA

REM transparent application failover alias...
REM this connection uses whichever of primary or standby is available
connect sys/pwd@orad2.dbcool.com as SYSDBA
```

Redo Log Application

A simple shell script on the standby can be used to apply redo logs transferred from the primary in an infinite loop. It doesn't matter if the redo log transfer process from the primary isn't running. If the next archived redo log file that needs to be applied hasn't arrived yet, the RECOVER command simply returns an "ORA-00308: cannot open archived log" error until the file arrives. The following ksh script applies all available archived redo logs copied from the primary server by using the RECOVER command in SQL*Plus, exits SQL*Plus when no more logs are available or a problem occurs, and then waits for 10 minutes before repeating the process:

```
#!/bin/ksh
export ORACLE_SID=ORAD2
export ORACLE_HOME=/u01/app/oracle/product/8.1.7

while true ; do
  $ORACLE_HOME/bin/sqlplus "/ as SYSDBA" <<!
recover automatic standby database until cancel;
cancel
exit
!
  sleep 600
done
```

In this simple example, the redo log transfer process from the primary is not synchronized with the recovery process on the standby. The recovery process runs independently of any archived redo log transfer process. That leads to two possible problems:

- The standby might attempt to apply a redo log still in transit from the primary.

- The standby might attempt to apply an incomplete log transferred when the primary archive log area was full.

The good news is that the Oracle recovery process is extremely robust in both cases. In the first case, the RECOVER command detects that the physical size of the archived redo log is less than the size of the file (as stored in the archived redo log file header), and RECOVER stops with the following message:

```
ORA-00332: archived log is too small - may be incompletely archived
```

In the second case, Oracle uses a checksum on each redo block to determine whether the archived redo log is complete. If it's not, error messages are displayed in the alert log and RECOVER stops. If appropriate file system monitoring of the archive log area fullness is in place on the primary, this situation should never happen. If it does, it's useful to know that the original archived redo log can simply be resent from the primary, and RECOVER applies it the next time it runs, assuming that it's now complete because space was freed on the primary archive log area. The following code shows some sample output from the alert log on the standby for the second case:

```
Media recovery buffers written to disk due to log corruption.
Some changes at scn 42312326367 may be on disk
Media Recovery failed with error 368
ORA-283 signalled during: ALTER DATABASE RECOVER  automatic standby
database . . .
```

It would be considered good design to synchronize the archived redo log transfer and recovery process between the primary and server ends, but, strictly speaking, it's not necessary because the RECOVER command is robust enough to handle synchronization issues gracefully. That leads to the possibility of complete independence between the archived redo log transfer and apply processes, leading to a standby configuration that's exceptionally quick to implement and easy to manage, provided that the database structure doesn't change.

In some cases, there is a requirement to run the standby database a few hours (or maybe a whole day) behind the primary to provide a contingency for logical application errors, such as the failure of an overnight batch process. A gap between the changes applied on the standby compared to the primary can be introduced by using the following option of the RECOVER command on the standby, where a constant string value is required for the time value:

```
recover automatic standby database until time '14-FEB-2002 22:43:38';
```

This simple example ensures that changes on the standby always lag a specific time behind those on the primary, as long as the time used in RECOVER is generated relative to SYSDATE. For example, use of the time string equivalent to SYSDATE-1 in the RECOVER command ensures that all changes applied to the standby are at least 24-hours old. Rather than base the lag on a time, a more sophisticated approach is to explicitly determine the system change number (SCN) at a significant point in the transaction processing stream on the primary (for example, immediately before the batch starts) to identify the SCN that should be used in the RECOVER command on the standby. In Oracle8i, the USERENV('COMMITSCN') function can be used to identify the current SCN value. By saving this value at the appropriate point in the processing stream on the primary (into either a table or log file), the SCN value can be used on the standby to determine the lag between the primary and standby in terms of business transactions, rather than on a fixed time interval. The following example shows how to recover the standby database using the SCN of a known change on the primary, generated using USERENV('COMMITSCN'):

```
recover automatic standby database until change 4567890;
```

NOTE In Oracle9i, the GET_SYSTEM_CHANGE_NUMBER function in the DBMS_FLASHBACK package can be used to find the current SCN.

Redo Log Transfer

The implementation of a manual process to transfer archived redo logs from the primary to the standby has three simple requirements:

- You should be able to guarantee that the transfer of each log is successful.
- Each archived redo log should be transferred to the standby one time.
- Logs should be generated at a predetermined interval.

Keep in mind that if the log archive destination is the same for the primary and standby, the destination can be read on the primary from the Oracle data dictionary. This approach simplifies the configuration. In the example provided in this section, the archived redo log files are pushed from the primary to the standby. They could be pulled from the standby end. It doesn't matter which server the transfer originates from. To guarantee that the transfer of each log is successful, use the following pseudocode:

1. Transfer the archived redo log from the primary to the standby using UNIX rcp.

2. Generate a checksum of the archived redo log on the primary and standby.

3. Compare the checksums; if they match, the transfer was successful.

4. If the transfer was successful, record the log sequence number in a log file.

This procedure uses a checksum to ensure that the archived redo logs on each end are identical. Most UNIX operating systems use either the CKSUM or **CHECKSUM** command to generate a checksum on a file. Based on the preceding design, the existence of the sequence number in the log file after the transfer completes is the only method guaranteeing that the log transfer was successful. When the log file contains entries, the following pseudocode can be used to identify the archived redo logs to transfer each time the procedure is called:

1. Get the log sequence of the last log transferred successfully to the standby from the list of transferred logs.

2. Identify the next log to transfer by incrementing the last log sequence by 1.

3. Get the last archived redo log sequence using SELECT MAX(SEQUENCE#) FROM V$LOG_HISTORY. This identifies the last log written on the primary database.

4. Transfer all logs to standby in sequence based on the values in 2. and 3.

A script, dbcool_arch_to_standby.pl is available for download from the book's companion Web site. This script implements the end-to-end transfer process as defined by the preceding list of requirements. The script runs on the primary and uses the generic Perl routines described in Chapter 4. As a result, it logs useful information automatically on each invocation, and prevents more than one instance of the script from running against a specific Oracle database at any time. This is an example command line that transfers logs from the primary database ORAD2 (SYSTEM password *pwd*) to the standby server sb1:

```
$ dbcool_arch_to_standby.pl sid=ORAD2 system_pwd=pwd standby_host=sb1
```

The log file that holds the list of transferred logs contains lines like those in the following code. The lines identify the log sequence number that was transferred and the transfer completion time:

```
46232 Sat Feb 16 17:22:59 GMT 2002 OK
46233 Sat Feb 16 17:23:09 GMT 2002 OK
46234 Sat Feb 16 17:23:12 GMT 2002 OK
```

To ensure that archived redo logs are created at regular intervals on the primary for transfer to the standby, a database job can be used to switch the logs on a scheduled interval. This is requirement 3. from the original list. The following job switches logs every 15 minutes:

```
begin
sys.dbms_ijob.submit (
job=>100,
luser=>'SYSTEM',
puser=>'SYSTEM',
cuser=>'SYSTEM',
next_date=>to_date('2002-02-14:18:34:52','YYYY-MM-DD:HH24:MI:SS'),
interval=>'sysdate+15/(24*60)',
broken=>FALSE,
what=>'execute immediate ''alter system switch logfile'';',
nlsenv=>'NLS_LANGUAGE=''AMERICAN'' NLS_TERRITORY=''AMERICA'''||
'NLS_CURRENCY=''$'' NLS_ISO_CURRENCY=''AMERICA'''||
'NLS_NUMERIC_CHARACTERS=''.,'' NLS_DATE_FORMAT=''DD-MON-YYYY'''||
'NLS_DATE_LANGUAGE=''AMERICAN'' NLS_SORT=''BINARY''',
env=>'0102000200000000'
);
end;
/

commit;
```

NOTE In Oracle9*i*, you can automate the log switch process without a database job. Oracle9*i* provides the ARCHIVE_LAG_TARGET initialization parameter that allows you to force a log switch after a specified time (in seconds).

Addition of Datafiles to the Primary

When running a standby in manual mode, changes to the structure of the primary database need to be executed manually on the standby or the standby suspends the application of redo. Primary database changes, such as the addition of datafiles to a tablespace or the creation of a new tablespace, fall into this category. After addition of a tablespace on the primary, a new datafile appears in the Oracle control file on the standby, transmitted by the redo. However, the new file doesn't physically exist in the file system on the standby, and Oracle doesn't create it automatically. As a result, redo log application on the standby stops because there is no file to apply changes to, and errors appear in the alert log of the standby database when the RECOVER command is executed (see the following example):

```
ORA-01157: cannot identify/lock datafile 7 - see DBWR trace file
ORA-01110: datafile 7: '/u03/oradata/ORAD2/indexes01.dbf'
```

For the standby redo log application to resume, the following things need to happen:

1. The standby redo log application process needs to be stopped.

2. The new datafile needs to be created in the standby database.

3. The standby redo log application process needs to be restarted.

After creation, when the redo application starts again, all changes to the file since it was created on the primary are applied. The following SQL can be used on the primary to generate the SQL to add datafiles to the standby, in cases where datafiles are added to an existing tablespace and in cases where datafiles are created as part of a new tablespace:

```
REM example for file_id=7. Change this if you run it...
select 'alter database create datafile '||chr(10)||
       '   '''||file_name||''' as '||chr(10)||
       '   '''||file_name||''';' add_file
from dba_data_files where file_id = 7;

REM sample output from SQL...
alter database create datafile
  '/u03/oradata/ORAD2/indexes01.dbf' as
  '/u03/oradata/ORAD2/indexes01.dbf';
```

The DBA needs to provide the FILE_ID value (or values) for the datafile that has been added to the primary. This value appears in the alert log on the standby, as shown in the earlier error message. The generated ALTER DATABASE CREATE DATAFILE statement can then be executed remotely against the standby using SQL*Plus from the primary with a SYSDBA connection, or it can be transferred to the standby and executed locally. The following example shows a SQL*Plus script to run remotely on the primary against the standby, assuming that SQL*Plus on the primary has been started using the /NOLOG command-line option:

```
connect sys/pwd@orad2.standby.dbcool.com as SYSDBA
alter database create datafile
  '/u03/oradata/ORAD2/indexes01.dbf' as
  '/u03/oradata/ORAD2/indexes01.dbf';
```

It's important to emphasize that the original ORA-01157 error signifies that the new datafile appears in the standby control file, but doesn't physically exist on the standby server. The datafile is added to the standby control file through transferred redo information in the usual way. It's not possible to execute CREATE DATAFILE on the standby until the standby control file contains the new file. If the file doesn't exist in the standby control file yet, more redo needs to be applied until the new name appears. As a result, if you add several new files to the primary at one time, it might be necessary to run CREATE DATAFILE, and then apply redo on the standby more than once to resynchronize the standby with the primary. You can view datafiles that exist in either the primary or standby control file using the following SQL, to determine which files don't yet exist in the standby control file:

```
select name from v$datafile;
```

Starting the Standby in Read-Only Mode

Before starting the standby database in read-only mode, all recovery operations should be stopped. The following sequence of commands can be used to ensure that recovery operations are stopped first before starting in read-only mode.

```
shutdown immediate;
startup nomount;
alter database mount standby database;
alter database open read only;
```

If a query requires a sort operation and the TEMPORARY tablespace doesn't contain a tempfile, the following error is reported: "ORA-25153: Temporary Tablespace is Empty." It's quite safe to add a tempfile to any TEMPORARY tablespace on the standby, as follows, so that read-only queries that require sorts can complete:

```
alter tablespace TEMP
add tempfile  '/u02/oradata/ORAD2/temp01.dbf' size 100M;
```

If necessary, the database can be returned to standby mode so that more redo can be applied from the primary. The capability to return to standby mode is not affected by the addition of tempfile files to the standby while in read-only mode. The following commands return the database to standby mode:

```
shutdown immediate;
startup nomount;
alter database mount standby database;
```

Activating the Standby

The standby can take over the role of the primary by activating it. When activated, the standby can't return to standby mode. The following commands activate and open the standby database for normal use:

```
shutdown immediate;
startup nomount;
alter database mount standby database;
REM recover standby database until cancel;
alter database activate standby database;
alter database mount;
alter database open;
```

The commented command can be used to apply all available redo that has not yet been applied before activating the standby. Before making the activated database available to end users, remember to add any missing tempfile files to TEMPORARY table-spaces, and ANALYZE tables and indexes that might cause errors on use (due to NOLOGGING operations performed on them).

Running a Physical Standby Database Using Oracle Data Guard

The manual approach is easy to implement, and it provides a standby capability. It works in both Oracle8i and Oracle9i. However, it has several drawbacks. The most significant drawback is that there is a potential for data loss when the standby takes over the role of the primary. This is possible because only redo from complete archived redo logs on the primary is available on the standby. Therefore, the standby data is only current up to the last complete archived redo log, and committed data in the online redo logs of the primary is not available if the primary is suddenly lost. The manual approach is easy to manage as long as the primary database structure doesn't change. Manageability becomes an issue when the structure of the primary changes due to the addition of datafiles. In this case, manual intervention on the standby is required to ensure that redo can be applied after the changes. Finally, it's not possible to switch roles between the standby and the primary. This is potentially a very useful feature in situations where the primary and standby sites experience scheduled outages at different times.

Data Guard in Oracle9i provides solutions to all these issues. If you need to provide disaster recovery facilities for your Oracle databases, the features of Data Guard are a compelling reason to move up to Oracle9i. This section covers the implementation of a physical standby database using Data Guard. The configuration described assumes, up front, that the standby database is used as the primary at some stage, and that the primary might become the standby. As a result, the initial configuration on both sites is implemented with this in mind.

Operating in No-Data-Loss Mode

Data Guard provides the capability to run a standby database in no-data-loss mode. This capability is enabled through the use of standby redo logs. Oracle strongly recommends the creation of standby redo logs as a matter of routine in any primary database that might be operated with a standby in the future. When created in the primary database, standby redo logs are ignored. If present in the primary database when it's copied to the standby, they are available for use in the standby. Optionally, they can be added to the standby when required.

When standby redo logs are in operation, redo changes are transferred directly to them from the log writer process (LGWR) on the primary. The standby redo logs are archived on the standby, and then applied. There's no longer a requirement for the standby to wait for a complete archived redo log from the primary before applying redo. The old archived-redo-log-based approach is referred to as delayed mode in Data Guard and is no longer a user-selectable option in later releases of Oracle9i. Standby redo logs can be multiplexed in groups like regular online redo logs. There is no requirement for standby redo logs to exist in the same numbers, or the same size, as redo logs. However, the simplest approach is to create the same number of groups and members for standby redo logs. The following SQL shows the commands required to create two online redo log groups (1 and 2) with a single member in each, and two standby redo log groups (3 and 4) with a single member in each:

```
ALTER DATABASE ADD LOGFILE GROUP 1
(
  '/u02/oradata/ORAD2/redog1m1.log'
) SIZE 10M;

ALTER DATABASE ADD LOGFILE GROUP 2
(
  '/u02/oradata/ORAD2/redog2m1.log'
) SIZE 10M;

REM add sb_ prefix to standby logs to identify them clearly...
ALTER DATABASE ADD STANDBY LOGFILE GROUP 3
(
  '/u02/oradata/ORAD2/sb_redog3m1.log'
) SIZE 10M;

ALTER DATABASE ADD STANDBY LOGFILE GROUP 4
(
  '/u02/oradata/ORAD2/sb_redog4m1.log'
) SIZE 10M;
```

The use of standby redo logs alone doesn't guarantee no-data-loss operation. It's necessary to set the appropriate Data Guard data protection mode before no-data-loss operation can be guaranteed, and the use of standby redo logs is a prerequisite.

Data Guard Data Protection Modes

To guarantee that all changes made to the primary are available on the standby, Data Guard can run in a configuration where changes to redo on the primary are synchronized with redo changes on the standby. Before the primary writes its own redo, it sends the same redo to the standby, and requests that the standby write it to disk. The standby server sends an acknowledgement to the primary to notify it that redo was written on disk. This is referred to as no-data-loss mode. When running in no-data-loss mode, it's possible for the network between the primary and standby to drop, or the standby server to experience a failure. In this case, the primary needs to decide how to proceed when the redo can't be written to the standby in synch with the primary. The two capabilities that Oracle provides in this case are referred to using terminology that changed in later releases of Oracle9*i*:

- Maximize Protection mode (previously referred to as Guaranteed Protection mode)
- Maximize Availability mode (previously referred to as Instant Protection mode)

In Maximize Protection mode, a failure by the standby to confirm the redo write results in shutdown of the primary, unless more than one standby is in operation. No data divergence is allowed. Oracle, therefore, recommends that for systems with high availability (HA) requirements, multiple standby databases should be available in Maximize Protection mode. Maximize Protection mode provides a high level of protection of primary database data should the primary be lost because all committed transactions are available on the activated standby database.

In Maximize Availability mode, when the redo-write confirmation isn't received from the standby, the primary continues to operate without transferring redo to the standby redo logs until the problem on the standby is resolved. In effect, redo application switches from synchronous to asynchronous mode. When the standby becomes available, archived redo logs written on the primary during the outage are transferred to the standby and applied. When the gap in archived redo logs between sites has been resolved, redo is applied directly to the standby redo logs as before. The feature that enables gaps in archived redo logs between the primary and standby to be resolved is referred to as the Fetch Archive Logs (FAL) service. FAL services are enabled through initialization parameters, which will be described later in this chapter in the sections titled *Managed Standby Initialization Parameters* and *Logical Standby Initialization Parameters*.

Like Maximize Protection mode, Maximize Availability mode waits for confirmation from the standby before proceeding with its redo-write operation. Unlike Maximize Protection mode, Maximize Availability mode allows the primary to operate when the standby is temporarily unavailable, so data divergence is allowed. However, if the primary fails while the standby is unavailable, the activated standby might be missing transactions from the primary. Oracle provides an overwhelming number of options with respect to data protection modes. However, Maximize Protection and Maximize Availability are probably the two you are most likely to use. A third mode, known as the Maximize Performance mode (referred to as Rapid Protection in early versions of Oracle9i) writes redo to the standby in synch with the primary, but doesn't wait for an acknowledgement from the standby. Therefore, Maximize Performance provides less protection than the other two modes, but doesn't impact the performance of the primary to the same degree.

Both Maximize Protection and Maximize Availability increase the elapsed time of operations on the primary because each redo write waits for confirmation from the standby server. This overhead is the price to pay for enhanced data protection. Before you implement standby databases in either mode, be sure to test that time critical business transactions complete within the required times when standby databases are in operation.

Implementation of Data Guard Protection Modes

At this stage, the discussion has been limited to qualitative descriptions of the Data Guard features. This section describes how to specify log archive destinations on the primary database to implement no-data-loss protection. For a database in ARCHIVELOG mode running without a standby, a single archived redo log destination is often implemented. This is a typical initialization parameter in such a case:

```
log_archive_dest_1 = "location=/u04/oradata/ORAD2/arch MANDATORY"
```

The view V$ARCHIVE_DEST presents information on all log archive destinations in operation, which includes the following information for the preceding initialization parameter:

```
select status,binding,target,archiver,destination
from v$archive_dest;
```

```
STATUS     BINDING     TARGET     ARCHIVER    DESTINATION
---------  ----------  --------   ----------  ----------------------------
VALID      MANDATORY   PRIMARY    ARCH        /u04/oradata/ORAD2/arch
```

The V$ARCHIVE_DEST view contains many other columns, most of which only have meaning for standby databases. The MANDATORY parameter is relevant to both primary and standby log archive destinations. It's used to determine the policy for the reuse of online redo logs. If the log archive destination specifies MANDATORY, and archival of the online redo logs fails, the online log will not be overwritten. Instead, the database suspends until the problem preventing archiving of the log is resolved. As every DBA knows, if the local log archive area fills, Oracle suspends until space is freed. The following log archive destination specifies a remote destination (to identify the location of a standby database) based on the Oracle Net alias orad2.standby. dbcool.com:

```
log_archive_dest_2=
'SERVICE=orad2.standby.dbcool.com MANDATORY REOPEN=10 SYNC AFFIRM
 REGISTER LGWR'
```

This log destination contains the attributes required to implement no-data-loss standby in Maximize Availability mode. The REOPEN attribute (which is optional) specifies a time in seconds that Oracle waits before trying a failed log transfer to the standby site again. The SERVICE attribute identifies the Net Alias of a remote database instance running in standby mode. The use of SYNC and AFFIRM together mandate that redo log writes on the standby take place using synchronous network transmission and synchronous disk I/O. As a result, when the primary receives notification of the write, the redo is guaranteed to exist on at least one standby site. The REGISTER attribute ensures that registration of archived redo logs takes place on the standby database control file. The attribute LGWR indicates that redo transport takes place for standby redo log files on the standby site, and is carried out by the primary LGWR. In the LOG_ARCHIVE_DEST_1 example, shown at the start of this section, the archiver process is not specified. It's ARCH by default.

Maximize Protection mode requires the same style of log archive destination as shown in LOG_ARCHIVE_DEST_2. To place the configuration into Maximize Protection mode, an additional command needs to be executed on the *primary* database:

```
alter database set standby database to maximize protection;
```

Recall that Maximize Protection shuts down the primary database if a MANDATORY remote standby destination is not available. To prevent a single standby outage from shutting down the primary, it's necessary to have more than one standby location, and guarantee that at least one is available when running in Maximize Protection Mode.

Managed Standby Initialization Parameters

To configure the initialization parameters for the primary and standby databases so that each database can fulfill both the primary and standby roles after a switchover, it's necessary to ensure that specific parameters exist in both databases. Some of these parameters are identical in both databases, and some have different values in each database. Table 23.1 shows values common to both the primary and standby databases in a Data Guard environment, based on the ORAD2 database instance used in the previous examples.

When running in no-data-loss mode, redo is transmitted from the primary to the standby through standby redo logs when the standby is available. Before being applied to the standby, the standby redo logs are archived into the location specified by LOG_ARCHIVE_DEST_1. If the standby is not available, the archived redo log files generated on the primary during the standby outage are transferred to the standby by the FAL process, which resolves gaps in the log sequence between the primary and the standby when the standby becomes available. These archived redo logs from the primary are transported to the STANDBY_ARCHIVE_DEST directory on the standby.

In theory, STANDBY_ARCHIVE_DEST and LOG_ARCHIVE_DEST_1 can specify the same directory. In practice, it can be useful to distinguish between them. For that reason, it's helpful to define a naming standard for the STANDY_ARCHIVE_DEST location. In Table 23.1, the location is given by the "standby" subdirectory of LOG_ARCHIVE_DEST_1.

The REMOTE_ARCHIVE_ENABLE setting of TRUE allows the standby database to receive redo logs for archiving from the primary database. The STANDBY_FILE_MANAGEMENT setting AUTO enables automatic creation of new datafiles on the standby after they are added to the primary, which addresses one of the main drawbacks of the manual approach. If either database changes roles from primary to standby, or vice versa, the settings in Table 23.1 continue to work in all cases. It's useful to know which logs have been applied on the standby. In a standby database managed by Data

Table 23.1 Initialization Parameters Common to Primary and Standby Databases

PARAMETER NAME	VALUE
remote_archive_enable	TRUE
log_archive_dest_1	/u04/oradata/ORAD2/arch
standby_archive_dest	/u04/oradata/ORAD2/arch/standby
standby_file_management	AUTO
compatible	9.0.0.0.0 (or higher)

Guard, the V$ARCHIVED_LOG view contains information about the archived redo logs that have been applied on the standby from STANDBY_ARCHIVE_DEST. The following SQL statements show how to determine the applied logs on both a managed and manual standby:

```
REM managed Data Guard standby, logs applied...
select * from v$archived_log;

REM ...compare with manual standby, logs applied...
select * from v$log_history;
```

If the primary and standby databases switch roles, the Oracle Net aliases used to refer to them continue to refer to the original server. As a consequence, initialization parameters that refer to aliases need to be switched around on each server, as shown in Table 23.2.

Keep in mind that FAL parameters only apply to the database that is currently running in standby mode, and the log archive destination only applies to the primary database. After the changes have been made to the primary and standby database parameter files, the primary can be started. The V$ARCHIVE_DEST view can be utilized to show the status of the standby log archive destination used to transfer redo from the primary database to the standby database. The following example shows that the standby archive log destination (identified by DESTINATION='orad2.standby. dbcool.com' and TARGET='STANDBY') is not currently available because the Oracle Net listener isn't running on the standby server:

```
select status,archiver arch,fail_date,fail_sequence f_seq,error
from v$archive_dest where target='STANDBY'
and destination='orad2.standby.dbcool.com';



STATUS  ARCH              FAIL_DATE      F_SEQ ERROR
------- ----- ------------------- ------ --------------------------
ERROR   LGWR  16-FEB-2002 18:37:44  2426 ORA-12541: TNS:no listener
```

Table 23.2   Initialization Parameters Differing between Primary and Standby

STANDBY SERVER	PRIMARY SERVER
fal_client=orad2.standby.dbcool.com	fal_client=orad2.dbcool.com
fal_server=orad2.dbcool.com	fal_server=orad2.standby.dbcool.com
log_archive_dest_25	log_archive_dest_2=
'service=orad2.dbcool.com mandatory reopen=10 sync affirm register lgwr'	'service=orad2.standby.dbcool.com mandatory reopen=10 sync affirm register lgwr'

The ARCHIVER column value 'LGWR' shows that the standby is configured to use standby redo logs, and the FAIL_SEQUENCE column identifies the log sequence on the primary where the transfer error occurred. This value is used by FAL to transfer any archived redo logs generated on the primary while the standby database was unavailable. The sequence of archived redo logs generated during the downtime of the standby is known as a gap sequence.

Running Managed Recovery

To take advantage of the full range of Data Guard standby features, the standby database must be mounted in standby mode (identical to the manual recovery approach), and then recovery must be started in managed standby mode, as follows:

```
startup mount;
alter database mount standby database;
REM !! create standby redo logs now, if they don't exist yet
alter database recover managed standby database disconnect from session;

REM alternative managed recovery command running 4 parallel streams
alter database recover managed standby database disconnect parallel 4;
```

Use of the DISCONNECT FROM SESSION option runs the recovery in the background, and allows the DBA to exit from SQL*Plus after starting managed recovery. Managed recovery can be stopped with the following command:

```
alter database recover managed standby database cancel immediate;
```

The V$ARCHIVE_DEST view can be used on the primary database to confirm that the standby is operational. It if is, the destination has a VALID status:

```
select status,archiver arch,fail_date,fail_sequence f_seq,error
from v$archive_dest where target='STANDBY';
```

```
STATUS    ARCH    FAIL_DATE    F_SEQ ERROR
--------  ------  -----------  ------- -------
VALID     LGWR                     0
```

If the standby is unavailable and the standby log archive destination specified on the primary database uses the MANDATORY attribute, the potential exists for the primary to suspend. This occurs when the current online redo log cycles back to the one that couldn't be archived to the standby site. To keep the primary from suspending, the log archive destination state for the standby can be set to DEFER, as follows:

```
alter system set log_archive_dest_state_2 = 'DEFER';
```

The use of DEFER allows the primary to continue to operate, and changes the STATUS of the destination in V$ARCHIVE_DEST to DISABLED. In general, the use of DEFER is recommended to keep the nonavailability of the standby from impacting the primary. Using suitable monitoring, errors in V$ARCHIVE_DEST for standby log archive destinations can be detected, and the status can be changed to DEFER automatically until the standby is available. When the standby is available, the standby log destination can be enabled using the following command (followed by a log switch to manually initiate FAL to transfer logs in the gap immediately):

```
alter system set log_archive_dest_state_2 = 'ENABLE';


REM optional, but FAL only restarts on next switch, so force one now
alter system switch logfile;
```

The V$MANAGED_STANDBY view can be queried on the standby site to display the status of the standby. The following SQL displays the process names, process identification numbers (PIDs), and status values for a standby database operating in managed recovery mode:

```
select process,pid,client_pid,status from v$managed_standby;

PROCESS        PID CLIENT_PID   STATUS
------- ---------- -------------- ------------
MRP0         24490 N/A          WAIT_FOR_LOG
RFS          24502 12906        WRITING
RFS          24504 12914        ATTACHED
```

The CLIENT_PID value for the remote file server (RFS) process on the standby contains the UNIX PID of the ARCH process from the primary database (CLIENT_PID=12914) and the UNIX PID of the LGWR on the primary database (CLIENT_PID=12906). This output is good way to check that the standby redo logs are in use. If they aren't, the PID of the LGWR on the primary is missing. It's worth noting that if standby redo logs do not exist on the primary, or they aren't configured correctly, no error is reported. Instead, the standby runs in Deferred mode and applies redo from archived redo logs on the primary. The use of standby redo logs should always be checked because it's a requirement to use them for no-data-loss operation. Another way to confirm that standby redo logs are in use is to run the UNIX fuser command on the standby redo log files from the standby. This displays PIDs of standby database background processes that are accessing the logs. If no processes are accessing any of the logs, they aren't being used.

Switching Primary and Standby States

The managed physical standby configuration that has been presented in this chapter is designed for two purposes:

- To allow the standby database to take on the role of the primary database in the case of a disaster on the primary server site. This is referred to as a *failover*.
- To allow the standby and primary databases to switch roles under DBA control, for example in the case of a planned outage on the primary site. This is referred to as a *switchover*.

The standby initialization parameters shown in Table 23.2 are designed for a switchover scenario where the primary and standby switch roles. In a failover scenario, those initialization parameters for the old standby (as shown in Table 23.2) refer to a standby that no longer exists. These parameters should be removed before starting the old standby as the new primary. Table 23.3 shows the operations required on the primary and standby databases for failover and switchover.

Keep in mind that the managed standby example in this chapter assumes that the configuration is running in Maximize Availability mode, and that standby redo logs are in use. This ensures no data loss. It's still possible to activate the standby database with the manual method, using ALTER DATABASE ACTIVATE STANDBY DATABASE. This should be avoided if possible because it leads to the possibility of data loss on the standby when it's activated as the new primary. After the failover operations have been completed, a SHUTDOWN followed by a STARTUP starts the standby in normal operation as the new primary.

In order for switchover to succeed, there must be no active sessions on the primary database, and the standby database must mounted and running in managed recovery mode. If the error ORA-01903 is reported when running SWITCHOVER TO STANDBY on the primary, the problem might be due to a session related to the database job queue. If this is the case, set the parameter JOB_QUEUE_PROCESSES to 0, as follows, before trying the switchover again:

```
alter session set job_queue_processes=0;
```

The execution of SWITCHOVER TO STANDBY on the primary is essential for the switchover to succeed. This sends the End of Redo (EOR) record to the standby and ensures that all redo from the primary is applied to the standby before the roles are switched. If this step is omitted, it's possible to end up with two standby databases permanently! The alert logs on the primary and standby indicate that the EOR record has been generated on the primary and sent to the standby, where redo has been applied:

```
Incomplete recovery done UNTIL CHANGE 1165897
MRP0: Media Recovery Complete: End-Of-REDO
```

Table 23.3 Failover and Switchover Operations

OPERATION	PRIMARY DATABASE	STANDBY DATABASE
Database switchover	`alter database commit to switchover to standby;`	`alter database commit to switchover to primary;`
Database failover	`None: the primary database is lost`	`alter database recover managed standby database finish;` `alter database commit to switchover to primary;`

At this stage, the primary can be shut down and reopened as a physical standby database. The old primary is now a standby. Next, the old standby needs to be switched to the new primary using SWITCHOVER TO PRIMARY. For the operation to succeed, all redo from the log stream on the old primary must have been applied. If the error ORA-16139 is reported on the standby when you attempt SWITCHOVER TO PRIMARY, it is an indication that the database has not been recovered through the end of the log stream from the old primary, and graceful switchover is not possible. The best way to avoid this is to ensure that standby redo logs are in use on the standby, and that the EOR record appears in the standby alert log before switching states.

Running an Oracle9*i* Logical Standby Database

The logical standby option in Oracle9*i* enables the standby database to remain open for read-only use while redo transport and apply processing is in progress. This is not possible with a physical standby database. Additional indexes and materialized views can be created on the logical standby database to speed the performance of reports. Logical standby databases are commonly used to provide the capability to run reports on near-live data, without significantly impacting the performance of the primary database. The initialization parameters for database buffer sizes and sort areas can be increased on the standby if required.

Like physical standby, changes from the primary are still transported to the standby via redo in logical standby. However, they are first converted to SQL transactions before being applied to the standby. This contrasts with physical standby, where physical block changes are performed on the standby, based on ROWID values in the redo. Chapter 17 contains an example of how to use Oracle's LogMiner GUI tool to understand the relationship between redo data and the SQL transactions contained in it, as well as background information on the Oracle database recovery process.

Unlike a physical standby database, a logical standby database doesn't propagate data corruption from the standby. The standby is able to perform this check because it has access to both the primary and standby data values prior to applying redo.

Prerequisites for Running Logical Standby

Most of the prerequisite requirements for a physical standby still apply. Oracle Net aliases should exist for the primary database, the standby database, and a service name to enable transparent failover between the two for end-user applications. The primary must be running in ARCHIVELOG mode with automatic archiving in operation, as specified by the initialization parameter LOG_ARCHIVE_START=true.

Some types of primary database objects are not supported for logical standby databases. Unsupported objects in the primary are automatically excluded from the redo-apply process on the standby. These objects can be determined in advance on the primary using:

```
select * from dba_logstdby_unsupported;
```

All table rows in the primary for which log transport to the logical standby is required must be uniquely identifiable. This can be guaranteed by ensuring that all tables contain either a primary key constraint or a unique constraint based on NOT NULL columns. Tables that don't meet unique row requirements can be identified in advance on the primary with the following SQL:

```
select owner, table_name, bad_column from dba_logstdby_not_unique;
```

A BAD_COLUMN value of Y means that the table contains a column with a potentially unbounded size. Oracle doesn't store the column width in the dictionary for such types. For example, character large objects (CLOBs) are unbounded. In this case, rows must be unique across columns (with the exception of unbounded columns) for the table to be properly maintained on the standby.

A BAD_COLUMN value of N indicates that the table can be properly maintained on the standby using a feature known as supplemental logging. Supplemental logging adds extra column information to redo on the primary when table data is modified. Supplemental logging is a *mandatory* prerequisite for running a logical standby, and can be enabled explicitly on the primary with the following command:

```
alter database add
supplemental log data (primary key,unique index) columns;

REM use this SQL to check the values...
select supplemental_log_data_pk, supplemental_log_data_ui
from v$database;
```

For tables with primary keys or NOT NULL unique constraints, supplemental logging is minimal. For tables with columns identified by BAD_COLUMN='Y' supplemental logging causes all scalar values in the column to be added to the redo for the purpose of uniquely identifying the row at the standby. This can result in a very significant amount of extra redo generation for the row. The best way to resolve this is to add a primary key or NOT NULL unique constraint to the table. If this isn't possible, another solution is to add a primary key to the primary table in a RELY DISABLE state, for example:

```
alter table no_pk add primary key (keycol1, keycol2) rely disable;
```

Use of a RELY DISABLE primary key reduces the supplemental redo generated by changes to the table, without incurring the cost of maintaining the underlying index on the primary. It's essential that the chosen columns represent a unique combination that could form an enabled primary key. If they don't, redo isn't applied on the standby.

Finally, the logical standby uses segments owned by SYS and SYSTEM to maintain the standby. By default, these are located in the SYSTEM tablespace. If it's intended that the logical primary and standby databases might switch roles in the future, these segments should be relocated to a different tablespace on the standby, using the SET_TABLESPACE procedure in the DBMS_LOGMNR_D package. This operation should be performed on the *primary* before it is cloned to make the standby. This is an example:

```
create tablespace log_ts datafile '/u02/oradata/ORAD2/log_ts01.dbf'
size 100m autoextend on next 12800k maxsize unlimited
extent management local uniform size 128k;

begin sys.dbms_logmnr_d.set_tablespace('log_ts'); end;
/
```

Logical Standby Initialization Parameters

Probably the most significant difference between a logical and physical standby configuration is that the FAL_CLIENT and FAL_SERVER parameters in the standby parameter file are not specified. On the other hand, the use of ARCHIVE_LOG_DEST_1, LOG_ARCHIVE_FORMAT, and STANDBY_ARCHIVE_DEST applies to both logical and physical standby and can be set identically on both. Note that the ARCHIVE_LOG_DEST_2 parameter used on the primary to identify the standby database is enabled at the end of the configuration, after the logical standby is up and running in logical standby mode. If it's enabled before that point, the configuration doesn't work.

It's important to use server parameter files to hold database initialization parameters for the primary and standby, so the Oracle database management system (DBMS) can take control of changing and persisting any parameters needed to support logical standby as and when required. The following SQL*Plus command can be used on the primary to convert an existing init.ora file into a server parameter file (based on the use of default file names) when the command is executed from the $ORACLE_HOME/dbs directory:

```
REM in order to use the spfile afterwards, shutdown and restart dbms
create spfile from pfile;
```

The logical standby can be cloned from the primary either following a clean shutdown of the primary or while the primary database is up and running. If the primary is to remain up, the database Resource Manager must be running. This can be enabled using the following SQL:

```
alter system set resource_manager_plan=system_plan scope=both;
shutdown immediate;
startup;
```

Note that even though the primary database can remain up during creation of the logical standby, it's necessary to place the primary into a quiesced state during the process using ALTER SYSTEM QUIESCE. This requires that all existing transactions complete and causes new transactions to hang, which might appear to end users as a problem with the database. As a result, you might want to arrange for scheduled downtime while the logical standby is being created to avoid the unpredictability associated with waiting for existing transactions to complete.

To ensure the fastest application of redo on the standby, log-apply services require memory in the shared pool, and the use of parallel query. By default, 25 percent of SGA memory on the standby is allocated for redo-apply operations. Therefore, consideration should be given to increasing the SGA on the standby instance compared with that on the primary. The APPLY_SET procedure in the DBMS_LOGSTDBY package is used to control resource allocation. The following command restricts the SGA usage for redo log application on the standby to the specified limit:

```
begin dbms_logstdby.apply_set('MAX_SGA',50000000); end;
/
```

In order for log-apply services to run in parallel, a minimum value of 5 is required for the initialization parameter PARALLEL_MAX_SERVERS on the standby. By default, all available servers are used. The number of servers used can be limited by APPLY_SET:

```
begin dbms_logstdby.apply_set('MAX_SERVERS',7); end;
/

REM select * from DBA_LOGSTDBY_PARAMETERS show APPLY_SET values
REM unset the value if setting causes errors on the standby
begin dbms_logstdby.apply_unset('MAX_SERVERS'); end;
/
```

These changes can be carried out on the primary before cloning it to make the standby. This ensures that the values are in effect at all times, including after any role-switch operations between the primary and standby. They can be executed at any time on the standby.

Creating the Logical Standby

The logical standby database must be based on a copy of the primary. This copy can be taken either following a clean shutdown of the primary (using either SHUTDOWN or SHUTDOWN IMMEDIATE) or while the primary database is up.

Datafiles only (not tempfile files, online redo logs, or control files) must be copied to the standby. The following example makes the same assumptions as the physical standby example earlier in the chapter, namely that the standby is located on a separate server with an identical physical layout to the primary and uses the same database name and SID. The OFA environment, initialization file, and password need to be copied to the standby also, as before. The following SQL on the primary generates the list of datafiles that need to be copied manually to the standby site:

```
select f.file_name from dba_data_files f;
```

Alternatively, the dbcool_gen_standby.pl script (discussed previously with respect to physical standby creation) can be used to generate a script that transfers the database across the network in parallel, using compression. This can help to expedite the process of creating the logical standby. This is an example of usage, which specifies mode= logical as opposed to mode=physical during physical standby creation:

```
$ export ORACLE_SID=ORAD2
$ export ORACLE_HOME=/u01/app/oracle/product/9.2.0
$ dbcool_gen_standby.pl system_pwd=pwd mode=logical \
status=hot standby_host=sb1
```

The status=hot parameter specifies that the primary database is to remain up while the logical standby is being created. Alternatively, status=cold can be used to generate a script that performs a clean shutdown of the primary before copying the files to the standby. The examples in the rest of this section assume that the primary database is closed while the cloning of the logical standby takes place.

The Oracle Net listener for both the primary and standby should be running. After the transfer of database files to the standby is complete, and assuming that the password, initialization file, and OFA structure is in place on the standby, the following SQL*Plus commands must be executed on the primary:

```
startup mount

alter database backup controlfile to '/tmp/to_standby.ctl' reuse;

select checkpoint_change# from v$database;

select max(name) arch_start from v$archived_log
where standby_dest='NO';

alter database open;

begin dbms_logstdby.build; end;
/

alter system archive log current;

select max(name) arch_stop from v$archived_log
where dictionary_begin='YES' and standby_dest='NO';
```

It's important to be aware that a logical standby database is based on a regular control file backup, rather than a standby control file as used by a physical standby database. The BUILD procedure in the DBMS_LOGSTDBY package adds information to redo logs generated on the primary so that the standby can interpret them, and enables supplemental redo generation if it's not already enabled. It's critical that no DDL is executed during the time interval after the opening of the primary and before the execution of BUILD.

When the SQL is executed, the following output values need to be recorded because they are used subsequently in the initial processing on the logical standby, to synchronize the initial state of the logical standby before redo can be applied:

```
CHECKPOINT_CHANGE#
------------------
          261567
```

```
ARCH_START
------------------------------------------------
/u04/oradata/ORAD2/arch/T0001S0000000166.ARC

ARCH_STOP
------------------------------------------------
/u04/oradata/ORAD2/arch/T0001S0000000168.ARC
```

The backup control file identified by '/tmp/to_standby.ctl' must be copied to all the control file locations referenced in the server parameter file on the standby:

```
$ rcp -p /tmp/to_standby.ctl sb1:/u02/oradata/ORAD2/control01.ctl
$ rcp -p /tmp/to_standby.ctl sb1:/u03/oradata/ORAD2/control02.ctl
```

All archived redo logs in the range identified by ARCH_START and ARCH_STOP need to be copied to the standby, using an operating system command, such as rcp. When all file transfers are completed, processing switches to the standby where the CHECKPOINT_CHANGE# and ARCH_STOP values, recorded previously at the primary, are used:

```
startup mount

REM clear all logfile groups, 2 in our example...
alter database clear logfile group 1;
alter database clear logfile group 2;

REM recover using the CHECKPOINT_CHANGE# saved from the primary
alter database recover automatic from
'/u04/oradata/ORAD2/arch' database until change 261567
using backup controlfile
/

REM ensure that no changes can be made to the logical standby . . .
alter database guard all;
alter database open resetlogs;

REM recreate the tempfile used in the primary TEMP tablespace
alter tablespace TEMP
add tempfile '/u02/oradata/ORAD2/temp01.dbf'
size 20M reuse autoextend on;

REM register the ARC_STOP file transferred from the primary
alter database register logical logfile
'/u04/oradata/ORAD2/arch/T0001S0000000168.ARC';

REM begin standby apply at CHECKPOINT_CHANGE# save on primary . . .
alter database start logical standby apply initial 261567;
```

Applying Redo on the Logical Standby

At this stage, the standby and primary are up and running. The standby is ready to apply logs from the primary and has applied the initial logs transferred as part of the initial configuration. The final step is to set and enable an archived redo log destination on the primary to identify the location of the standby database for redo log transport:

```
alter system set log_archive_dest_2='service=orad2.standby.dbcool.com
lgwr'
 scope=both;


alter system set log_archive_dest_state_2=enable scope=both;
```

The role of the standby database can be confirmed from the contents of V$DATABASE after the process is complete, using the following SQL:

```
select database_role from v$database;


DATABASE_ROLE
----------------
LOGICAL STANDBY
```

Progress of redo log application on the standby can be found in the LOGSTDBY_PROGRESS view using the following SQL:

```
select applied_scn,applied_time,newest_time
from dba_logstdby_progress;


  APPLIED_SCN        APPLIED_TIME          NEWEST_TIME
------------- --------------------- ---------------------
        72646  17-FEB-2002 16:37:41  17-FEB-2002 16:41:10
```

The status of logs that have been applied can be determined from DBA_ LOGSTDBY_PROGRESS. Any gaps in log sequences are resolved automatically by the standby database. You need to be aware that a log switch on the primary is required before changes can take effect on the logical standby. When the standby apply-redo process is running, status information can be viewed in the V$LOGSTDBY view. This view includes the UNIX PID values for the standby processes that are performing the generation of SQL from the redo, and executing it against the standby. The following SQL shows the contents of V$LOGSTDBY for a logical standby database in the process of applying some redo:

```
select pid,type,status from v$logstdby;


PID    TYPE         STATUS
------ ------------ ----------------------------
28529  COORDINATOR  ORA-16116: no work available
```

```
28531  READER      ORA-16117: processing
28533  BUILDER     ORA-16117: processing
28535  PREPARER    ORA-16116: no work available
28537  ANALYZER    ORA-16116: no work available
28539  APPLIER     ORA-16117: processing
```

Additional indexes and materialized views can be created on the logical standby (for example, to speed up SQL reports) by preceding and following the DDL statements in SQL*Plus with the following commands:

```
SQL> execute dbms_logstdby.guard_bypass_on
REM create an extra index here...
SQL> execute dbms_logstdby.guard_bypass_off
```

If required, redo can be applied to selected objects on the standby only, by skipping the rest using the SKIP procedure in DBMS_LOGSTDBY.

Logical Standby Failover

Before failing over to the logical standby, all outstanding archived redo logs that need to be applied to the standby must be manually copied from the primary to the standby directory that is specified by the STANDBY_ARCH_DEST initialization parameter. After stopping the logical redo-apply process, manually copied archived redo logs can be registered and applied to the standby as follows:

```
alter database stop logical standby apply;

REM run this step for each archived redo log
REM manually copied from primary...
alter database register logical logfile 'filespec';

REM start apply
alter database start logical standby apply;

/*
 * check V$LOGSTDBY view for idle processes at this point,
 * to confirm all redo applied,then stop apply
 */
alter database stop logical standby apply;

REM now activate the standby as the primary
alter database activate logical standby database;
```

Like physical standby, logical standby also supports switchover operations (in a similar way). This requires the previous creation of database links between the primary and standby.

Enhancing Standby Management Using Oracle9*i* Data Guard Manager

The extensive new Data Guard features in Oracle9*i* can make command-line management of the configuration a challenge, whether physical or logical standby is used. Data Guard broker is the component that reduces the complexity of creating and managing standby database configurations when used in conjunction with the Data Guard Manager GUI in Oracle Enterprise Manager (OEM). To use Oracle Data Guard Manager for standby database configurations, you must first perform the following actions:

- Run an OEM Management Server. This requires an OEM Repository Database. Chapter 24 contains more information on installing and running OEM.

- Run the Oracle Intelligent Agent on each site.

- Find and register the primary and standby databases in the OEM Repository, using the Oracle Intelligent Agent. If you plan to create a new standby database, Data Guard Manager can add it to the configuration automatically.

- Register the operating system and Oracle-preferred credentials in OEM for the primary and standby server machines, and for the primary and standby databases. Oracle credentials require SYSDBA privileges, which in turn require the use of a password file on the primary and standby databases.

- Configure the Oracle listeners on each site to allow connections to the standby and primary databases.

When this configuration is in place, the following commands run Data Guard Manager:

```
$ export DISPLAY=your_X_display:0
$ oemapp dataguard
```

The manually performed examples (shown earlier in this chapter) become increasingly difficult if any of the following apply:

- Database file locations differ between the primary and standby.
- A different database name is required for the logical standby.
- A different instance name is required for the logical standby.
- Different database initialization parameters are required for the logical standby.

Keep in mind that Oracle recommends that a different database name and DBID value be generated for the logical standby database, to avoid the possibility of accidentally applying redo directly to the logical standby. (The examples in this chapter leave the name and DBID unchanged.) The recommended changes to DBID and the database name can be accomplished from the command line using the DBNEWID command. The following example uses DBNEWID (utility name nid on UNIX) to generate a new DBID for the ORAD2 database and changes its name to ORAD3:

```
$ nid target=sys/pwd dbname=ORAD3
```

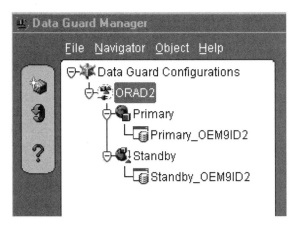

Figure 23.1   Data Guard Manager standby configuration.

At this stage, command-line configuration gets even more difficult because the use of DBNEWID requires re-creation of the password file, and additional database startup and shutdown operations. The solution for managing the complexity is using Data Guard Manager. Through the use of Data Guard Manager, all these changes to the logical standby can be performed automatically, including the re-creation of password files, listener.ora file changes, and oratab file changes. Data Guard Manager, therefore, massively reduces initial administration overhead for logical standby database creation, especially for more complex configurations.

Using Data Guard Manager, the standby can take on the primary role with a couple of mouse clicks; there's no need to consult any documentation to find the right commands to run and the order of execution. Data Guard Manager can create a standby configuration from scratch, including a standby database. Alternatively, a primary and standby configuration can be created manually (as shown in this chapter), and then registered with Data Guard Manager, which then takes on the responsibility for managing and monitoring the configuration. Data Guard Manager can also be started from the OEM Console by choosing Tools from the main menu, and then choosing Database Applications. If you add an existing standby database to a Data Guard Manager configuration, the Manager makes all necessary changes to initialization parameters provided that you are using a server parameter file, as recommended previously.

Data Guard broker creates a log file in the BACKGROUND_DUMP_DEST directory on both the primary and the standby, containing detailed status information about the configuration. The file name contains the name of the instance. For example, the log file for the instance OEM9ID2 is drcOEM9ID2.log. Figure 23.1 shows the Data Guard Manager screen for a primary and standby configuration named ORAD2.

Summary

Oracle9*i* builds on the physical standby database available in previous versions by adding logical standby and an increased number of options to balance data protection on the standby with data availability on the primary. The physical standby functionality in Oracle9*i* Data Guard, running in Maximize Availability mode, provides an extremely robust disaster recovery service that can be managed automatically by Oracle. The Maximize Protection mode means that a standby can provide a guaranteed no-data-loss solution.

Oracle9*i* provides enhanced automation of standby management by allowing datafiles to be added to the primary database without manual intervention on the standby. This is a major improvement compared to previous releases, where manual intervention was required. In Maximize Availability mode, standby log transport services can handle any outage on the standby with grace, and without impacting the primary availability. They can also automatically resolve gaps in the redo sequence between the sites when the standby service is restored. For scheduled outages, the primary and standby can switch roles with a few simple commands.

Oracle9*i* also provides the long-awaited logical standby database. This allows a standby database to remain open for reporting purposes while redo is applied from the primary, after having been translated to SQL first. Unlike physical standby, logical standby also provides protection from physical corruption on the primary. In addition, extra indexes and materialized views can be created on the standby, to enhance the performance of end-user reports.

With increasing functionality comes more complex administration. To address this, the combination of Data Guard broker and Data Guard Manager in OEM allows the Oracle9*i* primary and standby configurations to be managed as a single entity from a GUI, enabling primary and standby roles to be switched easily. If you are using logical standby, Data Guard Manager is probably the only way to set up and manage the system without a high DBA administration overhead. Due to its tight integration with OEM, Data Guard Manager can also generate events to identify runtime errors for both physical and logical standby configurations.

PART

Six

Maintaining the Oracle System

## CHAPTER 24

Guidelines for Health Checks and Monitoring

Health checks and monitoring are required to prevent and detect database outages and provide the highest availability for systems. Although several third-party products perform these tasks—such as BMC Patrol and Compuware EcoTOOLS—they are all extremely expensive. Oracle provides its own tools—the Oracle Intelligent Agent (OIA) and Oracle Enterprise Manager (OEM), which can perform the same functions. You should consider Oracle's offerings if you want to save money and reduce the number of third-party vendors that you have to manage.

When you have identified a problem through monitoring or health checks, a notification needs to be sent somewhere in order to alert the support person who needs to fix the problem. The routing of problems to the right place in combination with monitoring is called a *systems management framework*. Although OIA and OEM can provide the monitoring and notification, it's possible that your company already has a systems management framework in place based on an open standard such as the Simple Network Management Protocol (SNMP). In this case, any alerts that your OEM monitoring raises may need to be compatible with the framework. This doesn't prevent you from using OEM to raise alerts because OEM can raise standard SNMP traps against your existing SNMP-based framework.

This chapter offers guidelines for implementing health checks and monitoring databases. Health checks typically take the form of scripts that check to make sure databases are built to conform with the best practices for avoiding unscheduled outages. You can run them once a day.

> **NOTE** The Perl script dbcool_ora_healthcheck.pl, which automates the health checks covered in this chapter, is available for download from this book's companion Web site.

Monitoring consists of checks that run frequently to make sure your database is providing the ongoing performance and availability that end-user applications require. After providing a list of useful health checks, we will distinguish between monitoring requirements and monitoring implementation techniques. Monitoring requirements are covered in depth because understanding them is essential to avoid wasting valuable database administrator (DBA) time raising alerts that actually don't indicate critical problems that require immediate attention. The following is a list of topics covered in this chapter:

- Health checks for physical layout
- Health checks for tablespace and rollback segment definitions
- Defining monitoring requirements
- Implementing monitoring using database jobs
- Sending alerts from within the database using UNIX sendmail
- Implementing monitoring using OEM and OIA
- Creating customized monitoring scripts and Fixit Jobs in OEM

This chapter doesn't cover performance monitoring. Performance monitoring is a specialist subject with different requirements that requires specialized tools to achieve the best results. This topic is covered in Chapter 8 and 16.

Defining and Implementing Health Checks

Oracle database management system (DBMS) health checks are scripted checks that you can use to ensure that your Oracle databases conform to your organization's Oracle standards. The standards themselves are typically based on Oracle Corporation's own best practices for running an Oracle database. For example, Oracle provides the Optimal Flexible Architecture (OFA) standard for laying out an Oracle database for ease of management. If your organization bases Oracle physical layout on the Oracle OFA standard, then you should proactively check to make sure your databases conform to the standard. If they don't, the failure to adhere to the standard may result in outages that take longer to resolve than those in standards-based installations. All DBAs should be familiar with OFA, which is covered in detail in Oracle documentation.

The difference between health checks and monitoring is that health checks can be performed on a database with no connected users and are used to check database configuration settings that don't change frequently over time. In that respect, health checks are a special case of monitoring with low execution frequency and do not fix the detected problems automatically. You might consider running the health checks daily or twice a day for each database instance. Health checks that fail are problems waiting to happen rather than problems that will happen imminently or have already happened. The Perl script dbcool_ora_healthcheck.pl is available for download from this book's companion Web site to run all of the checks in this section.

Physical Layout Checks

The physical layout is based on Oracle's OFA standard (see Preface). Physical layout checks ensure that the following requirements are met:

- File names (for both user-managed files and Oracle-Managed Files [OMF]) meet naming standards.
- Each log group has at least two members, and all groups have the same size.
- A minimum of two control files are present.

In general, only violations of the health checks need to be reported. This keeps the amount of output generated to a minimum in order to draw attention to issues that need to be addressed. Perl is well suited for reading the contents of the Oracle data dictionary and matching the results against patterns to test for OFA naming-standard conformance. In addition, you might want to make sure that files are laid out in such a way that control files and log group members are on separate disks and that the disks are on separate disk controller interface cards. For the purposes of this chapter, the physical storage is assumed to be opaque to the DBA in the sense that the storage is provided to match performance and availability requirements through a storage area network (SAN), as discussed in Chapter 2. This means that issues related to the physical hardware are beyond the scope and no longer the DBA's responsibility. If this is not the case in your organization, the source code for the checks is provided on the companion Web site so you can modify them to meet your needs. In the examples in this section, databases conform to the OFA standard and may contain user-managed files or OMF for datafiles, redo logs, and control files. The following Structured Query Language (SQL) forms the basis for all file name checks:

```
select name,filename,decode(group#,0,null,group#) log_group
from
  (select 'redo' name,f.member filename,f.group#
  from v$log l,v$logfile f Where l.group# = f.group#)
union select 'control',name,0  from v$controlfile c
union select f.TABLESPACE_NAME,f.file_name,0 from dba_data_files f
union select tf.TABLESPACE_NAME,tf.file_name,0 from dba_temp_files tf);
```

The following output shows the results of the report for an Oracle9*i* database with a mixture of user-managed files and OMF. If the NAME column is uppercase, it contains the name of a tablespace. If it is lowercase, it specifies whether the file is a control file or redo log member:

```
NAME         FILENAME                                          LOG_GROUP
----------   -----------------------------------------------   -----------
LONGTSNAME   /u02/oradata/ORAD1/ora_longtsna_xzns8vj7.dbf
SYSTEM       /u02/oradata/ORAD1/ora_system_xwrk5w6p.dbf
TABAUTO      /u02/oradata/ORAD1/ora_tabauto_xwycbv70.dbf
```

```
TEMP            /u02/oradata/ORAD1/ora_temp_xzno1knn.tmp
UNDO1           /u02/oradata/ORAD1/ora_undo1_xwrk7gx3.dbf
USERS           /u02/oradata/ORAD1/users01.dbf
control         /u02/oradata/ORAD1/ora_xwrk4zgp.ctl
redo            /u02/oradata/ORAD1/ora_1_xwrk4zv2.log          1
redo            /u02/oradata/ORAD1/ora_2_xwrk5c4k.log          2
redo            /u03/oradata/ORAD1/ora_1_xwrk55gr.log          1
redo            /u03/oradata/ORAD1/ora_2_xwrk5jqg.log          2
```

Datafile Names

To check whether a datafile name matches the standard, two patterns are required. One pattern is required to check for user-managed files, and another is required to check for OMF. OMF datafile names begin with ora_ or o1_mf_ followed by the first eight characters of the tablespace name, and then by a unique string, followed by .dbf for datafiles and .tmp for TEMPORARY tablespace tempfiles. User-managed files are named using the tablespace name followed by a two-digit sequence number to uniquely identify the file name followed by .dbf.

> **NOTE** OMF names are internally generated by the DBMS and the naming format is not published. As such, Oracle may choose to change the generated names between releases.

The dbcool_ora_healthcheck.pl script uses the check_datafile() subroutine to check datafiles for name conformance. The variable $omf holds the OMF pattern to compare the file name against, and the $userf variable holds the user-managed pattern to compare the file against. The routine is passed to the datafile name and tablespace name from the previous query as follows:

```
check_datafile('TEMP','/u02/oradata/ORAD1/ora_temp_xzno1knn.tmp');
```

The complete definition of check_datafile() is:

```
sub check_datafile()
{
  my($pn,$ts) = @_;        # $pn is file path, ts is tablespace name

  $fn=basename($pn);       # pn is full pathname, $fn is filename
  $ts1=lc($ts);            # tablespace name in lowercase
  $ts8 = substr $ts1,0,8;# 1st 8 chars of tablespace name for OMF

  # $SID is the ORACLE_SID, passed as a command line argument

  # define regular expression for file name standards
  $omf="/u[0-9][0-9]/oradata/$SID/ora_". $ts8 . "_.*(\.dbf|\.tmp)\$";
  $userf="/u[0-9][0-9]/oradata/$SID/" . $ts1 . "[0-9][0-9]\.dbf\$";

  if (is_omf($fn) eq 'Y')
```

```
  {
    # check file $pn against OMF pattern
    # e.g. /u02/oradata/ORAD1/ora_temp_xzno1knn.tmp
    if ($pn !~ m/$omf/) { print "\nnon-standard OMF file: $pn"; }
  }
  else
  {
    # check file $pn against user file pattern
    # e.g. /u02/oradata/ORAD1/users01.dbf
    if ($pn !~ m/$userf/) { print "\nnon-standard datafile: $pn"; }
  }
}
```

In our sample database list, all the datafile names, both OMF and user-managed files, match the naming standard, so the output for the routine is empty. You can change the file patterns quite easily to meet your organization's naming standards. This small, self-contained routine nicely demonstrates Perl's powerful capability to make sure your database matches your naming standards.

The file names themselves should also be checked for uniqueness. Nothing prevents two files with identical names from belonging to the same tablespace. This can happen if the DBA accidentally forgets to increase the file sequence number by one when adding the second file. For example, the following two files with the same name could both be part of the USERS tablespace:

```
/u02/oradata/ORAD1/users01.dbf
/u03/oradata/ORAD1/users01.dbf
```

The dbcool_ora_healthcheck.pl script reports duplicate file names. These duplicate names don't prevent the database from running, but they can lead to confusion, especially when you are remapping backup files into different directories while performing a database restore. Uniqueness checks for OMF names are not required because Oracle guarantees uniqueness.

Redo Log Groups

The redo logs in the sample database have been created using OMF. There are two groups, with two member files in each group. The OMF names use the number after the ora_ to identify the log group, followed by a unique string, followed by .log. The names used in the example database all meet the naming standard:

```
/u02/oradata/omfd1/ora_1_xwrk4zv2.log
/u02/oradata/omfd1/ora_2_xwrk5c4k.log
/u03/oradata/omfd1/ora_1_xwrk55gr.log
/u03/oradata/omfd1/ora_2_xwrk5jqg.log
```

The check_redo() subroutine is used to perform the name conformance check for the redo log files. The code uses a Perl hash variable named $log_file_exists to check whether redo log file names are duplicated. The same test is not required for OMF redo log names because Oracle guarantees uniqueness. The complete definition of check_redo() is as follows:

```
sub check_redo()
{
  my($pn,$group) = @_;

  my($fn);

  $fn=basename($pn); # pn is full pathname

  $omf="/u[0-9][0-9]/oradata/$SID/ora_" . $group . "_.*(\.log)\$";
  $userf="/u[0-9][0-9]/oradata/$SID/redo[0-9][0-9]" .
         "_" . "[0-9]\.log\$";

  if (is_omf($fn) eq 'Y')
  {
      if ($pn !~ m/$omf/) { print "\nnon-standard OMF file: $pn"; }
  }
  else
  {
      # group 4 member 1/u03/oradata/ORAD1/redo04_1.log',

      if ($pn !~ m/$userf/) { print "\nnon-standard datafile: $pn"; }

      if ($log_file_exists{$fn}) { print "\nlog $fn already exists"; }
      else {  $log_file_exists{$fn} = 'Y'; }
  }
}
```

In addition to meeting naming standards, redo log groups should also be identically sized. The following SQL returns results only when groups of different sizes exist:

```
select count "DISTINCT LOG GROUP SIZES"
from
(select count(distinct(bytes)) count from v$log)
where count > 1;
```

Each redo log group should contain at least two members. Even when redo logs are protected against loss through software- or hardware-based Redundant Array of Independent Disks (RAID), multiplexed redo log groups can provide additional benefits by protecting against file corruption and the accidental removal of a single file in a duplexed group. The following SQL shows redo log groups that don't contain at least two members:

```
select group# "SINGLE MEMBER LOG GROUP"
from v$log where members=1;
```

Control Files

Control files store the structure of the database and various system change number (SCN) values. The availability of the control file is required at all times in order for the database to operate. Oracle can optionally maintain multiple copies of the control file, and this feature should always be implemented, regardless of any storage mirroring or redundancy that is in place. The following SQL returns a result set only when the database contains a single control file:

```
select count "SINGLE CONTROL FILE IN USE" from
(select count(*) count from v$controlfile)
where count=1;
```

The dbcool_ora_healthcheck.pl script checks the names of control files, in a similar way as redo logs and datafiles, to ensure that naming standards are followed.

Tablespace Checks

The following tablespace checks are performed by dbcool_ora_healthcheck.pl to ensure that tablespace definitions and usage meet the following requirements:

- Index and table data are in separate tablespaces.
- All application tablespaces use LOCAL extent allocation and uniform size.
- All datafiles for application tablespaces use the AUTOEXTEND option.
- Rollback segments are in a dedicated tablespace.
- Temporary tablespaces use tempfiles.
- All users use a tablespace with temporary contents as their temporary tablespace.
- Only system administration accounts have a default tablespace of SYSTEM.
- Only authorized users own segments in the SYSTEM tablespace.

Tablespaces That Contain Indexes and Tables

Indexes and tables should not be stored in the same tablespace as application data. Although the need to separate tables and indexes for performance reasons is not relevant to modern storage architectures like SAN, the tablespace is a basic unit of recovery, which is a good reason to keep table and index data apart. If you separate your indexes and tables into different tablespaces, you have the ability to offline the index data independently of table data. In the event of a media failure or corruption to a datafile storing an index, you can keep the table data online while you rebuild the index data. The following SQL shows application tablespaces that contain indexes and tables:

```
select * from
(
select tablespace_name,
    sum(decode(segment_type,'INDEX',1,0)) IND,
    sum(decode(segment_type,'TABLE',1,0)) TAB
    from dba_segments where tablespace_name <> 'SYSTEM'
    group by tablespace_name
)
where IND>0 and TAB>0;
```

DbCool makes it easy to relocate indexes from one tablespace to another, if you find application tablespaces that contain tables and indexes. Consider OEM. OEM creates all indexes and tables for the OEM repository schema by default in the same tablespace, which is called OEM_REPOSITORY. This breaks the rule that application table and index data should not reside in the same tablespace. If you first create a tablespace called OEM_INDEXES to hold the indexes, and run the following SQL in DbCool, the index relocate statements are loaded into the grid:

```
select 'alter index '||owner||'.'||segment_name||
       ' rebuild tablespace OEM_INDEXES' run_cool_sql
from dba_segments where segment_type='INDEX'
and tablespace_name='OEM_REPOSITORY';
```

The grid contents are shown in Figure 24.1.

Whenever you use RUN_COOL_SQL for a query in DbCool, the column contents in the results grid can be treated as Data Definition Language (DDL) statements. If you right-click the grid and choose Execute RUN_COOL_SQL column, then all the rebuild statements will be executed in order. You can use the RUN_COOL_SQL alias for more than one column, in which case the DDL in the columns is executed from left to right. If you change the grid selection mode to List Style first, you can select individual rows to run, rather than the whole grid, by using the standard Windows list selection keys. Alternatively, you can relocate indexes using a server-based procedural approach using the Procedural Language PL/SQL EXECUTE IMMEDIATE command, as in the examples covered in Chapter 13.

Application Tablespaces without LOCAL UNIFORM

The use of LOCAL extent management with uniform space allocation is a best practice that is recommended throughout this book for Oracle tablespace creation. It provides the following benefits:

- Avoids the Oracle data dictionary as a point of contention for tablespace space management
- Makes a tablespace transportable
- Ensures that all free space can be used

The following SQL shows tablespaces that don't use uniform extent allocation:

```
select tablespace_name from dba_tablespaces
where extent_management <>'LOCAL' and tablespace_name <> 'SYSTEM';
```

Using uniform extent allocation eliminates the fragmentation of tablespace free space and avoids space wastage. The following SQL shows LOCAL tablespaces that don't use management extent:

```
select tablespace_name from dba_tablespaces
where allocation_type <> 'UNIFORM' and tablespace_name <> 'SYSTEM' and
contents='PERMANENT';
```

```
RUN_COOL_SQL
alter index OEM.SYS_C001382 rebuild tablespace OEM_INDEXES
alter index OEM.SESSION__ID_PK rebuild tablespace OEM_INDEXES
alter index OEM.SMP_VDU_PRINCIPALS_PKEY rebuild tablespace OEM_INDEXES
alter index OEM.SYS_C001392 rebuild tablespace OEM_INDEXES
alter index OEM.SMP_VDU_OBJECTS_PKEY rebuild tablespace OEM_INDEXES
alter index OEM.SYS_C001398 rebuild tablespace OEM_INDEXES
alter index OEM.SMP_VDU_PRIVILEGE_PKEY rebuild tablespace OEM_INDEXES
alter index OEM.SMP_VDU_PRIV_INDEX rebuild tablespace OEM_INDEXES
alter index OEM.SMP_VDU_PRINCIPAL_NAME_INDEX rebuild tablespace OEM_IND
```

Figure 24.1 Index relocation using DbCool RUN_COOL_SQL.

Keep in mind that Oracle 9i Release 2 allows the SYSTEM tablespace to use LOCAL extent management for the first time, which means that you can omit *and tablespace _name <> 'SYSTEM'* from the WHERE clause.

Datafiles Not Using AUTOEXTEND

It's possible for an application outage to occur when there is insufficient space allocated in a tablespace to enable a table or index to grow, even when the underlying UNIX file system holding the tablespace datafiles has plenty of free space available. The AUTOEXTEND option on a datafile should be used to allow Oracle to add more space to a tablespace on demand by increasing the size of the underlying datafile automatically. Using AUTOEXTEND indicates that there is no reason for an object to fail to extend, unless there is no disk capacity remaining on the underlying UNIX file system. This doesn't mean that you no longer need to monitor space, but it does mean that you should monitor the space capacity on the UNIX file systems rather than the space capacity on the database.

To take full advantage of the higher availability made possible by autoextend, you need to use a few large file systems for your database so that all datafiles can take advantage of the total pool of free space. The use of AUTOEXTEND for rollback, undo, and temporary tablespaces needs more careful consideration. You might not want to use AUTOEXTEND in these cases because an unusually large workload carried out without careful planning can result in autoextended files filling the UNIX file system to capacity. The following SQL shows database files containing regular data without AUTOEXTEND enabled:

```
select file_name from dba_data_files
where autoextensible <> 'YES'
and tablespace_name in
(select tablespace_name from dba_tablespaces
 where contents='PERMANENT'
);
```

Rollback Segments Not in Dedicated Tablespaces

Oracle9*i* makes it possible to create an UNDO tablespace to enforce the use of a table-space for undo data only. If you still use regular rollback segments, you should make sure that rollback segments are in a dedicated tablespace to ensure that the space available for undo data is predictable and under control. The following SQL shows tablespaces that contain non-SYSTEM rollback segments and other segment types:

```
select tablespace_name,segment_type
from dba_segments where segment_type <> 'ROLLBACK'
and tablespace_name in
(  select tablespace_name from dba_segments
   where segment_type='ROLLBACK'
   and segment_name <> 'SYSTEM'
   group by tablespace_name
)
group by tablespace_name,segment_type;
```

Temporary Tablespaces That Don't Use Tempfiles

From Oracle8*i* on, Oracle has enabled tablespaces with temporary contents to use tempfiles. The use of tempfiles is a more efficient way to create temporary tablespaces, which are used to hold transient data during an Oracle sort operation performed during SQL execution. For example, tempfiles are never backed up by Recovery Manager (RMAN), which saves disk or tape space for the backup, and they never generate redo, which makes them a prerequisite for standby databases that need to be opened in read-only mode. The following SQL shows temporary tablespaces that don't use tempfiles:

```
select tablespace_name from dba_tablespaces
where contents='TEMPORARY'
and tablespace_name not in
(select tablespace_name from dba_temp_files);
```

Users Not Using a Temporary Tablespace for Sorts

Whenever an Oracle user account is created, a tablespace is assigned to the user through the temporary tablespace option for the purposes of sorting. This sort tablespace should always be a temporary tablespace. If a user is assigned the SYSTEM tablespace for sort operations, then sorts can fill up the SYSTEM tablespace. By default, SYSTEM is used as the sort tablespace if no tablespace is specified at user creation time. Oracle9*i* provides a solution to this problem by permitting the creation of a default temporary tablespace to be assigned to all users if no sort tablespace is specified for the user at the time of creation. This feature is strongly recommended. The following SQL shows users who don't use a tablespace with temporary contents as their sort tablespace:

```
select username,temporary_tablespace from dba_users
where temporary_tablespace not in
```

```
(select tablespace_name from dba_tablespaces
where contents='TEMPORARY');
```

In Oracle9*i*, the following SQL can be used to create and display a default temporary tablespace based on an existing tablespace that must have TEMPORARY contents:

```
alter database default temporary tablespace temp_default;
```

```
select property_name,property_value
from database_properties
where property_name = 'DEFAULT_TEMP_TABLESPACE';
```

```
PROPERTY_NAME            PROPERTY_VALUE
----------------------- ----------------
DEFAULT_TEMP_TABLESPACE  TEMP_DEFAULT
```

Users with a Default Tablespace of SYSTEM

Only Oracle-created administration accounts such as SYS, SYSTEM, and OUTLN should have a default tablespace of SYSTEM. If user accounts have a tablespace of SYSTEM, the possibility exists for those users to fill up the SYSTEM tablespace and cause an outage. The following SQL shows nonauthorized users who have a default tablespace of SYSTEM:

```
select username
from dba_users where default_tablespace='SYSTEM'
and username not in ('SYSTEM','SYS','OUTLN');
```

Users with UNLIMITED TABLESPACE Privileges

It's common practice for DBAs to grant the RESOURCE role to an Oracle account as a shortcut to give a user permission to create segments in his or her own schema. One side effect of granting RESOURCE is that the UNLIMITED TABLESPACE quota is granted explicitly to the user. This is not usually what is required, but it provides compatibility with previous versions of Oracle. You need to be aware that UNLIMITED TABLESPACE is a user attribute rather than a privilege. A user with an UNLIMITED TABLESPACE quota can create an object in any data tablespace, including the SYSTEM tablespace. This can result in outages if the SYSTEM tablespace or another application fills. The following SQL generates SQL statements to turn off an UNLIMITED tablespace quota for non-DBA accounts:

```
select 'revoke unlimited tablespace from '||grantee
from dba_sys_privs
where privilege='UNLIMITED TABLESPACE'
and grantee in (select username from dba_users
where username not in ('SYSTEM','SYS','OUTLN'));
```

Nonauthorized Users Owning SYSTEM Tablespace Segments

The SYSTEM tablespace holds the Oracle data dictionary and should not be used to store user segments. Allowing user segments in the SYSTEM tablespace makes it possible for user data to fill the SYSTEM tablespace and cause an outage. The following SQL shows nonauthorized users who store segments in the SYSTEM tablespace:

```
select distinct(owner)
from dba_segments where tablespace_name='SYSTEM'
and owner not in ('SYSTEM','SYS','OUTLN');
```

Miscellaneous Configuration Information

The dbcool_ora_healthcheck.pl script includes other checks to ensure that your database conforms to standards covered elsewhere in this book with respect to:

- Database and networking naming (Chapter 3)
- Auditing (Chapter 25)
- Recoverability (Chapter 17)

The following SQL checks to make sure that the database and network-naming standards described in Chapter 3 are followed and that the database is in ARCHIVELOG mode with auditing enabled:

```
select name,upper(value) from v$parameter
where name in ('audit_trail','global_names','instance_name',
'service_names','db_name','db_domain','log_archive_start')
union
select 'global_name',global_name from global_name
union
select 'log_mode',log_mode from v$database;
```

The following output shows the results of the previous SQL for a database instance called ORAP1 (which is accessed by end-user applications using the alias of orap1.dbcool.com) that conforms to the standards:

```
NAME                   UPPER(VALUE)
---------------        --------------
audit_trail            DB
db_domain              DBCOOL.COM
db_name                ORAP1
global_name            ORAP1.DBCOOL.COM
global_names           TRUE
instance_name          ORAP1
log_archive_start      TRUE
log_mode               ARCHIVELOG
service_names          ORAP1.DBCOOL.COM
```

In order to meet the standard, db_name needs to match both the instance_name and System ID (SID). The service_names value should match the Transparent Network Substrate (TNS) alias, the global_name, and the concatenation of db_name and db_domain. The global_names setting should be set to TRUE to enforce global database naming, and the audit_trail should be set to use the database. The database is in ARCHIVELOG mode, and automatic archiving is enabled. Finally, the activation of audit options associated with AUDIT ALL needs to be confirmed. The following SQL returns a result set only if AUDIT ALL has *not* been executed to enable a standard set of auditing options:

```
select audit_opts "AUDIT ALL not run" from
(
select count(*) audit_opts from dba_stmt_audit_opts
) where audit_opts=0;
```

Defining Monitoring Requirements

Monitoring involves running checks repeatedly—sometimes on a fairly short time interval such as every few minutes—to identify database-related problems that have happened or will happen soon if no action is taken. After a problem has been identified, the DBA group is notified—typically via email, cell phone (via Short Message Service [SMS]), or radio paging.

The Oracle-monitoring tools on the market have hundreds of options. They typically measure Oracle's low-level performance counters and raise an alert when a value falls or rises above a threshold. My experience is that such monitoring does not actually increase database availability. Often the contrary is true: If you overload a DBA with alerts that don't prove to be meaningful upon investigation over a period of time, then there is a danger that the DBA will end up ignoring an important alert. As a result, the monitoring covered in this section is restricted to those events that actually compromise availability or might compromise availability without immediate action. These events apply unconditionally to all Oracle databases and should result in the generation of alerts whenever the following conditions arise:

- The database is not available.
- Segments can't extend or invalid objects exist.
- Datafiles are in recovery mode or offline.
- Database jobs are failing or broken.
- Constraints or triggers are disabled.
- In-doubt distributed transactions exist.
- Rollback segments are full.
- Resumable space allocation errors occur in Oracle9*i*.
- Severe errors are reported in the Oracle alert log.

This section describes each condition and how each affects availability.

Database Not Available

You should check periodically to make sure your database is up and running, which is sometimes referred to as *checking for the database heartbeat*. There are various ways to check if the database is available. For example, you can check for the existence of the database processes and network listener. The simplest way to check if the database is up is to try connecting to it from a remote client. If the connection succeeds, then you implicitly confirm that the Oracle instance, the network listener, and all the required Oracle processes are present. You can use the dbcool_db_up.pl script covered in Chapter 4 to perform this check against a remote database as follows:

```
$ dbcool_db_up.pl tns=orap1.dbcool.com
```

The script returns 0 if the test succeeds.

Segments That Can't Extend

If the database has insufficient room for a table or index to extend and more space is required, an error is reported to the application and a message appears in the Oracle alert log to identify what happened. This situation is to be avoided at all costs as it can cause a very significant outage. For example, if the job in progress was a lengthy batch run, then failure might require the job to be repeated, resulting in the system being unavailable for business use.

Before Oracle8i, the identification of segments that didn't have sufficient space to extend was fairly straightforward. There are usually two reasons why a segment can't extend. Either there is no free extent of sufficient size to meet the segment's next extent or the segment has reached its maximum number of extents. These scenarios can be identified with SQL.

When identifying the largest available free extent in a tablespace, it's crucial that the SQL used performs an outer join with the DBA_DATA_FILES view in order to make sure that tablespaces having no free space are included in the result set. The following SQL shows the largest free extent available in all tablespaces, including a tablespace S1 that has no free space, which is included as a result of the outer join (+) condition:

```
select d.TABLESPACE_NAME,nvl(max(f.bytes),0) largest_free_extent
     from dba_free_space f,dba_data_files d
     where f.tablespace_name(+) = d.tablespace_name
     group by d.tablespace_name;


TABLESPACE_NAME       LARGEST_FREE_EXTENT
----------------      --------------------
LONGTSNAME                     104792064
S1                                     0
S3                             104792064
SYSTEM                            174080
TABAUTO                        104726528
UNDO1                           63832064
USERS                            5177344
```

The following SQL builds on the previous statement to show segments that can't extend, either because there is no existing free extent of sufficient size or the maximum extents limit has been reached, as determined by the OR clause predicate in the final parenthesis in the statement:

```
select * from dba_segments seg,
(
select d.TABLESPACE_NAME,nvl(max(f.bytes),0) largest_free_extent
      from dba_free_space f,dba_data_files d
      where f.tablespace_name(+) = d.tablespace_name
      group by d.tablespace_name
) ext
where seg.tablespace_name = ext.tablespace_name
and (seg.next_extent > ext.largest_free_extent or
      seg.extents = seg.max_extents)
```

This approach is not complete for Oracle8*i* and later in situations where LOCAL UNIFORM or LOCAL AUTOALLOCATE extent management options are used at tablespace creation time. The use of LOCAL UNIFORM in particular is strongly recommended to avoid space wastage. When these options are used, the value seg.next_ extent is always NULL, so it's meaningless to compare this to ext.largest_free_extent because the condition will always fail.

For Oracle8*i* and later, the SQL needs to be changed to include a reference to the ALLOCATION_TYPE column in DBA_TABLESPACES. If this column has the value USER, then the old space management applies, as shown in the previous statement. If ALLOCATION_TYPE contains the values SYSTEM or UNIFORM, then automatic extent management options are in place and the MIN_EXTLEN column in DBA_ TABLESPACES can be used to provide the value of the next extent that needs to be allocated for all segments in those tablespaces rather than each segment's NEXT_EXTENT value. The following SQL shows the changes required to enable space shortages to be detected when the new space allocation options are in use:

```
select owner,segment_name,segment_type,seg.tablespace_name,
decode(ext.allocation_type,'USER',next_extent,ext.min_extlen) next,
      ext.largest_free_extent,
      extents,max_extents
from dba_segments seg,
(select d.TABLESPACE_NAME,nvl(max(f.bytes),0) largest_free_extent,
      t.allocation_type,t.min_extlen
from dba_free_space f,dba_data_files d,dba_tablespaces t
      where f.tablespace_name(+) = d.tablespace_name
      and   d.tablespace_name=t.tablespace_name
group by d.tablespace_name,t.allocation_type,t.min_extlen) ext
where seg.tablespace_name = ext.tablespace_name and
(decode(ext.allocation_type,'USER',next_extent,ext.min_extlen) >
      ext.largest_free_extent
 or seg.extents = seg.max_extents);
```

If you use large file systems, auto-extensible datafiles, LOCAL uniform space allocation, and unlimited extents for your segments, you should never experience a space shortage unless the underlying UNIX file system has run out of space. The health checks described earlier in the chapter are designed to ensure that your database implementation follows these recommendations. The monitoring of UNIX file system capacity is a critical factor for this approach to succeed. This is usually a service provided by the UNIX SA group rather than the responsibility of the DBA because it's required for all file systems on a server, not just those holding the Oracle database. With the advent of modern storage architectures such as SAN combined with volume managers, it's possible to grow file systems on demand without an outage, should file system capacity thresholds be reached.

Invalid Objects

An object that is invalid may identify a genuine problem. For example, if a table has a view that is based upon it and the table is dropped, then the view becomes invalid. Any SQL that references the view will fail. Oracle tracks dependencies between objects automatically, and these are available through the DBA_DEPENDENCIES view. When an invalid is object is referenced, Oracle transparently attempts to recompile it on demand. If the recompile is successful, because the cause of the invalidation has subsequently been fixed, execution continues. If the recompile fails, the object remains invalid. A production database should not contain invalid objects, as they are potential or actual problems waiting to happen. The sudden appearance of invalid objects suggests that changes are being made to the database to cause the invalidation. These should be investigated as they occur. The following SQL displays invalid objects:

```
select * from dba_objects where status <> 'VALID';
```

Files in Recovery Mode

Files in recovery mode can appear suddenly—for example, due to a media failure or corruption. They won't necessarily prevent operation of the database until data is requested from the file itself. If the requested data is in the System Global Area (SGA) block buffer cache, then queries on objects stored in the missing or nonaccessible file can succeed even when the underlying file is no longer accessible. It's also possible to start up the database when a datafile is missing without receiving any errors. Files in recovery mode are always displayed in the V$RECOVER_FILE view after the next checkpoint, which fails for files that can't be checkpointed. The following SQL can be used to identify files in recovery mode:

```
select * from v$recover_file;
```

Datafiles Offline

After a file has been restored and after media recovery has been performed to recover the file, it's still possible for the file to remain offline. Any queries that reference data in the file will fail. The following SQL identifies the files that are offline:

```
select * from v$datafile where status='OFFLINE';
```

After successful recovery, the following SQL can be used to place an offline file online:

```
alter database datafile '/u02/oradata/ORAD1/ora_s1_xzobn3yj.dbf' online;
```

Failing and Broken Jobs

Many Oracle systems use the Oracle job queue subsystem implemented in the DBMS_JOB and DBMS_IJOB packages to submit and execute scheduled procedures. As these jobs execute asynchronously, errors are reported through the alert log and trace files. Jobs can fail up to 16 times, after which they are marked broken. Failures and broken jobs can be identified through the following SQL:

```
select * from dba_jobs
where broken='Y' or failures > 0;
```

It's also worth checking for scheduled jobs not currently executing and whose next execution date is in the past, as this indicates a problem with the job queue:

```
select * from dba_jobs
where broken='N'
and next_date < SYSDATE
and job not in (select job from dba_jobs_running);
```

Disabled Constraints and Triggers

Disabled constraints and triggers are problems waiting to happen. A production database should not contain disabled constraints and triggers. If present, they should be enabled or removed. If they are disabled temporarily for maintenance purposes and the DBA accidentally forgets to enable them, this check will find them. Leaving disabled objects in place leaves open the possibility that they will be accidentally enabled for whatever reason, resulting in production data integrity being compromised. If trigger behavior needs to be enabled and disabled during business processing, then it's better to make the process data-driven by having the trigger check data within the trigger text to determine whether it should execute. In this case, the trigger can remain enabled at all times. The following SQL statements identify triggers and constraints that are disabled:

```
select * from dba_triggers where status='DISABLED';
```

```
select * from dba_constraints where status='DISABLED';
```

Distributed Transactions Awaiting Recovery

If you use the Oracle transparent gateways (covered in Chapter 3) or database links to connect your Oracle databases to other systems, then there is a possibility that remote transactions can fail. These transactions can be identified from the DBA_2PC_PEND-ING view as follows:

```
select * from dba_2pc_pending;
```

Full Rollback Segments

When a rollback segment is marked with a status of FULL, no new transactions can use it. All transactions in the rollback segment must either commit or roll back before it can be used by other transactions. If all rollback segments become full, the database is effectively unavailable. The following SQL shows the IDs of full rollback segments:

```
select usn from v$rollstat where status='FULL';
```

Resumable Space Allocation Errors in Oracle9*i*

Oracle9*i* provides resumable space allocation features to suspend rather than termi-nate sessions that experience a space shortage, for example, due to the scenarios cov-ered in the previous section on segments that can't extend. Chapter 6 includes a detailed discussion of resumable space allocation features. The following SQL identi-fies sessions that are suspended, pending DBA action to address the space shortage so that the session can resume:

```
select * from dba_resumable where status <> 'NORMAL';
```

Alert Log Monitoring

Monitoring the alert log helps you identify some database problems as soon as they occur. From my experience, it doesn't produce the expected availability benefits unless the monitored messages are chosen very carefully so as not to create too many spurious alerts. Alert log monitoring is recommended for the Oracle errors shown in Table 24.1.

The ORA-00600 covers a multitude of possible causes and doesn't always indicate a problem that can be addressed in a meaningful way. Neither does ORA-07445. They should always be investigated and reported to Oracle Support if necessary.

Space shortages for rollback and temporary segments need to be treated differently from data space shortages because the techniques used to avoid data shortages, such as AUTOEXTEND, may not be considered appropriate in these cases. The ORA-1653 indicates that an actual data space shortage occurred during an index or table update. If you use the recommended techniques for avoiding such shortages (based on AUTOEXTEND and LOCAL uniform extent management), then this error should never occur. You still need to check for the problem just in case. The final three mes-sages should be trapped through the previous check for files in recovery mode, but there's no harm in checking for the same problem in more than one way if it leads to problems being detected sooner. The same reasoning applies to ORA-00257, which will also be detected by the dbool_db_up.pl test.

Table 24.1 Alert Log Error Monitoring

ERROR STRING	CAUSE
ORA-00257	archiver error. Connect internal only, until freed
ORA-00600	internal error code
ORA-00603	ORACLE server session terminated by fatal error
ORA-01157	cannot identify/lock datafile %s - see DBWR trace file
ORA-01578	ORACLE data block corrupted (file # %s, block # %s)
ORA-07445	exception encountered: core dump
ORA-01562	failed to extend rollback segment number %s
ORA-1650	unable to extend rollback segment
ORA-1652	unable to extend a temporary segment
ORA-1653	unable to extend table
ORA-27048	skgfifi: file header information is invalid

Keep in mind that errors reported in the alert log do not follow strict formatting rules. Some may indicate serious errors but not include the Oracle error number, such as the following messages that indicate problems with an archived redo log destination that may cause the database to suspend until fixed:

```
Archiving not possible: No primary destinations
I/O error 19502
```

Implementing Monitoring with Database Jobs

It's possible to carry out most of the monitoring in the previous section using database jobs running within the database itself. In effect, the database becomes self-monitoring. This approach has the advantage that the monitoring is completely controlled by the DBA, and doesn't require the additional complexity of managing and configuring external agents such as OIA.

Creating and Scheduling Jobs

In order to run scheduled jobs, you need to ensure that the job_queue_processes init.ora parameter is set. If it's not set, then your jobs won't run. You can set the parameter to use two queues without restarting the instance by using the following:

```
alter session set job_queue_processes=2;
```

If you're using a server parameter file, you can extend the setting so that it remains in place after the next database restart. If you're using the old-style init.ora file, then you need to remember to set the value in the file manually. Several database procedures are provided for submitting jobs to the job scheduler. In general, you are restricted to managing jobs in your own schema unless you use the DBMS_IJOB.SUBMIT procedure. This gives you full control over all jobs, including those in the schemas of other users. As a DBA, in general, I prefer to use the DBMS_IJOB interface for that reason.

To illustrate this, let's create a job to detect rows in DBA_2PC_PENDING. These rows identify distributed transactions awaiting recovery. This is one of the monitoring requirements described earlier. First, we need a stored procedure to schedule. This can be created as SYS using the following SQL:

```
create procedure sp_dba_2pc_pending as
begin
   for rec in (select * from dba_2pc_pending where rownum <=1) loop
       null; -- rows found, add notification code here later
   end loop;
end sp_dba_2pc_pending;
```

The simplest way to see how job submission works is to submit the job using the simplest interface and then reverse engineer the full definition from the database. The simplest interface for submitting a job is DBMS_JOB.SUBMIT, as shown in the following example:

```
declare
   job number;
begin
   sys.dbms_job.submit(job=>job,
                       next_date=>SYSDATE,
                       interval=>'sysdate+20/(24*60)',
                       what=>'sp_dba_2pc_pending;');
end;
```

The WHAT parameter is the job execution procedure. The semicolon in the WHAT parameter is required because the job queue executes the code in WHAT using an anonymous PL/SQL block, so the stored procedure call must be terminated just like any other PL/SQL procedure call. The NEXT_DATE value determines when the job will next execute, and the INTERVAL parameter is used to calculate the value of NEXT_DATE after execution completes. In this example, the job is scheduled to execute immediately and then every 20 minutes after it completes. For long-running jobs, this can cause the start time to drift from what is required. For example, if the job is intended to execute on the hour, at 20 minutes past the hour, and at 40 minutes past the hour, the interval shown won't meet the requirement because it's calculated after the previous execution completes. We address ways to avoid drift later.

NOTE You must execute a COMMIT after submitting your job in order for the job to run as scheduled. This is easy to overlook. If you don't commit, the job

will appear in DBA_JOBS for your session only, which can give the impression it's available to run through the job queues.

If you use DBMS_JOB.SUBMIT, Oracle generates the job ID for you. If you intend to run the same procedure on each server, it's better to standardize the job numbers so that a given function is performed using the same job ID on each database. To accomplish this, you have two options:

- Reverse engineer complete job definitions for existing jobs using the DBMS_IJOB.FULL_EXPORT procedure and then resubmit the jobs using job IDs of your choice.

- Use the DBMS_JOB.IJOB procedure to submit the job.

One way to accomplish this reverse engineering easily is to create a function around the FULL_EXPORT procedure as follows and execute the function via a query:

```
create function sp_export_job(p_job number) return varchar2 as
l_job varchar2(4000);
begin
    sys.dbms_ijob.full_export(p_job,l_job);
    return(l_job);
end;
/

REM select full job definitions using function...
select sp_export_job(job)||chr(10)
from dba_jobs;
```

The full definition of the original job is then available in the SQL result set for the query. The definition uses the full description specified by DBMS_IJOB.SUBMIT rather than the less flexible DBMS_JOB.SUBMIT that was used to submit the original job. In particular, the use of DBMS_IJOB.SUBMIT enables the DBA to specify the job number through the JOB parameter and choose the schema in which to run the job—through the LUSER, PUSER, and CUSER arguments.

To resubmit the job as the job number 1000, which we define to represent our standard job number for the DBA_2PC_PENDING check, it's necessary to first remove the original job using SYS.DBMS_IJOB.REMOVE(*jobid*) and resubmit the job with ID 1000, as follows, based on the reverse-engineered description:

```
begin
sys.dbms_ijob.submit(
job=>1000,
luser=>'SYS',puser=>'SYS',cuser=>'SYS',
next_date=>SYSDATE,
interval=>'sysdate+20/(24*60)',
broken=>FALSE,what=>'sp_dba_2pc_pending;',
nlsenv=>'NLS_LANGUAGE=''AMERICAN'' NLS_TERRITORY=''AMERICA''
NLS_CURRENCY=''$'' NLS_ISO_CURRENCY=''AMERICA''
NLS_NUMERIC_CHARACTERS=''.,'' NLS_DATE_FORMAT=''DD-MON-RR''
```

```
NLS_DATE_LANGUAGE=''AMERICAN'' NLS_SORT=''BINARY''',
env=>'0102000200000000'
);
end;
/
```

Once you have a template for DBMS_IJOB.SUBMIT, you can use it for all future job submissions. You can identify the cause of job failures through trace files in the background_dump_dest directory specified in the init.ora file. The trace files have names that identify the job queue processes—for example, ORAP1_snp0_468.trc.

Customizing Job Intervals

It's possible to be quite creative when providing the interval value in order to prevent the start time from drifting. For example, the following interval setting causes a job to start only on the next 20-minute interval past the hour:

```
interval=>'trunc(sysdate)+to_char(sysdate,''HH24'')/24+decode(mod(trunc(
to_char(sysdate,''M'')/20)+1,3),0,60/(24*60),1,20/(24*60),2,40/(24*60))'
```

This INTERVAL setting is somewhat difficult to follow. The requirement to escape the quote characters adds to the DBA burden, making it time consuming to get the syntax correct. Instead of specifying the NEXT_DATE using the INTERVAL parameter, you can set the NEXT_DATE for job submission *within the job procedure itself*. This enables the NEXT_DATE to be set in PL/SQL code, using complexity limited only by PL/SQL. In this case, when you submit the job, you use an INTERVAL of NULL. Ordinarily, this causes jobs to remove themselves from the job queue immediately after execution. However, if you pass the NEXT_DATE into the job as an IN OUT parameter and set the value within the procedure, it is used by the job scheduler to reset NEXT_DATE after the job execution completes. The following example shows how to submit a job that schedules itself to run only on Saturday or Sunday at 11:00. The WHAT procedure executed by the job scheduler looks like the following:

```
procedure sp_sat_and_sun_only(next_date in out date) as
begin
   -- do job processing

   -- set next_date for SAT 11:00 or SUN 11:00 only
   if TO_CHAR(sysdate,'DY') = 'SAT' then
      next_date := trunc(NEXT_DAY(SYSDATE,'SUNDAY'))+11/24;
   else
      next_date := trunc(NEXT_DAY(SYSDATE,'SATURDAY'))+11/24 ;
   end if;
end;
/
```

The call to DBMS_JOB.ISUBMIT requires the INTERVAL and WHAT parameters to be passed as follows, where NEXT_DATE is passed in:

```
        .
        .
        .
next_date=>SYSDATE
interval=>NULL
what=>'sp_sat_and_sun_only(next_date);'
        .
        .
        .
```

You can use a similar technique to pass in the job ID at job execution time. As a result, you can specify the job ID in any alerts you raise from within the job itself. If you use a standardized numbering scheme for all your jobs, then the job ID implicitly identifies the job that failed.

Alerting with Email

Once you have jobs up and running to monitor your database, the next step is to notify support staff whenever a problem occurs. Historically, it would have been necessary to write alert information to a file and have a process poll the file and raise alerts externally. If you are prepared to use email to raise alerts, then you can raise alerts from within the job process using the UTL_SMTP package. UTL_SMTP uses the Simple Mail Transfer Protocol (SMTP) to provide the facility to send email from within PL/SQL. If you use UNIX servers to run Oracle databases in your organization, then an SNMP-based mail program called sendmail is almost certainly running already. The sendmail program provides the SMTP-based email service required by UTL_SMTP. The following code provides a complete routine for sending email from PL/SQL:

```
procedure sp_sendmail
     ( p_sender     in varchar2,p_recipient in varchar2,
       p_subject    in varchar2,p_message   in varchar2,
       p_mailhost   in varchar2) as
   l_mail_conn utl_smtp.connection;
   l_open boolean := false;

  procedure send_header(name in varchar2, header in varchar2) as
  begin
     utl_smtp.write_data(
         l_mail_conn,name||':'||header||utl_tcp.CRLF);
  end;

begin
   l_mail_conn :=utl_smtp.open_connection(p_mailhost,25);
   l_open:=true;
   for rec in (select machine from v$session where sid=1) loop
      utl_smtp.helo(l_mail_conn,rec.machine);
   end loop;
   utl_smtp.mail(l_mail_conn,p_sender);
```

```
        utl_smtp.rcpt(l_mail_conn,p_recipient);
        utl_smtp.open_data(l_mail_conn);
        send_header('Subject',p_subject);
        send_header('To',p_recipient);
        utl_smtp.write_data(l_mail_conn, utl_tcp.CRLF||p_message);
        utl_smtp.close_data(l_mail_conn);
        utl_smtp.quit(l_mail_conn);
    exception
        when utl_smtp.transient_error or utl_smtp.permanent_error then
            if l_open then
                utl_smtp.quit(l_mail_conn);
            end if;
            raise_application_error(-20000,
            'mail send error: mailhost='||p_mailhost||' '||sqlerrm);
        when others then
            raise_application_error(-20000,
            'mail send error: mailhost='||p_mailhost||' '||sqlerrm);
    end;
```

A call to the SP_SENDMAIL procedure from our original procedure might look like this:

```
create procedure sp_dba_2pc_pending as
begin
    for rec in (select * from dba_2pc_pending where rownum <=1) loop
        -- send email alert when rows detected
        sp_sendmail(
            p_sender=>'OraAlert@dbcool.com',
            p_recipient=>'OracleDba@dbcool.com',
            p_subject=>'EMERGENCY in orad1.dbcool.com',
            p_message=>'rows found in DBA_2PC_PENDING',
            p_mailhost=>'srv1.dbcool.com');
    end loop;
end sp_dba_2pc_pending;
```

SMTP can run over the unreliable User Datagram Protocol (UDP), where there is no guarantee of delivery, or the Transmission Control Protocol/Internet Protocol (TCP/IP). You should make sure that TCP/IP is used. Most UNIX implementations use the file /etc/services to specify which port and protocol SMTP uses. The standard port number is 25. To ensure that email alerts reach their destination, you need to make sure that the P_MAILHOST server through which mail is delivered is available 24×7 and has monitoring in place to ensure that sendmail is operational at all times. To increase reliability, a good approach is to create a wrapper procedure around SP_SENDMAIL to send each email through two mail servers on different sites in order to ensure that emails are still delivered in the case of a single site outage.

As an aside, you can see from the PL/SQL code that SMTP is a simple protocol that is text based. This makes the protocol simple to use. The downside is that the P_SENDER does not have to be a real email address, and the machine passed to the procedure UTL_SMTP.HELO as the originating host for the email does not have to exist.

These are reasons why sendmail is so popular with senders of spam on the Internet because sendmail enables email senders and servers to be forged in the email headers.

It's worth mentioning that in some cases it's possible to generate an alert as soon as a problem occurs, without polling a database table or log file. The following trigger sends an email alert whenever an Oracle resumable space error occurs for sessions running on behalf of database accounts that have RESUMABLE privilege and ALTER SESSION ENABLE RESUMABLE set:

```
create or replace trigger trg_resumable_alert
after suspend on database
declare
   cur_sid number; cur_inst number;
   error_txt varchar2(4000); global_name varchar2(4000);
begin
   -- get session ID, instance ID (for RAC systems), global_name
   select sid,userenv('instance'),global_name
       into cur_sid,cur_inst,global_name
   from v$mystat,global_name where rownum<2;
   -- Identify space error
   select error_msg into error_txt from dba_resumable
   where session_id = cur_sid and instance_id = cur_inst;
   -- email the error/session/instance/database
   sp_sendmail(
      p_sender=>cur_sid||'_'||cur_inst||'@'||global_name,
      p_recipient=>'OracleDba@dbcool.com',
      p_subject=>'Resumable Space Alert',p_message=>error_txt,
      p_mailhost=>'srv1.dbcool.com');
end;
/
```

In this example, the p_sender parameter identifies the session, instance, and global_name of the database in which the problem occurred, rather than a real email account. This is useful information for the DBA that receives the email.

Implementing Monitoring with OEM

Monitoring a system yourself as demonstrated in the previous section is fine as far as it goes, but it doesn't go far enough. For example, if your Oracle job queue processing fails, then all of your monitoring is lost if you use database jobs to perform all of your monitoring. In that case, you need to monitor the job queues through a scheduled job that doesn't rely on the job queue for scheduling. Also, file system capacity monitoring is required, and this is something that is not typically performed within the database itself, although it is possible through the use of external procedures, as shown in Chapter 13.

An architecture is required for enterprise-wide monitoring, which is usually referred to as a *systems management framework*, to monitor database conditions throughout the network. There are several on the market, and they have similar architectures comprising a centralized management console and agent processes running on the monitored servers. The agent processes can be configured to run monitoring tests periodically and if exceptions are encountered, alert messages are sent to the management console to identify the location and nature of the problem. The management console software, which typically runs on a workstation with a color display, may contact support staff automatically by radio paging or email, or require human intervention to determine the escalation procedure. The escalation procedure often depends on whether the problem occurs during or after business hours, in which case the complexity of the process may require human intervention. The management console typically displays a graphical user interface (GUI), which provides a visual indication of the severity of the problem as alerts arrive. Alerts are usually classified into information, warning, and emergency severities, depending on the message content, source, and time of day. Red is usually used to indicate emergencies. The visual severity indicator remains in place until the problem is solved or acknowledged manually.

SNMP Frameworks

SNMP is an unreliable UDP-based open protocol that is used for the communication of information such as alerts (known as *traps* in the SNMP world) between managed nodes on an SNMP-based framework. The unreliability of the SNMP protocol has resulted in many solutions that use proprietary protocols, based on TCP, for communication between the managed nodes and the management console. Examples of such products are BMC Patrol, IBM Tivoli, and Oracle's OEM. These solutions also have the capability to raise alert events using SNMP in order to allow their agents to integrate with existing SNMP-based frameworks. The purchase of an enterprise-wide systems management framework needs to meet the monitoring required of all technology groups in an organization, including the DBA group. The software, hardware, and people costs of any systems management framework is high, and the choice of technology is a critical success factor for enabling support groups to meet service-level requirements.

The rest of this section describes the installation and use of the OIA as an example of how to perform enterprise-wide Oracle monitoring within the OEM framework. You're likely to use OIA in the future, even if you don't today, because it's essential in helping to automate the management of some of Oracle's more sophisticated and complex-to-manage products, such as Data Guard, which is covered in Chapter 23.

OIA Architecture

Figure 24.2 shows the processes and data flows for an OEM management framework using OIA to monitor five different databases on two servers. Oracle's framework enables multiple management consoles to register with the middle tier running Oracle Management Server (OMS). All process instances are shown as circles. One instance of OIA is required per managed server node, and this monitors all Oracle instances on the node. OEM can be used to connect directly from a console to an agent, but many features are not available in this configuration. In order to make full use of all OEM features, it is recommended that you use OMS and an OEM repository database to store information on the complete Oracle topology.

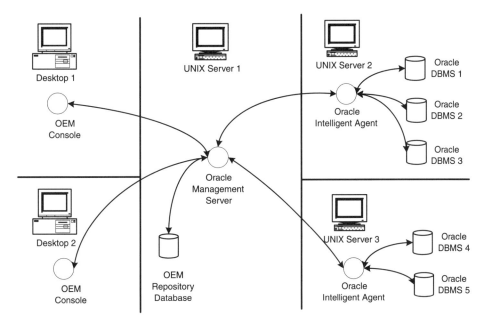

Figure 24.2 OIA framework.

Installing and Running OMS

Running the OEM framework in the most powerful configuration requires that you create an OMS and OEM Repository database. Before you begin, it's best to have a database already built to hold the repository. This database should be configured to use a password file because the credentials that are stored in the repository for connecting to it from OMS require SYSDBA privileges. Oracle can create a database for you as part of the installation process, but this won't meet the recommended database-naming standards proposed in this book.

To create a management server and OEM repository, you need to run the Enterprise Manager Configuration Assistant program (emca). During the installation, you should choose the options to configure a local management server and create a new repository, using the Custom option to install the OEM repository into an existing database. The schema takes a few minutes to install. Once the installation is complete, the management server can be started using the following command:

```
$ oemctl start oms
```

If you didn't configure an OEM repository first, you'll receive the following message: "Could not connect to the OMS: possible error in the configuration file." The default logon for the new management server is username system, password oem_temp. The first time you connect to the management server, you are prompted to change it.

OPTIONS FOR RUNNING OEM TOOLS

The examples in this section run the OEM tools from a UNIX server onto an X Windows display. To improve the responsiveness of the GUI, especially across a wide area network (WAN), you can install the tools onto a client such as a Windows PC and run them in client-server mode or within a Web browser. The OEM documentation provides full details.

The OraTcl Scripting Language

In order to take advantage of OIA's capabilities, it's necessary to have a basic understanding of Tool Control Language (Tcl) and OraTcl, an Oracle extension that provides an Oracle query and execution capability within the language. The Tcl script—nmiconf.tcl—is used to discover the Oracle services on a managed node. The version with the Oracle capability built in is called OraTcl. Although both jobs and event routines use Tcl, they are specified separately in the OEM console interface and are used for different purposes. Whereas jobs typically run tasks that can take a significant amount of time and affect the database state, such as the execution of a backup script or database shutdown, events typically need to run more frequently so they tend to be of a short duration.

Both Perl (as described in Chapter 4) and Tcl perform similar functions, albeit using a different syntax. If your heart is sinking at the thought of having to learn yet another new language, you'll find the move between Perl and Tcl, or vice versa, very straightforward. OEM also provides an interface for user-defined event procedures, so you can continue to use Perl or other languages if you want.

Event scripts can pass return codes back to the agent to specify the severity of the event, and it's even possible to pass information to a Fixit Job to fix the error without DBA intervention. Events have another significant difference from jobs in that they need to maintain the state between invocations to prevent the same event from being raised multiple times. This is provided through persistent global variables. The need to maintain state is most easily understood by looking at an example, along with some other code fragments to give a flavor of the Tcl language. The sample code leaves out error handling for clarity. In the real world, you should never do that.

Consider an OraTcl script that monitors the alert log for errors like ORA-00600 or ORA-00603. If an error has been detected and an alert has been raised, then on the next invocation, the job needs to search the alert log starting from the point it reached last time to avoid alerting the DBA of errors that were already detected. This requirement is implemented by saving the size of the alert log in a persistent variable using an initial value of –1 as a flag to indicate the first invocation of the job as follows:

```
oraeventpersist last_alert_size -1
```

An array is used to hold the errors to search the alert log, as follows:

```
set alert_errors {ORA-00600 ORA-00603}
```

One of the main benefits of OraTcl is that it has a built-in knowledge of Oracle databases, how they work, and what configuration settings DBAs need to access most frequently when writing event scripts. The alert log name is required in order to search the contents. The name can be assigned to a variable with trivial ease by reading the name from a preset array at the position given by ALERTFILE:

```
set alertfile [ALERTFILE]
```

OraTcl manages the population of the array completely transparently to the programmer. On the first invocation, the Tcl script detects that the file size is required, checks for the existence of the alert log, and reads the size of the file into the $last_alert_size variable using the following code:

```
if {$last_alert_size == -1}
{
    if { [file exists $alertfile] }
    {
        set last_alert_size [file size $alertfile]
    }
}
```

Tcl has many built-in commands, making it easy to access operating system routines for file processing and other services. It can test for a file's existence and size, open a file, seek to an offset within a file, read lines one at a time, and search for strings in the lines read. All these features are shown in the following code:

```
set fd [open $alertfile r]        # open the alert log file
seek $fd $last_alert_size start   # seek to byte offset from the start

while {[gets $fd line] >= 0}      # read lines from the file
{
    set alert_found 0
    foreach error $alert_errors    # for each error message in the array
    {
        if {[string first $error $line] >= 0}  # is it in the line read?
        {
            set alert_found 1                   # error found in log
            set ret_code $ALERT_EVENT
            incr number_of_errors               # increment error count
        }
    }
}
```

Discovering Databases and Services

Once you have a management server in place, you can use the OEM console to communicate with the OIA on any node to discover the databases installed on the node automatically. First, you need to start OIA on each node containing services that you want to discover:

```
$ agentctl start agent      # start 9i Intelligent Agent
$ lsnrctl dbsnmp_start      # start 8i Intelligent Agent
```

In both cases, the process dbsnmp is started. The process name is somewhat misleading because there is no requirement to have an SNMP agent running on the server. In this case, we aren't using an SNMP-based framework. Oracle9*i* has taken a significant step forward by including a watcher daemon process called dbsnmpwd, which starts at the same time as dbsnmp. The purpose of dbsnmpwd is to restart dbsnmp immediately, typically within a second, if it terminates without being shut down explicitly using agentctl stop agent. This guarantees that OIA runs at all times. If it terminates unexpectedly, you have lost your monitoring capability so in Oracle8*i* you need to monitor for the presence of an agent separately.

When the agent starts, it populates three files with information about discovered services that can be managed by OEM: snmp_ro.ora, snmp_rw.ora, and services.ora. They can be found in the TNS_ADMIN directory or in $ORACLE_HOME/network/admin. The read-only file (snmp_ro.ora) is overwritten when the agent starts so you shouldn't change it. The read write file (snmp_rw.ora) is updateable and you can add settings to it to enable tracing and logging through the following settings:

```
dbsnmp.trace_level = off      # other values: user, admin,16
dbsnmp.trace_file = agent     # default: dbsnmp.trc
dbsnmp.trace_directory = /tmp # default: $ORACLE_HOME/network/trace
nmi.trace_level = off         # Tcl trace, values as dbsnmp.trace_level
nmi.trace_directory = /tmp    # trace directory
```

The services.ora file contains all discovered services. The file contents are passed to OEM by the agent when node discovery is run on the OEM console. The OEM console is started up as follows and requires that you first set your UNIX DISPLAY environment variable to a valid X Windows display:

```
$ oemapp console
```

Errors and warnings encountered during the discovery process are written to the nmiconf.log file, which is located in $ORACLE_HOME/network/log. Although it's possible to add services manually to OEM, Oracle recommends that you use autodiscovery to let OIA find all the Oracle services on a node. In order to make the best use of autodiscovery, it's necessary to set up the Oracle configuration on the node explicitly to enable autodiscovery to take place.

One frustrating feature of the autodiscovery process—which is performed by the nmiconf.tcl script on the managed node and logged to nmiconf.log—is that is doesn't use an Oracle Names server to identify Oracle services on the node. Using Oracle Names to provide your Oracle name-to-address service is very strongly recommended in Chapter 3. As a result, a TNS alias orap1.dbcool.com on server dbsrv1.dbcool.com is likely to be identified in the OEM repository using the unique name orap1_dbsrv1 rather than the global name orap1.dbcool.com. The workaround to this problem is to specify GLOBAL_DBNAME=orap1.dbcool.com in the listener.ora entry for the database instance. Chapter 3 contains full details. It's a shame that Oracle doesn't integrate their own tools better to take advantage of their own naming services. Chapter 3 stated that you don't need a listener.ora file to connect to Oracle services. However, if you want to use autodiscovery, then you do need one because autodiscovery requires the static registration of the service name through GLOBAL_DBNAME. The dynamic registration features of the listener are not recognized by the registration process. If you are an enterprising DBA, you might want to investigate how nmiconf.tcl can be modified to identify local databases by querying an Oracle Names server.

Once you have restarted your listener using GLOBAL_DBNAME, followed by a restart of the agent, autodiscovery, performed through the Navigator main menu option on the OEM console, uses the contents of oratab, listener.ora, and sqlnet.ora to identify the Oracle services on the managed node. Once discovered, the names appear in the OEM console in the Network tree.

TIP The oratclsh utility can be used to report some information about the agent running on the local node by using the special Tcl orainfo verb at the prompt.

Creating Events

Once the managed nodes containing your databases are available in the OEM console, you can configure scheduled event tests on your database instances and raise alerts of different severities when the test conditions fail. You have a choice of using Oracle's supplied events or creating your own. To create an event, choose Event from the OEM console main menu and then choose Create Event. The Create Event tabbed dialog box appears with the options shown in Table 24.2.

Event creation steps should be followed in order from the top to bottom of Table 24.2. If you perform the steps out of order, Oracle will alert you of missing information when you attempt to register the event. After you have chosen a name for the event,

Table 24.2 Event Creation Steps

STEP NAME	PURPOSE
General	Choose event name and target database to run against.
Tests	Choose an Oracle-supplied event test or define your own SQL-based, on-script base test.
Parameters	Choose thresholds at which alert severities are generated.
Schedule	Choose how often the test runs.
Access	Choose who gets notified of the event.
Fixit Jobs	Choose an optional job to fix the problem that caused the event.

you need to add the databases in which you want to run the test from the Available Targets to the Monitored Targets list. The event name you choose is used to identify the event in email notifications and the OEM console alert list. Next, you need to choose which test type to use under the Tests tab. The available tests are shown in Figure 24.3.

The built-in tests are available as Tcl scripts, some of which can be located under $ORACLE_HOME/network/agent/events/oracle/rdbms. You can use these as templates for your own tests. In this example, the DBA_2PC_PENDING test used previously will be used to create a user-defined SQL test and a user-defined event test to demonstrate how you can integrate your own tests within OEM. The built-in tests probably won't do exactly what you want. To recap, the monitor test fails and an alert is required, if one or more rows exist in DBA_2PC_Monitoring, which is shown in the following SQL:

```
select count(*) from dba_2pc_pending;
```

User-Defined SQL Test

To create a user-defined test using the SQL of your choice, you need to choose User Defined SQL Test as the test type to use. Next, move to the Parameters tab and enter the SQL and threshold test criteria, as shown in Figure 24.4.

The SQL you use must return a single-column, single-row result set. In the example, if the column given by count(*) exceeds or matches the critical threshold of 1, a critical severity event is raised. In other words, if any rows appear in DBA_2PC_PENDING, a critical severity alert is generated. The Schedule tab schedules the test at 5-minute intervals by default, which you can modify. Under the Access tab, you should check

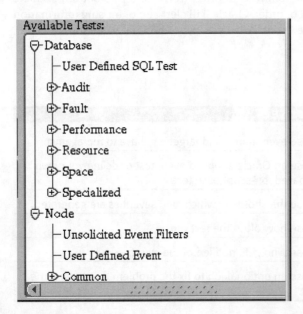

Figure 24.3   OEM event tests.

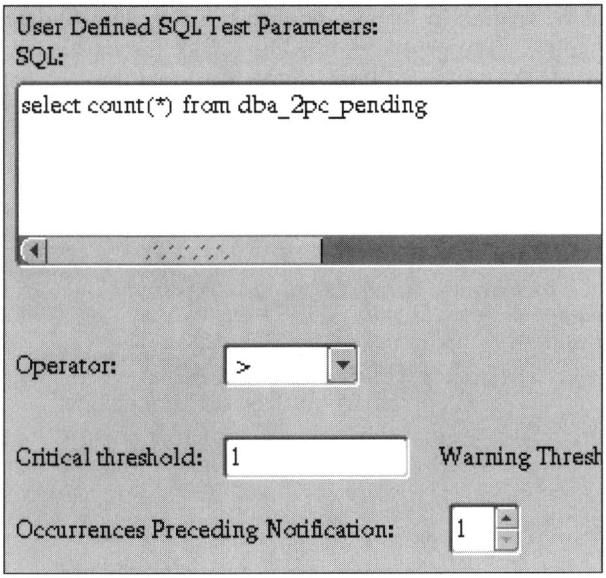

Figure 24.4 A user-defined SQL test.

the Notify box to ensure that alerts are sent to the notification targets, which are typically email accounts. Notification is covered in more detail in the section *Using Email Notification*. Finally, press Register, and the event is registered to run.

User-Defined Event Test

You can run scripts written in the language of your choice by selecting User Defined Event as the test type in the Tests tab. You must be running the Oracle9*i* agent to execute user-defined events. In this example, we use the Perl script dba_2pc_pending.pl to generate a critical severity alert whenever rows are found in DBA_2PC_PENDING. The full script can be downloaded from the companion Web site. When you register a script, you need to provide the script path and parameters in the Parameters tab, and ensure that the script is available on the monitored node in the location you specify. For example:

```
/u01/app/oracle/user_defined_events/dba_2pc_pending.pl sid=ORAD1
```

The script returns values back to OEM using a special tag containing the following predefined values that are recognized by OEM as event severities:

```
$OEM_SCRIPT_FAILURE=-2; $OEM_CLEAR=-1; $OEM_WARNING=1; $OEM_CRITICAL=2;
```

In order to treat the values as event severities, the Event State button *must* be pressed to identify the result as an event state in the Parameters tab. These severities are the same values returned by the Oracle-supplied Tcl scripts. In order to pass the value back to the OEM console, they must be written to UNIX standard output using the tag "<oraresult>*returncode*</oraresult>." The *returncode* must be one of the four listed. The following code fragment shows the section of the script that returns the count(*) values from the SQL select list along with severity information:

```
$the_sql="select count(*) from dba_2pc_pending";

# get a cursor for selecting the values
$c_files = &ora_open($session, $the_sql);
if ($ora_errno) { print "<oraresult>$OEM_SCRIPT_FAILURE</oraresult>";
                  goto EXIT;}

@column_vals = &ora_fetch($c_files); # fetch SQL results

# check if fetch failed...
if ($ora_errno) { print "<oraresult>$OEM_SCRIPT_FAILURE</oraresult>";
                  goto EXIT;}

# check count(*) value
if ($column_vals[0] == 0)
    {print "<oraresult>$OEM_CLEAR</oraresult>";}
else
    {print "<oraresult>$OEM_CRITICAL</oraresult>";}

EXIT:
    if ($ora_errno) {print "<oramessage>$ora_errstr</oramessage>";}
    if ($session) {&ora_logoff($session);}
```

If any part of the script fails, the $OEM_SCRIPT_FAILURE code is returned, and this value is treated by OEM as a critical event. If the count(*) value given by $column_vals[0] is not 0, then the $OEM_CRITICAL value 2 is returned to OEM and the event appears in the OEM event list as a critical event. If the count(*) value is 0, then the code $OEM_CLEAR is returned. This causes a notification event indicating that the problem is now fixed and causes any previous critical event to clear from the OEM alert list.

The special tag "<oramessage>*message*</oramessage>" can be executed multiple times and causes any user-defined messages within the tags to be returned as additional information to appear in the OEM console along with the alert itself. In the code example, the Oracle error message, if any, is returned.

Using Email Notification in OEM

If you perform your own problem notification using database jobs and UTL_SMTP, then emails will continue to be sent while the error condition exists. This can result in a flood of emails until the problem is fixed. OEM, on the other hand, sends a single notification when a critical event occurs and sends another when the event is cleared after the problem causing the event has been fixed. The body of the email can be customized to provide additional information on top of the default values shown in the following example. The following email subject and body are sent when the critical event is generated in the script dba_2pc_pending.pl:

```
Subject: OEM EVENT User Script DBA_2PC_PENDING CRITICAL

Name : User Script DBA_2PC_PENDING
Target Name : orap1.dbcool.com
Target Type : Database
Node Name : srv1.dbcool.com
Status : CRITICAL

User Defined Event
User Defined Event Execution has Current return value: 2
CRITICAL
```

The subject contains the event name (User Script DBA_2PC_PENDING) and severity (CRITICAL). The body contains details of the source of the event and node name, which in this case is given by the database TNS alias and the server where the problem occurred. The return value 2 corresponding to $OEM_CRITICAL in the script is also included. When the problem is fixed, the following email is sent to notify that the problem no longer exists:

```
Subject: OEM EVENT User Script DBA_2PC_PENDING CRITICAL

Name : User Script DBA_2PC_PENDING
Target Name : orap1.dbcool.com
Target Type : Database
Node Name : srv1.dbcool.com
Status : CLEARED

User Defined Event
User Defined Event Execution has Current return value: -1
CLEARED
```

To configure email notification, you need to provide details of an SMTP gateway (typically a UNIX server running sendmail) and an email account that appears to email recipients as the sender of the message. These are set by choosing Configure from the OEM console main menu and then choosing Configure Paging/Email. To set the recipient for email notification, you need to choose Configure and then Preferences from the main menu, followed by the Notification tab and then the Email node, and provide an email account for Receiver's Email. It's a good idea to use an email prefix of OEM in the email subject to make it easy for email-processing software to identify events generated by OEM. To ensure that notifications are generated, you need to choose the hours in which email events can be generated by using the Schedule tab.

TIP If email notification doesn't appear to be working, remember that by default all notification is *off*.

Fixit Jobs

It's possible to associate jobs with events in order to automate the process of fixing problems. This jobs are known as Fixit Jobs. For example, in certain cases, transactions in DBA_2PC_PENDING can be cleared using the PURGE_LOST_DB_ENTRY procedure. The following PL/SQL block, run as SYS, generates procedure calls based on the local transaction IDs of outstanding transactions and executes the generated calls to clear them:

```
begin
for rec in (select 'begin sys.dbms_transaction.purge_lost_db_entry('''||
            local_tran_id||'''); commit; end;' fix_sql
            from dba_2pc_pending) loop
    execute immediate rec.fix_sql;
end loop;
end;
```

By choosing the Fixit Jobs tab from Edit Event, you can create the previous PL/SQL block as a SQL*Plus job to clear the transactions and then choose the job from the list to associate it with the event. In order to identify Fixit Jobs in OEM, it's a good idea to prefix the names with a string, such as Fix, so that they stand out clearly in the list of jobs.

Summary

Database health checks should be performed regularly to ensure that all databases are configured to meet the organizational standard. If you build your databases according to the OFA standard, you can prevent many problems from occurring in the first place.

After the health checks are in place, you need to determine which events to monitor. Generally, the fewer events, the better. If you raise alerts on too many events that don't actually indicate critical problems, the DBA is likely to miss events that are really critical. The good news is that only a few events need to be monitored. Although you can perform monitoring yourself using database jobs and email notification, you should use an enterprise-wide systems management framework for a production environment. Oracle OEM and OIA are examples of frameworks that provide the network management and monitoring of all your Oracle resources. By using OEM, you can write your own event tests in languages of your choice, create jobs to fix problems automatically, receive events from external sources, and generate SNMP traps for external frameworks.

Auditing Techniques

In my experience, auditing is often overlooked or neglected in an Oracle database. Reasons given for not auditing usually include the presumed overhead of running it and the difficulty in setting it up and interpreting the results. This chapter explains why you should use auditing on all your Oracle databases, how to configure it, and how to report on the audit trail. The audit trail can provide a wealth of information not necessarily related to security, although that's the primary use for the information.

Basic Oracle auditing using the database audit trail enables you to automatically capture information on who is using your database and what operations they are performing on the database. In the case of database misuse, either accidental or deliberate, you have a record of who did what and when. For example, if a user accidentally drops an object, you can find the exact time the drop occurred by searching the audit trail. If necessary, you can restore the database and recover it by rolling forward to the point in time just before the drop, in order to restore the object to its original state. If you are using the Flashback Query feature in Oracle9*i*, you can access the table contents pre-drop in the open database without performing a restore. In both cases, you need information about the time that the drop occurred. You can also use the audit trail to detect unauthorized use of the system to validate your organization's security policies.

The facilities provided by the database audit trail are not sophisticated enough for more advanced auditing requirements. For example, a common requirement is to audit additional information for DELETE, INSERT, and UPDATE statements, such as the capture of values in deleted rows. This can be accomplished using database triggers and autonomous transactions. A long-requested feature required by database administrators (DBAs) to audit data access requests in SELECT statements has finally arrived in Oracle9*i* through fine-grained auditing.

This chapter begins with a discussion on the facilities provided by the database audit trail and how to use them. Following from that, more sophisticated, trigger-based auditing is shown that enables a complete history of data content changes to a table to be tracked over time. Finally, the fine-grained auditing features in Oracle9*i* are used to show how the auditing of access to data in tables and views—based on the content requested—can be performed. This chapter covers the following topics:

- Enabling the database audit trail
- Relocating the audit trail and changing ownership
- Understanding the audit session identifier
- Choosing audit options
- Identifying suspicious activity
- Using the audit trail to track input/output (I/O) trends
- Using triggers to audit data content changes
- Using fine-grained access control to audit SELECT statements in Oracle9*i*

Enabling the Database Audit Trail

You can store the audit trail in two places: the database or an operating system (OS) file. I prefer to use the database because the audit information is stored in tables, enabling you to run reports on the audit trail using the Structured Query Language (SQL) tools of your choice. To allow auditing, you need to set one of the following in your init.ora file and restart the database:

```
audit_trail=db             # audit into the SYS.AUD$ table or . . .

audit_trail=os             # ...audit to an Operating System file
audit_file_dest=directory  # optional location of OS audit file
```

If you choose to use the OS to store the audit trail and don't specify a directory, Oracle chooses the default location:

```
?/rdbms/audit
```

The "?" in the path is a shorthand for the $ORACLE_HOME of the database instance. The OS audit trail information for a CREATE TABLE statement that succeeded looks like this:

```
Sat Nov 10 18:47:28 2001
SESSIONID: "224" ENTRYID: "3" STATEMENT: "13" USERID: "SYSTEM" TERMINAL:
"PROTON2000" ACTION: "1" RETURNCODE: "0" OBJ$CREATOR: "SYSTEM" OBJ$NAME:
"Z" OS$USERID: "SmithJoh" PRIV$USED: 40
```

On Sun Solaris and most other UNIX systems, the Oracle audit information is written to a file whose name is associated with the Oracle server process that performs operations on behalf of the connected client session that is being audited. For a dedicated server process with PID 27790, the file might have a name like ora_27790.aud, whereas for a shared server configuration (see Chapter 3), the file might have a name like s000_27706.aud, where 27706 is the process ID (PID) of the shared server. This discussion of file names indicates how difficult it can be to find audit information using the OS option when you have possibly hundreds of files to search in order to locate the data. Finding information in a database-located audit trail is much easier, because you can find it with SQL.

If your auditing file system location fills, you can simply remove some files. If you hold audit trail information in the database and turn on auditing for connection requests (which is recommended), then database logons fail when the SYS.AUD$ table can't extend due to a lack of space. You can protect yourself against this possibility through appropriate monitoring. As a last resort, you can use CONNECT/AS SYSBA and truncate the SYS.AUD$ table to free up space. In general, Oracle does not support direct user modification of SYS-owned objects, but AUD$ is an exception.

Relocating the Audit Trail

It's not uncommon for DBAs to require the relocation of the audit trail into another tablespace. By default, the SYS.AUD$ table and its index reside in the SYSTEM tablespace, and they are probably the only objects in the data dictionary whose size is influenced by users through application usage patterns rather than controlled directly by the DBA. For that reason, it makes sense to relocate both objects into their own tablespaces. The following SQL creates tablespaces for both the audit trail and its index, using a storage layout based on the best practices covered earlier, and relocates them:

```
create tablespace audtab
datafile
  '/u02/oradata/OMFD1/audtab01.dbf' size 1M autoextend on
next 128k maxsize unlimited extent management local;
```

```
create tablespace audind
datafile
  '/u02/oradata/OMFD1/audind01.dbf' size 1M autoextend on
next 128k maxsize unlimited extent management local;
```

```
alter table sys.aud$ move tablespace audtab;
```

```
alter index sys.i_aud1 rebuild tablespace audind;
```

Be aware that moving the tablespace out of the SYSTEM tablespace is not supported by Oracle because of potential restore issues. During my own personal testing, I have not experienced any problems with restores of databases containing a relocated audit trail using Oracle8*i* or Oracle9*i*. You need to make a call on the costs and benefits of each approach.

Changing Audit Trail Ownership

Changing the ownership of the audit trail is not supported by Oracle. You might consider it if you want to put triggers in place on the SYS.AUD$ table to trap potentially harmful system activities (for example, NOT EXISTS audit entries) as they occur. DBAs often request this.

As it's not possible to create triggers on SYS-owned objects, the ability to create triggers on the audit trail requires that the ownership of the audit trail be changed from SYS to SYSTEM, for example. The step-by-step process required to do this is shown in Table 25.1, based on the separate auditing table and index tablespaces created in the previous section.

Once you have changed the audit trail ownership, you have the ability to raise alerts from SYS-owned triggers on the SYSTEM.AUD$ table to notify DBAs of security issues as soon as they occur rather than polling the audit trail views and detecting problems after they have occurred. The following trigger detects ORA-00942 "table or view does not exist" errors as soon as they occur:

```
CREATE OR REPLACE TRIGGER SYS.TRG_DETECT_942
AFTER INSERT ON SYSTEM.AUD$
FOR EACH ROW
BEGIN
```

Table 25.1 Steps for Changing Audit Trail Ownership

OPERATION	CODE
Restart database with auditing off	`audit_trail=none in init.ora`

Re-create audit trail and index in SYSTEM schema using SQL*Plus	`connect / as sysdba;`
	`create table system.aud$ tablespace AUDTAB`
	`as select * from aud$;`
	
	`create index system.i_aud1`
	`on system.aud$(sessionid, ses$tid) tablespace`
	`AUDIND;`
	
	`rename aud$ to aud$_temp;`
	`create view aud$ as select * from`
	`system.aud$;`
	
	`connect system/manager`
	`grant all on aud$ to sys with grant option;`
	`grant delete on aud$ to delete_catalog_role;`

Restart the database with auditing on	`audit_trail=db in init.ora`
Re-create the data dictionary views for auditing using SQL*Plus	`connect "/ as SYSDBA"` `@?/rdbms/admin/cataudit.sql`

```
    For rec in
      (select sys_context('USERENV','SESSIONID') id from dual) loop
      if :new.returncode=942 and user not in ('SYSTEM') then
         -- your alerting code here using rec.id to identify session
         null;
      end if;
    end loop;

EXCEPTION
   WHEN OTHERS THEN
      null;
END SYS.TRG_DETECT_942;
```

This example doesn't include details of the alerting mechanism to use. Chapter 24 on guidelines for monitoring and healthchecks includes a procedure, SP_SENDMAIL, which you can use to send an email.

Understanding the Audit Session Identifier

The AUD$.SESSIONID column is used to identify the audited session. The audit session identifier can be determined for the current session, to join with the audit trail, in three ways:

```
REM ------------------
REM 9i Only
REM ------------------
select SYS_CONTEXT('USERENV','SESSIONID') from dual;

SYS_CONTEXT('USERENV','SESSIONI
-------------------------------
346




REM -------------------------
REM requires SELECT priv on view
REM -------------------------
select audsid from v$session
where sid=
(select sid from v$mystat where rownum <=1);

  AUDSID
--------
     346




REM --------------------
REM works in all versions
REM --------------------
```

```
select userenv('sessionid') from dual;

 USERENV('SESSIONID')
 --------------------
                  346
```

These values can be useful if you want to perform additional custom auditing at log-on or log-off time, as shown later in the chapter, and if you need to relate the custom information to the data in SYS.AUD$. You should be aware that sessions connecting as SYSDBA have an AUDSID of 0, as do background database processes and processes spawned by the Oracle job queue.

Choosing Audit Options

After starting the database with auditing enabled in the init.ora file, you need to run some SQL to enable the auditing of database actions. The actions appear in the audit trail. There is a lot of flexibility in the various levels of auditing and options that you can allow. You can set auditing at the statement, option, and privilege levels. In order to understand auditing, you need to understand what actions can be audited, how you enable and disable them, and where audited information is stored. These prerequisites definitely make it somewhat complicated to get auditing up and running, especially if you are considering setting all the auditing levels individually. You can audit success-ful operations and unsuccessful operations independently.

Audit Trail Views

Information in the SYS.AUD$ table is somewhat user unfriendly in format and denor-malized. Actions that are audited appear as code numbers in the AUDIT# column rather than names. The AUDIT_OPTIONS table holds a mapping of the codes to strings. For example, the AUDIT# value 0 corresponds to CREATE TABLE. To make for easier reporting, Oracle provides several views on top of the audit trail. For reference purposes, Figure 25.1 shows the available views on the SYS.AUD$ trail using DbCool, based on information on the DBA_DEPENDENCIES dictionary view.

The tree in Figure 25.1 shows that the SYS.AUD$ table has a view, DBA_AUDIT_TRAIL, based upon it. The DBA_AUDIT_TRAIL decodes the numeric information into string values that DBAs can easily understand. Additional views are available based on DBA_AUDIT_TRAIL to show session, statement, and object audit information for the DBA, through the DBA views. Users can view audit information relevant to them-selves through the USER views.

Auditing BY ACCESS and BY SESSION

Oracle enables BY ACCESS or BY SESSION options to be specified when auditing is activated through AUDIT statements. Using BY SESSION is designed to reduce the auditing information generated by creating a single audit record for all statements of the same type in a given session. The BY ACCESS option creates an audit record for

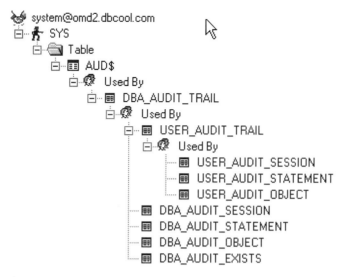

Figure 25.1 Views on SYS.AUD$.

each instance of the audited statement executed in a session. The default value is BY SESSION. However, DDL statements, such as CREATE TABLE, don't adhere to this rule. When you set auditing on for a DDL statement, such as CREATE TABLE, then BY ACCESS is used on whatever you specify. No error message is provided if you specify an incompatible option: The specified option is simply ignored.

Statement and Privilege Auditing

The options available for enabling statement auditing are held in the STMT_AUDIT_OPTION_MAP table, and the system privileges you can audit are held in the SYSTEM PRIVILEGE_MAP table. There is a very close correspondence between the two tables. The following SQL shows some of the statements you can audit:

```
select * from STMT_AUDIT_OPTION_MAP
where rownum <=4
order by option# asc;


  OPTION# NAME                PROPERTY
--------- ------------------- ----------
        3 ALTER SYSTEM               0
        4 SYSTEM AUDIT              0
        5 CREATE SESSION            0
        6 ALTER SESSION             0
```

Statement auditing can be performed at the user, session, and access level, or in a combination. These options are most easily understood by activitating some auditing, showing how the activation is recorded in the Oracle data dictionary, and reporting the audit trail information that is created as a result. The following statement generates an audit record for any CREATE TABLE statement executed by any user, for both successful and unsuccessful attempts:

```
audit create table;
```

As this is a DDL statement, BY ACCESS is always used. The DBA_STMT_AUDIT_OPTIONS view records the auditing action that was enabled as follows:

```
select USER_NAME,AUDIT_OPTION,SUCCESS,FAILURE
from DBA_STMT_AUDIT_OPTS;
```

```
USER_NAME    AUDIT_OPTION    SUCCESS     FAILURE
-----------  --------------  ----------  ----------
             CREATE TABLE    BY ACCESS   BY ACCESS
```

Very similar information is recorded in the DBA_PRIV_AUDIT_OPTIONS view because CREATE TABLE is both a privilege and a statement. The following information is an example of information that appears in the audit trail after a successful CREATE TABLE operation. The audit information can be viewed in DBA_AUDIT_TRAIL or DBA_AUDIT_OBJECT as follows:

```
select timestamp,action_name,owner,obj_name,returncode
from dba_audit_object;
```

```
           TIMESTAMP ACTION_NAME    OWNER   OBJ_NAME    RETURNCODE
--------------------- -------------- ------- ----------- ------------
 10-NOV-2001 13:50:41 CREATE TABLE   SYSTEM  T2                    0
```

Rather than generate audit records for all CREATE TABLE statements, you can audit CREATE TABLE statements for nominated users only. The following SQL audits the CREATE statements by SCOTT that are not successful, having turned off system-wide CREATE TABLE auditing first:

```
noaudit create table;
audit create table by scott whenever not successful;
```

The activation of this audit option is recorded as follows to indicate that successful statements by SCOTT are not audited, but failures are:

```
select USER_NAME,AUDIT_OPTION,SUCCESS,FAILURE
from DBA_STMT_AUDIT_OPTS WHERE AUDIT_OPTION='CREATE TABLE';
```

```
USER_NAME    AUDIT_OPTION    SUCCESS     FAILURE
-----------  --------------  ----------  ----------
SCOTT        CREATE TABLE    NOT SET     BY ACCESS
```

Subsequent CREATE TABLE statements for SCOTT that fail, for example, because SCOTT has no quota on the tablespace specific in the statement (error ORA-01536) are recorded along with the return code as follows:

```
select timestamp,action_name,owner,obj_name,returncode
from dba_audit_object where owner='SCOTT';
```

```
           TIMESTAMP ACTION_NAME    OWNER   OBJ_NAME    RETURNCODE
--------------------- -------------- ------- ---------- ------------
 10-NOV-2001 15:23:30 CREATE TABLE   SCOTT   A                 1536
```

So far, all auditing has been enabled BY ACCESS, which creates an audit record for each operation in each session. The following statement creates audit records BY SESSION for DELETE statements executed by all users:

```
audit delete table;
```

For the sake of example, assume that SCOTT logs on after the previous auditing command and runs the following operations:

```
delete from emp;
delete from emp;

delete from dept;

REM fails due to ORA-01031: insufficient privileges...
delete from all_users;
```

The DELETE statements result in the following entries in the audit trail, where the SESSIONID for the audit session has been identified using one of the techniques shown earlier in the chapter:

```
select action_name,owner,obj_name,ses_actions,statementid,entryid
from dba_audit_object WHERE sessionid=356;
```

ACTION_NAME	OWNER	OBJ_NAME	SES_ACTIONS	STATEMENTID	ENTRYID
SESSION REC	SYS	TS$	---F-----------	8	4
SESSION REC	SYS	USER$	---F-----------	8	3
SESSION REC	SYS	ALL_USERS	---F-----------	8	5
SESSION REC	SCOTT	DEPT	---S-----------	7	2
SESSION REC	SCOTT	EMP	---S-----------	5	1

Because auditing by session is in operation by default, each statement executed has a single audit entry for the whole session. For example, both DELETE statements on the EMP table result in a single session audit record. The SES_ACTIONS column represents a string of action types in the first 14 characters. Each character represents an action having the value S for success, F for failure, and B for both. The actions represented in order from left to right in SES_ACTIONS are ALTER, AUDIT, COMMENT,

DELETE, GRANT, INDEX, INSERT, LOCK, RENAME, SELECT, UPDATE, REFER-
ENCES, and EXECUTE. Therefore, the fourth character identifies the audited statement as a DELETE. The DELETE FROM ALL_USERS, which failed, has actually
generated three audit failure records identified by F because ALL_USERS is actually a
view-based SYS.TS$ and a SYS.USER$. It is possible to audit DELETE statements by
individual users and by access. For example, the following statements audit deletes by
SCOTT only, by session (the default), and by access:

```
audit delete table by scott;
audit delete table by scott by access;
```

Object Auditing

Auditing can be enabled for actions on specific objects. For example, you can enable
the auditing of DELETE statements on SCOTT.EMP and SCOTT.DEPT only by using:

```
audit delete on scott.emp by access;
audit delete on scott.dept by session whenever not successful;
```

Every object in the database has a set of object audit options held in a rather unusual
format, accessible though the DBA_OBJ_AUDIT_OPTS view. For each object privilege,
a three-character string is used to represent the state of the auditing requirement on the
object. As usual, an example based on the previous audit statements demonstrates best
how Oracle records the state of the auditing. The following SQL shows all object auditing that is enabled in the database:

```
select owner, object_name, object_type,
       alt,aud,com,del,gra,ind,ins,loc,ren,sel,upd,ref,exe
from dba_obj_audit_opts
where
alt !='-/-' or aud !='-/-' or com !='-/-' or del !='-/-' or gra !='-/-'
or ind !='-/-' or ins !='-/-' or loc !='-/-' or ren !='-/-' or sel !='-
/-' or
upd !='-/-' or ref !='-/-' or exe !='-/-';
```

Selecting only the DELETE privilege identified by the DEL column in this case
shows the state of the DELETE statement auditing for our example:

```
select owner, object_name, object_type,del
from dba_obj_audit_opts
where del !='-/-';

OWNER    OBJECT_NAME    OBJECT_TYPE    DEL
-------  -------------  -------------  -----
SYSTEM   EMP            TABLE          A/A
SCOTT    DEPT           TABLE          -/S
```

The first character in the DEL column identifies whether auditing should take place
whenever the DELETE action on the table is successful, and the third character identi-

fies whether unsuccessful deletes should be audited. For EMP, the two As show that DELETE BY ACCESS auditing should take place on successful and unsuccessful deletes on EMP. For DEPT, the S in the third character position shows that DELETE BY SESSION should take place only on unsuccessful deletes on DEPT. To specify all auditing options on an object, rather than setting them individually, you can use the AUDIT ALL shortcut, for example:

```
audit all on scott.emp;
```

It's possible to specify defaults for object audit options to take effect for newly created objects through the use of the ON DEFAULT clause. For example, to enable the DELETE statement auditing of all newly created objects, you would specify:

```
REM remember that BY SESSION is the default...
audit delete on default;
```

This has the effect of modifying the default object auditing options held in ALL_DEF_AUDIT_OPTS as follows (where BY SESSION is indicated by S as before):

```
select ALT,AUD,COM,DEL,GRA,IND,INS,LOC,REN,SEL,UPD,REF,EXE
from SYS.ALL_DEF_AUDIT_OPTS;

ALT AUD COM DEL GRA IND INS LOC REN SEL UPD REF EXE
--- --- --- --- --- --- --- --- --- --- --- --- ---
-/- -/- -/- S/S -/- -/- -/- -/- -/- -/- -/- -/- -/-
```

Recommended Auditing Options

There's no doubt that keeping track of audit options can be very difficult due to the multitude of tables and views that you need to be aware of. The easiest way to enable a meaningful set of auditing options is to use the following SQL shortcut:

```
AUDIT ALL;
```

Despite what the name might imply, this doesn't actually enable every possible auditing option available. For example, it actually *doesn't* enable any object-level auditing of data manipulation language (DML) statements. It *does* enable auditing for the most commonly used options that a DBA would want to track. For example, DROP USER, CREATE USER, and ALTER USER are all audited along with object DDL statements, such as CREATE TABLE, DROP TABLE, ALTER TABLE, and TRUNCATE TABLE, and session connection and disconnection. The full list can be found in the Oracle documentation. Auditing does add an overhead to database performance, due to the need to perform table inserts on the audit trail, but AUDIT ALL keeps the overhead within sensible limits and adds significant benefits for database security and potentially database availability by identifying the exact time of critical events that could harm the system.

Oracle recommends that you set options individually. However, using AUDIT ALL is much simpler. You need to be aware that after an Oracle upgrade, additional privileges may be included specific to the new version, so you should reexecute AUDIT ALL. To undo AUDIT ALL, you run NOAUDIT ALL.

SYSDBA Auditing

Connections that use the AS SYSDBA option are audited into operating files in the audit_file_dest location at all times, regardless of whether auditing is enabled in the init.ora file or not. This behavior can't be changed or turned off. It's not possible to audit any other actions performed as SYSDBA until Oracle9*i* Release 2 when SYSDBA auditing can be enabled through the use of the database initialization parameter AUDIT_SYS_OPERATIONS=TRUE. Even when SYSDBA auditing is enabled in Release 2, the operating system audit trail is always used, rather than SYS.AUD$. This is necessary because if SYSDBA connections and actions were audited into the database and the SYS.AUD$ table became full and could not extend, it would not be possible for a DBA to log on to the database to clear some space or perform other actions required to make the database available. The following examples show audit file output for an attempted SYS connection that failed due to ORA-28009 (connection to sys should be as sysdba or sysoper) and one that succeeded:

```
Sat Nov 10 10:33:05 2001
ACTION : 'connect SYS' OSPRIV : OPER
CLIENT USER: oracle
CLIENT TERMINAL: pts/3
STATUS: FAILED ( 28009 )

Sat Nov 10 10:33:32 2001
ACTION : 'connect sys' OSPRIV : DBA
CLIENT USER: oracle
CLIENT TERMINAL: pts/3
STATUS: SUCCEEDED ( 0 )
```

Identifying Suspicious Activity

Suspicious activities are easier to identify for a simple two-tier application because each application user typically has its own Oracle account. For applications that share Oracle accounts for multiple client application users, auditing is not so useful because the audit trail typically doesn't contain meaningful information about the client user. In this case, the application needs to provide an application-managed audit trail. Oracle Financials is a good example of an application that does this. For two-tier applications, account sharing is an example of suspicious activity. In this case, a given Oracle account may have multiple client users, suggesting that client users are sharing passwords or that users have unauthorized access to other users' accounts. The following SQL statement shows operating system accounts that have used more than one Oracle account and some results:

```
select s.os_username,username
from dba_audit_session s,
     (select os_username,count(distinct(username))
      from dba_audit_session where returncode=0 and action_name='LOGOFF'
      group by os_username
      having count(distinct(username)) > 1) o
where s.os_username = o.os_username and returncode=0 and
action_name='LOGOFF' group by s.os_username,username order by 1,2;


OS_USERNAME     USERNAME
-------------- -----------------
JonesSus        ALAN_S
JonesSus        BROWN_T
JonesSus        HALL_T
Administrator   HARMAN_S
Administrator   ADAMS_C
Administrator   TESTER
Administrator   FALL_G
Administrator   FLORENCE_S
```

In this case, the application is a two-tier Windows application, and OS_USERNAME is the Windows client account name of the connected user. The audit trail from DBA_AUDIT_SESSION shows that Windows user JonesSus has used three different Oracle accounts. More worrying still, the Windows NT Administrator account, which should not be accessible to business users, has been used to connect to Oracle accounts. This suggests flaws in the Windows security in the organization. This SQL shows similar information based on Oracle accounts using different Windows logons:

```
select s.username,os_username
from dba_audit_session s,
     (select username,count(distinct(os_username))
      from dba_audit_session where returncode=0 and action_name='LOGOFF'
      group by username
      having count(distinct(os_username)) > 1) o
where s.username = o.username
and returncode=0 and action_name='LOGOFF'
group by s.username,os_username
order by 1,2;
```

The use of AUDIT ALL enables the auditing of NOT EXISTS events, where a user performs an operation that fails because a table or other object does not exist. Such events can occur when a user tries to access an object for which he or she doesn't have access rights and may indicate an attempt to steal commercially sensitive information. The following SQL shows how to view the NOT EXISTS information:

```
select * from dba_audit_exists;
```

The next SQL statement shows AUDIT ALL activity for the user identified by the account given by the bind variable :username. If a user has performed a questionable activity, this report can be used to identify what happened from the audit trail:

```
select to_char(timestamp,'DY DD-MON-YY HH24:MI:SS')
timestamp,sessionid,logoff_time,username,os_username,action_name,obj_name,
terminal,returncode
from dba_audit_trail
where (username like upper(:username) or obj_name like upper(:username))
order by 1;
```

Other Uses of Audit Information

By using AUDIT ALL, you enable session connection and disconnection auditing that is made available through the DBA_AUDIT_SESSION view. This provides valuable security information, such as when a user logged on and off from the database, and the account and network host name that was used on the client. As well as security information, DBA_AUDIT_SESSION provides session I/O information that is extremely valuable for performing trend analysis and identification of the top database users in terms of I/O consumed. The following columns hold logical and physical I/O information for each audited session:

```
LOGOFF_LREAD
LOGOFF_PREAD
LOGOFF_LWRITE
```

The following report shows I/O information for weekly sessions in a format suitable for plotting graphs with Microsoft Excel:

```
select to_char(timestamp,'YYYY WW') weekno,sum(LOGOFF_LREAD)
logical_reads,
sum(logoff_pread) physical_reads,
sum(LOGOFF_LWRITE) logical_writes
from dba_audit_session
group by to_char(timestamp,'YYYY WW') order by 1;
```

WEEKNO	LOGICAL_READS	PHYSICAL_READS	LOGICAL_WRITES
2001 35	6236489352	174220084	219597881
2001 36	6454573741	190871110	207994254
2001 37	6213423627	203738383	190392777

The next SQL report shows the top user for each week of the year in the following categories: logical reads, physical reads, and logical writes. Such reports should be run with care as they scan the underlying audit table and can be very resource intensive. Output for week 43 is provided as an example:

```
select username,to_char(timestamp,'YYYY WW')
weekno,logoff_lread,logoff_pread,logoff_lwrite
from dba_audit_session,
(select to_char(timestamp,'YYYY WW') weekno,
        max(logoff_lread) max_lread,
        max(logoff_pread) max_pread,
        max(logoff_lwrite) max_lwrite
 from dba_audit_session
 group by to_char(timestamp,'YYYY WW')
) max_read
where (to_char(timestamp,'YYYY WW')=max_read.weekno
       and logoff_lread = max_read.max_lread)
or    (to_char(timestamp,'YYYY WW')=max_read.weekno
       and logoff_pread = max_read.max_pread)
or    (to_char(timestamp,'YYYY WW')=max_read.weekno
       and logoff_lwrite = max_read.max_lwrite) order by 2;


USERNAME        WEEKNO      LOGOFF_LREAD    LOGOFF_PREAD    LOGOFF_LWRITE
--------------  --------  --------------  --------------  ---------------
BATCH           2001 43         37533830          896053         26071933
DAY_R           2001 43        294275064           10117                6
SYSTEM          2001 43         15194188        10893261           767368
```

Viewing I/O by the user can be very helpful for Oracle performance management, as a follow-up study could identify why particular users consistently appear at the top of the list. In this case, the users should not be blamed for using too many resources. Instead, the focus should be on the business process being performed, along with an investigation of alternative ways to perform the same function to lower I/O costs. In some cases, where read-intensive reports are identified as the cause, the reports can sometimes be moved outside the main online processing periods to mitigate the effects of the I/O on other users. The information in the audit trail has other useful purposes. For example, you can count the number of distinct named sessions weekly to give an idea of the size of the database user base and how it changes over time, using the following SQL:

```
select to_char(timestamp,'YYYY WW') weekno,count(distinct(username))
from dba_audit_session
group by to_char(timestamp,'YYYY WW');


WEEKNO     COUNT(DISTINCT(USERNAME))
--------  ---------------------------
2001 34                           411
2001 35                           408
2001 36                           412
```

The previous report can be useful for showing that a system *isn't* being used. Every DBA should be aware of how usage patterns are changing over time in the databases they manage, and this report is one way to do it. Considerable expenditure on hardware and personnel can be wasted when used to manage and support applications that are not actually being used. It's also possible to identify sessions that failed to log off cleanly as follows:

```
select * from dba_audit_session
where action_name like 'LOGOFF BY CLEANUP';
```

Sessions that log off cleanly have an action name LOGOFF. Those that don't have an action name of LOGOFF BY CLEANUP, meaning that their resources were cleaned up later by Oracle's SMON process. Processes that don't disconnect cleanly should be followed up to identify the root cause. Sometimes sessions that terminate abnormally can cause core dumps on the database server, resulting in disk space shortages and potential database outages.

Using Database Triggers for Auditing

From Oracle8*i* on, you can use database triggers with autonomous transactions to perform the detailed tracking of changes in the data content of tables for auditing purposes. Using autonomous transactions guarantees that failed changes that were rolled back are still recorded in the change history. Autonomous transactions are sometimes referred to as nested transactions.

A simple trigger can be used to save rows deleted from the standard EMP table along with a timestamp when the delete occurred and the Oracle account that performed the deletion as follows:

```
/*
 * create empty copy of EMP with extra timestamp and user columns
 * to hold history of deletes
 */
create table emp_hist as
  select sysdate timestamp, user who,e.*
  from emp e where 1=2;

REM create a trigger to capture deleted rows...
create or replace trigger trg_emp_delete after delete on emp
  for each row
declare
  pragma autonomous_transaction;
begin
  insert into emp_hist values(
    sysdate,user,
    :old.empno,:old.ename,:old.job,:old.mgr,:old.hiredate,
    :old.sal,:old.comm,:old.deptno);
  commit;
end;
/

REM delete a row...
delete from emp where ename='SMITH';
```

Even though the row deletion has not yet been committed, the DELETE operation will show up in a query on the EMP_HIST table from another session due to the PRAGMA AUTONOMOUS_TRANSACTION statement in the trigger definition. The following SQL confirms that the DELETE has been recorded already:

```
select timestamp,who,ename from emp_hist;


            TIMESTAMP WHO     ENAME
-------------------- ------- -------
 05-APR-2002 18:21:47 SYSTEM  SMITH
```

Another example of trigger-based auditing is the use of a LOGOFF ON DATABASE trigger to capture all Oracle performance statistics and wait events in a table at session logoff time, which is done to provide more complete information than the database audit trail for use in performance trend analysis. The following example uses the LOGOFF_SAMPLE in the DBCOOL_MON package (downloadable from the companion Web site) to capture the information:

```
REM run as SYS
create trigger on_logoff before logoff on database
declare
begin

   sys.dbcool_mon.logoff_sample;

exception
  when others then
    null;
end;
```

Fine-grained Auditing in Oracle9*i*

Fine-grained auditing in Oracle9*i* provides a framework for the detailed capture and notification of SELECT statements on tables and views based on the content requested. For example, monitoring for the selection of specific columns and column values is possible. The detailed information available during the audited event includes:

- The full text of the SQL
- Bind variable values
- The current system change number (SCN)

Value-based policies are administered through the DBMS_FGA package based on an audit policy created by the DBA on the target table using the ADD_POLICY procedure. The audit policy contains an audit_condition argument that is used to specify rows that trigger an audit event when an end-user SQL statement returns rows that match the condition and include the column specified by the audit_column parameter. As part of the policy, an optional event handler—in the form of a PL/SQL procedure— can be provided to process an audited event.

The following SQL sets up a policy that audits SELECT statements on the SAL column of the EMP table for employees in the Sales department, and calls a procedure SYSTEM.SP_SENDMAIL_ALERT as the event handler:

```
begin
    dbms_fga.add_policy(
        policy_name          => 'scott_emp_sal',
        object_schema        => 'scott',
        object_name          => 'emp',
        audit_condition      => 'job = ''SALESMAN''',
        audit_column         => 'sal',
        handler_schema       => 'system',
        handler_module       => 'sp_sendmail_alert',
        enable               =>  true);
end;
/
```

The event handler routine SP_SENDMAIL_ALERT uses the SP_SENDMAIL procedure (described in Chapter 24) to send an email alert whenever an audit event matching the policy is generated. The definition of SP_SENDMAIL_ALERT is:

```
create procedure system.sp_sendmail_alert
    (p_schema varchar2, p_object varchar2, p_policy varchar2)
as
begin
    sp_sendmail(
        p_sender=>'OraAlert@dbcool.com',
        p_recipient=>'OracleDba@dbcool.com',
        p_subject=>'FGA ALERT:'||p_policy||'/'||p_schema||'/'||p_object,
        p_message=>'for your info',
        p_mailhost=>'srv1.dbcool.com');
end;
```

After creating the policy and the stored procedure for the event handler, the following statements generate audit events that result in the rows in the SYS.FGA_LOG$ table:

```
REM the * includes rows that match audit_condition and audit_column
select * from scott.emp;


REM use a value SALE% for bind variable :j to match audit_condition
REM Note: if you run this in DbCool, you can fill in the value in a form
select * from scott.emp where job like :j;
```

The following SQL shows some of the columns in the FGA_LOG$ for the two SQL SELECT statements on SCOTT.EMP, including the value supplied for the bind variable:

```
SQLTEXT                                   SQLBIND
----------------------------------------- -------------
select * from scott.emp
select * from scott.emp where job like :j   #1(5):SALE%
```

The complete list of audited information available in SYS.FGA_LOG$ is:

```
SESSIONID       NUMBER            NOT NULL
TIMESTAMP#      DATE              NOT NULL
DBUID           VARCHAR2(30)
OSUID           VARCHAR2(255)
OSHST           VARCHAR2(128)
CLIENTID        VARCHAR2(64)
EXTID           VARCHAR2(4000)
OBJ$SCHEMA      VARCHAR2(30)
OBJ$NAME        VARCHAR2(128)
POLICYNAME      VARCHAR2(30)
SCN             NUMBER
SQLTEXT         VARCHAR2(4000)
SQLBIND         VARCHAR2(4000)
COMMENT$TEXT    VARCHAR2(4000)
```

Summary

In order to provide a basic security auditing capability, a minimum level of database auditing can and should be enabled in all Oracle databases. This can be accomplished with a minimum of effort by using the AUDIT ALL shortcut command. This command provides a useful level of auditing without resulting in the overhead of thousands of audit records daily. Excessive use of audit options, such as auditing on individual objects, can have a significant overhead on database performance and must be considered carefully. Session auditing can help you identify I/O trends at no extra cost because AUDIT ALL enables session auditing. The audit trail can be relocated, and ownership of the underlying objects can be changed. Although unsupported, these options provide the potential for more flexible and proactive auditing. For situations where the database audit trail doesn't provide enough detail, more sophisticated auditing is available through trigger-based auditing from Oracle8*i* onwards and fine-grained auditing in Oracle9*i*.

Migration and Upgrade

Oracle Corporation uses the term *migration* for moving from Oracle7 to Oracle9*i*, and the term *upgrade* for moving from Oracle8*i* to Oracle9*i*. Although the terms are sometimes used interchangeably, migration is intended to convey that the task involves greater preparation than the simpler upgrade.

This chapter covers how to perform a migration or upgrade. Oracle provides Oracle Data Migration Assistant (ODMA) to perform the migration itself, so our emphasis will be on the migration prerequisites and post-migration checks. Failure to address all the prerequisites is much more likely to cause problems than ODMA itself. Post-migration checks are used to ensure that the migrated database is ready to run in a production environment. Keep in mind that ODMA provides migration and upgrade from Oracle 7.3.4, Oracle 8.0.6, and Oracle8*i*. This chapter covers the following topics:

- Migration prerequisites checklist

- Using ODMA to perform migration

- Post-migration tasks

NOTE ODMA becomes Database Upgrade Assistant (DBUA) in Oracle9*i*
Release 2, although the functionality is essentially the same. You should also
be aware that from Oracle9*i* Release 2 onwards, the second digit, rather than
the third, in the version number now refers to the maintenance release.

Migration Prerequisites

A document titled "Using Oracle Change Manager" is available for download from the companion Web site to this book. The document covers some generic and Oracle-specific information about change management. These same principles apply to a migration exercise, just like any other change. In particular, the implementation plan should be fully documented, the change success test criteria should be clearly defined, and the backout plan should be realistic.

Decision to Upgrade

Due to the risk of side effects resulting from the migration and upgrade process, the decision to implement these procedures should be based on business reasons, rather than the database administrator's (DBA's) requirement to get experience in the latest Oracle release in a production environment. Upgrading because the current Oracle release is out of its support life cycle is a sound reason for upgrading because it guarantees better levels of support. By definition, migration is performed against Oracle7. There aren't many valid reasons for running applications on Oracle7 when Oracle9*i* is available, and Oracle7 has long been unsupported by Oracle.

Third-Party Software

Before migration, you need to check that all the software needed to support your Oracle infrastructure is available and certified on the new version of Oracle. This might include backup software, performance management software, and monitoring software. If your Oracle database runs an application from a third-party vendor, then you should check that their software is certified against the new Oracle release.

Oracle9*i* Installation

To save time, Oracle9*i* software should be preinstalled on the database server containing the database to be migrated, including all the options installed in the original database. For example, if replication is installed in the original database, then replication needs to be installed in the migrated database. The required set of products should be confirmed by performing test runs of the complete end-to-end migration process, including end-user application testing after completion. If you've followed the suggestions in Chapter 1, then the Oracle software should be available already via a centralized Network File System (NFS) server.

Resolution of Alerts

All outstanding alerts, such as those due invalid objects, files in recovery mode, and failed distributed transactions, should be fixed before migration begins. Even if you don't systematically execute the minimal recommended monitoring in Chapter 24, you should refer to the checks in that chapter and run them manually.

During a migration, the Oracle data dictionary catalog is rebuilt. This can potentially invalidate objects. Before you begin a migration, you should ensure that no invalid objects exist before migration. That way you can be sure that any invalid objects after migration were introduced by the migration process and are not due to some preexisting condition.

Replication

If you are using symmetric replication, then replication must be quiesced and disabled, or migration will fail. The Oracle replication documentation should be consulted for any special requirements imposed on migration by replication. After quiescing has been completed, the DEF$_ERROR table needs to be checked for errors. These errors need to be resolved before migration.

ARCHIVELOG Mode

Migration and upgrades generate lots of redo logging. One option for reducing the need to manage the extra logs is to turn off ARCHIVELOG mode on the database following the premigration backup and restore it afterward, before the post-migration backup.

Files in AUTOEXTEND Mode

In order to provide the highest chance of success, database files related to the SYSTEM, undo, rollback, and temporary tablespaces should be placed into AUTOEXTEND mode before migration. The Oracle dictionary typically grows to at least 250MB during a migration and executes some large transactions.

Operating System Versions

Oracle's Metalink Web site should be checked in order to ensure that the original and migrated versions of Oracle are both supported on the operating system in place on the server. If they aren't, the operating system needs to be patched to the required release, and existing testing repeated. Metalink also contains alert information on problems involving migration. A thorough search of all the available information should be carried out to preempt possible problems.

Hard-Coded Oracle Environments

Any scripts that hard code the $ORACLE_HOME variable need to be identified in advance. These need to be changed to reflect the new $ORACLE_HOME setting after migration. A better design approach is to set all script environments at run time using the contents of the /var/opt/oracle/oratab (or /etc/oratab) file. That way scripts pick up any changes in the environment automatically without needing to change the script itself.

Plan Stability

When you migrate to a new version of Oracle, the Oracle release contains a new version of the Oracle optimizer. That leads to the potential for application Structured Query Language (SQL) Data Manipulation Language (DML) execution plans to change silently after migration. Although you might expect that the new plans would provide reduced elapsed times, that can't be guaranteed. The safest way to guarantee plan stability is to use stored outlines. Stored outlines are described in Chapter 9.

Database Character Set

The database character set needs to be set in the UNIX environment in which migration takes place. This should be saved for future reference and can be found using the following SQL:

```
select value from nls_database_parameters
where parameter='NLS_CHARACTERSET';
```

Test Runs

Test runs should always be carried out in advance to ensure that the migration of a production database is completed without problems and within the time available. The test machine should be checked in advance to confirm that the operating system release is identical to the production server and that UNIX kernel configuration parameters are large enough to meet requirements and are no larger than the production server.

Compatibility and Parameters

Oracle enables the control of database compatibility with the COMPATIBLE initialization parameter. By default, if the COMPATIBLE initialization parameter is not set in the init.ora parameter file, it defaults to the lowest possible setting for the release. For Oracle9i Release 1, COMPATIBLE defaults to *8.1.0*.

The decision on whether to change the COMPATIBLE setting is an important one. If your decision to upgrade is based on a requirement to take advantage of new Oracle features, then you need to change COMPATIBLE to the version number of the new release. In this case, testing and QA procedures must have been carried out using the new release. You should never change COMPATIBLE to a higher version during migration unless you tested with that version.

If your migration is part of a regular maintenance cycle, possibly due to support lapsing for your current version of Oracle, then you still need to perform QA and testing of Oracle9i even if you don't use the new features. In this case, the default behavior is adequate. The bottom line is that you should ensure that COMPATIBLE at migration time is set to whatever version you tested with.

Values should be set explicitly for the USER_DUMP_DEST, BACKGROUND_DUMP_DEST, and CORE_DUMP_DEST parameters to avoid their location changing after migration, based on the new $ORACLE_HOME value. If the Optimal Flexible Architecture (OFA) standard, which is recommended, is in use, then this isn't an issue.

The JOB_QUEUE_PROCESSES parameter should be set to 0 to ensure that no jobs start immediately or during migration. This needs to be reinstated after migration.

If a password file is in use, as discussed earlier, then it's a good idea to disable its use during migration by setting REMOTE_LOGIN_PASSWORD_FILE=NONE before migration and re-creating it afterward. In this case, existing SYSDBA and SYSOPER accounts will need to have their privileges regranted after migration. If you use Recovery Manager (RMAN) to perform your Oracle backups, RMAN is probably one of the accounts. The following SQL shows the accounts before migration:

```
select * from v$pwfile_users;
```

Timings

If your end-to-end migration needs to be completed in a fixed window, then you should note the time taken for each stage of the process. This should include the time for the following:

- Premigration checks
- Premigration backup
- Test restore of premigration backup
- Migration
- Post-migration backup and checks
- Application testing

Backup and Restore

A backup *and restore* is a prerequisite for a migration. If the migration goes wrong, your fallback position is dependent on the validity of the premigration backup. The only way to be 100 percent sure that your backup worked is to restore it onto another server and open the restored database, all before you perform the migration itself. The ability to open the database after the backup guarantees that you backed up every required file. Oracle can, of course, use a previous backup to restore the old database in the unlikely event that the premigration backup failed. If you include this in your contingency plan, then you need to factor in the extra time to roll the earlier backup forward.

The most reliable tool to use when performing the database backup is RMAN, which is covered in Chapter 18. Keep in mind that RMAN does not back up the online redo logs because they are never required for a recovery to a previous point in time. If you require the RMAN database incarnation to remain the same after a recovery following a failed migration, then you should back up the online redo logs separately. The online redo log backup should take place while the database is in a mounted state during the RMAN closed backup or after a clean shutdown. The following SQL can be used to generate a list of files to back up manually:

```
select l.member from v$logfile l
union select name from v$controlfile c
union select f.file_name from dba_data_files f
union select tf.file_name from dba_temp_files tf;
```

The following additional files need to be backed up manually before migration:

The init.ora file.   Some of the parameters used may be obsolete or deprecated in the migrated version.

The database password file.   This is backed up if database password files are used.

You can check whether a password file is in use by attempting a remote connection such as SYS using AS SYSDBA. If this works, the database uses a password file:

```
$ sqlplus /nolog

SQL> connect sys@orap1.dbcool.com as sysdba
```

As an alternative to using an RMAN backup and restore, if you use a standby database, you can open it in read-write mode, having applied all the changes from your primary database before migration starts. The standby database serves as a ready-made database that you can use to restore the primary to the premigration state if the migration goes wrong, thus saving the time for an RMAN backup and restore. Standby databases are covered in Chapter 23.

Migration Using ODMA

The simplest way to perform a migration or upgrade is to use ODMA. It is possible to perform manually the same steps that ODMA takes, although this is not recommended due to the additional complexity introduced. In two specific situations, ODMA can't be used. ODMA does not support the migration of systems with Oracle Parallel Server (OPS) installed. If you have OPS installed, then you must use another method to migrate your database. Other methods include the command-line migration utility (MIG) or export and import. Also, ODMA does not support the migration of systems that use raw devices.

   If you can't use ODMA, you can perform a migration by taking a full premigration export, followed by a full import into a database precreated using the Oracle version you are migrating to. In the past, this approach was sometimes taken in order to defragment the database as part of the migration process. If the requirement is to defragment data, Chapter 13 shows how to do that with Oracle9i. It's no longer necessary to perform an export and import. If the export and import approach is required, Chapter 19 contains the best practices for running import and export. It needs to be emphasized that a full export does *not* include SYS-owned objects; the database creation process creates these. In the unlikely event that your application installs objects into SYS, these need to be re-created manually after database creation.

It is strongly recommended that you use ODMA. Before beginning the migration process itself, ODMA will perform a SHUTDOWN IMMEDIATE of the instance. If the database is already down, ODMA will start it first and then perform SHUTDOWN IMMEDIATE. ODMA is a Java application and requires a valid X Windows display as follows:

```
$ xhost +yourdisplay

$ DISPLAY=yourdisplay:0.0; export DISPLAY
```

The migration utility needs to be executed in the environment of the *migrated* version. It's not necessary to set the ORACLE_SID at this stage because ODMA asks for it. The usual Oracle environment symbols can be set as follows, based on the *set_env* command described in Chapter 4:

```
$ set_env 9.0.1

$ export NLS_LANG=american_america.US7ASCII

$ odma &
```

Figure 26.1 shows the ODMA screen from which the target database for migration is selected.

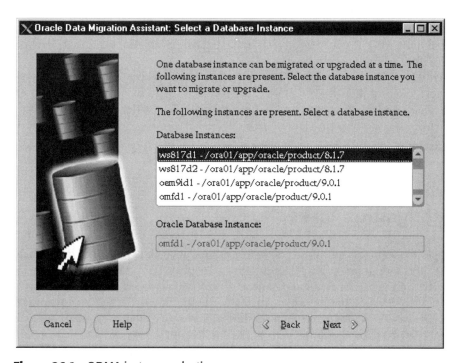

Figure 26.1 ODMA instance selection screen.

After starting ODMA, choose a custom upgrade, choose PL/SQL modules to be validated post-upgrade, and don't request a backup if you have already performed one. As recommended in the prerequisites, it's better to perform a backup *and validate it with a restore* before migration. Migration can modify the listener.ora file for the migrated version automatically. I prefer to do that manually afterward to avoid unexpected changes, and then only if necessary. If you are using dynamic listener registration, as covered in Chapter 3, then no change to listener.ora will be required because the migrated database will automatically register itself with the listener using the correct (migrated) version.

After the migration is complete, the init.ora file for the migrated version is placed in the $ORACLE_HOME/dbs directory. If you are using OFA for your software layout (which is strongly recommended), then your init.ora file in the new $ORACLE_ HOME/dbs directory *should be* a link from the pfile directory. Before overwriting the pfile version with the new version, it's essential to compare them to check for any differences in parameters. The new version may have parameters added by the migration process, such as the following:

```
#Parameter added by Data Migration Assistant
shared_pool_size = 52428800
```

Once you have compared the old and new files and made any changes, you should copy the new version over the pfile version and re-create the link from the pfile version to $ORACLE_HOME/dbs. It's easy to forget to do this and end up with two init.ora files, one in the pfile directory and one in the $ORACLE_HOME/dbs directory. The first sign that you've done this is that when you make changes to the pfile version, they apparently have no effect when you restart the database because the one in $ORACLE _HOME/dbs is actually being used.

Immediately after the migration is completed, it's a good idea to remove or rename the init.ora file or link in the old $ORACLE_HOME/dbs to make absolutely certain that the database can't be started under the old version by accident.

> **NOTE**   Later releases of Oracle9*i* use a directory called scripts in preference to pfile.

Post-Migration Tasks

If ARCHIVELOG mode was turned off before migration, it should be turned on immediately following migration. Any datafiles that were placed into AUTOEXTEND mode specifically for the migration should have AUTOEXTEND turned off. Before any non-DBA access is allowed after migration, the database should be checked for any invalid objects. The causes of these need to be identified, and recompilations or fixes applied. Any that can't be fixed should be investigated at Metalink or reported to Oracle Support Services (OSS). The JOB_QUEUE_PROCESSES value should be reinstated to its premigration setting, and REMOTE_LOGIN_PASSWORD_FILE should be reenabled if required. This requires the creation of a new password file and the regranting of

SYSDBA and SYSOPER privileges to those accounts that had the privileges before migration. A remote SYSDBA test connection should be performed to ensure that the password file is correct. The premigration checks contain an example of how to do this.

After migration to Oracle9*i*, connections using SYS must be performed using AS SYSDBA or AS SYSOPER, or the connection will fail. This new behavior provides enhanced protection of the data dictionary. The old-style behavior can be reinstated by setting the init.ora parameter O7_DICTIONARY_ACCESSIBILITY=TRUE, although this is not recommended for security reasons covered in Chapter 5.

The init.ora COMPATIBILITY setting, the oratab file, and the listener.ora file (if you're not using dynamic registration) should be checked to ensure that they reflect the version of the migrated database. If dynamic registration is not in use, the post-upgrade listener.ora file should contain an entry like this:

```
(SID_DESC =
  (SID_NAME = ws817d1
  (ORACLE_HOME = /ora01/app/oracle/product/9.0.1)
)
```

If you have multiple versions of Oracle on the server, and you run a single listener, then you should run the listener executable associated with the latest version of Oracle. This also applies when the listener is restarted on machine boot. If you're using the methods in Chapter 4 for standardization of your Oracle environment, then the listener to start on machine boot can be changed to the new version simply by changing the entry in the oratab file.

Application support personnel should perform the tasks specified in the change implementation to check that the application is working correctly after migration is completed. In particular, any application scripts that contain a hard-coded $ORACLE_HOME setting need to be changed to reflect the new version, or they will fail. Testing should include the following:

- Functionality testing
- Client connectivity testing, including testing database links
- Performance testing

The enforcement of plan stability through the use of stored outlines is probably the best approach to guarantee similar levels of performance compared to premigration, although generating them requires more preparation.

Once all testing is complete, a backup should be performed. This should take place immediately after completion of the migration and before application testing.

If you intend to remove the old version of the Oracle software, you should ensure that no files are currently in use by any existing database, and that no database files themselves are located there. If you follow the OFA standard, there won't be any, but you need to be absolutely certain. It's often best to leave the old software in place for a few days. You can then use the UNIX find command to check for files accessed or modified within the last few days to confirm that the files under the old version are not in use before you remove them.

Keep in mind that if you need to restore to a point in time associated with the old version for any reason following an upgrade or migration, then you need to have the old software release available. The following examples show how to check for files modified and accessed within the last seven days:

```
$ find $ORACLE_HOME -type f -mtime -7 -print  # modified . . .

$ find $ORACLE_HOME -type f -atime -7 -print  # accessed . . .
```

Summary

ODMA makes the process of migration or an upgrade to Oracle8*i* or 9*i* a fairly simple process. Migration failure is more likely to result from an incomplete premigration checklist or failure to carry out a comprehensive post-migration analysis than from ODMA itself. Using the pre- and post-migration checks in this chapter will increase the odds of a successful migration.

## CHAPTER 27

Working Effectively with Oracle Support

As a professional Oracle database administrator (DBA) or developer, you should be familiar with the support provided by Oracle Support Services (OSS) through the Metalink Web site (www.metalink.com). Metalink has some clearly stated goals from Oracle's point of view, and it's useful to evaluate customer experiences against those goals, and identify if and why they are not met. Oracle also publishes information on how customers can work effectively with OSS, and this chapter discusses the OSS-customer relationship both from the customer and the OSS analyst's point of view. All DBAs, developers, and managers should have a thorough understanding of the roles and responsibilities in this relationship, in particular, Oracle's expectation of customers, in order to exploit it fully.

You should always consult the extensive information that is available at Metalink and carefully read the documentation before requesting the services of an OSS analyst to investigate your problem. According to recent figures available from OSS, around 50 percent of Technical Assistance Requests (TARs) relate to customer-caused issues and requests for more information. If these could be reduced, then all customers could benefit from the increased amount of analysts' time available to solve real business problems. That doesn't mean the customer is always at fault in such situations. The need to request further information could relate to incompleteness or lack of clarity in Oracle's documentation, as well as customers' failure to read what's available.

Before you choose to deploy any Oracle technology, you need to take a look at all the factors that affect supportability, such as the maturity of the technology and the likely availability of OSS expertise. The implications are likely to influence the Oracle product set you deploy in a production environment.

This chapter covers the following topics:

- Using Metalink to meet customer requirements for support
- The benefits and drawbacks of problem reporting via the Web
- Oracle's goal of single point of ownership for TARs
- The availability of 24×7 support on the Web
- The OSS view of the customer's role in the support process
- The escalation process
- Using Oracle STATSPACK and Remote Diagnostic Agent to standardize support
- Choosing your Oracle product set for supportability

Using Metalink to Meet Support Requirements

Oracle Corporation is increasingly highlighting the availability of online support. If you have an active support contract for your Oracle licenses, you can take advantage of Oracle's Metalink Web site at www.metalink.com for the provision of online support. The biggest benefit of using Metalink over traditional telephone-based support is that it saves you time in the following ways:

- You avoid wasting time waiting for an analyst to take your call.
- Because the service is available 24×7, you can research issues yourself. The electronic method for tracking TARs is referred to as iTAR.

Customer requirements for Oracle support—actually, support for any purchased product—can probably be summarized in a single sentence: "Please fix my problem in the shortest time possible." It's interesting to analyze the degree to which Metalink meets its own stated goals and those of the customer.

Problem Reporting via the Web

Submission via the Web is the fastest way to report a problem because you don't need to wait for an analyst, and you can speed up TAR creation by cloning existing ones and changing the contents. Despite these benefits, I sometimes choose to use the telephone hotline to report a problem to OSS rather than submit one electronically via the Web. Hotline calls always involve a couple of minutes of an analyst's time spent telling me that electronic submission gets results faster. This is usually followed by an explanation from me on why a hotline call can get results faster (which is why I chose to make the call instead).

Although it's inconvenient to wait around for an analyst to take the call, the goal is to *fix* the problem in the shortest time, not necessarily to report the problem in the shortest time. The benefit of a phone call is that you can often avoid the long email thread that iTARs sometimes produce in the initial stages of problem resolution. This preamble usually occurs when the OSS analyst is unfamiliar with the product you are using and doesn't actually understand the problem. In this scenario, you can expect to receive potential solutions to your problem that actually aren't relevant, and the use of iTAR actually increases the time until problem resolution. Using a phone call, you can usually determine the analyst's level of knowledge and cut short the wasted time. The phone call also helps the analyst to understand that you are an experienced Oracle user who has already researched the problem, as a matter of due diligence, and not a beginner.

Single Point of Problem Ownership

The best support is provided when a problem has a single point of ownership, as this minimizes the customer's time spent having the problem directed to the right person. That means that the routing of a problem to the appropriate point of expertise should not be the customer's responsibility, but the vendor's. Oracle's official position is that Metalink is intended to provide this single point of ownership. To quote directly from the Metalink Web site (www.oracle.com/support/metalink/index.html, April 2002), "TARs submitted electronically are automatically matched to the right technical resource within Oracle Support Services."

My experience of iTAR is that too often when a difficult problem could be related to more than one Oracle technology area, the customer is deemed to be responsible for submitting it to exactly the right group and is blamed for delays when it isn't. Of course, if you didn't explain your problem clearly enough, then delays can't be blamed on the support analyst. But if the OSS analyst says something like "investigation was delayed because you didn't submit the problem to the correct support group" despite your best endeavors, then that's a sign that the support process is not meeting the goals defined by Oracle. It's a fact of life in the IT industry that users of graphical tools often get blamed for deficiencies in the user interface design of the application. As a user, if you think that the Web problem-reporting process could be improved, you can provide feedback on Metalink through the feedback feature and your Oracle account manager.

24×7 Availability of Metalink

Another one of Oracle's stated goals for Metalink is to provide 24×7 online access. Metalink undoubtedly contains a fantastic knowledge base of Oracle resources and access to highly skilled support staff through forums. Keep in mind that use of the forums comes without guaranteed response times. Personally, I can spend up to several hours a day on Metalink for research purposes, and rarely a day goes by without requiring access at some stage. In this respect, Metalink delivers fantastic support capabilities without requiring the input of an analyst and saves on both Oracle's time as well as the customer's time.

However, this makes 24×7 availability even more important. During the fall of 2001, Metalink suffered outages of several hours. One outage was apparently caused by a lightning strike in California. As a customer, you should never experience a service outage due to such a failure when the service states 24×7 availability as one of its features. As a database company, you could reasonably expect that Oracle would use its own technology to enhance the availability of its own services. During the writing of this book, one weekend I decided to review several of the TARs I had submitted in the past. This was the message I received:

```
Due to technical reasons TAR search for this country could not be
performed.
```

Here's another error that resulted in a significant outage in April 2001:

```
ORA-04031: unable to allocate 2550012 bytes of shared memory ("large
pool","unknown object","session heap","bind var buf")

    DAD name: plsql
    PROCEDURE  : ml2_gui.startup
    USER       : jsmith
    URL        :
http://metalink.oracle.com:80/metalink/plsql/ml2_gui.startup
```

As of early 2002, the necessary infrastructure to provide 24×7 availability for Metalink was not in place, although Oracle was planning to offer a new system to address the problem.

From the error messages returned by Metalink in the second half of 2001, it would seem that the database underlying Metalink was not monitored with the same diligence that a customer would apply to an Oracle production system. Errors include failure to extend the database due to a lack of space, which demonstrates that inadequate monitoring was in place.

Oracle does not publish service levels actually provided by Metalink. They would certainly make for interesting reading. What's obvious is that the levels of availability provided by Metalink fall short of 24×7. The good news is that such availability issues will be addressed in the near future. Oracle Corporation certainly has the tools to do so, and many customers deploy them with success. For example, monitoring can be provided by Oracle Enterprise Manager (OEM) and the Intelligent Agent (refer to Chapter 24), and Oracle Data Guard (refer to Chapter 23) provides protection against site disasters.

Oracle Expectations of Customers

An article that received widespread computer press coverage in December 2000 stated that many, if not most, Oracle customers in the United Kingdom overstated the severity of their problems in order to receive the support they required.

Oracle publishes information on how to work effectively with OSS on the Metalink Web site. According to Oracle's own information published in "Working with Support" (Doc ID 166650.1), nearly 50 percent of TARs reported in a recent year fell into two categories: those caused by customers themselves and those resulting from requests for additional information. Customer-related problems include things like misconfiguration of the server and database, incorrect installation, lack of training, and misunderstanding the documentation. This information highlights that working with OSS should be viewed as a collaboration between Oracle and the customer.

Customers should always search the Web, Metalink, and the Oracle Metalink forums before submitting a TAR and adhere to guidelines for all installations and configurations. OSS works under the assumption that customers only request support because the problem wasn't easy to solve in the first place. Given the percentage of TARs associated with customer-caused issues, the implication seems to be that customers are not doing all they can to make the best use of Oracle support resources.

For a more proactive approach, OSS provides scripts that can preempt problems in the first place. For example, OSS provides the InstallPrep.sh script to perform a check of the environment before you attempt to create an Oracle9*i* database on the most popular flavors of UNIX such as Solaris, Linux, and HP-UX. If you run this first, you're less likely to experience problems that lead to support calls.

Role of the Support Analyst and Escalation

According to Oracle, all OSS analysts undergo several weeks of boot-camp-style training to prepare them for support work, which consists of two mutually exclusive tasks:

- Taking new support calls
- Addressing existing issues from a prioritized queue of TARs owned by the analyst

Given the analysts' level of training, there's a good chance that the support you receive should meet your needs, but the job of the analyst is not without its challenges, especially for cases when customers overstate problem severities. Unfortunately for the customer, the support function is generally viewed as an overhead in many companies, and support analysts tend to be less respected than consultants who generate revenue income. However, none of those factors should be used as an excuse for poor support.

If you are not satisfied with the attention your problem receives, you should follow the official process for escalating the request. Almost by definition, the need to escalate a TAR means that the support process has failed in some way, either because the OSS analyst has not appreciated or accepted the severity of an issue, or because the customer has not made the severity clear. If you're not satisfied with the support you have received, *after* a problem has been resolved—possibly because Oracle has not met their stated support goals in some way—then there is no easy way today to indicate that fact. The requirement to escalate a problem is different, and covered by an explicit procedure.

Oracle's evidence that 29 percent of total TARs were related to customer requests for additional information suggests two possibilities: One is that customer's don't do sufficient research or read the documentation first, and the other is that Oracle's documentation and support infrastructure is not up to the job. Both definitely apply. My own personal experience, as an Oracle user who researches every possibility before reporting a TAR, is that incomplete documentation and how-to examples for new products are the root cause of many TARs. Also, the OSS's lack of knowledge of those products is the reason those TARs often seem to take a long while to reach a conclusion. Although both Metalink and the free Oracle Technology Web site (otn.oracle.com) contain many how-to examples, it can take many months for articles to appear related to new products. The Oracle forums can be a useful source for resolving such issues, but not when you need a guaranteed response within a fixed timescale.

Given that so many requests are for additional information, it's perhaps surprising that Oracle's iTAR system does not allow the customer to indicate such a request explicitly in order to make it clear that the issue is in no way business critical.

Need for a Reproducible Test Case

When a customer reports a problem to OSS for which a ready solution does not exist, the customer needs to provide OSS with a reproducible test case. The reproducible test case is a precise set of instructions that the customer can use to demonstrate the problem—on demand—on his or her own system. OSS can then follow the same instructions in house to reproduce the problem. Because OSS analysts have access to Oracle product development teams, the development teams can debug reproducible problems at the source-code level, enabling code fixes to be made.

According to an ex-Oracle support colleague, the area that was a source of much customer antagonism was the need to provide a reproducible test case. The issue from the customer's perspective is that the major part of the effort to identify the root cause of a problem is down to the customer's efforts in such a case. If the test case can only be reproduced in a 40GB production database on the customer site, then it's somewhat impractical to expect Oracle to set up your production environment in house. That said, it's surprising how often OSS appears to scramble for hardware resources when you need to send data of a reasonable size.

It's beyond dispute that it can take several hours of customer effort to reduce a complex situation to a simpler one of a manageable size that can be sent to OSS and reproduced at Oracle. Unfortunately for the customer, that's life. For a complex problem with myriad possible root causes, there is no shortcut. After the initial creation of a TAR via phone or iTAR, all information should be logged via iTAR to ensure that both the OSS analyst and customer have a common view of what's been agreed on and the progress to date.

As a customer, you have a right to expect OSS to formulate a plan at the outset of your problem. That's a stated goal of OSS. So if you experience a situation where the OSS analyst appears to be reacting to a problem without a clear plan, such as requesting that you supply huge amounts of trace files with no apparent value, don't be afraid to ask where it's leading. The analyst should always keep you in the picture regarding the direction of any investigation, particularly if collecting the information makes heavy demands on your time. Professional respect works both ways. If your problem turns out to be the result of a software bug, be sure that any workarounds suggested by OSS are practical and that your problem has a genuine business impact before requesting a code patch. Always be absolutely sure that the root cause of the problem is 100 percent solved by the patch. If any uncertainty as to the root cause remains, don't take the risk of installing a patch.

Don't underestimate the effort required by Oracle to code and regression test a patch: It's huge. You also need to consider the regression-testing implications of any in-house applications that require the patch. Always keep in mind that installing any patch on your site includes a risk of unwanted side effects. The introduction of faults into the Oracle database management system (DBMS) as a result of such one-off patches, and even as a result of major regression-tested patches, is definitely not unknown. If you can avoid a patch in any way, even if it involves modifying application code to work around it, consider that as a lower-risk option.

Using STATSPACK to Address Performance Issues

Many TARs relating to DBMS performance issues for the root cause can be difficult to identify. Too often performance problems on a database server are not related to the configuration of the database at all. Instead, a hardware resource issue on a server (often due to a CPU or memory shortfall) manifests itself as poor database performance.

If you're a long-time Oracle user, you're aware of the legendary utlbstat.sql and utlestat.sql scripts that take a snapshot of Oracle performance metrics over a period of time. In the past, you could expect OSS to ask you to run these scripts several times and send output in any situation when you reported database performance problems. OSS would then analyze the output for indicators of performance problems.

In order to formalize the method for collecting statistics on performance, OSS now recommends that you install and run the STATSPACK package on your databases. This package is compatible with Oracle 8.1.6 databases and later. You should install STATSPACK as a standard on your systems in order to supply performance metrics to OSS in a format familiar to them. The STATSPACK package, which you can download from Oracle's Web site, differs most fundamentally from utlbstat.sql and utlestat.sql in the following ways:

- More statistics are collected.
- The level of detail can be controlled.
- Sampled data is stored in database tables.

The persistent storage of performance metrics makes it available for graphical presentation and Structured Query Language (SQL) reports using the tools of your choice.

Details on Oracle STATSPACK can be found at Metalink, and there is even a book dedicated to it. The basic premise of STATSPACK is that Oracle performance metrics are sampled on a timer interval, typically through a database job, and stored in tables in the PERFSTAT schema, created when you install STATSPACK. Each collection is assigned a SNAP_ID generated from an Oracle SEQUENCE. Here are a few:

```
STATS$LATCH
STATS$LATCH_CHILDREN
STATS$ROLLSTAT
STATS$SESSION_EVENT
STATS$SESSTAT
```

If you're familiar with the Oracle data dictionary, then you'll recognize these tables as those found in the dictionary, along with a STATS$ prefix. In general, STATSPACK tables contain the columns in the original Oracle dictionary table with three additional columns, shown here, to identify the database, instance number (for collections on Oracle Parallel Server [OPS] and Real Application Clusters [RAC]), and collection ID for which the sample was collected:

```
SNAP_ID              NUMBER(6)       NOT NULL
DBID                 NUMBER          NOT NULL
INSTANCE_NUMBER      NUMBER          NOT NULL
```

The STATS$SNAPSHOT table contains the complete list of snapshots taken, along with the sample time. Generation of the standard STATSPACK performance report requires that you run an Oracle-supplied SQL*Plus script, whose name depends on the version of Oracle, and that you pass two collection IDs to identify the start and end samples for the snapshot. The following output shows part of the report that displays session statistics between two consecutive samples:

```
Instance Activity Stats for DB: ORAP1  Instance: orap1  Snaps:  667-668

Statistic                           Total    per Second    per Trans
--------------------------  ----------------  ------------  ------------
CPU used by this session            2,544         0.7          848.0
CPU used when call started          2,541         0.7          847.0
CR blocks created                     138         0.0           46.0
```

Using the Remote Diagnostic Agent

Whenever you report a TAR to Oracle via phone or iTAR, you need to provide details of your Oracle environment so that the analyst can ensure that any problem investigation is limited to the appropriate operating system, server platform, and Oracle version. This is a necessary, though tedious, part of the process. If you report problems using iTAR, then you can clone an existing TAR to save time on this stage. In the interests of proactive problem management, OSS released the Remote Diagnostic Agent (RDA) towards the end of 2001. RDA is a set of UNIX shell scripts designed to gather detailed information on the Oracle environment with a goal of collecting information to aid in problem diagnosis for OSS. However, the information is generically useful and will probably become a standard part of the DBA tool set in the future and run on a regular basis. After downloading the RDA tar file from OSS, it's installed by running the setup.sh script. This prompts the installer for information about database instances, including the following:

```
Enter your: Oracle Home to be Analyzed
Hit Return to Accept Default: /u01/app/oracle/product/8.1.7
=============================>


Enter your: Oracle SID to be analyzed
Hit Return to Accept Default: ORAP1
=============================>
```

```
Enter your: Prefix for all the Files Generated
Hit Return to Accept Default: RDA
=============================>


Enter your: OUT_DIR used for all the Files Generated
Hit Return to Accept Default: /opt/oracle/software/u01/app/oracle/rda
=============================>
```

After the initial configuration, running the rda.sh script generates an output file that can be sent to OSS for diagnostic purposes. Here's an example:

```
/u01/app/oracle/rda/RDA.rda.tar.Z
```

The most detailed information can be gathered if the script runs under the UNIX root account. At the very least, it should run as the Oracle DBA UNIX group (usually dba). The simplest way for the customer to view the output is to open the file RDA_Index.htm either by running a browser from the UNIX server or by making the information available via a virtual directory if Apache Web Server is running. Basic Apache configuration is covered in Chapter 4. Alternatively, the files can be copied to a PC and viewed locally using a Web browser.

Choosing Your Oracle Product Set

You might be wondering what your choice of Oracle products has got to do with support. I believe there is a very close connection. If you choose to run a nonmainstream Oracle product, then you're likely to receive poor levels of support because OSS analysts that have experience with the product in question won't be readily available. Without support available, your outages will be longer, and depending on the exact nature of the product and the circumstances of its use, the outage could become business critical. Many examples from real life can be used to back up this view.

For example, if you've used Oracle standby database technology in the past, then the superior features of Oracle Data Guard available in the Oracle9i version have probably caught your eye. Oracle Data Guard is covered in depth in Chapter 23. An early problem with the technology of the production release showed up when the product failed to create a standby database automatically based on a primary database containing redo log groups with more than one member. In reality, most production databases would contain more than one member per group. Oracle testing, performed by the development team, had simply not covered this scenario, possibly because the development team didn't run the tool in a production configuration likely to be used by a customer.

Another problem manifested itself with LogMiner, which refused to mine logs for a database containing standby redo log files; LogMiner simply didn't understand them. Finally, automatic standby registration was likely to fail on the standby site. This last scenario took the local Oracle support organization a while to process because the support analyst had to learn about Oracle standby database technology from scratch and then convince product development that there was a problem. In themselves, such problems might appear insignificant, but reading between the lines, the message is that Oracle Data Guard testing is not yet fully complete, and that support is not readily available. These issues take on much more significance on a production system.

If you've experienced Oracle's marketing for Oracle9*i*, then you're aware that Oracle Corporation's stated goal is to run your end-to-end technology stack. If you're like me, this gives you cause to question whether or not Oracle can provide the support required to back up this position. In reality, the answer is definitely "not yet." If Oracle is really serious about this proposition, then the infrastructure to support the tools needs to be proactively put in place first, not as a result of customers experiencing problems. The standby database scenario is one example. The smaller the customer base for the product you use, the more likely you are to experience problems using it, suffer from lack of documentation, and receive inadequate support. It can be difficult to protect yourself from this kind of risk because Oracle doesn't publish information about users taking up specific technologies, but you can try other approaches.

You should always approach Oracle for reference sites when considering using new Oracle technology, as reference sites can give you a good view of supportability issues experienced, and the frequency of problem occurrence. If no information is available, you need to draw your own conclusions from that. IBM famously used the lack of reference sites on OPS to question the viability of that product in press advertising in 2001. Although it might simply appear to be clever marketing, it has a basis in reality from my own experience.

On the other hand, Oracle RAC, the successor of OPS, appears to have a real and exciting future. Although cynics have said that RAC is simply a rebadging of OPS as part of an image makeover, RAC is actually a different entity that addresses the problems of OPS and adds much more. The evidence is clear that RAC has a different future. For example, when the CEO of Intel cites Oracle RAC as a key technology for delivering the benefits of macroprocessing to an organization, clearly RAC is something that has a big future. Intel CEO Craig Barrett did just this during a keynote speech at Oracle OpenWorld in December 2001. If RAC support is not of the highest quality today, the stated support for the technology from major industry players suggests that it will be in the near future. Oracle RAC is covered in Chapter 22.

The lesson is that before you take up a new Oracle technology in your organization, you should do extensive research in as many areas as possible before you deploy it. Supportability is a critical success factor for deployment; you need to look into supportability today and probable improvements in the future, and understand why those improvements are likely to take place. In some cases, such as the Oracle Intelligent Agent, it's clear that the product is becoming a must-have in order to simplify the management of some of Oracle's more complex technologies, such as the standby database covered in Chapter 23. As such, you need to make a call on when, rather than if, you should deploy it. The old saying that you should avoid deploying the point zero release of a product seems to be a good one, although it's a continual source of irritation for early adopters who want to take advantage of new features immediately.

The support part of the equation is critical and ultimately determines the availability of your Oracle systems. Oracle positions the single point of ownership available from Oracle9*i* as an advantage from a support perspective because you only have to deal with one company for all your needs. But this needs to be balanced against the likelihood of experiencing problems in the first place, and the real availability of support if you do.

The alternative approach that many companies take is to invest in best-of-breed technologies for all parts of the technology infrastructure. For example, you might choose to implement queuing based on the IBM MQ Series rather than Oracle Advanced Queuing. Or you might choose to use Microsoft's Active Directory as your Lightweight Directory Access Protocol (LDAP)-compliant enterprisewide directory, rather than Oracle Internet Directory (OID).

The challenge in this best-of-breed scenario becomes one of integrating technologies from different vendors into one seamless whole. As technologies become standards driven over time, these integration issues diminish, but they are certainly significant. The question you need to answer is whether problems are more likely from integration of the technology with the rest of the infrastructure or the technology itself. Integration problems can be a nightmare to manage, where the many companies involved simply pass the buck from one to another. On the other hand, if the problem is the technology itself, is better support likely to come from a world leader focused on that technology or from a company where the technology has a lower profile and competes for resources with many others?

In the real world, the problems you experience with a technology appear to correlate closely with whether you are an early adopter and how many other users are using the same technology. If you are an early adopter of a product with a small user base, then the chances are that when you experience a problem, you are the first one to hit it, and any fix will have to be created from scratch within the product development team. This poses a risk to the business using the technology because a fix could take too long to organize before money is lost. Implementing the fix itself can be risky because you need to be sure that a full regression test of the product has been performed with the fix in place. The opposite approach means that if you experience a problem, then a fix is likely to be available already because someone has experienced the problem before you have. Being an early adopter has some advantages as well as drawbacks. If you can deploy the technology successfully, then you may gain a business advantage over your competitors. As an early adopter, it's also likely that Oracle will be interested in your view of the product, potentially providing you with the opportunity to influence its future design.

If you are a user of Microsoft's Office suite of products, then you probably haven't experienced many bugs with those products for several reasons. These include the high quality of Microsoft's software engineering, the extensive Beta programs for the products, and, last but probably most important, the existence of millions of users around the world, any one of which has probably hit an individual problem before you did.

Sometimes you need to make a judgment call to use an Oracle technology in spite of an apparently small user base, where the alternatives introduce risks of their own and the Oracle benefits outweigh the risks. I would place Oracle Names and Recovery Manager (RMAN) in this category. Several years ago, neither was considered mainstream, and a decision to deploy them required a careful analysis of costs and benefits alongside extensive testing. Today they are both robust and mainstream. RMAN in particular has a bright future and has gained an increasingly high profile over time with the need to back up and recover increasingly large databases.

Once a product reaches a critical mass in terms of its user base, then you can feel comfortable deploying it because the support infrastructure at Oracle is likely to be in place. Unfortunately, that's no guarantee that the product will be viable in the long term. For example, Oracle Names will no longer exist after Oracle9*i*. However, that doesn't mean you should necessarily use the alternative product OID, now or in the future. Today I would place OID into the high-risk category due to supportability issues and the enterprisewide nature of any deployment. Oracle Names will continue to run for some time to come, and Microsoft's Active Directory should be carefully evaluated as an alternative solution. If your organization runs Windows 2000, or plans to, you potentially have an LDAP-compliant directory available already that is certified compatible by Oracle. Active Directory is a business-critical and central part of Windows 2000, with a large user base and the might of Microsoft behind it.

Summary

Oracle Metalink is a fantastic resource for Oracle support and troubleshooting. Although 24×7 availability has not yet been delivered, the service is due to improve as Oracle implements its own high-availability features on Metalink.

Oracle views the support relationship with the customer as one of collaboration, and this is certainly the best way to get results. As a customer, you need to understand Oracle's requirements of you to get the most from the relationship. If you understand the OSS analyst role, that can help. Don't forget that it works both ways: OSS also needs to proactively check that your needs are being met and what your requirements are as the customer. Always make sure that an analyst provides a clear plan of action at the outset of any problem you report, and that recommendations to apply patches are based on facts and not hunches. Consider following OSS recommendations for the installation of add-on packages that enable Oracle to provide support in a more standard way, such as through STATSPACK and RDA.

Always keep in mind that Oracle Corporation's goal is for Oracle9*i* to provide your whole technology stack through its ever-expanding product set. Inevitably, some of the newer—and therefore less mature and less widely used—products may be less stable and trouble free than long-standing products like the relational DBMS (RDBMS). Problems with these newer products are likely to take longer to fix due to a smaller OSS knowledge base and lesser availability of analyst expertise to support them. If you use early releases of such products, then you might find the support infrastructure is not in place to meet your requirements.

## CHAPTER 28

Troubleshooting Oracle DBMS Problems

As a database administrator (DBA), you'll be expected to identify and solve all kinds of problems quickly: database configuration, server configuration, application logic, and network issues, to name a few. As the person with the broadest knowledge of the end-to-end system, you will probably be best suited to start investigations. This chapter provides some techniques and tools for troubleshooting different types of Oracle problems and covers the following topics:

- Understanding the UNIX system log
- Identifying Oracle shared memory
- Using UNIX kernel tracing
- Using Oracle and operating system network tracing
- Using Oracle event tracing
- Operating system performance diagnostics

Understanding the UNIX System Log

The UNIX system log should always be checked by the DBA whenever a database problem is reported. The system log contains messages that indicate UNIX server problems that might affect the operation of the database. Here are some examples:

```
Nov 10 08:19:12 dbcoolsrv1 unix: NOTICE: alloc: /var: file system full
Nov 10 15:06:50 dbcoolsrv1 unix: NOTICE: /u01: out of inodes
```

The location of the log file is operating-system dependent. For example, on Solaris the log file is /var/adm/messages and on Linux the file is /var/log/messages. On a production server, you might expect the UNIX system administrator (SA) group to be responsible for generating alerts based on the contents of the log. However, any information that the DBA can provide to expedite the problem-resolution process can only reduce potential and actual outages.

Identifying Oracle Shared Memory

If you are running many database instances on a consolidated server, it's sometimes necessary to be able to identify the shared memory segment associated with the System Global Area (SGA) of each instance. This is useful if your server is short of memory or a shutdown has failed to remove the shared memory segment preventing the database from restarting. The following command shows all the shared memory segments currently allocated on a Solaris server, along with their owners and size:

```
$ ipcs -mb
IPC status from <running system> as of Sat Nov 10 11:38:29 2001
T          ID      KEY        MODE        OWNER    GROUP    SEGSZ
Shared Memory:
m           0    0x50000ff7 --rw-r--r--    root     root        68
m         201    0x6605adb8 --rw-r-----  oracle      dba   54714368
m         202    0x5ebba7d8 --rw-r-----  oracle      dba  252207104
```

In the past, it was difficult to associate the shared memory IDs with each Oracle instance. Oracle has recognized this problem and now provides a command-line utility, sysresv, in recent versions to display the shared memory segment ID and semaphores allocated for each instance. If you have multiple versions of Oracle on your server, you need to run sysresv for that version. You can use a Korn shell alias as follows to generate a list of Oracle System IDs (SIDs) that appear to be up on the server, and pass them to sysresv to give the following results:

```
$ alias sids='ps -deaf|grep dbw0|grep -v grep|sed s=.*dbw0_==|xargs'

$ sids
ORAD1 ORAD2

$ sysresv -d on -l 'sids'
IPC Resources for ORACLE_SID "ORAD1" :
Shared Memory:
ID              KEY
201             0x6605adb8
Semaphores:
ID              KEY
196608          0x1fd35560
1               0x1fd35561
2               0x1fd35562
Oracle Instance alive for sid "ORAD1"
```

```
IPC Resources for ORACLE_SID "ORAD2" :
Shared Memory:
ID              KEY
202             0x5ebba7d8
Semaphores:
ID              KEY
196611          0x372bd3e0
4               0x372bd3e1
5               0x372bd3e2
Oracle Instance alive for sid "ORAD2"
```

Using UNIX Kernel Tracing

UNIX kernel tracing enables you to log all UNIX system calls made by a process. System calls are the low-level operating system kernel calls that program code makes to access operating system services, such as those required to open files and read their contents. Kernel tracing can be used at program startup time or act on an existing process. For the case of the Oracle executable itself, system calls include those used to allocate operating system resources such as shared memory and semaphores that are required to start up an Oracle instance.

For obscure Oracle startup problems, tracing can be very useful. It's also useful when Oracle doesn't seem to be locating files where you expect, such as sqlnet.ora. In this case, file open() calls can be traced to show you exactly what files Oracle searched for, in what order, and what was found.

Finally, tracing can be very useful for situations where access to an underlying Oracle service passes through several layers of code, possibly even in different processes. Code that uses Oracle's external procedures is a good example. This section shows examples of all three cases, but there are many other potential uses. The examples are all real-world problems solved by tracing system calls on Solaris, which uses the TRUSS command for this purpose. Other UNIX systems have similar utilities. For example, HP-UX 11 uses TUSC, and Linux provides STRACE.

Tracing Database Startup Problems

During startup of an Oracle instance, the following error occurred:

```
SQL> startup
ORA-24323: value not allowed
ORA-03113: end-of-file on communication channel
```

Whenever an Oracle error is reported, your first action should be to check the cause and action provided by the Oracle oerr utility:

```
$ oerr ora 24323
24323, 00000, "value not allowed"
// *Cause:  A null value or a bogus value was passed in for a mandatory
//          parameter.
```

```
// *Action: Verify that all mandatory parameters are properly
initialized.
```

In this case, no trace files were produced in the trace directory identified by the user_dump_dest initialization parameter, and no additional information was found in the Oracle alert log, which is located in the directory given by the background_dump_dest initialization parameter. Oracle database management system (DBMS)-generated trace information can often identify the cause of a problem immediately.

The challenge in this case was to identify the parameter causing the problem when no additional trace or alter log information was available. A search of Metalink suggested a problem with some UNIX limits in the kernel without being specific about which and without pinpointing the init.ora parameter causing the problem. At this point, the STARTUP command was reexecuted using the following TRUSS command to trace the SQL*Plus command that was used to start up the instance:

```
$ truss -wall -rall -o /tmp/truss.log -f sqlplus "/ as sysdba"
```

Truss output can be very verbose, especially when used with the -rall and -wall commands that display the first few hundred bytes read and written by every read() and write() system call. Reads and writes include those on network interfaces, not just files. In the example, truss output is logged to the file /tmp/truss.log. The -f option causes any forked processes to be traced also. In this case, -f is crucial to identifying the problem because SQL*Plus doesn't actually start the database. In fact, the $ORACLE_HOME/bin/oracle executable is spawned by SQL*Plus, and the spawned process starts the database.

Based on Metalink information about possible causes, the system calls reported in the truss output can be searched for lines that identify a possible UNIX kernel resource shortage. System calls return errors from a standard set, which on most UNIX systems can be found in the file /usr/include/sys/errno.h. Additional information can be found in the UNIX manual pages using man errno. For example, the return code that identifies a resource shortage related to disk space, semaphores, and shared memory has the following from /usr/include/sys/errno.h:

```
#define ENOSPC   28      /* No space left on device            */
```

Conveniently, the truss output reports the same #define string as the one defined in the header file. A search of the truss output for the string ENOSPC shows the following, where the string of digits followed by a colon at the start of each line is the process ID of the process being traced:

```
9120: semget(-224336631, 77, 0640|IPC_CREAT|IPC_EXCL) Err#a28 ENOSPC
9120: semctl(3145728, 0, IPC_RMID, 0)        = 0
9120: close(9)           = 0
9120: shmctl(3001, IPC_RMID, 0)        = 0
9120: shmdt(0x80000000)          = 0
9120:     Incurred fault #6, FLTBOUNDS  %pc = 0xEF5D8AA0
9120:       siginfo: SIGSEGV SEGV_MAPERR addr=0xEF7FFDB4
9120:     Received signal #11, SIGSEGV [caught]
```

```
9120:         siginfo: SIGSEGV SEGV_MAPERR addr=0xEF7FFDB4
9120:     *** process killed ***
```

The startup problem appears to be related to a failure to allocate a semaphore because the semget() system call has failed, returning an ENOSPC error, with the result that the oracle process has been killed instead of starting up the database as planned. Semaphores are data structures (provided by the UNIX kernel) that applications can use to synchronize access to data. The number of semaphores required is related to the PROCESSES parameter in the init.ora file, which in this case is 500. The number of available semaphores that can be created is limited by settings in the /etc/system file that control the total number of semaphores that the UNIX kernel can allocate systemwide.

In this example, the UNIX kernel settings did not follow the recommendations in Chapter 1, and two other database instances were already started, causing some of the available semaphores to be allocated already. Rather than increasing the available semaphores, which would require a server reboot, the PROCESSES parameter was reduced to 30 in the init.ora file and the database started without a problem. Resolving this problem required expertise in understanding the relationship between the init.ora PROCESSES parameter and UNIX semaphore allocation. You might reasonably expect a professional Oracle DBA to have such expertise, but the problem would not have been solved quickly without the ability to identify the underlying cause through system call tracing. Once you have analyzed a few traces, inspecting the output is straightforward.

Locating the Legato Media Interface in Oracle9*i*

In Oracle8*i* on Solaris, if you wanted to stream backup data from Recovery Manager (RMAN) to a Legato tape library, it was necessary to remove the Oracle-supplied test library $ORACLE_HOME/lib/libobk.so and re-create it as a link to the Legato media management interface in /usr/lib/libobk.so. This is covered in Chapter 18.

In Oracle9*i*, no such instructions are provided, and no test library is installed into $ORACLE_HOME/lib/libobk.so. On the face of it, it might appear that the Legato interface is no longer available. This is, of course, not the case. Oracle has actually improved the design of the DBMS so that the default location of the Legato interface is searched by default, without the need to create the link.

Oracle provides the sbttest program to enable a simple backup of a named file to a Legato server through the media management software interface, without the need for a full database backup. This is useful for confirming that your Oracle-to-Legato interface is working correctly. The following SBTTEST command can be traced with TRUSS to show exactly where and how Oracle locates the Legato media management software:

```
$ truss -wall -rall -o /tmp/truss.log -f $ORACLE_HOME/bin/sbttest
symfind
.
.
.
9816: open("/u01/prod/9.0.1/lib/libobk.so", O_RDONLY) Err#2 ENOENT
9816: open("/opt/SUNWcluster/lib/libobk.so", O_RDONLY) Err#2 ENOENT
```

```
9816: open("/u01/prod/9.0.1/lib/libobk.so", O_RDONLY) Err#2 ENOENT
9816: open("/usr/lib/libobk.so", O_RDONLY)        = 4
.
.
.
```

In this case, the trace output shows exactly the order in which Oracle searches for the Legato library libobk.so in Oracle9*i*. The library is first searched for under $ORACLE_HOME/lib. The return code ENOENT from the file open() system call indicates that the file couldn't be found there, as shown from the description of the error code in errno.h:

```
#define ENOENT  2       /* No such file or directory          */
```

After searching in the default Solaris SUNWcluster directory, the file is eventually found in /usr/lib, where it is opened in read-only mode. The return code 4 is the file handle used to reference the library in any subsequent read() system calls. A similar approach can be useful when determining the search path for Oracle's network software configuration files. This example demonstrates that Oracle attempts to locate a Lightweight Directory Access Protocol (LDAP) server first in the ldap.ora file, which in this case isn't present, and then searches for sqlnet.ora, which is found in /var/opt/oracle:

```
9119: access("/u01/prod/8.1.7/network/admin/ldap.ora", 0) Err#2 ENOENT
9119: access("/var/opt/oracle/sqlnet.ora", 0)     = 0
9119: open("/var/opt/oracle/sqlnet.ora", O_RDONLY) = 8
```

Tracing External Procedures

This final example shows a failed attempt to call an external procedure in a shared library, and uses tracing to identify where the error occurred. You can see a complete example of linking external procedures into the Oracle DBMS using dbcool_utl.so, which can be downloaded from the companion Web site for this book. The following Structured Query Language (SQL) was used to create the library reference:

```
create or replace library LIB_DBCOOL_UTL as
'/u01/app/oracle/lib/dbcool_utl.so';
```

Next, the following SQL was run to call routines in the shared library in order to display the UNIX mount point and free disk space on the mount point for all the database files:

```
select file_name,
       dbcool_utl.disk_free(file_name),
       dbcool_utl.mount_point(file_name)
from dba_data_files;
```

An error, "ORA-28576: lost RPC connection to external procedure agent," was returned. This error has several possible causes. To identify the root cause, the first step is to trace the call from the SQL executed in the client session through to the shared library on the server. In this case, you need to trace an existing process, the Transparent Network Substrate (TNS) listener, and any processes it spawns by providing the process ID after the -p argument. The listener process, PID 2162, contacts the external procedure via the external process listener, and it can be traced as follows, with some trace output provided:

```
$ truss -wall -rall -o /tmp/truss.log -f -p 2162

2162:   poll(0x00127B64, 5, -1)          (sleeping...)
13410:  execve("/u01/app/oracle/product/9.0.1/bin/extproc", 0x00146580,
0x001835C0)  argc = 2
13410:  open("/u01/app/oracle/lib/dbcool_utl.so", O_RDONLY) = 5
13412:  execve("/bin/sh", 0xEFFFE4E0, 0xEFFFFC28)  argc = 3
13414:  execve("/usr/sbin/df", 0x000386B4, 0x00038784)  argc = 3
```

The trace output shows that the listener was originally in a sleeping state awaiting connection requests. Upon receiving the call to the external procedure dbcool_utl. disk_free, the listener then spawned the extproc process, which opened the shared library dbcool_utl.so. The shared library ran a shell to execute the UNIX df command to find the mount point and the disk for the first file name returned from dba_data_files. In this example, the df command should have executed once for each file in dba_data_files, and the failure to display subsequent calls to df indicates that the shared library contains a code bug that caused the process to crash. This problem needs to be fixed by the developer of the shared library. Incidentally, because Oracle runs external procedures in a separate address space from the database shadow process (as shown), any crashes that occur in external procedure calls can't cause the database or even the client session to crash.

Using Network Tracing

Network tracing is an extremely useful technique for investigating both Oracle connectivity and performance issues. Oracle provides an extensive tracing capability built in to Oracle Net. To analyze performance issues, it can be useful to view the actual Transmission Control Protocol/Internet Protocol (TCP/IP) network packet. This can be achieved through the use of an operating system network trace tool.

Operating System Network Tracing

All Oracle DBAs on UNIX should familiarize themselves with the tools in this section. With the increasing prevalence of multitiered applications that include Oracle in the technology stack, it's essential that the DBA has a basic understanding of how to trace network problems.

The Netstat Utility

Netstat displays the contents of various network-related data structures in various formats, depending on the command-line options chosen. For example, "netstat -a" shows the state of all TCP/IP sockets. If you want to confirm that the Oracle network listener is operating on the default listener port of 1521, you can check the status of it using the following command:

```
$ netstat -an|grep LISTEN |grep 1521

      *.1521              *.*           0     0    0    0 LISTEN
```

The wildcard *.* shows that the listener will accept connections from any client, and LISTEN shows that the port is in a listening state. It's a good idea to always use the -n argument in combination with -a. The -n argument ensures that any named network services in the /etc/services file are displayed by port number rather than name. So, if the following appeared in /etc/services, then the oracle listener would appear in the netstat -a output by name rather than by port if the -n option was not provided:

```
$ grep listen /etc/services

listener        1521/tcp                    # Oracle Listener V2

$ netstat -a|grep LISTEN

      *.listener          *.*           0     0    0    0 LISTEN
```

If you are running any product, not just Oracle related, that listens on a network port, then netstat is useful for checking if the port is already in use by another application. One limitation of netstat is that it can show whether a port is in use, but it doesn't show the UNIX process that has opened the port. If a port is in use by another application, you probably need to know what that is. To find the process holding a port open, you need lsof.

The lsof Utility

Lsof is a UNIX utility that lists open files. It's available free for many UNIX systems, such as HP, Solaris, and Linux. However, the name doesn't do justice to its full capabilities. Lsof includes network ports in its list of open files. So if you discover that another process appears to be holding a port open according to netstat, you can use lsof to find the process. Lsof can identify if a port is in use on its own. However, as it can take a while to run, it's best to use netstat first to confirm that the port is in use. The following command shows all TCP open sockets, and the process ID owning the socket:

```
$ lsof -i tcp
```

Sometimes netstat and lsof output don't match. This is because lsof retrieves its information from open file system objects, such as sockets, while netstat usually gets its output from kernel lookup tables. Occasionally, netstat may report on sockets that don't exist in lsof if those sockets are open at the network level but closed at the application level. For example, sockets reported in the FIN_WAIT_1 and FIN_WAIT_2 state in netstat can occur after an application has closed a socket. As result, the socket disappears from the lsof list. However, if the FIN packet sent to the remote machine during the close-socket procedure has not been acknowledged because the remote machine has crashed, for example, the UNIX kernel will hold the sockets in FIN_WAIT_1 and FIN_WAIT_2 states and retransmit for a few minutes. The sockets will only disappear from the netstat output after a timeout period has elapsed. It is possible to modify TCP/IP settings to change the timeout values, but this is not recommended without a complete understanding of the side effects of any changes.

The Snoop Utility

Solaris snoop is a command utility that captures packets from the network and displays their contents in real time or saves them to a file for later inspection. Other UNIX variants (including Linux) have similar utilities, such as tcpdump. Snoop is a very useful program, but at the same a very dangerous program because it can run in what is referred to as promiscuous mode, which reports on all TCP/IP traffic, not just traffic intended for the host where it runs. Running "snoop -P" can disable promiscuous mode. By default, snoop requires root privileges to run. The following command captures all traffic passing in or out of the current server into the file net.text:

```
$ snoop -o net.txt
```

After a period of time, the command can be cancelled and the file contents inspected using the following command:

```
$ snoop -i net.txt -V -x 0 -t a >net.text.snoop
```

The -V and -x 0 arguments cause the full contents of each packet to be saved to the file net.text.snoop along with the wallclock time reported by -t a. The following output from net.text.snoop shows the first part of the TCP/IP packet resulting from the SQL query SELECT * FROM EMP. This shows the result set exactly as it appears in the network packet, along with the TCP/IP header that identifies the source and destination machine addresses, and the wallclock time:

```
106 21:51:29.26136     dbcoolpc1 -> 198.231.35.23 ETHER Type=0800 (IP),
size = 1010 bytes
106 21:51:29.26136     dbcoolpc1 -> 198.231.35.23 IP   D=198.231.35.23
S=172.28.142.128 LEN=996, ID=36272
106 21:51:29.26136     dbcoolpc1 -> 198.231.35.23 TCP D=2857 S=1521
Ack=202482359 Seq=3406210470 Len=956 Win=9520

        0: 0000 0c07 ac02 0800 2089 653f 0800 4500    . . . . . . . . .e?..E.
       16: 03e4 8db0 4000 ff06 b4b6 ac1c 9f91 c6e7    . . . . .@ . . . . . . .
```

```
 32: 2317 05f1 0b29 cb06 a5a6 0c11 a2b7 5018  # . . . .) . . . . . . .P.
 48: 2530 dc10 0000 03bc 0000 0600 0000 0000  %0 . . . . . . . . . .
 64: 0602 0108 0001 d700 0000 0704 3733 3639  . . . . . . . . . . 7369
 80: 0000 0553 4d49 5448 0000 0543 4c45 524b  . . . SMITH . . . CLERK
 96: 0000 0437 3930 3200 0009 3137 2d44 4543  . . . 7902 . . . 17-DEC
112: 2d38 3000 0003 3830 3000 0000 8101 0205  -80 . . . 800 . . . . .
128: 7d02 3230 0000 0704 3734 3939 0000 0541  }.20 . . . .7499 . . . A
144: 4c4c 454e 0000 0853 414c 4553 4d41 4e00  LLEN . . . SALESMAN.
```

Chapter 9 shows how Oracle network performance can be improved by the appropriate choice of array size.

Oracle Net Tracing

Oracle provides a sophisticated and extensive network tracing facility for diagnosing Oracle connectivity problems on both the client and server. For example, consider a situation where a company has suffered a site disaster, resulting in the relocation of databases to different servers on a disaster recovery (DR) site. An old application that has been running for years is no longer able to connect, and connection attempts return "ORA-12535 TNS:operation timed out" errors. In this case, the challenge is to identify the database that the application is attempting to connect to because the Oracle TNS alias used to connect to the database is embedded in the application executable rather than supplied by the user at logon time. The client's sqlnet.log file always contains sufficient information to identify the server and database instance to which the connection was attempted, through the HOST= and SID= log information. Connection attempts that fail always log information to sqlnet.log, as in this case:

```
**************************************************************************
Fatal OSN connect error 12203, connecting to:
 (DESCRIPTION=(ADDRESS_LIST=(ADDRESS=(PROTOCOL=tcp)
HOST=dbcoolsrv1.dbcool.com)(PORT=1521)))(CONNECT_DATA=(SID=ORAD1)(CID=
(PROGRAM=OraApp.exe)(HOST=DBCOOLPC1)(USER=IngramG))))

  VERSION INFORMATION:
     TNS for 32-bit Windows: Version 2.3.4.0.0 - Production
     Windows NT TCP/IP NT Protocol Adapter for 32-bit Windows: Version
2.3.4.0.0 - Production
  Time: 29-OCT-01 13:08:28
  Tracing not turned on.
  Tns error struct:
    nr err code: 12203
    TNS-12203: TNS:unable to connect to destination
    ns main err code: 12535
    TNS-12535: TNS:operation timed out
```

As recommended in Chapter 3 on network configuration, you should always provide an explicit path for the location of the sqlnet.log file on the client PC from where the connection request originates through the use of the following setting in the sqlnet .ora file:

```
log_directory_client=C:\temp
```

If you fail to set the directory explicitly, the sqlnet.log file is created in the directory from which the application is launched, which can make locating the log a chore when a client PC uses many different Microsoft network shares to launch applications. As well as logging data on simple connectivity problems, Oracle Net can log and trace information on network name resolution and client-server data traffic through the following parameters in sqlnet.ora:

```
trace_level_client=16          # values USER|ADMIN|OFF|16
trace_directory_client=c:\trc  # use an explicit directory for files
trace_unique_client=true       # create a new file for each session
```

The next section on Oracle event tracing shows a nice example of how you can use the client trace information to identify the location of PL/SQL code errors. Oracle9*i* has an enhancement that means you can determine the TNS alias resolution method used for Oracle network names by running tnsping, which now reports the name resolution method. In previous versions of the Oracle client, it was necessary to enable client-side tracing to determine if a name was resolved locally through tnsnames.ora or through an Oracle Names or LDAP server. The tnsping output in Oracle9*i* reports the location of the sqlnet.ora file used and the resolution method as follows:

```
Used parameter files:
/var/opt/oracle/sqlnet.ora

Used ONAMES adapter to resolve the alias
```

The 9*i* tnsping program provides an additional benefit by reporting on the CONNECT_DATA component of the service name. In previous versions, the CONNECT_DATA value wasn't provided, meaning that you had to search your tnsnames.ora file or query the full details from the Names server. On the server, similar trace and logging facilities are provided to help diagnose connectivity issues at the server end through the following settings in the listener.ora file:

```
log_directory_listener = /tmp/trc
trace_directory_listener = /tmp/trc
trace_level_listener=16
```

Unlike the client settings, the server log and trace settings can be displayed and modified while the listener is running, as shown in the following examples:

```
$ lsnrctl show trc_directory  # or trc_level or trc_file
$ lsnrctl show log_directory  # or log_status or log_file
```

```
$ lsncrtl set trc_level 4      # set level 4 trace
$ lsnrctl set trc_directory /tmp
$ lsnrctl set log_status off
$ lsnrctl save_config_on_stop # save dynamic settings on stop
```

Using Oracle Event Tracing

Oracle event tracing can be used both for determining the code location of errors and for additional performance tracing of SQL statements above and beyond the basic trace you get with ALTER SESSION SET SQL_TRACE TRUE. Basic SQL tracing is covered in Chapter 9.

Event Tracing for Errors

Oracle event tracing enables you to trigger the dumping of trace information into text files in the user_dump_dest directory when specific Oracle errors occur in order to identify exactly what caused an Oracle error. Here's a real-life example, with a few details changed to protect the guilty, that demonstrates the power of Oracle event tracing. In this example, a developer has created an application that doesn't follow the recommendations made in Chapter 6 on designing supportable applications. The application calls an Oracle procedure that generates an error, "ORA-06502: PL/SQL: numeric or value error," along with an error stack that provides the procedure name that caused the problem and the exact line in the code.

Unfortunately, the Oracle error reported to the user by the application is simply "ORA-06502: a serious error occurred" without identification of the routine and line number where the error occurred. In this case, the developer decided to report only on the error code. The challenge is to find out exactly where in the code the error occurred, what SQL caused it, and why. Given that a typical application may call many different packages and procedures, and execute thousands of lines of code, at first sight this problem is akin to finding a needle in a haystack. An example follows that simulates the real-world problem based on a procedure that takes a single parameter as follows:

```
procedure my_procedure(p_in number) as
    l_number number(3);
begin
    l_number := p_in;
end;
```

One way to identify the error is to enable Oracle Net tracing on the client, as demonstrated earlier in the chapter. Oracle always returns unhandled errors to the client application, even if the application chooses not to report the complete message passed back from the server. The error information can be viewed in the network trace on the client. When MY_PROCEDURE is called with parameter 12345, the level-16 network trace on the client contains the following:

```
nsprecv:  87 4F 52 41 2D 30 36 35  |.ORA-065|
nsprecv:  30 32 3A 20 50 4C 2F 53  |02: PL/S|
nsprecv:  51 4C 3A 20 6E 75 6D 65  |QL: nume|
nsprecv:  72 69 63 20 6F 72 20 76  |ric or v|
nsprecv:  61 6C 75 65 20 65 72 72  |alue err|
nsprecv:  6F 72 3A 20 6E 75 6D 62  |or: numb|
nsprecv:  65 72 20 70 72 65 63 69  |er preci|
nsprecv:  73 69 6F 6E 20 74 6F 6F  |sion too|
nsprecv:  20 6C 61 72 67 65 0A 4F  | large.O|
nsprecv:  52 41 2D 30 36 35 31 32  |RA-06512|
nsprecv:  3A 20 61 74 20 22 53 59  |: at "SY|
nsprecv:  53 54 45 4D 2E 4D 59 5F  |STEM.MY_|
nsprecv:  50 52 4F 43 45 44 55 52  |PROCEDUR|
nsprecv:  45 22 2C 20 6C 69 6E 65  |E", line|
nsprecv:  20 34 0A 4F 52 41 2D 30  | 4.ORA-0|
nsprecv:  36 35 31 32 3A 20 61 74  |6512: at|
nsprecv:  20 6C 69 6E 65 20 35 0A  | line 5.|
```

So far, so good. This output in the network trace clearly identifies the exact location of the problem as line 5 in the procedure MY_PROCEDURE. This approach is fine for a two-tier client server application, when the user and client PC details are known in advance. The problem becomes several degrees more difficult to trap when the application is a three-tier application, the database client middleware runs on an NT server, and the middleware uses connection pooling. Through connection pooling, the middleware routes all client requests through one of several application queues that all use an Oracle account named APPWARE.

In this case, the DBA can't access the sqlnet.ora file to add tracing because the middleware server is on a remote site without remote access available. Also, the actual middleware connection to the database for a given client user can't be identified in advance due to the use of connection pooling. Connection pooling shares Oracle resources for a single server process between several end-user sessions at once. This has the advantage of making better use of server resources, at the cost of making it more difficult to trace the flow of data from an end-user request through to the database session that executed it. Even in complex scenarios like this, the DBA can dump Oracle trace information to identify the code location through the use of event tracing. Oracle states that event tracing should only be enabled on the instructions of Oracle Support. Of course, you can do it yourself if you understand the implications. The following SQL statements show how to trigger trace dumps whenever the error 6502 occurs in the *current* session:

```
REM smaller trace than systemstate level 10...
alter session set events '6502 trace name errorstack level 3';

REM more detailed trace...
alter session set events '6502 trace name systemstate level 10';
```

This solution is inadequate in our example because our requirement is to set the event trace in all sessions owned by the account APPWARE because we don't know the problematic session in advance. The unsupported procedure SYS.DBMS_SYSTEM. SET_EV allows the DBA to enable event tracing for other sessions. As usual, unsupported doesn't mean the procedure doesn't work. It actually means that Oracle Support won't answer questions on the procedure behavior or provide support if it doesn't work. It works fine for Oracle8*i* and 9*i*. The following SQL generates PL/SQL calls to set 6502 tracing on sessions with the owner APPWARE:

```
select 'begin dbms_system.set_ev('||sid||','||serial#||','
                          ||6502||','||3||','||
                          '''ERRORSTACK''); end;' run_cool_sql
from v$session where username='APPWARE';


RUN_COOL_SQL
-------------------------------------------------------------
begin dbms_system.set_ev(7,1069,6502,3,'ERRORSTACK'); end;
begin dbms_system.set_ev(8,160,6502,3,'ERRORSTACK'); end;
begin dbms_system.set_ev(9,87,6502,3,'ERRORSTACK'); end;
begin dbms_system.set_ev(10,10,6502,3,'ERRORSTACK'); end;
begin dbms_system.set_ev(11,30,6502,3,'ERRORSTACK'); end;
begin dbms_system.set_ev(12,6,6502,3,'ERRORSTACK'); end;
begin dbms_system.set_ev(13,9,6502,3,'ERRORSTACK'); end;
begin dbms_system.set_ev(14,7,6502,3,'ERRORSTACK'); end;
```

The PL/SQL blocks need to be executed as SYS to enable the trace. If you use DbCool, you can execute the SQL to deliver results to the grid, then right-click the grid, and use the RUN_COOL_SQL feature to execute all the generated calls with minimal effort. Here are two fragments of the trace information in one of the generated trace files in the server trace file directory (identified by the user_dump_dest initialization parameter) that identify exactly where the ORA-06502 error occurred, and the value of the bind variable passed in that caused the overflow:

```
*** SESSION ID:(13.25) 2001-11-10 10:15:49.529
*** 2001-11-10 10:15:49.529
ksedmp: internal or fatal error
ORA-06502: PL/SQL: numeric or value error: number precision too large
Current SQL statement for this session:
declare
begin
SYSTEM.MY_PROCEDURE(P_IN=>:P_IN);
end;
----- PL/SQL Call Stack -----
  object     line  object
  handle   number  name
81c3e30c       4  procedure SYSTEM.MY_PROCEDURE
81c459ec       5  anonymous block
.
```

```
        .
        .
Cursor 13 (25d8790): CURBOUND  curiob: 25ef0cc
 curflg: 44 curpar: 0 curusr: 0 curses 82dbc0bc
 cursor name: declare
begin
SYSTEM.MY_PROCEDURE(P_IN=>:P_IN);
end;
 child pin: 8278c554, child lock: 8277aaa8, parent lock: 827950c4
 xscflg: 110664, parent handle: 81c4726c, xscfl2: d100000
 lng hand: 25d9e00
  nxt: 1.0x000000f8
Cursor frame allocation dump:
frm: -------- Comment --------  Size  Seg Off
 bind 0: dty=1 mxl=4000(4000) mal=00 scl=00 pre=00 oacflg=01 oacfl2=0
size=4000 offset=0
   bfp=025ebdf0 bln=4000 avl=05 flg=05
   value="12345"
```

This information should be sufficient to identify the root cause of the problem and fix it. In this simulation, we know the value passed was 12345. In the real-world scenario that this example simulates, the procedure call actually took place several levels down the call stack from the procedure executed by the user, and the input value wasn't known until the trace was generated. The tracing technique enables the underlying problem to be identified in all cases. Chapter 6 contains tips on how to prevent such problems occurring in the first place. It's interesting to analyze how such problems are caused. In the real-world problem that this example simulates, the application generated internal numeric IDs for user accounts. Over a period of years, the IDs grew from two digits in length to eventually require five digits, resulting in the value extending beyond a four-digit PL/SQL number variable used in the code, causing the ORA-06502. As a result, the application continued to work for older users and stopped working for users created after a certain date. Bizarre problems like this usually have a perfectly simple explanation once you find where the problem occurred. Finding the location of the problem is the hard part.

It's absolutely critical that any trace is disabled as soon as possible after information has been collected. The trace files can grow very large, very quickly, and impact the performance of the DBMS. Disabling the trace for a session can be achieved by passing a value of 0 for the error level and reexecuting the call to SET_EV as follows:

```
select 'begin dbms_system.set_ev('||sid||','||serial#||','
                    ||6502||','||0||','||
                    '''ERRORSTACK''); end;' run_cool_sql
from v$session where username='APPWARE';
```

Alternatively, the SID and SERIAL# arguments can be passed as NULL values to disable trace for all sessions.

Event Tracing for Performance Problems

You're no doubt familiar with using standard SQL trace to enable the tracing of SQL statements for performance analysis as shown in Chapter 9. You can use SET_EV to trace the values of bind variables and session waits, in addition to the standard trace that is generated with ALTER SESSION SET SQL_TRACE TRUE. This is enabled through the 10046 event. The following example shows PL/SQL calls to SET_EV using the event 10046 and various trace levels for the session identified by SID 8 and SERIAL# 149:

```
REM identical to ALTER SESSION SET SQL_TRACE TRUE, level 1
begin SYS.DBMS_SYSTEM.SET_EV(SI=>8,SE=>149,EV=>10046,LE=>1,NM=>'');end;

REM trace SQL with bind variables, level 5
begin SYS.DBMS_SYSTEM.SET_EV(SI=>8,SE=>149,EV=>10046,LE=>5,NM=>'');end;

REM trace SQL with event waits, level 9
begin SYS.DBMS_SYSTEM.SET_EV(SI=>8,SE=>149,EV=>10046,LE=>9,NM=>'');end;

REM trace SQL with bind variables, event waits, level 13
begin SYS.DBMS_SYSTEM.SET_EV(SI=>8,SE=>149,EV=>10046,LE=>13,NM=>'');end;

REM trace off for one session, level 0
begin SYS.DBMS_SYSTEM.SET_EV(SI=>8,SE=>149,EV=>10046,LE=>0,NM=>'');end;
```

Don't forget that you must disable the trace as soon as possible, as the files can grow very large, very quickly, slowing DBMS performance and filling the user_dump_dest directory. To disable trace manually, you need to repeat the original calls for each session using a value of LE=>0. Alternatively, the SID and SERIAL# arguments can be passed as NULL values to disable trace for all sessions. DbCool provides a user-friendly interface for enabling and disabling trace levels, accessible from the Debug main menu, as shown in Figure 28.1.

Determining Which Events Are Enabled

In order to turn trace off for all those events you have enabled, it would be useful if Oracle provided a procedure to report on this information, in case you accidentally forget to turn it off. Unfortunately, it's only possible to report on enabled events in the current session, which has limited use in the real world, as you'll probably be using the facility to trace other sessions. The following is a widely published method to report on events enabled in the current session using SQL*Plus:

```
set serveroutput on
declare
  event_level number;
begin
```

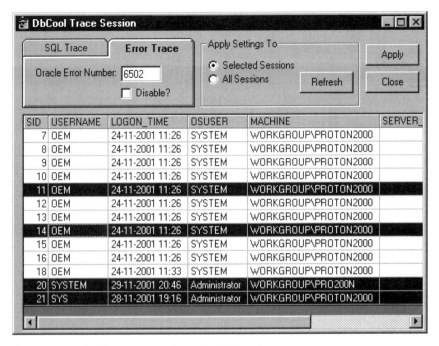

Figure 28.1   Setting event tracing using DbCool.

```
-- for each possible event
for i in 10000..10999 loop
    sys.dbms_system.read_ev(i,event_level);
    if (event_level > 0) then
        dbms_output.put_line('Event '||to_char(i)||' level '||
                            to_char(event_level));
    end if;
end loop;
end;
/
```

DbCool can disable event tracing for the 10046 event, as shown in the previous section, by generating calls to disable the trace, which the user can apply in all sessions via the graphical user interface (GUI). This approach could be extended to generate calls to disable all events in all sessions by iterating over each possible event for each session and executing a SET_EV cal using a level (LE parameter) value of 0.

Operating System Performance Diagnostics

Strictly speaking, host performance management and monitoring should be a service provided by the UNIX SA group in your organization using procedures and tools to meet a set of requirements. As a DBA, it's useful to have at least a basic understanding of how to diagnose server performance problems and their relationship with database performance. This section covers tools—some are Solaris specific—that enable the DBA to identify server resource usage in terms of central processing unit (CPU), input/output (I/O), memory, and network utilization. These tools are typically used to diagnose the cause of problems in response to a report that the system is running slow.

Identification of Top CPU Processes

The UNIX top utility is a free program (available for all popular UNIX systems) that displays a process list ordered by top CPU consumption typically over the previous few seconds. To report CPU usage for each process on Solaris, a percentage value is displayed, where the total CPU capacity on a server is 100 percent. This means that on a four-processor machine, a single process may consume up to 25 percent of the CPU, or 50 percent on a two-processor machine. For each Oracle process, the RES column (indicating the memory resident set size of a process) should be viewed with care as the value includes the size of the SGA shared memory segment, which is actually allocated once only and attached to each Oracle process as a shared resource. Figure 28.2 shows a top snapshot for a two-processor server during an Oracle import.

Memory Utilization

All modern UNIX systems use virtual memory to enable a server to provide more memory to applications than is physically available. Blocks are paged in and out to disk on demand, using the swap partition as a backing store. When excessive paging takes place, the I/O demands on the system can cause a severe performance degradation because disk blocks are orders of magnitude slower than memory to access. On

```
last pid:  5491;  load averages:  1.12,  1.11,  1.15
98 processes:  95 sleeping, 1 running, 2 on cpu
CPU states: 31.0% idle, 52.0% user, 10.8% kernel,  6.2% iowait,  0.0% swap
Memory: 1024M real, 30M free, 691M swap in use, 1142M swap free

  PID USERNAME THR PRI NICE   SIZE   RES STATE    TIME    CPU COMMAND
29018 oracle    13   8    4   340M  320M run    492:22  47.87% oracle
 5491 oracle     1  22    0   840K  624K cpu/1    0:00   0.89% cksum
 5482 oracle     1  58    0  2176K 1696K cpu/0    0:00   0.10% top
 1610 oracle     1  58    0  2176K 1648K sleep    0:49   0.09% top
 5490 root       1  48    0  2760K 1424K sleep    0:00   0.07% in.rshd
  471 root       4  58    0  2848K 1944K sleep    5:18   0.05% tibhawkhma
28168 oracle    18  59    0   217M  191M sleep    0:45   0.04% oracle
28166 oracle    11  59    0   219M  191M sleep    9:02   0.04% oracle
28164 oracle   215  58    0   221M  194M sleep    8:03   0.04% oracle
  205 root       1  48    0  1904K 1376K sleep    0:02   0.03% inetd
```

Figure 28.2 Output from the UNIX top utility.

many UNIX systems, the vmstat command-line utility is available to report on virtual memory usage as shown in the following example on Solaris:

```
$ vmstat 5
procs     memory            page            disk          faults      cpu
 r b w   swap free re mf pi po fr de sr s0 s1 s2 s3  in  sy  cs us sy id
 0 0 0 11456 4130  1 41 19  1  3  0  2  0  4  0  0  48 112 130  4 14 82
 0 0 1 10132 4200  0  4 44  0  0  0  0  0 23  0  0 211 230 144  3 35 62
 0 0 1 10132 4610  0  0 20  0  0  0  0  0 19  0  0 150 172 146  3 33 64
```

A high value in the sr column, representing the page scan rate in pages per second, is usually accepted to be the best indicator of excessive paging. If the sr column contains values on the order of thousands, then the server may be experiencing a real RAM shortage that is impacting overall server performance. This awk script displays the scan rate every five seconds:

```
$ vmstat -S 5 | awk '{ print $12 }'
sr
73
1351
1041
1000
1516
```

Excessive paging is caused by a shortage of real memory required by applications running on the server. Real memory shortages can be caused by applications, including Oracle's own, that leak memory over time, causing a gradual increase in memory requirements on the system. Memory leaks are usually caused by code bugs where a programmer allocates memory dynamically at run time, doesn't free the memory, and then overwrites the original pointer. This dynamic memory is allocated from what is referred to as the heap, or the total pool of available memory on the server. Memory leaks may individually be small, as little as a few hundred bytes at a time. For a middleware server process that remains up and running for weeks at a time, these small wasted allocations can grow into hundreds of MB of wasted memory. On Solaris, the SZ column in the output of the ps -l command shows the total virtual memory size of each process in machine pages. The top command can provide similar information. Solaris also provides a suite of extremely useful programs in /usr/proc/bin (Solaris 2.6) and /usr/bin (Solaris 2.8) to report on detailed process information. The pmap program produces a detailed map of process memory, showing the type of memory allocated to the process in various categories. The following output shows pmap information from the Oracle Java Runtime Engine (JRE) used by Oracle Enterprise Manager (OEM), which includes a dynamic memory allocation of 11MB out of a total of 30MB:

```
# /usr/proc/bin/pmap 14658
14658:  /jre/1.1.8/bin/../bin/sparc/native_threads/jre -nojit
00010000      16K read/exec
```

```
/jre/1.1.8/bin/sparc/native_threads/jre
00022000     16K read/write/exec
/jre/1.1.8/bin/sparc/native_threads/jre
00026000  11304K read/write/exec      [ heap ]
  .
  .
  .

total     30112K
```

Linux also provides a very similar facility through /proc, which is a pseudo file system used as an interface to kernel data structures related to per-process memory, file, and CPU use. For example, to display status information for the process with PID you would run:

```
$ cat /proc/20552/status
```

Disk I/O

The iostat command-line utility reports disk read and write rates as well as service times, and it is very useful for the diagnosis of disk performance problems. It can be found on Solaris and Linux amongst others. The following example shows some sample output:

```
# iostat -xc 10
                                extended device statistics           cpu
 device    r/s  w/s    kr/s    kw/s wait actv  svc_t  %w  %b  us sy wt id
 md0       0.1  0.2    0.8     1.6  0.0  0.0   39.8   0   0   8  1  2 89
 md1       1.2  0.2    9.8     7.4  0.0  0.0   21.6   0   1
 md5       0.0  0.0    0.0     0.0  0.0  0.0   36.1   0   0
 md10      0.0  0.2    0.4     1.5  0.0  0.0   26.7   0   0
 md11      0.6  0.2    4.9     7.4  0.0  0.0   24.1   0   1
 md20      0.0  0.2    0.4     1.5  0.0  0.0   20.4   0   0
 md21      0.6  0.2    4.9     7.4  0.0  0.0   16.2   0   1
```

The average service time in milliseconds, svc_t, is probably the best indicator of the performance of your disks. The previous example indicates a possible disk-bound system, although the exact interpretation of values is system dependent.

Network Performance

The netstat utility referenced earlier in the chapter can report on many low-level UNIX performance counters. For example, the -i option can report on network packet transfer information along with collisions and errors, as shown in this example:

```
Name  Mtu   Net/Dest   Address     Ipkts     Ierrs Opkts    Oerrs Collis Queue
lo0   8232  loopback   localhost   838440        0 838440   0     0      0
hme0  1500  dbcools1   dbcools1    31550446      0 2532080 0     0      0
```

SymbEL

I strongly believe that the power and usability of the available performance management tools have a massive influence on the ability to deliver Oracle production systems that meet performance and availability requirements. You can usually fix any problem once it has been identified, but the hardest challenge is actually to identify the problem in the first place. This is made more difficult if you only have access to a collection of command-line tools and need to analyze their output yourself. Root cause analysis requires great tools.

In the Solaris environment, Adrian Cockcroft and Rich Pettit approach legendary status for creating an expert system to report on Solaris performance issues. Rich Pettit is the creator of se, which is the interpreter and runtime for the SymbEL language. SymbEL is an interpreted language based on C and was created to address the need for simplified access to data residing in the Solaris kernel. The Solaris kernel contains all the UNIX performance counters that are required to identify performance problems. Adrian Cockcroft is the author of an essential book on Solaris performance tuning "Sun Performance and Tuning." The zoom component of se presents a color-coded GUI based on Adrian Cockcroft's tuning rules to provide alerts on CPU, I/O, RAM, and network resource shortages for a user-defined time interval. The software is free and available for download from the Internet. Just like an Oracle database, UNIX provides many performance counters, and as usual the challenge is to interpret them correctly. The zoom.se component does just that. Be sure to read the disclaimers carefully before you run zoom on a production system. The software is unsupported, but in use at thousands of sites. The main screen is shown in Figure 28.3.

When resource usage exceeds thresholds, the user interface components change color, and as usual, red indicates a severe resource shortage. You can click the resource to find more details. Figure 28.4 shows the detailed information reported for a RAM shortage.

The software is delivered as a Solaris package, RICHPse. It requires an X server display to run and is started using the following command line:

```
/opt/RICHPse/bin/se zoom.se
```

If you try and run the utility without root privileges, you'll receive an error:

```
Fatal: cannot open /dev/ip
```

DBA Access to Server Performance Metrics

Many UNIX performance counters are accessible to root only, as are the tools required to access them. The primitive UNIX security model doesn't provide fine-level access to the counters, so DBAs are typically prevented from accessing them. This need not be a problem because the sudo utility exists to solve it. Sudo is a free program available on all popular UNIX systems, including Linux and Solaris, to enable secure access to

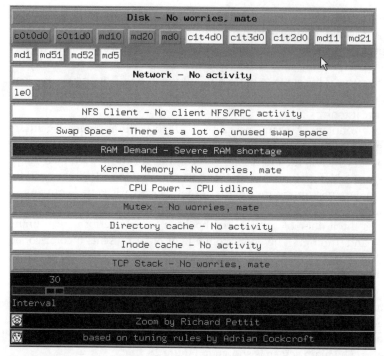

Figure 28.3 Rich Pettit's zoom utility.

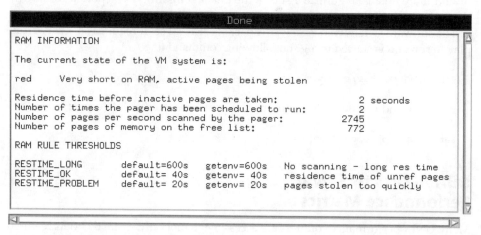

Figure 28.4 A RAM shortage identified with zoom.

root-privileged programs that are required to access the data structure such as /dev/ip. In the previous example, the UNIX SA would configure sudo to enable the Oracle UNIX account to run /opt/RICHPse/bin/se zoom.se as the root user. Configuration is trivially simple, and the user can be forced to provide the regular account password if necessary to enforce security on each execution.

Summary

This chapter provides a sample of the potential problems that can occur when using Oracle. Often the first view the DBA has of such problems is an end-user report of a slow database or a complete lockup. In order to resolve problems fast, the DBA needs to use all the available tracing and monitoring techniques to identify whether the problem is related to server hardware problems or resource shortages, the network, the Oracle database itself, or a combination of them. This means that DBAs must have a basic understanding of server performance metrics, as the DBA is often the first port of call when performance degrades or obscure problems occur.

If the basic techniques covered in this chapter don't identify the root cause of your problem, the Web is a fantastic source of tips, tools, and techniques for troubleshooting Oracle DBMS problems. My first port of call is Oracle's Metalink Web site, followed by a Web search using the Google search engine at www.google.com. In many cases, you're not the first person to experience a particular problem, and the fantastic knowledge base that is the Web can often provide the cause and the solution.

Index